COMPOSERS and their Music

To those who speak the only truly international language,
between whom there are no barriers of space or
time, race or creed; to the makers of music, this book
is humbly dedicated.

THE DICTIONARY OF
COMPOSERS
and their Music
EVERY LISTENER'S COMPANION
Arranged Chronologically and Alphabetically

ERIC GILDER
JUNE G. PORT

PADDINGTON
PRESS LTD
NEW YORK & LONDON

Library of Congress Cataloging in Publication Data

Gilder, Eric, 1911–
      The Dictionary of Composers and their music.

      1. Music—Bibliography. 2. Music—Chronology.
I. Port, June G., 1930–   joint author.
II. Title.
ML113.G4   016.78   77-15998
ISBN 0-448-22364-3

Filmset in England by Servis Filmsetting Ltd., Manchester.
Printed and bound in Scotland by
Morrison & Gibb Ltd., Edinburgh.
Designed by Pete Pengilley

IN THE UNITED STATES
PADDINGTON PRESS
Distributed by
GROSSET & DUNLAP

IN THE UNITED KINGDOM
PADDINGTON PRESS

IN CANADA
Distributed by
RANDOM HOUSE OF CANADA LTD.

IN SOUTHERN AFRICA
Distributed by
ERNEST STANTON (PUBLISHERS) (PTY.) LTD.

ERIC GILDER is a composer, teacher, conductor, pianist and musicologist. Trained at London's Royal College of Music, he studied under such gifted men as John Ireland, Ralph Vaughan Williams, Constant Lambert and Sir Malcolm Sargent. A prolific composer, Gilder has written for the orchestra, voices, the theater and television. He has served as a choral conductor and appeared at London's Royal Festival Hall both as a conductor and as a pianist.

He began his career as a teacher at a private London music college, which was some years later renamed the Eric Gilder School of Music. He continues to teach and lecture on a variety of music subjects.

JUNE G. PORT is a guitarist, cellist, teacher and musicologist. She is currently the administrator of the Eric Gilder School of Music in London and a lecturer on the history of music.

Preface

We have lectured for many years on music appreciation and history. We found that we needed to carry to the classroom about twenty bulky volumes in order to answer most of the questions thrown at us. Biographies of composers are legion, but in years of searching we could find no one book that contained all the information required. Many others to whom we spoke all admitted the same difficulty.

What was obviously required was complete factual information about who wrote what, and when, all between the covers of one book. This would be of lasting value as a permanent reference, not only to the academic student, but also to the vast numbers of interested laymen—the music-lovers, the concert-goers, the record-collectors, the listeners.

Our original intention has now become Part One of the present book. This is an alphabetical list of composers with their music arranged chronologically. Each composition is dated and the composer's age is supplied.

To have called this "A Complete List of Everything Ever Composed by Anybody" would have been far too rash a boast. All composers must have their jottings, tentative pieces, trifling things that have been discarded as unworthy, mere exercises. Some of these have been preserved, and may be seen in museums in the composer's own handwriting; but their contribution to the world's musical treasury is too inconsiderable to make them worthy of special mention. There are some works that composers themselves would not wish to be immortalized. (Dukas, for example, who was his own severest critic, burned all his un-published compositions when in his early forties and, although still composing, published no more.)

Omissions are therefore inevitable, and we have used our own discretion. However, we feel that every work of importance by the 275 composers represented is included. There are count-less others, but in such a book as this the line must be drawn somewhere, and the reader must forgive us if some favorite composer or work does not appear. The composers chosen are those whose works may be heard in the concert hall, the opera or ballet house, and the church. Many of these composers have also written incidental music and music for the theater which is included here; but a complete list of works for the theater could fill a large book by itself and, in general, composers who wrote for that medium alone have been omitted.

Where does such a book begin? Not until the sixteenth century did composers emerge who began to develop music as a serious art form, and music as we know it can be said to date from this time. An exact date cannot be provided, for there was a long period of evolution; but one can say definitely that the birth of "modern" music took place in Europe, and the first composer mentioned in this book is Thomas Tallis, who was born about 1505.

It was during the compiling of Part One that the ideas for Parts Two and Three emerged, and for us these became the most fascinating sections in some respects.

Part Two is a chronological survey, enabling the reader to turn to any year from 1554 through 1975 and see exactly what music was written, which composers were born and which died. Such an historical overview can perhaps best be appreciated if one sticks a pin somewhere in the calendar. Take the year 1847. That was the year Mendelssohn died. Spontini the indestructible was still prolifically writing opera in the classical mold. Bizet, Dvořák, Fauré, Grieg, Mussorgsky, Rimsky-Korsakov, Sullivan and Tchaikovsky were toddlers. Donizetti, whose operas were well rooted in tradition, still had a year to live, whereas in that year Verdi wrote *Macbeth* and Wagner was already working on *Lohengrin*, to be produced three years later. It was a good year for opera, contributions coming from Balfe, Dargomizhsky, Flotow and Schumann. Berwald, Meyerbeer and Rossini were all writing with middle-aged maturity, while the fourteen-year-old Borodin produced his Flute Concerto. Glinka, called the Father of Russian Music, wrote *Greetings to the Fatherland*, Berlioz was in his forties, Liszt his thirties, and Chopin was an ailing man of thirty-seven with only two years to live. Offenbach and Franck were both twenty-five years of age and already established as powers in the musical world. Lalo, the elegant Frenchman of Spanish descent, was already writing the music of Spanish flavor which was to influence Falla, Debussy and Ravel. Smetana was twenty-three and was later to establish the great nationalist school of Czech music, and to conduct the Czech Opera in which Dvořák played the viola. Brahms, Saint-Saëns and Balakirev were as yet unfledged children.

When Spontini was born, Boyce was still alive; when Boyce was born, Corelli was still alive; and Corelli was born a mere ten years after Monteverdi died. In this year of 1847 Spontini still had four more years to live; by the time he died, d'Indy was born, and *he* lived until 1931, by which time Boulez was very much alive. So with the names of five men—Corelli, Boyce,

Spontini, d'Indy and Boulez—who could just have met each other, we span the whole of musical composition from the glees, motets and madrigals to the music of today, a matter of something over three hundred years. Music as we know it is a very young art indeed.

Part Three of this book is a timeline, enabling one to see at a glance which composers were contemporaries, when each was born and died. It is a visual aid to gaining a clear perspective of musical history.

Research for this book brought up copious anomalies. Standard books on the subject have often been at variance with each other in the matter of dates. This is sometimes quite understandable. Certain modern composers, for example, were only accepted by publishers or by performing or copyright organizations quite late in their composing careers, and a large collection of early works bears only the date of such acceptance. Not all manuscripts bear a date in the composer's handwriting. If one of the present compilers, himself a composer, were asked the date of a certain one of his works, he might easily say, "Oh, about twenty years ago," and be unable to be any more accurate.

Many composers did not give their works opus numbers, and some who did seemed to be unable to count! Köchel's catalog of the works of Mozart can be accepted as definitive. For the rest, we have been ruled by the greatest consensus of opinion.

There has been a great variety of spellings of the names and works of Russian composers. The only accurate way to spell them, of course, is in the original Russian; any other spelling must be purely phonetic. This book incorporates spellings that are generally accepted in the Western world. In a similar way, the titles of works given are the titles by which they are best known, be they translated or in the original language.

Special mention must be made of the list of works by Johann Sebastian Bach. To begin with, his works can generally only be dated according to the years he spent in various appointments; i.e., during the nine years between 1708 and 1717 while at Weimar, as court organist, chamber musician and finally Concert-meister, he composed most of his great organ works. Then at Cöthen, between 1717 and 1723 as Kapellmeister and conductor of the court orchestra, he wrote the Brandenberg Concerti, the suites for orchestra, the violin concerti and much chamber music. From 1723 until his death in 1750, he was Cantor of the Leipzig Thomasschule, and there he composed approximately 265 church cantatas, as well as compositions for one of the Leipzig musical societies of which he was conductor.

Our obvious sources of information were such standard works as Grove's *Dictionary of Music and Musicians*, the Oxford *Histories*, Scholes's *Oxford Companion to Music*, the *International Cyclopaedia of Music and Musicians*, and Anderson's *Contemporary American*

Composers, from all of which we had to choose a mere handful from the thousands listed. The British *Performing Rights Society* and the American *ASCAP* contributed much information on contemporary British and American composers; for the rest, the reference books in French, German and Italian, and the biographies of composers, have been too numerous for us to be able to remember them. However, to all these and to the many composers who took the time to answer our letters of inquiry, for the great excitement over years of research, we give our grateful thanks.

Eric Gilder
June G. Port

Part One

In this alphabetical listing of composers, their music is arranged in chronological order. The dates, next to which appear the composers' ages, are those when the music is first mentioned. It is not always possible to ascertain whether these dates refer to the commencement or to the completion of a piece of music. Where possible, both dates are given, as Stravinsky: *Les Noces* (1917–1923). In some cases, the first information available is a mention of a first performance, in which case the name of the work is prefaced with the letters *f.p.*; in others, the first information may refer to the date of publication, when the letter *p.* is used. For some works, the letter *c.* for *circa* prefaces the nearest approximation. *Posthumous* in the age column indicates that the work was published, or first performed, after the composer's death. When dates of some of a composer's music cannot be traced, those works are listed at the end of the entry and undated.

Collections of short works are sometimes not listed individually. Consider the five hundred chamber cantatas of Alessandro Scarlatti, or the two hundred songs of Charles Ives: to list all such music would require many volumes. Instead, in such cases, works are referred to as so many "songs," "piano pieces," "cantatas," etc.

Key signatures are generally given in full, such as, *Rhapsody in C♯ minor*. However, if a number of works of the same kind were written in any one year, keys are abbreviated: e.g., Four string quartets in Dm: C: A: F♯m, indicating works in D minor, C major, A major and F♯ minor.

In the section for Bach, a number of works bear the suffix (*& continuo*). This indicates that the continuo is not generally used in modern performance.

A few composers, although generally considered as being of a particular nationality, were born in another country. In these instances both countries are listed: e.g., U.S.A. (b. Germany). In cases where the country of a composer's birth no longer exists, the modern equivalent is also included: Bohemia (Czechoslovakia).

As explained in the preface, works are given the names by which they are best known to English-speaking people.

ADAM, Adolphe/1803–1856/France

1832 (29) *Faust*, ballet
1834 (31) *Le Châlet*, opera
1836 (33) *Le Postillon de Longjumeau*, opera
1839 (36) *La Jolie fille de Gand*, ballet
1841 (38) *Giselle*, ballet
1849 (46) *Le Toreador*, opera
1852 (49) *Si J'etais roi*, opera
1856 (53) *Le Corsaire*, ballet
Adam also composed a total of 39 operas, as well as many ballets, choruses, songs and much church music.

ALBÉNIZ, Isaac/1860–1909/Spain (For details see page 218)

ALBINONI, Tommaso/1671–1750/Italy

1694 (23) *Zenobia, regina di Palmireni*, opera
1707 (36) Sinfonie e Concerti a 5
1710 (39) Concerti a 5
*c.***1716** (*c*.45) 12 Concerti a 5
*c.***1722** (*c*.51) 12 Concerti a 5
Albinoni composed many works of concerto grosso type, as well as more than 50 operas.

ALFVÉN, Hugo/1872–1960/Sweden

1896 (24) "Sonata" and "Romance", for violin and piano
1897 (25) Symphony No. 1 in F minor
1898–99 (26) Symphony No. 2 in D major
                Elegy, for horn and organ
1904 (32) Swedish Rhapsody No. 1, *Midsommervaka*
1905 (33) Symphony No. 3 in E major
                En Skargardssagen, symphonic poem
1907 (35) Swedish Rhapsody No. 2, *Uppsalarapsodi*
1912 (40) *Sten Sture*, cantata for male voices
1918–19 (46) Symphony No. 4 in C minor
1923 (51) *Bergakungen*, pantomime drama
1928 (56) *Manhem*, cantata for male voices
1932 (60) *Spamannen*, incidental music
                Vi, incidental music
1937 (65) Swedish Rhapsody No. 3, *Dalarapsodi*
1942 (70) Symphony No. 5 in A minor
Between 1898 and 1937 Alfvén wrote a number of piano pieces, and between 1900 and 1928 he wrote 10 cantatas, for solo voices, chorus and orchestra.

ALWYN, William/b. 1905/Great Britain

1927 (22) Five Preludes for orchestra
1930 (25) Piano Concerto
1936 (31) *Marriage of Heaven and Hell*, choral work
1939 (34) Violin Concerto

Rhapsody, for piano quartet
Sonata-Impromptu, for violin and viola
1940 (35) Masquerade, overture
Divertimento for solo flute
1942 (37) Concerto Grosso No. 1
1943 (38) Pastoral Fantasia, for viola and strings
1945 (40) Concerto for oboe, harp and strings
1946 (41) Suite of Scottish Dances
1947 (42) Manchester Suite, for orchestra
Three Songs (Louis MacNeice)
Piano Sonata
1948 (43) Three Winter Poems, for string quartet
1949 (44) Symphony No. 1
1951 (46) Festival March
Concerto Grosso No. 2
1953 (48) Symphony No. 2
The Magic Island, symphonic prelude
1954 (49) Lyra Angelica, for harp and strings
1955 (50) Autumn Legend, for English horn and strings
1956 (51) Symphony No. 3
1957 (52) Elizabethan Dances, for orchestra
1959 (54) Symphony No. 4
1964 (59) Concerto Grosso No. 3
1966 (61) Derby Day, overture
1970 (65) Sinfonietta for strings
1973 (68) Symphony No. 5, Hydriotaphia

ANTHEIL, George/1900–1959/U.S.A.

1922 (22) Airplane Sonata, for piano
Sonata Sauvage, for piano
Symphony No. 1
1923 (23) Ballet Mecanique (1923–24, revised 1953)
Violin Sonata No. 1
1926 (26) Jazz Symphonietta, for twenty-two instruments
1928–29 (28) Transatlantic, opera
1931 (31) Helen Retires, opera
1935 (35) Dreams, ballet
1936 (36) Course, dance score
1942 (42) Symphony No. 4
1947–48 (47) Symphony No. 5
1948 (48) Symphony No. 6
McKonkey's Ferry, overture for orchestra
Serenade, for string orchestra
Piano Sonata No. 4
Songs of Experience (Blake poems), for voice and piano
1950 (50) Volpone, opera
1951 (51) Eight Fragments from Shelley, for chorus
1953 (53) Capital of the World, ballet
1955–56 (55) Cabezza de Vacca, cantata

ARENSKY, Antony/1861–1906/Russia (For details see page 218)

ARNE, Thomas (Dr. Arne)/1710–1778/Great Britain

1733 (23) *Rosamund*, opera
           Opera of Operas, opera
           Dido and Aenas, opera
1736 (26) *Zara*, incidental music
1738 (28) *Comus*, a masque
1740 (30) *Alfred*, a masque (in which occurs "Rule, Britannia")
           The Judgment of Paris, opera
1743 (33) *Eliza*, opera
           Britannia, a masque
1744 (34) *Abel*, oratorio
1750 (40) *p.* Seven trio sonatas for two violins with figured bass
1762 (52) *Artaxerxes*, opera
           Love in a Village, pasticcio
1764 (54) *Judith*, oratorio (possibly 1761)
           Olimpiade, opera
1775 (65) *Caractacus*

ARNELL, Richard/b.1917/Great Britain

1939 (22) String Quartet No. 1
1940 (23) Violin Concerto
1941 (24) String Quartet No. 2
1942 (25) Symphony No. 2
1943 (26) Symphony No. 1
1944 (27) Symphony No. 3
1945 (28) String Quartet No. 3
1946 (29) Piano Trio
           Piano Concerto
1947 (30) *Punch and the Child*, ballet
           Harpsichord Concerto
1948 (31) Symphony No. 4
1950 (33) Symphony No. 5
           String Quintet
1951 (34) *Harlequin in April*, ballet
           String Quartet No. 4
1953 (36) *The Great Detective*, ballet
           Lord Byron, a symphonic portrait
1955 (38) *Love in Transit*, opera
1956 (39) *Landscape and Figures*, for orchestra
1957 (40) *The Angels*, ballet
1958 (41) *Moonflowers*, opera
1959 (42) *Paralyzed Princess*, operetta
1961 (44) Brass Quintet
1962 (45) String Quartet No. 5
1963 (46) *Musica Pacifica*
1966 (49) *Robert Flaherty*, a symphonic portrait
1967 (50) *Sections*, for piano and orchestra
1968 (51) *Food of Love*, overture
           Nocturne "Prague-1968", for mixed media
1971 (54) *I Think of All Soft Limbs*, for mixed media
1973 (56) *Astronaut One*, for mixed media

ARNOLD, Malcolm/b.1921/Great Britain

1943 (22) *Beckus the Dandipratt*, overture
Larch Trees, symphonic poem
1944 (23) Horn Concerto
Variations on a Ukrainian Folksong, for piano
1946 (25) Symphony for strings
1947 (26) Violin Sonata No. 1
Viola Sonata
Children's Suite, for piano
1948 (27) *The Smoke*, overture
Festival Overture
Symphonic Suite
Sonatina for flute and piano
1949 (28) Clarinet Concerto
1950 (29) Symphony No. 1
Serenade for small orchestra
Eight English Dances
String Quartet No. 1
1951 (30) *Sussex*, overture
Concerto for piano duet and strings
Sonatina in three movements for clarinet and piano
Sonatina in three movements for oboe and piano
1952 (31) *Curtain Up*
Three Shanties for wind quintet
1953 (32) Symphony No. 2
Oboe Concerto
Homage to the Queen, ballet
Violin Sonata No. 2
Sonatina for recorder and piano
1954 (33) Harmonica Concerto
Concerto for organ and orchestra
Concerto for flute and strings
Sinfonietta No. 1, for two oboes, two horns and strings
"The Tempest", incidental music
1955 (34) *Tam O'Shanter*, overture
Little Suite for Orchestra, No. 1
John Clare Cantata, for voices and piano duet
Serenade for guitar and strings
1956 (35) *The Dancing Master*, opera
The Open Window, opera
Solitaire, ballet suite
A Grand Overture, for orchestra
1957 (36) *Toy Symphony*
Four Scottish Dances, for orchestra
Symphony No. 3
1958 (37) Sinfonietta No. 2, for flutes, horns and strings
1959 (38) Guitar Concerto
Oboe Quartet
"Five Songs of William Blake", for voice and strings
1960 (39) Symphony No. 4
Rinaldo and Armida, ballet
Song of Simeon, nativity play, with chorus, brass, harp,

		percussion, celesta and strings
1961	(40)	Symphony No. 5
		Divertimento No. 2, for full orchestra
1962	(41)	Concerto for two violins and strings
1963	(42)	Little Suite for Orchestra, No. 2
1964	(43)	Sinfonietta No. 3, for strings and wind
		Water Music
1965	(44)	Fantasy, for bassoon
		Fantasy, for clarinet
		Fantasy, for horn
		Fantasy, for flute
		Fantasy, for oboe
1967	(46)	Symphony No. 6
		Peterloo, for orchestra
		Trevelyan Suite, for wind band
		Concert Piece, for piano and percussion
1973	(52)	Symphony No. 7

AUBER, Daniel/1782–1871/France

1828	(46)	*Muette de Portici* (also called *Masaniello*), opera
1830	(48)	*Fra Diavolo*, opera
1835	(53)	*The Bronze Horse*, opera (revised 1857)
1837	(55)	*Domino Noir*, opera
1841	(59)	*Les Diamants de la couronne*, opera
1846	(64)	*fp. Manon Lescaut*, opera
1858	(76)	*p.* Piano Trio in D major, Op. 1

AUBERT, Louis/1877–1969/France

1892	(15)	"Sous bois", song
1894	(17)	"Vielle chanson Espagnole"
1896	(19)	*Rimes tendres*, song cycle
1897	(20)	*Les Noces d'Apollon et d'Urainie*, cantata
1899	(22)	Fantaisie for piano and orchestra
1900	(23)	"Suite Brève", for two pianos (orchestrated and revised 1913)
		"Trois esquisses", for piano
		"La Lettre", vocal work
1902	(25)	*La Légende du Sang*
1903	(26)	*La Momie*, ballet
1904	(27)	*Chrysothemis*, ballet
		The Blue Forest, opera (1904–10)
1908	(31)	*Crépuscules d'Automne*, song cycle
1911	(34)	*Nuit Mauresque* (possibly 1907)
1913	(36)	*Sillages*, three pieces for piano
1917	(40)	*Six poèmes Arabes* (possibly 1907)
		Tu es Patrus, for chorus and organ
1919	(42)	*La Habanera*, symphonic poem
1921	(44)	*Dryade*, symphonic poem
1923	(46)	*La nuit ensorcelée*, ballet
1925	(48)	*Capriccio*, for violin and orchestra

1927 (50)   p. *Noel Pastoral*, for piano and orchestra
            p. Violin Sonata in D minor and D major
1930 (53)   *Feuilles d'images*
1937 (60)   *Les fêtes d'été*
1947 (70)   *Offrande*
1948 (71)   *Le Tombeau de Chateaubriande*
1952 (76)   *Cinéma*

BACH, Carl Phillip Emmanuel/1714–1788/Germany

1731 (17)   Trio in B minor
1742 (28)   *Prussian* Sonata
1743 (29)   Clavier Sonata, *Wurtemburgian*
1747 (33)   Sonata in D major
1762 (48)   Harp Sonata in B minor
1770 (56)   *Passion Cantata*
            Solfeggio in C minor
            Duo in E minor
1773 (59)   Fantasia in C minor
1775 (61)   *The Israelites in the Wilderness*, oratorio
1780 (66)   Symphony in F major
1787 (73)   *The Resurrection and Ascension of Jesus*, oratorio
1788 (74)   Concerto in E♭, for harpsichord, fortepiano and strings
            Quartet in G major
C.P.E. Bach's works include 210 solo clavier pieces, 52 concertos with
orchestral accompaniment, 22 passions, many cantatas, sonatas for
violin and piano, and trios.

BACH, Johann Christian/1735–1782/Germany

1761 (26)   *fp. Artaserse*, opera
            fp. Catone in Utica, opera
1762 (27)   *fp. Allessandro nell'Indie*, opera
1763 (28)   *Orione*, opera
            Zanaida, opera
1765 (30)   *Adriano in Siria*, opera
1767 (32)   *Carattaco*, opera
1770 (35)   *Gioas, re di Giuda*, oratorio
1772 (37)   *Endimione*, cantata
            Temisocle, opera
1776 (41)   *Lucio Silla*, opera
1779 (44)   *Amadis des Gaules*, opera
J.C. Bach also composed symphonies, opera overtures, concertos,
sextets, quintets, quartets, trios, piano and violin sonatas, violin duets,
piano sonatas, military marches, etc.

BACH, Johann Sebastian/1685–1750/Thuringia (Germany)

1700–08 (15–23) Five Fantasies in Bm: C: Cm: G: G for organ
            Fantasy and Fugue in A minor for organ
            Three Fugues in Cm: D: G for organ
            Four Preludes in Am: C: C: G for organ

Four Preludes and Fugues in Am: C: Cm: Em (Short) for
    organ
Toccata and Fugue in E for organ
Variations on Chorales (Partitas) for organ:
    1) "Christ, der du bist der helle Tag"
    2) "O Gott, du frommer Gott"
    3) "Sei gegrüsset, Jesu gütig"
Fantasy in C minor for clavier
Fantasy (on a Rondo) in C minor for clavier
Fughetta in C minor for clavier
Five Fugues in C: Cm: Dm: Dm: Em for clavier
Two Preludes (Fantasies) in Am: Cm for clavier
Four Preludes and Fughettas in Dm: Em: F: G for clavier
Prelude and Fugue in A minor for clavier
Sonata in A minor (one movement) for clavier
Five Toccatas in D: Dm: Em: G: Gm for clavier
*c.*1704 (*c.*19) Sonata in D for clavier
*c.*1705 (*c.*20) *Quodlibet,* for four voices and continuo
1708–17 (23–32) "Alla breve pro organo pleno" in D for organ
Four organ concertos (after Vivaldi and others) in Am:
    C: C: G
Two Fantasies and Fugues in Cm: Gm for organ
Fantasy in C minor for organ
Four Fugues in Bm: Cm: G "Jig": Gm for organ
"Passacaglia" in C minor for organ
"Pastorale" in F for organ
Nine Preludes and Fugues in A: Am (Great): C: Cm
    (Great): D: Fm: G (Great): Gm for organ
Eight Short Preludes and Fugues in C: Dm: Em: F: G:
    Gm: Am: B♭ for organ
Four Toccatas and Fugues in C: Dm (Dorian): Dm: F for
    organ
Three Trios in Cm: Dm: F (Aria) for organ
Fantasy in G minor for clavier
Fantasy (Prelude) in A minor for clavier
Five Fugues in A: A: A (on a theme by Albinoni): Am:
    Bm for clavier
Suite in A minor for clavier
Suite in E♭ for clavier
Suite ("Ouverture") in F for clavier
*c.*1714 (*c.*29) "Canzona" in D minor for organ
1717 (32) Orgelbüchlein, for organ
1717–23 (32–38) Violin Concerto in A minor with strings (& continuo)
Violin Concerto in D with strings (& continuo)
Concerto in D minor for two violins with strings (& continuo)
Fugue in G minor for violin and continuo
Sonata in E minor for violin and continuo
Sonata in G for violin and continuo
Three sonatas for flute and continuo:
    No. 1 in C. No. 2 in E minor. No. 3 in E
Sonata in C for two violins and continuo
Sonata in C minor for flute, violin and continuo (?1717–23)

Sonata in G for flute, violin and continuo
Sonata in G for two flutes and continuo
Three Sonatas for clavier and flute:
No. 1 in B minor. No. 2 in E♭. No. 3 in A minor
Three Sonatas for clavier and viola da gamba:
No. 1 in G. No. 2 in D. No. 3 in G minor
Six Sonatas for clavier and violin:
No. 1 in B minor. No. 2 in A. No. 3 in E. No. 4 in
C minor. No. 5 in F minor. No. 6 in G
Suite in A for clavier and violin
Fantasy and Fugue in A minor for clavier
Twelve Little Preludes, for clavier
Prelude and Fugue in A minor for clavier
Six Preludes for Beginners, for clavier
Suite in D for clavier (possibly not by Bach)
Two Toccatas in Cm: F♯m for clavier

*c.*1720 (*c.*35) Six Sonatas (Partitas) for solo violin:
No. 1 in G minor. No. 2 in A minor. No. 3 in C.
No. 4 in B minor. No. 5 in D minor. No. 6 in E
Six Suites (Sonatas) for solo cello:
No. 1 in G. No. 2 in D minor. No. 3 in C. No. 4 in E♭.
No. 5 in C minor. No. 6 in D

1720 (35) "Clavierbüchlein vor Wilhelm Friedemann Bach"

1720–23 (35–38) Chromatic Fantasy and Fugue, in D minor for
clavier

1721 (36) The "Brandenburg" Concerti:
No. 1 in F for violino piccolo, three oboes, two horns,
bassoon, strings (& continuo)
No. 2 in F for violin, flute, oboe, trumpet, strings
(& continuo)
No. 3 in G for strings (& continuo)
No. 4 in G for violin, two flutes, strings (& continuo)
No. 5 in D for clavier, violin, flute, strings (& continuo)
No. 6 in B♭ for strings (without violins and continuo)

1722 (37) "Clavierbüchlein vor Anna Magdalena Bachin"
Six Suites ("French"), in Dm: Cm: Bm: E♭: G: E for
clavier (*c.*1722)
The Well-Tempered Clavier, Book I

1723 (38) Magnificat in D, for solo voices, chorus, orchestra and
continuo (?1723)
Motet: "Jesu, meine Freunde", for five-part chorus
Passion according to St. John, for soprano, contralto,
tenor and bass soli, chorus, organ and continuo
"Sanctus" in D, for eight-part chorus, orchestra and
organ (*c.*1723)
Five Preludes and Fugues, in Bm (Great): C (Great): Dm:
E♭ (St. Anne): Em (Great or "The Wedge") (1723–39)
Variations on Chorale (Partita) "Vom Himmel hoch da
Komm' ich her" (1723–50)

1725 (40) "Notenbuch vor Anna Magdalena Bachin", for clavier
Five songs from Anna Magdalena Bach's "Notenbuch"
Six Suites ("English"), in A: Am: Gm: F: Em: Dm for clavier

*c.*1726 (*c.*41)   Motet: "Fürchte dich nicht", for eight-part chorus
1727–36 (42–51) Concerto in C for two claviers with strings
　　　　　Concerto in C minor for two claviers with strings
　　　　　(identical to the concerto for two violins in D minor,
　　　　　1717–23)
　　　　　Concerto in C minor for two claviers with strings
1729 (44) Motet: "Der Geist hilft unsrer Schwachheit auf", for
　　　　　eight-part chorus with accompaniment
　　　　　Passion according to St. Matthew, for soprano, contralto,
　　　　　tenor and bass soli, double chorus, double orchestra
　　　　　and continuo
1729–33 (44–48) Six sonatas (trios) in E♭: Cm: Dm: Em: C: G for
　　　　　organ
1729–36 (44–51) Clavier Concerto in A with strings (& continuo)
　　　　　Clavier Concerto in D with strings (& continuo) (identical
　　　　　to violin concerto in E)
　　　　　Clavier Concerto in D minor with strings (& continuo)
　　　　　(probably originally a violin concerto)
　　　　　Clavier Concerto in E with strings (& continuo)
　　　　　Clavier Concerto in F with two flutes, strings (& continuo)
　　　　　(identical to Brandenburg Concerto No. 4 in G)
　　　　　Clavier Concerto in F minor with strings (& continuo)
　　　　　Clavier Concerto in G minor with strings (& continuo)
　　　　　(identical to violin concerto in A minor)
*c.*1730 (*c.*45) Concerto in A minor for clavier, flute and violin with
　　　　　strings
1731 (46) Six Partitas for clavier, in B♭: Cm: Am: D: G: Em
*c.*1733 (*c.*48) Concerto in C for three claviers with strings
　　　　　Concerto in D minor for three claviers with strings
　　　　　Concerto in A minor for four claviers with strings
　　　　　(transcription of Concerto for four violins by Vivaldi)
1733–?38 (48–?53) Mass in B minor for two sopranos, contralto,
　　　　　tenor, bass, chorus, orchestra and continuo
1734 (49) Christmas Oratorio (six cantatas) for solo voices, chorus,
　　　　　orchestra and organ
1735 (50) Concerto in the Italian Style, for clavier, in F
　　　　　Ascension Oratorio (Cantata No. 11 "Lobet Gott in seinen
　　　　　Reichen") (1735–36)
　　　　　Partita (Ouverture) in B minor for clavier
1736 (51) Easter Oratorio for solo voices, chorus, orchestra and organ
*c.*1737–40 (*c.*52–55) Lutheran Masses for solo voices, chorus,
　　　　　orchestra and organ: No. 1 in F: No. 2 in Gm: No. 3
　　　　　in Am: No. 4 in G
*c.*1738 (*c.*53) Fantasy (with unfinished Fugue) in C minor for clavier
1739 (54) Catechism Preludes (Clavierübung, Vol. III):
　　　　　1) Kyrie: Christie: Kyrie
　　　　　2)   do.   ("alio modo")
　　　　　3) Allein Gott in der Höh' sei Ehr'
　　　　　4)   do.
　　　　　5)   do. (fughetta)
　　　　　6) Dies sind die heil'gen zehn Gebot'
　　　　　7)   do. (fughetta)

    8) Wir glauben all' an einem Gott
    9)   do. (fughetta "Giant" fugue)
  10) Vater unser in Himmelreich
  11)   do.
  12) Christ unser Herr zum Jordan kam
  13)   do.
  14) Aus tiefer Not schrei ich zu dir
  15)   do.
  16) Jesus Christ unser Heiland
  17)   do. (fugue)
       Clavier Duets (two-part pieces for one player)

1742 (57) Aria with thirty variations, "Goldberg Variations" for
         double-keyboard harpsichord
1744 (59) *The Well-Tempered Clavier*, Book II
1747 (62) *A Musical Offering*, for flute and violin, with continuo:
         "Ricercare a tre voci"
         "Canon perpetuus super thema regium"
         "Canones diversi 1–5"
         "Fuga canonica in Epidiapente"
         "Ricercare a sei voci"
         Two canons
*c.***1747–50** (*c.*62–65) Schübler's Book, for organ
1748–50 (63–65) *The Art of Fugue*, for unspecified instruments:
         1–14 Contrapunctus I–XIV
         15–18 Four Canons
         19–20 Two Fugues for two keyboards
         21 Unfinished Fugue on three subjects
dates unknown: Overtures (Suites):
         1) in C for woodwind, strings (& continuo)
         2) in B minor for flute, strings (& continuo)
         3) in D for oboes, bassoons, trumpets, timpani, strings
           (& continuo)
         4) in D for oboes, bassoons, trumpets, timpani, strings
           (& continuo)
Bach also composed:
2 psalms:
  "Lobet den Herrn, alle Heiden", for four-part chorus
  "Singet dem Herrn ein neues Lied", for eight-part chorus
Fantasy and Fugue in A minor for clavier, after 1717
Prelude and Fugue in E♭ for clavier, after 1723
198 church cantatas
23 secular cantatas
Shorter keyboard works, including 15 two-part inventions and 15
"symphonies", known today as three-part inventions.

BALAKIREV, Mily/1837–1910/Russia

1852 (15) *Grand Fantaisie on Russian Folksongs*, for piano and
         orchestra
         Septet for flute, clarinet, strings and piano
1854 (17) String Quartet, *Quatour original russe* (1854–55)
*c.***1855** (*c.*18) Piano Concerto No. 1 in F♯ minor

"Three Forgotten Songs"
1855–6 (18) Octet for flute, oboe, horn, strings and piano
1858 (21) Overture on Russian Themes
1858–65 (21–28) Twenty songs
1861 (24) Piano Concerto No. 2 begun; resumed 1909; completed
      by Liadov
1866–98 (29–61) Symphony No. 1 in C major
1867 (30) *Overture on Czech themes*
      Thamar, symphonic poem (1867–82)
1869 (32) *fp. Islamey*, for piano
1884 (47) *Russia*, symphonic poem
1895–96 (58) Ten songs
1903–04 (66) Ten songs
1905 (68) Piano Sonata in B minor
1907–08 (70) Symphony No. 2 in D minor
1910 (73) Suite on pieces by Chopin

BALFE, Michael/1808–1870/Great Britain

1829 (21) *I rivali de se stesso*, opera
1830 (22) *Un avvertimento ai gelosi*, opera
1833 (25) *Enrico IV al Passo della Marna*, opera
1835 (27) *The Siege of Rochelle*, opera
1836 (28) *Maid of Artois*, opera (based on *Manon Lescaut*)
1837 (29) *Catherine Grey*, opera
      Joan of Arc, opera
1838 (30) *Falstaff*, opera
      Diadeste, opera
1841 (33) *Keolanthe*, opera
1843 (35) *The Bohemian Girl*, opera
      Geraldine, opera
1844 (36) *The Castle of Aymon*, opera
      Daughter of St. Mark, opera
1845 (37) *The Enchantress*, opera
1846 (38) *The Bondman*, opera
1847 (39) *Maid of Honour*, opera
1852 (44) *The Devil's in it*, opera
      The Sicilian Bride, opera
1857 (49) *Rose of Castille*, opera
1860 (52) *Bianca*, opera
1861 (53) *The Puritan's Daughter*, opera
1863 (55) *The Armourer of Nantes*, opera
      Blanche de Nevers, opera
1864 (56) *The Sleeping Queen*, opera
1874 (posthumous) *fp. Il Talismano*, opera

BANTOCK, Sir Granville/1868–1946/Great Britain

1892 (24) *Aegypt*, ballet
      Fire Worshippers
1899 (31) String Quartet in C minor
1900 (32) Tone Poem No. 1, *Thalaba the Destroyer*

1901 (33) Tone Poem No. 2, *Dante*
              Tone Poem No. 3, *Fifine at the Fair*
1902 (34) Tone Poem No. 4, *Hudibras*
              Tone Poem No. 5, *Witch of Atlas*
              Tone Poem No. 6, *Lalla Rookh*
              The Time Spirit
1903 (35) Serenade for four horns
1906 (38) *Omar Khayyam*
1915 (47) *Hebridean* Symphony
1918 (50) *Pibroch*, for cello and piano (or harp)
1919 (51) Viola Sonata in F major, *Colleen*
1922 (54) *Song of Songs*
1923 (55) *Pagan* Symphony
1924 (56) *The Seal-woman*, opera
1928 (60) *Pilgrim's Progress*
1937 (69) *King Solomon*
1938 (70) *Aphrodite in Cyprus*, symphonic ode
Bantock also composed a setting of Swinburne's "Atalanta in
Calydon"; "Fantastic Poem" and "Celtic Poem", for cello and piano;
"Hamabdil", for cello and harp (or piano).

BARBER, Samuel/b.1910/U.S.A.

1929 (19) Serenade for string orchestra, or string quartet
1931 (21) *School for Scandal*, overture
              Dover Beach, for voice and string quartet
1932 (22) Cello Sonata
1933 (23) *Music for a Scene from Shelley*
1936 (26) Symphony No. 1, in one movement
              String Quartet No. 1
              Adagio for Strings, arranged from String Quartet No. 1
1937 (27) First Essay for Orchestra
1939 (29) Violin Concerto
1940 (30) *A Stop-watch and an Ordnance Map*, for male chorus and
                  orchestra
1942 (32) Second Essay for Orchestra
1944 (34) Symphony No. 2 (revised 1947)
              Capricorn Concerto, for flute, oboe, trumpet and strings
              Excursions, for piano
1945 (35) Cello Concerto
1946 (36) *Medea: The Cave of the Heart*, ballet
1947 (37) *Knoxville: Summer of 1915*, ballet suite for voice and
                  orchestra
1948 (38) Piano Sonata
              String Quartet No. 2
1953 (43) *Souvenirs*, ballet suite
1954 (44) *Prayers of Kiekegaard*, for soprano, chorus and orchestra
1956 (46) *Summer Music*, for woodwind quintet
1958 (48) *Vanessa*, opera (libretto by Gian-Carlo Menotti, *q.v.*)
1959 (49) *A Hand of Bridge*, opera, for four solo voices and chamber
                  orchestra
1960 (50) *Toccata Festiva*, for organ and orchestra

1961 (51)   *Dies Natali*, choral preludes for Christmas on "Silent
            Night"
1962 (52)   Piano Concerto
            Andromache's Farewell, for soprano and orchestra
1966 (56)   *Antony and Cleopatra*, opera
1969 (59)   *Despite and Still*, song cycle
1971 (61)   *The Lovers*, for baritone, chorus and orchestra
1973 (63)   *fp*. String Quartet

BARTÓK, Béla/1881–1945/Hungary

1902 (21)   Scherzo for orchestra
1903 (22)   *Kossuth*, tone poem
            Violin Sonata
1904 (23)   *Rhapsody*, for piano and orchestra
            Burlesca
            Piano Quintet
1905 (24)   Suite No. 1
            Suite No. 2 (1905–07, revised 1943)
1907 (26)   Hungarian Folksongs, for piano
1908 (27)   *Portraits*, for orchestra (1907–08)
            Violin Concerto No. 1
            String Quartet No. 1 in A minor
1909 (28)   *For Children*, for piano
1910 (29)   Four Dirges, for piano
            Deux Images, for orchestra
1911 (30)   *Duke Bluebeard's Castle*, opera
            Allegro Barbaro, for piano
            Three Burlesques, for piano
1912 (31)   Four Pieces for Orchestra
1914 (33)   Fifteen Hungarian Peasant Songs (1914–17)
            The Wooden Prince, ballet (1914–16)
1915 (34)   Roumanian Folk Dances, for piano
            Twenty Roumanian Christmas Songs
            String Quartet No. 2 in A minor (1915–17)
1916 (35)   Suite for piano
1918–19 (37)   *The Miraculous Mandarin*, ballet
1920 (39)   Eight Improvisations on Peasant Songs
1921 (40)   Violin Sonata No. 1 (Atonal)
1922 (41)   Violin Sonata No. 2
1923 (42)   Dance Suite, for orchestra
1924 (43)   *Five Village Scenes* (Slovak folk songs), for female voices
            and piano
1926 (45)   Piano Concerto No. 1
            Cantata Profana, for tenor and baritone soli, mixed chorus
            and orchestra
            Piano Sonata
            Nine Little Pieces, for piano
            Out of Doors, suite
            Three Village Scenes, for chorus and orchestra
            Mikrokosmos, Books I–VI, 150 small pieces for piano,
            arranged in order of technical difficulty (1926–37)

1927 (46) String Quartet No. 3
1928 (47) *Rhapsody No. 1 and No. 2*, for violin and orchestra
           Rhapsody No. 1, for cello and piano
           String Quartet No. 4
1930–31 (49) Piano Concerto No. 2
1931 (50) Forty-four Duos for two violins
1934 (53) String Quartet No. 5
1936 (55) *Music for Strings, Percussion and Celesta*
           Petite Suite, for piano
1938 (57) Violin Concerto No. 2
           Sonata for two pianos and percussion
           Contrasts, trio for clarinet, violin and piano, the violinist
                using two instruments, one of normal tuning, the
                other tuned: G♯, D, A, E♭
1939 (58) Divertimento for strings
           String Quartet No. 6
1941 (60) Concerto for two pianos and percussion (also orchestra)
1943 (62) *Concerto for Orchestra*
1944 (63) Sonata for unaccompanied violin
1945 (64) Piano Concerto No. 3
           Viola Concerto

BAX, Sir Arnold/1883–1953/Great Britain

1906 (23) Piano Trio in E major, in one movement
1907 (24) *Fatherland*, for two sopranos, chorus and orchestra
1908 (25) *Lyrical Interlude*, for string quartet
1909 (26) Christmas Carol
           Enchanted Summer, for tenor, chorus and orchestra
1910 (27) *In the Faery Hills*, symphonic poem
           Violin Sonata No. 1 (1910–15)
1912 (29) *Christmas Eve on the Mountains*, for orchestra
           Nympholept, for orchestra
1913 (30) Scherzo for orchestra
1914–15 (31) Piano Quintet in G minor
1915 (32) *Légende*, for violin and piano
           Violin Sonata No. 2
           The Maiden with the Daffodils, for piano
           Winter Waters, for piano
1916 (33) *Ballade*, for violin and piano
           Dream in Exile, for piano
           Elegy, trio for flute, viola and harp
1917 (34) Symphonic Variations for piano and orchestra
           Tintagel, symphonic poem
           November Woods, symphonic poem
           An Irish Elegy, for English horn, harp and strings
           Moy Well (An Irish Tone Poem), for two pianos
           Between Dusk and Dawn, ballet
1918 (35) String Quartet No. 1 in G major
           Folk Tale, for cello and piano
1919 (36) Piano Sonata No. 1 in F♯ minor
           Piano Sonata No. 2 in G major

Harp Quintet in F minor
What the Minstrel Told Us, for piano
1920 (37) *The Truth About Russian Dancers*, ballet
The Garden of Fand, symphonic poem
Summer Music, for orchestra
Phantasy, for viola and orchestra
Four pieces for piano: "Country Tune", "Hill Tune",
    "Lullaby" and "Mediterranean"
1921 (38) Mater Ora Filium, for unaccompanied chorus
Of a Rose I Sing, for small chorus, harp, cello and bass
Viola Sonata
Symphony No. 1 in E♭ major and minor (1921–22)
1922 (39) *The Happy Forest*, symphonic poem
1923 (40) *Romantic Overture*, for small orchestra
Saga Fragment, for piano, strings, trumpet and cymbals
Piano Quartet
Oboe Quintet in G
Cello Sonata in E minor
1924 (41) *Cortège*, for orchestra
Symphony No. 2 in E minor and C major (1924–25)
String Quartet No. 2 in E minor (1924–25)
1927 (44) Violin Sonata No. 3 in G minor
1928 (45) Sonata for viola and harp
Sonata for two pianos
Symphony No. 3 in C major (1928–29)
1929 (46) *Legend*, for viola and piano
Overture, Elegy and Rondo, for orchestra
1930 (47) Symphony No. 4 in E♭ (1930–31)
Winter Legends, for piano and orchestra
Overture to a Picaresque Comedy, for orchestra
1931 (48) *The Tale the Pine Trees Knew*, symphonic poem
Nonet for flute, oboe, clarinet, harp and strings
String Quintet in one movement
Symphony No. 5 in C♯ minor (1931–32)
1932 (49) *A Northern Ballad*, for orchestra (1932–33)
Sinfonietta
Cello Concerto in G minor
Piano Sonata No. 4 in G major
1933 (50) Sonatina in D, for cello and piano
1934 (51) Symphony No. 6 in C major
Concerto for flute, oboe, harp and string quartet
Octet for horn, strings and piano
Clarinet Sonata in D major
1935 (52) *The Morning Watch*, for chorus and orchestra
Overture to Adventure, for orchestra
1936 (53) Concerto for bassoon (or viola), harp and string sextet
String Quartet No. 3 in F major
1937 (54) Violin Concerto
A London Pageant, for orchestra
Northern Ballad No. 2, for orchestra
1939 (56) Symphony No. 7 in A♭
1943 (60) *Work in Progress*, overture

1944 (61) *Legend*, for orchestra
1945 (62) *Legend-Sonata*, for cello and piano in F♯ minor
1946 (63) Te Deum, for chorus and organ
⠀⠀⠀⠀⠀⠀⠀Gloria, for chorus and organ
1947 (64) *Epitholamium*, for chorus and organ
⠀⠀⠀⠀⠀⠀⠀Two Fanfares for the wedding of Princess Elizabeth and
⠀⠀⠀⠀⠀⠀⠀⠀⠀Prince Philip
⠀⠀⠀⠀⠀⠀⠀*Morning Song*, for piano and small orchestra
1950 (67) Concertante for orchestra with piano (left hand), written
⠀⠀⠀⠀⠀⠀⠀⠀⠀for Harriet Cohen
1953 (70) Coronation March

BEDFORD, David/b.1937/Great Britain

1963 (26) *Two Poems*, for chorus
⠀⠀⠀⠀⠀⠀⠀*Piece for Mo*, for percussion, vibraphone, accordion, three
⠀⠀⠀⠀⠀⠀⠀⠀⠀violins, cello and double bass
1964–65 (27) *A Dream of the Seven Lost Stars*, for mixed chorus and
⠀⠀⠀⠀⠀⠀⠀⠀⠀chamber ensemble
1965 (28) *This One for You*, for orchestra
⠀⠀⠀⠀⠀⠀⠀*Music for Albion Moonlight*, for soprano and instruments
⠀⠀⠀⠀⠀⠀⠀"O Now the Drenched Land Awakes", for baritone and
⠀⠀⠀⠀⠀⠀⠀⠀⠀piano duet
1966 (29) *That White and Radiant Legend*, for soprano, speaker and
⠀⠀⠀⠀⠀⠀⠀⠀⠀instruments
⠀⠀⠀⠀⠀⠀⠀*Piano Piece I*
1967 (30) *Five*, for two violins, viola and two cellos
⠀⠀⠀⠀⠀⠀⠀*Trona for 12*, for instrumental ensemble
⠀⠀⠀⠀⠀⠀⠀*18 Bricks Left on April 21st*, for two electric guitars
1968 (31) *Gastrula*, for orchestra
⠀⠀⠀⠀⠀⠀⠀*Pentomino*, for wind quintet
⠀⠀⠀⠀⠀⠀⠀*Piano Piece II*
⠀⠀⠀⠀⠀⠀⠀"Come In Here Child", for soprano and amplified piano
1969 (32) *The Tentacles of the Dark Nebula*, for tenor and instruments
1970 (33) *The Garden of Love*, for instrumental ensemble
⠀⠀⠀⠀⠀⠀⠀*The Sword of Orion*, for instrumental ensemble
1971 (34) *Star Clusters, Nebulae and Places in Devon*, for mixed
⠀⠀⠀⠀⠀⠀⠀⠀⠀double chorus and brass
⠀⠀⠀⠀⠀⠀⠀*Nurse's Song with Elephants*, for ten acoustic guitars and
⠀⠀⠀⠀⠀⠀⠀⠀⠀singer
⠀⠀⠀⠀⠀⠀⠀*With 100 Kazoos*, for instrumental ensemble and one
⠀⠀⠀⠀⠀⠀⠀⠀⠀hundred kazoos played by the public
⠀⠀⠀⠀⠀⠀⠀"Some Stars Above Magnitude 2.9", for soprano and
⠀⠀⠀⠀⠀⠀⠀⠀⠀piano
1972 (35) *Holy Thursday with Squeakers*, for soprano and
⠀⠀⠀⠀⠀⠀⠀⠀⠀instruments
⠀⠀⠀⠀⠀⠀⠀*When I Heard the Learned Astronomer*, for tenor and
⠀⠀⠀⠀⠀⠀⠀⠀⠀instruments
⠀⠀⠀⠀⠀⠀⠀*An Easy Decision*, for soprano and piano
⠀⠀⠀⠀⠀⠀⠀*Spillihpnerak*, for viola
1973 (36) *A Horse, His Name Was Hunry Fencewaver Walkins*, for
⠀⠀⠀⠀⠀⠀⠀⠀⠀instruments

Jack of Shadows, for solo viola and instruments
Pancakes, with Butter, Maple Syrup and Bacon and the T.V. Weatherman, for wind quintet
Variations on a Rhythm by Mike Oldfield, for percussion (three players, eighty-four instruments and conductor)

1974 (37) *Star's End*, for rock instruments and orchestra
Twelve Hours of Sunset, for mixed choir and orchestra
The Golden Wine is Drunk, for sixteen solo voices
Because He Liked to be at Home, for tenor (doubling recorder) and harp

BEETHOVEN, Ludwig van/1770–1827/Germany

1780 (10) Nine variations on a March by Dressler, in C minor for piano, Op. 176
1781 (11) "Schilderung eines Mädchen", song, Op. 229
1782–1802 (12–32) Seven Bagatelles for piano, in E♭: C: F: A: C: D: A♭, Op. 33
1783 (13) Menuet in E♭ for piano, Op. 165
p. Three piano sonatas, in E♭: Fm: D, Op. 161 (composed very early)
1784 (14) *p.* "An einem Säugling", song, Op. 230
p. Rondo, allegretto in A major, for piano, Op. 164
1785 (15) Piano Quartets No. 1–3 in E♭: D: C, Op. 152
Piano Trio No. 9 in E♭, Op. 153
Prelude in F minor, for piano, Op. 166
1786 (16) Trio in G major, for piano, flute and bassoon, Op. 259
1789 (19) Two preludes through all twelve major keys, for piano or organ, Op. 39
1790 (20) "Musik zu einem Ritterballet", Op. 149
Twenty-four variations on Righini's air "Venni amore", for piano, Op. 177
Cantata on the death of Emperor Joseph II, Op. 196a
Cantata on the ascension of Leopold II "Er schlummert", Op. 196b
1791 (21) Thirteen variations on Dittersdorf's air "Es war einmal", Op. 178
1792 (22) Allegro and menuetto in G major, for two flutes, Op. 258
1793 (23) *p.* Twelve variations in F major on "Se vuol ballare", for violin and piano, Op. 156
1794 (24) Trio for two oboes and English horn, Op. 87
Rondo allegro in G major, for violin and piano, Op. 155
p. Variations in G major on a theme by Count von Waldenstein, for piano (four hands), Op. 159
1795 (25) *p.* Three piano trios, in E♭: G: Cm, Op. 1
Piano Concerto No. 2 in B♭, Op. 19
"Adelaide", song, Op. 46
p. Twelve Deutsche Tänze, Op. 140
Six minuets for piano, Op. 167
Six allemandes for violin and piano, Op. 171
p. Nine variations on Paisello's air "Quant è più bello", Op. 179

Twelve variations on minuet from ballet "Le nozze disturbate", Op. 181

"Der Freie Mann", song, Op. 233

"Die Flamme lodert", opferlied, Op. 234

"Seufer eines Ungeliebten" and "Gegenliebe", songs, Op. 254

1796 (26) Twelve variations on a Russian Dance from Wianizky's "Waldmachen", Op. 182

"Ah, perfido", scena and aria for soprano and orchestra, Op. 65

p. Six variations on Paisello's duet "Nel cor più", for piano, Op. 180

"Farewell to Vienna's citizens", song, Op. 231

1797 (27) *p.* Piano Sonatas No. 1–3 in Fm: A: C, Op. 2

p. String Trio in E♭, Op. 3

p. String Quintet in E♮, Op. 4

p. Cello Sonatas No. 1 and 2, Op. 5

p. Sonata in D, for piano (four hands), Op. 6

p. Piano Sonata No. 4 in E♮, Op. 7

p. Serenade in D for string trio, Op. 8

Quintet for piano, oboe, clarinet, bassoon and horn, Op. 16

p. Rondo for piano, Op. 51

p. Twelve variations in G on "See, the conquering hero comes", for cello and piano, Op. 157

War Song of the Austrians, Op. 232

Symphony in C, *Jena* (authenticity doubtful), Op. 257

1798 (28) *p.* Three string trios, in G: D: Cm, Op. 9

p. Piano Sonatas Nos. 5–7, in Cm: F: D, Op. 10

p. Trio in E♮ for piano, clarinet (or violin) and cello, Op. 11

p. Twelve variations on "Ein Mädchen" for violin and piano, Op. 66

p. Twelve minuets, Op. 139

p. Six easy variations in F on a Swiss air, for piano or harp, Op. 183

p. Eight variations in C on Grétry's air "Une fièvre brûlante", Op. 184

1799 (29) *p.* Violin Sonatas Nos. 1–3, Op. 12

p. Piano Sonata No. 8 in Cm, *Pathétique*, Op. 13

p. Piano Sonatas Nos. 9–10 in E: G, Op. 14

p. Seven Ländler Dances, in D, Op. 168

Ten Variations on Salieri's air "La stessa, la stessissima", Op. 185

p. Seven variations on Wonter's "Kind, willst du", Op. 186

Eight variations on Sussmayer's Trio "Tandeln und scherzen", Op. 187

"Der Wachtelschlag", song, Op. 237

1800 (30) Sonata for piano and horn (or violin), Op. 17

String Quartets No. 1–6 in F: G: D: Cm: A: B♭, Op. 18

Septet in E♮, for violin, viola, horn, clarinet, bassoon, cello and double-bass, Op. 20

Symphony No. 1 in C

Piano Sonata No. 11 in B♮, Op. 22
Sonata for piano, violin and viola, Op. 23
Mount of Olives, oratorio, Op. 85
Piano Concerto No. 3 in C minor, Op. 37
Air with six variations on "Ich denke dein", Op. 160
Six Very Easy Variations on an original theme, for piano,
   Op. 188

1801 (31) *p.* Piano Concerto No. 1 in C, Op. 15
p. Violin Sonata No. 5 in F, *Spring*, Op. 24
String Quintet in C, Op. 29
fp. The Creatures of Prometheus (Numbers 1–16) ballet,
   Op. 43

1802 (32) *p.* Serenade for flute, violin and viola, Op. 25
p. Piano Sonata No. 12 in A♭, Op. 26
p. Piano Sonata No. 13 in E♭, *Sonata quasi una fantasia*,
   Op. 27
p. Piano Sonata No. 14 in C♯ minor, *Moonlight*, Op. 27
p. Piano Sonata No. 15 in D, *Pastoral*, Op. 28
Violin Sonatas No. 6–8 in A: Cm: G, Op. 30
Six variations in F on an original theme, for piano, Op. 32
Fifteen variations with a fugue on a theme from
   "Prometheus" for piano, Op. 35
Symphony No. 2 in D, Op. 36
Violin Sonata No. 9, *Kreutzer*, Op. 47
Two Easy Sonatas (Nos. 19–20) in Gm: C for piano,
   Op. 49
p. Rondo for piano, Op. 51
Terzetto, *Tremate*, Op. 116
Opferleid, Op. 121b
p. Seven variations on "Bei Mannern" for cello and piano,
   Op. 158
p. Six Ländler Dances in D (No. 4 in D minor), Op. 169
Piano Sonatas No. 16–18 in C: D: E♭, Op. 31 (1802–4)

1803 (33) Romance in G, for violin and orchestra, Op. 40
p. Six songs for soprano, Op. 48
Fidelio, opera (commenced 1803, last revision 1814),
   Op. 72
p. "Das Glück der Freundschaft", song, Op. 88
p. Twelve Kontretänze for orchestra, Op. 141
p. "Zartliche Liebe", song, Op. 235
p. "La Partenza", song, Op. 236
Six songs, Op. 75 (1803–10)

1804 (34) *p.* Fourteen variations in E♭ for piano trio, Op. 44
p. Three Grand Marches, for piano four hands, Op. 45
Piano Sonata No. 21, *Waldstein*, Op. 53
Symphony No. 3, *Eroica*, Op. 55
Triple Concerto in C for piano, violin, cello and
   orchestra, Op. 56
Piano Sonata No. 23 in F minor, *Appassionata*, Op. 57
Andante favori in F, for piano, Op. 170
p. Seven variations on "God save the King", for piano,
   Op. 189

	p. Five variations on "Rule, Britannia" for piano, Op. 190
1805 (35)	*p.* "An die Hoffnung", song, Op. 32
	p. Romance in F for violin and orchestra, Op. 5
	p. Eight songs, Op. 52
	Piano Concerto No. 4 in G, Op. 58
	Symphony No. 5 in C minor, Op. 67
1806 (36)	*p.* Piano Sonata No. 22 in F, Op. 54
	Symphony No. 4 in B♭, Op. 60
	Violin Concerto in D (also same arranged for piano and orchestra), Op. 61
	Thirty-two variations in C minor for piano, Op. 191 (1806–07)
1807 (37)	*Coriolanus*, overture, Op. 62
	Mass in C, Op. 86
	Leonore No. 1 overture, Op. 138
	"In questa tomba oscura", arietta, Op. 239
	String Quartets Nos. 7–9, *Rassumovsky* in F: Em: C, Op. 59
1808 (38)	*p.* "Sehnsucht", songs with piano, Op. 241
1809 (39)	*p.* Symphony No. 6 in F, *Pastoral*, Op. 68
	p. Cello Sonata No. 3 in A, Op. 69
	p. Trios Nos. 4–5, for piano, violin and cello, Op. 70
	Piano Concerto No. 5 in E♭, *Emperor*, Op. 73
	String Quartet No. 10 in E♭, *Harp*, Op. 74
	Military March in F, Op. 145
	p. "Als die Geleibt sich trennan wollt", song, Op. 238
	"Als mir hoch", song, Op. 242
	"Turteltaube", song, Op. 255
1810 (40)	*p.* Wind Sextet, Op. 71 (early work)
	p. Six variations in D for piano, Op. 76
	p. Fantasy in G minor for piano, Op. 77
	p. Piano Sonata No. 24 in F♯, Op. 78
	p. Piano Sonata No. 25 in G, Op. 79
	p. Sextet in E♭ for two violins, viola, cello and two horns, Op. 81b
	p. Three songs for soprano and piano, Op. 83
	Egmont, incidental music, Op. 84
	String Quartet No. 11 in Fm, *Quartett serioso*, Op. 95
	p. "Andenken", song, Op. 240
	p. "Welch ein wunderbares Leben", song, Op. 243
	p. "Der Frühling entbluhet", song, Op. 244
	"Gedenke mein! ich denke dein", song, Op. 256
1811 (41)	*p.* Choral Fantasia in C minor for piano, orchestra and chorus (theme Beethoven's song "Gegenliebe"), Op. 80
	p. Piano Sonata No. 26 in E♭, *Les Adieux*, Op. 81a
	p. Four ariettas and duet, for soprano and tenor with piano, Op. 82
	Piano Trio No. 6 in B♭, *Archduke*, Op. 97
	The Ruins of Athens, overture and eight numbers, Op. 113
	King Stephen, overture and nine numbers, Op. 117
	"O dass ich dir", song, Op. 247
1812 (42)	Symphony No. 7 in A, Op. 92
	Symphony No. 8 in F, Op. 93

Violin Sonata No. 10 in G, Op. 96
Piano Trio No. 10 in B♭, Op. 154

1813 (43) *Wellington's Victory* (or *Battle of Vittoria*), for orchestra,
Op. 91
Triumphal March in C, for orchestra, Op. 143
"Dort auf dem hohen Felsen", song, Op. 248

1814 (44) Polonaise in C, for piano, Op. 89
Piano Sonata No. 27 in E minor, Op. 90
"Merkenstein", duet, Op. 100
Overture in C, *Namensfeier*, Op. 115
Elegiac Song, Op. 118
Der glorreiche Augenblick, cantata, Op. 136
p. "Germania", bass solo, Op. 193
Leonore Prohaska, incidental music, Op. 245
p. Twenty-five Irish songs, Op. 223 (1814–16)
p. Twenty Irish songs, Op. 224 (1814–16)
p. Twelve Irish songs, Op. 225 (1814–16)

1815 (45) Cello Sonatas Nos. 4–5 in C: D, Op. 102
Calm Sea and Prosperous Voyage, for chorus and
orchestra, Op. 112
Three Duos, for clarinet and bassoon, Op. 147
p. "Es ist vollbracht", bass solo, Op. 194
Twelve Songs of varied nationality, Op. 228
"Wo bluht das Blumchen", song, Op. 250
Twenty-five Scotch songs for one and sometimes two
voices and small orchestra, Op. 108 (1815–16)
"Der stille Nacht", song, Op. 246 (1815–16)

1816 (46) "An die Hoffnung", song, Op. 94
"Wenn ich ein Voglein war", song, Op. 249
An die ferne Geliebt, song cycle, Op. 98
p. "Der Mann van Wort", song, Op. 99
Military March in D, Op. 144

1817 (47) *p.* Piano Sonata No. 28 in A, Op. 101
String Quintet in Cm, (arranged from Op. 1, No. 3),
Op. 104
Fugue in D, Op. 137
Song of the Monks, from "William Tell", Op. 197
p. Twenty-six Welch Songs, Op. 226
"Nord oder Sud", song, Op. 251
"Lisch aus, mein Licht", song, Op. 252
Symphony No. 9, *Choral*, Op. 125 (1817–23)

1818 (48) *Missa Solemnis* in D, Op. 123
"Ziemlich Lebhaft" in B♭ for piano, Op. 172
Six very easy themes varied, for piano, flute or violin,
Op. 105 (1818–19)
Piano Sonata No. 29 in B♭, *Hammerklavier*, Op. 106
(1818–19)
Ten National Themes with Variations, for flute or violin
and piano, Op. 107 (1818–20)

1820 (50) Piano Sonata No. 30 in E, Op. 109
Allegro con brio in C, for violin and orchestra, Op. 148
"Wenn die Sonne nieder sinket", song, Op. 253

1821 (51) Piano Sonata No. 31 in A♭, Op. 110
           p. Bagatelles for piano, Op. 119
1822 (52) *Consecration of the House,* overture, Op. 124
           "The Kiss", arietta, Op. 128
           "Bundeslied", Op. 122 (1822–23)
1823 (53) Piano Sonata No. 32 in C minor, Op. 111
           Bagatelles for piano, Op. 126
           p. Bagatelles for piano, Op. 119
           Variations on a Waltz by Diabelli, Op. 120
           "Minuet of Congratulations", Op. 142
           Cantata in E♭, Op. 199
1824 (54) *p. The Ruins of Athens,* march and chorus, Op. 114
           p. Variations on "Ich bin der Schneider Kakadu",
              Op. 121a
           String Quartet No. 12 in E♭, Op. 127
1825 (55) Great Fugue in E♭ for violins, viola and cello, Op. 133
           Rondo a capriccio in G, for piano, Op. 129 (1825–26)
           String Quartet No. 13 in B♭, *Scherzoso,* Op. 130
1826 (56) String Quartet No. 14 in C♯ minor, Op. 131
           String Quartet No. 15 in A minor, Op. 132
           String Quartet No. 16 in F, Op. 135
           Andante maestoso in C for piano, Op. 174

Other works:
Op. 38   Trio, arranged from Op. 25
Op. 41   Revision of Op. 25
Op. 42   Notturno in D, arranged from Op. 8
Op. 63   Arrangement of Op. 4 for piano trio
Op. 64   Arrangement of Op. 3 for cello and piano
Op. 134   Great Fugue in B♭ for piano (four hands), arrangement of
           Op. 133
Op. 150   (MS) Sonatina and Adagio in C minor, for mandolin and
           cembalo
Op. 163   Two sonatinas for piano (doubtful authenticity)
Op. 173   *Für Elise* in A minor, for piano
Op. 195   (no details)
Op. 198   "O Hoffnung", chorus (4 bars), *c.*1818
Op. 201   (no details)
Ops. 203–222 Canons and small incidental pieces
Op. 247a Another setting of Op. 247
Published posthumously:
1828 Op. 119 Bagatelles for piano
1829 Op. 151 Rondo in B♭ for piano and orchestra
      Op. 146 Rondino in E♭ (composed very early)
1830 Op. 162 Piano Sonata in C, called "Easy"
1831 Op. 192 Eight variations in E♭ on "Ich habe ein kleines
                Huttchen nur"
1834 Op. 103 Octet in E♭, for two oboes, two clarinets, two horns,
                two bassoons (original of Op. 4)
1836 Op. 175 Ten cadenzas to the piano concertos
1841 Op. 227 Twelve Scottish Songs
1865 Op. 200 Cantata in E♭, "Graf, graf, lieber graf"

BELLINI, Vicenzo/1801–1835/Italy

1825 (24) *Adelson e Salvina*, opera
           Bianca e Fernando, opera
1827 (26) *Il Pirata*, opera
1829 (28) *La Straniera*, opera
           Zaira, opera
1830 (29) *I Capuleti ed i Montecchi*, opera
1831 (30) *La Sonnambula*, opera
           Norma, opera
1833 (32) *Beatrice di Tenda*, opera
1835 (34) *I Puritani*, opera

BENJAMIN, Arthur/1893–1960/Australia

1920 (27) "Three Impressions", for voice and string quartet
1924 (31) *Pastoral Fantasy*, for string quartet
           Sonatina for violin and piano
1925 (32) *Three mystical Songs*, for unaccompanied chorus
1928 (35) *Concerto quasi una fantasia*, for piano and orchestra
1931 (38) *The Devil Take Her*, comic opera
1932 (39) Violin Concerto
1933 (40) *Prima Donna*, comic opera
1935 (42) *Heritage*, for orchestra
           Romantic Fantasy, for violin, viola and orchestra
1937 (44) *Nightingale Lane*, for two voices and piano
           Overture to an Italian Comedy, for orchestra
1938 (45) Two Jamaican Pieces for Orchestra, "Jamaican Song"
               and "Jamaican Rumba"
           Sonatina for cello and piano
           Cotillon Suite of English Dance Tunes, for orchestra
1940 (47) Sonatina for chamber orchestra
1942 (49) Concerto for oboe and strings
1944–45 (51) Symphony No. 1
1945 (52) *From San Domingo*, for orchestra
           Red River Jig, for orchestra
           Elegy, Waltz and Toccata, for viola and orchestra
1946 (53) *Caribbean Dance*, for orchestra
1947 (54) Ballade for strings
1949 (56) *The Tale of Two Cities*, opera (1949–50)
           Valses Caprices, for clarinet (or viola) and piano
1951 (58) *Orlando's Silver Wedding*, ballet

BENNETT, Richard Rodney/b.1936/Great Britain

1954 (18) Piano Sonata
           Sonatina for flute
1957 (21) Five Pieces for orchestra
           String Quartet No. 3
           Violin Sonata
           Sonata for solo violin
           Sonata for solo cello
           "Four Improvisations", for violin

1959 (23) *The Approaches of Sleep*
1960 (24) *Journal*, for orchestra
              Calendar, for chamber ensemble
              Winter Music, for flute and piano (also for orchestra)
1961 (25) *The Ledges*, one-act opera
              Suite Française, for small orchestra
              Oboe Sonata
1962 (26) *London Pastoral Fantasy*, for tenor and chamber orchestra
              Three Elegies, for chorus
              Fantasy for piano
              Sonata No. 2 for solo violin
1964 (28) *The Mines of Sulphur*, opera
              Jazz Calendar, ballet in seven scenes
              Aubade, for orchestra
              String Quartet No. 4
              Nocturnes for piano
1965 (29) Symphony No. 1
              Trio for oboe, flute and clarinet
              Diversions for piano
1966 (30) *Epithalamion*, for voices and orchestra
              Childe Rolande, for voice and piano
1967 (31) *A Penny for a Song*, opera
              Symphony No. 2
              Wind Quintet
              The Music That Her Echo Is, song cycle
1968 (32) Piano Concerto
              All the King's Men, children's opera
              Crazy Jane, for soprano, clarinet, cello and piano
1969 (33) *A Garland for Marjory Fleming*, for soprano and piano
1970 (34) Guitar Concerto
1972 (36) *Commedia* II, for flute, cello and piano
1973 (37) Concerto for Orchestra
              Viola Concerto, for viola and chamber orchestra
              Commedia III, for flute/piccolo, oboe/English horn, bass
                  clarinet, horn, trumpet, two percussion, piano/celesta,
                  violin and cello
              Commedia IV, for two trumpets, horn, trombone and tuba
              Alba, for organ
              Scena I, for piano
              Scena II, for cello
1974 (38) *Spells*, for soprano, chorus and orchestra
              Love Spells, for soprano and orchestra
              Sonnet Sequence, for tenor and strings
              Four-piece Suite, divertimento for two pianos
              Time's Whiter Series, for counter-tenor and lute
1975 (39) Violin Concerto in two movements
              Oboe Quartet

BERG, Alban/1885–1935/Austria

1905–08 (20–23) Seven "Frühe-Lieder" for soprano and piano, or
                    orchestra

1906–08 (21–23) Piano Sonata
1908 (23) *An Leukon*
1909–10 (24) Four Songs for medium voice and piano
1910 (25) String Quartet
1912 (27) Five Orchestra Songs to Picture Postcard Texts by Peter
　　　　　　Altenberg
1913 (28) Four pieces for clarinet and piano
　　　　　　Three orchestral pieces (1913–14)
1917–21 (32–36) *Wozzeck*, opera
1923–25 (38–40) Chamber Concerto, for piano, violin and thirteen
　　　　　　wind instruments
1925–26 (40) *Lyric Suite*, for string quartet
1928–34 (43–49) *Lulu*, opera
1929 (44) Three pieces for orchestra
　　　　　　Der Wein, concert aria for soprano and orchestra
　　　　　　(possibly 1920)
1935 (50) Violin Concerto, "in memory of an angel" (i.e. Manon
　　　　　　Gropius, eighteen-year-old daughter of Mahler's widow
　　　　　　by her second husband)

BERIO, Luciano/b.1925/Italy

1936 (11) Pastorale
1946–47 (21) Four Popular Songs, for female voice and piano
1947 (22) Petite Suite for piano
1949 (24) *Magnificat*, for two sopranos, mixed chorus and instruments
1950 (25) Concertino for solo clarinet, solo violin, harp, celeste and
　　　　　　strings
　　　　　　Opus Number Zoo, for woodwind quintet and narrator
　　　　　　(revised 1970)
1951 (26) Two pieces for violin and piano
1952 (27) *Allez Hop—story for voice, mime and dance*, for mezzo-
　　　　　　soprano, eight mimes, ballet and orchestra
　　　　　　Five variations for piano (1952–53)
1953 (28) *Chamber Music*, for female voice, clarinet, cello and harp
1954 (29) *Nones*, for orchestra
　　　　　　Variations for chamber orchestra
　　　　　　Mutations, electronic music
1956 (31) *Allelujah* I, for orchestra
　　　　　　Allelujah II, for orchestra
　　　　　　String Quartet
　　　　　　Perspectives, electronic music
1957 (32) Divertimento for orchestra (with Bruno Maderna)
　　　　　　Serenata, for flute and fourteen instruments
　　　　　　El Mar la Mar, for soprano, mezzo-soprano and seven
　　　　　　instruments
　　　　　　Momenti, for electronic sound
1958 (33) *Tempi Concertati*, for flute, violin, two pianos and other
　　　　　　instruments (1958–59)
　　　　　　Differences, for five instruments and tape
　　　　　　Sequence I, for flute
　　　　　　Theme (Homage to Joyce), electronic music

1959 (34)   *Quaderni* I, II and III from "Epifanie", for orchestra
(1959–63)
1960 (35)   *Circles,* for female voice, harp and two percussion
1961 (36)   *Visage,* electronic music with voice
1962 (37)   *Passaggio,* messa in scena for soprano, two choirs and
instruments
1963 (38)   *Sequence* II, for harp
Sincronie, for string quartet (1963–64)
1965 (40)   *Laborintus* II, for voices, instruments and tape
Rounds, for cembalo
Sequence III, for solo voice
1966 (41)   *Il cambattimento di Tancredi e Clorinda,* for soprano,
baritone, tenor, three violins and continuo
Sequence IV, for piano
Sequence V, for trombone
1967 (42)   *Rounds,* for piano
Sequence VI, for viola
O King, for voice and five players
1968 (43)   Sinfonia
Questo vuol dire che, for three female voices, small choir
and tape
1969 (44)   *Opera,* opera in four acts
Sequence VII, for oboe
"The Modification and Instrumentation of a Famous
Hornpipe as a Merry and Altogether Sincere Homage
to Uncle Alfred", for five instruments
1970 (45)   *Memory,* for electric piano and electric cembalo
1971 (46)   *Bewegung,* for orchestra
Bewegung II, for baritone and orchestra
Ora, for soprano, mezzo-soprano, flute, English horn,
small chorus and orchestra
Amores, for sixteen vocalists and fourteen instrumentalists
Agnus, for two sopranos and three clarinets
Autre Fois — Berceuse Canonique pour Igor Stravinsky, for
flute, clarinet and harp
1972 (47)   *E Vó — Sicilian Lullaby,* for soprano and instruments
Concerto for two pianos and orchestra (1972–73)
Recital I (for Cathy), for mezzo-soprano and seventeen
instruments
1973 (48)   *Still,* for orchestra
Eindrücke, for orchestra
. . . Points on the Curve to Find . . . , for piano and
twenty-two instruments
Linea, for two pianos, vibraphone and marimbaphone
1974 (49)   *Per la dolce memoria di quel giorno,* ballet
Apres Visage, for orchestra and tape
Chorus, for voices and instruments
Calmo, for soprano and instruments
1975 (50)   *Il Malato Immaginario,* incidental music
La Ritirata Notturna di Madrid, for orchestra
Sequence VIII, for percussion
Sequence IX, for violin

BERKELEY, Sir Lennox/b.1903/Great Britain

1925 (22) "The Thresher", for medium voice and piano
*c.*1933 (*c.*30) Violin Sonata No. 2
1934 (31) Polka, for piano
           Three pieces for two pianos (Polka, Nocturne, Capriccio)
           (1934–38)
1935 (32) *Jonah*, oratorio
           Overture for Orchestra
           String Quartet No. 1
           "How Love Came In", for medium voice and piano
           Étude, Berceuse and Capriccio, for piano
1936 (33) Five short pieces for piano
1937 (34) *Domini est Terra*, for chorus and orchestra
           Mont Juic — Suite of Catalan Dances, for orchestra (with
           Britten *q.v.*)
1938 (35) *The Judgement of Paris*, ballet
           Introductions and Allegro, for two pianos and orchestra
1939 (36) Serenade for string orchestra
           Five songs for solo voice and piano (1939–40)
1940 (37) Symphony No. 1
           Sonatina for recorder (flute) and piano
           Four Concert Studies, Set I, for piano
           Five Housman Songs, for tenor and piano
1942 (39) String Quartet No. 2
           Sonatina for violin and piano
1943 (40) Divertimento for orchestra
           String Trio
1944 (41) "Lord, when the Sense of Thy sweet Grace", for mixed
           choir and organ
1945 (42) Piano Sonata
           Violin Sonata
           Six Preludes for piano
           Festival Anthem for mixed choir and organ
1946 (43) Introduction and Allegro, for solo violin
           Nocturne, for orchestra
           Five Songs (de la Mare) for high voice and piano
1947 (44) Piano Concerto
           Four Poems of St. Teresa of Avila, for contralto and
           strings
           Stabat Mater, for six solo voices and twelve instruments
           "The Lowlands of Holland", for low voice and piano
1948 (45) Concerto for two pianos and orchestra
1949 (46) *Colonus' Praise*, for chorus and orchestra
           Three Mazurkas for piano
           Scherzo for piano
1950 (47) Sinfonietta for orchestra
           Elegy for violin and piano
           Toccata for violin and piano
           Theme and variations for solo violin
1951 (48) *Gibbons Variations*, for tenor, chorus, strings and organ
           Three Greek Songs, for medium voice and piano
1952 (49) Flute Concerto

Four Ronsard Sonnets, Set 1, for two tenors and piano
1953 (50) Suite for orchestra
*c.*1954 (*c.*51) *A Dinner Engagement*, opera in one act
           Nelson, opera in three acts
           Trio for violin, horn and piano
           Sonatina for piano duet
1955 (52) Concerto for flute, violin, cello and harpsichord (or piano)
           Suite from "Nelson", for orchestra
           Sextet for clarinet, horn and string quartet
           Crux fidelis, for tenor and mixed choir
           Salve regina, for unison voices and organ
           Look up sweet Babe, for soprano and mixed choir
           Concert study in E♭ for piano
1956 (53) *Ruth*, opera in three scenes
1957 (54) Sonatina for guitar
           "Sweet was the song", for mixed choir and organ
1958 (55) Concerto for piano and double string orchestra
           Five poems of W.H. Auden, for medium voice and piano
1959 (56) Overture for Light Orchestra
           Sonatina for two pianos
           "So sweet Love seemed", for medium voice and piano
1960 (57) *A Winter's Tale*, suite for orchestra
           Improvisation on a Theme of Falla, for piano
           Prelude and Fugue, for clavichord
           Missa Brevis, for mixed choir and organ
           "Thou hast made me", for mixed choir and organ
1961 (58) Concerto for violin and chamber orchestra
           Five pieces for violin and orchestra
1962 (59) Sonatina for oboe and piano
           Batter my Heart, for soprano, mixed choir, organ and
              chamber orchestra
           "Autumn's Legacy", for high voice and piano
1963 (60) *Four Ronsard Sonnets — Set 2*, for tenor and orchestra
           Justorum Animae, for mixed choir
           "Counting the Beats", for high voice and piano
           "Automne", for medium voice and piano
1964 (61) *Diversions*, for eight instruments
           "Songs of the Half-light", for high voice and guitar
           Mass for five voices
1965 (62) Partita for chamber orchestra
           Three songs for four male voices
1966–68 (63–65) Three pieces for organ
1967 (64) *Castaway*, opera in one act
           Signs in the Dark, for mixed choir and strings
           Oboe Quartet
           Nocturne for harp
1968 (65) "The Windhover", for mixed choir
           Theme and Variations for piano duet
1969 (66) Symphony No. 3
           Windsor Variations, for piano duet
1970 (67) *Dialogues*, for cello and chamber orchestra
           String Quartet No. 3

Theme and variations for guitar
1971 (68) "Palm Court Waltz", for orchestra/piano duet
In Memoriam Igor Stravinsky, for string quartet
"Duo", for cello and piano
Introduction and Allegro, for double-bass and piano
"Chinese Songs", for medium voice and piano
1972 (69) *Four Concert Studies, Set II*, for piano
Three Latin Motets, for five-part choir
"Hymn for Shakespeare's Birthday", for mixed choir and
    organ
1973 (71) Sinfonia Concertante for oboe and orchestra
Antiphon, for string orchestra
Voices of the Night, for orchestra
1974 (72) Suite for strings
Guitar Concerto
Herrick Songs, for high voices and harp
1975 (73) Quintet for piano and wind

BERLIOZ, Hector/1803–1869/France

1827 (24) *Waverley*, overture
Les Francs-Juges, overture
La Mort d'Orphée, cantata
1828 (25) *Herminie*, cantata
1829 (26) *Cléopâtra*, cantata
Huit scènes de Faust, cantata
Irlande, five songs with piano (1829–30)
1830 (27) *Symphonie Fantastique* (revised 1831)
Sardanapale, cantata
1831 (28) *Le Corsaire*, overture (revised 1855)
King Lear, overture
1832 (29) *Le Cinq Mai*, cantata (1830–32)
1834 (31) *Harold in Italy*, for viola and orchestra
Sara la baigneuse, for three choirs, with orchestra
Le Nuits d'été, song cycle for soprano and orchestra
1837 (34) *Grande Messe des Morts*, requiem
1838 (35) *Benvenuto Cellini*, opera (1834–38)
Roméo et Juliette, dramatic symphony for solo voices and
    chorus (1838–39)
1839 (36) *Rêverie and Caprice*, for violin and orchestra
1840 (37) *Symphonie Funèbre et Triomphale*, for chorus, strings and
    military band
1844 (41) *Roman Carnival*, overture (from material from "Benvenuto
    Cellini")
1846 (43) *Damnation of Faust*, dramatic cantata (in which occurs
    Berlioz's arrangement of the Rákóczy March)
1848 (45) *La Mort d'Ophelie*, for two-part female chorus (also for
    voice and piano)
1854 (51) *L'Enfance du Christ*, oratorio (1850–54)
1856–59 (53–56) *The Trojans*, opera (Part II produced 1863; Part I
    produced 1890)
1862 (59) *Béatrice et Bénédict*, opera (1860–62)

BERNSTEIN, Leonard/b.1918/U.S.A.

1941 (23)   Clarinet Sonata (1941–42)
           Symphony No. 1, *Jeremiah* (1941–44)
1942–43 (24)   *Seven Anniversaries*, for piano
1943 (25)   *I Hate Music*, song cycle for soprano
1944 (26)   *Fancy Free*, ballet
           On the Town, dance episodes
1945 (27)   *Hashkivenu*, for cantor, chorus and organ
1946 (28)   *Facsimile*, ballet
1947 (29)   Five Pieces for piano (1947–48)
           Symphony No. 2, *The Age of Anxiety*, for piano and
               orchestra (1947–49)
1948 (30)   *Four Anniversaries*, for piano
1949 (31)   *La Bonne Cuisine*, song cycle
           Two Love Songs
1950 (32)   *Prelude, Fugue and Riffs*, for jazz combo and orchestra
1951 (33)   "Afterthought", song
1952 (34)   *Trouble in Tahiti*, one-act opera
           Wonderful Town
1954 (36)   Serenade for violin, strings and percussion
           Five Anniversaries, for piano
           On the Waterfront, film score
1956 (38)   *Candide*
1957 (39)   *West Side Story*, score for stage musical and film
1960 (42)   *Symphonic Dances* on "West Side Story"
1963 (45)   Symphony No. 3, *Kaddish*
1965 (47)   *Chichester Psalms*, for chorus and orchestra
1971 (53)   *Mass*, a theater piece for singers, players and dancers
1974 (56)   *Dybbuk*, ballet
1975 (57)   Suite No. 1 from "Dybbuk"
           Seven Dances from "Dybbuk"

BERWALD, Franz Adolf/1796–1868/Sweden

1816 (20)   Theme and Variations, for violin and orchestra
1817 (21)   Double Concerto, for two violins and orchestra (now lost)
           Septet, for violin, viola, cello, clarinet, bassoon, horn and
               oboe
1819 (23)   Quartet, for piano, clarinet, bassoon and horn
1820 (24)   Symphony No. 1
           Violin Concerto in C♯ minor
1825 (29)   Serenade, for tenor and six instruments
1827 (31)   *Gustav Wasa*, opera
           Concertstücke, for bassoon and orchestra
1842 (46)   Symphony No. 2, *Sérieuse*
           Symphony No. 3
           (Symphony No. 4 is lost)
1844 (48)   *A Country Wedding*, for organ, four hands
1845 (49)   Symphony No. 5, *Singulière*
           Symphony No. 6
           Five piano trios
1852–54 (56–58)   Three piano trios

1855 (59) Piano Concerto in D major
1856–58 (60–62) Two piano quintets (possibly 1853–54)
1859 (63) *p.* Cello Sonata
1862 (66) *Estrella de Soria*, opera
1887 (posthumous) *p.* String Quartet in E♭ major
1905 (posthumous) *p.* String Quartet in A minor
Berwald also composed Violin Sonata in E♭.

BIRTWHISTLE, Harrison/b.1934/Great Britain

1957 (23) *Refrains and Choruses*, for flute, oboe, clarinet, bassoon
and horn
1959 (25) *Monody for Corpus Christi*, for soprano, flute, horn and
violin
Preçis, for piano
1960 (26) *The World is Discovered*, for instrumental ensemble
1962–63 (28) Chorales for orchestra
1964 (30) Three Movements with Fanfares, for orchestra
Entr'Actes and Sappho Fragments, for soprano and
instruments
Description of the Passing of a Year, narration for mixed
choir a cappella
1965 (31) *Tragoedia*, for instrumental ensemble
Ring a Dumb Carillon, for soprano, clarinet and percussion
Motet: *Carmen Paschale*, for mixed choir and organ
1966 (32) *Verses*, for clarinet and piano
Punch and Judy, opera (1966–67)
1968 (34) *Nomos*, for four amplified wind instruments and orchestra
Linoi, for clarinet and piano
1969 (35) *Down By The Greenwood Side*, dramatic pastoral
Verses for Ensembles, for instrumental ensemble
Ut Heremita Solus, arrangement of instrumental motet
Hoquetus David (Double Hoquet), arrangement of
instrumental motet
Medusa, for instrumental ensemble (1969–70)
Cantata, for soprano and instrumental ensemble
1970 (36) *Prologue*, for tenor and instruments
Nenia on the Death of Orpheus, for soprano and instruments
Four Interludes from a Tragedy, for clarinet and tape
1971 (37) *An Imaginary Landscape*, for orchestra
Meridian, for mezzo-soprano, six-part choir and ensemble
The Fields of Sorrow, for two sopranos, eight-part mixed
choir and instruments
Chronometer, for eight-track electronic tape
1972 (38) *The Triumph of Time*, for orchestra
Tombeau—in memoriam Igor Stravinsky, for flute, clarinet,
harp and string quartet
Dinah and Nick's Love Song, for three soprano saxophones
and harp (or three English horns and harp)
La Plage—Eight Arias of Remembrance, for soprano, three
clarinets, piano and marimba
Epilogue—"Full Fathom Five", for baritone and instruments

1973 (39) *Grimethorpe Aria*, for brass band
           Chanson de Geste, for solo sustaining instrument and tape
           Five Choral Preludes arranged from Bach, for soprano
               and instrumental ensemble
1974 (40) *Chorales from a Toyshop*, in five parts with variable
               orchestration

BIZET, Georges/1838—1875/France

1854 (16) *La Prêtresse*, one-act opera
1855 (17) Symphony in C (was not performed until 1935)
1857 (19) *Le Docteur Miracle*, operetta
           Clovis et Clothilde, cantata
1859 (21) *Don Procopio*, opera
1863 (25) *The Pearl Fishers*, opera
1865 (27) *Chasse Fantastique*, for piano
           Ivan the Terrible, opera (withdrawn, thought lost,
               recovered 1944, produced 1946 in Würtemburg)
1866 (28) Trois esquisses musicales, for piano or harmonium
1867 (29) *The Fair Maid of Perth*, opera
1868 (30) Symphony in C, *Roma*
           Marche Funèbre, for orchestra
           Variations Chromatiques, for piano
           Marine, for piano
1869 (31) *Vasco da Gama*, symphonic ode with chorus
1871 (33) Petite Suite d'Orchestre
           Jeux d'enfants, twelve pieces for piano duet (later five were
               made into an orchestral suite)
1872 (34) *L'Arlésienne*, incidental music
           Djarmileh, opera
1873 (35) *Patrie*, overture
1875 (37) *fp. Carmen*, opera

BLISS, Sir Arthur/1891—1975/Great Britain

*c.*1915 (*c.*24) Piano Quartet in A minor
           String Quartet in A major
1916 (25) Two pieces for clarinet and piano
1918 (27) *Madam Noy*, for soprano, flute, clarinet, bassoon, harp,
               viola and double-bass
1919 (28) *As You Like It*, incidental music for two solo violins,
               viola, cello and singers
           Rhapsody, (wordless) for mezzo-soprano, tenor, flute,
               English horn, string quartet and double-bass
           Piano Quintet (unpublished, MS lost)
1920 (29) *Rout*, for soprano and chamber orchestra (revised version
               for full orchestra written at the invitation of
               Diaghilev, *fp.* 1921)
           Conversations, for chamber orchestra
           Two Studies for orchestra
           Concerto for piano and tenor voice, strings and percussion
               (revised 1923; revised as Concerto for two pianos and

orchestra, 1924)
1920–21 (29) *The Tempest*, overture and interludes
1921 (30) *Mêlée Fantasque*, for orchestra (revised 1965)
  A Colour Symphony (1921–22, revised 1932). Movements are headed Purple, Red, Blue and Green, and are interpreted in the light of their heraldic associations
1923 (32) *Ballads of the Four Seasons* (Li-Po), for medium voice and piano
  String Quartet (1923–24) (MS lost)
  The Women of Yueh (Li-Po), song cycle for voice and chamber ensemble
1924 (33) *Masks I–IV*, for piano
1926 (35) Introduction and Allegro for orchestra, revised 1937
  Hymn to Apollo, for orchestra, revised 1965
1927 (36) Four Songs, for high voice and violin
  Oboe Quintet
1928 (37) *Pastoral: Lie Strewn the White Flocks*, for mezzo-soprano, chorus, flute, drums and string orchestra
1929 (38) *Serenade*, for baritone and orchestra
1930 (39) *Morning Heroes*, symphony for orator, chorus and orchestra
  Fanfares for Heroes, for three trumpets, three trombones, timpani and cymbals
1931 (40) Clarinet Quintet
1933 (42) Viola Sonata
1934–35 (43) *Things to Come*, suite for orchestra from music for the film
1935 (44) Music for Strings
1936 (45) *Kenilworth Suite*, for brass
1937 (46) *Checkmate*, ballet
1938 (47) Piano Concerto
1940 (49) *Seven American Poems*, for low voice and piano
1941 (50) String Quartet in B♭ major
1943 (52) Three Jubilant and Three Solemn Fanfares, for three trumpets, three trombones and tuba, or full military band
1944 (53) *Miracle in the Gorbals*, ballet
  The Phoenix "Homage to France—August 1944", orchestral march
  "Auvergnat" for high voice and piano
1945 (54) *Baraza*, concert piece for piano and orchestra with men's voices ad lib
1946 (55) *Adam Zero*, ballet
1948–49 (57) *The Olympians*, opera
1950 (59) String Quartet No. 2
1952 (61) *The Enchantress*, scena for contralto and orchestra
  Piano Sonata
1953 (62) Processional, for full orchestra and organ (composed for performance in Westminster Abbey at the Coronation of Her Majesty Queen Elizabeth II)
1954 (63) *A Song of Welcome*, for soprano, baritone, chorus and orchestra

1955 (64) Violin Concerto
           Meditations on a Theme of John Blow, for orchestra
           Elegiac Sonnet, for tenor, string quartet and piano
1956 (65) *Edinburgh Overture*, for full orchestra
1957 (66) *Discourse*, for orchestra (recomposed 1965)
1958 (67) *The Lady of Shalott*, ballet
1960 (69) *Tobias and the Angel*, opera in two acts
1962 (71) *The Beatitudes*, cantata for soprano, tenor, chorus,
              orchestra and organ
1963 (72) *Mary of Magdala*, cantata for contralto, bass, chorus and
              orchestra
           Belmont Variations, for brass band
           A Knot of Riddles, for baritone and eleven instruments
1964 (73) *Homage to a Great Man (Winston Churchill)*, march for
              orchestra
           The Golden Cantata, for tenor, mixed chorus and orchestra
1966 (75) Fanfare Prelude, for orchestra
1967 (76) *River Music*, for unaccompanied choir
1969 (78) *The World is Charged with the Grandeur of God*, for chorus
              and wind instruments
           Angels of the Mind, song cycle for soprano and piano
           Miniature Scherzo for piano
1970 (79) Cello Concerto
1971 (80) Two Ballads, for women's chorus and small orchestra
           Triptych, for piano
1972 (81) Three Songs for voice and piano
           Metamorphic Variations, for orchestra
1974 (83) *Prelude "Lancaster"*, for orchestra
1975 (84) *Shield of Faith*, cantata for soprano, baritone, chorus and
              organ

BLOCH, Ernest/1880–1959/Switzerland

1900–29 (20–49) *Helvetia*, a symphonic fresco for orchestra
1901–02 (21) Symphony in C♯ minor
1904–05 (24) *Hiver*, symphonic poem
              Printemps, symphonic poem
1906 (26) *Poèmes d'Automne*, for voice and orchestra
1910 (30) *fp. Macbeth*, opera (written possibly 1903–9)
1912 (32) Prelude and Two Psalms, for high voice (1912–14)
           Israel Symphony, with two sopranos, two altos and bass
              (1912–16)
1913 (33) *Trois Poèmes Juifs*, for orchestra
1915–16 (35) *Schelomo—Hebrew Rhapsody*, for cello and orchestra
1916 (36) String Quartet No. 1 in B minor
1918–19 (38) Suite for viola
           Suite for viola and piano
1920 (40) Violin Sonata No. 1
1921–23 (41–43) Piano Quintet
1922 (42) *In the Night*, for piano
           Poems of the Sea, for piano (1922–24)
1923 (43) *Baal Shem*, for violin and piano

Melody, for violin and piano
Enfantines, for piano
Five Sketches in Sepia, for piano
Nirvana, for piano

1924 (44) Concerto Grosso for strings with piano obbligato
(1924–25)
In the Mountains (Haute Savoie), for string quartet
Night, for string quartet
Three Landscapes, for string quartet
Three Nocturnes for piano trio
Violin Sonata No. 2, *Poème mystique*
Exotic Night, for violin and piano
From Jewish Life, for cello and piano
Méditation Hébraïque, for cello and piano

1925 (45) *Prélude (Recuillement)*, for string quartet
1926 (46) *America: an Epic Rhapsody*, for orchestra
Four Episodes, for chamber orchestra
1929 (49) *Abodah*, for violin and piano
1933 (53) *Avodath Hakodesh*, sacred service, for baritone, chorus and
orchestra
1934–36 (54–56) *A Voice in the Wilderness*, symphonic poem for
cello and orchestra
1935 (55) Piano Sonata
1937 (57) *Evocations*, symphonic suite
Violin Concerto (1937–38)
1938 (58) Piece for string quartet
1944 (64) Suite Symphonique
1945 (65) String Quartet No. 2
1946–48 (66–68) *Concerto Symphonique*, for piano
1949 (69) *Scherzo fantasque*, for piano
1950 (70) Concertino for viola, flute and strings
Piece for string quartet
1951 (71) *Cinq pièces Hébraïque*, for viola and piano
String Quartet No. 3 (1951–52)
1952 (72) Sinfonia Brève
Concerto Grosso for string quartet and string orchestra

BLOW, John/1649–1708/Great Britain

*c.*1684 (*c.*35) *Venus and Adonis*, a masque
Ode for St. Cecilia's Day — "Begin the Song"
1697 (48) "My God, my God, look upon me", anthem
1700 (51) *Amphion Anglicus*, collection of songs and vocal chamber
music
Blow also composed many harpsichord pieces, odes for state occasions,
secular songs and catches, 110 anthems, 13 services, etc.

BOCCHERINI, Luigi/1743–1806/Italy

1765 (22) *La Confederazione*, opera
1786 (43) *La Clementina*, opera
1801 (58) Stabat Mater

Boccherini also composed:
4 cello concerti
20 symphonies, including 8 concertantes
21 sonatas for piano and violin
6 sonatas for violin and bass
6 sonatas for cello and bass
6 duets for two violins
48 trios for two violins and cello
12 trios for violin, viola and cello
18 quintets for flute or oboe, violins, viola and cello
12 quintets for piano, two violins, viola and cello
112 quintets for two violins, viola and two cellos
12 quintets for two violins, two violas and cello
16 sextets for various instruments
2 octets for various instruments
Vocal works, totaling 467 in all, including a Mass for four voices and
    instruments; a Christmas cantata; and 14 concert arias and duets
    with orchestra
1 suite for full orchestra
102 string quartets

BOËLLMANN, Léon/1862–1897/France

1877 (15) Piano Quartet
Boëllmann wrote many works for organ, including:
Fantaisée dialogue, for organ and orchestra
Gothic Suite for organ
Fantasia in A major, for organ
Heures mystiques, for organ
Boëllmann also composed:
Symphony in F major
Symphonic Variations, for cello and orchestra
Piano Trio
Cello Sonata

BOÏELDIEU, François/1775–1834/France

1793 (18) *La Fille coupable*, opera
1795 (20) Harp Concerto in G major
1800 (25) *Calife de Bagdad*, opera
1803 (28) *Ma Tante Aurore*, opera
1812 (37) *Jean de Paris*, opera
1825 (50) *La Dame blanche*, opera

BORODIN, Alexander/1833–1887/Russia

1847 (14) Concerto for Flute in D major and minor, with piano
1862–67 (29–34) Symphony No. 1 in E♭ major
1867 (34) *The Bagotirs*, opera-farce
1869–76 (36–43) Symphony No. 2 in B minor
1869–87 (36–54) *Prince Igor*, opera (left unfinished and completed
        by Rimsky-Korsakov and Glazunov, *q.v.*)

1875–79 (42–46) String Quartet No. 1 in A major
1880 (47) *In the Steppes of Central Asia*, orchestral "picture"
1881 (48) String Quartet No. 2 in D major
1885 (52) Petite Suite, for piano
Scherzo in A♭, for piano
1886 (53) *Serenata alla Spagnola*, a movement for the string quartet "B-la-F" (the other movements were by Rimsky-Korsakov, Liadov and Glazunov, *q.v.*)

BOULEZ, Pierre/b.1925/France

1946 (21) *Visage Nuptial*, for soprano, alto and chamber orchestra (first version)
Piano Sonata No. 1
Sonatina for flute and piano
1947–48 (22) *Soleil des eaux*, for voices and orchestra
Piano Sonata No. 2
1949 (24) *Livre pour cordes*, for string orchestra
Livre pour quatour, for string quartet
1951 (26) *fp. Polyphonie* X, for eighteen instruments
Second version of *Visage Nuptial*, for soprano, alto, choir and orchestra
1952 (27) *fp. Structures*, Book I, for two pianos
1954 (29) *Le Marteau sans maître*, for alto voice and six instruments
1955 (30) *Symphonie Mecanique*, music for the film
1957 (32) *Doubles*, for three orchestral groups divisi
Poésie pour pouvoir, for reciter, orchestra and tape
Deux Improvisations sur Mallarmé, for soprano and instrumental ensemble
Piano Sonata No. 3
1959 (34) *fp. Tombeau*, for orchestra
1960 (35) *fp. Pli selon pli*, Portrait de Mallarmé (Don; Improvisations I, II, III; Tombeau), for soprano and orchestra
1961 (36) Structures, Book II, for two pianos
1964 (39) *fp. Figures-Doubles-Prismes*, for orchestra
Éclat, for fifteen instruments
1968 (43) *fp. Domaines*, for clarinet and twenty-one instruments
1970 (45) *Multiples*, for orchestra
fp. Cummings ist der Dichter, for sixteen mixed voices and instruments
1972–74 (47–49) *. . . Explosante-Fixe . . . .*, for ensemble and live electronics
1974–75 (49) *Rituel, in memoriam Maderna*, for orchestra in eight groups

BOYCE, William/1710–1779/Great Britain

c.1750 (c.40) *p.* Eight Symphonies in Eight Parts . . . Opera Seconda
1758 (48) Ode to the New Year
1769 (59) Ode to the King's Birthday
1772 (62) Ode to the New Year
1775 (65) Ode to the King's Birthday

*c.*1785 (posthumous) *p.* Ten voluntaries for organ or harpsichord
1786 (posthumous) *p.* Ode to the King's Birthday
1790 (posthumous) *p.* "Oh where shall wisdom be found?", anthem
Boyce also composed church and stage music and songs.

BRAHMS, Johannes/1833–1897/Germany

1851 (18) Scherzo in E♭ minor, for piano, Op. 4
           Six songs for tenor or soprano, Op. 7 (1851–53)
1852 (19) Piano Sonata No. 1 in C major, Op. 1 (1852–53)
           Piano Sonata No. 2 in F♯ minor, Op. 2
           Six songs for tenor or soprano, Op. 3 (1852–53)
           Six songs for tenor or soprano, Op. 6 (1852–53)
1853 (20) Piano Sonata No. 3 in F minor, Op. 5
           Piano Trio No. 1 in B major, Op. 8 (1853–54)
1854 (21) Variations on a Theme by Schumann, for piano, Op. 9
           Four Ballades for piano, in Dm: D: B: Bm, Op. 10
           Piano Concerto No. 1 in D minor, Op. 15
1855–68   Seven Songs, Op. 48
1855–75   Piano Quartet No. 3 in C minor, Op. 60
1855–76   Symphony No. 1 in C minor, Op. 68
1856 (23) "Lass dich nur nichts dauern", sacred song, Op. 30
           Variations on an original theme, for piano, Op. 21/1
           Variations on a Hungarian theme, for piano, Op. 21/2
1857–58 (24) Serenade for orchestra in D major, Op. 11
1857–60   Serenade for orchestra in A major, Op. 16
1857–68   Four Songs, Op. 43
           German Requiem, Op. 45
1858 (25) "Ave Maria", for women's chorus, orchestra and organ,
              Op. 12
           "Funeral Hymn", for mixed chorus and wind orchestra,
              Op. 13
           Eight Songs and Romances, Op. 14
1858–59   Five Songs, Op. 19
1858–60   Three Duets for soprano and alto, Op. 20
1858–68   Five Songs, Op. 47
1859 (26) *Marienlieder*, for four-part mixed choir, Op. 22
           The 13th Psalm, for three-part women's chorus and
              organ, Op. 27
1859–60   Three Quartets for solo voices with piano, Op. 31
1859–61   Three Songs, Op. 42
1859–63   Three Sacred Choruses, Op. 37
           Twelve Songs and Romances, Op. 44
1859–73   String Quartet No. 1 in C minor, Op. 51
           String Quartet No. 2 in A minor
1860 (27) Part-Songs, for women's chorus, two horns and harp,
              Op. 17
           String Sextet No. 1 in B♭ major, Op. 18
           Two Motets, for five-part mixed choir a cappella, Op. 29
1860–62   Four Duets for alto and baritone, Op. 28
1861 (28) Variations and Fugue on a theme by Handel, for piano,
              Op. 24

Piano Quartet No. 1 in G minor, Op. 25

Piano Quartet No. 2 in A major, Op. 26

1861–62   "Soldaten Lieder", five songs, Op. 41

1861–68   Fifteen Romances from "Magelone", Op. 33

1862–63 (29)   Piano Studies (Variations on a theme by Paganini) Books I and II, Op. 35

1862–65   Cello Sonata No. 1 in Em, Op. 38

1962–74   Three Quartets for solo voices, Op. 63

1863 (30)   Song, for alto, viola and piano, Op. 91

1863–68   *Rinaldo*, cantata, Op. 50

1863–77   Two Motets, Op. 74

1863–90   Thirteen Canons, Op. 113

1864 (31)   Fourteen German folk songs, for four-part choir

Piano Quintet in F minor, Op. 34

Four Songs, Op. 46

1864–65   String Sextet No. 2 in G major, Op. 36

1864–68   Five Songs, Op. 49

1865 (32)   Trio for piano, violin and horn, in E♭ major, Op. 40

1869 (36)   *Liebeslieder Waltzer* (words, Daumer), Op. 52

p. Piano Studies in Five Books, Books I–II

1870 (37)   Alto Rhapsody, for alto, male chorus and orchestra, Op. 53

1870–71   *Triumphlied*, for chorus and orchestra, Op. 55

1871 (38)   *Schicksalied (Song of Destiny)*, Op. 54

Eight Songs, Op. 57

Eight Songs, Op. 58

1871–73   Eight Songs, Op. 59

1871–78   Eight piano pieces in two books: Nos. 1, 2, 5 and 8 are Capriccios. Nos. 3, 4, 6 and 7 are Intermezzi, Op. 76

1873 (40)   Variations on a theme by Haydn, *St. Anthony*, for orchestra, Op. 56a

1873–74   Nine Songs, Op. 63

1874 (41)   Four Duets for soprano and alto, Op. 61

Seven Songs, Op. 62

1875 (42)   String Quartet No. 3 in B♭ major, Op. 67

Fifteen Neues Liebeslieder, for piano duet, Op. 65

1875–77   Four Songs, Op. 70

1876–77 (43)   Five Songs, Op. 72

1877 (44)   Nine Songs, Op. 69

Five Songs, Op. 71

Symphony No. 2 in D major, Op. 73

1877–78   Four Ballads and Romances for two voices, Op. 75

Six Songs, Op. 86

1877–79   Six Songs, Op. 85

1877–84   Four vocal quartets, Op. 92

1878 (45)   Violin Concerto in D major, Op. 77

1878–79   Violin Sonata No. 1 in G major, *Regen Sonate*

1878–81   Piano Concerto No. 2 in B♭ major, Op. 83

Five Songs and Romances for one or two voices, Op. 84

1879 (46)   Two Rhapsodies for Piano, No. 1 in Bm: No. 2 in Gm, Op. 79

p. Piano Studies in Five Books, Books III–V

1880 (47) *Academic Festival Overture*, Op. 80
1880–81 *Tragic Overture*, Op. 81
1880–82 Piano Trio No. 2 in C, Op. 87
1882 (49) *Nanie*, Op. 82
　　　　　　String Quintet No. 1 in F major, Op. 88
　　　　　　"Gesang de Parzen", Op. 89
1883 (50) Symphony No. 3 in F major, Op. 90
1883–84 Six Songs and Romances, Op. 93a
1884 (51) "Tagelied (Dank der Damen)", Op. 93b
　　　　　　Five Songs, Op. 94
　　　　　　Seven Songs, Op. 95
　　　　　　Four Songs, Op. 96
　　　　　　Six Songs, Op. 97
1884–85 Symphony No. 4 in E minor, Op. 98
1886 (53) Cello Sonata No. 2 in F major, Op. 99
　　　　　　Violin Sonata No. 2 in A major, *Meistersinger*, Op. 100
　　　　　　Five Songs, Op. 105
　　　　　　Five Songs, Op. 106
　　　　　　Five Songs, Op. 107
1886–88 Violin Sonata No. 3 in D minor, *Thuner-Sonate*, Op. 108
　　　　　　Deutsche Fest- und Gedenkspruche, Op. 109
1887 (54) Double Concerto for violin, cello and orchestra in A
　　　　　　　　minor, Op. 102
　　　　　　Zigeunerliede, Op. 103
1888 (55) Five Songs, Op. 104
1888–91 Six Vocal Quartets, Op. 112
1889 (56) Three Motets, Op. 110
1890 (57) String Quintet No. 2 in G major, Op. 111
1891 (58) Trio for piano, violin and clarinet in A minor, Op. 114
　　　　　　Clarinet Quintet in B minor, Op. 115
1892 (59) *Fantasien*, for piano, in two books, Op. 116
　　　　　　Three Intermezzi for piano, Op. 117
　　　　　　Six Piano Pieces (intermezzi, ballade, romance), Op. 118
　　　　　　Four Piano Pieces (three intermezzi, one rhapsody), Op. 119
1894 (61) Sonata No. 1 in F minor, for piano and clarinet, or viola,
　　　　　　　　Op. 120
　　　　　　Sonata No. 2 in E♭ major, for piano and clarinet, or
　　　　　　　　viola, Op. 120
1896 (63) Four Serious Songs, Op. 121

BRIDGE, Frank/1879–1941/Great Britain

1902 (23) *Berceuse*, for violin and small orchestra
1904 (25) *Novelleten*, for string quartet
　　　　　　Violin Sonata
1905 (26) Piano Quintet
　　　　　　Phantasie Quartet in F♯ minor
　　　　　　Norse Legend, for violin and piano
1906 (27) Three Idylls for string orchestra
　　　　　　String Quartet in E minor
　　　　　　Nine Miniatures, for cello and piano
1907 (28) *Isabella*, symphonic poem

Trio No. 1 in C minor, *Phantasie*
1908 (29) *Dance Rhapsody*, for orchestra
Suite for strings
1909 (30) *Dance Poem*, for orchestra
1911 (32) *The Sea*, suite for orchestra
1912 (33) String Sextet
1914 (35) *Summer*, tone poem
1915 (36) *The Open Air*, poem for orchestra
The Story of My Heart, poem for orchestra
Lament, for strings
String Quartet in G minor
1916 (37) "A Prayer", for chorus
1917 (38) Cello Sonata in D minor and D major
1919–29 (40–50) *The Christmas Rose*. opera
1922 (43) *Sir Roger de Coverley*, for string quartet or orchestra
Piano Sonata (1922–25)
1926 (47) String Quartet No. 3
1927 (48) *Enter Spring*, for orchestra
1928 (49) *Rhapsody*, for two violins and viola
1929 (50) Trio No. 2
1930 (51) *Oration "concert elegiaco"*, for cello and orchestra
1931 (52) *Phantasm*, rhapsody for piano and orchestra
1937 (58) String Quartet No. 4
1940 (61) *Rebus*, for orchestra
Vignettes de Danse, for small orchestra
Divertimento for flute, oboe, clarinet and bassoon

BRITTEN, Benjamin/1913–1976/Great Britain

1930 (17) Hymn to the Virgin
1932 (19) Sinfonietta, for chamber orchestra
Phantasy Quartet, for oboe and string trio
1933 (20) *A Boy Was Born*, choral variations for men's, women's
and boy's voices unaccompanied with organ ad lib
Two Part-songs for chorus and piano
Friday Afternoons, twelve children's songs with piano
(1933–35)
1934 (21) *Simple Symphony*, for string orchestra (based entirely on
material which the composer wrote between the ages
of 9 and 12)
Suite, for violin and piano (1934–35)
Holiday Diary, suite for piano
Te Deum in C major
1936 (23) *Our Hunting Fathers*, song cycle
Soirées musicales, suite
1937 (24) *Mont Juic, suite of Catalan Dances*, for orchestra (with
Berkeley, *q.v.*)
Variations on a Theme of Frank Bridge, for strings
On This Island, song cycle
1938 (25) Piano Concerto No. 1 (revised 1945)
1939 (26) Violin Concerto (revised 1958)
Canadian Carnival, for orchestra

Ballad of Heroes, for high voice, choir and orchestra
Les Illuminations, song cycle
1940 (27) Diversions on a Theme, for piano (left hand) and orchestra
Paul Bunyan, operetta (c.1940–41, revised 1974)
Sinfonia da Requiem
Seven Sonnets of Michelangelo, for tenor and piano
1941 (28) Scottish Ballad, for two pianos and orchestra
Matinées musicales, for orchestra
String Quartet No. 1
1942 (29) Hymn to St. Cecilia, for five-part chorus with solos
unaccompanied
A Ceremony of Carols, for treble voices and harp
1943 (30) Rejoice in the Lamb, a Festival Cantata
Prelude and Fugue, for strings
Serenade, song cycle for tenor, horn and strings
1944 (31) Festival Te Deum, for chorus and organ
1945 (32) Peter Grimes, opera
The Holy Sonnets of John Donne, for high voice and piano
String Quartet No. 2
1946 (33) Variations and Fugue on a Theme of Purcell (Young
Person's Guide to the Orchestra), for speaker and
orchestra
The Rape of Lucretia, opera
1947 (34) Albert Herring, opera
Canticle No. 1, "My Beloved is Mine"
Prelude and Fugue on a Theme of Vittoria, for organ
1948 (35) St. Nicholas, for tenor, choir, strings, piano and percussion
The Beggar's Opera, by John Donne realized from original
airs
1949 (36) The Little Sweep (Let's Make an Opera)
Spring Symphony, for three solo singers, mixed choir,
boys' choir and orchestra
A Wedding Anthem, for soprano, tenor, chorus and organ
1950 (37) Lachrymae, for viola and piano
Five Flower Songs, for unaccompanied chorus
1951 (38) Billy Budd, opera
Six Metamorphoses After Ovid, for solo oboe
1952 (39) Canticle No. 2, "Abraham and Isaac", for contralto, tenor
and piano
1953 (40) Gloriana, opera
Winter Words, songs
1954 (41) The Turn of the Screw, opera
Canticle No. 3, "Still Falls the Rain", for tenor, chorus and
piano
1955 (42) Alpine Suite, for recorder trio
Hymn to St. Peter, for choir and organ
1956 (43) The Prince of the Pagodas, ballet
Antiphon, for mixed choir and organ
1957 (44) Noye's Fludde, mystery play with music
Songs from the Chinese, for high voice and guitar
1958 (45) Nocturne, song cycle for tenor, seven obbligato instruments
and strings

	Sechs Hölderlin-Fragmente, song cycle
1959 (46)	Missa Brevis
	Cantata Academica, Carmen Basiliense, for soprano, alto, tenor and bass soli, chorus and orchestra
1960 (47)	*A Midsummer Night's Dream*, opera
1961 (48)	*War Requiem*, for soprano, tenor and baritone soli, chorus, orchestra, chamber orchestra, boys' choir, and organ
	Cello Sonata in C major
1963 (50)	Symphony for cello and orchestra
	Cantata misericordium, for tenor, baritone, string quartet, string orchestra, piano, harp and timpani
	Nocturnal, after John Dowland, for guitar
1964 (51)	*Curlew River*, parable for church performance
	Cello Suite No. 1
1965 (52)	*Gemini Variations*, for flute, violin and piano (four hands)
	Songs and Proverbs of William Blake
	Voices for Today, anthem for chorus
	The Poet's Echo, for high voice and piano
1966 (53)	*The Burning Fiery Furnace*, parable for church performance
	The Golden Vanity, for boys and piano
1967 (54)	Cello Suite No. 2
	The Building of the House, overture, with or without chorus
1968 (55)	*The Children's Crusade*, for children's voices and orchestra
	The Prodigal Son, parable for church performance
1969 (56)	Suite for harp
	"Who are these children?", for tenor and piano
1970 (57)	*Owen Wingrave*, opera
1971 (58)	Cello Suite No. 3
	Canticle No. 4, "Journey of the Magi"
1973 (60)	*Death in Venice*, opera
1974 (61)	Canticle No. 5, "The Death of St. Narcissus", for tenor and harp
	Suite on English folk tunes, for orchestra
	A Birthday Hansel, for voice and harp
1975 (62)	*Phaedra*, dramatic cantata for mezzo-soprano and small orchestra
	String Quartet No. 3

BROWN, Earle/b.1926/U.S.A.

1952 (26)	*Folio and Four Systems*, for piano and orchestra
	Music for violin, cello and piano
1953 (27)	Twenty-five Pages —from one to twenty-five pianos
1961 (35)	*Available Forms* II, for ninety-eight players and two conductors
1962 (36)	*Novara*, for instrumental ensemble
1963 (37)	*From Here*, for chorus and twenty instruments (chorus optional)
	Times Five, for flute, trombone, harp, violin, cello and four-channel tape
1964 (38)	*Corroborree*, for two or three pianos

1965 (39) *Nine Rarebits*, for one or two harpsichords
           String Quartet
1966 (40) *Modules 1 and 2*, for orchestra
1967–68 (41) *Event-Synergy II*, for instrumental ensemble
1969 (42) *Modules 3*, for orchestra
1970 (43) *Syntagm III*, for instrumental ensemble
1972 (45) *Time Spans*, for orchestra
           New Piece: Loops, for choir and/or orchestra
           Sign Sounds, for instrumental ensemble
1973 (46) *Centering*, for solo violin and ten instruments

BRUCH, Max/1838–1920/Germany

1856 (18) String Quartet in C minor
1857 (19) Piano Trio in C minor
1858 (20) *Scherz, List und Rache*, opera
1860 (22) String Quartet in E major
1863 (25) *Die Lorely*, opera
c.1864 (c.26) *Frithjof-Scenen*, for solo voices, chorus and orchestra
1868 (30) Violin Concerto No. 1 in G minor
1870 (32) Symphony No. 1 in E♭ major
           Symphony No. 2 in F minor
1872 (34) *Hermione*, opera
           Odysseus, cantata
1878 (40) Violin Concerto No. 2 in D minor
1881 (43) *p. Kol Nidrei*, for cello and piano, or orchestra
1887 (49) Symphony No. 3 in E major
1891 (53) Violin Concerto No. 3 in E major
1905 (67) Suite on a popular Russian melody
1911 (73) Concertstücke for violin, in F♯ minor

BRUCKNER, Anton/1824–1896/Austria

1849 (25) Requiem in D minor
1854 (30) Solemn Mass in B♭ major
1863 (39) Symphony in F minor (known as No. 00)
           Overture in G minor
           Germanenzug, for chorus and brass
1864 (40) Symphony in D minor (known as No. 0, revised 1869)
           Mass No. 1 in D minor
           "Um Mitternacht", for male-voice chorus
1866 (42) Symphony No. 1 in C minor (revised 1891)
           Mass No. 2 in E minor
1868 (44) Mass No. 3 in F minor, *Grosse Messe* (revised 1871 and
           1890)
1869 (45) "Locus iste", motet
1871 (47) "Os uisti", motet
1872 (48) Symphony No. 2 in C minor (revised 1891)
1873 (49) Symphony No. 3 in D minor, *Wagner* (revised 1877 and
           1888)
1874 (50) Symphony No. 4 in E♭ major, *Romantic* (revised 1880)
1877 (53) Symphony No. 5 in B♭ major (revised 1878)

1878 (54) *Abendzauber*, for baritone and male chorus
1879 (55) String Quartet
1881 (57) Symphony No. 6 in A major
1883 (59) Symphony No. 7 in E major
1884 (60) Symphony No. 8 in C minor, *Apocalyptic* (possibly 1887, revised 1890)
           Te Deum
1894 (70) Symphony No. 9 in D minor (unfinished, *fp*. 1903)

BULL, John/1563–1628/Great Britain

No details of Bull's works are available. He is included in this book because of his importance in the history of music as a composer for the virginals, and because he ranks as one of the founders of the keyboard repertory.

BUSONI, Ferruccio/1866–1924/Italy

1880–81 (14–15) String Quartet No. 1 in C major
1882 (16) *Spring, Summer, Autumn, Winter*, for male voice and orchestra
           Il Sabato del villagio, for solo voices, chorus and orchestra
           Serenata, for cello and piano
1883 (17) Piano Sonata in F minor
1886 (20) String Quartet in C minor
           Little Suite, for cello and piano
1888 (22) Symphonic Suite
           Konzert-Fantasie, for piano and orchestra; later (1892) called "Symphonisches Tongedicht"
1889 (23) String Quartet No. 2 in D minor
1890 (24) Konzertstücke for piano
           Violin Sonata No. 1
1895 (29) Orchestral Suite No. 2
1896–97 (30) Violin Concerto in D major
1897 (31) *Comedy Overture*
1898 (32) Violin Sonata No. 2
1903–04 (37) Piano Concerto (using male choir)
1907 (41) *Élégien*, for piano
1908–11 (42–45) *The Bridal Choice*
1909 (43) *Berceuse élégiaque*
1912 (46) *Nocturne Symphonique*
1913 (47) *Indian Fantasy*, for piano and orchestra
1914–16 (48–50) *Arlecchino*, opera
1916–24 (50–58) *Doktor Faust*, opera (completed by Jarnach after Busoni's death and produced in Dresden in 1925)
1917 (51) *Turandot*, opera
           Die Brautwahl, orchestral suite
1919 (53) Concertino for clarinet and small orchestra
1920 (54) Divertimento for flute and orchestra
           Sonatina No. 6 for piano (chamber fantasy on Bizet's *Carmen*)
1921 (55) Romance and Scherzo for piano

Elegy for clarinet and piano
1923 (56) Ten variations on a Chopin prelude
Busoni also composed many piano solos and a *Fantasia
Contrappuntista* for two pianos, based on Bach's *Art of Fugue.*

BUTTERWORTH, George/1885–1916/Great Britain

1909 (24) "I Fear Thy Kisses", song
1911 (26) Six Songs from Housman's "A Shropshire Lad"
Two English Idylls, for small orchestra
"Requiescat", song
1912 (27) *A Shropshire Lad*, rhapsody for orchestra
On Christmas Night, for chorus
We Get Up In The Morn, arranged for male chorus
In The Highlands, arranged for female voices and piano
"Bredon Hill" and other songs
Eleven folk songs from Sussex
p. "Love Blows as the Wind Blows", for baritone and
string quartet
1913 (28) *Banks of Green Willow*, idyll for orchestra

BUXTEHUDE, Dietrich/1637–1707/Denmark

1671 (34) Wedding Arias
1678 (41) Wedding Arias
1692 (55) Sonata in D major, for viola da gamba, cello and
harpsichord
1696 (59) Seven Trio Sonatas for violin, gamba and basso continuo,
Op. 1
Seven Trio Sonatas for violin, gamba and basso continuo,
Op. 2
1705 (68) Wedding Arias

BYRD, William/1543–1623/Great Britain

1575 (32) *p.* Seventeen Motets
*c.***1586** (*c.*43) *p.* A Printed Broadside for six voices
1588 (45) *p.* Psalmes, Sonnets and Songs
1589 (46) *p.* Cantiones sacrae, Book I: twenty-nine motets for five
voices
p. Songs of Sundrie Natures
1591 (48) *p.* Cantiones sacrae, Book II: twenty motets for five voices;
twelve motets for six voices
1605 (62) *p.* Gradualia, Book I: thirty-two motets for five voices;
twenty motets for four voices; eleven motets for three
voices
1607 (64) *p.* Gradualia, Book II: nineteen motets for four voices;
seventeen motets for five voices, nine motets for six
voices
1611 (68) *p.* Psalmes, Songs and Sonnets

CAGE, John/b.1912/U.S.A.

1933 (21) Sonata for solo clarinet
1934 (22) Six Short Inventions for seven instruments
1938 (26) *Metamorphosis*, for piano
1939 (27) *First Construction (In Metal)*, for percussion sextet
           Imaginary Landscape No. 1, for two variable-speed phono-
               turntables, frequency recordings, muted piano and
               cymbal
1941 (29) *Double Music*, for percussion
1942 (30) *Wonderful Widow of 18 Springs*, for voice and closed
               piano
1943 (31) *She is Asleep*, for twelve tom-toms, voice and prepared
               piano
           Amores, for prepared piano and percussion
           Perilous Night, suite for prepared piano (1943–44)
1944 (32) *A Book of Music*, for two prepared pianos
           Three Dances for two amplified prepared pianos
               (1944–45)
1946–48 (34–36) Sonatas and Interludes for prepared pianos
1950 (38) String Quartet in Four Parts
1951 (39) Concerto for prepared piano and chamber orchestra
           Music of Changes, for piano
           Imaginary Landscape No. 4, for twelve radios, twenty-four
               players and conductor
1952 (40) *Water Music*, for pianist with accessory instruments
           Williams Mix, for eight-track tape
           4' 33" (tacet), for piano, in four movements
1953–56 (41–44) *Music for piano "4–84 for 1–84 pianists"*
1954 (42) *34' 46.776" for a pianist*, for prepared piano
1955 (43) *26' 1.1499" for a string player*
1957 (45) *Winter Music*, for one to twenty pianists
           Concerto for piano and orchestra, for piano and one to
               thirteen instrumental parts
1958 (46) *Variations* I, for any kind and number of instruments
           Fontana Mix: a) a score for the production of one or
               more tape tracks or for any kind and number of
               instruments
               b) prerecorded tape material to be performed in any
               way
1960 (48) *Cartridge music*
           Theater Piece, for one to eight performers
1961 (49) *Music for Carillon*, No. 4
           Variations II
           Atlas eclipticalis, for orchestra
1963 (51) *Variations III*
           Variations IV
1965 (53) *Variations V*
1966 (54) *Variations VI*
1967–69 (55–57) *H P S C H D*, for seven harpsichords and fifty-two
               computer-generated tapes (with Lejaren Hiller)
1969 (57) *Cheap Imitation*, for piano

CAMPIAN (CAMPION), Thomas/1562–1620/Great Britain

1601 (39) *p.* A Book of Airs to be Sung to the Lute
1607 (45) *p.* Songs for a Masque to celebrate the Marriage of Sir
               James Hay
1613 (51) *p.* Songs for a Masque to celebrate the marriage of
               Princess Elizabeth
Campian composed more than 100 songs to lute accompaniment.

CARPENTER, John Alden/1876–1951/U.S.A.

1904 (28) "Improving Songs for Anxious Children"
1912 (36) Violin Sonata
1913 (37) *Gitanjali*, song cycle on poems of Tagore
1915 (39) *Adventures in a Perambulator*, for orchestra
               Concertino for piano and orchestra (revised 1947)
1917 (41) Symphony No. 1
1918 (42) Four Negro Songs
1919 (43) *Birthday of the Infanta*, ballet
1920 (44) *A Pilgrim Vision*, for orchestra
1921 (45) *Krazy Kat*, ballet
1925 (49) *Skyscrapers*, ballet
1928 (52) String Quartet
1932 (56) *Patterns*, for piano and orchestra
               Song of Faith, for chorus and orchestra
1933 (57) *Sea Drift*, symphonic poem
1934 (58) Piano Quintet
1935 (59) *Danza*, for orchestra
1936 (60) Violin Concerto
1940 (64) Symphony No. 2
1941 (65) *Song of Freedom*, for chorus and orchestra
1942 (66) Symphony No. 3
1943 (67) *The Anxious Bugler*, for orchestra
1945 (69) *The Seven Ages*
1948 (72) *Carmel Concerto*

CASELLA, Alfredo/1883–1947/Italy

1901 (18) *Pavana*, for piano
1903 (20) *Variations sur une chaconne*, for piano
1904 (21) Toccata for piano
1905–6 (22) Symphony No. 1
1907 (24) Cello Sonata No. 1
1908 (25) Sarabande for piano, or harp
               Symphony No. 2 (1908–09)
1909 (26) *Italia*, orchestral rhapsody
               Notturnino, for piano
               Berceuse Triste, piano
               Orchestral Suite in C major (1909–10)
1910 (27) *Barcarola*, for piano
1912–13 (29) *Le Couvent sur l'eau*, ballet
1913 (30) *Notte di Maggio*, for voice and orchestra
1914–17 (31–34) *Siciliana* and *Burlesca*, for piano trio

1916 (33) *Pupazzetti*, for nine instruments
           Pagine di Guerra
           Elegia eroica
1920 (37) Five pieces for string quartet
1921 (38) *A Notte alta*
1923–24 (40) Concerto for string quartet
1924 (41) *La Giara*, ballet
           Partita for piano
1926 (43) *Concerto Romano*, for organ and orchestra
           Introduction, Aria and Toccata, for orchestra
           Adieu à la vie, for voice and orchestra
           Scarlattiana
1927 (44) Cello Sonata No. 2
           Concerto for Strings
1928 (45) Violin Concerto in A minor
           La Donna Serpente, opera (1928–31)
1930 (47) Serenade for small orchestra
1931–35 (48–52) *Introduction, corale e marcia*, for woodwind
1932 (49) *La Favola d'Orfeo*, opera
           Sinfonia for clarinet, trumpet and piano
1933 (50) Concerto for violin, cello, piano and orchestra
1934 (51) *Notturno e Tarantella*, for cello
           Cello Concerto
1937 (54) Concerto for Orchestra
           Il Deserto Tentato, oratorio
1939–40 (56) Sinfonia
1942 (59) *Paganiniana*
1943 (60) Concerto for strings, piano and percussion
           Harp Sonata
1944 (61) Missa Solemnis "Pro Pace"

CASTELNUOVO-TEDESCO, Mario/1895–1968/Italy

1915 (20) *Copias*, for guitar (orchestra version 1967)
1920 (25) *Cipressi*
           La Mandragola, opera
1921–25 (25–29) Thirty-three Shakespeare Songs
1925 (29) *Le Danze del re David*, for piano
1927 (32) Piano Concerto No. 1
1933 (38) Sonata for Guitar, *Homage to Boccherini*
1936 (41) Tarantella
           Concerto for two guitars and orchestra
           Concertino for harp and chamber orchestra
1938 (43) *Auvassin et Nicolette*, for voice, instruments and marionettes
1939 (44) Guitar Concerto
           Violin Concerto No. 2, *The Prophets*
1956 (61) *All's Well that Ends Well*, opera
1958 (63) *The Merchant of Venice*, opera
           Saul
1963 (68) *Song of Songs*
1966 (71) Sonata for cello and harp
Castelnuovo-Tedesco also composed:

Violin Concerti Nos. 1 and 3
Piano Concerto No. 2
Concerto Italiano
Symphonic Variations for violin and orchestra
An American Rhapsody
In Toscana, opera
Many oratorios.

CATALANI, Alfredo/1854–1893/Italy

1883 (29) *Dejanire*, opera
1886 (32) *Edmea*, opera
1890 (36) *Lorely*, opera
1892 (38) *La Wally*, opera

CHABRIER, Emanuel/1841–1894/France

1860 (19) Impromptu in C, for piano
1877 (36) *L'Étoile*, opera
1879 (38) *Une Éducation manquée*
1880 (39) Dix pieces pittoresques, for piano
1883 (42) *fp. España*, orchestral rhapsody
               Trois Valses romantiques, for piano duo
1885 (44) *Habanera*, for piano
1886 (45) *Gwendoline*, opera
1887 (46) *Le Roi malgré lui*, opera
1888 (47) *Marche Joyeuse*, for orchestra

CHAMINADE, Cécile/1857–1944/France

1888 (31) *Callirhoe*, ballet
Chaminade also composed:
Concertstücke, for piano and orchestra
2 orchestral suites
Le Sevillane, opera-comique
2 piano trios
Many songs and piano pieces.

CHARPENTIER, Gustave/1860–1956/France

1890 (30) *Impressions d'Italie*, orchestral suite
1892 (32) *La Vie du poète*, cantata
1894 (34) *Poemès chantées*, for voice and orchestra
1895 (35) *Impressions fausses*, for voice and orchestra
1896 (36) *Sérénade à Watteau*, for voice and orchestra
1900 (40) *Louise*, opera
1913 (53) *Julien*, opera

CHAUSSON, Ernest/1855–1899/France

1880 (25) *Les Caprices de Marianne*, opera
               Joan of Arc, for chorus

1882 (27) *Viviane*, symphonic poem
Piano Trio in G minor
Poème de l'amour et de la mer, for voice and piano
(1882–92)
1884–85 (29) *Hélène*, opera
1886 (31) *Hymne Védique*, for chorus and orchestra
Solitude dans les bois, for orchestra
1887 (32) *Chant Nuptial*
1890 (35) Symphony in B♭ major
1891 (36) Concerto for piano, violin and string quartet
1896 (41) *Poème*, for violin and orchestra
1897 (42) *Chant Funèbre*
Ballata
Piano Quartet in A major
1898 (43) *Soir de fête*
1899 (44) String Quartet in C minor, unfinished
1903 (posthumous) *fp. Le Roi Arthus*

CHÁVEZ, Carlos/b.1899/Mexico

1920 (21) Symphony
Piano Sonata No. 1
1921 (22) *El Fuego Nuevo*, ballet
String Quartet No. 1
1923 (24) Piano Sonata No. 2
1924 (25) Sonatina for violin and piano
Sonatina for cello and piano
1925 (26) *Energia*, for nine instruments
1926 (27) *Los cuatro soles*, ballet
1927 (28) *H.P.* (*i.e.,* Horsepower), ballet
1930 (31) Sonata for horns
1932 (33) String Quartet No. 2
1933 (34) Symphony No. 1, *Sinfonia di Antigone*
Cantos de Mexico
Soli No. 1, for oboe, clarinet, trumpet and bassoon
1935 (36) Symphony No. 2, *Sinfonia India*
Obertura Republicana
1938 (39) Concerto for four horns
1939 (40) Four Nocturnes for voice and orchestra
1940 (41) Piano Concerto
Antigona, ballet
Xochipili-Macuilxochitl (the Aztec God of Music), for
Mexican orchestra
1942 (43) Toccata for percussion instruments
1944 (45) *Hija de Colquide* (Daughter of Colchis), ballet
1945 (46) *Piramide*
1948–50 (49–51) Violin Concerto, in eight sections played without
a break (revised 1962)
1951 (52) Symphony No. 3
1953 (54) Symphony No. 4, *Sinfonia Romantica*
Symphony No. 5, *Symphony for Strings*
1958 (59) *Inventions* No. 1, for piano

1960 (61) *Love Propitiated*, opera
1961 (62) Symphony No. 6
                Soli No. 2, for wind quintet
1964 (65) *Resonancias*, for orchestra
                Tambuco, for six percussion
1965 (66) *Soli* No. 3, for bassoon, trumpet, viola, timpani and
                    orchestra
                Violin Concerto No. 2
                Inventions No. 2, for violin, viola and cello
1966 (67) *Soli* No. 4, for brass trio
1967 (68) *Inventions* No. 3, for harp
1969 (70) *Clio*, symphonic ode
                Discovery, for orchestra
                Fuego Olimpico, suite for orchestra

CHERUBINI, Luigi/1760–1842/Italy

1778 (18) *Demophon*, opera
1788 (28) *Ifigenia in Aulide*, opera
1797 (37) *Médée*, opera
1800 (40) *Les Deux journées*, opera
1803 (43) *Anacreon*, opera
1814 (54) String Quartet No. 1 in E♭ major
1815–29 (55–69) String Quarter No. 2 in C major
                String Quartet No. 3 in D minor
1833 (73) *Ali Baba*, opera
1835 (75) String Quartet No. 4 in E major
                String Quartet No. 5 in F major
                String Quartet No. 6 in A minor
1836 (76) Requiem Mass in D minor
1837 (77) String Quartet in E minor

CHOPIN, Frederic/1810–1849/Poland

1817 (7) Polonaises No. 13 in G minor, and No. 14 in B♭ major
1821 (11) Polonaise No. 15 in A♭ major
1822 (12) Polonaise No. 16 in G minor
1825 (15) Polonaise No. 8, Op. 71/1
1826 (16) Three écossaises
                Polonaise No. 11 in B♭ minor
                Introduction and variations in E minor, on *Der
                    Schweizerbub*
1827 (17) Nocturne No. 19, Op. 72
1828 (18) *Krakowiak*, concert rondo for orchestra
                Fantasia on Polish Airs, in A major, for piano and
                    orchestra
                Rondo in C major, for two pianos
                Piano Sonata No. 1 in C minor
                Polonaises Nos. 9 and 10, Op. 71
1829 (19) Piano Concerto No. 2 in F minor
                Introduction and Polonaise in C major, for cello and piano
                Twelve Grande Studies for piano (No. 5 "Black Keys",

1844 (34) Piano Sonata No. 3 in B minor
1845–46 (35) Cello Sonata in G minor
         Barcarolle in F♯ minor
         Polonaise No. 7
1846 (36) Nocturnes, Nos. 17–18
1846–47 (36) Waltzes, Nos. 6–8

CILÈA, Francesco/1866–1950/Italy

1886 (20) Piano Trio
1887 (21) Suite for orchestra
1889 (23) *Gina*, opera
1892 (26) *La Tilda*, opera
1894 (28) Cello Sonata
1897 (31) *L'Arlesiania*, opera
1902 (36) *Adriana Lecouvreur*, opera
1907 (41) *Gloria*, opera
1913 (47) *Il Canto della vita*, for voice, chorus and orchestra
1931 (65) Suite for orchestra

CIMAROSA, Domenico/1749–1801/Italy

1772 (23) *Le stravaganze del conte*, opera
1778 (29) *L'Italiana in Londra*, opera
1780 (31) *Giuditta*, oratorio
1781 (32) *Il pittore parigino*, opera
         Il Convito, opera
1782 (33) *La ballerina amante*, opera
         Absalon, oratorio
1784 (35) *L' Olimpiade*, opera
         Artaserse, opera
1786 (37) *L'Impresario in Angustie*, opera
1789 (40) *Cleopatra*, opera
1792 (43) *Il matrimonio segreto*, opera (this won wide fame for its
         combination of dramatic and musical values, in a
         style near Mozart's)
1793 (44) *I Traci amanti*, opera
         Concerto for two flutes and orchestra
1794 (45) *Penelope*, opera
1796 (47) *Gli Orazi e Curiazi*, opera

CLEMENTI, Muzio/1752–1832/Italy

1773–1832 (21–80) One hundred sonatas, including sixty for piano

COLERIDGE-TAYLOR, Samuel/1875–1912/Great Britain

1896 (21) Symphony in A minor
1898 (23) *Hiawatha's Wedding Feast*, cantata (words by Longfellow)
         Ballade in A minor, for orchestra
1899 (24) *Death of Minnehaha*, cantata (Longfellow)
         Solemn Prelude

1900 (25) *Hiawatha's Departure*, cantata (Longfellow)
1901 (26) *The Blind Girl of Castel-Cuille*
           Toussaint l'ouverture, concert overture
           Idyll
1902 (27) *Meg Blane*
1903 (28) *The Atonement*, oratorio
1905 (30) Five Choral Ballads
1906 (31) *Kubla Khan*
1909 (34) *Bon-Bon* suite
1910 (35) *Endymion's Dream*, for chorus
1911 (36) *A Tale of Old Japan*, cantata
           Bamboula, rhapsodic dance
           Violin Concerto in G minor
Coleridge-Taylor also composed chamber music and many piano solos.

COPLAND, Aaron/b.1900/U.S.A.

1923 (23) *As it Fell Upon a Day*, for soprano, flute and clarinet
1924 (24) Symphony for organ and orchestra
1925 (25) *Grogh*, ballet
           Dance Symphony (1922—25)
           Music for the Theater, suite for small orchestra
1926 (26) Piano Concerto
1928 (28) Symphony No. 1 (an orchestral version of the Symphony
           for organ, minus organ)
1929 (29) Symphonic Ode (revised 1955)
           Vitebsk, study on a Jewish theme, for piano trio
1930 (30) Piano Variations
1933 (33) Symphony No. 2, *Short Symphony*
1934 (34) *Statements*, for orchestra
           Hear Ye! Hear Ye!, ballet
1936 (36) *El Salon Mexico*, for orchestra
1938 (38) *An Outdoor Overture*
           Billy the Kid, ballet (also orchestral suite)
1940 (40) *Quiet City*, orchestral suite for trumpet, English horn and
           strings
1941 (41) Piano Sonata
1942 (42) *Danzon Cubano*
           Rodeo, ballet
           fp. A Lincoln Portrait, for narrator and orchestra
1943 (43) Violin Sonata
1944 (44) *Appalachian Spring*, ballet (also orchestral suite)
1946 (46) Symphony No. 3
1948 (48) Concerto for clarinet and strings, with harp and piano
1950 (50) Piano Quartet
           Twelve Poems of Emily Dickinson, for voice and piano
1951 (51) *Pied Piper*, ballet
1954 (54) *The Tender Land*, opera in three acts
1955 (55) Symphonic Ode
           A Canticle of Freedom, for mixed chorus and orchestra
           (revised 1965)
1957 (57) Orchestral Variations

Piano Fantasy
1959 (59) *Dance Panels*, ballet in seven sections (revised 1962)
1960 (60) Nonet for strings
1962 (62) *Connotations*, for orchestra
          Down a Country Lane, for orchestra
1964 (64) *Music for a Great City*, for orchestra
          Emblems for a Symphonic Band
1967 (67) *Inscape*, for orchestra
1971 (71) Duo for flute and piano
1972 (72) Three Latin-American Sketches

CORELLI, Arcangelo/1653–1713/Italy

1681 (28) *p.* Sonatas in three parts (Twelve Sonatas da Chiesa)
1685 (32) *p.* Sonatas in three parts (Twelve Sonatas da Camera)
1689 (36) *p.* Sonatas in three parts (Twelve Sonatas da Chiesa)
1694 (41) *p.* Sonatas in three parts (Twelve Sonatas da Camera)
1700 (47) *p.* Sonatas for violin and violone or harpsichord. The first
          six of these are "da Chiesa"; the next five, "da
          Camera"; and the last, the famous set of variations on
          "La Folia"
*c.***1714** (*c.*54) *p.* Concerti Grossi

COUPERIN, François/1668–1733/France

1690 (22) Pièces d'orgue en deux messes:
          Messe pour les Paroisses, twenty-one organ pieces
          Messe pour les Couvents, twenty-one organ pieces
          Messe Solenelle
1692 (24) Trio Sonata, *La Steinkerque*
1709 (41) Messe à l'usage des Couvents
1713 (45) Harpsichord Works, Book I
1715 (47) Leçons de ténèbres, for one and two voices
1717 (49) Harpsichord Works, Book II
1722 (54) Harpsichord Works, Book III
          Four "Concerts Royeaux" for harpsichord, strings and
          wind instruments
1724 (56) *Les Goûts-Réunis*, ten concerts for various instruments
1730 (62) *p.* Harpsichord Works, Book IV

CUI, César/1835–1918/Russia

1857 (22) Scherzo for orchestra, Nos. 1 and 2
1858 (23) *The Caucasian Prisoner*, opera
1859 (24) Tarantella
          The Mandarin's Son, opera
1869 (34) *William Ratcliffe*, opera
1875 (40) *Angelo*, opera
1881 (46) Marche Solenelle
1883 (48) *Suite Concertante*, for violin and orchestra
1886 (51) *Deux Morceaux*, for cello and orchestra
1888–89 (53) *Le Filibustier*, opera

1890 (55) String Quartet in C minor
           String Quartet in D major
           String Quartet in E♭ major
1897 (62) p. Five Little Duets, for flute and violin with piano
1899 (64) *The Saracen*, opera
1903 (68) *Mlle. Fifi*, opera
1907 (72) *Matteo Falcone*, opera
1911 (76) *The Captain's Daughter*, opera
           p. Violin Sonata in D major
Cui also composed:
Petite Suite for violin and piano
12 miniatures for violin and piano.

DALLAPICCOLA, Luigi/1904–1975/Italy

1937–38 (33) *Volo di Notte*, opera
1938–41 (34–37) *Canti di Prigionia*, for chorus and instruments
1942 (38) *Cinque Frammente di Saffo*, for soprano and chamber
           orchestra
           Marsia, ballet
1943 (39) *Sex carmina Alcaei*, for soprano and instruments
1944–45 (40) *Due liriche di Anacreonte*, for soprano and instruments
1944–48 *Il Prigioniero*, opera
1945 (41) Ciaccona, Intermezzo e Adagio, for cello
1946–47 (42) Two pieces for orchestra
1948 (44) *Quattro liriche di Antonio Machado*, for soprano and piano
1949 (45) *Tre poemi*, for soprano and chamber orchestra
1949–50 *Job*, mystery play, for narrator, solo voices, chorus and
           orchestra
1951–55 (47–51) *Canti di Liberazione*, for chorus and orchestra
1952 (48) *Quaderno musicale di Annalibera*, for piano
           Goethe-Lieder, for mezzo-soprano and three clarinets
           (1952–53)
1954 (50) *Piccola musica notturna*, for orchestra
1955 (51) *An Mathilde*, cantata
1956 (52) *Cinque canti*, for baritone and eight instruments
           Concerto per la notte di natale dell'anno, for soprano and
           chamber orchestra
1957–58 (53) *Requiescat*, for chorus and orchestra
1959–60 (55) *Dialoghi*, for cello and orchestra
1960–68 (56–64) *Ulisse*, opera
1962 (58) *Preghiere*, for baritone and chamber orchestra
1964 (60) *Parole di San Paolo*, for voice and instruments
           Quattro liriche di Antonio Machado, version for soprano
           and orchestra
1970 (66) Sicut umbra, for mezzo-soprano and twelve instruments
           Tempus aedificandi
1971 (67) Tempus destruendi

DARGOMIZHSKY, Alexander/1813–1869/Russia

1847 (34) *Esmeralda*, opera (possibly *c.*1839)

1856 (43) *fp. Rusalka*, opera
1861–63 (48–50) *Baba-Yaga*, fantasy for orchestra
1867 (54) *The Triumphe of Bacchus*, opera-ballet
1872 (posthumous) *fp. The Stone Guest*, opera (completed by Cui,
    orchestrated by Rimsky-Korsakov, *q.v.*)
Dargomizhsky also composed:
About 90 songs
15 vocal duets
Tarentelle Slav, for piano, four hands
Finnish Fantasy
Kosachok, Ukrainian Dance
The Dance of the Mummers

DAVIES, Peter Maxwell/b.1934/Great Britain

1955 (21) Trumpet Sonata
    Stedman Doubles, for clarinet and percussion (revised
        1967)
1956 (22) Five Pieces for Piano
1957 (23) *St. Michael* Sonata, for seventeen wind instruments
    Alma redemptoris Mater, for six wind instruments
1958 (24) Sextet
    Stedman Caters, for chamber ensemble (revised 1968)
1959 (25) *Prolation*, for orchestra
    Five motets, for soloists, choir and instruments
    Ricercare and Doubles on "To Many a Well", for eight
        instruments
1960 (26) *O Magnum Mysterium*, four carols for chorus, with
        instrumental sonatas and a fantasia for organ
1961 (27) Te Lucis Ante Terminium, for choir and chamber
        orchestra
    String Quartet
1962 (28) First Fantasia on an "In Nomine" of John Taverner, for
        orchestra
    Leopardi Fragments, for soprano, contralto and instruments
    Sinfonia for chamber orchestra
1963 (29) Veni Sancte Spiritus, for soloists, chorus and small
        orchestra
    Seven "In Nomine", for instruments (1963–65)
1964 (30) Second Fantasia on John Taverner's "In Nomine", for
        orchestra
    Shakespeare Music, for chamber ensemble
1965 (31) *The Shepherd's Calender*, for young singers and
        instrumentalists
    Revelation and Fall, for soprano solo and instruments
    Ecce Manus Tradentis, for mixed choir and instruments
    Shall I Die for Mannes Sake, carol for soprano and alto
        voices and piano
1966 (32) Five Carols for soprano and alto voices unaccompanied
    Notre Dame des Fleurs, for soprano, mezzo-soprano,
        counter-tenor and instruments
1967 (33) *Antechrist*, for chamber ensemble

Hymnos, for clarinet and piano
1968 (34) *L'Homme Armé*, for speaker (or singer) and chamber
ensemble (revised 1971)
1969 (35) *St. Thomas Wake*, Foxtrot for orchestra on a Pavan by
John Bull
Eight Songs for a Mad King, for male singer and chamber
ensemble
Worldes Bliss, for orchestra
Eram quasi Agnus, instrumental motet
Vesalii Icones, for dancer, solo cello and ensemble
1970 (36) *Taverner*, opera
1971 (37) *From Stone to Thorn*, for mezzo-soprano and instrumental
ensemble
1972 (38) *Blind Man's Buff*, a masque
Fool's Fanfare, for speaker and instrumental ensemble
Hymn to St. Magnus, for soprano and chamber ensemble
Tenebrae super Gesualdo, for mezzo-soprano, guitar and
chamber ensemble
Canon in memory of Igor Stravinsky, for instrumental
ensemble
1973 (39) *Stone Litany*, for mezzo-soprano and orchestra
Scottish Dances for instrumental ensemble
Fiddlers at the Wedding, for mezzo-soprano and chamber
orchestra (1973–74)
1974 (40) *Dark Angels*, for soprano and guitar
Miss Donnithorne's Maggot, for mezzo-soprano and
chamber ensemble
All Sons of Adam, motet for instrumental ensemble
1975 (41) Ave Maris Stella, for instrumental ensemble

DEBUSSY, Claude/1862–1918/France

1876–79 (14–17) Trio in G minor
1880 (18) *Danse bohémienne*, for piano
Andante for piano
La Belle au bois dormant, song (1880–83)
1881 (19) Fugue for piano
1882 (20) Two four-part fugues, for piano
Triomphe de Bacchus, for piano duet
Intermezzo, for orchestra
Printemps, for women's choir and orchestra
1883 (21) *Invocation*, for male voice choir and orchestra
Le Gladiateur, cantata
1884 (22) *L'Enfant prodigue*, cantata
Diane au bois, for chorus
Divertissement I, for orchestra
Suite for Orchestra, No. 1
1885 (23) *Almanzor*, for chorus
1887–88 (25) *The Blessed Damozel (La Damoiselle élue)*, cantata (on
a French translation of Rosetti's poem)
1887–89 Cinq poèmes de Baudelaire, songs
1888 (26) *Petite Suite*, for piano, four hands :

    "En bateau"
    "Cortège"
    "Menuet"
    "Ballet"
    Arabesques I and II, for piano
    Ariettes oubliées, songs

1889–90 (27) *Fantaisie*, for piano and orchestra

1890 (28) *Suite Bergamasque*, for piano:
    "Prélude"
    "Menuet"
    "Clair de Lune"
    "Passepied"
    Tarentelle Styrienne (Danse), for piano
    Ballade, for piano
    Rêverie, for piano
    Valse romantique, for piano

1891 (29) *Mazurka*, for piano
    Marche écossaise
    Trois mélodies de Verlaine, songs
    Deux Romances, songs
    Rodrigue et Chimène, opera in three acts (unfinished)

1892 (30) *Fêtes galantes*, songs (first series)

1893 (31) String Quartet in G minor
    Proses lyriques, songs

1894 (32) *Prélude à l'après-midi d'un faune*, for orchestra

1897 (35) *Chansons de Bilitis*, songs

1900 (38) *Nocturnes*, for orchestra:
    "Nuages"
    "Fêtes"
    "Sirenes", with wordless female chorus

1901 (39) *Pour le piano*: (possibly 1896)
    "Prélude"
    "Sarabande"
    "Toccata"

1902 (40) *Pelléas et Mélisande*, opera

1903 (41) *Estampes*:
    "Pagodas"
    "Soirée dans Grenade"
    "Jardins sous la pluie"
    Danse sacrée et danse profane, for harp and strings
    D'un cahier d'esquisses, for piano
    Le Diable dans le beffroi, libretto and musical sketches

1903–05 (41–43) *Rhapsodie*, for saxophone, contralto and orchestra

1904 (42) *L'Isle Joyeuse*, for piano
    Trois chansons de France
    Masques, for piano
    La Mer, three symphonic sketches
    Fêtes Galantes, songs (second series)

1905 (43) *Images*, for piano, Book I:
    "Reflets dans l'eau"
    "Hommage à Rameau"
    "Mouvement"

1907 (45) *Images*, for piano, Book II:
    "Cloches à travers les feuilles"
    "Et la lune descend sur la temple qui fut"
    "Poissons d'or"
1908 (46) *Children's Corner*, for piano:
    "Doctor Gradus ad Parnassum"
    "Jumbo's Lullaby"
    "Doll's Serenade"
    "Snow is Dancing"
    "Little Shepherd"
    "Golliwog's Cake-walk"
    Ibéria, (No. 2 of *Images* for orchestra)
    Trois chansons de Charles d'Orléans, for unaccompanied chorus
    The Fall of the House of Usher (sketches for libretto and vocal score, unfinished, 1908—10)
1909 (47) *Rondes de Printemps* (No. 3 of *Images* for orchestra)
    Homage à Haydn, for piano
1909—10   Préludes for piano, Book I (12 préludes)
    Trois ballades de François Villon, songs
    Petite piece en B♭, for clarinet and piano
    La plus qui lente, for piano
    Le Promenoir des deux amants, three songs
    Rhapsody for clarinet, No. 1
1911 (49) *Martyrdom of St. Sebastian*, incidental music to d'Annunzio's mystery-play
1912 (50) *Gigues* (No. 1 of *Images* for orchestra)
    Jeux, poème dansé, for orchestra
    Khamma, ballet
    Syrinx, for solo flute
1913 (51) *La Boîte à Joujoux*, ballet music for piano
    Préludes for piano, Book II (12 préludes)
    Trois poèmes de Mallarmé, songs
1914 (52) *Berceuse héroïque*, for piano
1915 (53) Cello Sonata in D minor
    En Blanc et noir, piano duet
    Twelve Etudes for piano
    Six Épigraphes Antiques
    Noël des enfants, for chorus
1916 (54) Sonata for flute, viola and harp, in G minor
    Ode à la France, for chorus (1916—17)
1917 (55) Violin Sonata in G minor and G major

DELIBES, Léo/1836—1891/France

1866 (30) *La Source (Nalla)*, ballet
1870 (34) *Coppélia*, ballet
1876 (40) *Sylvia*, ballet
1882 (46) *Le Roi s'amuse*, incidental music
1883 (47) *Lakmé*, opera

DELIUS, Frederick/1862–1934/Great Britain

1886 (24) *Florida Suite*, for orchestra
1888 (26) *Marche Caprice*, for orchestra
             Sleigh Ride, for orchestra
1892 (30) *Irmelin*, opera
1895 (33) *Over the Hills and Far Away*, tone poem
1899 (37) *Paris — The Song of a Great City*, nocturne for orchestra
1902 (40) *Appalachia*, for orchestra, with final chorus
1903 (41) *Sea Drift*, for baritone, chorus and orchestra
1904 (42) *Koanga*, opera
1905 (43) *A Mass of Life*, for soloists, chorus and orchestra, text
             from Nietzsche's *Thus Spake Zarathustra*
1906 (44) Piano Concerto in C minor
1907 (45) *Brigg Fair — an English Rhapsody*, for orchestra
             Songs of Sunset
             A Village Romeo and Juliet, opera (from which comes the
             "Walk to the Paradise Garden")
1908 (46) Dance Rhapsody No. 1, for orchestra
             In a Summer Garden
1912 (50) *On Hearing the First Cuckoo in Spring*, for orchestra
             Summer Night on the River, for orchestra
             Song of the High Hills, for wordless chorus and orchestra
1914 (52) *North Country Sketches*, for orchestra
1916 (54) Violin Concerto
             Dance Rhapsody No. 2, for orchestra
1917 (55) *Eventyr*, for chorus and orchestra
1918 (56) *A Song Before Sunrise*
1919 (57) *Fennimore and Gerda*, opera
1920 (58) *Hassan*, incidental music
1922 (60) *A Pagan Requiem* (possibly 1914–16)
1925 (63) *Caprice and Elegy*, for cello and orchestra
1930 (68) *A Song of Summer*
1932 (70) *Prelude to Irmelin* (based on themes from the earlier
             opera)
1934 (72) *Songs of Farewell*, for choir and orchestra

DIAMOND, David/b.1915/U.S.A.

1935 (20) Partita, for oboe, bassoon and piano
1936 (21) *Psalm*, for orchestra
             Sinfonietta
             TOM, ballet
             Concerto for string quartet
             Violin Concerto No. 1
             Cello Sonata
1937 (22) Variations for small orchestra
             Quintet for flute, string trio and piano
1938 (23) *Heroic Piece*, for small orchestra
             Elegy in memory of Ravel, for brass, harps and percussion
             Music, for double string orchestra, brass and timpani
             Cello Concerto
             Piano Quartet

1940 (25) Concerto for small orchestra
           Symphony No. 1
           Quartet No. 1
1941 (26) *The Dream of Audubon*, ballet
1942 (27) Symphony No. 2
           Concerto for two solo pianos
1943 (28) Quartet No. 2
1944 (29) *The Tempest*, incidental music
           Rounds, for string orchestra
1945 (30) Symphonies Nos. 3 and 4
1946 (31) Quartet No. 3
           Violin Sonata
1947 (32) Violin Concerto No. 2
           Romeo and Juliet, incidental music
           Piano Sonata
1948 (33) *Chaconne*, for violin and piano
1949 (34) *L'Âme de Debussy*, song cycle
           Timon of Athens, symphonic portrait
1950 (35) Piano Concerto
           Chorale for chorus
           Quintet for two violas, two cellos and clarinet
1951 (36) Quartet No. 4
           Symphony No. 6
           Mizmor l'David, sacred service for tenor, chorus, orchestra
              and organ
           The Midnight Meditation, song cycle
           Piano Trio
1954 (40) Sinfonia Concertante
           Sonata for solo violin
1956 (41) Sonata for solo cello
1957 (42) *The World of Paul Klee*
1958 (43) Woodwind Quintet
1959 (44) Symphony No. 7
1960 (45) Symphony No. 8
           Quartet No. 5
1961 (46) Nonet for three violins, three violas and three cellos
1962 (47) *This Sacred Ground*, for baritone, chorus, children's chorus
              and orchestra
           Quartet No. 6
1963 (48) Quartet No. 7
1964 (49) Quartet No. 8
           We Two, song cycle
1966 (51) Quartets Nos. 9 and 10
1967 (52) *To Music*, choral symphony for tenor, bass-baritone,
              chorus and orchestra
           Hebrew Melodies, song cycle
           Violin Concerto No. 3
1969 (54) Music for chamber orchestra
1974 (59) *fp.* Quartet No. 10

DITTERSDORF, Carl Ditters von/1739–1799/Germany

1767 (28) *Amore in Musica*, opera
1770 (31) *Il Viaggiatore americano*, opera
1771 (32) *L'Amore disprezzato*, opera
1773 (34) *Il Tutore e la Pupilla*, opera
1774 (35) *Il tribunale de Giove*, opera
1775 (36) *Il finto pazzo per amore*, opera
           Il maniscalco, opera
           Lo Sposo burlato, opera
1776 (37) *La contadina felice*, opera
           La moda, opera
           Il barone di Rocca Antica, opera
1777 (38) *L'Arcifanfano, re de' matti*, opera
1786 (47) *Doktur und Apotheker*, opera
           Betrug durch Aberglauben, opera
1787 (48) *Democrito corretto*, opera
           Die Liebe in Narrenhaus, opera
1789 (50) *Hieronimus Knicker*, opera
1790 (51) *Das rote Käppchen*, opera
1791 (52) *Hokus Pokus*, opera
1794 (55) *Des Gespeust mit de Trommel*, opera
1795 (56) *Don Quixote der Zeite*, opera
           Gott Mars, opera
           Schach vom Schiras, opera
1796 (57) *Ugolino*, opera
           Die Lustigen Weiber von Windsor, opera
           Der Durchmarsch, opera
1797 (58) *Der Terno secco*, opera
           Der Mädchenmarkt, opera
Dittersdorf also composed church music, symphonies, and string
quartets.

DOHNÁNYI, Ernst von/1877–1960/Hungary

1895 (18) *fp.* Piano Quintet in C minor (Op. 1, published 1902)
1896 (19) *Zrinyi*, overture
1897 (20) Symphony No. 1 in F major
1903 (26) *p.* String Quartet in A major
           p. Cello Sonata in B♭ minor
1904 (27) *p.* Serenade in C major, for string trio
1907 (30) *p.* String Quartet in D major
1910 (33) *Der Schlier der Pierette*, ballet
           p. Piano Quintet in E♭ major
1913 (36) *p.* Violin Sonata in C♯ minor
           Tante Simona, opera
1915 (38) Violin Concerto No. 1
1916 (39) *Variations on a Nursery Song*, for piano and orchestra
1919 (42) Suite in F♯ minor
1920 (43) *Hitvallas*, for tenor, choir and orchestra
1922 (45) *The Tower of the Voivod*
1929 (52) *A Tenor*, opera
1941? (?64) Cantus Vitae, cantata

1946 (69) Piano Concerto No. 2
1950 (73) Twelve Studies for Piano
1952 (75) Violin Concerto No. 2
            Harp Concerto
1953 (76) Stabat Mater
1954 (77) *American Rhapsody*
Dohnányi also composed:
Symphony No. 2 in D minor, (Op. 9)
Concertstücke for Cello, (Op. 12)
Ruralia Hungarica, for piano (later orchestrated) (Op. 33)
Symphony No. 3 in E major
No details are available of Dohnányi's work from 1929 until
he went to the United States in 1946.

DONIZETTI, Gaetano/1797–1848/Italy

1830 (33) *Anna Bolena*, opera
1832 (35) *L'Elisir d'Amore*, opera
1833 (36) *Lucrezia Borgia*, opera
1834 (37) *Rosmonda d'Inghilterra*, opera
1835 (38) *Lucia di Lammermoor*, opera
1840 (43) *La Favorita*, opera
            La Fille du régiment, opera
1842 (45) *Linda de Chamounix*, opera
1843 (46) *Maria de Rohan*, opera
            Don Pasquale, opera
            Don Sébastien, opera
Donizetti composed more than 60 operas, some in French.

DOWLAND, John/1563–1626/Great Britain

1597 (34) *p.* First book of Songes or Ayres
1600 (37) *p.* Second book of Songes
1603 (40) *p.* Third book of Songes or Ayres
1604 (41) *p. Lachrymae*
1612 (49) *p.* Fourth book of Songes, *A Pilgrimes Solace*

DUKAS, Paul/1865–1935/France

1892 (27) *Polyeucte*, overture
1896 (31) Symphony in C major
1897 (32) *The Sorcerer's Apprentice*, symphonic poem
1901 (36) Piano Sonata in E♭ minor
1903 (38) Variations, Interlude and Finale on a Theme by Rameau,
            for piano
1906 (41) *Villanelle*, for horn and piano
1907 (42) *Ariadne and Bluebeard*, opera
1909 (44) *Prélude élégiaque*, for piano
            Vocalise
1912 (47) *La Péri—poème dansé*, for orchestra (possibly 1921)
1921 (56) *La Plainte, au loin, du faune*, for piano
1924 (59) *Sonnet de Ronsard*, for voice and piano

DURUFLÉ, Maurice/b.1902/France

1926 (24) Scherzo, for organ
1927 (25) *Triptyque*, for piano
1928 (26) *Prélude, récitatif et variations*, for flute, viola and piano
1929 (27) Prélude, Adagio and Chorale Variations on "Veni, Creator", for organ
1930 (28) Suite (Prélude, Sicilienne and Toccata) for organ
1935 (33) Three Dances for orchestra
1940 (38) Andante and Scherzo, for orchestra
1942 (40) *Prélude et Fugue sur l'nom Alain*, for organ
1947 (45) *Requiem*, for mezzo-soprano, bass, choir, orchestra and organ
1960 (58) Four Motets on Gregorian themes, for choir a cappella
1967 (65) Mass "Cum Jubilo", for baritone solo, choir, orchestra and organ

---

DVOŘÁK, Antonin/1841–1904/Bohemia (Czechoslovakia)

1857–9 (16–18) Mass in B♭ major
1861 (20) String Quintet in A minor
1862 (21) String Quartet No. 1 in A major
1865 (24) Symphony No. 1 in C minor
           Symphony No. 2 in B♭ major
           Cello Concerto in A major
           Clarinet Quintet
           The Cypresses, ten love songs for string quartet
1870 (29) *Alfred*
           Dramatic (Tragic) Overture
           Notturno, in B major, for strings
           String Quartet in B♭ major
           String Quartet in D major
           String Quartet in E minor
1871 (30) *King and Charcoal Burner*, opera (1st version)
           Rosmarine
           Overture in F major
           Piano Trios, Nos. 1 and 2
           Cello Sonata
1872 (31) Patriotic Hymn
           May Night, Nocturne for orchestra
           Piano Quintet in A major
1873 (32) Symphony No. 3 in E♭ major
           Romance, for violin and orchestra
           String Quartet in F minor
           String Quartet in A minor
           Octet *Serenade*
           Violin Sonata in A minor
1874 (33) Symphony No. 4 in D minor
           Rhapsody for orchestra, in A minor
           String Quartet in A minor
1875 (34) Symphony No. 5 in F major (old numbering: No. 3)
           Serenade for strings, in E major
           String Quintet, with double-bass, in G major

Piano Quartet in D major
Piano Trio in B♭ major
Moravian Vocal Duets
1876 (35) Piano Concerto in G minor
Stabat Mater
String Quartet in E major
Piano Trio in G minor
Four songs for mixed choir
1877 (36) *The Cunning Peasant*, opera
Symphonic Variations for orchestra
String Quartet in D minor
1878 (37) *Slavonic Dances*, for orchestra (first series)
Slavonic Rhapsodies, for orchestra
Serenade in D minor, for orchestra
String Sextet in A major
Bagatelles, for two violins, cello and harmonium (or
      piano)
1879 (38) Violin Concerto in A minor (1879–80)
Festival March
Czech Suite in D major
Mazurka, for violin and orchestra
String Quartet in E♭ major
Polonaise in E♭ major
1880 (39) Symphony No. 6 in D major (old numbering: No. 1)
Violin Sonata in F major
Gipsy Songs
1881 (40) *Legends*, for orchestra
String Quartet in C major
1882 (41) *My Home*, overture
1883 (42) *Husitska*, overture
Scherzo Capriccioso, for orchestra
Piano Trio in F minor
1885 (44) Symphony No. 7 in D minor (old numbering: No. 2)
The Spectre's Bride, cantata
1886 (45) *Slavonic Dances* for orchestra (second series)
St. Ludmila, oratorio
1887 (46) Piano Quintet in A major
Piano Quartet in E♭ major
Terzetto for two violins and viola
1889 (48) Symphony No. 8 in G major (old numbering: No. 4)
1890 (49) Gavotte, for three violins
Piano Trio, *Dumka* (1890–91)
1891 (50) *Nature, Life and Love*, cycle of overtures:
      "Amid Nature"
      "Carnival"
      "Othello" (1891–92)
Rondo, for cello and orchestra
Forest Calm, for cello and orchestra
1892 (51) Te Deum
1893 (52) Symphony No. 9 in E minor, *From the New World*
      (old numbering: No. 5)
String Quartet in F major, *American*

         String Quartet in E♭ major
1895 (54) Suite for orchestra
         Cello Concerto in B minor
         String Quartet in A♭ major
         String Quartet in G major
1896 (55) Four Symphonic Poems:
             The Watersprite
             The Noonday Witch
             The Wood Dove
             The Golden Spinning-wheel
1897 (56) Heroic Song
1901 (60) *fp. Rusalka*, opera

ELGAR, Sir Edward/1857–1934/Great Britain

1878 (21) *Romance*, for violin and piano (also arrangement for
            violin and orchestra)
         Promenades, six pieces for wind instruments
1879 (22) *Harmony Music*, seven pieces for wind instruments (No. 7
            1881)
         Intermezzos for Wind, five pieces
1883 (26) *Une Idyll*, for violin and piano (c.1883)
         Fugue in D minor, for oboe and violin
1890 (33) *Froissart*, concert overture
1891 (34) *La Capriceuse*, for violin and piano
1892 (35) *Serenade for Strings*
         The Black Knight, cantata
1894–5 (37) *Scenes from the Saga of King Olaf*, cantata
1895 (38) Organ Sonata in G major
1896 (39) *The Light of Life (Lux Christi)*, oratorio
1897 (40) Imperial March
         The Banner of St. George, a ballad for soprano, chorus and
            orchestra
         Sea Pictures, five songs for contralto and orchestra
1898 (41) *Caractacus*, cantata for soprano, tenor, baritone and bass
            soli, chorus and orchestra
         Variations on an Original Theme, *Enigma*, for orchestra
            (1898–9)
1899 (42) *Sérénade Lyrique*, for orchestra
         In the South (Alassio), concert overture
1900 (43) *The Dream of Gerontius*, oratorio
1901 (44) *Cockaigne* overture *(In London Town)*
         Concerto allegro for piano
         Introduction and Allegro for strings (1901–5)
         Pomp and Circumstance Marches 1–4 (1901–07)
1902 (45) Coronation Ode
         Dream Children, two pieces for piano or small orchestra
         Falstaff, symphonic study in C minor (1902–13)
1903 (46) *The Apostles*, oratorio
*c.***1903–10** (c.46–53) Symphony No. 2 in E♭ major
1906 (49) *The Kingdom*, oratorio
         The Wand of Youth, Suites 1 and 2, for orchestra —final

version 1906–07 (begun in 1867, 1869, or 1871;
revised 1879–81; revised again *c*.1902)
1907 (50)   Symphony No. 1 in A♭ major (1907–08)
1909 (52)   Violin Concerto (*c*.1909–10)
Elegy, for string orchestra
1910 (53)   *Romance*, for bassoon and orchestra
1912 (55)   *The Music Makers*, for contralto, chorus and orchestra
1914 (57)   *Carillon*, recitation with orchestra
p. Sospiri, for orchestra
1915 (58)   *Polonia*, symphonic prelude
Une Voix dans le desert, recitation with orchestra
1917 (60)   *fp. The Spirit of England*, three pieces for voices and
orchestra:
No. 1 *The Fourth of August* (finished 1917)
No. 2 *To Women* (1915)
No. 3 *For the Fallen* (1915)
Le Drapeau Belge, recitation with orchestra
Fringes of the Fleet, song cycle
1918 (61)   Violin Sonata in E minor
String Quartet in E minor
Piano Quintet in A minor (1918–19)
1919 (62)   Cello Concerto in E minor
1923 (66)   *fp. King Arthur*, incidental music
1924 (67)   *fp. Pageant of Empire*
1928 (71)   *fp. Beau Brummel*, incidental music
1930 (73)   *Severn Suite*, for brass band, also arranged for orchestra
Pomp and Circumstance, March No. 5 for orchestra
1931 (74)   *p. Nursery Suite* for orchestra (dedicated to H.R.H.
Princesses Elizabeth and Margaret Rose)

ENESCO, Georges/1881–1955/Rumania

1895 (14)   *Ouverture tragica e ouverture trionfale*
Four *Sinfonie scolastiche* (1895–96)
1897 (16)   *Rumanian Poem*
1898 (17)   *p.* Violin Sonata No. 1
1899 (18)   *Fantaisie Pastorale*
1901 (20)   *Rumanian Rhapsody*, No. 1
Symphonie Concertante, for cello and orchestra
p. Violin Sonata No. 2
1902 (21)   *Rumanian Rhapsody*, No. 2
1903 (22)   Suite for orchestra
1905 (24)   Symphony No. 1 in E♭ major
p. String Octet in C major
1911 (30)   Symphony No. 2 in A major
1915 (34)   Suite for Orchestra
1919 (38)   Symphony No. 3 with organ and chorus
1921 (40)   Violin Concerto
Oedipus, opera (begun *c*.1921)
1937 (56)   *Suite Villageoise*, for orchestra
1950 (69)   *Vox Maris*, symphonic poem

FALLA, Manuel de/1876–1946/Spain

1908 (32) *Pièces espagnoles*, for piano
1909 (33) *Trois mélodies*, songs
           Nights in the gardens of Spain, for piano and orchestra
           (1909–15)
1913 (37) *fp. La Vida brève*, opera
1915 (39) *fp. El Amor Brujo*, ballet
1919 (43) *fp. The Three-cornered Hat*, ballet
           Fantasia bética, piano solo
1921 (45) *Homage pour la Tombeau de Debussy*, for guitar
1922 (46) *El Retablo de Maese Pedro*, opera
           Seven Spanish Popular Songs
1923–26 (47–50) Concerto for harpsichord, flute, oboe, clarinet,
           violin and cello
1934 (58) Fanfare for wind and percussion
1935 (59) *Pour le Tombeau de Paul Dukas*, for piano
1940 (64) *Homenajes*, orchestral version of "Homage pour le
           Tombeau de Debussy"

FARNABY, Giles/*c.*1560–*c.*1600/Great Britain

1598 (*c.*38) Canzonets to Foure Voyces
Farnaby also composed over 50 pieces in the Fitzwilliam Virginal
Book.

FAURÉ, Gabriel/1845–1924/France

1870 (25) "Puisqu'ici-bas", duet for two sopranos
           "Tarentella", duet for two sopranos
1873 (28) *Cantique de Jean Racine*
1875 (30) *Les Djinns*, for chorus and orchestra
           Suite for Orchestra
           Allegro Symphonique, for orchestra
1876 (31) Violin Sonata in A major
1878 (33) Violin Concerto
1879 (34) Piano Quartet No. 1 in C minor
1880 (35) *Berceuse*, for violin and piano
1881 (36) Ballade, for piano and orchestra
           Le Ruisseau
1882 (37) *Romance*, for violin and orchestra
           Le Naissance de Venus
1883 (38) *Élégie* in C minor
           Four Valse-Caprices, for piano (1883–94)
           Five Impromptus (1883–1910)
           Thirteen Nocturnes (1883–1922)
           Thirteen Barcarolles (1883–1921)
1884 (39) Symphony in D minor (unpublished)
1886 (41) Piano Quartet No. 2 in G minor
1887 (42) Requiem
           Pavane, with chorus ad lib
1888 (43) *Caligula*, incidental music
1889 (44) *Shylock*, incidental music

Petite Pièce, for cello and piano
1890 (45) Cinq mélodies de Verlaine, songs
1891–92 (46) *La Bonne Chanson*, nine songs
1893 (48) *Dolly Suite*, for piano duet
1895 (50) *Romance*, for cello and piano
1897 (52) Theme and variations for piano
1898 (53) *Pelléas et Mélisande*, incidental music
Andante for violin and piano
Papillon, for cello and piano
Sicilienne, for cello and piano
Fantasia for flute and piano
1900 (55) *Promethée*, lyric tragedy
1901 (56) *La Voile du bonheur*, incidental music
1904 (59) Impromptu for harp
1906 (61) Piano Quintet in D minor
Le Chanson d'Eve, song cycle (1906–10)
1908 (63) *Sérénade*, for cello and piano
1910 (65) Nine Préludes
1913 (68) *Pénélope*, opera
1915–18 (70–73) *Le Jardin clos*, eight songs
1917 (72) Violin Sonata No. 2 in E minor and E major
1918 (73) Cello Sonata No. 1 in D minor
Une Châtelaine et sa tour, for harp
1919 (74) Fantaisie for piano and orchestra
Mirages, four songs
1920 (75) *Masques et Bergamasques*, suite
1921 (76) Piano Quintet No. 2 in C minor
1922 (77) Cello Sonata No. 2 in G minor
L'Horizon chimerique, songs
1923 (78) Piano Trio in D minor
1924 (79) String Quartet

FELDMAN, Morton/b.1926/U.S.A.

1951 (25) *Projections* 1 and 2, for flute, trumpet, violin and cello
Intersection I
1957 (31) Pieces for four pianos
1959 (33) *Atlantis*, for chamber orchestra
1960–61 (34) *Durations* I–V
1962 (36) *Last Pieces*, for piano
The Swallows of Salangan, for chorus and sixteen instruments
1963 (37) *Christian Wolff in Cambridge*
1965 (39) *Journey to the End of Night*, for soprano and four wind
instruments
De Kooning, for piano trio, horn and percussion
Four Instruments
1966–67 (40) *First Principles*
1967 (41) *Chorus and Instruments*
In Search of an Orchestration
1968 (42) *Vertical Thoughts 2*
False Relationships and the Extended Ending, for two
chamber groups

1969 (43) *On Time and the Instrumental Factor*, for orchestra
1970 (44) *Madame Press Died Last Week at 90*, for instrumental
            ensemble
            The Viola in My Life I and II, for solo viola and
            instruments
            The Viola in My Life III, for viola and piano
1971 (45) *The Viola in My Life* IV, for viola and orchestra
            Chorus and Orchestra
            Three Clarinets, Cello and Piano
            Rothko Chapel, for solo viola, soprano, alto, chorus,
            percussion and celeste
            I Met Heine on the Rue Fürstenberg, for voice and
            chamber ensemble
1972 (46) *Cello and Orchestra*
            Voice and Instruments
            Chorus and Orchestra II
            Voices and Instruments
            Piano and Voices, for five pianos (pianists also hum)
            Pianos and Voices II, for five pianos and five voices
1973 (47) *String Quartet and Orchestra*
            For Frank O'Hara, for instrumental ensemble
            Voices and Cello
1974 (48) *Instruments* I
            Voice and Instruments II
1975 (49) *Piano and Orchestra*
            Instruments II
            Four Instruments II

FIELD, John/1782–1837/Great Britain

1814 (22) Three Nocturnes, for piano
1832 (50) *fp.* Piano Concerto No. 1 in E♮ major
Field also composed:
7 concertos
4 sonatas
20 nocturnes (invented the name and style of *Nocturne*)
6 rondos
2 divertissements
2 fantasias
2 piano quintets
4 romances, etc.

FINE, Irving/1914–1962/U.S.A.

1942 (28) *Alice in Wonderland*, incidental music
1944 (30) *The Choral New Yorker*, cantata
1946 (32) *Fantasia*, for string trio
            Violin Sonata
1948 (34) *Toccata Concertante*, for orchestra
            Partita for wind quintet
1949 (35) *The Hour-glass*, choral cycle
1952 (38) String Quartet

                      Mutability, song cycle
1955 (41) *Serious Song and Lament*, for string orchestra
1960 (46) *Diversion*, for orchestra
1961 (47) *Romanza*, for wind quintet
1962 (48) Symphony No. 2

FINZI, Gerald/1901–1956/Great Britain

1924 (23) *Severn Rhapsody*
1933 (32) *A Young Man's Exhortation*, song cycle
1934–37 (33–36) Seven Part-Songs (Bridges) for unaccompanied
              chorus
1935 (34) *Introit*, for violin and orchestra, revised 1945
1936 (35) *Earth, Air and Rain*, song cycle
              Three Short Elegies, for unaccompanied chorus
              Five Two-part Songs (Christina Rossetti) and Five Unison
                Songs
              Two Sonnets by John Milton, for high voice and small
                orchestra
              Interlude, for oboe and string quartet
1940 (39) *Dies Natalis*, cantata
1942 (41) *Let us Garlands Bring*, five songs
              Prelude and Fugue for violin, viola and cello
1945 (44) *Farewell to Arms*, for tenor and small orchestra
              Five Bagatelles for clarinet and piano
1946 (45) "Lo, the full and final sacrifice", festival anthem
1947 (46) *Ode for St. Cecilia's Day* (possibly 1950)
1948 (47) *Love's Labours Lost*, incidental music
1949 (48) Clarinet Concerto
              Before and After Summer, song cycle
1950 (49) *Intimations of Immortality*, for tenor, chorus and
                orchestra
1952 (51) *Love's Labours Lost*, orchestral suite
1954 (53) *Grand Fantasia and Toccata*, for piano and orchestra
1955 (54) Cello Concerto
1956 (55) *In Terra Pax*, for chorus and orchestra
              Eclogue, for piano and string orchestra
1958 (posthumous) *p. The Fall of the Leaf*, for orchestra
1959 (posthumous) *p. To a Poet*, song cycle

FLOTOW, Friedrich/1812–1883/Germany

1847 (35) *Martha*, opera
Flotow composed a great many operas, only one of which has survived.

FOSS, Lukas/b.1922/U.S.A. (b.Germany)

1938 (16) Four two-part Inventions for piano
              Drei Goethe-Lieder
1940 (18) Music for *The Tempest*
              Two Symphonic Pieces
              Four Preludes, for flute, clarinet and bassoon

1941 (19) *Allegro Concertante*, for orchestra
Dance Sketch, for orchestra
Duo for cello and piano
1942 (20) *The Prairie*, for chorus with soloists and orchestra
Clarinet Concerto (later revised as Piano Concerto No. 1)
1943 (21) *Paradigm*, for percussion
1944 (22) *The Heart Remembers*, ballet
Within These Walls, ballet
Symphony
Ode, for orchestra (revised 1958)
1945 (23) *Song of Anguish*, for voice and piano, or orchestra
1946 (24) *Song of Songs*, for voice and orchestra
Composer's Holiday, for violin and piano
1947 (25) String Quartet
1948 (26) Oboe Concerto
Ricordare, for orchestra
Capriccio, for cello and piano
1949 (27) *The Jumping Frog of Calaveras County*, opera
Piano Concerto No. 2
1952 (30) *Parable of Death*, for tenor, narrator and orchestra
1955 (33) *Griffelkin*, opera
The Gift of the Magi, ballet
1956 (34) Psalms, for chorus and orchestra
1957 (35) *Behold! I Build an House*, for chorus
1958 (36) *Symphony of Chorales*
1959 (37) *Introductions and Goodbyes*, opera
1960 (38) *Time Cycle*, four songs with orchestra
1963 (41) *Echoi*, for clarinet, cello, piano and percussion
1964 (42) *Elytres*, for orchestra
1965 (43) *Fragments of Archilochos*, for chorus, speaker, soloists and
chamber ensemble
1966 (44) *Discrepancy*, for twenty-four winds
1967 (45) Cello Concerto
Phorion, for orchestra, electric organ, harpsichord and
guitar
Baroque Variations, for orchestra
1969 (47) *Geod*, for orchestra with optional voices
1972 (50) *Ni, bruit, ni vitesse*, for two pianos, two percussion and
inside piano
Cave of the Winds, for wind quintet
1973 (51) *MAP*, a musical game for an entire evening, any four
musicians can play
1974 (52) *fp. Orpheus*, for viola, cello or guitar and orchestra

FRANCK, César/1822–1890/Belgium

1840 (18) Three Piano Trios, in F♯m: B♭: Bm
1842 (20) Piano Trio No. 4 in B major
1843 (21) Andante quietoso, for violin and piano, in A major
1846 (24) *Ruth*
Ce qu'on entend sur la montagne, symphonic poem
(c.1846)

1851–52 (29) *Le Valet de Ferme*, opera
1858 (36) Ave Maria, motet
1865 (43) *The Tower of Babel*, oratorio
1872 (50) *Panis Angelicus*
1874 (52) *Redemption*, cantata with symphonic interlude
1876 (54) *Les Éolides*, symphonic poem
1878 (56) Cantabile for organ
        Fantasie in A major, for organ
        Pièce héroïque, for organ
1879 (57) *Béatitudes*, cantata
        Piano Quintet in F minor
1880 (58) *L'Organiste*, fifty-five pieces for harmonium
1881 (59) *Rebecca*
1882 (60) *Le Chasseur maudit*, symphonic poem
        Hulda, opera (1882–85)
1884 (62) *Les Djinns*, symphonic poem for piano and orchestra
        Prélude, Chorale et Fugue, for piano
        Nocturne, vocal
1885 (63) *Symphonic Variations*, for piano and orchestra
1886 (64) Violin Sonata in A major
1887 (65) Prélude, Chorale et Finale, for piano
1888 (66) Symphony in D minor (1886–88)
        Psyche, symphonic poem
        Ghisele, opera (1888–90)
1889 (67) Quartet in D major
1890 (68) Chorales for organ

FRESCOBALDI, Girolamo/1583–1643/Italy

1615 (32) *p.* Toccate d'Involatura
        p. Ricercare e canzone francesi
1624 (41) *p.* Capricci sopra diversi soggetti
1627 (44) *p.* Second Book of Toccate
1628 (45) *p.* Libro delle canzoni
1635 (52) *p.* Fiori musicali
Frescobaldi composed many toccatas, fugues, ricercari, etc., for organ
and harpsichord; also madrigals and motets.

FRICKER, Peter Racine/b.1920/Great Britain

1941–44 (21–24) Three Preludes for piano
1946 (26) Four Fughettas for two pianos
1947 (27) Sonata for Organ
        Two Madrigals
        Wind Quintet
        Three Sonnets of Cecco Angiolieri, for tenor and seven
            instruments
        String Quartet in one movement
1948 (28) Symphony No. 1 (1948–49)
        Rondo Scherzoso, for orchestra
1949 (29) *Prelude, Elegy and Finale*, for string orchestra
        Concerto for Violin and small orchestra, No. 1

(1949–50)
1950 (30) Violin Sonata
            Concertante No. 1, for English horn and strings
            Symphony No. 2 (1950–51)
            Four Impromptus, for piano
1951 (31) Concertante No. 2, for three pianos, strings and timpani
            Canterbury Prologue, ballet
            Viola Concerto (1951–53)
1952 (32) String Quartet No. 2 (1952–53)
            Concerto for piano and small orchestra (1952–54)
1953–54 (33) Violin Concerto No. 2, *Rapsodia Concertante*
1954 (34) *Dance Scene*, for orchestra
            Nocturne and Scherzo for piano, four hands
1955 (35) Horn Sonata
            The Tomb of St. Eulalia, elegy for counter-tenor, gamba and
                harpsichord
            Litany, for double string orchestra
            Musick's Empire, for chorus and small orchestra
1956 (36) Cello Sonata
            Suite for Harpsichord
1957–58 (37) *The Vision of Judgment*, oratorio
            Octet for flute, clarinet, bassoon, horn, violin, viola,
                cello and double-bass
            Variations for piano
1958 (38) *Comedy Overture*, for orchestra
            Toccata for piano and orchestra (1958–59)
1959 (39) Serenade No. 1, for flute, clarinet, bass-clarinet, viola,
                cello and harp
            Serenade No. 2, for flute, oboe and piano
1960 (40) Symphony No. 3
1961 (41) Cantata for tenor and chamber ensemble (1961–62)
            Twelve studies for piano
1963 (43) *O Longs désirs*, five songs for soprano and orchestra
1964–66 (44–46) Symphony No. 4
1965 (45) Ricercare for organ
            Four *Dialogues*, for oboe and piano
            Four Songs for soprano and piano (also orchestrated)
1966 (46) Fantasy for viola and piano
            Three Scenes, for orchestra
            The Day and the Spirits, for soprano and harp (1966–67)
1967 (47) Seven Counterpoints for orchestra
            Ave Maris Stella, for male voices and piano
            Episodes I, for piano (1967–68)
            Cantilena and Cabaletta, for solo soprano
1968 (48) *Refrains*, for solo oboe
            Magnificat, for solo voices, choir and orchestra
            Concertante No. 4, for flute, oboe, violin and strings
            Gladius Domini, toccata for organ
            Some Serious Nonsense, for tenor, flute, oboe, cello and
                harpsichord
1969 (49) Saxophone Quartet
            Praeludium for organ

1970 (50) *Paseo*, for guitar
           The Roofs, for coloratura soprano and percussion
1971 (51) *Sarabande in memoriam Igor Stravinsky*
           Nocturne, for chamber orchestra
           Intrada, for organ
           A Bourrée for Sir Arthur Bliss, for cello
           Concertante No. 5 for piano and string quartet
1972 (52) *Introitus*, for orchestra
           Come Sleep, for contralto, alto flute and bass clarinet
           Fanfare for Europe, for trumpet
           Ballade, for flute and piano
           Seven Little Songs for chorus
1973 (53) Gigue, for cello
           The Groves of Dodona, for six flutes
1974 (54) *Spirit Puck*, for clarinet and percussion
           Two Petrach Madrigals
           Trio-Sonata for organ
1975 (55) String Quartet No. 3
           Symphony No. 5

GABRIELI, Andrea/c.1510–1586/Italy

1562–5 (52–55) *p.* Sacrae cantiones, a 5 v.v.
1576 (66) *p.* Cantiones ecclesiaticae, a 4 v.v.
1578 (68) *p.* Cantiones sacrae
1589 (posthumous) *p.* Madrigali e ricercare a 4
1605 (posthumous) *p.* Canzoni all francese et ricercare Arlosi

GABRIELI, Giovanni/1557–1612/Italy

1587 (30) *p.* Concerti a 6–16 voci
           p. Madrigali e ricercare
1597 (40) *p.* Sacrae symphoniae, Book I
1608 (51) *p.* Canzona (La Spiritosa)
1615 (58) *p.* Canzoni e sonate
           p. Sacrae Symphoniae, Book II

GADE, Niels Vilhelm/1817–1890/Denmark

1840 (23) *Faedrelandets Muser*, ballet
           Echoes from Ossian, overture
           Piano Sonata
1841 (24) Symphony No. 1 in C minor
1842 (25) *Napoli*, ballet
           Violin Sonata No. 1 in A major
1844 (27) *In the Highlands*, overture
1846 (29) *p.* String Quintet in E minor
1847 (30) Symphony No. 3 in A minor
1849 (32) *p.* String Octet in F major
1850 (33) *Mariotta*, a play with music
           Symphony No. 4 in B♭ major
           p. Violin Sonata No. 2 in D minor

1852 (35) Symphony No. 5 in D minor
Spring Fantasy, for voices and orchestra
1855 (38) *p. Novelleten*, for piano trio
*c.***1856** (*c.*39) Symphony No. 6 in G minor
1861 (44) *Hamlet*, concerto overture
Michelangelo, overture
1864 (47) Symphony No. 2 in E major
Symphony No. 7 in F major
Fantasies for clarinet
p. Piano Trio in F major
p. Fantasiestücke for cello and piano
1865 (48) *p.* String Sextet in D minor
1871 (54) Symphony No. 8 in B minor
1874 (57) *Noveletten*, for string orchestra
1879 (62) *En Sommertag paa Landet*, five pieces for orchestra
1880 (63) Violin Concerto
1884 (67) *Holbergiana Suite*
1887 (70) *p.* Violin Sonata No. 3 in B♭ major
1888–90 (71–73) *Ulysses*, march
1890 (73) *p.* String Quartet in D major

GERHARD, Roberto/1896–1970/Spain

1918 (22) *L' Infantament Meravellos de Shahrazade*, for voice and
piano
Piano Trio
1922 (26) Seven Hai-Ku, for voice and five instruments
1928 (32) Wind Quintet
1934 (38) *Ariel*, ballet
1940–41 (44) *Don Quixote*, ballet
1941 (45) *Hommaje a Pedrell*, symphony
1942–45 (46–49) Violin Concerto
1944 (48) *Alegrias*, ballet suite
Pandora, ballet (1944–45)
1945–47 (49–51) *The Duenna*, opera
1950 (54) Impromptus for piano
1951 (55) Concerto for piano and strings
1952–53 (56) Symphony No. 1
1955–56 (59) Concerto for harpsichord, strings and percussion
String Quartet No. 1
1956 (60) Nonet for eight winds and accordion
1957 (61) *Don Quixote*, suite
1959 (63) Symphony No. 2
1960 (64) Symphony No. 3, *Collages*, for tape and orchestra
String Quartet No. 2 (1960–62)
1962 (66) *Concert for Eight*, for flute, clarinet, guitar, mandolin,
double-bass, accordion, piano and percussion
1963 (67) *Hymnody*, for eleven players
The Plague, for speaker, chorus and orchestra (1963–64)
1965 (69) Concerto for orchestra
1966 (70) *Epithalium*, for orchestra
Gemini, for violin and piano

1967 (71) Symphony No. 4, *New York*
1968 (72) *Libra*, for flute, clarinet, violin, guitar, piano and
                 percussion
1969 (73) *Leo*, chamber symphony for ten players

GERMAN, Sir Edward/1862—1936/Great Britain

1886 (24) *The Rival Poets*, operetta
1889 (27) *Richard III*, incidental music
1890 (28) Symphony No. 1 in E minor
1891 (29) Funeral March
1892 (30) *Gipsy Suite*
                 Henry VIII, incidental music
1893 (31) *The Tempter*, incidental music
                 Romeo and Juliet, incidental music
                 Symphony No. 2 in A minor
1895 (33) Symphonic Suite in D minor
1896 (34) *As You Like It*, incidental music
1897 (35) *In Commemoration*, fantasia
                 Hamlet, symphonic poem
1899 (37) *The Seasons*, symphonic suite
1900 (38) *Nell Gwynne*, incidental music
1901 (39) *The Emerald Isle*, operetta (unfinished, completed by
                 Sullivan, *q.v.*)
1902 (40) *Merrie England*, operetta
1903 (41) *A Princess of Kensington*, operetta
1904 (42) *Welsh Rhapsody*, for orchestra
1907 (45) *Tom Jones*, operetta
1909 (47) *Fallen Fairies*
1911 (49) Coronation March and Hymn (for the coronation of
                 George V)
1919 (57) Theme and Six Variations, for orchestra

GERSHWIN, George/1898—1937/U.S.A.

1924 (26) *Rhapsody in Blue*, for piano and orchestra (orchestrated
                 by Grofé, *q.v.*)
1925 (27) Piano Concerto
1928 (30) *An American in Paris*, for orchestra
1931 (33) Second Rhapsody
1934 (36) *Cuban Overture*
1935 (37) *Porgy and Bess*, opera
1936 (38) Three Preludes for piano
Gershwin also composed many popular songs.

GIBBONS, Orlando/1583—1625/Great Britain

1612 (29) *p*, Madrigals and Mottets of Five Parts: Apt for viols and
                 voyces
Gibbons other works include about 40 anthems and other church
music, music for viols, keyboard pieces, and expressive madrigals,
such as "The Silver Swan".

1936 (24) *Four Moods in Three Keys*, for chamber orchestra
1937 (25) *The Woolyworm*, symphonic satire
            The Panhandle, suite for orchestra
            Thoughts Provoked on Becoming a Prospective Papa, suite
               for orchestra
            The Crucifixion, for solo voices, narrator, chorus and
               orchestra
1938 (26) *The Raven*, for narrator and orchestra
1939–40 (27) *An American Symphony*, Symphony No. 1
1940 (28) *Portrait of a Frontier Town*, suite for orchestra
            Symphony Of Faith, Symphony No. 2
            A Symphony of Free Men, Symphony No. 3 (1940–41)
1941 (29) *The Night Before Christmas*, for narrator and orchestra
1942 (30) Three Sketches for Strings
1943 (31) *Prairie Poem*
            Symphony No. 4
1944 (32) *A Short Overture to an Unwritten Opera*, for orchestra
            The Alamo, symphonic poem
            Symphony No. 5 (1944–45)
1945 (33) *To an Unknown Soldier*, symphonic poem
1946–47 (34) Symphony No. $5\frac{1}{2}$ (*A Symphony for Fun*)
1947 (35) Symphony No. 6
            Dude Ranch
            Three Short Pieces for Strings
1948 (36) *Saga of a Prairie School*
Gillis also composed:
Symphonies Nos. 7–12
A Short, short, symphony
Shindig, ballet
The Park Avenue Kids, opera
The Gift of the Magi, opera
Pep Rally, opera
The Legend of Star Valley Junction, opera
The Nazarene, opera
Behold the Man, opera
Atlanta, orchestral suite
Twinkletoes, suite for orchestra
Four Scenes from Yesterday, suite for orchestra
Tulsa — A symphonic Portrait in Oil, for orchestra
Amarillo — A Symphonic Celebration, for orchestra
The Man Who Invented Music, for narrator and orchestra
Alice in Orchestralia, for narrator and orchestra
Thomas Wolfe, American, for narrator and orchestra
Toscannini: a portrait of a century, for narrator and orchestra
A Ceremony of Allegiance, for narrator and orchestra
His Name Was John, for narrator and orchestra
The Answer, for narrator and orchestra
Piano Concertos Nos. 1 and 2
Chamber music
Choral music.

GIORDANO, Umberto/1867–1948/Italy

1889 (22) *Marina*, opera
1892 (25) *Mala Vita*, opera
1894 (27) *Regina Diaz*, opera
1896 (29) *Andrea Chénier*, opera
1898 (31) *Fedora*, opera
1904 (37) *Siberia*, opera
1907 (40) *Marcella*, opera
1910 (43) *Mese Mariano*, opera
1915 (48) *Madame Sans-Gêne*, opera
1921 (54) *Giove a Pompeii*, opera
1924 (57) *La Cena delle Beffe*, opera
1929 (62) *Il re*, opera

GLAZUNOV, Alexander/1865–1936/Russia

1881 (16) Symphony No. 1 (first performed under the baton of
            Balakirev, *q.v.*)
            Overture on Greek Themes, No. 1 (1881–84)
1882 (17) String Quartet in D major
            Overture on Greek Themes, No. 2 (1883–85)
1883 (18) Serenade No. 1
            String Quartet in F major
1884 (19) Serenade No. 2
1885 (20) *Stenka Razin*, tone poem
1886 (21) Symphony No. 2
1887 (22) *Suite Caractéristique* (possibly 1884)
            Lyric Poem
1889 (24) *The Forest*, fantasia (possibly 1887)
1890 (25) *Wedding March*
            Un Fête Slav
            The Sea
1891 (26) *Oriental Rhapsody*
1892 (27) Symphony No. 3 (possibly 1890)
            The Kremlin (possibly 1890)
            Le Printemps
            String Quartet in A major
1893 (28) Symphony No. 4
1894 (29) *Carnival*, overture
            Chopiniana Suite
            String Quartet in A minor
1895 (30) Symphony No. 5
            Cortège Solenelle
1896 (31) Symphony No. 6
1899 (34) String Quartet in D minor
1900 (35) *Solenne Overture*
1901 (36) *The Seasons*, ballet (possibly earlier)
1902 (37) Symphony No. 7
            Ballade
1904 (39) Violin Concerto
1905 (40) *Scéne Dansante*
            Symphony No. 8

1907 (42) *Canto di destino*, overture
1909 (44) Symphony No. 9 (begun, left unfinished, first performed
           1948)
1911 (46) Piano Concerto
1933 (68) *Epic Poem*
1936 (71) Saxophone Concerto

GLIÈRE, Reinhold Moritzovich/1875–1956/Russia

1899–1900 (24) Symphony No. 1
1900 (25) String Octet in D major
           String Sextet No. 1
           String Quartet No. 1 in A major
1902 (27) String Sextet No. 2
1904 (29) String Sextet No. 3 in C major
1905 (30) String Quartet No. 2 in G minor
1907 (32) Symphony No. 2
1908 (33) *The Sirens*, symphonic poem
1909–11 (34–36) Symphony No. 3, *Ilya Murometz*
1912 (37) *Chrysis*, ballet
1915 (40) *Trizna*, symphonic poem
1919 (44) *Imitation of Jezekiel*, symphonic poem for narrator and
           orchestra
1921 (46) *Cossacks of Zaporozh*, symphonic poem
1922, 1930 (47, 55) *Comedians*, ballet
1923–25 (48–50) *Shakh-Senem*, opera
1924 (49) Two Poems for soprano and orchestra
           For the Festival of the Comintern, fantasy for wind
               orchestra
           March of the Red Army, for wind orchestra
1925 (50) *Cleopatra*, ballet
1926–27 (51) *Red Poppy*, ballet
1928 (53) String Quartet No. 3
1938 (63) Harp Concerto in E♭ major
1942 (67) Concerto for coloratura soprano
Glière also composed many songs and piano pieces.

GLINKA, Michail/1804–1857/Russia

1822 (18) Variations on a Theme of Mozart, for piano
1826 (22) Memorial Cantata
           Pathètique Trio, for piano, clarinet and bassoon, or piano,
               violin and cello (1826–27)
1830 (26) String Quartet in F major
1833–34 (29) Sextet for piano and strings
1836 (32) *A Life for the Tsar*, opera (called *Ivan Sussanin* in Russia)
           The Moldavian Gipsy, incidental music
1839 (35) *Valse-fantaisie*, for orchestra (revised 1856)
1840 (36) *Farewell to Petersburg*, song cycle
1842 (38) *Russlan and Ludmilla*, opera
1845 (41) Spanish Overture No. 1, *Jota Aragonesa*
1847 (43) *Greeting to the Fatherland*, for piano

1848 (44) *Wedding Song (Kamarinskaya)*, fantasia for orchestra
Glinka also composed many piano pieces and songs.

GLUCK, Christoph Willibald (von)/1714–1787/Bavaria (Germany)

1741 (27) *Artaserse*, opera
1742 (28) *Demetrio*, opera
1743 (29) *Il Tigrane*, opera
1745 (31) *Ippolito*, opera
1746 (32) *Artmene*, opera
     p. Six Sonatas for two violins and continuo
1747 (33) *Le Nozze d'Ercole e d'Ebe*, opera
1750 (36) *Ezio*, opera
1752 (38) *Issipile*, opera
1753 (39) Nine Symphonies
1755 (41) *Les Amours champêtres*, opera
     Alessandro, ballet
1756 (42) *Antigono*, opera
     Le Chinois poli en France, opera
1758 (44) *L'Isle de Merlin, ou, le Monde renversé*, opera
1759 (45) *L'Arbe enchanté*, opera
1761 (47) *La Cadi dupé*, opera
     Don Juan, ballet
1762 (48) *Orfeo ed Euridice*, opera
1764 (50) *Poro*, opera
     La Rencontre imprévue, opera
1765 (51) *Semiramide*, ballet
1766 (52) *L'Orfano della China*, ballet
1767 (53) *Alkestis*, opera
1770 (56) *Paride ed Elena*, opera
1774 (60) *Iphigénie en Aulide*, opera
1777 (63) *Armide*, opera
1779 (65) *Iphigénie en Tauride*, opera
?   (?) Seven Sonatas for two violins and bass

GODARD, Benjamin/1849–1895/France

1876 (27) Violin Concerto No. 2, *Concerto romantique*
1878 (29) Piano Concerto
     La Tasse, dramatic symphony for solo voices, chorus and
       orchestra
     Les Bijoux de Jeanette, one-act opera
1879 (30) *Scènes poétiques*
1880 (31) Symphony
     Diane: poème dramatique
1882 (33) *Symphonie*, ballet
1883 (34) *Symphonie Gothique*
1884 (35) *Symphonie Orientale*
     Pedro de Zalamea, four-act opera
1886 (37) *Symphonie Légendaire*
1888 (39) *Jocelyn*, opera
1890 (41) *Dante*, opera

Godard also composed:
3 string quartets
3 violin sonatas
1 piano trio
Suite de trois morceaux, for flute
Over 100 songs.

GOEHR, Alexander/b.1932/Germany

1951 (19) *Songs of Babel*
           Piano Sonata (1951–52)
1954 (22) Fantasias for clarinet and piano
           Fantasia for orchestra (revised 1958)
1956–57 (24) String Quartet No. 1
1957 (25) Capriccio for piano
           The Deluge, cantata for soprano, contralto, flute, horn,
               trumpet, harp, violin, viola, cello and double bass
1958 (26) *La Belle Dame sans merci*, ballet
1959 (27) Variations for flute and piano
           Four Songs from the Japanese, for high voice with
               orchestra or piano
           Sutter's Gold, cantata for bass solo, chorus and orchestra
               (1959–60)
           Hecuba's Lament, for orchestra (1959–61)
1961 (29) Suite for flute, clarinet, horn, harp, violin (doubling
               viola) and cello
           Violin Concerto (1961–62)
1962 (30) A Little Cantata of Proverbs
           Two Choruses, for mixed chorus a cappella
1963 (31) *Virtutes*, cycle of songs and melodramas for chorus,
               piano duet and percussion
           Little Symphony (In memory of Walter Goehr), for small
               orchestra
           Little Music for Strings
1964 (32) Five Poems and an Epigram of William Blake, for mixed
               chorus
           Three Pieces for Piano
1965 (33) Pastorals for Orchestra
1966 (34) *Arden muss sterben*, opera
1967 (35) *Warngedichte*, for low voice and piano
           String Quartet No. 2
1968 (36) *Romanza*, for cello and orchestra
           Naboth's Vineyard, a dramatic madrigal
1969 (37) *Konzertstücke*, for piano and small orchestra
           Nonomiya, for piano
           Paraphrase on the Madrigal "Il combattimento de
               Tancredi e Clorinda" by Monteverdi, for solo clarinet
1970 (38) Symphony in one movement
           Shadowplay-2, music theater for tenor, alto flute, alto
               saxophone, horn, cello and piano
           Sonata about Jerusalem
           Concerto for eleven instruments

GOLDMARK, Karl/1830–1915/Hungary

1875 (45) *The Queen of Sheba*, opera
1876 (46) *Rustic Wedding*, symphony
1886 (56) *Merlin*
1896 (66) *The Cricket on the Hearth*
1908 (78) *A Winter's Tale*

GOSSEC, François Joseph/1734–1829/Belgium

1760 (26) Requiem Mass
1761 (27) *Le Tonnelier*, opera
1765 (31) *Le Faux Lord*, opera
1766 (32) *Les Pêcheurs*, opera
1767 (33) *Toinon et Toinette*, opera
           Le Double déguisemente, opera
1774 (40) *Sabinus*, opera
           La Nativité, oratorio
1775 (41) *Alexis et Daphné*, opera
1776 (42) *Hylas et Sylvie*, incidental music
1778 (44) *Le Fête du village*, opera
1779 (45) *Les Scythes enchaînes*, ballet
           Mirsa, ballet
1781 (47) *L'Arche d'alliance*, oratorio
1782 (48) *Thesée*, opera
1786 (52) *Rosine*, opera
1796 (62) *La Reprise de Toulon*, opera
1803 (69) *Les Sabots et le Cerisier*, opera
1813 (79) *Dernière Messe des vivants*

GOULD, Morton/b.1913/U.S.A.

1932 (19) Chorale and Fugue in Jazz
1936 (23) Little Symphony
           Symphonette No. 2
1937 (24) Piano Concerto
           Spirituals for orchestra
1939 (26) Symphonette No. 3
           Jericho, for concert band
1940 (27) *A Foster Gallery*
           Latin-American Symphonette
1941 (28) *Lincoln Legend*
1943 (30) Symphony No. 1
           Symphony No. 2 (on marching tunes)
           Concertette for viola and orchestra
           Viola Concerto
           Interplay, for piano and orchestra
1944 (31) Concerto for orchestra
1945 (32) *Harvest*, for vibraphone, harp and strings
           Ballade for band
1946 (33) *Minstrel Show*
           Symphony No. 3
1947 (34) *Fall River Legend*, ballet

1948 (35) Serenade of Carols
1950 (37) *Family Album*
1951 (38) *Battle Hymn of the Republic*
1952 (39) *Dance Variations*, for two pianos and orchestra
1953 (40) Inventions for four pianos and orchestra
1955 (42) *Jekyll & Hyde Variations*
               Derivations, for clarinet and band
1956 (43) *Dialogue*, for piano and strings
               Santa Fe Saga
1957 (44) *Declaration Suite*
1958 (45) *Rhythm Gallery*, for narrator and orchestra
               St. Lawrence Suite, for band
1964 (51) *Festive Music*, for off-stage trumpet and orchestra
               Marches: Formations
               World War I: Revolutionary Prelude, Prologue (1964–65)
1966 (53) *Venice*, audiograph for two orchestras
               Columbia
1967 (54) *Vivaldi Gallery*, for string quartet and divided orchestra
1968 (55) *Troubador Music*, for four guitars and orchestra
1969 (56) *Soundings*
1971 (58) Suite for tuba and three horns

GOUNOD, Charles/1818–1893/France

1837 (19) Scherzo for orchestra
1840 (22) *Marche militaire suisse*, for orchestra
1851 (33) *Sappho*, opera
1852–54 (34–36) *La Nonne sanglante*, opera
1852–59 (34–41) *Faust*, opera
1855 (37) Symphony No. 1 in D major
               Symphony No. 2 in E♭ major
               Messe Solenelle à St. Cécile
1857 (39) *Le Médecin malgré lui*, opera
1860 (42) *Philémon et Baucis*, opera
1862 (44) *La Reine de Saba*, opera
1864 (46) *Mireille*, opera
1865 (47) Chant des Compagnons
1867 (49) *Roméo et Juliette*, opera
1871 (53) Saltarello for orchestra
1873 (55) *Funeral March of a Marionette*, for orchestra
1876–77 (58) *Cinq-Mars*, opera
1878 (60) *Marche Religieuse*, for orchestra
1879 (61) *The Redemption*, oratorio
1881 (63) *Le Tribut de Zamora*, opera
1884 (66) *fp. Mors et Vita*, oratorio
1888 (70) Petite Symphonie, for ten wind instruments

GRAINGER, Percy/1882–1961/Australia

1916 (34) *In a Nutshell*, suite for piano and orchestra
1918 (36) *Children's March*
1921 (39) *Molly on the Shore*

1922 (40) *Shepherd's Hey*
1925 (43) *Country Gardens*
1927 (45) *Shallow Brown*
          Irish Tune from County Derry (Londonderry Air)
1928 (46) Colonial Songs
          Over the Hills and Far Away
1929 (47) *English Dance*
1930 (48) *Lord Peter's Stable Boy*
          Spoon River
          To A Nordic Princess
1931 (49) *The Nightingale and the Two Sisters*
1932 (50) *Blithe Bells*

GRANDJANY, Marcel/1891–1975/U.S.A. (b. France)

(dates unknown) *Poème*, for harp, horn and orchestra
                Aria in Classic Style, for harp and strings
                Children's Hour Suite, for harp
                Colorado Trail, for harp
                Divertissement, for harp
                Rhapsody, for harp
                Fantasia on a Theme of Haydn
                The Erie Canal

GRÉTRY, André Ernest Modeste/1742–1813/Belgium

1769 (27) *Le Tableau parlant*, opera-comique
1771 (29) *Zemire et Azor*, opera-comique
1778 (36) *L'Amant jaloux*, opera-comique
1784 (42) *L'Épreuve villageoise*, opera-comique
          Richard Coeur-de-Lion

GRIEG, Edvard Hagerup/1843–1907/Norway

1865 (22) *In Autumn*, concert overture
          Violin Sonata No. 1
1867 (24) Lyric Pieces for piano, Book I
          Violin Sonata No. 2
1869 (26) Piano Concerto in A minor
1872 (29) *Sigurd Jorsalfar*, incidental music
1875 (32) *Peer Gynt*, incidental music
1880 (37) Two Elegiac Melodies
1881 (38) Norwegian Dances
1883 (40) Lyric Pieces for piano, Book II
1884 (41) Lyric Pieces for piano, Book III
1885 (42) *Holberg Suite*, for strings
1887 (44) Violin Sonata, No. 3
1888 (45) Lyric Pieces for piano, Book IV
1891 (48) Lyric Pieces for piano, Book V
1893 (50) Lyric Pieces for piano, Book VI
1895 (52) Lyric Pieces for piano, Book VII
1896 (53) Lyric Pieces for piano, Book VIII

1898 (55)   Lyric Pieces for piano, Book IX
Symphonic Dances
1901 (58)   Lyric Pieces for piano, Book X
1906 (63)   *Moods*
Grieg also composed other piano works and many songs.

GRIFFES, Charles Tomlinson/1884–1920/U.S.A.

1912 (28)   *Tone Images*, for mezzo-soprano and piano
The Pleasure Dome of Kubla Khan, symphonic poem
(1912–16)
1915 (31)   Three Tone Pictures for piano:
The Lake at Evening
The Vale of Dreams
The Night Wind
Fantasy Pieces for piano:
Barcarolle
Notturno
Scherzo
1916 (32)   *The Kairn of Koridwen*, dance drama for woodwinds, harp,
celesta and piano
Two Sketches on Indian Themes, for string quartet
Roman Sketches:
The White Peacock
Nightfall
The Fountain of Acqua Paolo
Clouds
1917 (33)   *Sho-Jo*, pantomimic drama for four woodwinds, four
strings, harp and percussion
1918 (34)   *Poem*, for flute and orchestra
Piano Sonata
1919 (35)   Nocturnes for orchestra
Griffes also composed many choral works and songs.

GROFÉ, Ferde/1892–1972/U.S.A.

1931 (39)   *Grand Canyon Suite*, for orchestra
1937 (45)   *Broadway at Night*
Symphony in Steel (uses four pairs of shoes, two brooms,
locomotive bell, pneumatic drill and compressed air
tank)
1964 (72)   *World's Fair Suite*
Grofé also wrote: *Tabloid, Death Valley Suite, Mississippi Suite, Mark
Twain Suite, Hollywood Suite, Milk, Wheels, Three Shades of Blue, New
England Suite, Metropolis, Aviation Suite.*

HAMILTON, Ian/b.1922/Great Britain

1948 (26)   Quintet for clarinet and string quartet
Symphonic Variations for string orchestra
1949 (27)   Symphony No. 1
String Quartet No. 1

1950 (28) Clarinet Concerto
1951 (29) Symphony No. 2
Clerk Saunders, ballet
Flute Quartet
Piano Sonata (revised 1971)
1952 (30) Violin Concerto
Bartholomew Fair, overture
1954 (32) String Octet
Four Border Songs and the Fray of Suport
Songs of Summer, for soprano and piano
1956 (34) Scottish Dances
Sonata for chamber orchestra
1957 (35) Cantata for tenor and piano
Five Love Songs, for tenor and orchestra
1958 (36) *Overture 1912*
Concerto for jazz trumpet and orchestra
Sonata for solo cello
1959 (37) Sinfonia for two orchestras
Écossaise, for orchestra
1960 (38) Piano Concerto (revised 1967)
1962 (40) Arias for small orchestra
Sextet
1963 (41) *Sonatas and Variants*, for ten wind instruments
Nocturnes with Cadenza, for piano
1964 (42) Organ Concerto
Cantos, for orchestra
Jubilee, for orchestra
1965 (43) *Dialogues*, for soprano and five instruments
Aubade, for solo organ
String Quartet No. 2
1966 (44) *Threnos — In Time of War*, for solo organ
Five Scenes, for trumpet and piano
Flute Sonata
1967–69 (45–47) *Agamemnon*, opera
The Royal Hunt of the Sun, opera
1968 (46) *Pharsalia*, opera
1969 (47) *Circus*, for two trumpets and orchestra
1970 (48) *Epitaph for This World and Time*, for three choruses and
three organs
Alastor, for orchestra
Voyage, for horn and chamber orchestra
1971 (49) Violin Concerto No. 2, *Amphion*
1972 (50) *Commedia*, concerto for orchestra
Descent of the Celestial City, for chorus and organ
Palinodes, for solo piano
1974 (52) *The Cataline Conspiracy*, opera
Piano Sonata No. 2
1975 (53) Te Deum
Violin Sonata No. 1
Cello Sonata No. 2
Sea Music, for chorus and string quartet

HANDEL, George Frederick/1685–1759/Germany

1707 (22) "Laudate pueri Dominum", aria
            Rodrigo, opera (c.1707)
1708 (23) *La Resurrezione*, Easter oratorio
1711 (26) *Rinaldo*, opera
1712 (27) *Il Pastor fido*, opera (first version)
1713 (28) *Teseo*, opera
            Te Deum and Jubilate, for the Peace of Utrecht
1715 (30) *Amadigi de Gaule*, opera
            The *Water Music* (1715–17)
c.1720 (c.35) The *Chandos Anthems*
            Acis and Galatea, secular cantata
            Radamisto, opera
            Huit Suites de pièces, for harpsichord
1721 (36) *Floridante*, opera
1723 (38) *Ottone*, opera
1724 (39) *Giulio Cesare*, opera
            Fifteen Chamber Sonatas
1725 (40) *Rodelinda*, opera
            Trio Sonata in D minor
1727 (42) *Zadok the Priest*, coronation anthem
            Admeto, opera
1728 (43) *Tolomeo*, opera
c.1731 (c.46) Nine sonatas for two violins and continuo
1732 (47) *Esther*, English Biblical oratorio
            Sosarme, opera
            Ezio, opera
1733 (48) *Orlando*, opera
            Huit Suites de pièces, for harpsichord
1734 (49) *Persichore*, ballet
            Il Pastor fido (second and third versions)
            Arianna, opera
            p. Six concerti grossi
1735 (50) *Alcina*, opera
1736 (51) *Atalanta*, opera
            Alexander's Feast, secular cantata
            Six fugues for harpsichord
1737 (52) *Berenice*, opera
            Concerto grosso in C major
1738 (53) *Xerxes*, opera (which includes "Ombra mai fu", known
                as "Handel's Largo")
            Six organ concerti
1739 (54) *Israel in Egypt*, oratorio
            Saul, oratorio (which includes the "Dead March")
            Ode for St. Cecilia's Day
            Twelve concerti grossi
            Seven trio sonatas
1740 (55) p. Concerti for oboe and strings
            p. Six organ concerti
            Three double concerti (1740–50)
1741 (56) *Messiah*, oratorio (composed in under four weeks)
            Five concerti grossi

1742 (57) *Forest Music*
1743 (58) *Samson*, oratorio
          The *Dettingen* Te Deum
1744 (59) *Semele*, secular oratorio
1745 (60) *Belshazzar*, oratorio
1746 (61) *Occasional Oratorio*
1747 (62) *Judas Maccabaeus*, oratorio
1748 (63) *Joshua*, oratorio
1749 (64) *Music for the Royal Fireworks*
          Solomon, oratorio
          Susanna, oratorio
1750 (65) *Theodora*, oratorio
1752 (67) *Jephtha*, oratorio
1760 (posthumous) *p.* Six organ concerti

HANSON, Howard/b.1896/U.S.A.

1915 (19) Prelude and Double Fugue, for two pianos
1916 (20) Symphonic Prelude
          Piano Quintet
1917 (21) Symphonic Legend
          Concerto da Camera, for piano and string quartet
1919 (23) Symphonic Rhapsody
1920 (24) *Before the Dawn*, symphonic poem
          Exaltation, symphonic poem with piano obbligato
1921 (25) Concerto for organ, strings and harp
1922 (26) Symphony No. 1 in E minor, *Nordic*
1923 (27) *North and West*, symphonic poem
          Lux Aeterna, symphonic poem with viola obbligato
          String Quartet
1925 (29) *The Lament of Beowulf*, for chorus
1926 (30) Organ Concerto
          Pan and the Priest, symphonic poem
1927 (31) *Heroic Elegy*, for chorus and orchestra
1930 (34) Symphony No. 2, *Romantic*
1933 (37) *The Merry Mount*, opera
1935 (39) *Drum Taps*, for baritone, chorus and orchestra
1938 (42) Symphony No. 3
1943 (47) Symphony No. 4, *Requiem* (in memory of his father)
1945 (49) *Serenade*, for flute, strings, harp and orchestra
1948 (52) Piano Concerto
1951 (55) *Fantasia on a Theme of Youth*, for piano and strings
1955 (59) Symphony No. 5, *Sinfonia sacrae*
1956 (60) *Elegy in memory of Serge Koussevitsky*, for orchestra
1958 (62) *Mosaics*, for orchestra
1959 (63) *Summer Seascapes*
1961 (65) *Bold Island Suite*
1963 (67) *For the First Time*, for orchestra
1967 (71) *Dies Natalis*, for orchestra
1968 (72) Symphony No. 6

HARRIS, Roy Ellsworth/b.1898/U.S.A.

1926 (28) *Impression of a rainy day*, for string quartet
1927 (29) Concerto for clarinet and string quartet
1928 (30) Piano Sonata
1929 (31) *American Portraits*, for orchestra
1930 (32) String Quartet No. 1
1931 (33) *Toccata*, for orchestra
1932 (34) *Chorale*, for strings
              Fantasy, for piano and woodwind quintet
              String Sextet
1933 (35) Symphony No. 1
              String Quartet No. 2
1934 (36) Symphony No. 2
              When Johnny comes marching home, overture
              Songs for Occupations, for chorus
              Piano Trio
1936 (38) *Symphony for Voices*
              Time Suite, for orchestra
              Prelude and fugue for string orchestra
              Piano Quintet
1937 (39) Symphony No. 3
              String Quartet No. 3
1938 (40) *Soliloquy and Dance*, for viola and piano
1939 (41) Symphony No. 4
              String Quartet
1940 (42) *Western Landscape*, ballet
              Challenge, for baritone, chorus and orchestra
              American Creed, for orchestra
              Evening Piece, for orchestra
              Ode to Truth, for orchestra
              String Quintet
1941 (43) *From This Earth*, ballet
              Acceleration, for orchestra
              Violin Sonata
1942 (44) Piano Concerto, with band
              Symphony No. 5
              What so proudly we hail, ballet
1943 (45) Cantata for chorus, organ and brass
              Mass, for male chorus and organ
1944 (46) Symphony No. 6
1945 (47) Piano Concerto No. 1
1946 (48) Concerto for two pianos
              Accordion Concerto
1947 (49) *Quest*, for orchestra
1948 (50) *Elegy and Pæan*, for viola and orchestra
1949 (51) *Kentucky Spring*, for orchestra
1951 (53) *Cumberland Concerto*, for orchestra
              Symphony No. 7
1953 (55) Piano Concerto No. 2
              Abraham Lincoln walks at midnight, chamber cantata
1954 (56) *Fantasy*, for piano and orchestra
1956 (58) *Folk Fantasy* for festivals, for piano and choir

1959 (61) *Give me the splendid silent sun*, cantata for baritone and
           orchestra
1961 (63) *Canticle to the sun*, cantata for soprano and chamber
           orchestra
1962 (64) Symphony No. 8
           Symphony No. 9
1963 (65) *Epilogue to Profiles in Courage: J.F.K.*, for orchestra
           Salute to Death
1964 (66) Duo for cello and piano
           Horn of Plenty, for orchestra
1965 (67) Symphony No. 10
           Rhythm and Spaces, for string orchestra
1967 (69) Symphony No. 11
1968 (70) Concerto for amplified piano, brasses and percussion
           Piano Sextet
1969 (71) Symphony No. 12
?   ?   Symphony No. 13
1975 (77) Symphony No. 14

HAYDN, (Franz) Joseph / 1732 – 1809 / Austria

1755 (23) String Quartets Nos. 1–13
1756 (24) Organ Concerto No. 1 in C major
           Piano Concerto in C major
1759 (27) Symphony No. 1 in D major
1760 (28) Organ Concerto No. 2 in C major
           Symphony No. 2 in C major (*c.*1760)
*c.*1761 (*c.*29) Symphony No. 3 in G major
           Symphony No. 4 in D major
           Symphony No. 5 in A major
           Symphony No. 6 in D major, *Le matin*
           Symphony No. 7 in C major, *Le midi*
           Symphony No. 8 in G major, *Le soir, ou la têmpete*
           Symphony No. 19 in D major
1762 (30) Symphony No. 9 in C major
before 1763 Symphony No. 10 in D major
           Symphony No. 11 in E♭ major
           Piano Sonata No. 3 in A major
1763 (31) Symphony No. 12 in E major
           Symphony No. 13 in D major
before 1764 Symphonies Nos. 14 and 15
*c.*1764 (*c.*32) Symphonies Nos. 16–18
1764 (32) Symphony No. 22 in E♭ major, *Der Philosoph*
1765 (33) Symphony No. 30 in C major, *Alleluia*
           Symphony No. 31 in D major, *Horn Signal*
           String Quartets Nos. 14–19
           Symphony No. 26 in D minor, *Lamentations* (*c.*1765)
1766 (34) Mass No. 4, in E♭, *Great Organ*
           Piano Sonatas Nos. 4–7
           Piano Sonatas Nos. 8–12 (1766–67)
*c.*1767 (*c.*35) Piano Sonatas Nos. 13–16
1767 (35) Piano Sonata No. 17

before **1769**   Violin Concerto in C major
              Violin Concerto in G major
1769 (37)   String Quartets Nos. 20–25
before **1770**   Violin Concerto in D major
1770 (38)   Mass No. 5 in B♭, *Little Organ* or *St. John*
after **1770**   Piano Concerto in G major
before **1771**   Piano Concerto in F major
              Violin Concerto in A major
1771 (39)   String Quartets Nos. 26–31
              Piano Sonata No. 18 in C minor
before **1772**   Symphony No. 43 in E♭ major, *Mercury*
              Symphony No. 44 in E minor, *Trauersymphonie*
1772 (40)   Symphony No. 45 in F♯ minor, *Farewell*
              Symphony No. 46 in B major
              Symphony No. 48 in C major, *Maria Teresa*
              Mass No. 3, *St. Cecilia*
              String Quartets Nos. 32–37, *Sun* or *Great*
              Symphony No. 52 in C minor (1772–74)
before **1773**   Symphony No. 49 in F minor, *The Passion*
1773 (41)   Violin Sonatas Nos. 2–4 (without violin, Piano Sonatas
                 Nos. 22–24)
              Piano Sonatas Nos. 19–24
before **1774**   Symphony No. 53 in D major, *The Imperial*
1774 (42)   Symphony No. 55 in E♭ major, *The Schoolmaster*
before **1776**   Symphony No. 59 in A major, *Feuersymphonie*
1776 (44)   Symphony No. 60 in C major, *Il Distratto*
              Piano Sonatas Nos. 25–30
1777 (45)   Symphony No. 63 in C major, *La Roxolane*
              Piano Sonatas Nos. 31 and 32 (1777–78)
1779 (47)   Symphony No. 69 in C major, *Laudon*
              Piano Sonatas Nos. 33–37 (1779–80)
1781 (49)   Symphony No. 73 in D major, *La Chasse*
              Concerto for horn and strings, No. 2
              String Quartets Nos. 38–43, *Russian* or *Jungfern*
1783 (51)   Cello Concerto in D major
before **1784**   Piano Sonatas Nos. 38–40
1784 (52)   *Armida*, opera
              String Quartets Nos. 44–50, dedicated to the King of
                 Prussia (1784–87)
*c.***1785** (*c.*53)   Piano Sonata No. 41 in A♭ major
1785 (53)   Piano Sonata No. 42 in G minor (1785–86)
              Piano Sonata No. 44 in A♭ major (1785–86)
              Symphony No. 87 in A major (with Symphonies Nos.
                 82–86 comprise the *Paris* symphonies)
1786 (54)   Symphony No. 82 in C major, *The Bear*
              Symphony No. 83 in G minor, *La Poule*
              Symphony No. 84 in E♭ major
              Symphony No. 85 in B♭ major, *La Reine*
              Symphony No. 86 in D major, *The Miracle*
1787 (55)   Symphony No. 88 in G major
              Symphony No. 89 in F major
              String Quartets Nos. 51–57, *The Seven Words*, arranged

for quartet
Piano Sonata No. 45 in F major (1787–88)
1788 (56) Symphony No. 90 in C major
Symphony No. 91 in E♭ major
Symphony No. 92 in G major, *Oxford*
Toy Symphony in C major, for two violins, double-bass, keyboard and toy trumpet, drum, rattle, triangle and bird-warblers
1789 (57) String Quartets Nos. 58 and 59
Piano Sonata No. 46 in C major
Piano Sonata No. 47 in E♭ major (1789–90)
before 1790 Violin Sonata No. 1
1790 (58) Piano Sonata No. 48 in C major (*c.*1790)
Seven Nocturnes for the King of Naples
1791 (59) Symphony No. 93 in D major
Symphony No. 94 in G major, *Surprise*
Symphony No. 95 in C minor
Symphony No. 96 in D major, *Miracle*
1792 (60) Symphony No. 97 in C major
Symphony No. 98 in B♭ major
The Storm, oratorio
before 1793 String Quartets Nos. 60–69
1793 (61) Symphony No. 99 in E♭ major
String Quartets Nos. 70–75, dedicated to Count Apponyi
1794 (62) Symphony No. 100 in G major, *Military*
Symphony No. 101 in D major, *Clock*
before 1795 Piano Sonata No. 49 in D major
1795 (63) Symphony No. 102 in B♭ major
Symphony No. 103 in E♭ major, *Drum Roll*
Symphony No. 104 in D major
1796 (64) Trumpet Concerto in E♭ major
Mass No. 9 in B♭, *Heiligenmesse*
Mass No. 10 in C major, *Paukenmesse*
1797–98 (65) *The Creation*, oratorio
String Quartets Nos. 76–81
1798 (66) Mass No. 11 in D minor, *Nelson* or *Imperial*
Piano Sonata No. 50 in E♭ major
The Seasons, oratorio (1798–1801)
1799 (67) String Quartets Nos. 82–83
Mass No. 12 in B♭ major, *Theresienmesse*
1800 (68) Te Deum
1803 (71) String Quartet No. 84
Haydn's last 12 symphonies are known as the *Salomon* symphonies. He also composed: 125 trios with barytone, more than 20 Italian and German operas, many songs, some in English.

HENZE, Hans Werner/b.1926/Germany

1946 (20) Chamber Concerto, for solo piano, solo flute and strings
Violin Sonata
1947 (21) Symphony No. 1, first version
Violin Concerto No. 1

Concertino for piano and wind orchestra, with percussion
Five Madrigals for small mixed choir and eleven solo
   instruments
String Quartet No. 1

1948 (22) *Chorus of the Captured Trojans*, for mixed choir and large
   orchestra
The Reproach, concert aria for baritone, trumpet, trombone
   and string orchestra
Lullaby of the Blessed Virgin, for boys' choir and nine solo
   instruments
Whispers from Heavenly Death, cantata for high voice and
   eight solo instruments
The Magic Theater, one-act opera for actors (new version
   for singers, 1964)
Chamber Sonata, for piano, violin and cello (revised 1963)

1949 (23) *Jack Pudding*, ballet
Ballet Variations
Symphony No. 2
Symphony No. 3 (1949–50)
Apollo et Hyazinthus, improvisations for harpsichord,
   contralto and eight solo instruments
Variations for piano
Serenade, for solo cello

1950 (24) *Symphonic Variations*, for piano and orchestra
Piano Concerto No. 1
Rosa Silber, ballet

1951 (25) *Labyrinth*, Choreographic Fantasy
The Sleeping Princess, ballet
Boulevard Solitude, lyric drama
A Country Doctor, radio opera (stage version 1964)

1952 (26) *The Idiot*, ballet-pantomime
King Stag, opera (1952–55)
Quintet for wind instruments
String Quartet No. 2

1953 (27) *Ode to the Westwind*, for cello and orchestra
The End of a World, radio opera

1955 (29) Symphony No. 4 (in one movement)
Three Symphonic Studies for orchestra (revised 1964)
Quattro Poemi, for orchestra

1956 (30) *Maratona*, ballet
Ondine, ballet (1956–57)
Concerto per il Marigny, for piano and seven instruments
Five Neapolitan Songs, for medium voice and chamber
   orchestra

1957 (31) *Nocturnes and Arias*, for soprano and orchestra
Sonata per Archi (1957–58)

1958 (32) *Three Dithyrambs*, for chamber orchestra
Chamber Music
Der Prinz von Homburg, opera
Three Tentos, for guitar

1959 (33) *The Emperor's Nightingale*, ballet
Elegy for Young Lovers, opera (1959–61)

Piano Sonata
1960 (34) *Antifone*, for orchestra
1961 (35) *Six Absences pour le Clavecin*, for harpsichord
1962 (36) Symphony No. 5
          Les Caprices de Marianne, incidental music
          In re cervo (or *The Errantries of Truth*), opera
          Novae de Infinito Laudes, cantata
1963 (37) *Los Caprichos*, fantasia for orchestra
          Ariosi, for soprano, violin and orchestra
          Adagio, for clarinet, horn, bassoon and string quintet
          Lucy Escott Variations, for piano (also for harpsichord)
          Being Beauteous, cantata
          Cantata della Fiaba Estrema
1964 (38) *Tancredi*, ballet
          The Young Lord, comic opera
          Choral Fantasy
          Divertimenti for two pianos
1965 (39) *The Bassarids*, opera
          In Memoriam: The White Rose, for chamber orchestra
1966 (40) Double Concerto for oboe, harp and strings
          Fantasia for strings
          Muses of Sicily, concerto for choir, two pianos, wind
            instruments and timpani
1967 (41) Piano Concerto No. 2
          Telemanniana, for orchestra
          Moralities, three scenic cantatas for soli, speaker, choir
            and small orchestra
1968 (42) *Essay on Pigs*, for voice and orchestra
          The Raft of the "Medusa", oratorio vulgare e militare in
            due parti—per Che Guevara, for soprano, baritone,
            speaker, mixed choir with nine boys' voices and
            orchestra
1969 (43) Symphony No. 6 for two chamber orchestras
          Compases (viola concerto) for viola and twenty-two
            players (1969–70)
          El Cimarrón, recital for four musicians (1969–70)
1971 (45) Violin Concerto No. 2
          Heliogabalus Imperator, for orchestra (1971–72)

HINDEMITH, Paul/1895–1963/Germany

before **1917** Cello Concerto No. 1
1917 (22) Three pieces for cello and piano
1918 (23) Violin Sonata No. 1 in E♭ major
          Violin Sonata No. 2 in D major
          String Quartet No. 1 in F minor
1919 (24) Violin Sonata in F major
          Sonata for solo viola
          Cello Sonata
1921–22 (26) *Chamber Music*, No. 1
1922 (27) String Quartet No. 2 in C major
          String Quartet No. 3

Suite for Klavier
Sonata for solo viola
Die Junge Magd, six songs
1923 (28) String Quartet No. 4
Kleine Sonata für viola d'amore und klavier
Sonata for solo cello
1924 (29) Piano Concerto
Chamber Music, No. 2
Sonata for solo violin
Das Marienleben, song cycle
1925 (30) Concerto for orchestra
Chamber Music, Nos. 3 and 4
1926 (31) *Cardillac*, opera
1927 (32) *Chamber Music*, No. 5
1928 (33) Concerto for organ and chamber orchestra
Chamber Music, No. 6
1930 (35) *Concert Music*, for piano, harps and brass
1931 (36) *The Unceasing*, oratorio
1932 (37) *Philharmonic Concerto*
1934 (39) *Mathis der Maler*, opera, also symphony
1935 (40) Viola Concerto, *Der Schwanendreher*
Concerto for orchestra
1937 (42) *Symphonic Dances*, for orchestra
Organ Sonatas, Nos. 1 and 2
1938 (43) *Nobilissima Visione*, ballet
1939 (44) Violin Concerto
1940 (45) Symphony in E♭ major
Cello Concerto No. 2
Theme and Variations for piano and strings, *The Four
   Temperaments*
Harp Sonata
1943 (48) *Symphonic Metamorphoses* on a Theme by Weber, for
   orchestra
Cupid and Psyche, overture
Ludus Tonalis, for piano
1944 (49) *Hérodiade*, for speaker and chamber orchestra
1945 (50) Piano Concerto
1946 (51) *When Lilacs in the Dooryard Bloomed—an American
   Requiem* (for Walt Whitman)
1947 (52) *Symphonia Serena* (possibly 1946)
Clarinet Concerto
1948 (53) Concerto for trumpet, bassoon and strings
Septet for wind instruments
1949 (54) Horn Concerto
Concerto for woodwind, harp and orchestra
Organ Sonata No. 2
1950 (55) Sinfonietta
Requiem for Those We Love (possibly 1946)
1951 (56) *Der Harmonie der Welt*, symphony
1952 (57) Symphony in E♭ for military band
Sonata for four horns
1958 (63) Octet

HODDINOTT, Alun/b.1929/Great Britain

1953 (24)   *fp. Fugal Overture*, for orchestra
             fp. Nocturne, for orchestra
1954 (25)   *fp.* Concerto for clarinet and string orchestra
1955 (26)   *fp.* Symphony No. 1
1956 (27)   *fp.* Septet for wind, strings and piano
1957 (28)   *Rondo Scherzoso*, for trumpet and piano
1958 (29)   *fp.* Harp Concerto
             fp. Serenade for string orchestra
             fp. Concertino for viola and small orchestra
             fp. Four Welsh Dances, for orchestra
1959 (30)   *fp. Nocturne and Dance*, for harp and orchestra
             fp. Piano Sonata No. 1
1960 (31)   *fp.* Concerto No. 1 for piano, wind and percussion
             fp. Sextet for flute, clarinet, bassoon, violin, viola and
                cello
1961 (32)   *fp.* Concerto No. 2 for piano and orchestra
             fp. Violin Concerto
1962 (33)   *fp. Rebecca*, ballad for unaccompanied mixed voices
             fp. Variations for flute, clarinet, harp and string quartet
             fp. Symphony No. 2
1963 (34)   *fp.* Divertimento for oboe, clarinet, horn and bassoon
             fp. Sinfonia for string orchestra
1964 (35)   *fp. Danegeld*, six episodes for unaccompanied mixed voices
             fp. Jack Straw, overture
             fp. Harp Sonata
             fp. Toccata all Giga, for organ
             fp. Intrada, for organ
             fp. Sarum Fanfare, for organ
1965 (36)   *fp. Dives and Lazarus*, cantata
             fp. Concerto Grosso No. 1
             fp. Aubade and Scherzo, for horn and strings
1966 (37)   *fp.* String Quartet No. 1
             fp. Concerto No. 3 for piano and orchestra
             fp. Pantomime, overture
             fp. Concerto Grosso No. 2
             fp. Variants, for orchestra
             fp. Piano Sonata No. 4
1967 (38)   *fp. Night Music*, for orchestra
             fp. Clarinet Sonata
             fp. Organ Concerto
             fp. Suite for harp
1968 (39)   *fp.* Symphony No. 3
             fp. Nocturnes and Cadenzas, for clarinet, violin and piano
             fp. Roman Dream, scena for solo soprano and instrumental
                ensemble
             fp. An Apple Tree and a Pig, scena for unaccompanied
                mixed voices
             fp. Sinfonietta 1
             fp. Piano Sonata No. 5
             fp. Divertimenti for eight instruments
             fp. Fioriture, for orchestra

1969 (40) *fp. Black Bart*, ballade for mixed voices and orchestra
             fp. Nocturnes and Cadenzas, for cello and orchestra
             fp. Violin Sonata No. 1
             fp. Horn Concerto
             fp. Investiture Dances, for orchestra
             fp. Sinfonietta 2
             fp. Divertimento for orchestra
             fp. Symphony No. 4
1970 (41) *fp.* Fantasy for harp
             fp. Sinfonietta 3
             fp. Violin Sonata No. 2
             fp. Cello Sonata
             fp. The Sun, the Great Luminary of the Universe, for
               orchestra
1971 (42) *fp.* Concerto for oboe and strings
             fp. Concertino for trumpet, horn and orchestra
             fp. Out of the Deep, motet for unaccompanied mixed voices
             fp. Violin Sonata No. 3
             fp. Horn Sonata
             fp. The Tree of Life, for soprano and tenor, chorus, organ
               and orchestra
1972 (43) *fp. Aubade*, for small orchestra
             fp. The Hawk is Set Free, for orchestra
             fp. Piano Sonata No. 6
1973 (44) *fp. The Floore of Heav'n*, for orchestra
             fp. Symphony No. 5
1974 (45) *fp. The Beach of Falesa*, opera
             fp. Ritornelli, for solo trombone, wind instruments and
               percussion
1975 (46) *fp. Landscapes*, for orchestra
Hoddinott also composed *Welsh Dances*, Suite No. 2, for orchestra.

HOLST, Gustav (von)/1874–1934/Great Britain

1895 (21) *The Revoke*, one-act opera
1896 (22) *Fantasiestücke*, for oboe and string quartet
             Quintet for wind and piano
             Four songs
1897 (23) *A Winter Idyll*, for orchestra
             Clear and Cool, for choir and orchestra
1898 (24) *Ornulf's Drapa*, for baritone and orchestra
1899 (25) *Walt Whitman*, overture
             Five part-songs for mixed voices (1899–1900)
             Sita, opera (1899–1906)
1900 (26) *Cotswolds Symphony*
             Suite de Ballet, in E♭
             Ave Maria for eight-part female choir
1902 (28) *The Youth's Choice*, opera
             Four part-songs for mixed voices
             Six songs for baritone
             Six songs for soprano
1903 (29) *Indra*, symphonic poem

King Estmere, for choir and orchestra
Quintet for wind

1904 (30) *The Mystic Trumpeter*, for soprano and orchestra

1905 (31) *Song of the Night*, for violin and orchestra
Four carols for mixed voices
Song from "The Princess"

1906 (32) *Songs of the West*, for orchestra
Two Songs Without Words, dedicated to Vaughan
    Williams (*q.v.*)

1907 (33) *Somerset Rhapsody*, for orchestra
Nine Hymns from the Rig-Veda (1907–08)

1908 (34) *Savitri*, opera
Choral Hymns from the Rig-Veda, Group 1

1909 (35) *A Vision of Dame Christian*, incidental music
First Suite for Military Band, in E♭ major
Choral Hymns from the Rig-Veda, Group 2

1910 (36) *Beni Mora*, Oriental Suite
The Cloud Messenger, ode
Choral Hymns from the Rig-Veda, Group 3

1911 (37) *Invocations*, for cello and orchestra
Oh England My Country, for choir and orchestra
Hecuba's Lament, for choir and orchestra
Second Suite for Military Band, in F major

1912 (38) *Choral Hymns from the Rig-Veda*, Group 4

1913 (39) *St. Paul's Suite*, for strings
Hymn to Dionysus, for choir and orchestra

1914–16 (40–42) *The Planets*, orchestral suite in seven movements

1915 (41) *Japanese Suite*

1916 (42) Five part-songs
Four songs for voice and violin
Three festival choruses

1917 (43) *Hymn of Jesus*, for two choruses, semi-chorus and
    orchestra
A Dream of Christmas

1919 (45) *Festival Te Deum*
Ode to Death

1921 (47) *The Perfect Fool*, opera
The Lure, ballet

1922 (48) Fugal Overture, No. 1

1923 (49) Fugal Overture, No. 2
Choral Symphony (1923–24)

1924 (50) *At the Boar's Head*, opera
Terzetto, for flute, oboe and viola
Two Motets for mixed voices

1925–26 (51) Seven part-songs (Bridges)

1926 (52) *The Golden Goose*, choral ballet
Chrissemas Day in the Morning, for piano

1927 (53) *Egdon Heath*, symphonic poem
The Morning of the Year, choral ballet
The Coming of Christ, mystery play
Two folk song arrangements, for piano

1928 (54) *Moorside Suite*, for brass band

1929 (55) Concerto for two violins
           The Tale of the Wandering Scholar, opera
           Twelve songs
1930 (56) Choral Fantasia
           Hammersmith, Prelude and Scherzo, for orchestra
1933 (59) *Lyric Movement*, for viola and strings
           Brook Green Suite, for strings

HONEGGER, Arthur/1892–1955/Switzerland (b. France)

1916–17 (24) String Quartet No. 1
1916–18 (24–26) Violin Sonata No. 1
1919 (27) Violin Sonata No. 2
           Dance of the Goat, for flute
1920 (28) *Pastorale d'été*
           Viola Sonata
           Cello Sonata
1921 (29) *King David*, oratorio with spoken narration
           Horace Victorieux, "mimed symphony"
           Sonatina for clarinet and piano (1921–22)
1923 (31) *Chant de Joie*
1924 (32) *Pacific 231*, Mouvement Symphonique No. 1, for orchestra
1925 (33) *Judith*, opera
           Concertino for piano and orchestra
1927 (35) *Antigone*, lyric drama
1928 (36) *Rugby*, Mouvement Symphonique No. 2, for orchestra
1930 (38) Symphony No. 1
           Les Aventures du Roi Pausole, light opera
1931 (39) *Cries of the World*, choral-orchestral
           Amphion
           1001 Nights
1932 (40) Mouvement Symphonique No. 3, for orchestra (1932–33)
           Sonatina for violin and cello
1934 (42) Cello Concerto
           Sémiramis, ballet, using voice and Ondes Martenot
           String Quartet No. 2 (1934–36)
1936 (44) *Nocturne*
           String Quartet No. 3
1937 (45) *L'Aiglon*, opera (with Ibert, *q.v.*)
1938 (46) *La Famille Cardinal*, opera (with Ibert)
           Joan of Arc at the Stake, incidental music
           La Danse des Morts, for solo voices, chorus and orchestra
1941 (49) Symphony No. 2, for strings and trumpet
1943 (51) *Jour de fête suisse*, suite
1946 (54) Symphony No. 3, *Liturgique*
           Symphony No. 4, *Deliciae Basiliensis*
1949 (57) Concerto da Camera
1951 (59) Symphony No. 5, *Di Tre Re*
           Monopartita, for orchestra; a suite whose movements are
              linked and intended to form a single musical structure
1952 (60) *Suite Archaïque*
1953 (61) *Christmas Cantata*

HUMPERDINCK, Engelbert/1854–1921/Germany

1880 (26) *Humoreske*
1893 (39) *Hänsel und Gretel*, opera
1895 (41) *Die Sieben Geislein*, opera
1898 (44) *Moorish Rhapsody*, for orchestra
1902 (48) *Dornroschen*
1905 (51) *Die Heirat wieder Willen*
1910 (56) *Koenigskinder*, opera
1911 (57) *The Miracle*
1914 (60) *Die Marketenderin*
1919 (65) *Gaudeamus*

IBERT, Jacques/1890–1962/France

1922 (32) *Ports of Call (Escales)*, orchestral suite
              Ballad of Reading Gaol, ballet
1925 (35) *Scherzo féerique*
              Concerto for cello and wind instruments
1926 (36) *Jeux*, for orchestra
1927 (37) *Angélique*, opera
1929 (39) *Persée et Andromedée*, opera
1930 (40) *Le Roi d'Yvetot*, opera
              Divertissement, for chamber orchestra
1932 (42) *Donogoo*, for orchestra
              Paris, symphonic suite
1934 (44) *Diane de Poitiers*, ballet
              Concertino da Camera, for alto saxophone and small
                orchestra
1935 (45) *Gonzaque*, opera
1937 (47) *L'Aiglon*, opera (with Honegger, q.v.)
1938 (48) *La Famille Cardinal*, opera (with Honegger)
              Capriccio for ten instruments
1943 (53) String Quartet in C major
1944 (54) Trio for violin, cello and harp
              Suite Elisabethaine, for orchestra
1949 (59) *Étude-Caprice, pour un Tombeau de Chopin*, for solo cello
1951 (61) Sinfonia Concertante

d'INDY, Vincent/1851–1931/France

1874 (23) *Max et Thecla*, symphonic overture (Part 2 of
                Wallenstein Trilogy)
              Jean Hunyade, symphony (1874–75)
1876 (25) *Anthony and Cleopatra*, overture
              Attendez-moi sous l'orme, opera (1876–78)
1878 (27) *The Enchanted Forest*, ballad-symphony
              Piano Quartet (1878–88)
1879–83 (28–32) *Le Chant de la cloche*, opera
1880 (29) *Le Camp de Wallenstein*, symphonic overture (Part 1 of
                Wallenstein Trilogy)
1882 (31) *La Mort de Wallenstein*, symphonic overture (Part 3 of
                Wallenstein Trilogy)

1884 (33) *Saugesfleure*, orchestral legend
Lied for cello (or viola) and orchestra
1886 (35) *Symphony on a French Mountain Air*
Suite in D major, for trumpet, two flutes and string
quartet
1887 (36) *Serenade and Valse*, for small orchestra
Trio for clarinet, cello and piano
1888 (37) *Fantasie*, for oboe and orchestra
1890 (39) *Karadec*, incidental music
String Quartet No. 1, in B♭
1891 (41) *Tableaux de voyage*
1896 (45) *Istar*, symphonic variations for orchestra
1897 (46) *Fervaal*
String Quartet No. 2, in E
1898 (47) *Medée*, incidental music
Chansons et danses, for seven wind instruments, in B♭
L'Étranger, lyric drama (1898–1901)
1902–03 (51) Symphony No. 2 in B♭
1903 (52) *Choral Varié*, for saxophone and orchestra
1904 (53) Violin Sonata in C
1905 (54) *Jour d'été à la montagne*
1906 (55) *Souvenirs*, tone poem
1916–18 (65–67) Sinfonia brève de ballo Gallico
1918 (67) *Sarabande et Minuet*, for piano, flute, oboe, clarinet, horn
and bassoon
1920 (69) *Légende de St. Christophe*
Le Poème des Rivages (1920–21)
1922–23 (71) *Le Rêve de Cynias*
1924 (73) Piano Quintet in G minor
1925 (74) Cello Sonata in D major
Diptyque méditerranéen (1925–26)
1927 (76) Concert for piano, flute, cello and string quartet
"Suites en parties", for harp, flute, viola, and cello
1929 (78) String Sextet in B♭
1930 (79) String Quartet No. 4 in D♭
Piano Trio No. 2, in the form of a suite
Suite for flute obbligato, violin, viola, cello and harp

IPPOLITOV-IVANOV, Mikhail/1859–1935/Russia

1882 (23) *Yar-Khmel*, for orchestra
1887 (28) *Ruth*, opera
p. Violin Sonata
1890 (31) *Asra*, opera
1894–95 (35) *Armenian Rhapsody*
1895 (36) *Caucasian Sketches*, suite for orchestra
1897 (38) *p.* String Quartet in A minor
1898 (39) *p.* Piano Quartet in A♭ major
1900 (41) *Assia*
1907 (48) Symphony
1909 (50) *Treachery*
1912 (53) *The Spy*

1916 (57) *Ole the Norseman*
1923–24 (64) *Mtzyry*
1928 (69) *Episodes from Schubert's Life*
1933–34 (74) *The Last Barricade*
1934 (75) *Catalan Suite*

IRELAND, John/1879–1962/Great Britain

1895 (16) Two pieces for piano
1905 (26) *Songs of a Wayfarer*
1906 (27) Piano Trio No. 1, *Phantasy Trio*
1909 (30) Violin Sonata No. 1
1912 (33) *Greater Love Hath No Man*, motet
1913 (34) *Forgotten Rite*, for orchestra
          Decorations, for piano:
              The Island Spell
              Moonglade
              Scarlet Ceremonies
          Three Dances for piano
          Sea Fever, song (words Masefield)
          Marigold, song
          Impressions, song
1915 (36) Preludes for piano
1917 (38) Piano Trio No. 2
          Violin Sonata No. 2
          The Cost, songs
1918 (39) *Leaves from a child's sketchbook*
1919 (40) *Summer Evening*
          The Holy Boy
1920 (41) Three *London Pieces*, for piano
          Piano Sonata
1921 (42) *Mai-Dun*, symphonic rhapsody
          Land of Lost Content, song cycle
1923 (44) Cello Sonata
1927 (48) *Sonatina*, for piano
1929 (50) *Ballade*, for piano
1930 (51) Piano Concerto in E♭ major
1931 (52) *Songs Sacred and Profane*
1932 (53) *A Downland Suite*, for brass band
1933 (54) *Legend*, for piano and orchestra
1934 (55) *A Comedy Overture*, for brass band
1936 (57) *London Overture*, for orchestra
1937 (58) *These Things Shall Be*, for baritone, choir and orchestra
          Green Ways, for piano
1938 (59) Piano Trio No. 3
1939 (60) *Concertino Pastorale*, for strings
1941 (62) *Sarnia*, for piano
          Three Pastels, for piano
          O Happy Land, song
1942 (63) *Epic March*
1943 (64) *Fantasy Sonata*, for clarinet and piano
1944 (65) *A Maritime Overture*, for military band

1946 (67) *fp. Satyricon Overture*
Ireland also composed:
Minuet and Elegy, for string orchestra
Equinox, for piano
Many songs and piano compositions.

IVES, Charles Edward/1874–1954/U.S.A.

1891 (17) Variations on "America", for organ
1896 (22) Quartet No. 1, *Revival Service*
Symphony No. 1 in D minor (1896–98)
1897–1902 (23–28) Symphony No. 2
1898–1907 (24–33) *Calcium Light Night*, for chamber orchestra
Central Park in the dark, for orchestra
1900–06 and **1914–15** *Children's Day at the Camp Meeting*, three pieces for violin and piano
1901–04 (27–30) Symphony No. 3
1902–10 (28–36) Violin Sonata No. 2
1903–08 (29–34) Violin Sonata No. 1
1903–14 (29–40) *Three Places in New England*, for orchestra
1904 (30) *Thanksgiving, and/or Father's Day* (Part 4 of *Holidays Symphony*)
1904–11 (30–37) Theater Orchestra Set No. 1:
In the Cage
In the Inn
In the Night
1906 (32) *The Pond*
1908 (34) *The Unanswered Question*
1910–16 (36–42) Symphony No. 4
1911 (37) *Browning overture*
Hallowe'en, for piano and strings
The Gong on the Hook and Ladder
Tone-Roads, No. 1 for chamber orchestra (1911–15)
1912 (38) *Decoration Day* (Part 2 of *Holidays Symphony*)
Lincoln, the great commoner, for chorus and orchestra
1913 (39) *Washington's Birthday* (Part 1 of *Holidays Symphony*)
Fourth of July (Part 3 of *Holidays Symphony*)
Over the pavements, for chamber orchestra
1914 (40) *Protests*, piano sonata
1915 (41) *Concord*, piano sonata (1909–15)
Orchestral Set No. 2
Tone-Roads, No. 3 for chamber orchestra
1919–27 (45–53) Orchestral Set No. 3
Ives also composed:
11 volumes of chamber music
The celestial country, for chorus
3 *Harvest home chorales*
General Booth's entrance into heaven, with brass band and chorus
Many psalm settings and other choral works
About 200 songs
Many piano pieces.

JACOB, Gordon/b.1895/Great Britain

	Up to and including
1936 (41)	*The Jar in the Bush*, ballet
	Uncle Remus, ballet
	Symphony in C
	Oboe Concerto
	Piano Concerto
	Viola Concerto
	Violin Concerto
	The Piper at the Gates of Dawn, tone poem
	Variations on an Original Theme, for orchestra
	Variations on an Air by Purcell, for string orchestra
	Denbigh Suite, for strings
	Donald Caird, for chorus and orchestra
	William Byrd Suite, for military band
	Serenade, for five wind instruments
	Quartets Nos. 1 and 2
1945 (50)	Symphony No. 2
	Clarinet Concerto
1950 (55)	Sinfonietta in D major
	A Goodly Heritage, cantata
1951 (56)	Flute Concerto
	Fantasia on Songs of the British Isles
1956 (61)	Piano Concerto No. 2
	Sextet
	Piano Trio
1958 (63)	Suite for recorder and string quartet
	Diversions, for woodwind and strings
	Miniature String Quartet
	Old Wine in New Bottles, for wind instruments
1961 (66)	Fantasia on Scottish Tunes
	Improvisations on a Scottish Tune, for orchestra
	Trombone Concerto
1962 (67)	*News from Newtown*, cantata
1963 (68)	Suite for brass band
1965 (70)	*Festival Te Deum*, for chorus and orchestra
1966 (71)	Oboe Sonata
	Variations on a Theme of Schubert
1967 (72)	Concerto for Band
	Animal Magic, cantata for children
	Six miniatures
1968 (73)	Suite for bassoon and string quartet
	Divertimento in E♭
1969 (74)	*Redbridge Variations*
	Piano Quartet
1970 (75)	*A York Symphony*
	Pride of Youth, for brass band
	A Joyful Noise, for brass band
1971 (76)	*Rhapsody for Three Hands*, for piano
1972 (77)	Double-bass Concerto
	Tuba Suite, with orchestra or piano
	Psalm 103 for chorus

1973 (78) Saxophone Quartet
1974 (79) Quartet for Clarinets
           Sinfonia Brevis
           Havant Suite, for chamber orchestra
1975 (80) Concerto for organ, strings and percussion
           Fantasy Sonata for organ
           Rhapsody, for piano

JANÁČEK, Leos/1854–1928/Czechoslovakia

1877 (23) Suite for strings
1880 (26) *Dumka*, for violin and piano
1887 (33) *Sarka*, opera
1889 (35) Six Lach Dances
1891 (37) *The Beginning of a Romance*, opera
           Rákos Rákóczy, ballet
1894–1903 (40–49) *Jenůfa*, opera
1904 (50) *Osud (Fate)*, opera
1908–17 (54–63) *Mr. Brouček's Excursion to the Moon*, opera
1915–18 (61–64) *Taras Bulba*, rhapsody for orchestra
1919 (65) *Katya Kabanova*, opera (1919–21)
           Diary of a Young Man who disappeared, song cycle
1920 (66) *Ballad of Blanik*, symphonic poem
1921 (67) Violin Sonata
1923 (69) String Quartet No. 1 in E minor
1924 (70) *The Cunning Little Vixen*, opera
           The Makropoulos Affair, opera (1924–26)
           Miade (Youth), suite for wind
1925 (71) Sinfonietta (1925–26)
           Concertino for piano, two violins, viola, cello, bassoon
              and horn
1926 (72) *Capriccio*, for piano and wind instruments
           Festliche Messe
1927 (73) *From the House of the Dead*, opera (1927–28)
           Glagolitic Mass
1928 (74) String Quartet No. 2, *Intimate Pages*

JONGEN, Joseph/1873–1953/Belgium

1893–1905 (20–32) Piano Trio in B minor
           Violin Sonata No. 1 in D major
1894 (21) *p.* String Quartet No. 1 in C minor
1898 (25) *Fantaisie*, for violin and orchestra
1899 (26) Symphony
           Violin Concerto
1902 (29) *Fantaisie sur deux Noëls wallons*, for orchestra
           Piano Quartet in E♭ major
1904 (31) *Lalla Rookh*, symphonic poem
1907 (34) *Félyane*, opera (unfinished)
after 1905 and
before 1909   Piano Trio in F♯ minor
1909 (36) Violin Sonata No. 2 in E major

1911 (38) *S'Arka*, ballet
           Cello Sonata (1911–12)
1912 (39) *Deux rondes wallons*, for orchestra
1913 (40) *Impressions d'Ardennes*, for orchestra
1915 (42) *Suites en deux parties*, for viola and orchestra
1916 (43) String Quartet No. 2 in A major
1917 (44) *Tableaux pittoresques*, for orchestra
1918 (45) *p. Serenade Tendre* and *Serenade Triste*, for string quartet
1919 (46) *Poème héroïque*, for violin and orchestra
1922 (49) *Rhapsody*, for piano, flute, oboe, clarinet, horn and
           bassoon
1928 (55) *Pièce symphonique*, for piano and orchestra
1929 (56) *Passacaille et Gigue*, for orchestra
           Suite for viola and orchestra
1930 (57) *Sonata Eroica*
1933 (60) *La Légende de Saint-Nicholas*, for children's choir and
           orchestra
           Symphonie Concertante, for organ and orchestra
1936 (63) *Triptyque*, three suites for orchestra
1938 (65) *Hymne à la Meuse*, for chorus and orchestra
1939 (66) *Ouverture-Fanfare*, for orchestra
1941 (68) *La Cigale et le fourmi*, for children's chorus
           Ouverture de fête, for orchestra
1943 (70) Piano Concerto
1944 (71) *Bourée*, for orchestra
Jongen also composed:
Concerto for harp
Concerto for wind quintet.

KABALEVSKY, Dimitri/b.1904/Russia

1929 (25) Piano Concerto No. 1 in A minor
           String Quartet in A minor
1930 (26) *Poem of Struggle*, for chorus and orchestra
1932 (28) Symphony No. 1, *Proletarians Unite!*, for chorus and
           orchestra
           Symphony No. 2 in E minor
1933 (29) Symphony No. 3, *Requiem for Lenin*, for chorus and
           orchestra
1936 (32) Piano Concerto No. 2 in G minor
1938 (34) *Colas Breugnon*, opera, revised 1968–69
           Vasilek, ballet
1939 (35) Symphony No. 4, *Shchors*, for chorus and orchestra
1940 (36) *The Golden Spikes*, ballet
           The Comedians, suite for small orchestra
1942 (38) *Peoples Avengers*, suite for chorus and orchestra
           Before Moscow, opera
           Our Great Fatherland, cantata
c.1944 (c.40) *The Family of Taras*, opera
1948 (44) Violin Concerto
1949 (45) Cello Concerto
1952 (48) Piano Concerto No. 3

Cello Sonata
1955 (51) *Nikita Vershinin*, opera
1956 (52) Symphony No. 5
          Romeo and Juliet, symphonic suite
1960 (56) *Overture Pathétique*, for orchestra
          The Spring, symphonic poem
          Camp of Friendship, six children's songs (begun 1935)
          Gasts in the kitchen-garden, play for children
          Major-minor études, for solo cello
          Three Dancing Songs for children
1961 (57) Rondo for violin and piano
1962 (58) *Requiem*, for two soloists, children's and mixed choirs
              and orchestra (1962–63)
          Cello Sonata
1963 (59) Three Songs of Revolutionary Cuba
          Three Songs
          Five Songs (1963–64)
1964 (60) Rhapsody for piano and orchestra, *School Years*
          Cello Concerto No. 2
1965 (61) *Symphonic Prelude in memory of heroes of Gorlovka*
          Rondo for cello and piano
          Twenty easy pieces for violin and piano
          Spring Plays and Dances, for piano
1966 (62) *The Motherland*, cantata for children's choir and orchestra
1967 (63) *Recitative and Rondo*, for piano
1968–69 (64) *Sisters*, lyric opera

KHACHATURIAN, Aram/b.1903/Armenia (Russia)

1927 (24) *Poèm*, for piano
1932 (29) Violin Sonata
          String Quartet in C major
          Trio in G minor, for clarinet, violin and piano
1933 (30) Symphony No. 1 (1933–34)
          Dance Suite
1936 (33) Piano Concerto
1937 (34) *Song of Stalin*, for chorus and orchestra
1939 (36) *Happiness*, ballet
          Masquerade, incidental music
1940 (37) Violin Concerto
1942 (39) *Gayane*, ballet
          Symphony No. 2
1944 (41) Concerto for violin and cello
          Masquerade suite
1945 (42) Solemn Overture *To the End of the War*
1947 (44) *Symphonie-Poème*
1950 (47) Cello Concerto
1954 (51) *Spartacus*, ballet
1955 (52) Three Suites for Orchestra
1956 (53) *Ode of Joy*, for soloist, chorus and orchestra
1957 (54) *Lermontov Suite*
1958 (55) Sonatina for piano

1960 (57) Rhapsody for violin and orchestra
           Ballade, for bass with orchestra
1961 (58) Piano Sonata
1962 (59) Cello Sonata
1965 (62) *Concerto-Rhapsody*, for cello and orchestra
1966 (63) Suite for Orchestra, No. 4

KODÁLY, Zoltán/1882–1967/Hungary

1897 (15) Overture for orchestra
1901 (19) Adagio for violin (or viola) and piano
1906 (24) *Summer Evening*
1908 (26) String Quartet No. 1 in C minor
1909–10 (27) Cello Sonata (Atonal)
1914 (32) Duo for violin and cello (Atonal)
1915 (33) Sonata for unaccompanied cello
1916–17 (34) String Quartet No. 2 in D major
1917–18 (35) Seven piano pieces
1919–20 (37) *Serenade*, for two violins and viola
1923 (41) *Psalmus Hungaricus*, for tenor, chorus and orchestra
1925 (43) *Meditation on a theme of Debussy*, for piano
1926 (44) *Háry János*, opera
1930 (48) *Dances of Marosszeck*, for piano (afterwards orchestrated)
1931 (49) *Theater Overture*
           The Spinning Room, lyric scenes (1931–32)
           Pange lingua, for mixed choir and organ
1933 (51) *Dances of Galanta*, orchestral suite
1934 (52) *Jesus and the Merchants*, for chorus and orchestra
1936 (54) Te Deum for chorus and orchestra
1938–39 (56) *Variations on a Hungarian Folk-song*, for orchestra
1939 (57) Concerto for orchestra
           The Peacock Variations
1945 (63) Missa Brevis
1947 (65) Viola Concerto
           String Quartet
1948 (66) *Czinka Panna*, opera
1954 (72) *Spartacus*, ballet
1960 (78) Symphony in C major
1965 (83) Variations for piano
1967 (85) *Laudes Organi*, fantasia on twelfth-century sequence, for
              mixed choir and organ

KORNGOLD, Erich Wolfgang/1897–1957/U.S.A. (b. Austria)

1910–13 (13–16) Piano Trio
1916 (19) *Der Ring des Polykrates*, opera buffe
1919 (22) *Much Ado About Nothing*, incidental music
1920 (23) *The Dead City*, opera
1939 (42) *Die Kathrin*, opera
1940 (43) *Songs of the Clown*
           Four Shakespeare Songs
1941 (44) *Psalm*, for solo, chorus and orchestra

1942 (45) *Prayer*, for tenor, chorus and orchestra
           Tomorrow, song
1945 (48) Violin Concerto
           String Quartet No. 3
1946 (49) *The silent serenade*, comedy with music
           Cello Concerto
1947 (50) *Symphonic serenade*, for strings
           Five songs for middle voice
1951 (54) Symphony in F♯ major
1952 (55) *Sonnet to Vienna*, song
1953 (56) Theme and Variations for orchestra
           Straussiana, for orchestra

KORTE, Karl/b.1928/U.S.A.

1948 (20) String Quartet No. 1
1955 (27) *Concertato on a Choral Theme*, for orchestra
1958 (30) *Story of the Flutes*, symphonic poem
1959 (31) *For a Young Audience*, for orchestra
           Fantasy, for violin and piano
1960 (32) Quintet for oboe and strings
1961 (33) Symphony No. 2
           Four Blake Songs, for women's voices and piano
1962 (34) *Nocturne and March*, for band
           Ceremonial Prelude and Passacaglia, for band
1963 (35) *Southwest*, a dance overture
           Prairie Song, for trumpet and band
           Introductions, for brass quintet
           Mass for Youth, with orchestra or keyboard
1964 (36) *Diablerie*, for woodwind quintet
1965 (37) *Aspects of Love*, seven songs on various texts
           String Quartet No. 2
1968 (40) Symphony No. 3
           Matrix, for woodwind quartet, piano, percussion and
               saxophone
           May the Sun Bless Us, four settings of texts of Tagore, for
               male voices, brass and percussion
1969 (41) *Facets*, for saxophone quartet
           Dialogue, for saxophone and tape
1970 (42) *Gestures*, for electric brass, percussion, piano and band
           Psalm XIII, for chorus and tape
1971 (43) *I Think You Would Have Understood*, for stage band, solo
               trumpet and two-channel tape
           Remembrances, for flute and tape
1974 (46) Four Songs, *Libera me*

LALO, Édouard/1823–1892/France

1855 (32) String Quartet in E♮
1872 (49) *Deux Aubades*, for small orchestra
           Violin Concerto in F major
           Divertissement, for small orchestra

1873 (50) *Symphonie Espagnole*, for violin and orchestra, in five movements
1875 (52) *Allegro Symphonique*
1876 (53) Cello Concerto
1881 (58) *Rapsodie Norvégienne*
1882 (59) Ballet Suites Nos. 1 and 2, *Namouna*
1884 (61) Scherzo
1886 (63) Symphony in G minor
1888 (65) *Le Roi d'Ys*, opera
1889 (66) Piano Concerto in G minor

LAMBERT, Constant/1905–1951/Great Britain

1925–26 (20–21) *Romeo and Juliet*, ballet
1926 (21) *Pomona*, ballet
Poems by Li-Po
1927 (22) Music for Orchestra
Elegiac Blues
1928–29 (23) Piano Sonata
1929 (24) *The Rio Grande*, for chorus, orchestra and piano solo
1931 (26) Concerto for piano and nine instruments
1936 (31) *Summer's Last Will and Testament*, for chorus and orchestra
1937 (32) *Horoscope*, ballet
1940 (35) *Dirge*, for male voices and strings
1942 (37) *Aubade héroïque*, for orchestra
1950 (45) *Tiresias*, ballet

LECLAIR, Jean-Marie/1697–1764/France

1723 (26) *p.* Sonatas for Violin Alone, with a Bass, Book I
1728 (31) *p.* Sonatas for Violin Alone, with a Bass, Book II
1734 (37) *p.* Sonatas for Violin Alone, with a Bass, Book III
1737 (40) *p.* Six concertos for violin
1746 (49) *Scylla et Glaucus*, opera

LEHÁR, Franz (Ferencz)/1870–1948/Hungary

1905 (35) *The Merry Widow*, operetta
1909 (39) *Count of Luxemburg*, operetta
1928 (58) *Frederica*, operetta
1929 (59) *The Land of Smiles*, operetta
Lehár also composed many other operettas and a violin concerto.

LEONCAVALLO, Ruggero/1858–1919/Italy

1892 (34) *I Pagliacci*, opera
1894 (36) *Serafita*, symphonic poem
1897 (39) *La Bohème*, opera (this failed whereas Puccini's on the same subject succeeded)
1900 (42) *Zaza*, opera

LIADOV, Anatol/1855–1914/Russia

1876 (21) *Birulki*, for piano
1879 (24) *Arabesque*, for piano
1887 (32) *Scherzo*, for orchestra
1888 (33) *Mazurka*, for orchestra
1890 (35) *Dal Tempo Antico*, for piano
1892 (37) *Kukalki*, for piano
1893 (38) *Une tabatière à musique*, for piano
1899 (44) *Slava*, for women's chorus, two harps and two pianos
1900 (45) *Polonaise*, for orchestra
1904 (49) *Baba Yaga*, symphonic poem
1906 (51) *Eight Popular Russian Songs*, for orchestra
1909 (54) *The Enchanted Lake*, symphonic poem
1910 (55) *Kikimora*, symphonic poem
           Dance of the Amazons, for orchestra
1914 (59) *Naenia (Dirge)*

LIGETI, György/b.1923/Hungary

1953 (30) String Quartet
1958 (35) *Artikulation*, for tape
           Apparitions, for large orchestra (1958–59)
1960 (37) *Atmospheres*, for large orchestra
1961 (38) *Fragment*, for eleven instruments
           Volumina, for organ (1961–62)
1962 (39) *Poème Symphonique*, for one hundred metronomes
           Aventures, for three singers and seven instruments
           Nouvelles Aventures, for three singers and seven
               instruments (1962–65)
1963–65 (40–42) *Requiem*
1966 (43) Cello Concerto
           Lux Aeterna
1967 (44) *Lontana*, for large orchestra
           Two studies for organ (1967–69)
1968 (45) *Ramifications*, for string orchestra (1968–69)
           Ten pieces for wind quintet
           String Quartet No. 2
           Continuum, for harpsichord
1969–70 (46) Chamber Concertato for thirteen instruments
1971 (48) *Melodien*, for orchestra
           Horizont, for recorder
1972 (49) *Kylwiria*, opera
           Double Concerto for flute, oboe and orchestra

LISZT, Franz (Ferencz)/1811–1886/Hungary

1830–49 (19–38) Piano Concerto No. 1 in E♭ major
1831 (20) *Harmonies poétiques et religieuses*, for piano and orchestra
1835–83 *Anneés de pèlerinage*, for piano
1839 (28) Piano Concerto No. 2 in A minor
c.1840 (c.29) *Malediction*, for piano and strings
1843 (32) *Valse Impromptu*, in A♭ major

1849–50 (38) *Héroïde funèbre*, for orchestra
1850 (39) *Consolations*, for piano
　　　　　　Prometheus, symphonic poem
　　　　　　Liebestraüme, nocturnes for piano
1852 (41) *Hungarian Rhapsodies*, Nos. 1–15
1854 (43) *Orpheus*, tone poem
　　　　　　Les préludes, symphonic poem
　　　　　　Hungaria, symphonic poem
*c.***1855** (*c.*44) *Totentanz*, for piano and orchestra
1856 (45) *Tasso*, symphonic poem
　　　　　　Die Hunnenschlacht, symphonic poem
1857 (46) *Mazeppa*, symphonic poem
　　　　　　Faust, symphony (possibly 1854–57)
　　　　　　Dante, symphony (possibly 1855–56)
1859 (48) *Hamlet*, symphonic poem
　　　　　　Die Ideale, for orchestra
*c.***1860** (*c.*49) *Fantasy on Hungarian Folktunes*, for piano and orchestra
1863 (52) Two Concert Studies for piano
1866 (55) *Deux Légendes*, for piano
1867 (56) *Legend of St. Elizabeth* (possibly 1857–62)
1879 (68) *Via Crucis*
*c.***1880** (*c.*69) *Hungarian Rhapsodies*, Nos. 16–20
1881 (70) *Mephisto Waltz*

LOEFFLER, Charles/1861–1935/Alsace

1891 (30) *The Nights in the Ukraine*, for violin and orchestra
1894 (33) *Fantasy Concerto*, for cello and orchestra
1895 (34) *Divertimento*, for violin and orchestra
1901 (40) *Divertissement Espagnol*, for saxophone and orchestra
1902 (41) *Poem*, for orchestra
1905 (44) *La Mort de Tintagiles*, symphonic poem for two viola
　　　　　　d'amore and orchestra
　　　　　　La Villanelle du Diable, symphonic fantasy for organ and
　　　　　　orchestra
　　　　　　A Pagan Poem, for piano, English horn and three trumpets
1916 (55) *Hora Mystica*, symphony with men's chorus
1923 (62) "Avant que tu ne t'en ailles", poem
1925 (64) *Memories of my childhood*, for orchestra
1928 (67) *Clowns*, intermezzo

LULLY, Jean/1632–1687/Italy

1658 (26) *fp. Ballets d'Alcidiane*
1659 (27) *fp. Ballets de la raillerie*
1660 (28) *fp. Ballet de Xerxes*
1661 (29) *fp. Ballet de l'Impatience*
　　　　　　fp. Ballet des Saisons
　　　　　　fp. Ballet de l'Ercole amante
1663 (31) *fp. Ballets des Arts*
　　　　　　fp. Ballets des noces de village
1664 (32) *fp. Ballet des amours déguises*

fp. La Mariage forcé, comedy ballet
fp. La Princesse d'Elide, comedy ballet
fp. Entr'actes for Corneille's *Oedipe*
Miserere, concert setting of "Miserere mei Deus", psalm
1665 (33) *fp. La Naissance de Venus*, ballet
           fp. Ballet des Gardes
           fp. L'Amour médecin, comedy ballet
1666 (34) *fp. Ballet des Muses*
           fp. Le Triomphe de Bacchus dans les Indes, ballet
1667 (35) *fp. Le Sicilien*, comedy ballet
1668 (36) *fp. Le Carnaval, ou Mascarade de Versailles*, ballet
           fp. Georges Dandin, comedy ballet
           fp. Plaude Laetare
1669 (37) *fp. Ballet de Flore*
           fp. Monsieur de Pourceaugnac, comedy ballet
1670 (38) *fp. Les Amants magnifiques*, comedy ballet
           fp. Le Bourgeois gentilhomme, comedy ballet
1671 (39) *fp. Ballet des Ballets*
           fp. Psyche, tragi-comedy
1673 (41) *fp. Cadmus et Hermione*, opera
1674 (42) *fp. Alceste*, opera
1675 (43) *fp. Thesée*, opera
1676 (44) *fp. Atys*, opera
1677 (45) *fp. Isis*, opera
           fp. Te Deum
1678 (46) *fp. Psyche*, opera
1679 (47) *fp. Bellérophon*, opera
1680 (48) *fp. Prosperine*, opera
1681 (49) *fp. Le Triomphe de l'amour*, ballet
1682 (50) *fp. Persée*, opera
1683 (51) *fp. Phaéton*, opera
           fp. De Profundis
1684 (52) *fp. Amadis de Gaule*, opera
           fp. Motets for two choirs
1685 (53) *fp. Roland*, opera
           fp. Le Temple de la Paix, ballet
1686 (54) *fp. Armide et Renaud*, opera
           fp. Acis et Galathée, opera

LUTOSLAWSKI, Witold/b.1913/Poland

1934 (21) Piano Sonata
1938 (25) *Symphonic Variations*, for orchestra
1941 (28) *Variations on a Theme of Paginini*, for two pianos
           Symphony No. 1 (1941–47)
1949 (36) *Overture for Strings*
1950–54 (37–41) *Concerto for Orchestra*
1951 (38) *Little Suite*, for orchestra
           Silesian Triptych, for soprano and orchestra
1954 (41) *Dance Preludes*, first version for clarinet and piano
1955 (42) *Dance Preludes*, second version for clarinet and instruments
1957 (44) Five Songs

1958 (45) *Funeral Music*, for strings
           Three Postludes for orchestra (1958–63)
1959 (46) *Dance Preludes*, third version, for instruments
1961 (48) *Jeux Vénitiens*
1962–63 (49) *Trois poèmes d'Henri Michaux*, for mixed chorus of
           twenty voices, wind instruments, two pianos, harp and
           percussion
1964 (51) String Quartet
1965 (52) *Paroles Tissées*, for voice and instruments
1967 (54) Symphony No. 2
1968 (55) *Livre pour orchestre*
1969–70 (56) Cello Concerto
1972 (59) *Preludes and fugue*, for thirteen solo strings

LUTYENS, Elisabeth/b.1906/Great Britain

1938 (32) String Quartets Nos. 1 and 2
           Partita for two violins
           Sonata for solo viola
1939 (33) *Three Pieces for Orchestra*
           String Trio
1940 (34) Chamber Concerto No. 1, for nine instruments
           Chamber Concerto No. 2, for clarinet, tenor saxophone,
           piano, concertante and string orchestra (1940–41)
           Midas, ballet for string quartet and piano
1941 (35) *Five Intermezzi for Piano*
1942 (36) Three Symphonic Preludes
           Nine Bagatelles, for cello and piano
           Two Songs (Auden) for voice and piano
1944 (38) *Suite Gauloise*, for small orchestra
1945 (39) Chamber Concerto No. 3, for bassoon, string orchestra
           and percussion
           Five Little Pieces for Clarinet and Piano
1947 (41) Viola Concerto
           Chamber Concerto No. 4, for horn and small orchestra
           Chamber Concerto No. 5, for string quartet and small
           orchestra
           The Pit, dramatic scene for tenor and bass soli, women's
           chorus and orchestra
1948 (42) Chamber Concerto No. 6, for oboe, harp and string
           orchestra
           Aptote, for solo viola
           Three Improvisations for piano
           Nine Songs, for voice and piano
1949 (43) String Quartet No. 3
1950 (44) *Concertante*, for five players
1951 (45) *Requiem for the Living*
           Penelope, music drama for violin, cello and piano soli,
           choir and orchestra
           Nativity, for soprano and strings
1952 (46) String Quartets Nos. 4–6
1953 (47) Three songs and incidental music, for Group Theater's

    Homage to Dylan Thomas
1954 (48) *Infidelio*, seven scenes for soprano and tenor soli and
    seven instruments
    Valediction, for clarinet and piano
1955 (49) *Music for Orchestra I*
    Capriccii, for two harps and percussion
    Nocturnes, for violin, guitar and cello
    Sinfonia for organ
1956 (50) *Chorale for Orchestra (Hômmage à Stravinsky)*
    In the Temple of a Bird's Wing, for baritone and piano
    (also 1965)
1956–57 *Three Duos:*
    1) Horn and piano
    2) Cello and piano
    3) Violin and piano
1957 (51) *Six Tempi for Ten Instruments*, for flute, oboe, clarinet,
    bassoon, horn, trumpet, violin, viola, cello and piano
    De Amore, cantata for soprano and tenor soli, choir and
    orchestra
    Variations, for solo flute
1958 (52) *Piano e Forte*, for solo piano
1959–60 (53) *Quincunx*, for soprano and baritone soli and orchestra
1960 (54) Wind Quintet
1961 (55) *Symphonies for solo piano, wind, harps and percussion*
    Catena, cantata for soprano and tenor soli and twenty-one
    instruments
1962 (56) *Music for Orchestra II*
    Five Bagatelles for piano
1963 (57) *Music for Orchestra III*
    Encomion "Let us now praise famous men . . .", for
    chorus, brass and percussion
    String Quintet
    Wind Trio, for flute, clarinet and bassoon
    Fantasie Trio, for flute, clarinet and piano
    Présages, for solo oboe
    The Country of the Stars, motet
1964 (58) *Music for Piano and Orchestra*
    Music for Wind, for double wind quintet
    Scena, for violin, cello and percussion
1965 (59) *The Numbered*, opera in prologue and two acts (1965–67)
    The Valley of Hatsu-Se, for soprano solo, flute, clarinet,
    cello and piano
    Magnificat and Nunc Dimittis, for unaccompanied chorus
    The Hymn of Man, motet for unaccompanied male chorus
    (revised for mixed chorus 1970)
1966 (60) *And Suddenly It's Evening*, for solo tenor and eleven
    instruments
    Akapotik Rose, for solo soprano, flute, two clarinets, string
    trio and piano
    The Fall of the Leafe, for solo oboe and string quartet
    Music for Three, for flute, oboe and piano
1967 (61) *Novenaria*, for orchestra

Time Off? Not a Ghost of a Chance, charade in four scenes
and three interruptions, for baritone, actor, vocal
quartet, two mixed choruses and instruments
Scroll for Li-Ho, for violin and piano
Helix, for piano (four hands)

1968 (62) *Essence of Our Happiness*, for solo tenor, chorus and
orchestra
Horai, for violin, horn and piano
Epithalanium, for organ (soprano solo optional)
A Phœnix, for solo soprano, violin, clarinet and piano
The Egocentric, for tenor or baritone and piano
The Tyme Doth Flete, for unaccompanied chorus, prelude
and postlude for two trumpets and two trombones
optional

1969 (63) *Isis and Osiris*, lyric drama for eight voices and small
orchestra (1969–70)
Temenos, for organ
The Dying of the Sun, for solo guitar
Trois pièces brêve, for chamber organ
The Tides of Time, for double-bass and piano
String Trio

1970 (64) *Anerca* (Eskimo poetry), for speaker/actress, ten guitars
and percussion
Visions of Youth, for soprano, three clarinets, piano and
percussion
Oda a la Tormenta, for mezzo-soprano and piano
In the Direction of the Beginning, for bass and piano
Verses of Love, for mixed choir unaccompanied

1971 (65) *Islands*, for soprano, tenor, narrator and instrumental
ensemble
The Tears of Night, for counter-tenor, six sopranos and
three instrumental ensembles
Dirge for the Proud World, for soprano, counter-tenor,
harpsichord and cello
Requiescat (Igor Stravinsky 1971), for soprano and string
trio
Driving Out the Death, for oboe and string trio

1972 (66) *The Linnet from the Leaf*, music/theater for five singers
and two instrumental groups
Voice of Quiet Waters, for chorus and orchestra
Counting Your Steps, for chorus, four flutes and four
percussion
Chimes and Cantos, for baritone solo, two trumpets, two
trombones, four violins, two double-basses and
percussion
Plenum I, for piano solo
Dialogo, for tenor and lute

1973 (67) *One and the Same*, scena for soprano, speaker, two female
mimes, male mime and instrumental ensemble
The Waiting Game, three scenes for mezzo-soprano,
baritone and small orchestra
Roads, for two sopranos, counter-tenor, baritone and bass

Rape of the Moone, for wind octet
Laudi, for soprano, three clarinets, piano and percussion
Tre, for solo clarinet
Plenum II, for solo oboe
Plenum III, for string quartet
1974 (68) *The Winter of the World*, for orchestras
Kareniana (for Karen Phillips), for instrumental ensemble
1975 (69) *Eos*, for small orchestra
Fanfare for a Festival, for three trumpets and three
    trombones
Pietá, for harpsichord
Ring of Bone, for solo piano

MACDOWELL, Edward/1861–1908/U.S.A.

1882 (21) Piano Concerto No. 1 in A minor
1883 (22) *Modern Suite*, for piano, No. 1
1884 (23) *Forest Idylls*, four pieces for piano
1885 (24) *p. Hamlet and Ophelia*, symphonic poem
1887 (26) Six Idylls after Goethe, for piano
Six Poems after Heine, for piano
1888 (27) *Lancelot and Elaine*, symphonic poem
Marionettes, eight pieces for piano
Romance, for cello
1889 (28) *Les Orientales*, after Hugo, for piano
Lamia, symphonic poem
1890 (29) Piano Concerto No. 2 in D minor
Twelve Studies for piano, Books I and II
1891 (30) Suite No. 1 for orchestra
The Saracens, symphonic poem
The Lovely Alda, symphonic poem
1893 (32) Piano Sonata No. 1, *Tragica*
1894 (33) Twelve Virtuoso Studies, for piano
1895 (34) Piano Sonata No. 2, *Eroica*
1896 (35) *Indian Suite* (Suite No. 2), for orchestra
Woodland Sketches, for piano
1898 (37) *Sea Pieces*
1900 (39) Piano Sonata No. 3, *Norse* (dedicated to Grieg, *q.v.*)
1901 (40) Piano Sonata No. 4, *Keltic*
1902 (41) *Fireside tales*
New England Idylls

MAHLER, Gustav/1860–1911/Austria (b. Bohemia)

1880 (20) Klagende Lieder
1882 (22) Lieder und Gesänge aus der Jugendzeit
1883 (23) Lieder eines fahrenden Gesellen, for voice and orchestra
1888 (28) Lieder aus des *Knaben Wunderhorn*, song cycle for voice
    and orchestra
Symphony No. 1 in D major
1894 (34) Symphony No. 2 in C minor, *Resurrection*, with final
    movement for soprano and contralto soloists, choir

and orchestra
1895 (35) Symphony No. 3 in D minor, with final movement for
contralto, boys' and female choruses and orchestra
1900 (40) Symphony No. 4 in G major, with final movement for
soprano and orchestra
1902 (42) Symphony No. 5 in C♯ minor
Five Rückert Songs
1904 (44) Symphony No. 6 in A minor
1905 (45) Symphony No. 7 in E minor
Kindertotenlieder, song cycle for voice and orchestra
1907 (47) Symphony No. 8 in E♭ major, *Symphony of a Thousand*,
with eight vocal soloists, two chor· ses, boys' chorus,
organ and orchestra
1908 (48) *Das Lied von der Erde* (The Song of the Earth), song cycle
of symphonic dimensions
1909 (49) Symphony No. 9 in D major
1910 (50) Symphony No. 10 begun, unfinished at Mahler's death
(A completion was made in 1964 by Deryk Cooke
which is now used as the performing version)

MALIPIERO, Gian Francesco/1882–1973/Italy

1906 (24) *Sinfonia del Mare*
1908 (26) Cello Sonata
1910 (28) *Sinfonia del Silenzio e della Morte*
Impressioni dal Vero, I (1910–11)
1914–15 (32) *Impressioni dal Vero, II*
1917 (35) *Ditirambo Tragico*
Armenia
1918 (36) *Grottesco*, for small orchestra
Pantea, ballet
L'Orfeide, opera (1918–21)
1919–21 (37–39) *Tre Commedie Goldiane*, opera
1920 (38) *Oriente Immaginario*
1921–22 (39) *Impressioni dal Vero, III*
1925 (43) *Filomela e l'Infatuato*, opera
Merlino maestro d'organi, opera (1925–28)
Il Mistero di Venezia, opera (1925–28)
1926 (44) *L'Esilio dell'Eroe*, five symphonic impressions
1929 (47) *Torneo Notturno*, opera
1930 (48) *La Bella e il Mostro*, opera
1931 (49) Concerto for Orchestra
1932 (50) Violin Concerto
Sette Invenzione
Inni
1933 (51) *La favola del figlio cambiato*, opera
1934 (52) Symphony No. 1
Piano Concerto No. 1
1936 (54) *Julius Caesar*, opera
Symphony No. 2, *Elegiaca*
1937 (55) Piano Concerto No. 2
Cello Concerto

1938 (56) *Anthony and Cleopatra*, opera
           Triple Concerto, for violin, cello and piano
1939 (57) *Ecuba*, opera
1940 (58) *La Vita e'Sogno*, opera
1941–42 (59) *I Capriccio di Callot*, opera
1942 (60) *Minnie la Candida*, opera
1943 (61) *L' Allegra Brigata*, opera
1944 (62) Symphony No. 3, *delle Campane*
1946 (64) Symphony No. 4, *In Memoriam*
1947 (65) Symphony No. 5, *Concertante in eco*, with two pianos
           Symphony No. 6, *Degli archi*, for strings
1948 (66) Symphony No. 7, *delle Canzoni*
           Piano Concerto No. 3
           Mondi Celeste e Infernali, opera (1948–49)
1950 (68) Symphony in one movement
           Piano Concerto No. 4
1951 (69) *Sinfonia del Zodiaco*
1952 (70) Violin Concerto
1957 (75) Quintet for piano and strings
1959 (77) *Musica da Camera*, for wind quintet
           Six poesie di Dylan Thomas, for soprano and ten
              instruments
1960 (78) String Quartet No. 3
1964 (82) *In Time of Daffodils*, for soprano, baritone, flute, clarinet,
              bass-clarinet, viola, double-bass, guitar and percussion
           Symphony No. 8
1965 (83) *Costellazioni*, for piano
1966 (84) Symphony No. 9
1967 (85) *Carnet de Notes*, for chamber orchestra
           Cassazione, for string sextet
           Symphony No. 10
1968 (86) *Gli Eroi di Bonaventura*
           Flute Concerto
1970 (88) Symphony No. 11

MARTIN, Frank/1890–1974/Switzerland

1926 (36) *Rythmes*, three symphonic movements
1931 (41) Violin Sonata
           Chaconne, for cello and piano
1933 (43) Four Short Pieces, for guitar
1934 (44) Piano Concerto No. 1
1935 (45) *Rhapsody*, for two violins, two violas and double-bass, or
              string orchestra
1936 (46) Symphony for full orchestra (1936–37)
           Danse de la peur, for two pianos and small orchestra
           String Trio
1938 (48) *Ballade*, for alto saxophone, string orchestra, piano,
              timpani and percussion
           Le Vin herbe, opera
           Sonata da Chiesa, for viola d'amore and organ
1939 (49) *Ballade*, for piano and orchestra

    Ballade, for flute, string orchestra and piano
    Ballade, for flute and piano
1941 (51) Sonata da Chiesa, for flute and string orchestra
1942–43 (52) *Die Weise von Liebe und Tod des Cornets Christoph
    Rilke,* for high voice and orchestra
1943 (53) *Sechs Monologe aus Jedermann,* for baritone and piano
1944 (54) Petite Symphonie Concertante (1944–45)
    In Terra Pax, oratorio
    Passacaglia for organ
1945–48 (55–58) *Golgotha,* oratorio
1946 (56) Overture to Racine's *Athalie,* for orchestra
1947 (57) *Trois chants de Noël,* for high voice, flute and piano
1948 (58) *Ballade,* for cello and piano
    Eight Piano Preludes
1949 (59) Concerto for seven wind instruments
1950 (60) Violin Concerto (1950–51)
    Five Ariel Songs, for mixed chamber choir
1951 (61) Concerto for cembalo and small orchestra (1951–52)
1952–55 (62–65) *La Tempête,* opera
1955–56 (65) *Études,* for string orchestra
1956 (66) *Overture in Homage to Mozart,* for orchestra
1957–59 (67–69) *La Mystère de la Nativité,* oratorio
1958 (68) *Overture in Rondo,* for orchestra
    Pseaumes de Genève, for mixed choir, children's voices,
    organ and orchestra
1960 (70) *Drey Minnelieder,* for soprano and piano
1961–62 (71) *Monsieur de Pourceaugnac,* opera
1963–64 (73) *Les Quatre élements,* symphonic studies: Earth, Water,
    Air, Fire
1964 (74) *Pilate,* cantata
1965–66 (75) Cello Concerto
1967 (77) String Quartet
1968 (78) *Maria-Triptychon* (Ave Maria—Magnificat—Stabat
    Mater), for soprano, solo violin and orchestra
    Piano Concerto No. 2
1969 (79) *Erasmi Monumentum,* for orchestra and organ
    Poèmes de la mort, for tenor, baritone, bass and three
    electric guitars (1969–71)
1970 (80) *Three Dances,* for oboe, harp, string quintet and string
    orchestra
1971–72 (81) *Requiem,* for soprano, contralto, tenor and bass soli,
    mixed choir, orchestra and organ
1972 (82) *Ballade,* for viola, wind orchestra, cembalo, harp and
    timpani
1973 (83) *Polyptique,* for violin and two small string orchestras
    Fantasy on Flamenco rhythms, for piano
1974 (84) *Et la vie l'emporta,* chamber cantata

MARTINŮ, Bohuslav/1890–1959/Bohemia (Czechoslovakia)

1918 (28) *Czech Rhapsody,* for chorus
1921 (31) *Istar,* ballet

1922 (32) *The Grove of the Satyrs*, symphonic poem
          Shadows, symphonic poem
          Vanishing Midnight, symphonic poem
1925 (35) *Half Time*, symphonic poem
          Piano Concerto No. 1
          On tourne, ballet
1927 (37) *La Bagarre*, symphonic poem
          La Revue de cuisine, ballet
          Le Raid merveilleux, ballet (1927–28)
1928 (38) *The Soldier and the Dancer*, opera
          Les Lames du Couteau, opera
          Échéc au roi, ballet
          La Rapsodie
          Entr'acte
          Concertino for piano (left hand) and chamber orchestra
1929 (39) *Journée de Bonte*, opera
          The Butterfly that Stamped, ballet
1930 (40) *Serenade*, for chamber orchestra
          Violin Sonata No. 1
1931 (41) Cello Concerto
          Partita (Suite No. 1)
          Spaliček, ballet
1932 (42) *Les Rondes*
          Sinfonia for two orchestras
          Overture for the Sokol Festival
1933 (43) *The Miracle of Our Lady*, opera
1934 (44) *Inventions*
1935 (45) *The Suburban Theater*, opera
          Le Jugement de Paris, ballet
          Concertino for piano, No. 2
1936–37 (46) *Juliette, or The Key to Dreams*, opera
1937 (47) *Alexandre bis*, opera
          Comedy on the Bridge, opera
1938 (48) Concerto for two string orchestras, piano and timpani
          Concerto Grosso, for orchestra
          Tre Ricercare, for orchestra
          Quartet No. 5
          Madrigals for women's voices
1939 (49) Field Mass
1940 (50) Military March
1942 (52) Symphony No. 1
1943 (53) Symphony No. 2
          Concerto for two pianos
          Violin Concerto
          In Memory of Lidice
1944 (54) Symphony No. 3
          Cello Concerto (1944–45)
1945 (55) Symphony No. 4
          Thunderbolt P-47
1947 (57) Quartet No. 7
1948 (58) Piano Concerto No. 3
1953 (63) *The Marriage*, opera

1955 (65) *Three Frescoes*

MASCAGNI, Pietro/1863–1945/Italy

1879 (16) Symphony in C minor
1881 (18) Symphony in F major
           In Filanda, for voices and orchestra
1890 (27) *Cavalleria Rusticana*, opera
1891 (28) *L'Amico Fritz*, opera
           Solemn Mass
1892 (29) *I Rantzau*, opera
1895 (32) *Guglielmo Ratcliff*, opera
           Silvano, opera
1896 (33) *Zanetto*, opera
1898 (35) *Iris*, opera
1901 (38) *Le Maschera*, opera
1905 (42) *Amica*, opera
1911 (48) *Isabeau*, opera
1913 (50) *Parisina*, opera
1917 (54) *Lodoletta*, opera
           Satanic Rhapsody
1919 (56) *Si*, opera
1921 (58) *Il Piccolo Marat*, opera
1932 (69) *Pinotta*, opera
1935 (72) *Nero*, opera

MASSENET, Jules/1842–1912/France

1863 (21) Overture de Concert
           David Rizzio, cantata
1865 (23) Suite for Orchestra, No. 1
1871 (29) Suite for Orchestra, No. 2, *Scènes hongroises*
1873 (31) Suite for Orchestra, No. 3, *Scènes dramatiques*
           Phedre, concert overture
1874 (32) Suite for Orchestra, No. 4, *Scènes pittoresques*
1875 (33) *Eve*, oratorio
1876 (34) Suite for Orchestra, No. 5, *Scènes napolitaines*
1877 (35) *Le Roi de Lahore*, opera
           Narcisse, cantata
1879 (37) Suite for Orchestra, No. 6, *Scènes de féerie*
1880 (38) *La Vierge*, oratorio
1881 (39) Suite for Orchestra, No. 7, *Scènes alsaciennes*
           Hérodiade, opera
1884 (42) *Manon*, opera
1885 (43) *Le Cid*, opera
1887 (45) *Parade Militaire*
1890 (48) *Visions*, symphonic poem
1892 (50) *Werther*, opera
1894 (52) *Thaïs*, opera
           La Navarraise
1897 (55) *Marche Solenelle*
           Fantaisie, for cello and orchestra

Sappho, lyric play
Devant la Madone
1899 (57) *Brumaire*, overture
Cendrillon, opera
1900 (58) *La Terre promisé*, oratorio
1902 (60) Piano Concerto
Le Jongleur de Notre Dame
1910 (68) *Don Quixote*, opera

MAW, Nicholas/b.1935/Great Britain

1957 (22) *Sonatina*, for flute and piano
1958 (23) *Nocturne*, for mezzo-soprano and chamber orchestra
1960 (25) *Five Epigrams*, for mixed unaccompanied voices
1961 (26) *Essay*, for organ (revised 1963)
1962 (27) *Scenes and Arias*, for soprano, mezzo-soprano, contralto
and orchestra (revised 1966)
Chamber Music, for oboe, clarinet, horn, bassoon and
piano
Our Lady's Song, carol for unaccompanied mixed voices
1963 (28) *Round*, for children's chorus, mixed chorus and piano
The Angel Gabriel, carol for unaccompanied mixed chorus
1964 (29) *One Man Show*, comic opera in two acts
Balulalow, carol for unaccompanied mixed voices
Corpus Christi Carol
1965 (30) String Quartet
1966 (31) *Sinfonia*, for small orchestra
The Voice of Love, song cycle for mezzo-soprano and piano
1967 (32) Sonata for strings and two horns
Double Canon for Igor Stravinsky on his 85th birthday, for
various instruments
1969–70 (34) *The Rising of the Moon*, opera
1971 (36) *Epitaph—Canon in memory of Igor Stravinsky*, for flute,
clarinet and harp
1972 (37) *Concert Music for Orchestra* (derived from the opera,
Rising of the Moon)
Five Irish Songs, for mixed chorus
1973 (38) *Serenade*, for chamber orchestra
Life Studies, for fifteen solo strings
Personae, for piano

MEDTNER, Nicholas/1880–1951/Russia

1904 (24) Nine Songs (Goethe)
1907 (27) Three Songs (Heine)
1908 (28) Twelve Songs (Goethe)
1910 (30) Three Songs (Nietzsche, etc.)
Violin Sonata
1912 (32) Three *Nocturnes*, for violin and piano
1916–18 (36–38) Piano Concerto No. 1 in C minor
1921 (41) Sonata-Vocalise No. 1
1924 (44) Violin Sonata

1926–27 (46) Piano Concerto No. 2 in C minor
1936 (56) Violin Sonata, *Sonata Epica*
1942–43 (62) Piano Concerto No. 3 in E minor, *Ballade*

MENDELSSOHN (-Bartholdy), Felix/1809–1847/Germany

1821 (12) Piano Sonata No. 2 in G minor
1822 (13) Piano Quartet No. 1 in C minor
1823 (14) Piano Quartet No. 2 in F minor
           Violin Sonata in F minor
1824 (15) Piano Quartet No. 3 in B minor
           Symphony No. 1 in C minor
1825 (16) *Wedding of the Camacho*, comic opera
           Trumpet Overture, for orchestra
           String Octet in E♭ major
           Capriccio in F♯ minor, for piano
1826 (17) *A Midsummer Night's Dream*, overture
           String Quintet in A major
           Piano Sonata No. 1 in E major
           Six Songs (1826–27)
1827 (18) String Quartet No. 2 in A minor
           Fugue in E♭ major, for string quartet
           Piano Sonata No. 3 in B♭ major
           p. Seven pieces for piano
1829 (20) *Die Heimkehr aus der Fremde*, operetta
           String Quartet No. 1 in E♭ major
           Variations concertantes, for cello and piano, in D major
           Three Fantasies for piano
           Twelve Songs
1830 (21) Symphony No. 5, *Reformation*
           Hebrides, concert overture
           Twelve Songs
           Six Songs
1831 (22) Piano Concerto No. 1 in G minor
           Die erste Walpurgisnacht, for solo voices, chorus and
              orchestra
           Song
1832 (23) *Meerstille (Calm Sea and Prosperous Voyage)*, concert
              overture
           Capriccio Brillant, in B minor, for piano and orchestra
           Six Preludes and Fugues for piano (1832–37)
1833 (24) Symphony No. 4, *Italian*
           Die Schöne Melusine, overture
           Fantasy in F♯ minor, for piano
           Three Capriccios for piano (1833–34)
1834 (25) *Rondo Brillant* in E♭, for piano and orchestra
           p. Songs Without Words, Book I, for piano
           Piano Sextet in D major
           Three Studies for piano (1834–36)
           Two Romances of Byron
           Six Songs (1834–37)
           Song

1835 (26) *p. Songs Without Words*, Book II, for piano
Two Sacred Songs
Two Songs after Eichendorff
1836 (27) *St. Paul*, oratorio
Étude in F minor, for piano
1837 (28) Piano Concerto No. 2 in D minor
Three Organ Preludes and Fugues
Capriccio in E major, for piano
Gondellied in A major, for piano
String Quartets Nos. 3–5 in D: Em: E♭ (1837–38)
Six Songs (1837–42)
1838 (29) Serenade and Allegro Gioioso in B minor, for piano and
    orchestra
Cello Sonata No. 1 in B♭ major
Piano Trio No. 1 in D minor
Andante Cantabile, and Presto Agitato, in B major, for
    piano
1839 (30) *Ruy Blas*, overture
Songs Without Words, Book III, for piano
Six Songs
Song
1840 (31) *Lobegesang (Hymn of Praise)*, symphony-cantata
    (Symphony No. 2)
Festgesang, for male chorus and orchestra
1841 (32) *Cornelius March*
Songs Without Words, Books IV and VII, for piano
Allegro Brillant in A major, for piano
Variations in B♭ major
Variations in E♭ major
Variations serieuses
Six Songs (1841–45)
1842 (33) Symphony No. 3, *Scotch*
Cello Sonata in D major (1842–43)
Songs Without Words, Book VIII, for piano
Kinderstücke (Christmas Pieces), for piano
1843 (34) *Athalie*, incidental music
Andante in E major, for string quartet
Scherzo in A minor, for string quartet
Capriccio in E minor, for string quartet
Songs Without Words, Books V and VI, for piano
1844 (35) Violin Concerto in E minor
Hear My Prayer, for soprano, chorus and organ
p. Six Organ Sonatas (1844–45)
1845 (36) Piano Trio No. 2 in C minor
String Quintet in B♭ major
Songs Without Words, for cello and piano
1846 (37) String Quartet No. 6, in F minor
fp. Elijah, oratorio
Lauda Sion, cantata
1847 (38) *Lorely*, opera (unfinished)
1852 (posthumous) *fp.* Christus, oratorio (unfinished)
Mendelssohn also composed:

1827–47   Four pieces for string quartet
1827–41   Prelude and Fugue in E minor, for piano

MENNIN, Peter/b.1923/U.S.A.

1945 (22)   Concertino for flute, strings and percussion
1946 (23)   Symphony No. 3
1947 (24)   Fantasia for string orchestra
1949 (26)   Symphony No. 4, *The Cycle*, for choir and orchestra
             The Christmas Story, cantata
1950 (27)   Symphony No. 5
             Violin Concerto
             Canto and Toccata, for piano
             Five pieces for piano
1951 (28)   *Canzona*, for band
1952 (29)   Concertato for orchestra, *Moby Dick*
             Quartet No. 2
1953 (30)   Symphony No. 6
1956 (33)   Cello Concerto
             Sonata Concertante for violin and piano
1958 (35)   Piano Concerto
1963 (40)   Symphony No. 7 (1963–64)
             Canto, for orchestra
1967 (44)   Piano Sonata
1968–69 (45)   *Cantata de Virtute*, for chorus and orchestra, children's
             chorus, soloists and narrator
1971 (48)   *Sinfonia for Orchestra*
1973 (50)   *fp.* Symphony No. 8

MENOTTI, Gian-Carlo/b.1911/U.S.A. (b.Italy)

1931 (20)   *Variations on a theme of Schumann*, for piano
1936 (25)   *Trio for a housewarming party*, for flute, cello and piano
1937 (26)   *Amelia al Ballo*, opera (the only one Menotti wrote in
             Italian)
1939 (28)   *The Old Maid and the Thief*, opera
1942 (31)   *The Island God*, opera
1944 (33)   *Sebastian*, ballet
1945 (34)   Piano Concerto in A minor
1946 (35)   *The Medium*, opera
1947 (36)   *The Telephone*, opera
             Errand into the Maze, ballet
1950 (39)   *The Consul*, opera
1951 (40)   *Amahl and the Night Visitors*, opera
             Apocalypse, for orchestra
1952 (41)   Violin Concerto
1954 (43)   *The Saint of Bleeker Street*, opera
1956 (45)   *The Unicorn, the Gorgon and the Manticore*, ballet
1958 (47)   *Maria Golovin*, opera
1963 (52)   *Labyrinth*, opera
             The Last Savage, opera
             Death of the Bishop of Brindisi, cantata

1964 (53) *Martin's Lie*, opera
1967 (56) *Canti della Lontananza*, song cycle
1968 (57) *Help, Help, the Globolinks*, children's opera
1970 (59) *The Leper*, drama
           Triplo Concerto a Tre, symphonic piece
1971 (60) *fp. The Most Important Man in the World*, opera
1973 (62) *fp.* Suite for two cellos and piano

MESSAGER, André Charles/1853–1929/France

1875 (22) Symphony
1877 (24) *Don Juan et Haydée*, cantata
1878 (25) *Fleur d'Oranger*, ballet
1885 (32) *Le Béarnasie*, operetta
1886 (33) *Les deux pigeons*, ballet
1888 (35) *Isoline*, opera
1890 (37) *La Basoche*, operetta
1893 (40) *Madame Chrysanthème*, operetta
1894 (41) *Mirette*, operetta
1896 (43) *Le Chavalier d'Harmenthal*, operetta
1897 (44) *Les P'tites Michu*, operetta
1898 (45) *Véronique*, operetta
1907 (54) *Fortuno*, operetta
1914 (61) *Béatrice*, operetta
1919 (66) *Monsieur Beaucaire*, operetta

MESSIAEN, Olivier/b.1908/France

1928 (20) Fugue in D minor, for orchestra
           Le Banquet Eucharistique
           Le Banquet Céleste, for organ
1929 (21) *Préludes*, for piano
1930 (22) *Simple chant d'une âme*
           Les Offrandes oubliées
           Diptyque, for organ
1931 (23) *Le Tombeau resplendissant*
1932 (24) *Hymne au Saint Sacrement*, for orchestra
           Fantaisie Burlesque, for piano
           Apparition de l'Eglise éternelle, for organ
1933 (25) *L'Ascension*, for organ
           Mass, for eight sopranos and four violins
1935 (27) *La Nativité du Seigneur*, nine meditations for organ
1937 (29) *Poèmes pour mi*, for voice and orchestra
1939 (31) *Les Corps glorieux*, for organ
1941 (33) *Quatour pour la fin du temps*, for violin, clarinet, cello and
                piano
1943 (35) *Visions de l'Amen*, for two pianos
           Rondeau, for piano
1944 (36) *Vingt regards sur l'enfant Jésus*, for piano
1947 (39) *Turangalîla*, symphony for orchestra, piano and Ondes
                Martenot
1950 (42) *Le Merle noir*, for piano and flute

Messe de la Pentecôte
1953 (45) *Reveil des oiseaux*, for piano and orchestra
1956 (48) *Oiseaux exotiques*, for piano, wind instruments and
              percussion
1960 (52) *Chronochromie*
1963 (55) *Sept Haï-Kaï*
1964 (56) *Couleurs de la cité céleste*
1965 (57) *La Transfiguration de notre Seigneur Jésus-Christ*
              (1965—69)

MEYERBEER, Giacomo/1791—1864/Germany

1831 (40) *Robert le diable*, opera
1836 (45) *Les Huguenots*, opera
1849 (58) *Le Prophète*, opera
1854 (63) *L'Étoile du nord*, opera
1859 (68) *Dinorah*, opera
1865 (posthumous) *fp. L'Africaine*, opera

MILHAUD, Darius/1892—1974/France

1910—15 (18—23) *La Brèbis égarée*, opera
1911 (19) Violin Sonata
1912 (20) String Quartet No. 1 in A minor
1913—14 (21) Suite Symphonique No. 1
1914 (22) Sonata for two violins and piano
              Printemps, for violin and piano
              String Quartet No. 2, (atonal) (1914—15)
1916 (24) String Quartet No. 3
1917 (25) Symphony for small orchestra, No. 1, *Le Printemps*
1918 (26) Symphony for small orchestra, No. 2, *Pastorale*
              Sonata for flute, oboe, clarinet and piano
              L'Homme et son desir, ballet
              String Quartet No. 4
1919 (27) Suite Symphonique No. 2, *Protée*
              Machines agricoles, six pastoral songs for middle voice
                 and instruments
1920 (28) *Le Boeuf sur le toit*, ballet
              Ballade, for piano and orchestra
              Five Studies for piano and orchestra
              Sérénade (1920—21)
              Printemps, six piano pieces
              String Quartet No. 5
1921 (29) *Saudades de Brasil*, dance suite
              Symphony for small orchestra, No. 3, *Sérénade*
              Symphony for strings, No. 4, *Ouverture, Choral, Étude*
1922 (30) Symphony for small wind orchestra, No. 5
              La Creation du monde, ballet, using jazz idiom
                 (1922—23)
              Three *Rag-Caprices*
              String Quartet No. 6
1923 (31) Symphony No. 6 for soprano, contralto, tenor, bass, oboe

and cello
1924 (32) *Les Malheurs d'Orphée*, opera
Esther de Carpentras (1924–25)
1925 (33) String Quartet No. 7
Deux Hymnes
1926 (34) *Le Pauvre matelot*, opera
1927 (35) Violin Concerto No. 1
Carnival of Aix, for piano and orchestra
1928 (36) *Christophe Columb*, opera (revised 1956)
Cantate pour louer le Seigneur
1929 (37) Viola Concerto
Concerto for percussion and small orchestra
1930 (38) *Maximilien*, opera
1932 (40) String Quartet No. 8
1933 (41) Piano Concerto No. 1
1935 (43) Cello Concerto No. 1
String Quartet No. 9
1936 (44) *Suite provençale*
1937 (45) *Cantate de la paix*
1938 (46) *Medée*, opera
1939 (47) Symphony No. 1 for full orchestra
King Renée's chimney, for wind quartet
1940 (48) String Quartet No. 10, *Birthday Quartet*
1941 (49) Piano Concerto No. 2
Clarinet Concerto
Concerto for two pianos
Four Sketches
1942 (50) String Quartet No. 11
1943 (51) *Bolivar*, opera
1944 (52) Symphony No. 2 for full orchestra
Jeux de printemps
Suite Française
1945 (53) *The Bells*, ballet
Cello Concerto No. 2
String Quartet No. 12, *In memory of Fauré*
1946 (54) Symphony No. 3 for full orchestra and chorus, *Hymnus Ambrosianus*
Piano Concerto No. 3
Violin Concerto No. 2
String Quartet No. 13
1947 (55) Symphony, *1848*
Concerto for marimba and vibraphone
1949 (57) Piano Concerto No. 4
String Quartets Nos. 14 and 15, to be played together as octet, or separately
1951 (59) *The Seven-branched Candelabra*
1953 (61) *David*, opera
1954 (62) Harp Concerto
1955 (63) Symphonies Nos. 5 and 6
1956 (64) Symphony No. 7
1957 (65) Symphony No. 8, *Rhodanienne*
Oboe Concerto

Aspen Serenade
1958 (66) Violin Concerto No. 3, *Concerto royal*
1960 (68) Symphony No. 10
  ?   ?   Symphony No. 11
1962 (70) Symphony No. 12
1963 (71) *Pacem in terris*, for chorus and orchestra
1964 (72) *La Mère coupable*, opera
        String Septet

MOERAN, Ernest/1894–1950/Great Britain

1919 (25) Three piano pieces
1920 (26) Theme and variations for piano
        Piano Trio in E minor
        Ludlow Town, song cycle
1921 (27) *In the Mountain Country*, symphonic impression
        On a May Morning, for piano
1922 (28) Rhapsody No. 1 in F major
        Three Fancies, for piano
1924 (30) Rhapsody No. 2 in E major
1925 (31) *Summer Valley*, for piano
1926 (32) *Irish Love Song*, for piano
1932 (38) *Farrago*, suite for orchestra
1934 (40) *Nocturne*, for baritone, chorus and orchestra
1937 (43) Symphony in G minor
1942 (48) Violin Concerto
1943 (49) Rhapsody No. 3 in F♯ major, for piano and orchestra
1944 (50) Sinfonietta
        Overture for a Masque
1945 (51) Cello Concerto
1946 (52) *Fantasy Quartet*, for oboe and strings
1948 (54) *Serenade*, in G major

MONTEVERDI, Claudio/1567–1643/Italy

1584 (17) *p.* Canzonettas for three voices
1587 (20) *p.* Madrigals, for five voices, Book I
1590 (23) *p.* Madrigals, for five voices, Book II
1592 (25) *p.* Madrigals, for five voices, Book III
1603 (36) *p.* Madrigals, for five voices, Book IV
1605 (38) *p.* Madrigals, for five voices, Book V
1607 (40) *p.* Scherzi Musicali for three voices
        fp. Orfeo, opera
1608 (41) *Ballo delle Ingrate*
        fp. L'Arianna, opera
1610 (43) Vespers
        p. Masses
1614 (47) *p.* Madrigals, for five voices, Book VI
1615 (48) *fp. Tirsi e Clori*, ballet
1617 (50) *La Maddalena*, opera
1619 (52) *p.* Madrigals, for one, two, three, four and six voices,
        Book VII

1627 (60) *Armida*, opera
1628 (61) *Mercurio e Marte*, opera
1632 (65) *p.* Scherzi Musicali, for one or two voices
1638 (71) *p.* Madrigals, of war and love (Madrigali guerrieri e
                amorosi) Book VIII
1640 (73) Selve Morale e Spirituale
1641 (74) *Il ritorno d'Ulisse in patria*, opera
1642 (75) *L'Incoronazione di Poppea*, opera
1650 (posthumous) *p.* Masses for four voices and psalms
1651 (posthumous) *p.* Madrigals and Canzonettes, for two or three
                voices, Book IX

MOORE, Douglas/b.1893/U.S.A.

1924 (31) *The Pageant of P.T. Barnum*, suite for orchestra
1928 (35) *A Symphony of Autumn*
           Moby Dick, for orchestra
1929 (36) Violin Sonata
1930 (37) *Overture on an American theme*
1933 (40) String Quartet
1935 (42) *White Wings*, opera (possibly 1948)
1936 (43) *The Headless Horseman*, opera
1938 (45) *Dedication*, for chorus
1939 (46) *The Devil and Daniel Webster*, opera
1941 (48) *Village Music*, suite for small orchestra
1942 (49) Quintet for woodwinds and horn
1943 (50) *In Memoriam*, symphonic poem
1944 (51) *Down East Suite*, for violin with piano or orchestra
1945 (52) Symphony in A major
1946 (53) Quintet for clarinet and strings
1947 (54) *Farm Journal*, suite for chamber orchestra
1948 (55) *The Emperor's New Clothes*, opera for children
1950 (57) *Giants in the Earth*, opera
1952 (59) *Cotillion*, suite for string orchestra
1953 (60) Piano Trio
1956 (63) *The Ballad of Baby Doe*, opera
1957 (64) *Gallantry*, a soap opera
1961 (68) *Wings of the Dove*, opera
1962 (69) *The Greenfield Christmas Tree*, a Christmas entertainment
1966 (73) *Carry Nation*, opera

MORLEY, Thomas/1557–1603/Great Britain

1593 (36) *p.* Canzonets, or Little Short Songs to Three Voyces
1594 (37) *p.* Madrigalls to Foure Voyces
1595 (38) *p.* The First Booke of Balletts to Fiue Voyces
           p. The First Booke of Canzonets to Two Voyces
1597 (40) *p.* Two songs in "Canzonets or Little Short Songs to
           Foure Voyces. Celected out of the best and approved
           Italian Authors"
           p. Canzonets or Little Short Aers to Fiue and Sixe Voices
           p. A Plaine and Easie Introduction to Practicall Musicke

1598 (41)   *p.* Madrigalls to Fiue Vouces. Celected out of the best
approved Italian Authors
1599 (42)   *p.* The First Booke of Consort Lessons, made by diuerse
exquisite Authors for six Instruments
1600 (43)   *p.* The First Booke of Ayres or Little Short Songs; to sing
and play to the Lute with the Base Viole
1601 (44)   *p.* Two madrigals in *"The Triumphs of Oriana,* to five and
six voices, composed by diuerse seuerall authors"

MOZART, Wolfgang Amadeus/1756—1791/Austria

1762–64 (6–8)   Sonata in C major for violin and piano, K.6
1763–64 (7–8)   Sonata in D major for violin and piano, K.7
              Sonata in B♭ major for violin and piano, K.8
1764 (8)   Sonata in G major for violin and piano, K.9
              Sonata in B♭ major for violin and piano, K.10
              Sonata in G major for violin and piano, K.11
              Sonata in A major for violin and piano, K.12
              Sonata in F major for violin and piano, K.13
              Sonata in C major for violin and piano, K.14
              Sonata in B♭ major for violin and piano, K.15
              Symphony No. 1 in E♭ major, K.16
              Symphony No. 4 in D major, K.19
1765 (9)   Piano Sonatas (four hands) in C major, K.19d
                (unpublished)
              Three Sonatas by J.C. Bach arranged as Concertos with
                string orchestra, K.107
              Symphony No. 5 in B♭ major, K.22
1766 (10)   Sonata in E♭ major for violin and piano, K.26
              Sonata in G major for violin and piano, K.27
              Sonata in C major for violin and piano, K.28
              Sonata in D major for violin and piano, K.29
              Sonata in F major for violin and piano, K.30
              Sonata in B♭ major for violin and piano, K.31
1767 (11)   Piano Concerto in F major, K.37
              Piano Concerto in B♭ major, K.39
              Piano Concerto in D major, K.40
              Piano Concerto in G major, K.41
              Symphony No. 6 in F major, K.43
              Sonata for Organ and Strings in E♭ major, K.62
              Sonata for Organ and Strings in B♭ major, K.68
              Sonata for Organ and Strings in D major, K.69
              Symphony No. 43 in F major, K.76
1768 (12)   *Bastien und Bastienne,* opera
              Symphony No. 7 in D major, K.45
              Symphony No. 8 in D major, K.48
1769 (13)   Mass in C major, K.66
              Symphony No. 9 in C major, K.73
              Symphony No. 42 in F major, K.75
1770 (14)   String Quartet in G major, K.80
              Symphony No. 10 in G major, K.74
              Symphony No. 11 in D major, K.80

Symphony No. 45 in D major, K.95
Symphony No. 47 in D major, K.97
Symphony No. 12 in G major, K.110
1771 (15) Symphony No. 46 in C major, K.95
Symphony No. 13 in F major, K.112
Symphony No. 14 in A major, K.114
Symphony No. 50 in D (finale only, to the Overture of
    Asanio in Alba), K.120
Overture of *La finta giardinera*
1772 (16) Piano Sonata (four hands) in D major, K.381
String Quartet in D major, K.155
String Quartet in G major, K.156
String Quartet in C major, K.157
String Quartet in F major, K.158
String Quartet in B♭ major, K.159
String Quartet in E♭ major, K.160
Sonata for organ and strings, in D major, K.144
Sonata for organ and strings, in F major, K.145
Mass in C minor and C major, K.139
Symphony No. 15 in G major, K.124
Symphony No. 16 in C major, K.128
Symphony No. 17 in G major, K.129
Symphony No. 19 in E♭ major, K.132
Symphony No. 20 in D major, K.133
Symphony No. 21 in A major, K.134
Symphony in D major (first two movements identical
    with the overture *Il sogno di Scipiona*, K.126), K.161
Symphony No. 22 in C major, K.162
Symphony No. 51 in D major (finale only, to the overture
    of *Il sogno di Scipiona*), K.163
Lucio Silla, opera
1773 (17) Piano Concerto in D major, K.175
Concertone in C major for two violins, K.190
String Quartet in F major, K.168
String Quartet in A major, K.169
String Quartet in C major, K.170
String Quartet in E♭ major, K.171
String Quartet in B♭ major, K.172
String Quartet in D minor, K.173
String Quintet in B♭ major, K.174
Symphony No. 23 in D major, K.181
Symphony No. 24 in B♭ major, K.182
Symphony No. 25 in G minor, K.183
Symphony No. 26 in E♭ major, K.184
1774 (18) Bassoon Concerto in B♭ major, K.191
Symphony No. 27 in G major, K.199
Symphony No. 28 in C major, K.200
Symphony No. 29 in A major, K.201
Symphony No. 30 in D major, K.202
Piano Sonata in C major, K.279
Piano Sonata in F major, K.280
Piano Sonata in B♭ major, K.281

Piano Sonata in E♭ major, K.282
Piano Sonata in G major, K.283
Piano Sonata in D major, K.284
Piano Sonata (four hands) in B♭ major, K.358

1775 (19)   *La finta giardinera*, opera
Il re pastore, opera
Symphony No. 49 in C major (finale only, to the overture of *Il re pastore*), K.102
Violin Concerto in B♭ major, K.207
Violin Concerto in D major, K.211
Violin Concerto in G major, K.216
Violin Concerto in D major, K.218
Violin Concerto in A major, K.219
Sonata for organ and strings, in B♭ major, K.212

1776 (20)   Piano Concerto in B♭ major, K.238
Piano Concerto in F major, for three pianos, K.242
Piano Concerto in C major, K.246
Adagio to K.219 Violin Concerto, K.261
Rondo Concertante to K.207 Violin Concerto, K.269
Piano Trio in B♭ major, K.254
Sonata for organ and strings in F major, K.224
Sonata for organ and strings in A major, K.225
Sonata for organ and strings in G major, K.241
Sonata for organ and strings in F major, K.244
Sonata for organ and strings in D major, K.245
Mass in C major, K.257

1777 (21)   Piano Concerto in E♭ major, K.271
Violin Concerto in D major, K.271a
Piano Sonata in C major, K.309
Sonata for organ and strings in G major, K.274

1778 (22)   Concerto in C major for flute and harp, K.299
Concerto in G major for flute, K.313
Concerto in D major for flute, K.314
Andante in C major for flute, K.315
Sinfonia Concertante in E♭ for flute, oboe, horn and bassoon (app. K.9)
Piano Sonata in A minor, K.310
Piano Sonata in D major, K.311
Piano Sonata in C major, K.330
Piano Sonata in A major, K.331
Piano Sonata in F major, K.332
Piano Sonata in B♭ major, K.333
Violin Sonata in C major, K.296
Violin Sonata in G major, K.301
Violin Sonata in E♭ major, K.302
Violin Sonata in C major, K.303
Violin Sonata in E minor, K.304
Violin Sonata in A major, K.305
Violin Sonata in D major, K.306
Symphony No. 31 in D major, *Paris*, K.297

1779 (23)   Sinfonia Concertante in E♭ for violin and viola, K.364
Sonata for organ and strings in C major. K.328

Mass in C major, K.317
Symphony No. 32 in G major, K.318
Symphony No. 33 in B♭ major, K.319
1780 (24) Violin Concerto in E♭ major, K.268 (1780–81)
      (authenticity doubtful)
    Sonata for organ and strings in C major, K.336
    String Quartet in B♭, K.46 (arrangement of K.361
      Serenade, may be spurious)
    Symphony No. 34 in C major, K.338
    Six variations for violin and piano on *Helas, j'ai perdu
      mon amant* K.360
1781 (25) *Idomeneo*, opera
    Rondo in C major, for violin, K.373
    Concerto Rondo in E♭ for horn, K.371
    Twelve variations on *La bergere Celimene*, for violin and
      piano, K.359
    Violin Sonata in F major, K.376
    Violin Sonata in F major, K.377
    Violin Sonata in B♭ major, K.378
    Violin Sonata in G minor and G major, K.379
    Violin Sonata in E♭ major, K.380
    Sonata for two pianos in D major, K.448
1782 (26) *Il Seraglio*, opera
    Concerto Rondo in D minor to K.175 Piano Concerto,
      K.382
    Concerto Rondo in A major, (discarded from K.414
      Piano Concerto), K.386
    Piano Concerto in F major, K.413
    Piano Concerto in A major, K.414
    Piano Concerto in C major, K.415
    Horn Concerto in D major, K.412
    Violin Sonata in A major and A minor (finished by
      Stadler), K.402
    Violin Sonata in C major, unfinished, K.403
    Violin Sonata in C major, unfinished, K.404
    String Quartet in G major (Haydn Set, No. 1), K.387
    Five fugues from Bach's *Well-Tempered Clavier*, for string
      quartet, K.405
    Symphony No. 35 in D major, *Haffner*, K.385
1783 (27) Oboe Concerto in F major, fragment, K.293
    Votive Mass
    Horn Concerto in E♭ major, K.417
    Horn Concerto in E♭ major, K.447
    String Quartet in D minor (Haydn Set, No. 2), K.421
    String Quartet in E♭ major (Haydn Set, No. 3), K.428
    Piano Trio in D minor and D major (completed by
      Stadler), K.442
    Symphony No. 36 in C major, *Linz*, K.425
    Symphony No. 37 in G major, K.444 (introduction only,
      the rest by M. Haydn)
1784 (28) Piano Concerto in E♭ major, K.449
    Piano Concerto in B♭ major, K.450

Piano Concerto in D major, K.451
Piano Concerto in G major, K.453
Piano Concerto in B♭ major, K.456
Piano Concerto in F major, K.459
Violin Sonata in B♭ major, K.454
Piano Sonata in C minor, K.457
String Quartet in B♭ major (Haydn Set, No. 4), K.458

1785 (29) Piano Concerto in D minor, K.466
Piano Concerto in C major, K.467
Piano Concerto in E♭ major, K.482
Andante for a Violin Concerto, in A major, K.470
Violin Sonata in E♭ major, K.481
String Quartet in A major (Haydn Set, No. 5), K.464
String Quartet in C major (Haydn Set, No. 6), K.465
Piano Quartet in G minor, K.478

1786 (30) *Impresario*, opera
Marriage of Figaro, opera
Piano Concerto in A major, K.488
Piano Concerto in C minor, K.491
Piano Concerto in C major, K.503
Horn Concerto in E♭ major, K.495
Piano Sonata (four hands) in G major, K.357
Piano Sonata (four hands) in F major, K.497
String Quartet in D major, K. 499
Piano Quartet in E♭ major, K.493
Piano Trio in G major, K.496
Piano Trio in B♭ mjaor, for piano, clarinet and viola,
    K.498
Piano Trio in B♭ major, K.502
Symphony No. 38 in D major, *Prague*, K.504

1787 (31) *Don Giovanni*, opera
Piano Sonata (four hands) in C major, K.521
Violin Sonata in A major, K.526
String Quintet in C minor, K.406 (arrangement of
    Serenade, K.388)
String Quintet in C major, K.515
String Quintet in G minor, K.516
Eine Kleine Nachtmusik, for strings

1788 (32) Piano Concerto in D major, *Coronation*, K.537
Piano Sonata (Sonatina) in C major, K.545
Violin Sonata in F major, K.547
String Quartet in D minor, Adagio and Fugue (fugue
    identical with K.426 for two pianos), K.546
Piano Trio in E major, K.542
Piano Trio in C major, K.548
Piano Trio in G major, K.564
Symphony No. 39 in E♭ major, K.543
Symphony No. 40 in G minor, K.550
Symphony No. 41 in C major, *Jupiter*, K.551

1789 (33) Piano Sonata in B♭ major (better known as a violin
    sonata, but the violin part is not by Mozart), K.570
Piano Sonata in D major, K.576

String Quartet in D major (King of Prussia Set, No. 1),
   K.575
1790 (34) *Cosi fan tutte*, opera
String Quartet in B♭ major (King of Prussia Set, No. 2),
   K.589
String Quartet in F major (King of Prussia Set, No. 3),
   K.590
String Quintet in D major, K.593
1791 (35) *Clemenza di Tito*, opera
The Magic Flute, opera
Piano Concerto in B♭ major, K.595
Clarinet Concerto in A major, K.622
String Quintet in E♭ major, K.614

MUSGRAVE, Thea/b.1928/Great Britain

1953 (25) *A Tale for Thieves*, ballet in one act
A Suite of Bairnsangs, for voice and piano
1954 (26) *Cantata for a Summer's Day*
1955 (27) *The Abbot of Drimock*, chamber opera in one act
Five Love Songs, for soprano and guitar
1958 (30) *Obliques*, for orchestra
String Quartet
A Song for Christmas, for high voice and piano
1959 (31) *Triptych*, for tenor and orchestra
1960 (32) *Colloquy*, for violin and piano
Trio for flute, oboe and piano
Monologue, for piano
1961 (33) *Serenade*, for flute, clarinet, harp, viola and cello
Sir Patrick Spens, for tenor and guitar
1962 (34) Chamber Concerto No. 1
The Phoenix and the Turtle, for small choir and orchestra
1963 (35) *The Five Ages of Man*, for chorus and orchestra
1964–65 (36) *The Decision*, opera in three acts
1965 (37) *Festival Overture*, for orchestra
Excursions, for piano (four hands)
1966 (38) *Nocturnes and Arias*, for orchestra
Chamber Concerto No. 2, *In Homage to Charles Ives*
Chamber Concerto No. 3
1967 (39) Concerto for Orchestra
Impromptu, for flute and oboe
Music for Horn and Piano
1968 (40) Concerto for Clarinet and Orchestra
Beauty and the Beast, ballet in two acts for chamber
   orchestra and tape (1968–69)
1969 (41) *Night Music*, for chamber orchestra
Soliloquy, for guitar and tape
Memento Vitae (Concerto in Homage to Beethoven), for
   orchestra
1970 (42) *Elegy*, for viola and cello
Impromptu No. 2, for flute, oboe and clarinet
From One to Another, for viola and tape

1971 (43) Concerto for Horn and Orchestra
           Primavera, for soprano and flute
1972–73 (44) *The Voice of Ariadne*, chamber opera in three acts
1973 (45) Viola Concerto
1974 (46) *Space Play*, a concerto for nine instruments
1975 (47) *Orfeo I*, an improvisation on a theme, for flute and tape
           Orfeo II, for solo flute and fifteen strings

MUSSORGSKY, Modeste/1839–1881/Russia

1857 (18) *Souvenir d'enfance*, for piano
1858 (19) Scherzo for orchestra
           Edipo, for mixed chorus (1858–60)
1859 (20) *Marcia di Sciamie*, for soloists, choir and orchestra
           Impromptu passione, for piano
1861 (22) *Alla marcia notturna*, for orchestra
           Scherzo and Finale, for a symphony in D major
           (1861–62)
1867 (28) *St. John's Night on the Bare Mountain*
           La disfatta di Sennacherib, first version for choir and
           orchestra
           Symphonic Intermezzo "in modo classico"
1868 (29) *fp. Zenitha* (The Marriage), opera (private performance)
           The Nursery, song cycle (1868–72)
1869 (30) *Boris Godunov*, opera, first version with piano (rewritten
           1872)
1872 (33) *Khovantschina*, opera
1874 (35) *Pictures from an Exhibition*, for piano
           Sunless, song cycle
           Sorochinsky Fair, opera (a passage from this work was
           freely arranged and orchestrated as *Night on the Bare
           Mountain* by Rimsky-Korsakov, q.v.)
           Jesus Navin, for contralto, bass, choir and piano
           (1874–77)
1875–77 (36–38) *Songs and Dances of Death*, song cycle
1879 (40) "Song of the Flea", setting of Mephistophiles' song in
           Goethe's *Faust*
1880 (41) Five Popular Russian Songs, for male chorus
           Turkish March, for orchestra
           Meditation, for piano
           Une larme, for piano
           Au village, for piano

NICOLAI, Karl Otto/1810–1849/Germany

1831 (21) Symphony
1832 (22) Mass
1835 (25) Symphony
           Funeral March (for the death of Bellini)
1838 (28) *Von Himmel Hoch*, overture
1839 (29) *Henry II*, opera
1840 (30) *Il Templario*, opera

Gildippe ed Odoardo, opera
1841 (31) *Il Proscritto*, opera
1844 (34) *Ein Feste Burg*, overture with chorus
1849 (39) *fp. The Merry Wives of Windsor*, opera

NIELSEN, Carl/1865–1931/Denmark

1888 (23) Little Suite in A minor, for strings
              Quintet
1888–1907 String Quartet in F minor
              String Quartet in G minor (1890)
              String Quartet in E♭ major (1897)
              String Quartet in F major
1889 (24) *Symphonic Rhapsody*
1891–92 (26) Symphony No. 1 in G minor
1894 (29) Symphonic Suite for piano
1902 (37) Symphony No. 2, *Four Temperaments*
              Saul and David, opera
1903 (38) *Helios*, overture
1906 (41) *fp. Maskarade*, opera
1907–08 (42) *Saga-Drøm*
1910 (45) *At A Young Artist's Bier*
              Symphony No. 3, *Espansiva* (1910–11)
1911 (46) Violin Concerto
1914 (49) *Serenate in vano*
1916 (51) Symphony No. 4, *Inextinguishable*
              Chaconne, for piano
              Theme and Variations for piano
1918 (53) *Pan and Syrinx*
1922 (57) Symphony No. 5
              Quintet for Wind
1925 (60) Symphony No. 6, *Simple*
1926 (61) Flute Concerto
1927 (62) *En Fantasirejse til Faerøerne*, rhapsodic overture
1928 (63) Clarinet Concerto
1931 (66) *Commotio*, for organ

NILSSON, Bo/b.1937/Sweden

*c.***1956** (*c.*19) *Frequenzen*, for eight players
1957 (20) *Kreutzungen*, for instrumental ensemble
              Buch de Veränderungen
              Mädchentotenlieder (1957–58)
1958 (21) *Quantitaten*, for piano
              Zwanzig Gruppen für Blaser, for piccolo, oboe, clarinet (1958–59)
              Stunde eines Blocks, for soprano and six players
1959 (22) *Und die Zeiger seiner Augen wurden langsam zurückgedreht*,
                   for solo voices, chorus and mixed media
              Ein irrender Sohn, for high voice and instruments
1960 (23) *Szene I*
              Reaktionen, for four percussionists
1961 (24) *Szene II*

1962 (25) *Szene III*
           Entree, for large orchestra and tape
1963 (26) *Versuchungen*, for large orchestra
1964 (27) *La Bran*, for mixed choir and orchestra
1965 (28) *Litanei uber das verlorene Schlagzeug*
1967 (30) *Revue*, for orchestra
1970 (33) *Attraktionen*, for string quartet

OFFENBACH, Jacques/1819−1880/Germany

1853 (34) *Le Mariage aux lanternes*, operetta
1858 (39) *Orpheus in the Underworld*, operetta
1864 (45) *La Belle Hélène*, operetta
1866 (47) *Bluebeard*, operetta
           La Vie parisienne, opera
1867 (48) *La Grande Duchesse de Gérolstein*, operetta
1868 (49) *La Perichole*, operetta
1878 (59) *Madame Favart*, operetta
1881 (posthumous) *fp. The Tales of Hoffman*, operetta

ORFF, Carl/b.1895/Germany

1925 (30) Prelude for Orchestra
1927 (32) *Concertino* for wind
1928 (33) *Entrata* (revised 1940)
1930 (35) *Catulli Carmina*, choral setting of poems of Catallus
           (revised 1943)
1934 (39) *Bayerische Musik*
1935 (40) *Carmina Burana*, scenic cantata on Latin texts
1936 (41) *Olympischer Reigen*
1937−38 (42) *Der Mond*, opera
1941−42 (46) *Die Kluge*, opera
1944 (49) *Die Bernauerin* (1944−45)
1945−46 (50) *Astutuli*
1947−48 (52) *Antigone*, opera
1950−51 (55) *Trionfo di Afrodite*
1955 (60) *Der Sänger der Vorwelt*
           Comoedia de Christi resurrectione
1956 (61) *Nanie und Dithyrambe*, choral work
1958 (63) *Oedipus, der Tyrann*
1960 (67) *Ludus de nato Infante mirificus*
1962 (67) *Ein Sommernachtstraum*
1969−71 (74−76) *De Temporum fine comoedia*, dramatic cantata
1973 (78) *Rota*, for chorus and instruments

PADEREWSKI, Ignacy/1860−1941/Poland

1880 (20) Violin Sonata
1884 (24) Polish Dances for Piano, Books I and II
1888 (28) Piano Concerto in A minor
1893 (33) *Polish Fantasy on Original Themes*, for piano and
           orchestra

1901 (41) *Manru*, opera
1903–07 (43–47) Symphony in B minor

PALESTRINA, Giovanni Pierluigi da/*c.*1525–1594/Italy

1554 (*c.*29) *p.* First Book of Masses
1563 (*c.*38) *p.* First Book of Motets
1567 (*c.*42) *Missa Papae Marcelli*
1569 (*c.*44) *p.* Second Book of Masses
1570 (*c.*45) *p.* Third Book of Masses
             Missa Brevis
1584 (*c.*59) *p.* Settings of *The Song of Solomon*
1590 (*c.*65) *p. Aeterna Christi Munera*, mass
             Stabat Mater (*c.*1590)
Palestrina also composed many motets and madrigals.

PENDERECKI, Krzysztof/b.1933/Poland

1958 (25) *Epitaphium on the Death of Artur Malawski*, for string
             orchestra and timpani
           Emanations, for two string orchestras
           The Psalms of David, for mixed choir and instruments
1959 (26) *Strophes*, for soprano, narrator and ten instruments
1960 (27) *Anaklasis*, for strings and percussion groups
           String Quartet No. 1
1961 (28) *Fluorescences*, for orchestra
           Dimensions of Time and Silence, for choir and orchestra
           Threnody, for fifty-two stringed instruments
           Kanon, for strings and electronic tape
           Polymorphia
1962 (29) *Stabat Mater*, for three sixteen-part choirs
1964 (31) Sonata for cello and orchestra
1965 (32) *Capriccio*, for oboe and strings
1967 (34) *Dies Irae*, oratorio for soprano, tenor and bass soli,
             chorus and orchestra
           Pittsburgh Overture, for winds and percussion
1968 (35) *The Devils of Loudon*, opera (1968–69)
           String Quartet No. 2
           Capriccio for Seigfried Palm, for solo cello
1969–71 (36–38) *Utrenja*, for soprano, contralto, tenor, bass and
             basso profundo soli, two mixed choirs and orchestra
1970 (37) *Kosmogonia*, for soprano, tenor and bass soli, chorus and
             orchestra
1971 (38) *De Natura Sonoris II*, for wind, percussion and strings
           Prélude (1971), for wind, percussion and contrabasses
           Actions, for jazz ensemble
1972 (39) *Canticum Canticorum Salomonis (Song of Songs)*, for
             sixteen-voice chorus, chamber orchestra and dance
             pair
           Partita, concerto for harpsichord, five solo instruments
             electronically amplified and orchestra
1973 (40) Symphony

1974 (41)   *The Dream of Jacob*

PERGOLESI, Giovanni/1710–1736/Italy

1731 (21)   *Salustia*, opera
1732 (22)   *Lo Frate innamorato*, opera
            La Serva padrona, opera
1733 (23)   *Il Prigionier superbo*, opera
1734 (24)   *Adriano in Siria*, opera
            La Contadina astuta, opera
1735 (25)   *L'Olimpiade*, opera
            Flamincio, opera
1736 (26)   *Stabat Mater*, for female voices
Pergolesi also composed: 8 other operas, 12 cantatas, over 30
sonatas, symphonies, concertos.

PIERNÉ, Gabriel/1863–1937/France

1882 (19)   *Edith*, cantata
1883 (20)   *Le Chemin de l'amour*, opera-comique
            Trois pièces formant suite de concert, for orchestra
1885 (22)   Symphonic Overture
            Fantaisie-Ballet, for piano and orchestra
1886 (23)   *Don Luis*, opera-comique
1887 (24)   Piano Concerto in C minor
1889 (26)   *Marche Solenelle*
            Pantomime, for orchestra
1890 (27)   *Scherzo Caprice*, for piano and orchestra
1891 (28)   *Le Colliers de saphire*, ballet
1892 (29)   *Les Joyeuses commères de Paris*, ballet
1893 (30)   *Lizarda*, opera-comique (1893–94)
            Bouton d'or, ballet
            Le Docteur Blanc, ballet
1895 (32)   *La Coupe enchantée*, opera-comique
            Salomé, ballet
1897 (34)   *Vendée*, opera-comique
            L'An mil, symphonic poem with chorus
1900 (37)   Violin Sonata
1901 (38)   *La Fille de Tabarin*, opera-comique
            Poème Symphonique, for piano and orchestra
            Concertstücke, for harp
1902 (39)   *The Children's Crusade*, oratorio
1907 (44)   *Canzonetta*, for clarinet
1908 (45)   *The Children of Bethlehem*, oratorio
1919 (56)   Piano Quintet
            Cello Sonata
1920 (57)   *Paysages franciscains*, for orchestra
1923 (60)   *Cydalise and the Satyr*, ballet
1927 (64)   *Sophie Arnould*, opera-comique
1931 (68)   *Divertissement sur un thème pastorale*, for orchestra
            Fantaisie basque, for violin
1934 (71)   *Giration*, ballet

   Fragonard, ballet
1935 (72) *Images*, ballet
1937 (74) *Gulliver in Lilliput*

PISTON, Walter/b.1894/U.S.A.

1926 (32) Three pieces for flute, clarinet and bassoon
   Piano Sonata
1927 (33) Symphonic Piece
1929 (35) Suite No. 1 for orchestra
1930 (36) Flute Sonata
1931 (37) Suite for oboe and piano
1933 (39) Concerto for Orchestra
   String Quartet No. 1
1934 (40) Prelude and Fugue for Orchestra
1935 (41) String Quartet No. 2
   Piano Trio No. 1
1937 (43) Symphony No. 1
   Concertino, for piano and chamber orchestra
1938 (44) *The Incredible Flutist*, ballet
1939 (45) Violin Concerto No. 1
   Violin Sonata
1940 (46) Chromatic Study for Organ
1941 (47) *Sinfonietta*, for orchestra
1942 (48) *Fanfare for the Fighting French*
   Quintet for flute and strings
   Interlude, for viola and piano
1943 (49) Symphony No. 2
   Prelude and Allegro, for organ and strings
   Passacaglia, for piano
1944 (50) *Fugue on a Victory Tune*
   Partita, for violin, viola and organ
1945 (51) Sonata for violin and harpsichord
1946 (52) *Divertimento*, for nine instruments
1947 (53) Symphony No. 3
   String Quartet No. 3
1948 (54) Suite No. 2 for Orchestra
   Toccata, for orchestra
1949 (55) Piano Quintet
   Duo for violin and cello
1950 (56) Symphony No. 4
1951 (57) String Quartet No. 4
1952 (58) *Fantasy*, for English horn, harp and strings
1954 (60) Symphony No. 5
1955 (61) Symphony No. 6
1956 (62) *Serenata*, for orchestra
   Quintet for Wind
1957 (63) Viola Concerto
1958 (64) *Psalm and Prayer of David*, for chorus and seven
    instruments
1959 (65) *Three New England Sketches*, for orchestra
   Concerto for two pianos and orchestra

1960 (66) Violin Concerto No. 2
           Symphony No. 7
1961 (67) Symphonic Prelude
1962 (68) *Lincoln Center*, Festival overture
           String Quartet No. 5
1963 (69) *Variations on a theme by Edward Burlingame Hill*, for orchestra
           Capriccio, for harp and string orchestra
1964 (70) Sextet for stringed instruments
           Piano Quartet
1965 (71) Symphony No. 8
           Pine Tree Fantasy, for orchestra
           Ricercare, for orchestra
1966 (72) Variations for cello and orchestra
           Piano Trio No. 2
1967 (73) Concerto for clarinet and orchestra

PIZZETTI, Ildebrando/1880—1968/Italy

1904 (24) Three Symphonic Preludes to *Oedipus Rex*
1906 (26) String Quartet in A major
1909—12 (29—32) *Phaedra*, opera
1914 (34) *Sinfonia del fuoco*
1915—21 (35—41) *Deborah and Jael*, opera
1918 (38) Violin Sonata in A minor and A major
1921 (41) Cello Sonata in F major
1922 (42) *Lo Straniero*, opera
           Requiem
1925—27 (45—47) *Fra Gherardo*, opera
1928 (48) *Concerto dell'estate*
1929 (49) *Rondo veneziano*, for orchestra
1930 (50) Piano Concerto
1931—35 (51—55) *Orseolo*, opera
1933—34 (53) Cello Concerto
1938—42 (58—62) *L'Oro*, opera
1940 (60) Symphony in A major
1942 (62) Piano Sonata
1944 (64) Violin Concerto
1949 (69) *Vanna Lupa*, opera
1950 (70) *Ifigenia*, opera
1953 (73) *Cagliostro*, opera
1958 (78) *Murder in the Cathedral*, opera (on T.S. Eliot's play)

PONCHIELLI, Amilcare/1834—1886/Italy

1861 (27) *La Savoiarda*, opera
1863 (29) *Roderico*, opera
1872 (38) *I Promessi Sposi*, opera
1873 (39) *Il Parlatore Eterno*, opera
           Le Due Gemelle, ballet
1874 (40) *I Lituani*, opera (revised as *Aldona*)
1875 (41) *A Gaetano Donizetti*, cantata

1876 (42)   *La Giaconda*, opera (from which comes the *Dance of the Hours*)
1880 (46)   *Il Figliuol Prodigo*, opera
1882 (48)   *In Memoria di Garibaldi*, cantata
1885 (51)   *Marion Delorme*, opera

PORPORA, Niccolò Antonio/1686–1766/Italy

1708 (22)   *Agrippina*, opera
1711 (25)   *Flavio Amicio Olibrio*, opera
            Il Martirio di S. Giovanni Nepomuceno, oratorio
1713 (27)   *Basilio, re d'Oriente*, opera
1714 (28)   *Arianna e Teseo*, opera
1718 (32)   *Temistocle*, opera
1719 (33)   *Faramondo*, opera
1721 (35)   *Il Martirio di Santa Eugenia*, oratorio
1723 (37)   *Adelaide*, opera
1724 (38)   *Griselda*, opera
1726 (40)   *Imeneo in Atene*, opera
1727 (41)   *Ezio*, opera
1729 (43)   *Semiramide riconosciuta*, opera
1730 (44)   *Mitridate*, opera
1731 (45)   *Poro*, opera
1732 (46)   *Germanico in Germania*, opera
1733 (47)   *Arianna in Nasso*, opera
1734 (48)   *Enea nel Lazio*, opera
            Davide e Bersabea, oratorio
1735 (49)   *Polifemo*, opera
            Ifigenia in Aulide, opera
1737 (51)   *Lucio Papirio*, opera
1738 (52)   *Carlo il Calvo*, opera
1739 (53)   *Il Barone di Zampano*, opera
1740 (54)   *Il Trionfo di Camilla*, opera
1742 (56)   *Statira*, opera
1743 (57)   *Temistocle*, opera
1747 (61)   *Filandro*, opera
Porpora also wrote songs, chamber music, harpsichord music, etc.

POULENC, Francis/1899–1963/France

1917 (18)   *Rapsodie nègre*, for cello, piano, flute and string quartet
1918 (19)   Sonata for two clarinets
            Sonata for piano (four hands)
            Trois mouvements perpetuelles, for piano
            Toréador, songs (1918–32)
1919 (20)   *Valse*, for piano
            Le Bestaire au cortège d'Orphée, songs
            Cocardes, songs
1920 (21)   Cinq Impromptus, for piano
            Suite in C major, for piano
1921 (22)   *La Baigneuse de Trouville* and *Discours du General*: two

numbers of a group work composed by all members
of "les Six" (except Louis Durey) for a play by Jean
Cocteau

1922 (23)   Sonata for trumpet, horn and trombone
Sonata for clarinet and bassoon
Chanson à boire, for a cappella male choir

1923 (24)   *Les Biches*, ballet

1924 (25)   *Promenade*, for piano
Poèmes de Ronsard (1924–25)

1925 (26)   *Napoli Suite*, for piano

1926 (27)   Trio for oboe, bassoon and piano
Chansons gaillardes

1927–28 (28) *Concert champêtre*, for harpsichord and orchestra
Deux novelettes, for piano
Airs chantés

1928 (29)   *Trois pièces*, for piano

1929 (30)   *Aubade*, for piano and eighteen instruments
Hommage à Roussel, for piano
Huit Nocturnes, for piano (1929–38)

1930 (31)   *Épitaphe*, song

1931 (32)   *Bagatelle*, for violin and piano
Trois poèmes de Louise Lalanne, songs
Four songs
Five songs

1932 (33)   Concerto in D major, for two pianos and orchestra
Sextet for piano and wind quintet (1932–40)
Improvisations for piano (1932–43)
Intermezzo, in D minor, for piano
Le Bal masqué, cantata

1933 (34)   *Feuillets d'album*, for piano (Ariette, Rêve, Gigue)
Villageoises, children's piano pieces

1934 (35)   *Intermezzo*, in D♭ major, for piano
Intermezzo, in C major, for piano
Presto, Badinage and *Humoresque*, for piano
Huit chansons polonaises
Quatre chansons pour enfants (1934–35)

1935 (36)   *Suite française*, for chamber orchestra
Cinq poèmes (Paul Eluard)
A sa guitare, song
Margot, incidental music (in collaboration with Auric)

1936 (37)   Sept chansons, for a cappella mixed choir
Litanies à la Vierge noire, for women's or children's
voices and organ
Petites voix, five choruses for three-part a cappella
children's choir
Les Soirées de Nazelles, for piano

1937 (38)   *Deux marches et un intermède*, for chamber orchestra
Mass in G major
Secheresses, cantata
Bourée d'Auvergne, for piano
Tel jour telle nuit, songs

1938 (39)   Concerto in G major, for organ, strings and timpani

Four penitential Motets (1938–39)
1939 (40) *Fiançailles pour rire*, songs
1940 (41) *Mélancolie*, for piano
           Banalities, songs
           Histoire de Babar le petit éléphant, for piano and narrator
              (1940–45)
           Cello Sonata (1940–48)
1941 (42) Salve regina, for four-part a cappella mixed choir
           Exultate Deo, for four-part a cappella mixed choir
           Les Animaux modèles, ballet
           La Fille du jardinier, incidental music
1942 (43) Violin Sonata (1942–43)
           Chansons villageoises, songs
1943 (44) *Figure humaine*, cantata
           Metamorphoses, songs
           Deux poèmes, songs
           Montparnasse, song
1944 (45) *La Mamelles de Tiresias*, opera buffe
           La Voyageur sans bagage, incidental music
           La Nuit de la Saint-Jean, incidental music
           Un Soir de neige, cantata
1945 (46) *Chansons françaises*, for a cappella mixed choir
           Le Soldat et la Sorciére, incidental music
1946 (47) Two songs
1947 (48) Flute Sonata
1948 (49) *Quatre petites prières (St. Francis)*, for a cappella male choir
1949 (50) Piano Concerto
1950 (51) *Stabat Mater*, for soprano, mixed choir and orchestra
1953 (54) Sonata for two pianos
           Dialogues des Carmelites, opera (1953–56)
1954 (55) *La Guirlande de Compra (Matelote provençal)*, for orchestra,
              in collaboration with other composers
           Variations sur le nom de Marguerite Long (Bucolique), for
              orchestra, in collaboration with other composers
1956 (57) *Le Travail du peintre*, song cycle
           Deux mélodies, songs
1957 (58) *Elegy*, for horn and piano
1958 (59) *La Voix humaine*, lyric tragedy, monodrama for soprano
1959 (60) *Gloria*, for soprano, mixed choir and orchestra
1960 (61) *Elegy*, for two pianos
1961 (62) *La Dame de Monte Carlo*, monologue for soprano and
              orchestra
1962 (63) *Sept Repons des ténèbres*, for soprano, choir and orchestra
           Oboe Sonata
           Clarinet Sonata

PREVIN, André/b.1929/U.S.A. (b. Germany)

1960 (31) *Overture to a Comedy*, for orchestra
Previn also composed:
Invitation to the Dance, ballet
Guitar Concerto

Portrait, for strings
String Quartet
Flute Quintet
Cello Sonata
Impressions, for piano.

PROKOFIEV, Sergei/1891–1953/Russia

1907–09 (16–18) Piano Sonata No. 1 in F minor
1907–11 (16–20) Four pieces for piano
1908–12 (17–21) Four pieces for piano
1909 (18) Four Études, for piano
             Sinfonietta in A major (final version 1929) (1909–14)
             Two poems for female voices and orchestra (1909–10)
1910 (19) *Dreams*, symphonic poem
             Autumnal Sketch, for orchestra (revised 1934)
             Deux Poèmes, for voice and piano (1910–11)
1911–12 (20) Piano Concerto No. 1 in D♭ major
1911–13 *Magdalene*, opera
1912 (21) Piano Concerto No. 2 in D minor
             Ballade, for cello and piano
             Piano Sonata No. 2 in D minor
             Toccata, in C major, for piano
             Sarcasms, for piano (1912–14)
1914 (23) Violin Concerto No. 1
             Scythian Suite (Ala et Lolly), for orchestra (1914–15)
             The Ugly Duckling, for voice and piano
1915 (24) *The Gambler*, opera (revised 1928)
             Chout, ballet (revised 1920)
             Visions fugitives, for piano
             Cinq Poésies, for voice and piano
1916 (25) Symphony No. 1, *Classical* (1916–17)
             Cinq Poésies d'Anna Akhmatova, for voice and piano
1917 (26) Piano Sonata No. 3 in A minor (begun in 1907)
             Piano Sonata No. 4 in C minor (begun in 1908)
             Seven, they are seven, Akhadian Incantation for tenor, chorus and orchestra
             Piano Concerto No. 3 in C major (1917–21)
1919 (28) *The Love of Three Oranges*, opera (Symphonic Suite of the same name composed 1919–24)
             The Fiery Angel, opera (1919–27)
             Overture on Hebrew Themes, for piano, clarinet and string quartet
1920 (29) *Five Songs Without Words*, for voice and piano
1921 (30) Five Songs
1923 (32) Piano Sonata No. 5 in C major
1924 (33) Symphony No. 2 in D minor (1924–25)
             Quintet in G minor, for oboe, clarinet, violin, viola and double-bass
1925 (34) *Pas d'Acier*, ballet (1925–26)
             Divertimento for orchestra (1925–29)
1928 (37) *The Prodigal Son*, ballet

Symphony No. 3 in C minor
1929–30 (38) Symphony No. 4 in C major (second version 1947)
1930 (39) *Sur le Borysthène (On the Dnieper)*, ballet
Four Portraits, symphonic suite from the opera *The Gambler* (1930–31)
String Quartet No. 1
1931 (40) Piano Concerto No. 4 in B♭ major, for the left hand
1932 (41) Piano Concerto No. 5 in G major
1933 (42) *Chant Symphonique*, for orchestra
Cello Concerto in E minor (1933–38)
1934 (43) *Egyptian Night*, symphonic suite
Lieutenant Kijé, symphonic suite for orchestra and baritone voice ad lib
1935 (44) *Romeo and Juliet*, ballet (1935–36)
Violin Concerto No. 2 in G minor
Musique d'enfants, for piano
1936 (45) *Peter and the Wolf*, for orchestra and narrator
Russian Overture
Cantata for the Twentieth Anniversary of the October Revolution, for double chorus, military band, accordions and orchestra (1936–37)
1938–39 (47) *Alexander Nevsky*, cantata for mezzo-soprano, chorus and orchestra
1939 (48) *Simeon Kotko*, opera
Zdravitsa, cantata for chorus and orchestra
Piano Sonata No. 6 in A major (1939–40)
Piano Sonata No. 7 in B♭ major (1939–42)
Piano Sonata No. 8 in B♭ major (1939–44)
1940 (49) *The Duenna*, opera (1940–41)
Cinderella, ballet (1940–44)
1941 (50) *War and Peace*, opera (1941–42)
Symphonic March
Suite for Orchestra, *1941*
A Summer's Day, suite for small orchestra (transcribed from the *Musique d'enfants* of 1935)
String Quartet No. 2 in F major
1942–43 (51) Flute Sonata in D major
Ballad of an Unknown Boy, cantata
1944 (53) Symphony No. 5 in B♭ major
1945–47 (54–56) Piano Sonata No. 9 in C major
Symphony No. 6 in E♭ minor
1947–48 (56) *The Story of a Real Man*, opera
1948–53 (57–62) *The Stone Flower*, ballet
1949 (58) Cello Sonata in C major
Winter Bonfire, suite for narrator, boys' chorus and orchestra (1949–50)
1950–52 (59–61) *Sinfonia Concertante* in E minor, for cello and orchestra (this is a reworking of the 1933–38 cello concerto)
1951–52 (60–61) Symphony No. 7 in C♯ minor
1952 (61) Cello Concertino in G minor
Prokofiev left unfinished a Concerto for two pianos and strings; a

Cello Sonata in C♯ minor; a second version of the Symphony No. 2; and sketches for a 10th and 11th piano sonata.

PUCCINI, Giacomo/1858—1924/Italy

1884 (26) *Le Villi*, opera
1889 (31) *Edgar*, opera
1893 (35) *Manon Lescaut*, opera
1896 (38) *La Bohème*, opera
1900 (42) *Tosca*, opera
1904 (46) *Madama Butterfly*, opera
1910 (52) *Girl of the Golden West (La Fanciulla del West)*, opera
1917 (59) *La Rondine*, opera
1918 (60) *Il Trittico*, three contrasted one-act operas to be produced
in a single evening:
      Suor Angelica
      Il Tabarro
      Gianni Schicchi
1926 (posthumous) *fp. Turandot*, opera

PURCELL, Henry/1659—1695/Great Britain

1680 (21) Nine fantasias of four parts
*c.***1682** (*c.*23) Anthem: Hear my prayer
1683 (24) Twelve sonatas of three parts
1688 (29) *How pleasant is this flowery plain*, secular cantata
1689 (30) *Dido and Aeneas*, opera
      Musick's Handmaid, for harpsichord
1690 (31) *The Prophetess* or *The History of Dioclesian*, opera
1691 (32) *King Arthur* or *The British Worthy*, opera
      The Wives' Excuse, incidental music
1692 (33) *The Faery Queen*, opera
      The Libertine, incidental music
      Oedipus, incidental music
1693 (34) *Epsom Wells*, incidental music
1694 (35) *The Married Beau*, incidental music
1695 (36) *The Indian Queen*, opera
      The Tempest, or *The Enchanted Island*, opera
      Bonduca, incidental music
1696 (posthumous) *p*. A choice collection of Lessons for the
      Harpsichord or Spinet
      p. Harpsichord Suites Nos. 1—8
Purcell also composed much church music, stage music, chamber music, complimentary odes to royalty, harpsichord pieces, etc.

QUILTER, Roger/1877—1953/Great Britain

1906 (29) *To Julia*, song cycle
1907 (30) *Serenade*, for orchestra
1908 (31) *Songs of Sorrow*
1909 (32) Seven Elizabethan Lyrics
1910 (33) Three English Dances

Four songs
1911 (34) *Where the Rainbow Ends*, incidental music
Three Songs of the Sea
1914 (37) *A Children's Overture*
Four Child Songs
1916 (39) Three Songs of William Blake
1921 (44) Five Shakespeare Songs
Three Pastoral Songs
1922 (45) *As You Like It*, incidental music
1925 (48) *The Rake*, ballet suite
Five Jacobean Lyrics
1936 (59) *Julia*, opera
1946 (69) *Tulips*, for chorus and orchestra
1948 (71) *The Sailor and His Lass*, for soloist, choir and orchestra
1949 (72) *Love at the Inn*, opera

RACHMANINOV, Sergei/1873–1943/Russia

1890–91 (17–18) Piano Concerto No. 1 in F♯ minor
1890–93 (17–20) Six songs
1891 (18) Scherzo for strings
1892 (19) *Prélude* and *Danse orientale*, for cello and piano
Five *Morceaux de Fantaisie*, for piano (includes the
C♯ minor prélude)
Intermezzo
1893 (20) *Aleko*, opera
The Rock, fantasy
Trio élégiaque, in D minor
Romance and *Danse hongroise*, for violin and piano
Suite No. 1, *Fantasy*, for two pianos
Six songs
1894 (21) *Caprice bohémien*, for orchestra
Seven piano pieces
Six piano duets
1895 (22) Symphony No. 1 in D minor
1896 (23) Six *Moments musicaux*, for piano
Twelve songs
Six songs for female, or boys', voices
1900–06 (27–33) Twelve songs
1901 (28) Piano Concerto No. 2 in C minor
Suite No. 2 for two pianos
Cello Sonata in G minor
1902 (29) *The Spring*, cantata
1903 (30) Variations on a theme by Chopin, for piano
Ten preludes for piano
1906 (33) *Francesca da Rimini*, opera
The Miserly Knight, opera
Fifteen songs
1907 (34) Symphony No. 2 in E minor
The Isle of the Dead, symphonic poem
Piano Sonata No. 1 in D minor
1909 (36) Piano Concerto No. 3 in D minor

1910 (37) *The Bells*, choral symphony (after Poe)
           Thirteen piano preludes
           Liturgy of St. John Chrystostum
1911 (38) Six *Études-Tableaux*, for piano
1912 (39) Fourteen songs
1913 (40) Piano Sonata No. 2 in B♭ minor
1915 (42) Vesper Mass
1916 (43) Six songs
           Nine *Études-Tableaux*, for piano (1916—17)
1927 (54) Piano Concerto No. 4 in G minor
1930 (57) Three Russian Folk-songs, for chorus and orchestra
           (possibly 1927)
1932 (59) Variations on a theme by Corelli, for piano
1934 (61) *Rhapsody on a theme by Paganini*, variations for piano and
           orchestra
1936 (63) Symphony No. 3 in A minor
1941 (68) *Three Symphonic Dances*, for orchestra

RAMEAU, Jean/1683—1764/France

1706 (23) *p.* Harpsichord Works, Book I
1728 (45) *p.* Harpsichord Works, Book II
1733 (50) *Hippolyte et Aricie*, opera
1735 (52) *Les Indes galantes*, opera-ballet
1737 (54) *Castor et Pollux*, opera-ballet
1739 (56) *Dardanus*, opera
           Les Fêtes d'Hebe, ballet
1741 (57) *p.* Harpsichord Works, Book III
1745 (62) *Platée*, ballet
1748 (65) *Pigmalion*, ballet
           Zais, ballet
1754 (71) *Zephyre*, ballet
1760 (78) *Les Paladins*, opera-ballet
Rameau composed more than 20 operas and opera-ballets, church
music, chamber music, cantatas, etc.

RAVEL, Maurice/1875—1937/France

1893 (18) *Sérénade grotesque*, for piano
1895 (20) *Menuet antique*
1896 (21) *Sainte*, song
1899 (24) *Pavane pour une Infante défunte*, for piano
1901 (26) *Jeux d'eau*, for piano
           Myrrha, cantata
1902 (27) *Alcyone*, cantata
1903 (28) *Schéhérezade*, three songs with orchestra
           String Quartet in F major
           Alyssa, cantata
1905 (30) *Miroirs*, for piano
           Sonatina, for piano
1906 (31) Introduction and Allegro for harp, flute, clarinet and
           string quartet

1907 (32) *Rhapsodie espagnole*, for orchestra
           Cinq Mélodies populaires greques
           Piece en forme de Habanera
           Sur le herbe, song
1908 (33) *Ma mère l'oye*, suite for piano
           Gaspard de la nuit, for piano
1909 (34) *Menuet sur le nom d'Haydn*, for piano
1911 (36) *L'Heure espagnole*, opera
           Valses nobles et sentimentales, for piano or orchestra
1912 (37) *Daphnis et Chloé*, ballet with chorus
1914 (39) *Two Hebrew Songs*, for soprano and orchestra
           Piano Trio in A minor
1915 (40) Three songs for unaccompanied choir
1917 (42) *Le Tombeau de Couperin*, for piano
1920 (45) *La Valse*, choreographic poem for orchestra
           Sonata for violin and cello
1922 (47) *Berceuse sur le nom Fauré*
1924 (49) *Tzigane*, for violin and piano
1925 (50) *L'Enfant et les sortilèges*, opera
1926 (51) *Chansons madécasses*, for voice, flute, cello and piano
1928 (53) *Bolero*, for orchestra
1931 (56) Piano Concerto in G major
           Piano Concerto for the left hand

RAWSTHORNE, Alan/1905–1971/Great Britain

1935 (30) Viola Sonata (revised 1954)
1936 (31) Concerto for clarinet and string orchestra
1937 (32) Theme and variations, for two violins
1938 (33) Symphonic Studies, for orchestra
1939 (34) String Quartet No. 1, *Theme and Variations*
1941 (36) *The Creel*, suite for piano duet
1942 (37) Piano Concerto No. 1
1944 (39) *Street Corner Overture*
1945 (40) *Cortèges*, fantasy overture
1946 (41) *Prisoner's March*, for orchestra
1947 (42) Concerto for oboe and strings
1948 (43) Violin Concerto No. 1
           Clarinet Quartet
1949 (44) Concerto for string orchestra
           Cello Sonata
1950 (45) Symphony No. 1
1951 (46) Piano Concerto No. 2
           Concertante Pastorale, for flute, horn and strings
1952 (47) *Canticle of Man*, chamber cantata for baritone, mixed
               chorus, flute and strings
1954 (49) *Practical Cats*, for speaker and orchestra
           String Quartet No. 2
1955 (50) *Madame Chrysanthème*, ballet
1956 (51) Violin Concerto No. 2
1957 (52) Violin Sonata
1958 (53) *Halle Overture*

1959 (54) Symphony No. 2, *A Pastoral Symphony*
1961 (56) *Improvisations on a theme by Constant Lambert*, for
                   orchestra
                   Concerto for ten instruments
1962 (57) *Medieval Diptych*, for baritone and orchestra
                   Divertimento for chamber orchestra
                   Quintet for piano and wind
                   Piano Trio
1963 (58) *Carmen Vitale*, for soprano solo, mixed chorus and
                   orchestra
1964 (59) Symphony No. 3
                   Elegiac Rhapsody, for strings
1965 (60) *Tankas of the Four Seasons*, for tenor and chamber
                   ensemble
                   Concertante, for violin and piano
1966 (61) Cello Concerto
                   Sonatine, for flute, oboe and piano
                   String Quartet No. 3
1967 (62) *Overture for Farnham*
                   Theme, Variations and Finale, for orchestra
                   The God in the Cave, cantata for mixed chorus and
                   orchestra
                   Scena Rustica, for soprano and harp
1968 (63) Concerto for two pianos and orchestra
                   Trio for flute, viola and harp
1969 (64) *Triptych*, for orchestra
1970 (65) Oboe Quartet
1971 (66) Quintet for piano, clarinet, horn, violin and cello

REGER, Max/1873–1916/Germany

1891 (18) Piano Trio in B minor
                   Violin Sonata in D major
1892 (19) Cello Sonata in F minor
1897–8 (24) Piano Quintet in C minor
                   Cello Sonata in G minor
                   Violin Sonata in A major
1900 (27) Two *Romances*, for solo instruments and orchestra
                   Clarinet Sonata in A♭ major
                   Clarinet Sonata in F♯ minor
                   String Quartet in G minor (1900–01)
                   String Quartet in A major (1900–01)
1902 (29) Piano Quintet in C minor
                   Violin Sonata in C major
1903 (30) *Gesang der Verklärten*, for voice and orchestra
1904 (31) String Quartet in D minor
                   Serenade, for flute, violin and viola, or two violins and
                   viola
                   String Trio in A minor
                   Cello Sonata in F major
                   Variations and Fugue on a theme of Beethoven, for two
                   pianos

Violin Sonata in F♯ minor
1905 (32) *Sinfonietta*, for orchestra
Suite in the Old Style, for violin and piano, in F major
1906 (33) *Serenade*
1907 (34) Variations and Fugue on a theme of Hiller
1908 (35) *Symphonic Prologue to a Tragedy*
Violin Concerto
Sonata for clarinet (or viola) and piano
Piano Trio
1909 (36) *The 100th Psalm*, for voice and orchestra
Die Nonnen, for voice and orchestra
String Quartet in E♭ major
1910 (37) Piano Concerto
String Sextet in F major
Piano Quartet in D minor
Cello Sonata in A minor
1911 (38) *Die Weihe der Nacht*, for chorus and orchestra
Eine Lustspielouverture
String Quartet in F♯ minor
Violin Sonata in E minor
1912 (39) *Konzert im Alten Stil*
Romischer Triumphgesang, for voice and orchestra
A Romantic Suite
1913 (40) *Vier Tondichtunger nach A. Böcklin*
Eine Ballettsuite
1914 (41) *Eine Vaterländische Ouverture*
Three canons, duets and fugues in ancient style, for two
violins
Variations and Fugue on a theme of Mozart
Piano Quartet in A minor
Piano Sonata in C minor
Cello Sonata in C minor
1915 (42) *Serenade*, for flute, violin and viola (or two violins and
viola) in G major
String Trio in D minor
Der Einsiedler, for chorus and orchestra
1916 (43) Quintet in A major

RESPIGHI, Ottorino/1879–1936/Italy

1902 (23) Piano Concerto
1905 (26) *Re Enzo*, comic opera
Notturno, for orchestra
Burlesca
Suite in G major, for string orchestra and organ
1907 (28) *Fantasy*, for piano and orchestra
String Quartet in D major
String Quartet in D minor
1908 (29) *Concerto in the old style*, for violin and orchestra
1909 (30) *Chaconne* by Vitali, transcribed for violin, strings and
organ
1910 (31) *Semirama*, lyric tragedy

1913 (34) *Carnival*, overture
1914 (35) Suite for strings and organ
1915 (36) *Sinfonia Drammatica*
1917 (38) *The Fountains of Rome*, symphonic poem
           Old Airs and Dances for Lute, transcribed for orchestra,
              Series I
           Violin Sonata in B minor
1918 (39) *Il Tramonto*, for mezzo-soprano and string quartet
1919 (40) *La Boutique Fantasque*, ballet music arranged from
              pieces by Rossini
1920 (41) *Scherzo Veneziano*, choreographic comedy
           Dance of the Gnomes
1921 (42) *Adagio with Variations*, for cello and orchestra
1922 (43) *The Sleeping Beauty*, musical fable in three acts
           Concerto Gregoriano, for violin and orchestra
1923 (44) *Belfagor*, lyric comedy
           La Primavera, lyric poem for soloists, chorus and
              orchestra
1924 (45) *Concerto in the Mixo-Lydian Mode*, for orchestra
           The Pines of Rome, symphonic poem
           Old Airs and Dances for Lute, Series II
           Doric String Quartet
1927 (48) *The Sunken Bell*, opera
           Three Botticelli Pictures, for orchestra:
              Spring (Primavera)
              The Adoration of the Magi
              The Birth of Venus
           The Birds, suite for small orchestra based on seventeenth-
              and eighteenth-century bird-pieces for lute and for
              harpsichord:
              Prelude
              Dove
              Hen
              Nightingale
              Cuckoo
           Church Windows, four symphonic impressions for
              orchestra
           Brazilian Impressions, for orchestra
1928 (49) *Toccata*, for piano and orchestra
1929 (50) *The Festivals of Rome*, orchestral suite
1930 (51) *Metamorphosen modi XII*, theme and variations for
              orchestra
           Bach's *Prelude and Fugue in D major*, transcribed for
              orchestra
1932 (53) *Belkis, Queen of Sheba*, ballet
           Mary of Egypt, mystery in one act and three episodes
           Old Airs and Dances for Lute, Series III
1934 (55) *La Fiamma*, melodrama in three acts
           Concerto for oboe, horn, violin, double-bass, piano and
              string orchestra
           Passacaglia in C minor (Bach), orchestral interpretation
1937 (posthumous) *fp. Lucrezia*

RIMSKY-KORSAKOV, Nikolas/1844—1908/Russia

1861—65 (17—21) Symphony No. 1 in E♭ major
1866 (22) Overture on Russian Themes
               Symphony No. 3 in C major (1866—73)
1867 (23) *Sadko*, tone poem (later developed into a ballet-opera)
               Fantasia on Serbian Themes, for orchestra
1868—72 (24—28) *The Maid of Pskov (Ivan the Terrible)*, opera
1869 (25) *Antar*, symphonic suite (originally Symphony No. 2)
1875 (31) Quartet No. 1
               Three Pieces for piano
               Six fugues
1876 (32) Sextet for strings
               Quintet for piano and wind
1878 (34) *May Night*, opera
               Variations on BACH, for piano
               Four pieces for piano
1879 (35) *Sinfonietta on Russian Themes*
               Legend, for orchestra (1879—80)
1880—81 (36) *The Snow Maiden*, opera
1882—83 (38) Piano Concerto in C♯ minor
1886 (42) *Fantasia Concertante on Russian Themes*, for violin and
                 orchestra
1887 (43) *Capriccio Espagnol*, for orchestra
1888 (44) *Russian Easter Festival Overture*
               Schéhérezade, symphonic suite
1892 (48) *fp. Mlada*, opera
1895 (51) *Christmas Eve*, opera
1897 (53) Three song-cycles:
                   In Spring
                   To the Poet
                   By the Sea
               Piano Trio
1898 (54) *Mozart and Salieri*, opera
1899 (55) *The Tsar's Bride*, opera
1900 (56) *The Legend of Tsar Sultan*, opera
1902 (58) *fp. Kaschey the Immortal*, opera
1903 (59) *Souvenir de trois chants polonaise*, for violin and orchestra
               Serenade, for cello and piano
               The Invisible City of Kitezh, opera (1903—05)
1905 (61) *fp.* Orchestral Variations on a Russian people's song
1906—07 (62) *Coq d'Or*, opera
Rimsky-Korsakov also wrote a cantata, *Ballad of the Doom of Oleg*.

ROBERTSON, Leroy/1896—1971/U.S.A.

1923 (27) *Endicott Overture*
1938 (42) Piano Quintet
1940 (44) Prelude, Scherzo and Ricercare for Orchestra
               String Quartet
1944 (48) Rhapsody for Piano and Orchestra
               American Serenade, for string quartet
1945 (49) *Punch and Judy Overture*

1947 (51) *Trilogy*, for orchestra
1948 (52) Violin Concerto
1953 (57) *The Book of Mormon*, oratorio
1966 (70) Piano Concerto
Robertson also composed:
Cello Concerto
Fantasia for Organ
Come, Come, Ye Saints, for chorus
Hatikva, for chorus
From the Crossroads, for chorus
The Lord's Prayer, for chorus
Passacaglia for Orchestra.

ROCHBERG, George/b.1918/U.S.A.

1949 (31) *Night Music*, for chamber orchestra
Symphony No. 1
1952 (34) Twelve Bagatelles for piano
String Quartet No. 1
1953 (35) Chamber Symphony for nine instruments
1954 (36) Three Psalms for Chorus
David the Psalmist, cantata
1955 (37) Duo Concertante for Violin and Cello
1956 (38) Sinfonia Fantasia
1958 (40) Symphony No. 2
Dialogues, for clarinet and piano
Cheltenham Concerto, for chamber orchestra
1959 (41) *La Bocca della verita*, for oboe and piano
String Quartet No. 2
1960 (42) *Time-Span*, for orchestra (revised 1962)
1961 (43) *Songs of Innocence and Experience*, for soprano and
chamber orchestra
1963 (45) Piano Trio
1965 (47) Music for the Magic Theater
Zodiac, orchestral version of the twelve Bagatelles
Contra mortem et tempus, for violin, flute, clarinet and
piano
Black Sounds, for winds and percussion
La bocca della verita, for violin and piano
1968 (50) *Tableaux*, for soprano and eleven players
Symphony No. 3, *A twentieth-century Passion*, for
orchestra, four solo voices, eight-part chamber choir
and double chorus
1970 (52) *Songs of Krishna*, for soprano and piano
Mizmor L'Piyus, for bass-baritone and small orchestra
1972 (54) *Electrikaleidoscope*
Ricordanza, for cello and piano
String Quartet No. 3
1974 (56) *Imago Mundi*, for orchestra
1975 (57) Violin Concerto
Rochberg also composed a Book of Songs (1937–69).

RODRIGO, Joaquín/b.1902/Spain

1934 (32) *Cantico de la Esposa*, for voice and piano
1939 (37) *Concierto de Aranjuez*, for guitar and orchestra
1942 (40) *Concierto Heroico*, for piano and orchestra
1943 (41) *Concierto de Estio*, for violin and orchestra
1947 (45) Four *Madrigales Amatorias*, for voice and piano (with
        orchestra, 1948)
1948 (46) *Ausencias de Dulcinea*, for bass, four sopranos and
        orchestra
1949 (47) *Concierto Galante*, for cello and orchestra
1952 (50) Four *Villancicos*, for voice and piano
        Four *Villancicos*, for chorus (*Canciones de Navidad*)
1954 (52) *Concert-Serenade*, for harp and orchestra
c.1955 (*c*.53) *Fantasia para un gentilhombre*, for guitar
1965 (63) *Sonata Pimpante*, for violin and piano (1965—66)
1967 (65) *Concierto Andaluz*, for four guitars and orchestra
1968 (66) *Concierto Madrigal*, for two guitars and orchestra
Rodrigo also composed:
Sones en la Giralda (Fantasia Sevillana), for harp and orchestra
Triptic de Mosen Cinto.

ROPARTZ, Guy (Joseph Marie Guy-Ropartz)/1864—1955/France

1887 (23) *La Cloche des morts*, for orchestra
1888 (24) *Les Landes*
        Marche de fête
1889 (25) *Cinq pièces brève*, for orchestra
        Carnaval
1892 (28) *Serenade*
1893 (29) *Le Diable Couturier*, opera
        Dimanche breton
        String Quartet No. 1 in G minor
1900 (36) Five motets
1904 (40) Cello Sonata No. 1 in E major
1907 (43) Violin Sonata No. 1 in D minor
        Pastorale and Dance, for oboe and orchestra
1911—12 (47) String Quartet No. 2 in D minor
        Serenade, for string quartet
1912 (48) *Le Pays*, opera
        À Marie endormie
        La Chasse du Prince Arthur
1913 (49) *Soir sur les Chaumes*
        Dans l'ombre de la montagne
1915 (51) Divertissement No. 1
1917 (53) Violin Sonata No. 2 in E major
        Musiques au jardin
1918 (54) Piano Trio in A minor
        Cello Sonata No. 2 in A minor
1924—25 (60) String Quartet No. 3 in G major
1926 (62) Romance and Scherzino, for violin and orchestra
1928 (64) *Rhapsody*, for cello and orchestra
1933 (69) *Sérénade champêtre*

1937 (73) *Requiem*, with orchestra
1942 (78) *De profundis*, with orchestra
1943 (79) *Indiscret*, ballet
           Petit Symphonie
1947 (83) Divertissement, No. 2
Ropartz also composed 5 symphonies (1895–1945), No. 3 with
soloists and chorus.

ROSSINI, Gioacchino/1792–1868/Italy

1808 (16) Sonatas for two violins, cello and double-bass
1809 (17) Variations for clarinet and orchestra, in C major
1810 (18) *La cambiale di matrimonio*, opera
1812 (20) *La Scala di seta (The Silken Ladder)*, opera
1813 (21) *L'Italiana in Algeri*, opera
           Tancredi, opera
1815 (23) *Elisabetta, Regina d'Inghilterra*, opera
1816 (24) *Otello*, opera
           The Barber of Seville, opera
1817 (25) *La Cenerentola*, opera
           La Gazza ladra (The Thieving Magpie), opera
1818 (26) *Mosè*, opera
1820 (28) *Maometto* II, opera
           Solemn Mass
1822 (30) *Zelmira*, opera
1823 (31) *Semiramide*, opera
1825 (33) *Il viaggio a Reims*, opera
1826 (34) *Le Siège de Corinthe*, opera (French-language version of
              Maometto II)
1827 (35) *Moïse*, opera (French-language version of *Mosè*)
1828 (36) *fp. Comte Ory*, comedy-opera
1829 (37) *William Tell*, opera
1863 (71) Petite Messe Solenelle
Rossini also composed:
Stabat Mater (1832–41)
Soirées musicales
Piano pieces, etc.

ROUSSEL, Albert/1869–1937/France

1902 (33) Piano Trio
1903 (34) *Resurrection*, for orchestra
           Violin Sonata
1904–06 (35) Symphony No. 1, *La poème de la forêt*
1905 (36) *Divertissement*, for piano, flute, oboe, clarinet, horn and
              bassoon
1910–11 (41) *Evocations*
1912 (43) *The Spider's Feast*, ballet
1919 (50) *Impromptu*, for harp
           Symphony No. 2 in B♭ major
1925 (56) *Pour une fête de Printemps*, tone poem
           Sérénade, for harp, flute, violin, viola and cello

Violin Sonata
Joueurs de flûte, four pieces for flute and piano
Segovia, for guitar
1927 (58) Piano Concerto in G major
1929–30 (60) Symphony No. 3 in G minor
1931 (62) *Bacchus and Ariadne*, ballet
1932 (63) Quartet
1934 (65) Symphony No. 4 in A major
Sinfonietta for strings
1936 (67) Concertino for Cello
Rhapsodie flamande
1937 (68) String Trio

RUBBRA, Edmund/b.1901/Great Britain

1921 (20) *The Secret Hymnody*, for mixed choir and orchestra
1924 (23) Double Fugue for orchestra
1925 (24) *La Belle Dame sans merci*, for mixed chorus and small
orchestra
Violin Sonata No. 1
1929 (28) Triple Fugue for orchestra
1931 (30) Piano Concerto
Violin Sonata No. 2
1933 (32) *Bee-Bee-Bei*, one-act opera
1934 (33) *Sinfonia Concertante*, for piano and orchestra
Rhapsody, for violin and orchestra
1936 (35) Symphony No. 1
1937 (36) Symphony No. 2
String Quartet in F minor
1938 (37) *Prism*, ballet music
1939 (38) Symphony No. 3
1941 (40) Symphony No. 4
The Morning Watch, for choir and orchestra
1944 (43) *Soliloquy*, for cello and orchestra
1946 (45) *Missa Cantuariensis*, for double choir unaccompanied
except for organ in the Credo
1947 (46) *Festival Overture*, for orchestra
Cello Sonata in G minor
Symphony No. 5 in B♭ major
1948 (47) *The Buddha*, suite for flute, oboe, violin, viola and cello
1951 (50) *Festival Te Deum*, for soprano, chorus and orchestra
String Quartet No. 2 in E♮ major
1952 (51) Viola Concerto in A major
1954 (53) Symphony No. 6
1955 (54) Piano Concerto in G major
1956 (55) Symphony No. 7 in C major
1957 (56) *In Honoram Mariae Matris Dei*, cantata
1958 (57) Oboe Sonata in C major
Pezzo Ostinato, for harp
1959 (58) Violin Concerto
1961 (60) *Cantata da Camera* (Crucifixus pro nobis)
1964 (63) String Quartet No. 3

Improvisation, for solo cello
1965 (64) *Inscape*, suite for chorus, strings and harp
1966 (65) Eight Preludes for Piano
1968 (67) Symphony No. 8
           Advent Cantata (Natum Maria Virgine), for baritone,
              chorus and small orchestra
           Violin Sonata No. 3
1969 (68) Missa Brevis, for treble voices and organ
1970 (69) Piano Trio No. 2
Rubbra also composed:
Sinfonia Sacra (The Resurrection) for soprano, contralto, baritone,
    mixed chorus and orchestra
Transformations, for solo harp
Chamber Symphony (No. 10)
Resurgam, overture
String Quartet No. 4
Much music for unaccompanied choir, anthems, part-songs and
    liturgical choral works.

SAINT-SAËNS, Camille/1835–1921/France

1855 (20) Symphony No. 1 in E♭ major
           Piano Quintet in A major, with double-bass ad lib
1857 (22) Organ Fantasia No. 1
1858 (23) Piano Concerto No. 1 in D major
1859 (24) Violin Concerto No. 1 in A minor
1863 (28) Piano Trio No. 1 in F major
1866 (31) Suite in D minor, for piano, cello (violin or viola)
1868 (33) Piano Concerto No. 2 in G minor
1869 (34) Piano Concerto No. 3 in E♭ major
1870 (35) *Introduction and Rondo Capriccioso*, for violin and orchestra
           Mélodies persanes, six songs
1871 (36) *Omphale's Spinning-Wheel*, symphonic poem
           Marche heroïque, for orchestra
1872 (37) *La Princesse jaune*, opera
1873 (38) Cello Concerto No. 1 in A minor
           Phaeton, symphonic poem
1874 (39) *Danse macabre*, symphonic poem
1875 (40) Piano Concerto No. 4 in C minor
1876 (41) *The Deluge*, oratorio
1877 (42) *Samson et Delilah*, opera
           La Jeunesse d'Hercule, symphonic poem
           Suite for Orchestra
1878 (43) Symphony No. 2 in A minor
1879 (44) Violin Concerto No. 2 in C major
           Suite algérienne
1880 (45) Violin Concerto No. 3 in B minor
1885 (50) Violin Sonata No. 1 in D minor
1886 (51) *Le Carnaval des animaux*, for piano and orchestra
           Symphony No. 3 in C minor, with organ and two pianos
1892 (57) Piano Trio No. 2 in E minor
1894 (59) Preludes and fugues for organ

1895 (60)   Piano Concerto No. 5 in F major
1896 (61)   Violin Sonata No. 2 in E♭ major
1897 (62)   Seven Improvisations for Grand Organ
1898 (63)   Preludes and fugues for organ
1900 (65)   String Quartet in E minor
1902 (67)   Cello Concerto No. 2 in D minor
                Coronation March
1913 (78)   *fp. The Promised Land*, oratorio
1915 (80)   *La Cendre Rouge*, ten songs
1918 (83)   *Fantasia* No. 3, for organ
Saint Saëns also composed:
Serenade, for piano, organ, violin, and viola (or cello)
Cello Sonata No. 1 in C minor
Piano Quartet in B♭ major
Septet in E♭ major for piano, trumpet, oboe and string quartet
Caprice on Danish and Russian Airs
Cello Sonata No. 2 in F major
Fantaisie, for harp and violin
La Muse et le poète, piano trio
String Quartet in G major
Clarinet Sonata in E♭ major
Bassoon Sonata in G major.

SARASATE, Pablo/1844–1908/Spain

1878 (34)   *Zigeunerweisen*, orchestra fantasy
Sarasate also composed:
Danses espagnoles: *Malaguena*
Danses espagnoles: *Habanera*
Romanza Andaluza
Jota Navarra
Playera
Zapateado
Caprice basque
Introduction and Tarantella, for violin and orchestra
Many works for violin.

SATIE, Erik/1866–1925/France

1886 (20)   *Ogives*, for piano
1887 (21)   Trois sarabandes, for piano
1888 (22)   *Trois Gymnopédies*, for piano
1890 (24)   *Trois Gnossiènnes*, for piano
1891 (25)   Trois Préludes from *Les Fils des étoiles*, for piano
1892 (26)   *Uspud*, ballet
                Sonneries de la Rose-Croix, for piano
1893 (27)   *Danses gothiques*, for piano
                Quatre Préludes, for piano
1894 (28)   *Prélude de la porte héroïque du ciel*, for piano
1895 (29)   Messe des Pauvres
1897 (31)   *Deux pièces froides*, for piano
1899 (33)   *Génévière de Brabant*, puppet opera

Jack-in-the-Box, ballet
1903 (37) Trois morceaux en forme de poire, for piano duet
1905 (39) Pousse l'amour, operetta
1906 (40) Prélude en tapisserie, for piano
Passacaille, for piano
1908 (42) Aperçus désagréables, for piano duet
1911 (45) En Habit de cheval, two chorales and two fugues, for orchestra
1912 (46) Choses vues à droite et à gauche (sans lunette), for violin and piano
1913 (47) Le Piège de Medusa, operetta
Descriptions automatiques, for piano
Embryons desséchés, for piano
Croquis et agarceries d'un gros bonhomme en bois, for piano
Chapitres tournés en tous sens, for piano
Enfantines, three sets of children's pieces for piano
1914 (48) Cinq Grimaces pour le songe d'une nuit d'été, for orchestra
Vieux Sequins et vielles cuirasses, for piano
Heures séculaires et instantées, for piano
Trois Valses du précieux dégoûte, for piano
Sports et divertissements, for piano
Les Pantins dansent, for piano
Trois Poemes d'amour, songs
1915 (49) Avant-dernières pensées, for piano
1916 (50) Parade, ballet
Trois mélodies, songs
1918 (52) Socrates, symphonic drama for four sopranos and chamber orchestra
1919 (53) Quatre petites pièces montées, for small orchestra
Nocturnes, for piano
1920 (54) La Belle Excentrique, for orchestra
Premier minuet, for piano
Trois petites mélodies, songs
1923 (57) Ludions, songs
1924 (58) Mercure, ballet
Relâche, ballet

SCARLATTI, Alessandro/1660–1725/Italy

1679 (19) fp. Gli equivoci nel sembiante, opera
1683 (23) fp. Pompeo, opera
fp. Psiche, opera
1690 (30) fp. Gli equivoci in amore, opera
1694 (34) fp. Pirro e Demetrio, opera
1698 (38) fp. Flavio cuniberto, opera
fp. La donna ancora e'fedele, opera
1699 (39) Two Sonatas for flute and continuo
1706 (46) Il sedecia, re di Gerusalemme, oratorio
1707 (47) fp. Mitridate eupatore, opera
fp. Il trionfo della libertà, opera
c.1710 (c.50) Motet: Est dies tropael
Informata vulnerate, cantata

1715 (55) *fp. Tigrone*, opera
           Twelve sinfonias
           Four quartets for two violins, viola and cello, without
               harpsichord
1718 (58) *fp. Telemaco*, opera
1719 (59) *fp. Marco Attilo Regolo*, opera
1720 (60) *fp. Tito o sempronio gracco*, opera
1721 (61) *fp. Griselda*, opera
Scarlatti also composed:
101 more operas
500 chamber cantatas
200 masses
14 oratorios

SCARLATTI, Domenico/1685–1757/Italy

1703 (18) *fp. Ottavia ristituta al trono*, opera
           fp. Giustina, opera
1704 (19) *fp. Irene*, opera
1710 (25) *fp. La Sylvia*, opera
1711 (26) *fp. Orlando*, opera
           fp. Tolomeo e Alessandro, opera
1712 (27) *fp. Tetide in sciro*, opera
1713 (28) *fp. Ifigenie in Aulide*, opera
           fp. Ifigenie in Tauride, opera
1714 (29) *fp. Amor d'un ombra*, opera
1715 (30) *fp. Ambleto*, opera
1718 (33) *fp. Berenice*, opera
1738 (53) *p. Essercizi per Gravicembalo*
1739 (54) *p. XLII Suites de pièces pour le Clavecin*
Scarlatti also wrote over 550 single-movement harpsichord sonatas.

SCHOECK, Othmar/1886–1957/Switzerland

1906–07 (20) *Serenade*, for small orchestra
1911 (25)   *Dithyrambe*, for double chorus and orchestra
             Violin Concerto (1911–12)
             Erwin und Elmire, incidental music (1911–16)
1915 (29)   *Trommelschlage*
1917–18 (31) *Don Ranudo de Colibrados*
1918 (32)   *Das Wandbild*
1919–20 (33) *Venus*, opera
1922–23 (36) *Élégie*, song cycle for voice and chamber orchestra
1924–25 (38) *Penthesiles*
1928–30 (42–44) *Vom Fischer und syner Fru*, dramatic cantata
1932 (46)   *Praeludium*
1937 (51)   *Massimilla Doni*, opera
1938–39 (52) *Das Schloss Durande*, opera
1945 (59)   *Sommernacht*
             Suite in A major, for strings
1947 (61)   Cello Concerto
1951 (65)   Horn Concerto

Festlichen Hymnus
1952 (66) *Befreite Sehnsucht*, song cycle for voice and orchestra
Schoeck also composed many songs.

SCHOENBERG, Arnold/1874–1951/Austria

1899 (25) *Verklaerte Nacht*, for string sextet (arranged for string
orchestra 1917; revised 1943)
1900–13 (26–39) *Gurre-Lieder*, for four solo singers, three male
choruses, one mixed chorus, large orchestra including
eight flutes and a set of iron chains
1903 (29) *Pelleas und Melisande*, suite for orchestra
1905 (31) String Quartet No. 1 in D minor
1906 (32) Chamber Symphonies Nos. 1 and 2
1907 (33) String Quartet No. 2 (transcribed for string orchestra
1917)
Friede auf Erden, for choir
1908 (34) *Buch der hängenden Gärten*, setting of fifteen poems by
Stefan George for solo voice and piano
1909 (35) *Ewartung*, monodrama, for soprano and orchestra
Five pieces for orchestra (revised 1949)
1910–13 (36–39) *Die Glückliche Hand*, music drama
1911 (37) *Herzgewächse*, for coloratura soprano, celesta, harmonium
and harp
1912 (38) *Pierrot Lunaire*, song cycle of twenty-one poems
1923 (49) *Serenade*, for septet and baritone
1924 (50) Quintet for wind instruments
1927 (53) String Quartet No. 3
1928 (54) Variations for orchestra
1929 (55) *Von Heute auf Morgen*, opera
1932 (58) *Moses und Aron*, two-act opera
1934 (60) Suite in G major for strings
1936 (62) Violin Concerto
1937 (63) String Quartet No. 4
1939 (65) *Kol Nidrei*
1941 (67) Variations and Recitative for organ
1942 (68) Piano Concerto
1943 (69) *Ode to Napoleon*, for speaker, strings and piano
1945 (71) Prelude to a *Genesis* Suite
1947 (73) *A Survivor from Warsaw*, cantata, for speaker, men's
chorus and orchestra
1949 (75) *Fantasia*, for violin and piano
1951 (77) De profundis, for a cappella choir

SCHUBERT, Franz/1797–1828/Austria

1811 (14) Quintet-overture
1812 (15) *Eine Kleine Trauermusik*, nonet
Quartet-overture
String Quartet Nos. 1–3 in B♭ : C: B♭
Sonata movement for piano trio, in B♭ major
1813 (16) Symphony No. 1 in D major

Minuet and Finale of a wind octet, in F major
String Quartets Nos. 4–6, in C: B♭ : D
Three Sonatinas for violin and piano, in D: Am: Gm
Five German Dances, with coda and seven trios
Five minuets with six trios
Des Teufels Lustschloss, opera
1814 (17) Quartet for flute, guitar, violin and cello, in G major
String Quartets Nos. 7 and 8, in D: B♭
"Gretchen at the Spinning-wheel", song
1815 (18) Symphony No. 2 in E♭ major
Symphony No. 3 in D major
String Quartet No. 9 in G minor
Piano Sonatas Nos. 1 and 2, in E: C
"Der Erlkönig", song
1816 (19) Symphony No. 4 in C minor, *Tragic*
Symphony No. 5 in B♭ major
Concertstücke, for violin and orchestra
Rondo for violin and string quartet
String Trio (one movement) in B♭ major
Piano Sonata No. 3 in E major, five movements
Adagio and Rondo Concertante, for piano quartet
1817 (20) String Quartet No. 10 in E♭ major (possibly 1813)
String Quartet No. 11 in E major
Violin Sonata in A major
Piano Sonata No. 4 in A♭, with finale in E♭
Piano Sonata No. 5 in E minor, two movements
Piano Sonata No. 6 in E♭ major
Piano Sonata No. 7 in F♯ minor
Piano Sonata No. 8 in B major
Piano Sonata No. 9 in E minor
"An die Musik" and "Tod und das Mädchen", songs
1818 (21) Symphony No. 6 in C major
Piano Sonatas Nos. 10 and 11, in C: Fm (unfinished)
1819 (22) Piano Quintet in A major, *Trout*
Piano Sonata No. 12 in C♯ minor (fragmentary)
Piano Sonata No. 13 in A major
1820 (23) *Die Zauberharfe*, melodrama
String Quartet No. 12 in C minor
1821 (24) Variation on a theme by Diabelli
Symphony No. 7 in E major (sketched only)
Alfonso und Estrella, opera (1821–22)
1822 (25) Symphony No. 8 in B minor, *Unfinished*
1823 (26) *Fierrabras*, opera
Die häusliche Krieg, opera
Rosamunde, incidental music
Piano Sonata No. 14 in A minor
Die Schöne Mullerin, song cycle
1824 (27) Octet in F major, for strings and wind instruments
String Quartet No. 13 in A minor
String Quartet No. 14 in D minor, *Death and the Maiden*
Cello Sonata in A minor, *Arpeggione*
Introduction and Variations for flute and piano, in E minor

1825 (28) Piano Sonata No. 15 in C major
           Piano Sonata No. 16 in A minor
           Piano Sonata No. 17 in D major
1826 (29) String Quartet No. 15
           Piano Trio in B♭ major
           Rondo Brilliant, for violin and piano, in B minor
           Piano Sonata No. 18 in G major
1827 (30) Piano Trio in E♭ major
           Phantasie, for violin and piano, in C major
           Die Winterreise, song cycle
1828 (31) Symphony No. 9, *The Great C major*
           String Quintet in C major
           Piano Sonata No. 19 in C minor
           Piano Sonata No. 20 in A major
           Piano Sonata No. 21 in B♭ major
           Schwanengesang, song cycle

Schubert also composed more than 600 songs.

SCHUMAN, William/b.1910/U.S.A.

1934 (24) *Choreographic Poem*, for seven instruments
1935 (25) Symphony No. 1, for eighteen instruments
1936 (26) String Quartet No. 1
1937 (27) Symphony No. 2
           String Quartet No. 2
           Choral étude
1939 (29) *American Festival Overture*
           Quartettino, for four bassoons
           String Quartet No. 3
           Prelude for Voices
1940 (30) Secular Cantata No. 1, *This is our time*
1941 (31) Symphony No. 3
           Symphony No. 4
           Newsreel Suite, for orchestra
1942 (32) Piano Concerto
           Secular Cantata No. 2, *A free song*
           Requiescat
1943 (33) *William Billings Overture*
           Symphony No. 5, for strings
           A prayer in time of war, for orchestra
1944 (34) *Circus Overture*
           Te Deum
1945 (35) *Undertow*, ballet
1947 (37) *Night Journey*, ballet
           Violin Concerto
1948 (38) Symphony No. 6
1949 (39) *Judith*, ballet
1950 (40) String Quartet No. 4
1953 (43) *The Mighty Casey*, baseball opera
           Voyage, for piano
1955 (45) *Credendum*, for orchestra
1956 (46) *New England Triptych*, for orchestra

1957 (47) *Prologues*, for chorus and orchestra
1959 (49) *Three Moods*, for piano
1960 (50) Symphony No. 7
1962 (52) *Song of Orpheus*, fantasy for cello and orchestra
1963 (53) Symphony No. 8
1964 (54) Symphony No. 9
　　　　　 String Trio
1969 (59) *In Praise of Shahn*, canticle for orchestra
1973 (63) *Concerto on Old English rounds*, for solo viola, women's
　　　　　　　chorus and orchestra

SCHUMANN, Robert/1810−1856/Germany

1829−31 (19−21) *Papillons*, twelve pieces for piano
1830 (20) *Theme and Variations on the name Abegg*, for piano
1832 (22) Six Concert Studies on Caprices by Paganini, Set I
1833 (23) Six Concert Studies on Caprices by Paganini, Set II
1834−35 (24) *Carnaval* (Scènes mignonnes), twenty-one piano pieces
1836 (26) *Phantasie* in C major, for piano
1837 (27) *Fantasiestücke*, for piano, Books I and II
　　　　　 p. *Études symphoniques*, twelve symphonic studies for
　　　　　　　piano
　　　　　 Davidsbündler-Tänze, eighteen piano pieces (revised 1850)
1838 (28) *Kinderscenen*, thirteen short piano pieces
　　　　　 Kriesleriana, for piano (dedicated to Chopin)
　　　　　 Novelleten, eight piano pieces
1839 (29) *Nachtstücke*, for piano
1840 (30) *Dichterliebe* (Poet's Love), song cycle
　　　　　 Frauenliebe und -leben, song cycle
　　　　　 Liederkreiss, nine songs (Heine)
1841 (31) Symphony No. 1, *Spring*, in B♭ major
　　　　　 Symphony No. 4 in D minor (withdrawn and revised in
　　　　　　　1851)
　　　　　 Overture, Scherzo and Finale, for orchestra (*Finale*
　　　　　　　revised 1845)
　　　　　 Piano Concerto in A minor (1841−45)
1842 (32) Piano Quintet in E♭ major
　　　　　 Piano Quartet in E♭ major
　　　　　 Four *Fantasiestücke* for piano trio, in Am: F: Fm: Am
　　　　　 Andante and Variations, for two pianos, two cellos and
　　　　　　　horn (best known as duet for two pianos) (1842?)
　　　　　 Three String Quartets, in Am: F: A
　　　　　 Liederkreiss, twelve songs (Eichendorff)
1843 (33) *Das Paradies und die Peri*, cantata
1845−46 (35) Symphony No. 2 in C major
1847 (37) *Genoveva*, opera (1847−48)
　　　　　 Piano Trio No. 1 in D minor and D major
　　　　　 Piano Trio No. 2 in F major
1849 (39) *Manfred*, dramatic poem
　　　　　 Three *Fantasiestücke*, for piano and clarinet with violin
　　　　　　　or cello ad lib, in Am: A: A
　　　　　 Adagio and Allegro, for piano and horn, in A♭ major

1850 (40) Symphony No. 3 in E♭ major, *Rhenish*
           Cello Concerto in A minor
1851 (41) Piano Trio No. 3 in G minor and G major
           Violin Sonata in A minor
           Violin Sonata in D minor
           Four *Marchenbilder*, for piano and viola (or violin)
1853 (43) Violin Concerto
           Märchenerzählungen, four pieces for piano, clarinet (or
           violin), and viola
           Introduction and Allegro, for piano
           Fantasy, for violin
1854 (44) *p. Albumblätter*, twenty pieces for piano

SCHÜTZ, Heinrich/1585–1672/Germany

1611 (26) *p.* Italian Madrigals
1619 (34) *p.* Psalms and Motets
           p. Psalmen Davids, for two, three or four choirs of voices
           and instruments
1623 (38) *Resurrection Oratorio*
           Easter Oratorio
           p. Historia der Auferstehung Jesu Christi, for voices and
           instruments
1625 (40) *p. Cantiones sacrae*, for four voices
1627 (42) *fp. Dafne*, opera
1629 (44) *p. Symphoniae sacrae*, Part I
1636 (51) *Musicalische exequien* (Funeral music)
           Kleine Geistliche Concerte, Book I
1638 (53) *fp. Orpheus and Euridice*, ballet
1639 (54) *Kleine Geistliche Concerte*, Book II
1645 (60) *The Seven Words from the Cross*, choral
1647 (62) *p. Symphoniae sacrae*, Part II
1648 (63) *p.* Musicali ad chorum sacrum
1650 (65) *p. Symphoniae sacrae*, Part III
1664 (79) *Christmas Oratorio*
1665–66 (80) Four Passions (*Matthew, Mark, Luke* and *John*)
1671 (86) *Deutsches Magnificat*

SEIBER, Mátyás/1905–1960/Hungary

1924 (19) String Quartet No. 1
           Sarabande and Gigue, for cello and piano
           Missa Brevis, for unaccompanied chorus
1925 (20) *Serenade*, for six wind instruments
           Sonata da Camera, for cello and violin
1926–28 (21–23) *Divertimento*, for clarinet and string quartet
1934 (29) *Eva spielt mit Puppen*, opera
           String Quartet No. 2 (1934–35)
1940 (35) *Besardo Suite No. 1*
1941 (36) *Besardo Suite No. 2*, for strings
           Transylvanian Rhapsody
           Fantasy, for cello and piano

Pastorale and Burlesque, for flute and strings (1941–42)
1942 (37) *Balaton*, opera
　　　　　　La Blanchisseuse, ballet music
1943–44 (38) *Fantasia Concertante*, for violin and strings
1944 (39) *Notturno*, for horn and strings
1945 (40) *Phantasy*, for flute, horn and strings
1948 (43) *Johnny Miner*, radio opera
　　　　　　String Quartet No. 3, *Quartetto lyrico* (1948–51)
1949 (44) *Ulysses*, cantata (possibly 1946–47)
　　　　　　Andantino and Pastorale, for clarinet and piano
1951 (46) *The Seasons*
　　　　　　Concertino, for clarinet and strings
1953 (48) Three pieces for cello and orchestra
1954 (49) *Elegy*, for violin and small orchestra
　　　　　　To Poetry, song cycle
1958 (53) *Permutazione a cinque*, for flute, oboe, clarinet, horn and
　　　　　　　bassoon
　　　　　　Portrait of the Artist as a Young Man, chamber cantata
1959 (54) *Improvisation for Jazz Band and Symphony Orchestra* (with
　　　　　　　Dankworth)
1960 (55) *Invitation*, ballet
　　　　　　A Three-cornered Fanfare
1962 (posthumous) *p.* Violin Sonata

SESSIONS, Roger/b.1896/U.S.A.

1923 (27) *The Black Maskers*, incidental music
1927 (31) Symphony No. 1
1930 (34) Piano Sonata No. 1
1935 (39) Violin Concerto, with orchestra which includes five
　　　　　　　clarinets but no violins
1936 (40) String Quartet No. 1
1938 (42) *Scherzino and March*, for orchestra
1939 (43) *Pages from a Diary* (From My Diary), for piano
1942 (46) Duo for violin and piano
1944–46 (48–50) Symphony No. 2
1946 (50) Piano Sonata No. 2
1947 (51) *fp. The Trial of Lucullus*, opera
1951 (55) String Quartet No. 2
1953 (57) Sonata for solo violin
1954 (58) *The Idyll of Theocritus*, for soprano and orchestra
1955 (59) Mass, for unison male voices and organ
1956 (60) Piano Concerto
1957 (61) Symphony No. 3
1958 (62) Symphony No. 4
　　　　　　String Quintet
1960 (64) *Divertimento*, for orchestra
1963 (67) *Psalm 140*, for soprano with organ or orchestra
1964 (68) Symphony No. 5
1965 (69) Piano Sonata No. 3
1966 (70) Symphony No. 6
　　　　　　Six pieces for cello

1967 (71) Symphony No. 7
1968 (72) Symphony No. 8
1970 (74) *Rhapsody*, for orchestra
           When Lilacs Last in the Dooryard Bloom'd, cantata
1971 (75) Concerto for viola and cello
1975 (79) Three choruses on Biblical texts
Sessions also composed *Montezuma*, an opera.

SHAPERO, Harold Samuel/b.1920/U.S.A.

1938 (18) *Three Pieces for Three Pieces*, for woodwind trio
1939 (19) Trumpet Sonata
1940 (20) String Quartet
1941 (21) *Nine-minute Overture*
           Piano Sonata (four hands)
1942 (22) Violin Sonata
1944 (24) *Three amateur sonatas*, for piano
1945 (25) *Serenade* in D major, for string orchestra
1947 (27) Piano Sonata No. 1
1948 (28) *Symphony for classical orchestra*
           The Travellers, for orchestra
1951–58 (31–38) Concerto for orchestra
1955 (35) *Credo*, for orchestra
1958 (38) *On Green Mountain*, for jazz combo
1960 (40) *Partita*, for piano and orchestra
Shapero also composed:
Pocahontas, ballet
The Minotaurs, ballet
The Defence of Corinth, for men's voices and piano (four hands)
Emblems, for men's voices
Hebrew Cantata
Sinfonia in C major
Variations in C major, for piano.

SHAPEY, Ralph/b.1921/U.S.A.

1946 (25) String Quartet No. 1
           Piano Sonata
1947 (26) Piano Quintet
1949 (28) String Quartet No. 2
           Three Essays on Thomas Wolfe, for piano
1950 (29) Violin Sonata
1951 (30) *Fantasy*, for orchestra
           String Quartet No. 3
           Cantata, for soprano, tenor, bass, narrator, chamber
               orchestra and percussion
1952 (31) Symphony No. 1
           Quartet for oboe and string trio
           Oboe Sonata
           Suite for piano
1953 (32) String Quartet No. 4
           Cello Sonata

1954 (33) Concerto for clarinet, with violin, cello, piano, horn,
                    tom-tom and bass drum
              Sonata-Variations, for piano
1955 (34) *Challenge — The Family of Man*, for orchestra
              Piano Trio
1956 (35) *Mutations No. 1*, for piano
1957 (36) String Quartet No. 5, with female voices (1957—58)
              Rhapsodie, for oboe and piano
              Duo for viola and piano
1958 (37) *Ontogeny*, for orchestra
              Walking Upright, eight songs for female voice and violin
1959 (38) Violin Concerto
              Rituals, for orchestra
              Soliloquy, for narrator, string quartet and percussion
              Evocation, for violin, piano and percussion
              Form, for piano
1960 (39) *Dimensions*, for soprano and twenty-three instruments
              De Profundis, for solo contrabass and instruments
              Movements, for woodwind quartet
              Five, for violin and piano
              This Day, for female voice and piano
1961 (40) *Incantations*, for soprano and ten instruments
              Discourse, for flute, clarinet, violin and piano
1962 (41) *Chamber Symphony*, for ten solo players
              Convocation, for chamber group
              Piece, for violin and instruments
              Birthday Piece, for piano
1963 (42) Brass Quintet
              String Quartet No. 6
              Seven, for piano (four hands)
1965 (44) String Trio
              Configurations, for flute and piano
1966 (45) *Partita*, for violin and thirteen players
              Poème, for violin and piano
              Mutations No. 2, for piano
              Partita, for solo violin
1967 (46) *Partita-Fantasy*, for cello and sixteen players
              Reyem, for flute, violin and piano
              Deux, for two pianos
              For Solo Trumpet
              Songs of Ecstasy, for soprano, piano, percussion and tape

SHOSTAKOVICH, Dmitri/1906—1975/Russia

1919 (13) Scherzo in F♯ minor, for orchestra
              Eight Preludes for piano
1920—21 (14—15) Five Preludes for piano
1921—22 (15—16) Theme with Variations, in B major, for orchestra
1922 (16) *Two Fables of Krilov*, for mezzo-soprano and orchestra
              Three Fantastic Dances, for piano
              Suite in F♯ minor, for two pianos
1923 (17) Piano Trio No. 1

1924 (18)   Symphony No. 1 in F minor (1924–25)
            Scherzo in E♭, for orchestra
            Prelude and Scherzo, for string octet (double string
               quartet) or string orchestra (1924–25)
1926 (20)   Piano Sonata No. 1
1927 (21)   *The Nose*, opera (1927–28)
            The Age of Gold, ballet (1927–30)
            Symphony No. 2 in B major, *October*, with chorus
            Aphorisms, ten pieces for piano
1928 (22)   *New Babylon*, for orchestra (film music)
            Six Romances on words by Japanese poets, for tenor and
               orchestra (1928–32)
1929 (23)   Symphony No. 3 in E♭ major, *The First of May*, with
               chorus
1930 (24)   *The Bolt*, choreographic spectacle (1930–31)
            Alone, film music (1930–31)
            Lady Macbeth of the Mtsensk District, opera (1930–32)
1931–32 (25)   *Hamlet*, incidental music
1932 (26)   *From Karl Marx to our own days*, symphonic poem for solo
               voices, chorus and orchestra
            Encounter, film music
            Twenty-four Preludes for piano (1932–33)
1933 (27)   Piano Concerto No. 1 in C minor, for piano, string
               orchestra and trumpet
            The Human Comedy, incidental music (1933–34)
1934 (28)   *Bright Stream*, comedy ballet (1934–35)
            Suite for Jazz Orchestra, No. 1
            Cello Sonata in D minor
            Girl Companions, film music (1934–35)
            Love and Hate, film music
            Maxim's Youth (The Bolshevik), film music (1934–35)
1935 (29)   Symphony No. 4 in C minor
            Five Fragments, for small orchestra
1936 (30)   *Salute to Spain*, incidental music
            Four Romances on Verses of Pushkin, for bass and piano
            Maxim's Return, film music
            Volochayevka Days, film music
1937 (31)   Symphony No. 5 in D minor
1938 (32)   Suite for Jazz Orchestra, No. 2
            String Quartet No. 1 in C major
            Friends, film music
            The Great Citizen, film music
            Man at Arms, film music
            Vyborg District, film music
1939 (33)   Symphony No. 6 in B minor
            The Great Citizen, Part II, film music
1940 (34)   Piano Quintet in G minor
            Three pieces for solo violin
            King Lear, incidental music
1941 (35)   Symphony No. 7 in C major, *Leningrad*
            The Gamblers, opera
1942 (36)   *Native Leningrad*, suite included in the theater show

"Motherland"
Piano Sonata No. 2
Six Romances on verses of English poets, for bass and piano
1943 (37) Symphony No. 8 in C minor
1944 (38) *Russian River*, suite
String Quartet No. 2, in A major
Piano Trio No. 2
Children's Notebook, six pieces for piano
Eight English and American Folk-songs, for low voice and
orchestra
Zoya, film music
1945 (39) Symphony No. 9 in E♭ major
Two Songs
Simple Folk, film music
1946 (40) String Quartet No. 3, in F major
1947 (41) Violin Concerto No. 1 (1947–48)
Poem of the Motherland, cantata
Pirogov, film music
Young Guards, film music
1948 (42) *From Jewish Folk poetry*, song cycle for soprano, contralto,
tenor and piano
Meeting on the Elbe, film music
Michurin, film music
1949 (43) Ballet Suite No. 1, for orchestra
String Quartet No. 4 in D major
The Song of the Forests, oratorio
The Fall of Berlin, film music
1950 (44) Twenty-Four Preludes and Fugues, for piano (1950–51)
Two Romances on verses by Mikhail Lermontov, for
male voice and piano
Byelinski, film music
1951 (45) Ballet Suite No. 2, for orchestra
Ten poems on texts by Revolutionary poets, for chorus a
cappella
The Memorable Year 1919, film music
1952 (46) Ballet Suite No. 3, for orchestra
String Quartet No. 5 in B♭ major
Four Monologues on verses of Pushkin, for bass and
piano
The Sun shines over our Motherland, cantata
1953 (47) Symphony No. 10 in E minor
Ballet Suite No. 4, for orchestra
Concertino, for two pianos
1954 (48) *Festival Overture*, for orchestra
Five Romances (Songs of our Days), for bass and piano
1955 (49) *The Gadfly*, film music
1956 (50) *Katerina Ismailova*, opera (new version of *Lady Macbeth
of Mtensk*)
String Quartet No. 6 in G major
Spanish Songs, for soprano and piano
The First Echelon, film music
1957 (51) Piano Concerto No. 2 in F major

Symphony No. 11 in G minor, *The Year 1905*
1958 (52) *Moscow, Cheremushki*, musical comedy
1959 (53) Cello Concerto No. 1 in E♭ major
1960 (54) *Novorossiysk Chimes* (The Fire of Eternal Glory), for
    orchestra
    String Quartet No. 7 in F♯ minor
    String Quartet No. 8 in C minor
    Satires (Pictures of the Past), for soprano and piano
    Five Days — Five Nights, film music
1961 (55) Symphony No. 12 in D minor, *1917*
1962 (56) Symphony No. 13 in B♭ minor, *Babi-Yar*, for bass solo,
    bass choir and orchestra
1963 (57) Overture on Russian and Kirghiz Folk Themes, for
    orchestra
    Hamlet, film music
1964 (58) String Quartet No. 9, in E♭ major
    String Quartet No. 10 in A♭ major
    The Execution of Stepan Razin, cantata
1965 (59) Five Romances on texts from *Krokodil* magazine, for bass
    and piano
1966 (60) Cello Concerto No. 2 in G major
    String Quartet No. 11 in F minor
    *Preface to the Complete Collection of my Works, and
    Brief Reflections apropos this Preface*, for bass and
    grand piano
1967 (61) Violin Concerto No. 2 in C♯ minor
    Funeral-Triumphal Prelude, for orchestra
    October, symphonic poem
    Spring, Spring, for bass and grand piano
    Sofya Perovoskaya, film music
    Seven Romances on poems of Alexander Blok, for soprano
    and piano trio
1968 (62) String Quartet No. 12 in D♭ major
    Sonata, for violin and grand piano
1969 (63) Symphony No. 14, for soprano, bass, string orchestra and
    percussion
1970 (64) *March of the Soviet Militia*, for wind orchestra
    String Quartet No. 13 in B♭ minor
    Loyalty, eight ballads for male chorus
    King Lear, film music
1971 (65) Symphony No. 15 in A major
1972–73 (66) String Quartet No. 14 in F♯ major
1973 (67) Six poems of Marina Tsvetaeva, suite for contralto and
    piano
1974 (68) String Quartet No. 15, in E♭ minor
    Suite on verses of Michelangelo Buonarroti, for bass and
    piano
    Four verses of Capitan Lebjadkin, for bass and piano
1975 (69) Sonata for viola and grand piano
    The Dreamers, ballet (largely drawn from *The Age of Gold*
    and *The Bolt*, with some new material)
It is believed that Shostakovich had completed two movements of

Symphony No. 16 just before his death, but this has not so far been confirmed by the Soviet authorities.

SIBELIUS, Jean/1865–1957/Finland

1881–82 (16–17) Piano Trio in F minor
Piano Quartet in E minor
1885 (20) Quartet in E♭ major
1888 (23) Theme and Variations for quartet, in C♯ minor
1889 (24) Piano Quintet
Quartet in B♭ major
Suite for violin, viola and cello
Violin Sonata in F major
1890–91 (25) Overture in A minor
Overture in E major
1891 (26) *Scène de ballet*
Piano Quartet in C major
1892 (27) *En Saga*, symphonic poem (revised 1901)
Kullervo, symphonic poem
1893 (28) *Karelia*, overture
Karelia, suite, for orchestra
The Swan of Tuonela, for orchestra (No. 3 of *Four Legends from Kalevala*)
1894 (29) *Spring Song*, symphonic poem
1895 (30) *Cassazione*
Lemminkäinen and the Maidens (No. 1 of the *Four Legends from Kalevala*)
Lemminkäinen in Tuonela (No. 2 of the *Four Legends from Kalevala*)
Lemminkäinen's Homecoming (No. 4 of the *Four Legends from Kalevala*)
1896 (31) *The Girl in the Tower*, opera (unpublished)
1898 (33) *King Christian II*, incidental music
Symphony No. 1 in E minor (1898–99)
1899 (34) *Scènes historiques*, Suite No. 1, three orchestral pieces
1900 (35) *Finlandia*, symphonic poem
1901 (36) Symphony No. 2 in D major
Cortège
Portraits, for strings
1903 (38) Violin Concerto in D minor (revised 1905)
Romance, for strings
1904 (39) *Kuolema*, incidental music, includes "Valse Triste"
Symphony No. 3 in C major (1904–07)
1905 (40) *Pelléas et Mélisande*, incidental music
1906 (41) *Pohjola's Daughter*, symphonic fantasia
1908 (43) String Quartet in five movements, *Voces Intimae*
1909 (44) *Night-ride and Sunrise*, tone poem
1911 (46) Symphony No. 4 in A minor
Rakastava Suite
Valse Romantique
Canzonetta, for strings
1912 (47) *Scènes historiques*, Suite No. 2, three orchestral pieces

Two *Serenades*, for violin
1913 (48) *Scaramouche*, pantomime
           Il Bardo, symphonic poem
1914 (49) *Oceanides*, symphonic poem
           Symphony No. 5 in E♭ major (1914–15)
1916 (51) *Everyman*, incidental music
1922 (57) *Suite caractéristique* (Vivo, Lento, Commodo)
1923 (58) Symphony No. 6 in D minor
1924 (59) Symphony No. 7 in C major, in one movement
1925 (60) *Tapiola*, symphonic poem
1926 (61) *The Tempest*, incidental music

SKRIABIN, Alexander/1872–1915/Russia

1894 (22) Piano Concerto
           Réverie, for orchestra
1895 (23) Symphony No. 1 in E major
1901 (29) Symphony No. 2 in C minor
1903 (31) Symphony No. 3 in C major, *The Divine Poem*
1908 (36) *Poem of Ecstasy*, for orchestra
1909–10 (38) *Poem of Fire — Prometheus*, for orchestra, piano,
              chorus "ad lib", organ and colour keyboard
Skriabin also composed:
10 piano sonatas (1892–1913)
84 preludes for piano
21 mazurkas for piano
8 impromptus for piano
23 studies for piano
15 "poems" for piano

SMETANA, Bedřich/1824–1884/Bohemia (Czechoslovakia)

1848–49 (24) *Festive Overture*, in D major
1853–54 (29) *Festive Symphony*, in E major
1855 (31) Piano Trio in G minor
1858 (34) *Richard III*, symphonic Poem
           Wallenstein's Camp, symphonic poem (1858–59)
1860–61 (36) *Haakon Jarl*, symphonic poem
1862 (38) *On the Sea-shore*, for piano
1863 (39) *The Brandenburgers in Bohemia*, opera
1866 (42) *The Bartered Bride*, opera
1868 (44) *fp. Dalibor*, opera
           Solemn Prelude in C major, for orchestra
1874 (50) *The Two Widows*, opera
           Ma Vlast, six symphonic poems:
               Vyšehrad (The High Castle)
               Vltava
               Sàrka
               From Bohemia's Woods and Fields
               Tabor
               Blanik
1876 (52) *The Kiss*, opera

String Quartet No. 1, *From My Life*, in E minor
1878 (54)   *The Secret*, opera
   Czech Dances
1881 (57)   *fp. Libuse*, opera
1882 (58)   String Quartet No. 2 in D minor
1883 (59)   *The Prague Carnival*
   String Quartet No. 2

SMYTH, Ethel/1858–1944/Great Britain

1887 (29)   Violin Sonata in A minor
1890 (32)   *Anthony and Cleopatra*, overture
   Serenade in D major, for orchestra
1891 (33)   Suite for strings
1893 (35)   Mass in D major
1898 (40)   *Fantastic*, opera
1901 (43)   *The Forest*, opera
1902 (44)   String Quartet in E minor (completed *c.*1912)
1906 (48)   *The Wreckers*, opera
1911 (53)   *March of the Women*, for orchestra
   Three Songs of Sunrise, for unaccompanied chorus
1916 (58)   *The Boatswain's Mate*, opera
1920 (62)   *Dreamings*
1923 (65)   *Fête galante*, opera
   Soul's Joy, for unaccompanied chorus
1926 (68)   *Entente Cordial*, opera
   A Spring Canticle, for chorus and orchestra
   Sleepless Dreams, for chorus and orchestra
1927 (69)   Concerto for Violin and Horn (also known as Horn
      Concerto)
1930 (72)   *The Prison*, for unaccompanied chorus

SOWERBY, Leo/1895–1968/U.S.A.

1916 (21)   Woodwind Quintet
1917 (22)   Piano Concerto No. 1 (revised 1919)
   Serenade, for string quartet
   Comes Autumn Time, for organ
1919 (24)   Trio for flute, viola and piano
1920 (25)   Cello Sonata
   The Edge of Dreams, song cycle
1921 (26)   Symphony No. 1
   Violin Sonata No. 1
1922 (27)   *From the Northland*, for piano
   Ballad of King Estmere, for two pianos and orchestra
1924 (29)   *Synconata*, for jazz orchestra
1925 (30)   *From the Northland*, for orchestra
   The Vision of Sir Launfal, for chorus and orchestra
   Monotony, for jazz orchestra
1926 (31)   *Mediaeval Poem*, for organ and orchestra
1928 (33)   Symphony No. 2
1929 (34)   Cello Concerto (1929–34)

                    Prairie, symphonic poem
                    Florida Suite, for piano
1930 (35)   Organ Symphony
1931 (36)   *Passacaglia, Interlude and Fugue*, for orchestra
1932 (37)   Piano Concerto No. 2
1936 (41)   Organ Concerto No. 1
1938 (43)   *Theme in Yellow*, for orchestra
                    Clarinet Sonata
1939 (44)   *Forsaken of Man*, cantata
1940 (45)   Symphony No. 3
1941 (46)   *Poem*, for viola with organ or orchestra
1944 (49)   *Classic Concerto*, for organ and strings
                    Violin Sonata No. 2
                    Canticle of the Sun, cantata
1945 (50)   Trumpet Sonata
1947 (52)   Symphony No. 4
1949 (54)   *Ballade*, for English horn and strings
1950 (55)   *Christ Reborn*, cantata
1951 (56)   *Concert Piece*, for organ and orchestra
1952 (57)   String Trio
1954 (59)   *All on a Summer's Day*, for orchestra
                    Fantasy, for trumpet and organ
1957 (62)   *The Throne of God*, for chorus and orchestra
1959 (64)   *Ask of the Covenant*, cantata
1964 (69)   Symphony No. 5
                    Piano Sonata
1965 (70)   *Solomon's Garden*, for chorus and orchestra
1966 (71)   *Symphonia Brevis*, for organ
1967 (72)   *Dialogue*, for organ and piano
                    Organ Concerto No. 2
                    Organ Passacaglia
Sowerby also composed over 300 songs.

SPONTINI, Gasparo/1774–1851/Italy

1807 (33)   *La Vestale*, opera
1809 (35)   *Ferdinand Cortez*, opera
1819 (45)   *Olympie*, opera
1821 (47)   *Nurmahal*, opera
1829 (55)   *Agnes von Hohenstaufen*, opera

STANFORD, Charles Villiers/1852–1924/Great Britain

1876 (24)   Symphony in B♭ major
1877 (25)   *Festival Overture*
1881 (29)   *The Veiled Prophet*, opera
1882 (30)   *Elegiac Symphony*, in D minor
                    Serenade, in G major, for orchestra
1884 (32)   *Canterbury Pilgrims*, opera
                    Savonarola, opera
1886 (34)   *The Revenge*, choral-ballad
1887 (35)   *Queen of the Seas*, overture

          Irish Symphony in F minor
          Prelude *Oedipus Rex*
1888 (36) Symphony in F major
1891 (39) *Eden*, oratorio
1894 (42) Symphony in D major, *L'Allegro ed il Pensiero*
1895 (43) Piano Concerto No. 1 in G major
          Suite of Ancient Dances
1896 (44) *Shamus O'Brien*, opera
1898 (46) Te Deum
1899 (47) Evening Service in C major
1901 (49) *Much Ado About Nothing*, opera
          Irish Rhapsody No. 1 in D minor
1904 (52) Violin Concerto No. 1 in D major
          Evening Service in G major
1907 (55) Stabat Mater
1911 (59) Symphony No. 7 in D minor
1914 (62) *Irish Rhapsody* No. 4 in A minor
1915 (63) Piano Concerto No. 2 in C minor
1916 (64) *The Critic*, opera
1925 (posthumous) *fp. The Travelling Companion*, opera

STOCKHAUSEN, Karlheinz/b.1928/Germany

1950 (22) *Chöre für Doris*, three movements for mixed choir a
          cappella
          Three Lieder, for voice and chamber orchestra: 1) Der
          Rebell, 2) Frei, 3) Der Saitenmann
          Choral, for mixed choir a cappella
1951 (23) *Sonatine*, for violin and piano
          Kreuzspiel, for oboe, bass-clarinet, piano and percussion
          Formel, for orchestra
1952 (24) *Étude*, musique concrète
          Spiel, for orchestra
          Schlagtrio, for piano and timpani
          Punkte, for orchestra
          Kontra-punkte, for ten instruments (1952–53)
          Klavierstücke I–IV (1952–53)
1953 (25) *Elektronische Studie I*, electronic music
1954 (26) *Elektronische Studie II*, electronic music
          Klavierstücke V–VIII (1954–55)
          Klavierstücke IX–X (revised 1961)
1955–56 (27) *Gruppen*, for three orchestras (1955–57)
          Zeitmasze, for oboe, flute, English horn, clarinet and
          bassoon
          Gesang der Jünglinge, electronic music
1956 (28) *Klavierstücke XI*
1959 (31) *Carré*, for four orchestras and four choirs (1959–60)
          Refrain, for piano, celesta and percussion
          Zyklus, for one percussionist
          Kontakte, for electronic sound (1959–60)
1962–64 (34–36) *Momente*, for soprano solo, four choral groups
          and thirteen instrumentalists

1963 (35)   *Plus Minus*, 2 x 7 pages "for working out"
1964 (36)   *Mikrophonie I*, for mixed media
           Mixtur, for five orchestral groups and electronics
1965 (37)   *Mikrophonie II*, for choir, Hammond organ, electronic
              instruments and tape
           Stop, for orchestra
           Solo (1965–66)
1966 (38)   *Telemusik*, electronic music
           Adieu, for flute, oboe, clarinet, horn and bassoon
           Hymnen, for electronics and music concrète (4-channel
              tape)
1967 (39)   *Prozession*, for Tam-tam, viola, elektronium, piano and
              electronics
1968 (40)   *Stimmung*, for six vocalists
           Kurzwellen, for piano, amplified instruments and
              electronics
           Aus den Sieben Tagen, fifteen compositions for ensemble
           Spiral, for one soloist with short-wave receiver
           Für Kommende Zeiten, seventeen texts for intuitive music
1969 (41)   *For Dr. K.*, for flute, bass clarinet, percussion, piano,
              viola and cello
           Fresco, for four orchestral groups
           Pole für 2 (1969–70)
           Expo für 3 (1969–70)
1970 (42)   *Mantra*, for two pianists
           Sternklang, for five groups
           Trans, for orchestra
1972 (44)   *Alphabet für Liège*
           Am Himmel Wandre Ich . . . . , Indianerlieder
           Ylem, for nineteen players/singers
1973–74 (45) *Inori*, for soloist and orchestra
1974 (46)   *Atmen gibt das leben . . . .* , for mixed choir
           Herbstmusik
           Vortrag uber Hu, for solo voice
1975 (47)   *Musik im Bauch*
           Tierkreis (Zodiac)

STRAUSS (Jr), Johann/1825–1899/Austria

1867 (42)   *Blue Danube Waltz*
1868 (43)   *Tales from the Vienna Woods*
1871 (46)   *Indigo und die vierzig Rauber*, operetta
1874 (49)   *Die Fledermaus*, operetta
1883 (58)   *Eine Nacht in Venedig*, operetta
1885 (60)   *Zigeunerbaron*, operetta
1887 (62)   *Simplizius*, operetta
1895 (70)   *Waldmeister*, operetta

STRAUSS, Richard/1864–1949/Germany

1876 (12)   *Festmarch*, for orchestra
1879 (15)   Overture in A minor

1880 (16)   Symphony in D minor
String Quartet in A major
1881–82 (17)   Violin Concerto in D minor
1882–83 (18)   Horn Concerto No. 1 in E♭ major
1883 (19)   *Concert Overture* in C minor
Piano Quartet in C minor (1883–84)
1884 (20)   Symphony in F minor
p. Serenade for Wind
p. Cello Sonata in F major
1886 (22)   *Aus Italien*, symphonic fantasia
Macbeth, symphonic poem (1886–90)
1888 (24)   *Don Juan*, symphonic poem
p. Violin Sonata in E♭ major
1889 (25)   *Tod und Verklaerung*, symphonic poem
1892–93 (28)   *Guntram*, opera (new version, 1940)
1894 (30)   *Also sprach Zarathustra*, symphonic poem
1895 (31)   *Till Eulenspiegel*, symphonic poem
1896 (32)   *Don Quixote*, fantasy variations for cello and orchestra
1898 (34)   *Ein Heldenleben*, symphonic poem
1901 (37)   *Feuersnot*, opera
1904 (40)   *Symphonia Domestica*
1905 (41)   *Salome*, opera
1906–08 (42–44)   *Elektra*, opera
1909–10 (45)   *Der Rosencavalier*, opera
1912 (48)   *Ariadne auf Naxos*, opera
1913 (49)   *Alpine Symphony*
1914 (50)   *Josephs-Legend*, ballet
Die Frau ohne Schatten, opera (1914–17)
1921 (57)   *Schlagobers*, ballet
1922–23 (58)   *Intermezzo*, opera
1924–27 (60–63)   *The Egyptian Helen*, opera
1930–32 (66–68)   *Arabella*, opera
1934 (70)   Symphony for wind instruments
1935 (71)   *The Silent Woman*, opera
Der Freidenstag, opera (1935–36)
1936–37 (72)   *Daphne*, opera
1938–40 (74–76)   *The Love of Danae*, opera (*fp*.1952)
1940–41 (76)   *Capriccio*, opera
1942 (78)   Horn Concerto No. 2 in E♭ major
1945 (81)   *Metamorphoses*, for twenty-three solo instruments
Oboe Concerto
1948 (84)   *Duet Concertino*, for clarinet, bassoon and strings
1950 (posthumous)   *fp.* Four Last Songs
Strauss also composed many songs.

STRAVINSKY, Igor/1882–1971/Russia

1905–07 (23–25)   Symphony in E♭ major
1908 (26)   *Scherzo fantastique*
Fireworks, for orchestra
Lament on the Death of Rimsky-Korsakov, for chorus and
orchestra

1910 (28)   *The Firebird*, ballet
           Petrouchka, ballet (1910–11, revised 1946–47)
1911 (29)   *The King of the Stars*, cantata
1913 (31)   *The Rite of Spring*, ballet
1914 (32)   *Le Rossignol* (The Nightingale), lyric tale in three acts
           (1908–14, revised 1962)
           Chansons plaisants, for voice and small orchestra
           Three pieces for string quartet
1915 (33)   *Rénard*, a burlesque
1916 (34)   *Berceuse du Chat*, for voice and three clarinets
1917 (35)   *Les Noces*, cantata-ballet (1917–23)
           Song of the Nightingale, symphonic poem
           The Soldier's Tale, opera-ballet
1918 (36)   *Ragtime*, for eleven instruments
           Four Russian Songs
1920 (38)   *Pulcinella*, ballet suite, after Pergolesi
           Symphonies for Wind Instruments
           Concertino, for string quartet
1921–22 (39)   *Mavra*, opera buffe in one act
1922–23 (40)   *Octet for Wind Instruments* (revised 1952)
1924 (42)   Concerto for piano and wind instruments
           Piano Sonata
1925 (43)   *Serenade* in A major, for piano
1927 (45)   *Oedipus Rex*, opera-oratorio
1928 (46)   *Apollo Musagetes*, ballet
           Le Baiser de la Fée, ballet
1929 (47)   *Capriccio*, for piano and orchestra
1930 (48)   *Symphony of Psalms*, for chorus and orchestra
1931 (49)   Violin Concerto in D major
1932 (50)   *Duo Concertante*, for violin and piano
1933 (51)   *Suite Italienne*, for cello and piano
1934 (52)   *Persephone*, melodrama for narrator, tenor, chorus,
           children's choir and orchestra
1935 (53)   Concerto for two pianos
1937 (55)   *Jeu des Cartes*, ballet
1938 (56)   *Dumbarton Oaks*, concerto for sixteen instruments, in E♭
           major
1940 (58)   Symphony in C major
1942 (60)   *Danses concertantes*
           Norwegian Moods
           Polka for Circus Elephants
1944 (62)   *Élégie*, for solo viola
           Sonata for two pianos
1945 (63)   *Symphony in Three Movements*
1946 (64)   *Ebony Concerto*, for clarinet and orchestra
           Concerto in D major for strings
1947 (65)   *Orpheus*, ballet
1948 (66)   *Mass*, for chorus and double wind quintet
1951 (69)   *The Rake's Progress*, opera
           Mass, for horns and orchestra
1952 (70)   Cantata on Old English Texts
1953 (71)   Septet

Three Songs from Shakespeare, for mezzo-soprano and
    piano
1954 (72) *In Memoriam Dylan Thomas*, for tenor, two tenor
    trombones, two bass trombones and string quartet
1955 (73) *Canticum sacrum*
1957 (75) *Agon*, ballet
    Threni (Lamentations of Jeremiah), for soloists, chorus
    and orchestra
1959 (77) *Movements*, for piano and orchestra
    Epitaphium, for flute, clarinet and harp
    Double Canon for string quartet
1960 (78) *Monumentus Pro Gesualdo*, for orchestra
1962 (80) *The Flood*, opera
    Abraham and Isaac, for baritone and orchestra
1963–64 (81) *In Memoriam Aldous Huxley*, variations for orchestra
1964 (82) *Elegy for J.F.K.*, for baritone or mezzo-soprano and three
    clarinets
    Fanfare for a new theater, for two trumpets
1966 (84) *Requiem Canticles*, for contralto and bass soli, chorus and
    orchestra

SUK, Josef/1874–1935/Czechoslovakia

1888 (14) Mass in B♮ major
1889 (15) *Fantasy*, for strings
    Piano Trio in C minor (1889–90)
1891 (17) *Dramatic Overture*
    Piano Quartet in A minor
1892 (18) *Serenade for Strings*
1893 (19) Piano Quintet in B minor
1896 (22) String Quartet No. 1 in B♮ major
1899 (25) Symphony No. 1 in E major
1903 (29) *Fantasy*, for violin and orchestra
1904 (30) *Prague*, symphonic poem
    Symphony No. 2 in C minor, *Asrael* (1904–06)
1907 (33) *A Summer Tale*, symphonic poem
1910–11 (36) String Quartet No. 2
1914 (40) *Meditation on a theme of an old Bohemian chorale*, for string
    quartet
1917 (43) *Harvestide*, symphonic poem
1919 (45) *Legend of Dead Victors*
    Towards a New Life
1931 (57) Mass in B♮ major

SULLIVAN, Sir Arthur/1842–1900/Great Britain

1862 (20) *The Tempest*, incidental music
1864 (22) *L'Ile enchantée*, ballet music
    Kenilworth, cantata
1866 (24) Cello Concerto
    Irish Symphony
    In Memoriam Overture

1867 (25) *Cox and Box*, operetta (libretto, Burnand)
1869 (27) *The Prodigal Son*, oratorio
1870 (28) *Overture di Ballo*, concert overture
1873 (31) *The Light of the World*, oratorio
1875 (33) *The Zoo*, operetta (libretto, Stephenson)
           Trial by Jury, operetta (libretto, Gilbert)
1877 (35) *The Sorcerer*, operetta (libretto, Gilbert)
           "The Lost Chord", song
1878 (36) *H.M.S. Pinafore*, operetta (libretto, Gilbert)
           Henry VIII, incidental music
           The Martyr of Antioch, oratorio
1880 (38) *The Pirates of Penzance*, operetta (libretto, Gilbert)
1881 (39) *Patience*, operetta (libretto, Gilbert)
1882 (40) *Iolanthe*, operetta (libretto, Gilbert)
1884 (42) *Princess Ida*, operetta (libretto, Gilbert)
1885 (43) *The Mikado*, operetta (libretto, Gilbert)
1886 (44) *The Golden Legend*, cantata
1887 (45) *Ruddigore*, operetta (libretto, Gilbert)
1888 (46) *The Yeomen of the Guard*, operetta (libretto, Gilbert)
1889 (47) *The Gondoliers*, operetta (libretto, Gilbert)
1891 (49) *Ivanhoe*, opera (libretto, Sturgis)
1892 (50) *Haddon Hall*, opera (libretto, Grundy)
1893 (51) *Utopia, Ltd.*, operetta (libretto, Gilbert)
1895 (53) *The Chieftan*, operetta (libretto, Burnand)
1896 (54) *The Grand Duke*, operetta (libretto, Gilbert)
1897 (55) Te Deum
1898 (56) *The Beauty Stone*, opera (libretto, Pinero and Conyers
           Carr)
1899 (57) *The Rose of Persia*, operetta (libretto, Hood)
1901 (posthumous) *The Emerald Isle*, operetta (libretto, Hood),
           completed by German (*q.v.*)

SWEELINCK, Jan/1562–1621/Holland

1592–94 (30–32) *p. Chansons françaises*, in three parts
1612 (50) *p. Rimes françoises et italiennes*
1619 (57) *p. Cantiones sacrae*
Sweelinck also composed:
Psaeumes mis en musique
Many organ, harpsichord and choral (sacred and secular) works.

SZYMANOWSKI, Karol/1883–1937/Poland

1905 (22) *Concert Overture*
1907 (24) Symphony No. 1 in F minor
1909 (26) Symphony No. 2 in B♭ major
1912–13 (29) *Hagith*, opera
1915–16 (32) Symphony No. 3, *Song of the Night*, with tenor and
           chorus
1917 (34) Violin Concerto No. 1
           String Quartet in C major
1920–24 (37–41) *King Roger*, opera

1924 (41) *Prince Potemkin*, incidental music
1926 (43) *Harnasie*, ballet
             Stabat Mater
1931–32 (48) *Symphonie Concertante*, for piano
1932–33 (49) Violin Concerto No. 2
Szymanowski also composed symphonic poems, piano music, choral
music and songs.

TALLIS, Thomas/*c*.1505–1585/Great Britain

1567 (*c*.62) *p*. Psalms tunes in "Archbishop Parker's Psalter"
Tallis composed many Latin masses, lamentations, motets (including
Spem in alium, for forty-part choir), pieces for keyboard, viols, etc.

TANSMAN, Alexandre/b.1897/Poland

1916 (19) Symphony No. 1
1922 (25) *Sextuor*, ballet
1924 (27) Sinfonietta
1925 (28) Symphony No. 2
             La Nuit Kurde, opera (1925–27)
1926 (29) Piano Concerto No. 1
1927 (30) Piano Concerto No. 2
1928 (31) *Lumières*
1929 (32) *Le cercle éternel*, ballet
1930 (33) *Triptych*, for string orchestra
1931 (34) Symphony No. 3, *Symphony Concertante* (1931–32)
             Concertino, for piano
1932 (35) *La Grande Ville*, ballet
             Two symphonic movements
1933 (36) *Partita*, for string orchestra
1936 (39) Viola Concerto
             Two Intermezzi
1937 (40) *Bric-a-Brac*
             Fantasy for violin
             Fantasy for cello
1938 (41) *Le toison d'or*
             Symphony No. 4
1942 (45) Symphony No. 5
1943 (46) Symphony No. 6, *In Memoriam*
             Symphonic études
1944 (47) Symphony No. 7
             Le roi qui jouait le fou
             Partita, for piano and orchestra
1945 (48) *Concertino*, for guitar and orchestra
1947 (50) *Isiah the Prophet*
             Music for Orchestra
1948 (51) *Music for Strings*
1949 (52) *Ricercari*
             Tombeau de Chopin, for strings
1950 (53) *Phèdre*, ballet
1951 (54) Symphony No. 8

1955 (58)   *Le Sermant*, opera
            Capriccio
            Concerto for orchestra
1961 (64)   *Psalms*, for tenor, chorus and orchestra
1962 (65)   *Resurrection*, for orchestra
            Six symphonic studies, for orchestra
1963 (66)   Six Movements for string orchestra
1964 (67)   *Il Usignolo di Boboli*, opera
1966 (69)   *Concertino*, for oboe and chamber orchestra
1968 (71)   Four Movements for orchestra
1969 (72)   *Concertino*, for flute and chamber orchestra
            Hommage à Erasme de Rotherdam, for orchestra

TAVENER, John/b.1944/Great Britain

1962 (18)   Piano Concerto (1962—63)
            Three Holy Sonnets, for voice and orchestra
1963—64 (19) *Three Sections*, from T.S. Eliot's "The Four Quartets",
            for tenor and piano
1964 (20)   *The Cappemakers*, for two narrators, two soloists, male
            chorus and instruments
1965 (21)   Chamber Concerto (revised 1968)
            Cain and Abel, dramatic cantata
            The Whale, for choir and orchestra (1965—66)
1967—68 (23) *Grandma's Footsteps*, for chamber orchestra
            Three surrealist songs, for mezzo-soprano, tape and piano
            doubling bongoes
1968 (24)   *In Alium*, for high soprano and orchestra
1969 (25)   *Celtic Requiem*, for voices and orchestra
1970 (26)   *Nomine Jesu*, for voices and orchestra
            Coplas, for voices and tape
1971 (27)   *In Memoriam Igor Stravinsky*, for two alto flutes, organ
            and bells
            Responsorium in Memory of Annon Lee Silver, for two
            soprano soli, mixed chorus and two flutes
1972 (28)   *Variations on "Three Blind Mice"*, for orchestra
            Ma fin est mon commencement, for voices and instruments
            Little Requiem for Father Malachy Lynch, for voices and
            instruments
            Ultimos Ritos, for voices and orchestra, including
            amplified instruments
            Canciones espanolas, for voices and instruments
1973 (29)   *Requiem for Father Malachy*, for choir and instruments
            Thérèse, opera (1973—76)

TAYLOR, (Joseph) Deems/1885—1966/U.S.A.

1912 (27)   *The Siren Song*, for orchestra
1914 (29)   *The Highwayman*, for baritone, women's voices and
            orchestra
            The Chambered Nautilus, for chorus and orchestra
1918 (33)   *The Portrait of a Lady*, for eleven instruments

1919 (34)   *Through the Looking-glass*, suite for chamber orchestra
            (version for full orchestra, 1922)
1923 (38)   *A Kiss in Xanadu*, pantomime in two scenes, for two
            pianos
1925 (40)   *Jurgen*, for orchestra
            Fantasy on Two Themes, for orchestra
            Circus Days, for jazz orchestra (version for full orchestra,
            1933)
1926 (41)   *The King's Henchman*, opera
1930 (45)   *Peter Ibbetson*, opera
1936 (51)   *Lucrece*, for string quartet
1937 (52)   *Ramuntcho*, opera
            Casanova, ballet
1941 (56)   *Processional*, for orchestra
1943 (58)   *Christmas Overture*, for orchestra
1945 (60)   *Elegy*, for orchestra
1950 (65)   *Restoration Suite*, for orchestra
1954 (69)   *The Dragon*, opera

TCHAIKOVSKY, Peter Ilych/1840−1893/Russia

1866 (26)   Symphony No. 1 in G minor, *Winter Daydreams*
1868 (28)   *Fate*, symphonic poem
1869 (29)   *Romeo and Juliet*, overture (final version 1880)
1871 (31)   String Quartet in D major
1872 (32)   Symphony No. 2 in C minor, *Little Russian*
1874−75 (34) Piano Concerto No. 1 in B♭ minor
            String Quartet in F major
1875 (35)   *Swan Lake*, ballet (*fp.* 1895)
            Symphony No. 3 in D major, *Polish*
            String Quartet in E♭ minor
1876 (36)   *Variations on a Rococo theme*, for cello and orchestra
            Slavonic March, for orchestra
1877 (37)   Symphony No. 4 in F minor
            Francesca da Rimini, symphonic fantasy
            Waltz-Scherzo, for violin and orchestra
1878 (38)   Violin Concerto in D major
1879 (39)   *Eugene Onegin*, opera
            Capriccio Italien, for orchestra
            Piano Concerto No. 2 in G major (1879−80)
1880 (40)   *Serenade for Strings*
1881 (41)   *Joan of Arc*, opera
1882 (42)   *1812 Overture*
            Piano Trio in A minor
1884 (44)   *Mazeppa*, opera
            Concert-Fantasy, for piano and orchestra
1885 (45)   *Manfred Symphony*
1888 (48)   *The Sleeping Beauty*, ballet
            Hamlet, overture
            Symphony No. 5 in E minor
1890 (50)   *The Queen of Spades*, opera
1892 (52)   *Iolanthe*, opera

Casse Noisette (The Nutcracker), ballet
p. String Sextet in D minor
1893 (53) Symphony No. 6 in B minor, *Pathétique*
Piano Concerto No. 3

TELEMANN, Georg/1681–1767/Germany

1708–12 (27–31) Trio Sonata in E♭ major
1715–20 (34–39) Concerto in A major
Suite in D minor
1716 (35) *Die Kleine Kammermusik*
Six suites for violin, querflute and piano
1718 (37) Six trios for two violins and cello, with bass continuo
1723 (42) *Hamburger Ebb und Fluht*, overture in C major
1725 (44) *Pimpinone*, opera
1728 (47) *Der getreuer Musikmeister*, cantata
1759 (78) St. Mark Passion
Telemann also composed:
40 operas
600 overtures
44 liturgical passions
Several oratorios
Innumerable cantatas and psalms.

THOMAS, Ambroise/1811–1896/France

1832 (21) *Hermann et Ketty*, cantata
1837 (26) *La Double échelle*, opera
1838 (27) *Le Perruquier de la Regence*, opera
1839 (28) *La Panier fleuri*, opera
La Gipsy, ballet
1840 (29) *Carlino*, opera
1841 (30) *Le Comte de Carmagnola*, opera
1842 (31) *Le Guerillero*, opera
1843 (32) *Angélique et Medor*, opera
Mina, opera
1846 (35) *Betty*, ballet
1849 (38) *Le Caïd*, opera
1850 (39) *Le Songe d'une nuit d'été*, opera
1851 (40) *Raymond*, opera
1853 (42) *La Tonelli*, opera
1855 (44) *La Cour de Célimène*, opera
1857 (46) *Psyché*, opera
Le Carnaval de Venise, opera
Messe solenelle
1860 (49) *Le Roman d'Elvire*, opera
1865 (54) *Marche religieuse*, for orchestra
1866 (55) *Mignon*, opera
1868 (57) *Hamlet*, grand opera
1874 (63) *Gille et Gillotin*, opera
1882 (71) *Françoise de Rimini*, opera
1889 (78) *La Tempête*, ballet

1923 (27) *Two Sentimental Tangoes*
1926 (30) *Sonata da Chiesa*, for five instruments
1928 (32) *Symphony on a Hymn Tune*
1929 (33) *Five Portraits*, for four clarinets
1930 (34) Violin Sonata
1931 (35) Quartet No. 1
            Serenade, for flute and violin
            Four Portraits, for violin and piano
            Stabat Mater
1932 (36) Quartet No. 2
1934 (38) *Four Saints in Three Acts*, opera
1937 (41) *Filling Station*, ballet
1941 (45) Symphony No. 2
1942 (46) *Canon for Dorothy Thomson*
            The Mayor La Guardia Waltzes
1943 (47) Flute Sonata
1944 (48) Suite No. 1, *Portraits*
            Suite No. 2
1947 (51) *The Mother of Us All*, opera
            The Seine at Night, for orchestra
1948 (52) *Wheatfield at Noon*, for orchestra
            Acadian Songs and Dances
1949 (53) Cello Concerto
1951 (55) *Five Songs of William Blake*, for baritone and orchestra
1952 (56) *Sea Piece with Birds*, for orchestra
1954 (58) Concerto for flute, strings and percussion
1957 (61) *The Lively Arts*, fugue
1959 (63) *Fugues and Cantilenas*, for orchestra
            Collected Poems
1960 (64) Mass, for solo voice and piano (version with orchestra, 1962)
            Missa pro defunctis (Requiem Mass), for men's chorus, women's chorus and orchestra
1961 (65) *A Solemn Music*, for orchestra (transcribed from original band score)
1962 (66) *A Joyful Fugue*, to follow *A Solemn Music*
            Pange lingua, for organ
1964 (68) *The Feast of Love*, for baritone and orchestra
            Autumn Concertino, for harp, strings and percussion
1966 (70) *Lord Byron*, opera (1966–68)
            Fantasy in Homage to an Earlier England, for orchestra
            The Nativity, for mixed chorus, soloists and orchestra (1966–67)
            Étude, for cello and piano
1967 (71) *Shipwreck and Love Scene*, from Byron's "Don Juan", for orchestra and tenor soloist
1973 (77) *Cantata based on Nonsense Rhymes*
Thomson also composed 4 piano sonatas.

TIPPETT, Sir Michael/b.1905/Great Britain

1934–35 (29) String Quartet No. 1 in A major (revised 1943)
1936–37 (31) Piano Sonata (revised 1942)
1937 (32) *A Song of Liberty*
1938–39 (33) Concerto for double string orchestra
1939–41 (34) *A Child of Our Time*, oratorio
        Fantasia on a Theme by Handel, for piano and orchestra
1941–42 (36) String Quartet No. 2
1942 (37) *The Source* and *The Windhover*, madrigals
1943 (38) *Boyhood's End*, song cycle
        Plebs angelica, motet for double chorus
1944 (39) Symphony No. 1 (1944–45)
        The Weeping Babe, motet for soprano solo and chorus
1945–46 (40) String Quartet No. 3
1946 (41) *Little Music*, for strings
1947–52 (42–47) *The Midsummer Marriage*, opera
1948 (43) Suite in D major
1950–51 (45) *Heart's Assurance*, song cycle for high voice and
        piano
1952 (47) *Dance Clarion Air*, madrigal
1953 (48) *Fantasia Concertante on a Theme by Corelli*, for strings
        Divertimento for chamber orchestra "Sellingers Round"
        (1953–54)
        Piano Concerto (1953–55)
1955 (50) Sonata for four horns
1956–57 (51) Symphony No. 2
1958 (53) *King Priam*, opera (1958–61)
        Crown of the Year, for chorus and orchestra
        Prelude, Recitative and Aria, for flute, oboe and harpsichord
1961 (56) *Three songs for Achilles*, for voice and guitar
        Magnificat and Nunc Dimittis
1962 (57) Concerto for orchestra (1962–63)
        Praeludium, for brass, bells and percussion
        Piano Sonata No. 2, in one movement
        Songs for Ariel
1964 (59) *Prologue and Epilogue*, for choir and orchestra
1965 (60) *Vision of St. Augustine*, for baritone, choir and orchestra
        The Shires Suite, for choir and orchestra (1965–70)
1966–70 (61–65) *The Knot Garden*, opera
1970 (65) Symphony No. 3, with soprano soloist (1970–72)
        Songs for Dov, for tenor solo and small orchestra
1972–73 (67) Piano Sonata No. 3

TURINA, Joaquín/1882–1949/Spain

1907 (25) Piano Quintet
1911 (29) Quartet
1912 (30) *La Procesion del Rocio*, symphonic poem
1914 (32) *Margot*, lyric comedy
1915 (33) *Evangelio*, symphonic poem
1916 (34) *Navidad*, incidental music
1917 (35) *La Adultera penitente*, incidental music

1918 (36) *Poema en forma de canciones*
1920 (38) *Sinfonia Sevillana*
           Danzas fantasticas
1921 (39) *Canto a Sevillana*, song cycle
1923 (41) *Jardin de Oriente*
1926 (44) *La oracion del torero*, for quartet
           Piano Trio
1928 (46) *Ritmos*, choreographic fantasy
1929 (47) *Triptico*
1931 (49) *Rapsodia sinfonica*, for piano and strings
           Piano Quartet
1933 (51) Piano Trio
1935 (53) *Serenade*, for quartet

VAUGHAN WILLIAMS, Ralph/1872–1958/Great Britain

1888 (16) Piano Trio
1900 (28) *Bucolic Suite*, for orchestra
1903 (31) *The House of Life*, song cycle (No. 2 is "Silent Noon")
1904 (32) Songs of Travel
1906 (34) *Norfolk Rhapsodies* Nos. 1–3, for orchestra (Nos. 2 and 3
           are lost)
1907 (35) *In the Fen country*, symphonic impression
           Towards the Unknown Region, song for chorus and
              orchestra
1908 (36) String Quartet in G minor
1909 (37) *A Sea Symphony* (Symphony No. 1), words by Walt
              Whitman, for soprano, baritone, chorus and orchestra
           The Wasps, incidental music
           On Wenlock Edge, song cycle
1910 (38) *Fantasia on a Theme by Thomas Tallis*, for strings (No. 9 in
              Archbishop Parker's Psalter, *p.* 1567)
1911 (39) *Five Mystical Songs*, for baritone, mixed chorus and
              orchestra
1912 (40) Fantasia on Christmas Carols
           Phantasy Quintet, for strings
1913 (41) *A London Symphony* (Symphony No. 2)
1920 (48) *Shepherd of the Delectable Mountains*, one-act opera (now
              also forms Act IV of *The Pilgrim's Progress*) (1920–21)
           The Lark Ascending, for violin and small orchestra
           Suite de Ballet, for flute and piano
           Mass in G minor (1920–21)
           Three Preludes for organ
1921 (49) *A Pastoral Symphony* (Symphony No. 3)
1923 (51) *Old King Cole*, ballet
1924 (52) *Hugh the Drover*, opera
1925 (53) *Concerto Accademico*, for violin and string orchestra
           Flos Campi, suite for viola, small wordless choir and small
              orchestra
           Sancta civitas, oratorio
1927 (55) *Along the Field*, eight songs (Housman) for voice and
              violin

1928 (56) *Sir John in Love*, opera
Te Deum, in G major
1929 (57) *Benedicite*, for soprano, mixed choir and orchestra
1930 (58) *Job, a Masque for Dancing*, for orchestra
Prelude and Fugue in C minor, for orchestra
1931 (59) Symphony No. 4 in F minor (1931–34)
Piano Concerto in C major
In Windsor Forest, cantata
1932 (60) *Magnificat*, for contralto, women's chorus, solo flute and
orchestra
1933 (61) *The Running Set*, for medium orchestra
1934 (62) *Fantasia on Greensleeves*, for orchestra
Suite for viola and small orchestra
1935 (63) *Five Tudor Portraits*, choral suite in five movements
1936 (64) *Riders to the Sea*, opera in one act
The Poisoned Kiss, romantic extravaganza with spoken
dialogue, for thirteen soloists, mixed chorus and
orchestra
Dona nobis pacem, cantata
1937 (65) Festival Te Deum, in F major
1938 (66) *The Bridal Day*, masque
Serenade to Music, for sixteen solo voices and orchestra
1939 (67) *Five Variants of Dives and Lazurus*, for strings and harp
1940 (68) *Six Choral Songs — to be sung in time of war*
Valiant for Truth, motet
1941 (69) *England, My England*, for baritone, double chorus, unison
voices and orchestra
1942 (70) *Coastal Command*, orchestral suite from the film
1943 (71) Symphony No. 5 in D major
1944 (72) Symphony No. 6 in E minor (1944–47)
Concerto for oboe and strings
A Song of Thanksgiving, for soprano, speaker, mixed choir
and orchestra
String Quartet No. 2, in A minor
1945 (75) *Story of a Flemish Farm*, orchestral suite from the film
1946–48 (74–76) *Partita*, for double string orchestra
Introduction and fugue, for two pianos
1949 (77) *Fantasia (quasi variazione) on the "Old 104th" Psalm Tune*,
for piano, chorus, organ (optional) and orchestra
An Oxford Elegy, for speaker, chorus and small orchestra
Folk-songs of the Four Seasons, cantata
1950 (78) Concerto Grosso, for string orchestra
The Sons of Light, cantata
Sun, Moon, Stars and Man, song cycle
1951 (79) *The Pilgrim's Progress*, a Morality in a Prologue, Four
Acts, and an Epilogue, for thirty-four soloists, chorus
and orchestra
Romance in D♭ major, for harmonica, strings and piano
1952 (80) *Sinfonia Antartica* (Symphony No. 7), in five movements
1954 (82) Concerto for Bass Tuba and Orchestra, in F minor
This Day (Hodie), a Christmas cantata
Violin Sonata in A minor

1955 (83) Symphony No. 8 in D minor (this was the first of the
             symphonies which Vaughan Williams allowed to be
             given a number)
1956 (84) *A Vision of Aeroplanes*, motet
             Symphony No. 9 in E minor (revised 1958)
             Two Organ Preludes, *Romanza* and *Toccata*
             Epithalamion, cantata (1956–57)
             Ten Blake Songs, for tenor and oboe
1958 (86) *The First Nowell*, nativity play for soloist, mixed chorus
             and small orchestra
             Vocalises, for soprano and B♭ clarinet
             Four Last Songs, for voice and piano
             Thomas the Rhymer, opera in three acts (uncompleted at
             Vaughan Williams death; exists in short score only)

VERDI, Guiseppe / 1813–1901 / Italy

1839 (26) *fp. Oberto*, opera
1842 (29) *fp. Nabucco*, opera
1843 (30) *fp. I Lombardi*, opera
1844 (31) *fp. Ernani*, opera
             fp. I Due Foscari, opera
1845 (32) *fp. Alzira*, opera
             fp. Giovanna d'Arco, opera
1846 (33) *fp. Attila*, opera
1847 (34) *fp. Macbeth*, opera
             fp. I Masnadieri, opera
1849 (36) *fp. Luisa Miller*, opera
1851 (38) *fp. Rigoletto*, opera
1853 (40) *fp. La Traviata*, opera
             fp. Il Trovatore, opera
1855 (42) *fp. I Vespri Siciliani*, opera
1857 (44) *fp. Araldo*, opera
             fp. Simon Boccanegra, opera
1859 (46) *fp. Un Ballo in Maschera*, opera
1862 (49) *fp. La Forza del Destino*, opera
             fp. Inno delle Nazioni, for chorus
1867 (54) *fp. Don Carlos*, opera
1871 (58) *fp. Aida*, opera
1873 (60) String Quartet in E minor
1874 (61) Requiem Mass
1887 (74) *fp. Otello*, opera
1889–98 (76–85) Four sacred pieces
1893 (80) *fp. Falstaff*, opera

VILLA-LOBOS, Heitor / 1887–1959 / Brazil

1908 (21) *Recouli*, for small orchestra
1910 (23) *Suite dos canticos sertanejos*, for small orchestra
1912 (25) *Aglaia*, opera
1913 (26) *Suite da terra*, for small orchestra
             Suite for piano

1914 (27) *Izaht*, opera
           Suite popular Brasiliera
           Ibericarabé, symphonic poem
           Dansas dos Indios Mesticos, for orchestra
           Suite for strings
1915 (28) String Quartets Nos. 1 and 2
1916 (29) Symphony No. 1, *The Unforseen*
           Centauro de Ouro, symphonic poem
           Miremis, symphonic poem
           Naufragio de Kleonica, symphonic poem
           Marcha religiosa No. 1, for orchestra
           Sinfonietta on a theme by Mozart
           Cello Concerto
           String Quartet No. 3
1917 (30) *Uirapurú*, ballet
           Amazonas, ballet for orchestra
           Symphony No. 2, *The Ascension*
           Fantasia, symphonic poem
           Iara, symphonic poem
           Lobishome, symphonic poem
           Saci Perêrê, symphonic poem
           Tédio de alvorado, symphonic poem
           Sexteto mistico, for flute, clarinet, saxophone, harp,
               celesta and double-bass
           String Quartet No. 4
1918 (31) *Jesus*, opera
           Marcha religiosa No. 3, for orchestra
           Marcha religiosa No. 7, for orchestra
           Vidapura, oratorio
1919 (32) *Zoé*, opera
           Symphony No. 3, *The War*
           Symphony No. 4, *The Victory*
           Dansa frenetica, for orchestra
1920 (33) Symphony No. 5, *The Peace*
           Dansa diabolica, for orchestra
           Chôros No. 1, for guitar
1921 (34) *Malazarte*, opera
           Quartet for harp, celesta, flute and saxophone, with
               women's voices
1923 (36) Suite for voice and viola
1924 (37) *Chôros No. 2*, for flute and clarinet
           Chôros No. 7, for flute, oboe, clarinet, saxophone, bassoon,
               violin and cello
1925 (38) *Chôros No. 3*, for clarinet, saxophone, bassoon, three
               horns and trombones, with male voice choir
           Chôros No. 8, for two pianos and orchestra
           Chôros No. 10, for choir and orchestra
1926 (39) *Chôros No. 4*, for three horns and trombones
           Chôros No. 5, for piano
           Chôros No. 6, for orchestra
           Chôros No. 6 bis, for violin and cello
1928 (41) *Chôros No. 11*, for piano and orchestra

Chôros No. 14, for orchestra, band and choir
1929 (42) *Suite sugestiva*, for voice and orchestra
Chôros No. 9, for orchestra
Chôros No. 12, for orchestra
Chôros No. 13, for two orchestras and band
Introdução aos Chôros, for orchestra
Twelve Studies for guitar
1930 (43) *Bachianas Brasilieras No. 1*, for orchestra: Preludio, Aria, Fuga
Bachianas Brasilieras No. 2, for orchestra: Preludio, Aria, Dansa, Tocata
1931 (44) String Quartet No. 5
1932 (45) *Caixinha de Bôas Festas*, ballet (also an orchestral suite)
1933 (46) *Pedra Bonita*, ballet
1936 (49) *Bachianas Brasilieras No. 4*, for piano: Preludio, Aria, Coral Dansa (1930–36)
1937 (50) *Currupira*, ballet
Sebastiao
Descobrimento do Brasil, four suites for chorus and orchestra
1938 (51) *Bachianas Brasilieras No. 3*, for piano and orchestra: Preludio, Aria, Tocata
Bachianas Brasilieras No. 6, for flute and bassoon: Aria, Fantasia
String Quartet No. 6
1939 (52) *New York Skyline*, for orchestra (Villa-Lobos "drew" the melody by following the outline of skyscrapers on graph paper. He then harmonized the resultant melodic line and scored it for orchestra.)
1940 (53) *Saudades da juventude*, Suite I
Preludes for guitar
1942 (55) *Bachianas Brasilieras No. 7*, for orchestra: Preludio, Giga, Tocata, Fuga
String Quartet No. 7
1944 (57) *Bachianas Brasilieras No. 8*, for orchestra: Preludio, Aria, Tocata, Fuga
String Quartet No. 8
1945 (58) *Bachianas Brasilieras No. 5*, for voice and orchestra of cellos: Aria, Dansa (1938–45)
Bachianas Brasilieras No. 9, for vocal orchestra
Piano Concerto No. 1
Fantasia for cello
Villa-Lobos also composed much chamber music and many songs.

VIVALDI, Antonio/*c*.1675–1741/Italy

1705 (*c*.30) *p.* Suonate da camera a tre, Op. 1
1709 (*c*.34) *p.* Sonate a violino e basso per il cambala, Op. 2
c.1712 (*c*.37) *p.* Twelve concerti, *L'Estro armonico*, Op. 3
p. Twelve concerti, *La Stravaganza*, Op. 4 (*c*.1712–13)
1713 (*c*.38) *fp.* Ottone in Villa, opera
1714 (*c*.39) *fp.* Orlando finto pazzo, opera

Moyses deus Pharaonis, oratorio
1715 (c.40) fp. Nerone fatto Cesare, opera
1716 (c.41) fp. Arsilda Regine di Ponto, opera
             Juditha triumphans, oratorio
             p. Six sonate; four for violin solo and bass, two for two
                violins and basso continuo, Op. 5
             p. Sei concerti a cinque, Op. 6 (1716–c.1717)
             p. Sette concerti a cinque, Books I and II, Op. 7
                (1716–c.1717)
1717 (c.42) fp. Tieteberga, opera
1718 (c.43) fp. Scanderbeg, opera
1720 (c.45) fp. La Verità in cimento, opera
1721 (c.46) fp. Silvia, opera
1722 (c.47) L' Adorazione delli tre Re Magi, oratorio
1724 (c.49) fp. Giustino, opera
c.1725 (c.50) p. Il cimento dell'Armonia e dell'Inventione, twelve
                concerti of which four are known as The Four Seasons,
                Op. 8
1726 (c.51) Cunegonda. opera
1727 (c.52) Ipermestra, opera
1728 (c.53) Rosilena ed Oronta, opera
             p. Twelve concerti, Le Cetra, Op. 9
1729–30 (c.54) p. Sei concerti a flauto traverso, due violini, alto
                (viola), organo e violoncello, Op. 10
             p. Sei concerti a violino principale, Op. 11
             p. Sei concerti a violino principale, Op. 12
1732 (c.57) fp. La fida ninfa, opera
1733 (c.58) fp. Motezuma, opera
1734 (c.59) fp. L'Olimpiade, opera
1735 (c.60) fp. Griselda, opera
             fp. Aristide, opera
1736 (c.61) fp. Ginevra, Principessa di Scozia, opera
1737 (c.62) fp. Catone in Utica, opera
             p. Il pastor fido, sonates pour la musette, viele, flute,
                hautbois, violon avec la Basso continuo, Op. 13
                (c.1737)
1738 (c.63) fp. L'Oracolo in Messenia, opera
1739 (c.64) fp. Feraspe, opera
c.1740 (c.65) p. Six sonates a violincelle et basse, Op. 14
Vivaldi's total output in the concerto genre numbers over 400,
including 220 solo concerti, some 60 concerti ripieni, 48 bassoon
concerti, 25 cello concerti, plus many works for various instruments.
There are about 46 known operas of the 100 that Vivaldi claimed to
have written.

WAGNER, Richard/1813–1883/Germany

1832 (19) Symphony in C major
1840 (27) Faust, overture
1842 (29) fp. Rienzi, opera
1843 (30) fp. The Flying Dutchman, opera
1845 (32) fp. Tannhäuser, opera

1851 (38) *fp. Lohengrin*, opera
1857–58 (44) The *Wesendonck Lieder*, five songs with orchestra
1865 (52) *fp. Tristan und Isolde*, music drama
1868 (55) *fp. Die Meistersinger von Nürnberg*, opera
1869 (56) *fp. Das Rheingold* (No. 1 of *Der Ring des Nibelungen*)
1870 (57) *fp. Die Walküre* (No. 2 of *Der Ring des Nibelungen*)
              Seigfried Idyll, for orchestra
1876 (63) *fp. Siegfried* (No. 3 of *Der Ring des Nibelungen*)
              fp. Götterdämmerung (No. 4 of *Der Ring des Nibelungen*)
1882 (69) *fp. Parsifal*, religious music drama

WALTON, Sir William/b.1902/Great Britain

1916 (14) Piano Quartet
1922 (20) *fp.* (privately) *Façade—An Entertainment*, for reciter and
              chamber ensemble
1925 (23) *Portsmouth Point*, overture
1926 (24) *Siesta*, for orchestra
1927 (25) Viola Concerto (soloist at *fp.* was Hindemith, *q.v.*)
              Sinfonia Concertante, for piano and orchestra
1931 (29) *fp. Belshazzar's Feast*, for baritone, chorus and orchestra
1934 (32) *fp.* Symphony No. 1 (first three movements only,
              performed in full 1935)
              Escape Me Never, ballet from the film
1937 (35) *Crown Imperial*, coronation march for orchestra
              In Honour of the City, for chorus and orchestra
1939 (37) Violin Concerto
1940 (38) *The Wise Virgins*, ballet (arranged from the music of
              J.S. Bach)
1941 (39) *Scapino*, overture
1942 (40) *Prelude and Fugue (The Spitfire)*, for orchestra
1943 (41) *Henry V*, incidental music for the film
              The Quest, ballet
1947 (45) *Hamlet*, incidental music for the film
              String Quartet in A minor
1949 (47) Violin Sonata
1953 (51) *Orb and Sceptre*, coronation march for orchestra
              Coronation Te Deum
1954 (52) *Troilus and Cressida*, opera
1955 (53) *Richard III*, incidental music for the film
              Johannesburg Festival Overture
1956 (54) Cello Concerto
1957 (55) *Partita*, for orchestra
1960 (58) Symphony No. 2
              fp. Anon. in Love, six songs for tenor and guitar
1961 (59) *Gloria*, for contralto, tenor and bass soli, mixed choir and
              orchestra
1962 (60) *fp. A Song for the Lord Mayor's Table*, cycle of six songs
              for soprano and piano
1963 (61) *Variations on a Theme of Hindemith*, for orchestra (theme
              from Hindemith's *Nobilissima Visione*)
1965 (63) *The Twelve*, for choir and orchestra, or organ

1966 (64)   Missa Brevis
1967 (65)   *The Bear*, one-act opera for three solo voices and chamber
             orchestra
1968 (66)   *Capriccio Burlesca*, for orchestra
1970 (68)   *Improvisations on an Impromptu of Benjamin Britten*, for
             orchestra
1972 (70)   *Jubilate Deo*, for double mixed chorus and organ
             Sonata for string orchestra, arranged from the String
               Quartet
             Five bagatelles for guitar
1974 (72)   *Cantico del Sole*
             Magnificat and *Nunc Dimittis*

WARLOCK, Peter (Philip Heseltine)/1894–1930/Great Britain

1917 (23)   *An Old Song*, for small orchestra
1922 (28)   *Serenade for Frederick Delius*, for orchestra
1923 (29)   *The Curlew*, song cycle for voice, flute, English horn and
             string quartet
1926 (32)   *Capriol Suite*, for strings (also arranged for full orchestra)

WEBER, Carl Maria von/1786–1826/Germany

1800 (14)   *Das Waldmädchen*, opera
1801 (15)   *Peter Schmoll und seine Nachbarn*, opera
1806–07 (20) Symphony No. 1 in C major
1807 (21)   Symphony No. 2 in C major
1810 (24)   Piano Concerto No. 1 in C major
1811 (25)   *Abu Hassan*, opera
             Bassoon Concerto
             Clarinet Concerto No. 1 in F minor
             Clarinet Concerto No. 2 in E♭ major
             Concertino for clarinet, in C minor and E♭ major
1812 (26)   Piano Concerto No. 2 in E♭ major
             Piano Sonata No. 1 in C major
1815 (29)   Concertino for horn, in E minor
             Quintet for clarinet and strings, in E♭ major
1816 (30)   Piano Sonata No. 2 in A♭ major
             Piano Sonata No. 3 in D minor
1819 (33)   *Invitation to the Dance*, for piano (orchestrated by
             Berlioz, 1841)
1821 (35)   *fp. Der Freischütz*, opera
             Concertstücke, for piano and orchestra, in E minor
1822 (36)   Piano Sonata No. 4, in E minor
1823 (37)   *fp. Euryanthe*, opera
1826 (40)   *fp. Oberon*, opera

WEBERN, Anton von/1883–1945/Austria

1908 (25)   *Passacaglia*, for orchestra, Op. 1
             Entfllieht auf Leichten Kahnan, for chorus, Op. 2
             Five Lieder, Op. 3

Five Lieder, Op. 4 (1908–09)
1909 (26)   Five Movements for string quartet, Op. 5
1910 (27)   Six pieces for large orchestra, Op. 6
Four pieces for violin and piano, Op. 7 (1910–15)
1911–12 (28)   Two Lieder, Op. 8
1913 (30)   Six Bagatelles for string quartet, Op. 9
Five pieces for orchestra, Op. 10 (1911–13)
1914 (31)   Three little pieces for cello and piano, Op. 11
1915–17 (32–34)   Four Lieder, Op. 12
1914–18 (31–35)   Four Lieder, with thirteen instruments, Op. 13
1917–21 (34–38)   Six Lieder, with violin, clarinet, bass clarinet,
viola and cello, Op. 14
1917–11 (34–39)   Five Geistliche Lieder, Op. 15
1924 (41)   Five canons, for voice, clarinet and bass clarinet, Op. 16
Six Volkstexte, Op. 17
1925 (42)   Three Lieder, Op. 18
1926 (43)   Two Lieder, Op. 19
1927 (44)   String Trio, Op. 20
1928 (45)   Symphony for small orchestra, Op. 21
1930 (47)   Quartet for violin, clarinet, saxophone and piano, Op. 22
1934 (51)   Three Gesänge from *Viae invaie*, Op. 23
Concerto for flute, oboe, clarinet, horn, trumpet, trombone,
violin, viola and piano, Op. 24
1935 (52)   Three Lieder, Op. 25
Das Augenlicht, for mixed chorus and orchestra, Op. 26
1936 (53)   Variations for piano, Op. 27
1938 (55)   String Quartet, Op. 28
1939 (56)   Cantata No. 1, *Jone*, Op. 29
1940 (57)   Variations for orchestra, Op. 30
1941–43 (58–60)   Cantata No. 2, *Jone*, Op. 31

WEINBERGER, Jaromir/1896–1967/Bohemia (Czechoslovakia)

1927 (31)   *Schwanda the Bagpiper*, opera
1929 (33)   *Christmas*, for orchestra
1930 (34)   *The Beloved Voice*, opera
Bohemian Songs and Dances, for orchestra
1931 (35)   *Passacaglia*, for orchestra
1932 (36)   *The Outcasts of Poker Flat*, opera
1934 (38)   *A Bed of Roses*, opera
1937 (41)   *Wallenstein*, opera
1938 (42)   Variations on *Under the Spreading Chestnut Tree*, for
orchestra
1940 (44)   *Song of the High Seas*, for orchestra
Saxophone Concerto
1941 (45)   *Lincoln Symphony*
Czech Rhapsody, for orchestra
The Bird's Opera, for orchestra
1957 (61)   *Préludes Religieuses et Profanes*, for organ
1960 (64)   *Aus Tirol*
1961 (65)   *Eine Walserouverture*
Weinberger also composed:

Overture to a Puppet Show, for orchestra
Overture to a Cavalier's Play, for orchestra
The Legend of Sleepy Hollow, for orchestra
Mississippi Rhapsody, for band
Prelude to the Festival, for band
Homage to the Pioneers, for band
Chamber music, choral works and songs.

WILLIAMSON, Malcolm/b.1931/Australia

1957 (26) First Piano Sonata
1958 (27) *Santiago de Espada*, overture
　　　　　　　Piano Concerto No. 1
1961 (30) Organ Concerto
1963 (32) *Our Man in Havana*, opera
　　　　　　　Elevamini Symphony
1964 (33) *Sinfonia Concertante*, for piano, three trumpets and string
　　　　　　　　orchestra
　　　　　　　Piano Concerto No. 3
　　　　　　　Variations for Cello and Piano
　　　　　　　The Display, a dance symphony in four movements
　　　　　　　The Merry Wives of Windsor, incidental music
　　　　　　　Elegy J.F.K., for organ
　　　　　　　Three Shakespeare Songs, for high voice and guitar (or
　　　　　　　　piano)
1965 (34) *The Happy Prince*, one-act opera
　　　　　　　Sinfonietta
　　　　　　　Symphonic Variations, for orchestra
　　　　　　　Concerto Grosso, for orchestra
　　　　　　　Violin Concerto
　　　　　　　Four North-Country Songs, for voice and orchestra
　　　　　　　Concerto for two pianos (eight hands) and wind quintet
1966 (35) *The Violins of St. Jacques*, opera
　　　　　　　Julius Caesar Jones, opera
　　　　　　　Sun Into Darkness, ballet
　　　　　　　Five Preludes for Piano
　　　　　　　Two Organ Epitaphs for Edith Sitwell
　　　　　　　Six English Lyrics, for low voice and piano
1967 (36) *Dunstan and the Devil*, one-act opera
　　　　　　　Pas de Quatre, music to the ballet *Nonet*, for flute, oboe,
　　　　　　　　clarinet, bassoon and piano
　　　　　　　Spectrum, ballet (music identical with the *Variations* for
　　　　　　　　cello and piano, 1964)
　　　　　　　The Moonrakers, cassation for audience and orchestra
　　　　　　　Serenade, for flute, piano, violin, viola and cello
　　　　　　　Sonata for two pianos
1968 (37) *The Growing Castle*, chamber opera for four singers
　　　　　　　Knights in Shining Armour, cassation for audience and
　　　　　　　　piano
　　　　　　　The Snow Wolf, cassation for audience and piano
　　　　　　　Piano Quintet
　　　　　　　From a Child's Garden, settings of twelve poems, for high

voice and piano
1969 (38)   *Lucky-Peter's Journey*, a comedy with music
Symphony No. 2
The Brilliant and the Dark, choral-operatic sequence for
women's voices
1971 (40)   *Genesis*, cassation for audience and instruments
The Stone Wall, cassation for audience and orchestra
Peace Pieces, six organ pieces in two volumes
Death of Cuchulain, for five male voices and percussion
instruments
In Place of Belief, setting of ten poems by Per Lagerqvist
for voices and piano duet
1972 (41)   *The Red Sea*, one-act children's opera
Symphony No. 3, *The Icy Mirror*, for soprano, mezzo-
soprano, two baritones, chorus and orchestra
Partita for Viola, on themes of Walton
The Musicians of Bremen, for six male voices
Love the Sentinel, for unaccompanied choir
1973 (42)   *The Winter Star*, cassation for audience and instruments
Concerto for two pianos and strings
Ode to Music, for chorus, echo chorus and orchestra
Pietà, four poems for soprano, oboe, bassoon and piano
Little Carols of the Saints, five organ pieces
The World at the Manger, Christmas cantata
Canticle of Fire, for chorus and organ
1974 (43)   *The Glitter Gang*, cassation for audience and orchestra

---

WOLF, Hugo/1860–1903/Austria

1877–78 (17+)   Lieder aus der Jugenzeit
1877–97 (17+)   Lieder nach verscheidenen Dichten
1879–80 (19)   String Quartet in D minor
1880–88 (20–28)   Eichendorff-Lieder
1883–85 (23–25)   *Penthesilea*, symphonic poem
1887 (27)   *Italian Serenade*, for string quartet (arranged for small
orchestra in 1892)
1888 (28)   Mörike-Lieder, fifty-three songs
Goethe-Lieder, fifty-one songs (1888–89)
1890 (30)   *Spanish Song-Book*, song settings of forty-four Spanish
poems
1891 (31)   *Italian Song-Book*, Book I, twenty-two songs
The Feast of Sulhaug, incidental music
1896 (36)   *fp. Der Corregidor*, opera
Italian Song-Book, Book II, twenty-four songs

WOLF-FERRARI, Ermanno/1876–1948/Italy

1895 (19)   Violin Sonata in G minor, Op. 1
1901 (25)   *p.* Piano Quintet in D♭ major, Op. 6
p. Piano Trio in F♯ major, Op. 7
1902 (26)   *p.* Piano Trio in D major, Op. 5
p. Violin Sonata in A minor, Op. 10

1903 (27) *p.* Chamber Symphony in B♭ major, Op. 8
           fp. Donne curiose, opera
           La Vita nuova, oratorio
1906 (30) *fp. School for Fathers,* opera
           fp. I quatro (sic) rusteghi, comedy-opera
1909 (33) *fp. Susanna's Secret,* opera
1911 (35) *fp. The Jewels of the Madonna,* opera
1936 (60) *fp. Il Campiello,* opera
1939 (63) *fp. Dama Boba,* opera

ALBÉNIZ, Isaac/1860–1909/Spain

(continued from page 12)
1893 (33) *The Magic Opal,* opera
1894 (34) *San Antonio de la Florida*
1895 (35) *Enrico Clifford,* opera
1896 (36) *Pepita Jiménez,* opera
1899 (39) *p. Catalonia,* orchestral rhapsody
1906–09 (46–49) *Iberia,* piano cycle
Albéniz also composed:
Merlin, opera
Piano Concerto
Navarra
Cantos de Espana
Espana
Recuerdof de Viaje
Suite Espanola
Torre Bermeja
Rapfodia Espana

ARENSKY, Antony/1861–1906/Russia

(continued from page 13)
1890 (29) *fp. A Dream on the Volga,* opera
1894 (33) *fp. Raphael,* opera
1899 (38) *Nal and Damayanti,* **opera** (completed)
Arensky also composed:
Egyptian Night, ballet
The Wolf, for bass voice and orchestra
2 Symphonies, in B minor and A minor
Nearly 100 piano pieces, including 3 suites for 2 pianos and
    6 pieces for four hands
Many string quartets, songs, vocal duets and cantatas, as well as
    music for unaccompanied chorus
Fantasia on Russian Folk Songs, for piano and orchestra.

Part Two

This chronologically arranged survey of compositions begins in 1554 and continues through 1975. Before 1554, four major composers were born: Tallis (*c.*1505), A. Gabrieli (1510), Palestrina (*c.*1525), and Byrd (1543).

Which composers were born, which died, and what music was written (or first performed or published) in any given year can be seen under the heading for that year. Within each year composers are listed chronologically, the oldest first. As in Part One, composers' ages are given beside each entry.

The entries in this section are sometimes condensed; for fuller details, cross-reference should be made to Part One.

1554	

        PALESTRINA (*c.*29)
        p. First Book of Masses

1557   MORLEY and GABRIELI, G. were born

1560   FARNABY was born

1562   CAMPIAN and SWEELINCK were born

        GABRIELI, A. (52)
        p. Sacrae cantiones a 5 v.v.,
           motets (1562–65)

1563   BULL and DOWLAND were born

        PALESTRINA (*c.*38)
        p. First Book of Motets

1567   MONTEVERDI was born

        TALLIS (*c.*62)
        p. Psalm Tunes printed in
           Archbishop Parker's Psalter
        PALESTRINA (*c.*42)
        Missa Papae Marcelli

1569	

        PALESTRINA (*c.*44)
        p. Second Book of Masses

1570	

        PALESTRINA (*c.*45)
        p. Third Book of Masses
        Missa Brevis

1575	

        BYRD (32)
        p. Seventeen Motets

1576	

        GABRIELI, A. (66)
        p. Cantiones ecclesiaticae a 4 v.v.,
           motets

	1578

GABRIELI, A. (68)
p. Cantiones sacrae, motets

FRESCOBALDI and GIBBONS were born	1583

	1584

PALESTRINA (*c.*59)
p. Settings of the *Song of Solomon*
MONTEVERDI (17)
Canzonettas for three voices

SCHÜTZ was born; TALLIS died	1585

GABRIELI, A. died	1586

BYRD (43)
p. A Printed Broadside for six
voices

	1587

GABRIELI, G. (30)
p. Concerti for six to sixteen
voices
p. Madrigali e ricercare
MONTEVERDI (20)
p. Madrigals, for five voices,
Book I

	1588

BYRD (45)
p. Psalmes, Songs and Sonnets

	1589

GABRIELI, A. (posthumous)
p. Madrigali e ricercare
BYRD (46)
p. Cantiones sacrae, Book I,
twenty-nine motets for five
voices
p. Songs of sundrie natures

1590

PALESTRINA (*c.65*)
p. Aeterne Christe Munera, mass
Stabat Mater (*c.1590*)
MONTEVERDI (23)
p. Madrigals, for five voices,
Book II

1591

BYRD (48)
p. Cantiones sacrae, Book II,
thirty-two motets

1592

MONTEVERDI (25)
p. Madrigals, for five voices,
Book III
SWEELINCK (30)
p. Chansons françaises, in three
parts (1592–94)

1593

MORLEY (36)
p. Canzonets, or Little Short
Songs to Three Voyces

1594   PALESTRINA died

MORLEY (37)
p. Madrigalls to Foure Voyces

1595

MORLEY (38)
p. The First Booke of Ballets to
fiue voyces
p. The First Booke of Canzonets
to two voyces

1597

MORLEY (40)
p. Two songs in "Canzonets or
Little Short Songs to foure
voyces"
p. Canzonets or Little Short Aers
to fiue and sixe voices
p. A Plaine and Easie Introduction
to Practicall Musicke

GABRIELI, G. (40)
p. Sacrae Symphoniae, Book I
DOWLAND (34)
p. First Book of Songes or Ayres

1598

MORLEY (41)
p. Madrigalls to fiue Voyces
FARNABY (38)
p. Canzonets to Foure Voyces

1599

MORLEY (42)
p. The Firste Booke of Consort
Lessons

FARNABY died **1600**

MORLEY (43)
p. The First Book of Ayres or
Little Short Songs to sing and
play to the Lute with the Base
Viole
DOWLAND (37)
p. Second Book of Songes

1601

MORLEY (44)
p. Two madrigals in *The
Triumphs of Oriana*
CAMPIAN (39)
p. A Book of Airs to be Sung to
the Lute

MORLEY died **1603**

MONTEVERDI (36)
p. Madrigals, for Five Voices,
Book IV
DOWLAND (40)
p. Third Book of Songes or Ayres

1604

DOWLAND (41)
p. *Lachrymae*

1605

GABRIELI, A. (posthumous)
p. *Canzoni alla francese et
Ricercare Arlosi*
BYRD (62)
p. Gradualia, Book I

MONTEVERDI (38)
p. Madrigals, for five voices,
Book V

1607

BYRD (64)
p. Gradualia, Book II
MONTEVERDI (40)
Scherzi Musicali for three voices
fp. Orfeo, opera
CAMPIAN (45)
p. Songs for a Masque

1608

GABRIELI, G. (51)
p. Canzona *La Spiritosa*
MONTEVERDI (41)
fp. L'Arianna, opera
Il Ballo delle ingrate, ballet

1610

MONTEVERDI (43)
p. Masses
p. Vespers

1611

BYRD (68)
p. Psalmes, Songs and Sonnets
SCHÜTZ (26)
p. Italian Madrigals

1612   GABRIELI, G. died

SWEELINCK (50)
Rimes françoises et italiennes
DOWLAND (49)
p. Fourth Book of Songes,
   A Pilgrimes Solace

GIBBONS (29)
p. Madrigals and Mottets of five
   parts: Apt for Viols and
   Voyces

1613

BULL (49)
p. Anthem for the marriage of
   Princess Elizabeth
CAMPIAN (51)
p. Songs for a Masque

1614

MONTEVERDI (47)
p. Madrigals, Book VI

	1615

GABRIELI, G. (posthumous)
p. Canzoni e sonate
p. Sacrae Symphoniae, Book II
MONTEVERDI (48)
fp. Tirsi e Clori, ballet

FRESCOBALDI (32)
p. Toccate d'Involatura
p. Ricercare e canzone francesi

	1617

MONTEVERDI (50)
La Maddalena, opera

	1619

MONTEVERDI (52)
p. Madrigals, Book VII
SWEELINCK (57)
p. Cantiones sacrae

SCHÜTZ (34)
p. Psalms and Motets

CAMPIAN died	1620

SWEELINCK died	1621

BYRD died	1623

SCHÜTZ (38)
Resurrection Oratorio
Easter Oratorio

	1624

FRESCOBALDI (41)
Capricci sopra diversi soggetti

GIBBONS died	1625

SCHÜTZ (40)
Cantiones sacrae, for four voices

DOWLAND died	1626

	1627

MONTEVERDI (60)
Armida, opera
FRESCOBALDI (44)
Second Book of Toccate
SCHÜTZ (42)
fp. Dafne, opera

1628	BULL died

MONTEVERDI (61)
fp. Mercurio e Marte, opera
FRESCOBALDI (45)
Libro delle canzoni

1629	

SCHÜTZ (44)
p. Symphoniae sacrae, Part I

1632	LULLY was born

MONTEVERDI (65)
p. Scherzi musicali, for one or
  two voices

1635	

FRESCOBALDI (52)
p. Fiori musicali

1636	

SCHÜTZ (51)
Musicalische exequien (Funeral
  music)
Kleine Geistliche Concerte, Book I

1637	BUXTEHUDE was born

1638	

MONTEVERDI (71)
p. Madrigali guerrieri e amorosi,
  Book VIII
SCHÜTZ (53)
fp. Orpheus and Euridice, ballet

1639	

SCHÜTZ (54)
Kleine Geistliche Concerte, Book II

1640	

MONTEVERDI (73)
Selva morale e spirituale

	1641

MONTEVERDI (74)
Il ritorno d'Ulisse in patria, opera

	1642

MONTEVERDI (75)
L'Incoronazione di Poppea, opera

MONTEVERDI and FRESCOBALDI died	1643

	1645

SCHÜTZ (60)
The Seven Words from the Cross,
  choral work

	1647

SCHÜTZ (62)
p. Symphoniae sacrae, Part II

	1648

SCHÜTZ (63)
p. Musicali ad chorum sacrum

BLOW was born	1649

	1650

SCHÜTZ (65)
p. Symphoniae sacrae, Part III
MONTEVERDI (posthumous)
p. Masses for four voices, and
  psalms

	1651

MONTEVERDI (posthumous)
p. Madrigals and Canzonettes,
  Book IX

CORELLI was born	1653

	1658

LULLY (26)
fp. Ballets d'Alcidiane

1659 PURCELL was born

LULLY (27)
fp. Ballet de la raillerie

1660 SCARLATTI, A. was born

LULLY (28)
fp. Ballet de Xerxes

1661

LULLY (29)
fp. Ballet de l'impatience
fp. Ballet des saisons
fp. Ballet de l'Ercole amante

1663

LULLY (31)
fp. Ballet des arts
fp. Ballet des noces de village

1664

SCHÜTZ (79)
Christmas Oratorio
LULLY (32)
fp. Ballet des amours déguises
fp. Entr'actes for Corneille's
  Oedipe
fp. Miserere, concert setting of
  "Miserere mei Deus"
fp. La mariage forcé, comedy
  ballet
fp. La Princesse d'Elide, comedy
  ballet

1665

LULLY (33)
fp. L'Amour médecin, comedy ballet
fp. La Naissance de Venus, ballet
fp. Ballet des Gardes
SCHÜTZ (80)
Four passions

1666

LULLY (34)
fp. Le triomphe de Bacchus dans
  les Indes, ballet
fp. Ballet des Muses

		1667

LULLY (35)
fp. Le Sicilien, comedy ballet

	COUPERIN was born	1668

LULLY (36)
fp. Georges Dandin, comedy ballet
fp. Le Carnaval, ou Mascarade de Versailles, ballet

		1669

LULLY (37)
fp. Monsieur de Pourceaugnac,
    comedy ballet
fp. Ballet de Flore

		1670

LULLY (38)
fp. Les amants magnifiques,
    comedy ballet
fp. Le Bourgeois gentilhomme,
    comedy ballet

	ALBINONI was born	1671

SCHÜTZ (86)
Deutches Magnificat
BUXTEHUDE (34)
Wedding Arias

LULLY (39)
fp. Psyche, tragi-comedy
fp. Ballet des Ballets

	SCHÜTZ died	1672

		1673

LULLY (41)
fp. Cadmus et Hermione, opera

		1674

LULLY (42)
fp. Alceste, ou Le Triomphe d'Alcide, opera

	VIVALDI was born (*c.* 1675)	1675

LULLY (43)
fp. Thésée, opera

1676	

LULLY (44)
fp. Atys, opera

1677	

LULLY (45)
fp. Isis, opera
fp. Te Deum

1678	

LULLY (46)
fp. Psyche, opera
BUXTEHUDE (41)
Wedding Arias

1679	

LULLY (47)
fp. Bellérophon, opera
SCARLATTI, A. (19)
fp. Gli equivoci nel sembiante,
    opera

1680	

LULLY (48)
fp. Proserpine, opera
PURCELL (21)
Nine fantasias of four parts

1681	TELEMANN was born

LULLY (49)
fp. Le Triomphe de l'Amour, ballet
CORELLI (28)
p. Sonatas in three parts (twelve
    sonatas da chiesa)

1682	

LULLY (50)
fp. Persée, opera
PURCELL (23)
Hear My Prayer, anthem (c.1682)

RAMEAU was born **1683**

LULLY (51)
fp. Phaéton, opera
De profundis
PURCELL (24)
Twelve sonatas of three parts

SCARLATTI, A. (23)
fp. Pompeo, opera
fp. Psiche, opera

1684

LULLY (52)
fp. Amadis de Gaule, opera
Motets for two choirs

BLOW (35)
Venus and Adonis, masque
Ode for St. Cecilia's Day "Begin
the Song"

BACH, J.S., HANDEL and SCARLATTI, D. were born **1685**

LULLY (53)
fp. Roland, opera
fp. Le Temple de la Paix, ballet

CORELLI (32)
p. Sonatas in three parts (twelve
sonatas da camera)

PORPORA was born **1686**

LULLY (54)
fp. Armide et Renaud, opera
fp. Acis de Galathée, opera

LULLY died **1687**

1688

PURCELL (29)
How pleasant is this flowery plain,
secular cantata

1689

CORELLI (36)
p. Sonatas in three parts (twelve
sonatas da chiesa)

PURCELL (30)
fp. Dido and Aeneas, opera
Musick's Handmaid, for
harpsichord

1690

PURCELL (31)
The Prophetess or *The History of
Dioclesian*, opera
SCARLATTI, A. (30)
fp. Gli equivoci in amore, opera

COUPERIN (22)
Pièces d'orgue en deux messes:
Messe pour les couvents,
twenty-one organ pieces
Messe pour les Paroisses,
twenty-one organ pieces
Messe solenelle

1691

PURCELL (32)
King Arthur or *The British Worthy*,
    opera
The Wives' Excuse, incidental
    music

1692   TARTINI was born

BUXTEHUDE (55)
Sonata in D major, for viola da
    gamba, cello and harpsichord
PURCELL (33)
The Faery Queen, opera
The Libertine, incidental music
Oedipus, incidental music

COUPERIN (24)
Trio Sonata, *La Steinkerque*

1693

PURCELL (34)
Epsom Wells, incidental music

1694

PURCELL (35)
The Married Beau, incidental
    music
SCARLATTI, A. (34)
fp. Pirro e Demetrio, opera

ALBINONI (23)
Zenobia, regina de Palmireni, opera
CORELLI (41)
p. Sonatas in three parts (twelve
    sonatas da camera)

1695   PURCELL died

PURCELL (36)
The Indian Queen, opera
The Tempest or *The Enchanted
    Island*, opera
Bonduca, incidental music

1696

BUXTEHUDE (59)
Seven Trio Sonatas, for violin,
    gamba and basso continuo, Op.1
Seven Trio Sonatas, for violin,
    gamba and basso continuo,
    Op. 2

PURCELL (posthumous)
p. A choice collection of Lessons
    for the Harpsichord or Spinet
p. Harpsichord Suites, 1–8

1697   LECLAIR was born

BLOW (48)
"My God, my God, look upon
    me", anthem

1698

SCARLATTI, A. (38)
fp. Flavio Cuniberto, opera
fp. La donna ancore e' fedele, opera

1699

SCARLATTI, A. (39)
Two sonatas for flute and
    continuo

1700

BLOW (51)
p. Amphion Anglicus, collection of
    songs and vocal chamber
    music

CORELLI (47)
p. Sonatas for violin and violone
    or harpsichord (six 'da chiesa';
    five 'da camera'; one
    Variations on "La Folia")

1703

SCARLATTI, D. (18)
fp. Ottavia ristituta al trono, opera
fp. Giustina, opera

*c.*1703–07
BACH, J.S. (18–22)
Prelude and Fugue in C minor,
    for clavier
Toccata and Fugue in C major,
    for clavier
Sonata in D major, for clavier
    (*c.*1704)

1704

SCARLATTI, D. (19)
fp. Irene, opera

1705

BUXTEHUDE (68)
Wedding Arias
VIVALDI (*c.*30)
p. Suonate da Camera. Op. 1

1706

SCARLATTI, A. (46)
Il sedecia, re di Gerusalemme,
    oratorio

RAMEAU (23)
p. Harpsichord Works, Book I

---

pre 1707

HANDEL
Sonata for viola da gamba

1707   BUXTEHUDE died

SCARLATTI, A. (47)
fp. Il trionfo della libertà, opera
fp. Mitridate eupatore, opera
ALBINONI (36)
Sinfonie e concerti a 5

HANDEL (22)
"Laudate pueri Dominum", aria
Rodrigo, opera (c.1707)

1708   BLOW died

TELEMANN (27)
Trio Sonata in E♭ major
    (1708–12)
BACH, J.S. (23)
Passacaglia and Fugue in C
    minor for organ (c.1708–17)
Most of the "Great" Preludes and
    Fugues (c.1708–17)
The Toccatas (c.1708–17)

HANDEL (23)
La Resurrezione, Easter oratorio
PORPORA (22)
Agrippina, opera

1709

COUPERIN (41)
Messe à l'usage des Couvents
VIVALDI (c.34)
p. Sonate a violini e bassi, Op. 2

1710   ARNE, BACH, W.F., BOYCE, PARADIES and PERGOLESI were born

SCARLATTI, A. (50)
Est dies tropael, motet (c.1710)
Informata vulnerate, cantata
    (c.1710)

ALBINONI (39)
Concerti a 5
SCARLATTI, D. (25)
fp. La Sylvia, opera

1711

SCARLATTI, D. (26)
fp. Tolomeo e Alessandro, opera
HANDEL (26)
Rinaldo, opera

PORPORA (25)
Flavio Anicio Olibrio, opera
Il martirio di S. Giovanni
    Nepomuceno, oratorio

1712

VIVALDI (c.37)
p. L'Estro harmonico, Op. 3,
    concertos (c.1712)
p. La stravaganza, Op. 4,
    concertos (1712–13)

SCARLATTI, D. (27)
fp. Tetide in sciro, opera
HANDEL (27)
Il Pastor Fido, opera (first
    version)

1713   CORELLI died

COUPERIN (45)
Harpsichord Works, Book I

VIVALDI (c.38)
fp. Ottone in Villa, opera

HANDEL (28)
Teseo, opera
Te Deum and Jubilate, for the
    Peace of Utrecht

SCARLATTI, D. (28)
fp. Ifigenia in Aulide, opera
fp. Ifigenia in Tauride, opera
PORPORA (27)
Basilio, re d'oriente, opera

BACH, C.P.E. and GLUCK were born   **1714**

CORELLI (posthumous)
p. Concerti Grossi
VIVALDI (*c.*39)
fp. Orlando finto pazzo, opera
Moyses deus Pharaonis, oratorio
SCARLATTI, D. (29)
fp. Amor d'un ombra, opera

PORPORA (28)
Arianna e Teseo, opera
TARTINI (23)
Violin Sonata in G minor,
    "Devil's Trill"

1715

SCARLATTI, A. (55)
fp. Tigrone, opera
Twelve sinfonias
Four string quartets (without
    harpsichord)
COUPERIN (47)
Leçons de ténèbres, for one and
    two voices
VIVALDI (*c.*40)
fp. Nerone fatto Cesare, opera

TELEMANN (34)
Concerto in A major (1715–20)
Suite in D minor (1715–20)
HANDEL (30)
Amadigi di Gaula, opera
Water Music (1715–17)
SCARLATTI, D. (30)
fp. Ambleto, opera

1716

ALBINONI (45)
Twelve concerti a 5 (*c.*1716)
VIVALDI (*c.*41)
fp. Arsilda Regina di Ponto, opera
Juditha, oratorio
p. Six sonate, Op. 5 (*c.*1716)
p. Six concerti a cinque, Op. 6
    (1716–*c.*17)
p. Seven concerti a cinque, Op. 7
    (1716–*c.*17)

TELEMANN (35)
Die Kleine Kammermusik
Six Suites for violin, querflute
    and piano

1717

COUPERIN (49)
Harpsichord Works, Book II
VIVALDI (*c.*42)
fp. Tieteberga, opera
BACH, J.S. (32–38)
English Suites (*c.*1717–23)
The Inventions, Little Preludes
    and Symphonies (*c.*1717–23)

The *Brandenburg* Concerti
    (*c.*1717–23)
The Suites (Overtures) for
    orchestra (*c.*1717–23)
The Violin Concerti (*c.*1717–23)
The Sonatas (Suites) for violin,
    flute, cello and viola da gamba
    (*c.*1717–23)

1718

SCARLATTI, A. (58)
fp. Telemaco, opera
VIVALDI (*c.*43)
fp. Scanderbeg, opera
TELEMANN (37)
Six Trios for two violins, cello
and bass continuo

SCARLATTI, D. (33)
fp. Berenice, opera
PORPORA (32)
Temistocle, opera

1719

SCARLATTI, A. (59)
fp. Marco Attilo Regolo, opera
PORPORA (33)
Faramondo, opera

1720

SCARLATTI, A. (60)
fp. Tito o sempronio gracco, opera
(completed version for Rome
production)
VIVALDI (*c.*45)
fp. La verità in cimento, opera
BACH, J.S. (35)
Chromatic Fantasia and Fugue,
for clavier (1720–23)

HANDEL (35)
Chandos Anthems (*c.*1720)
Huit Suites de pièces, for
harpsichord (*c.*1720)
Acis and Galatea, secular cantata
(*c.*1720)
Radamisto, opera (*c.*1720)

1721

SCARLATTI, A. (61)
fp. Griselda, opera
VIVALDI (*c.*46)
fp. Silvia, opera

HANDEL (36)
Floridante, opera
PORPORA (35)
Il martirio di Santa Eugenia,
oratorio

1722

COUPERIN (54)
Harpsichord Works, Book III
Four *Concerts Royaux*
ALBINONI (51)
Twelve concerti a cinque
(*c.*1722)

VIVALDI (*c.*47)
L'adorazione delle tre Re Magi,
oratorio
BACH, J.S. (37)
The Well-Tempered Clavier,
Part I
French Suites

1723

TELEMANN (42)
Hamburger Ebb und Fluht,
overture

BACH, J.S. (38)
St. John Passion
HANDEL (38)
Ottone, opera

PORPORA (37)
Adelaide, opera

LECLAIR (26)
p. Sonatas for Violin alone, with
  a Bass, Book I

1724

COUPERIN (56)
Les Goûts-Réunis, ten "concerts"
  for various instruments
VIVALDI (*c.*49)
fp. Giustino, opera

HANDEL (39)
Giulio Cesare, opera
Fifteen Chamber Sonatas
PORPORA (38)
Griselda, opera

SCARLATTI, A. died   **1725**

VIVALDI (*c.*50)
p. Concerto *The Seasons* (from
  Op. 8)
TELEMANN (44)
Pimpinone, opera

HANDEL (40)
Rodelinda, opera
Trio Sonata in D minor

1726

VIVALDI (*c.*51)
Cunegonda, opera
PORPORA (40)
Imeneo in Atene, opera

1727

VIVALDI (*c.*52)
Ipermestra, opera
HANDEL (42)
Zadok, the Priest, coronation
  anthem
Admeto, opera

PORPORA (41)
Ezio, opera

1728

VIVALDI (*c.*53)
Rosilena ed Oronta, opera
p. La Cetra concertos, Op. 9
TELEMANN (47)
Der getreuer Musikmeister,
  cantata
RAMEAU (45)
p. Harpsichord Works, Book II

HANDEL (43)
Tolomeo, opera
LECLAIR (31)
p. Sonatas for violin alone, with
  a Bass, Book II

1729

VIVALDI (*c*.54)
Concerti, Op. 10, 11 and 12
(1729–30)

BACH, J.S. (44)
St. Matthew Passion
The Clavier Concerti (1729–36)
PORPORA (43)
Semiramide riconosciuta, opera

1730

COUPERIN (62)
p. Harpsichord Works, Book IV
PORPORA (44)
Mitridate, opera

1731

BACH, J.S. (46)
St. Mark Passion
HANDEL (46)
Nine sonatas for two violins and
continuo (*c*.1731)
PORPORA (45)
Poro, opera

PERGOLESI (21)
Salustia, opera
BACH, C.P.E. (17)
Trio in B minor

1732   HAYDN was born

VIVALDI (*c*.57)
fp. La fida ninfa, opera
HANDEL (47)
Ezio, opera
Sosarme, opera
Esther, oratorio

PORPORA (46)
Germanico in Germania, opera
PERGOLESI (22)
Lo frate innamorato, opera
La serva padrona, opera

1733   COUPERIN died

VIVALDI (*c*.58)
fp. Motezuma, opera
RAMEAU (50)
Hippolyte et Aricie, opera
BACH, J.S. (48)
Mass in B minor
Christmas Oratorio
HANDEL (48)
Orlando, opera
Huit Suites de Pièces, for
harpsichord
PORPORA (47)
Arianna in Nasso, opera

ARNE (23)
Dido and Aenas, opera
The Opera of Operas, opera
Rosamund, opera
PERGOLESI (23)
Il Prigionier superbo, opera

1734

VIVALDI (c.59)
fp. L'Olimpiade, opera
HANDEL (49)
Persichore, ballet
Arianna, opera
Il Pastor fido, opera (second and
  third versions)
p. Six concerti grossi

PORPORA (48)
Enea nel Lazio, opera
Davide e Bersabea, oratorio
LECLAIR (37)
p. Sonatas for violin alone, with
  a Bass, Book III
PERGOLESI (24)
Adriano in Siria, opera
La Contadina astuta, opera

1735

VIVALDI (c.60)
fp. Griselda, opera
fp. Aristide, opera
RAMEAU (52)
Les Indes galantes, opera-ballet
BACH, J.S. (50)
Italian Concerto
Partita in B minor, for clavier
Ascension Oratorio (1735—36)

HANDEL (50)
Alcina, opera
PORPORA (49)
Ifigenia in Aulide, opera
Polifemo, opera
PERGOLESI (25)
L'Olimpiade, opera
Flamincio, opera

1736

VIVALDI (c.61)
fp. Ginevra, Principessa di Scozia,
  opera
BACH, J.S. (51)
Easter Oratorio

HANDEL (51)
Atalanta, opera
Alexander's Feast, secular cantata
Six Fugues for Harpsichord
ARNE (26)
Zara, incidental music
PERGOLESI (26)
Stabat Mater, for female voices

1737

VIVALDI (c.62)
fp. Catone in Utica, opera
p. Il Pastor Fido, sonatas
  (c.1737)
BACH, J.S. (52)
Masses, in F: A: Gm and G
  major (1737—40)

HANDEL (52)
Berenice, opera
Concerto grosso
PORPORA (51)
Lucio Papirio, opera
LECLAIR (40)
p. Six concertos for violin

1738

VIVALDI (c.63)
fp. L'Oracolo in Messenia, opera
HANDEL (53)
Xerxes, opera
Six organ concerti

SCARLATTI, D. (53)
p. Essercizi per Gravicembalo
PORPORA (52)
Carlo il Calvo, opera

CONTINUED

ARNE (28)
Comus, masque

PARADIES (28)
Alessandro in Persia, opera

1739   DITTERSDORF was born

VIVALDI (*c*.64)
fp. Feraspe, opera
RAMEAU (56)
Dardanus, opera
Les Fêtes d'Hebe, ballet
HANDEL (54)
Israel in Egypt, oratorio
Saul, oratorio
Ode for Saint Cecilia's Day
Twelve Concerti Grossi
Seven Trio Sonatas

SCARLATTI, D. (54)
*p. XLII Suites de pièces pour la
   Clavecin*
PORPORA (53)
Il Barone di Zampano, opera

1740

VIVALDI (*c*.65)
p. Six sonate a cello e basse,
   Op. 14 (*c*.1740)
HANDEL (55)
p. Concerti for oboe and strings
p. Six organ concerti
Three Double Concerti (1740–50)

PORPORA (54)
Il trionfo di Camilla, opera
ARNE (30)
Alfred, masque
The Judgement of Paris, opera

1741   VIVALDI died

RAMEAU (58)
p. Harpsichord Works, Book III
BACH, J.S. (56)
Six partitas for clavier

HANDEL (56)
Messiah, oratorio
Five concerti grossi
GLUCK (27)
Artaserse, opera

1742   GRÉTRY was born

BACH, J.S. (57)
The "Goldberg" Variations for
   clavier
HANDEL (57)
Forest Music
PORPORA (56)
Statira, opera

BACH, C.P.E. (28)
"Prussian" Sonata
GLUCK (28)
Demetrio, opera

1743   BOCCHERINI was born

HANDEL (58)
Samson, oratorio
The *Dettingen* Te Deum

PORPORA (57)
Temistocle, opera

ARNE (33)
Britannia, masque
Eliza, opera

BACH, C.P.E. (29)
Sonata for clavier, *Wurtemburgian*
GLUCK (29)
Il Tigrane, opera

1744

BACH, J.S. (59)
The Well-Tempered Clavier, Part II
HANDEL (59)
Semele, secular oratorio
ARNE (34)
Abel, oratorio

BACH, W.F. (34)
Clavier sonata No. 2, in A major
  (c.1744)

1745

RAMEAU (62)
Platée, ballet
HANDEL (60)
Balshazzar, oratorio

GLUCK (31)
Ippolito, opera

1746

HANDEL (61)
Occasional Oratorio
LECLAIR (49)
Scylla et Glaucus, opera

GLUCK (32)
Artamene, opera
p. Six sonatas for two violins and
  continuo

1747

BACH, J.S. (62)
A Musical Offering, for flute,
  violin and clavier
HANDEL (62)
Judas Maccabeus, oratorio
PORPORA (61)
Filandro, opera

BACH, C.P.E. (33)
Sonata in D major
GLUCK (33)
Le nozze d'Ercole e d'Ebe, opera

1748

RAMEAU (65)
Pigmalion, ballet
Zais, ballet

HANDEL (63)
Joshua, oratorio

CIMAROSA was born **1749**

BACH, J.S. (64)
The Art of Fugue

HANDEL (64)
Music for the Royal Fireworks
Solomon, oratorio
Susanna, oratorio

1750   BACH, J.S. and ALBINONI died

HANDEL (65)
Theodora, oratorio
ARNE (40)
Seven trio-sonatas for two
    violins with figured bass

BOYCE (40)
p. Eight Symphonies in Eight
    Parts . . . Opera seconda
    (*c*.1750)
GLUCK (38)
Ezio, opera

1752   CLEMENTI was born   1752

HANDEL (67)
Jephtha, oratorio
GLUCK (38)
Issipile, opera

1753

GLUCK (39)
Nine Symphonies

1754

RAMEAU (71)
Zephyre, ballet

1755

GLUCK (41)
Les Amours champêtres, opera
Alessandro, ballet

HAYDN (23)
String Quartets Nos. 1–13

1756   MOZART was born

GLUCK (42)
Antigono, opera
Le Chinois poli en France, opera

HAYDN (24)
Organ Concerto No. 1 in C major
Piano Concerto in C major

1757   SCARLATTI, D. died

1758

GLUCK (44)
*L'Isle de Merlin, ou Le Monde
    renversé*, opera

1759   HANDEL died

TELEMANN (78)
St. Mark Passion

GLUCK (45)
L'Arbre enchanté, opera
HAYDN (27)
Symphony No. 1 in D major

CHERUBINI was born **1760**

RAMEAU (78)
Les Paladins, opera-ballet
HANDEL (posthumous)
p. Six Organ Concerti

HAYDN (28)
Organ Concerto No. 2 in C major
Symphony No. 2 in C major
(*c.*1760)
GOSSEC (26)
Requiem Mass

1761

GLUCK (47)
Le Cadi dupé, opera
Don Juan, ballet
HAYDN (29)
Symphony No. 3 in G major
Symphony No. 4 in D major
Symphony No. 5 in A major
Symphony No. 6 in D major,
Le Matin
Symphony No. 7 in C major,
Le Midi
Symphony No. 8 in G major,
Le Soir, ou La Tempête
Symphony No. 19 in D major

GOSSEC (27)
Le Tonnelier, opera
BACH, J.C. (26)
Artaserse, opera
Catone in Utica, opera

1762

ARNE (52)
Artaxerxes, opera
Love in a Village, pasticcio
BACH, C.P.E. (48)
Harp Sonata in B minor
GLUCK (58)
Orfeo ed Euridice, opera

HAYDN (30)
Symphony No. 9 in C major
BACH, J.C. (27)
Alessandro nell'Indie, opera
MOZART (6)
Sonata in C major, for violin and
piano, K.6 (1762–64)

pre **1763**

HAYDN
Symphony No. 10 in D major
Symphony No. 11 in E♭ major
Piano Sonata No. 3 in A major

1763

HAYDN (31)
Symphony No. 12 in E major
Symphony No. 13 in D major
BACH, J.C. (28)
Orione, opera
Zanaida, opera

MOZART (7)
Violin Sonata in D major, K.7
Violin Sonata in B♭ major, K.8

---

pre **1764**

HAYDN
Symphonies Nos. 14 and 15

1764   RAMEAU and LECLAIR died

ARNE (54)
Judith, oratorio
L'Olimpiade, opera
GLUCK (50)
Poro, opera
La Recontre imprévue, opera
HAYDN (32)
Symphonies No. 16–18
   (c.1764)
Symphony No. 22 in E♭ major,
   Der Philosoph

MOZART (8)
Symphony No. 1 in E♭ major,
   K.16
Symphony No. 4 in D major,
   K.19
Seven Violin Sonatas, K.9 in G:
   K.10 in B♭: K.11 in G: K.12
   in A: K.13 in F: K.14 in C:
   K.15 in B♭

1765

GLUCK (51)
Semiramide, ballet
HAYDN (33)
Symphony No. 26 in D minor,
   Lamentations (c.1765)
Symphony No. 30 in C major,
   Alleluia
Symphony No. 31 in D major,
   Horn Signal
String Quartets Nos. 14–19
GOSSEC (31)
Le Faux Lord, opera

BACH, J.C. (30)
Adriano in Siria, opera
BOCCHERINI (22)
La confedarazione, opera
MOZART (9)
Symphony No. 5 in B♭ major,
   K.22
Piano Sonata in C major (four
   hands), K.19d
Three Sonatas by J.C. Bach
   arranged as concertos with
   string orchestra, K.107

1766

GLUCK (52)
L'Orfano della China, ballet
HAYDN (34)
Piano Sonatas Nos. 4–7
Piano Sonatas Nos. 8–12
   (1766–67)
Mass No. 4, *Great Organ*

GOSSEC (32)
Les Pêcheurs, opera
MOZART (10)
Six Violin Sonatas, K.26 in E♭:
   K.27 in G: K.28 in D: K.29 in
   D: K.30 in F: K.31 in B♭

1767

GLUCK (53)
Alkestis, opera
HAYDN (35)
Piano Sonatas Nos. 13–16
   (c.1767)
Piano Sonata No. 17

GOSSEC (33)
Le Double déguisemente, opera
Toinon et Toinette, opera
BACH, J.C. (32)
Carattaco, opera

DITTERSDORF (28)
Amore in musica, opera

MOZART (11)
Symphony No. 6 in F major,
K.43
Symphony No. 43 in F major,
K.76
Four Piano Concertos, K.37 in F:
K.39 in B♭: K.40 in D: K.41
in G
Three Sonatas for organ and
strings, K.62 in E♭: K.68 in
B♭: K.69 in D

PORPORA died   **1768**

MOZART (12)
Bastien und Bastienne, operetta
Symphony No. 7 in D, K.45
Symphony No. 8 in D, K.48

pre **1769**

HAYDN
Two Violin Concerti in C and G

TELEMANN died   **1769**

HAYDN (37)
String Quartets Nos. 20–25
GRÉTRY (27)
Le Tableau parlant, opera

MOZART (13)
Symphony No. 9 in C major,
K.73
Symphony No. 42 in F major,
K.75
Mass in C major, K.66

BEETHOVEN was born; TARTINI died   **1770**

BACH, C.P.E. (56)
Passion Cantata
Duo in E minor
Solfeggio in C minor
GLUCK (56)
Paride ed Elena, opera
HAYDN (38)
Violin Concerto in D major
(pre 1770)
Mass No. 5, *Little Organ*, or
St. John (1770–80)

BACH, J.C. (35)
Gioas Re di Giuda, oratorio
DITTERSDORF (31)
Il Viaggatore americano, opera
MOZART (14)
Five Symphonies, No. 10 in G,
K.74: No. 11 in D, K.80:
No. 45 in D, K.95: No. 47 in
D, K.97: No. 12 in G, K.110
String Quartet in G major, K.80

after **1770**

HAYDN
Piano Concerto in G major

---

pre **1771**

HAYDN
Piano Concerto in F major
Violin Concerto in A major

1771

HAYDN (39)
Piano Sonata No. 18 in C minor
String Quartets Nos. 26–31
DITTERSDORF (32)
L'amore disprezzato, opera
GRÉTRY (29)
Zémire et Azor, opera

MOZART (15)
Five Symphonies, No. 46 in C,
K.95: No. 13 in F, K.112:
No. 14 in A, K.114: No. 50
in D, finale only, to the
overture of *Asanio in Alba*,
K.120: Symphony in D, finale
only, to the overture of *La
finta giardinera*, K.121

---

pre **1772**

HAYDN
Symphony No. 43, *Mercury*
Symphony No. 44,
  Trauersymphonie

1772

HAYDN (40)
Symphony No. 45, *Farewell*
Symphony No. 46
Symphony No. 48, *Maria Teresa*
Symphony No. 52 (1772–74)
Mass No. 3, *St. Cecilia*
String Quartets Nos. 32–37,
  Sun or *Great* Quartets
BACH, J.C. (37)
Endimione, cantata
Temistocle, opera

CIMAROSA (23)
Le stravaganze del conte, opera
MOZART (16)
Lucio Silla, opera
Nine Symphonies, No. 15 in G,
K.124: No. 16 in C, K.128:
No. 17 in G, K.129: No. 19
in E♭, K.132: No. 20 in D,
K.133: No. 21 in A, K.134:
Symphony in D, K.161: No.
22 in C, K.162: No. 51 in D,
K.163

---

pre **1773**

HAYDN
Symphony No. 49, *The Passion*

1773

BACH, C.P.E. (59)
Fantasia in C minor
HAYDN (41)
Piano Sonatas Nos. 19–24 (Nos.
22–24 with violin parts are
Violin Sonatas No. 2–4)

DITTERSDORF (34)
Il Tutore e la Pupilla, opera

MOZART (17)
Four Symphonies, No. 23 in D,
  K.181: No. 24 in B♭, K.182:
  No. 25 in Gm, K. 183: No. 26
  in E♭, K.184
Piano Concerto in D major,
  K.175

"Concertone" in C major, for
  two violins, K.190
Six String Quartets, K.168 in F:
  K.169 in A: K.170 in C:
  K.171 in E♭: K.172 in B♭:
  K.173 in Dm
String Quintet in B♭, K.174

pre **1774**

HAYDN
Symphony No. 53, *The Imperial*

SPONTINI was born   **1774**

GLUCK (60)
Iphigénie en Aulide, opera
HAYDN (42)
Symphony No. 55, *The School-
master*
GOSSEC (40)
Sabinus, opera
La Nativité, oratorio
DITTERSDORF (35)
Il tribunale di Giove, opera

MOZART (18)
Four Symphonies, No. 27 in G,
  K.199: No. 28 in C, K.200:
  No. 29 in A, K.201: No. 30
  in D, K.202
Bassoon Concerto in B♭, K.191
Six Piano Sonatas, K.279 in C:
  K.280 in F: K.281 in B♭:
  K.282 in E♭: K.283 in G:
  K.284 in D
Piano Sonata in B♭ (four hands),
  K.358

BOÏELDIEU was born   **1775**

ARNE (65)
Caractacus, incidental music
BACH, C.P.E. (61)
The Israelites in the Wilderness,
  oratorio
GOSSEC (41)
Alexis et Daphné, opera
DITTERSDORF (36)
Il finto pazzo per amore, opera
Il maniscalco, opera
Lo sposo burlato, opera

MOZART (19)
La finta giardiniera, opera
Il re pastore, dramatic festival play
Symphony No. 49 in C, K.102
Five Violin Concerti, K.207 in
  B♭: K.211 in D: K.216 in G:
  K.218 in D: K.219 in A
Sonata in B♭, for organ and
  strings, K.212

pre **1776**

HAYDN
Symphony No. 59, *Feuersymphonie*

1776

GLUCK (62)
Alceste, opera
HAYDN (44)
Symphony No. 60 in C, *Il distratto*
Piano Sonatas, Nos. 25–30
GOSSEC (42)
Hylas et Sylvie, incidental music
BACH, J.C. (41)
Lucio Silla, opera
DITTERSDORF (37)
La contadina felice, opera
La moda, opera
Il barone di Rocco Antica, opera

MOZART (20)
Three Piano Concerti, K.238 in B♭: K.242 in F, for three pianos: K.246 in C
Piano Trio in B♭, K.254
Five Sonatas for organ and strings, K.224 in F: K.225 in A: K.241 in G: K.244 in F: K.245 in D
Mass in C major, K.257

1777

GLUCK (63)
Armide, opera
HAYDN (45)
Symphony No. 63, *La Roxolane*
Piano Sonatas Nos. 31 and 32 (1777–78)
DITTERSDORF (38)
L'Arcifanfano, re de' matti, opera

MOZART (21)
Piano Concerto in E♭, K.271
Violin Concerto in D, K.271a
Piano Sonata in C, K.309
Sonata for organ and strings in G, K.274

1778   ARNE died

GOSSEC (44)
La Fête du Village, opera
GRÉTRY (36)
L'amant jaloux, opera
CIMAROSA (29)
L'Italiana in Londra, opera
MOZART (22)
Symphony No. 31 in D, *Paris*, K.297
Concerto in C, for flute and harp, K.299
Two Flute Concerti, K.313 in G: K.314 in D

Sinfonia Concertante for wind instruments, app. K.9
Six Piano Sonatas, K.310 in Am: K.311 in D: K.330 in C: K.331 in A: K.332 in F: K.333 in B♭
Seven Violin Sonatas, K.296 in C: K.301 in G: K.302 in E♭: K.303 in C: K.304 in Em: K.305 in A: K.306 in D
CHERUBINI (18)
Demophon, opera

1779   BOYCE died

GLUCK (65)
Iphigénie en Tauride, opera
HAYDN (47)
Symphony No. 69, *Laudon*
Piano Sonatas Nos. 33–37 (1779–80)

GOSSEC (45)
Les Scythes enchaînés, divertissement
Mirsa, ballet
BACH, J.C. (44)
Amadis des Gaule's, opera

MOZART (23)
Symphony No. 32 in G, K.318
Symphony No. 33 in B♭, K.319
Sinfonia Concertante in E♭, for
violin and viola, K.364
Sonata for organ and strings in
C, K.328
Mass in C major, K.317

1780

BACH, C.P.E. (66)
Symphony in F major
CIMAROSA (31)
Giuditta, oratorio
MOZART (24)
Symphony No. 34 in C major,
K.338
Six Variations for violin and
piano on "Hélas, j'ai perdu
mon amant", K.360
Sonata for organ and strings in
C, K.336
BEETHOVEN (10)
Nine variations on a March by
Dressler

1781

HAYDN (49)
Symphony No. 73, *La Chasse*
Concerto No. 2 for Horn and
Strings
String Quartets Nos. 38–43,
Russian or *Jungfern* Quartets
GOSSEC (47)
L'Arche d'Alliance, oratorio
CIMAROSA (32)
Il convito, opera
Il pittore parigino, opera
MOZART (25)
Idomeneo, opera
Rondo for violin and orchestra in
C, K.373
Concerto Rondo in E♭ for horn,
K.371
Twelve Variations on "La
bergère célimène" for violin
and piano, K.359
Sonata for two pianos, K.448
Five Violin Sonatas, K.376 in F:
K.377 in F: K.378 in B♭:
K.379 in Gm and G: K.380
in E♭
BEETHOVEN (11)
"Schilderung eines Mädchen",
song

AUBER, FIELD and PAGANINI were born **1782**

GOSSEC (48)
Thésée, opera
CIMAROSA (33)
La ballerina amante, opera
Absalon, oratorio
MOZART (26)
Il Seraglio, opera
Symphony No. 35 in D,
Haffner, K.385
Three Piano Concerti, K.413 in
F: K.414 in A: K.415 in C
Horn Concerto, K.412
Three unfinished violin sonatas,
K.402–404
String Quartet, K.387
BEETHOVEN (12–32)
Bagatelles for piano (1782–1802)

1783

HAYDN (52)
Cello Concerto in D major
MOZART (27)
Symphony No. 36 in C, *Linz*,
  K.425
Two Horn Concerti, K.417 in
  E♭ : K.447 in E♭
Two String Quartets, K.421 in D:
  K.428 in E♭

BEETHOVEN (13)
p. Three Piano Sonatas
  (composed very early)
Minuet for piano

pre 1784

HAYDN
Piano Sonatas Nos. 38–40

1784   BACH, W.F. died

HAYDN (52)
Armida, opera
String Quartets Nos. 44–50
  (1784–87)
GRÉTRY (42)
L'Épreuve villageoise, opera
Richard Coeur de Lion, opera
CIMAROSA (35)
L'Olimpiade, opera
Artaserse, opera

MOZART (28)
Six Piano Concerti, K.449 in E♭ :
  K.450 in B♭ : K.451 in D:
  K.453 in G: K.456 in B♭ :
  K.459 in F
Violin Sonata in B♭, K.454
Piano Sonata in Cm, K.457
String Quartet in B♭, K.458
BEETHOVEN (14)
p. Rondo, allegretto for piano
p. "An einem Saugling", song

1785

HAYDN (53)
Symphony No. 87 in A major
Piano Sonata No. 41 in A♭
  (c.1785)
Piano Sonata No. 42 in G minor
  (1785–86)
Piano Sonata No. 44 in A♭
  (1785–86)

MOZART (29)
Three Piano Concerti, K.466 in
  Dm: K.467 in C: K.482 in E♭
Two String Quartets, K.464 in A:
  K.465 in C
Piano Quartet in Gm, K.478
Violin Sonata in E♭, K.481
BEETHOVEN (15)
Piano Quartets Nos. 1–3
Piano Trio No. 9
Prelude in F minor for piano

1786   WEBER was born

HAYDN (54)
Symphony No. 82, *The Bear*
Symphony No. 83, *La Poule*
Symphony No. 84

Symphony No. 85, *La Reine*
  (c.1786)
Symphony No. 86, *The Miracle*
  (c.1786)

GOSSEC (52)
Rosine, opera
DITTERSDORF (47)
Doktor und Apotheker, opera
Betrug durch Aberglauben, opera
BOCCHERINI (43)
La Clementina, opera
CIMAROSA (37)
L'impresario in Angustie, opera
MOZART (30)
The Impresario, opera
The Marriage of Figaro, opera
Symphony No. 38 in D, *Prague*,
   K.504
Three Piano Concerti, K.488 in

A: K.491 in Cm: K.503 in C
Horn Concerto in E♭, K.495
Two Piano Sonatas (four-hands),
   K.357 in G: K.497 in F
String Quartet in D, K.499
Piano Quartet in E♭, K.493
Three Piano Trios, K.496 in G:
   K.498 in B♭, for clarinet,
   viola and piano: K.502 in B♭
BEETHOVEN (16)
Trio for piano, flute and bassoon

GLUCK died **1787**

BACH, C.P.E. (73)
*The Resurrection and Ascension of
   Jesus*, oratorio
HAYDN (55)
Symphonies Nos. 88 and 89
String Quartets Nos. 51–57,
   Seven Words
Piano Sonata No. 45 (1787–88)
DITTERSDORF (48)
Die Liebe in Narrenhaus, opera
Democrito coretto, opera

MOZART (31)
Don Giovanni, opera
Eine Kleine Nachtmusik, for strings
Three String Quartets, K.406 in
   Cm: K.515 in C: K.516 in Gm
Piano Sonata in C (four hands),
   K.521
Violin Sonata in A, K.526

BACH, C.P.E. died **1788**

BACH, C.P.E. (74)
Concerto for harpsichord,
   fortepiano and strings
Quartet in G major
HAYDN (56)
Symphonies Nos. 90 and 91
Symphony No. 92, *Oxford*
Toy Symphony
MOZART (32)
Symphony No. 39 in E♭ major,
   K.543
Symphony No. 40 in G minor,
   K.550

Symphony No. 41 in C major,
   Jupiter, K.551
Piano Concerto in D major,
   Coronation, K.537
String Quartet in D minor,
   K.546
Three piano trios, K.542 in E:
   K.548 in C: K.564 in G
Piano Sonata in C (Sonatina),
   K.545
Violin Sonata in F, K.547
CHERUBINI (28)
Ifigenia in Aulide, opera

1789

HAYDN (57)
String Quartets Nos. 58–59
Piano Sonata No. 46
Piano Sonata No. 47 (1789–90)
DITTERSDORF (50)
Hieronimus Knicker, opera
CIMAROSA (40)
Cleopatra, opera

MOZART (33)
String Quartet in D, K.575
Two Piano Sonatas, K.570 in
  B♭: K.576 in D
BEETHOVEN (19)
Two Preludes through all twelve
  major keys, for piano or organ

pre 1790

HAYDN
Violin Sonata No. 1

1790

HAYDN (58)
Piano Sonata No. 48 (*c*.1790)
Seven Nocturnes for the King of
  Naples
DITTERSDORF (51)
Das rote Käppchen, opera
MOZART (34)
Così fan tutti, opera
String Quintet in D, K.593
Two String Quartets, K.589 in
  B♭: K.590 in F

BEETHOVEN (20)
"Musik zu einem Ritterballett",
  for orchestra
Twenty-four Variations on
  "Venni Amore", for piano
Two Cantatas

1791   MEYERBEER was born; MOZART died

HAYDN (59)
Symphony No. 93
Symphony No. 94, *Surprise*
Symphony No. 95
Symphony No. 96, *Miracle*
DITTERSDORF (52)
Hokus Pokus, opera

MOZART (35)
The Magic Flute, opera
La Clemenza di Tito, opera
Piano Concerto in B♭, K.595
Clarinet Concerto in A, K.622
String Quartet in E♭, K.614
BEETHOVEN (21)
Variations on "Es was einmal",
  for piano

1792   ROSSINI was born; PARADIES died

HAYDN (60)
Symphonies Nos. 97 and 98
The Storm, oratorio

CIMAROSA (43)
Il matrimonio segreto, opera
BEETHOVEN (22)
Allegro and menuetto for two
  flutes

1793

HAYDN (61)
Symphony No. 99
String Quartets Nos. 60–69
  (probably before 1793)
String Quartets Nos. 70–75
CIMAROSA (44)
I Traci amanti, opera
Concerto for two flutes and
  orchestra

BEETHOVEN (23)
p. Variations on "Se vuol ballare",
  for violin and piano
BOÏELDIEU (18)
La Fille coupable, opera

1794

HAYDN (62)
Symphony No. 100, *Military*
Symphony No. 101, *The Clock*
DITTERSDORF (55)
Das Gespeust mit der Trommel,
  opera
CIMAROSA (45)
Penelope, opera

BEETHOVEN (24)
Trio for two oboes and English
  horn
Rondo allegro for violin and
  piano
p. Variations on a Waldstein
  theme for piano (four hands)

---

pre 1795

HAYDN
Piano Sonata No. 49

1795

HAYDN (63)
Symphony No. 102
Symphony No. 103, *Drum Roll*
Symphony No. 104
DITTERSDORF (56)
Don Quixote der Zweite, opera
Gott Mars, opera
Schach vom Schiras, opera
BEETHOVEN (25)
p. Twelve *Deutsche Tänze*, for
  orchestra
Piano Concerto No. 2

Six allemandes for violin and
  piano
Six minuets for piano
p. Variations on "Quant' è più
  bello", for piano
Variations on minuet from *Le
  Nozze Disturbate*, for piano
"Die Flamme Iodert", opferlied
Four Songs
BOÏELDIEU (20)
Harp Concerto

BERWALD was born **1796**

HAYDN (64)
Trumpet Concerto
Mass No. 9, *Heiligenmesse*
Mass No. 10, *Paukenmesse*
GOSSEC (62)
La Reprise de Toulon, opera

DITTERSDORF (57)
Der Durchmarsch, opera
Die Lustigen Weiber von Windsor,
  opera
Ugolino, opera
CIMAROSA (47)
Gli Orazi e Curiazi, opera

CONTINUED

BEETHOVEN (26)
"Ah, perfido", scena and aria for
soprano and orchestra

p. Variations on "Nel cor più",
for piano
"Farewell to Vienna's citizens",
song

1797 SCHUBERT was born

HAYDN (65)
The Creation, oratorio (1797–98)
String Quartets Nos. 76–81
(1797–98)
DITTERSDORF (58)
Der Terno secco, opera
Der Mädchenmarkt, opera
CHERUBINI (37)
Médée, opera
BEETHOVEN (27)
Symphony in C, *Jena* (authenticity
doubtful)

Quintet for piano and wind
p. String Quintet
p. String Trio
p. Serenade for string trio
p. Piano Sonatas Nos. 1–4
p. Sonatas Nos. 1 and 2 for
cello and piano
p. Variations on "See, the
conquering hero comes", for
piano and cello
p. Sonata for piano (four hands)
p. Rondo, for piano
War Song of the Austrians, for
voices and piano

1798 DONIZETTI was born

HAYDN (66)
Mass No. 11, *Nelson*
The Seasons, oratorio
(1798–1801)
Piano Sonata No. 50
BEETHOVEN (28)
p. Three String Trios
p. Trio for clarinet (or violin),
cello and piano

p. Variations on "Ein Mädchen",
for piano and cello
p. Six variations on a Swiss Air,
for piano or harp
p. Piano Sonatas Nos. 5–7
p. Twelve minuets
p. Variations on "Une fièvre
brûlante", for piano

1799 DITTERSDORF died

HAYDN (67)
String Quartets Nos. 82 and 83
Mass No. 12, *Theresienmesse*
BEETHOVEN (29)
p. Violin Sonatas Nos. 1–3
p. Piano Sonata No. 8, *Pathétique*
p. Piano Sonatas Nos. 9 and 10
p. Seven Ländler Dances for piano

p. Variations on "Kind willst du",
for piano
Variations on "La stessa, la
Stessissima", for piano
Variation on "Tandeln und
Scherzen"
"Der Wachtelschlag", song

1800

HAYDN (68)
Te Deum
CHERUBINI (40)
Les Deux journées, opera

BEETHOVEN (30)
Symphony No. 1 in C major
Mount of Olives, oratorio
Piano Concerto No. 3

BEETHOVEN CONTINUED
Septet for strings and wind
String Quartets Nos. 1–6
Sonata for piano, violin and viola
Sonata for piano and horn (or
violin)
Piano Sonata No. 11
Air with six variations on "Ich
denke dein", for piano (four
hands)

Six very easy variations on an
original theme, for piano
BOÏELDIEU (25)
Le Calife de Bagdad, opera
WEBER (14)
Das Waldmädchen, opera

BELLINI was born; CIMAROSA died 1801

BOCCHERINI (58)
Stabat Mater
BEETHOVEN (31)
fp. The Creatures of Prometheus,
ballet

p. Piano Concerto No. 1
String Quintet
p. Violin Sonata No. 5, Spring
WEBER (15)
Peter Schmoll und seine Nachbarn,
opera

1802

BEETHOVEN (32)
Symphony No. 2
p. Serenade for flute, violin and
viola
p. Variations on "Bei mannern",
for cello and piano
p. Piano Sonatas Nos. 12 and 13
p. Piano Sonata No. 14, Moonlight
p. Piano Sonata No. 15, Pastoral
Piano Sonatas Nos. 16–20

Violin Sonatas Nos. 6–8
Violin Sonata No. 9, Kreutzer
p. Rondo, for piano
Variations on an original theme,
for piano
Variations and Fugue on a theme
from "Prometheus", for piano
Terzetto, Tremate
p. Six Ländler Dances
Opferlied

ADAM and BERLIOZ were born 1803

HAYDN (71)
String Quartet No. 84
GOSSEC (69)
Les Sabots et le Cerisier, opera
CHERUBINI (43)
Anacréon, opera
BEETHOVEN (33)
Fidelio, opera begun, (last

revision 1814)
Romance in G, for violin and
orchestra
p. Twelve Kontretänze, for
orchestra
p. Nine songs
Six songs (1803–10)
BOÏELDIEU (28)
Ma Tante Aurore, opera

GLINKA and STRAUSS, J. (Sr.) were born 1804

BEETHOVEN (34)
Symphony No. 3, Eroica
Triple Concerto in C major, for
violin, cello, piano and

orchestra
p. Fourteen variations in E♭, for
violin, cello and piano
p. Three Grand Marches, for
piano (four hands)   CONTINUED

BEETHOVEN CONTINUED
Piano Sonata No. 21, *Waldstein*
Piano Sonata No. 23,
  Appassionata
Andante favori, for piano

p. Seven Variations on "God Save
  the King", for piano
p. Five Variations on "Rule,
  Britannia", for piano

1805 BOCCHERINI died

BEETHOVEN (35)
Symphony No. 5
Piano Concerto No. 4

p. Romance in F, for violin and
  orchestra
p. Nine songs

1806

BEETHOVEN (36)
Symphony No. 4
Violin Concerto in D major
p. Piano Sonata No. 22

Thirty-two Variations in C minor,
  for piano (1806–07)
WEBER (20)
Symphony No. 1 (1806–07)

1807

BEETHOVEN (37)
Coriolanus, overture
Leonora No. 1, overture
String Quartets Nos. 7–9,
  Rassumovsky
Mass in C major
"In questa tomba oscura",
arietta

SPONTINI (33)
La Vestale, opera
WEBER (21)
Symphony No. 2

1808 BALFE was born

BEETHOVEN (38)
p. "Sehnsucht", songs with piano

ROSSINI (16)
Sonata for two violins, cello and
  double-bass

1809 MENDELSSOHN was born; HAYDN died

BEETHOVEN (39)
p. Symphony No. 6, *Pastoral*
Piano Concerto No. 5, *Emperor*
String Quartet No. 10, *Harp*
p. Trios Nos. 4 and 5, for violin,
  cello and piano
p. Cello Sonata No. 3
Military March in F
Three songs

SPONTINI (35)
Ferdinand Cortez, opera
ROSSINI (17)
Variations for clarinet and
  orchestra

CHOPIN, NICOLAI and SCHUMANN were born   1810

BEETHOVEN (40)
Egmont, incidental music
p. Sextet in E♭ for strings and
    horns
String Quartet No. 11, *Quartett*
    Serioso
p. Piano Sonatas Nos. 24 and 25

p. Fantasy in G minor, for piano
p. Six variations in D, for piano
p. Three songs for soprano
WEBER (24)
Piano Concerto No. 1
ROSSINI (18)
La cambiale di matrimonio, opera

LISZT and THOMAS were born   1811

BEETHOVEN (41)
The Ruins of Athens, overture and
    eight numbers
King Stephen, overture and nine
    numbers
p. Choral Fantasia, for chorus,
    piano and orchestra
Piano Trio No. 6, *The Archduke*
p. Piano Sonata No. 26, *Les
    Adieux*
p. Four ariettas and duet, for

soprano, tenor and piano
Song
WEBER (25)
Abu Hassan, opera
Bassoon Concerto
Clarinet Concertos Nos. 1 and 2
Concertino for clarinet
SCHUBERT (14)
Quintet-overture

FLOTOW and WALLACE were born   1812

BEETHOVEN (42)
Symphonies Nos. 7 and 8
Piano Trio No. 10
Violin Sonata No. 10
BOÏELDIEU (37)
Jean de Paris, opera
WEBER (26)
Piano Concerto No. 2
Piano Sonata No. 1

ROSSINI (20)
La Scala di seta (The Silken Ladder),
    opera
SCHUBERT (15)
Quartet-Overture
String Quartets Nos. 1–3
Eine Kleine Trauermusik, nonet

DARGOMIZHSKY, VERDI and WAGNER were born; GRÉTRY died   1813

GOSSEC (79)
Dernière Messe des vivants
BEETHOVEN (43)
Wellington's Victory, for orchestra
Triumphal March, for orchestra
Song
ROSSINI (21)
L'Italiana in Algeri, opera
Tancredi, opera

SCHUBERT (16)
Des Teufels Lustschloss, opera
    (1813–14)
Symphony No. 1
String Quartets Nos. 4–6
Three Sonatinas, for violin and
    piano
Five Minuets
Five German Dances

1814

CHERUBINI (54)
String Quartet No. 1
BEETHOVEN (44)
Leonore Prohanska, incidental
  music
Der Glorreiche Augenblick, cantata
Overture in C, *Namensfeier*
Piano Sonata No. 27
Polonaise in C, for piano
Markenstein, duet
p. Three books of Irish songs
p. "Germania", bass solo
Elegiac song

FIELD (22)
Three Nocturnes for piano
SCHUBERT (17)
String Quartets Nos. 7 and 8
Quartet for flute, guitar, viola
  and cello
"Gretchen am Spinnrade"
  (*Gretchen at the Spinning
  Wheel*), song

1815

CHERUBINI (55)
String Quartets Nos. 2 and 3
  (1815–29)
BEETHOVEN (45)
Calm Sea and Prosperous Voyage,
  for chorus and orchestra
Cello Sonatas Nos. 4 and 5
Three Duos, for clarinet and
  bassoon
Twenty-five Scotch songs
Twelve songs of varied nationality
Song

WEBER (29)
Quintet for clarinet and string
  quartet
Concertino for horn and
  orchestra
ROSSINI (23)
Elisabetta, Regina d'Inghelterra,
  opera
SCHUBERT (18)
Symphonies Nos. 2 and 3
String Quartet No. 9
Piano Sonatas Nos. 1 and 2
"Der Erlkönig", song

1816

BEETHOVEN (46)
An die ferne Geliebte, song cycle
Military March
Three songs
WEBER (30)
Piano Sonatas Nos. 2 and 3
ROSSINI (24)
Otello, opera
The Barber of Seville, opera
BERWALD (20)
Theme and Variations for violin
  and orchestra

SCHUBERT (19)
Symphony No. 4, *Tragic*
Symphony No. 5
Concertstücke, for violin and
  orchestra
Rondo, for violin and orchestra
Adagio and Rondo Concertante,
  for piano quartet
String Trio
Piano Sonata No. 3

1817   GADE was born

BEETHOVEN (47)
Symphony No. 9, *Choral*
  (1817–23)

String Quintet
p. Piano Sonata No. 28

ROSSINI (25)
La Cenerentola, opera
La Gazza Ladra (The Thieving Magpie), opera
BERWALD (21)
Double Concerto for two violins and orchestra (lost)
Septet for violin, viola, cello, clarinet, bassoon, horn and double-bass

SCHUBERT (20)
String Quartets Nos. 10 and 11
Piano Sonatas Nos. 4–9
Violin Sonata in A major
"An die Musik", song
"Tod und das Mädchen", song
CHOPIN (7)
Polonaises Nos. 13 and 24

GOUNOD was born **1818**

BEETHOVEN (48)
Six Themes Varied for piano, flute or violin (1818–19)
Ten National Themes with variations, for flute, or violin and piano
Piano Sonata No. 29, *Hammerklavier* (1818–19)
"Ziemlich lebhaft", for piano
Missa Solemnis in D major

ROSSINI (26)
Mosè, opera
SCHUBERT (21)
Symphony No. 6
Piano Sonatas Nos. 10 and 11

OFFENBACH was born **1819**

SPONTINI (45)
Olympie, opera
WEBER (33)
Invitation to the Dance, for piano
BERWALD (23)
Quartet for piano, clarinet, horn and bassoon

SCHUBERT (22)
Piano Quintet, *The Trout*
Piano Sonatas Nos. 12 and 13

1820

BEETHOVEN (50)
Allegro con Brio, for violin and orchestra
Piano Sonata No. 30
Song
WEBER (34)
Der Freischütz, opera
ROSSINI (28)
Maometto II, opera
Solemn Mass

BERWALD (24)
Symphony No. 1
Violin Concerto
SCHUBERT (23)
Die Zauberharfe, melodrama
String Quartet No. 12

1821

BEETHOVEN (51)
Piano Sonata No. 31
p. Bagatelles for piano
SPONTINI (47)
Nurmahal, opera
WEBER (35)
Concertstücke, for piano and
    orchestra

SCHUBERT (24)
Alfonso und Estrella, opera
    (1821–22)
Symphony No. 7 (sketched)
Variation on a Theme by Diabelli
MENDELSSOHN (12)
Piano Sonata No. 2
CHOPIN (11)
Polonaise No. 15

1822   FRANCK and RAFF were born

BEETHOVEN (52)
Consecration of the House,
    overture
Bundeslied (1822–23)
"The Kiss", arietta
WEBER (36)
Piano Sonata No. 4
ROSSINI (30)
Zelmira, opera

SCHUBERT (25)
Symphony No. 8, *Unfinished*
GLINKA (18)
Variations on a Theme of Mozart,
    for piano
MENDELSSOHN (13)
Piano Quartet No. 1, Op. 1
CHOPIN (12)
Polonaise No. 16

1823   LALO was born   1823

BEETHOVEN (53)
Piano Sonata No. 32
p. Bagatelles for piano
Variations on a Waltz by
    Diabelli
"Minuet of Congratulation"
Cantata E♭
WEBER (37)
fp. Euryanthe, opera
ROSSINI (31)
Semiramide, opera

SCHUBERT (26)
Fierrebras, opera
Der häusliche Kreig, opera
Rosamunde, incidental music
Piano Sonata No. 14
Die Schöne Mullerin, song cycle
MENDELSSOHN (14)
Piano Quartet No. 2
Violin Sonata

1824   BRUCKNER and SMETANA were born

BEETHOVEN (54)
String Quartet No. 12
p. The Ruins of Athens, March
    and Chorus
p. Variations on "Ich bin der
    Schneider Kakadu"
SCHUBERT (27)
Octet in F major, for strings and
    wind
String Quartet No. 13
String Quartet No. 14, *Death and*

the Maiden
Introduction and Variations for
    flute and piano
Arpeggione Sonata, for cello and
    piano
MENDELSSOHN (15)
Symphony No. 1
Piano Quartet No. 3

STRAUSS, J. (Jr.) was born **1825**

BEETHOVEN (55)
Great Fugue in B♭, for strings
String Quartet No. 13, *Scherzoso*
  (1825–26)
Rondo a capriccio, for piano
  (1825–26)
BOÏELDIEU (50)
La Dame blanche, opera
ROSSINI (33)
Il viaggio a Rheims, opera
BERWALD (29)
Serenade for tenor and six
  instruments

SCHUBERT (28)
Piano Sonatas Nos. 15–17
BELLINI (24)
Adelson e Salvina, opera
Bianca e Cernando, opera
MENDELSSOHN (16)
Wedding of the Camacho, comic
  opera
Trumpet Overture, for orchestra
String Octet
Capriccio, for piano
CHOPIN (15)
Polonaise No. 8

WEBER died **1826**

BEETHOVEN (56)
String Quartets Nos. 14–16
Andante maestoso in C major,
  for piano
WEBER (40)
fp. Oberon, opera
ROSSINI (34)
Siège de Corinthe, opera
SCHUBERT (29)
String Quartet No. 15
Piano Trio
Rondo Brillant, for violin and
  piano
Piano Sonata No. 18

GLINKA (22)
Memorial Cantata
Trio for piano, clarinet and
  bassoon, or piano, violin and
  cello, *Pathètique*
MENDELSSOHN (17)
A Midsummer Night's Dream,
  overture
String Quintet
Piano Sonata No. 1
Six songs (1826–27)
CHOPIN (16)
Polonaise No. 11
Three écossaises
Introduction and Variations on
  "Der Schweizerbub"

BEETHOVEN died **1827**

ROSSINI (35)
Moïse, opera (French version of
  Mosè)
BERWALD (31)
Gustav Wasa, opera
Concertstücke, for bassoon and
  orchestra
SCHUBERT (30)
Piano Trio
Phantasie, for violin and piano
Die Winterreise, song cycle
BELLINI (26)
Il Pirata, opera

BERLIOZ (24)
Les Francs-Juges, overture
Waverley, overture
La Mort d'Orphée, cantata
MENDELSSOHN (18)
String Quartet No. 2
Fugue for String Quartet
Piano Sonata No. 3
p. Seven pieces for piano
CHOPIN (17)
Nocturne No. 19

1828   SCHUBERT died

AUBER (46)
La Muette de Portici, opera
ROSSINI (36)
fp. Comte Ory, comedy-opera
SCHUBERT (31)
Symphony No. 9 in C major,
  The Great
String Quintet in C major
Piano Sonatas Nos. 19—21
Schwanengesang, song cycle

BERLIOZ (25)
Herminie, cantata
CHOPIN (18)
Krakowiak, concert rondo for
  orchestra
Fantasia on Polish airs, for piano
  and orchestra
Rondo for two pianos
Piano Sonata No. 1
Polonaises Nos. 9 and 10

1829   RUBINSTEIN was born; GOSSEC died

SPONTINI (55)
Agnes von Hohenstaufen, opera
ROSSINI (37)
William Tell, opera
BELLINI (28)
La Straniera, opera
Zaira, opera
BERLIOZ (26)
Cleopâtre, cantata
Huit Scènes de Faust, cantata
Irlande, five songs with piano
  (1829—39)
BALFE (21)
I rivali di se stesso, opera
SCHUMANN (19)
Papillons, twelve pieces for piano
  (1829—31)

MENDELSSOHN (20)
Die Heimkehr aus der Fremde,
  operetta
String Quartet No. 1
Variations Concertantes, for cello
  and piano
Three fantasies, for piano
Twelve songs
CHOPIN (19)
Piano Concerto No. 2
Introduction and Polonaise for
  cello and piano
Twelve Grand Studies for piano
  (1829—32); No. 5 "Black
  Keys", No. 12 "Revolutionary"
Polonaise No. 12
Waltzes Nos. 10 and 13
Variations on a Theme by
  Paganini

1830   GOLDMARK was born

AUBER (48)
Fra Diavolo, opera
DONIZETTI (33)
Anna Bolena, opera
BELLINI (29)
I Capuletti ed i Montecchi, opera
BERLIOZ (27)
Symphonie Fantastique (revised
  1831)
Sardanapale, cantata
GLINKA (26)
String Quartet
BALFE (22)
Un avvertimento ai gelosi, opera

MENDELSSOHN (21)
Hebrides, concert overture
Symphony No. 5, *Reformation*
Eighteen songs
CHOPIN (20)
Piano Concerto No. 1
Nine Mazurkas for piano
  (1830—31)
Nocturnes Nos. 4—6 for piano
  (1830—31)
SCHUMANN (20)
*Theme and Variations on the name
  "Abegg"*, for piano
LISZT (19—38)
Piano Concerto No. 1 (1830—49)

1831

MEYERBEER (41)
Robert le diable, opera
BELLINI (30)
La Sonnambula, opera
Norma, opera
BERLIOZ (28)
Le Corsaire, concert-overture
  (revised 1855)
King Lear, overture
MENDELSSOHN (22)
Piano Concerto No. 1
Die erste Walpurgisnacht, for
  solo voices, chorus and
  orchestra

CHOPIN (21)
Waltzes Nos. 1 and 3
Andante Spianoto, and Grand
  Polonaise Brillant (1831–34)
NICOLAI (21)
Symphony
LISZT (20)
Harmonies poétiques et religieuses,
  for piano and orchestra

CLEMENTI died **1832**

FIELD (50)
fp. Piano Concerto No. 1
ROSSINI (40)
Stabat Mater (1832–41)
DONIZETTI (35)
L'Elisir d'Amore, opera
ADAM (29)
Faust, ballet
BERLIOZ (29)
Le Cinq Mai, cantata
MENDELSSOHN (23)
Meeresstille (Calm Sea and
  Prosperous Voyage) concert-
  overture
Capriccio Brillant, for piano and

  orchestra
Six Preludes and Fugues for
  piano
CHOPIN (22–26)
Allegro de Concert
Scherzo No. 1
NICOLAI (22)
Mass
SCHUMANN (22)
Six Concert Studies on Caprices
  by Paganini, Set I
THOMAS (21)
Hermann et Ketty, cantata
WAGNER (19)
Symphony in C major

BORODIN and BRAHMS were born **1833**

CHERUBINI (76)
Ali Baba, opera
DONIZETTI (36)
Lucrezia Borgia, opera
BELLINI (32)
Beatrice di Tenda, opera
GLINKA (29)
Sextet for piano and strings
  (1833–34)
BALFE (25)
Enrico IV al passo della Marna,
  opera

MENDELSSOHN (24)
Symphony No. 4, *Italian*
Die schöne Melusine, overture
Fantasy in F♯ minor, for piano
Three capriccios for piano
CHOPIN (23)
Bolero in C major
Introduction and Variations on a
  theme by Hérold
SCHUMANN (23)
Six Concert Studies on Caprices
  by Paganini, Set II

1834   PONCHIELLI was born; BOÏELDIEU died

DONIZETTI (37)
Rosmonda d'Inghilterra, opera
ADAM (31)
Le Châlet, opera
BERLIOZ (31)
Harold in Italy, symphony with
   solo viola
Le Nuits d'été, song cycle for
   soprano and orchestra
Sara la baigneuse, choral ballad
MENDELSSOHN (25)
Rondo Brillant, for piano and
   orchestra
Piano sextet
p. *Songs Without Words*, Book I,
for piano
Three Studies for piano
   (1834–37)
Seven songs
CHOPIN (24)
Études Nos. 13–24 (1834–36)
Fantaisie Impromptu in C♯
   minor
Polonaises Nos. 1–2 (1834–35)
Prelude No. 26
SCHUMANN (24)
Carnaval, twenty-one pieces for
   piano (1834–35)

1835   CUI and SAINT-SAËNS were born; BELLINI died

CHERUBINI (78)
String Quartets Nos. 4–6
AUBER (53)
The Bronze Horse, opera
   (revised 1857)
DONIZETTI (38)
Lucia di Lammermoor, opera
BELLINI (34)
I Puritani, opera
BALFE (27)
The Siege of Rochelle, opera
MENDELSSOHN (26)
p. *Songs Without Words*, Book II,
   for piano
CHOPIN (25)
Ballade
Nocturnes, Nos. 7 and 8
Waltzes Nos. 2, 9 and 11
NICOLAI (25)
Symphony
Funeral March (for the death of
   Bellini)
LISZT (24)
Années de pèlerinage, for piano
   begun (completed 1883)

1836   DELIBES was born

CHERUBINI (79)
Requiem Mass
MEYERBEER (45)
Les Huguenots, opera
ADAM (33)
Le Postillon de Longjumeau, opera
GLINKA (32)
A Life for the Tzar, opera
The Moldavian Gipsy, incidental
   music
BALFE (28)
The Maid of Artois, opera
MENDELSSOHN (27)
St. Paul, oratorio
CHOPIN (26)
Ballade (1836–39)
Nocturnes Nos. 9 and 10
   (1836–37)
Twenty-four Preludes for piano
   (1836–39)
SCHUMANN (26)
Phantasie, for piano

BALAKIREV and WALDTEUFEL were born; FIELD died **1837**

CHERUBINI (80)
String Quintet
AUBER (55)
Le Domino noir, opera
BERLIOZ (34)
Grande Messe des Morts
BALFE (29)
Catherine Grey, opera
Joan of Arc, opera
MENDELSSOHN (28)
Piano Concerto No. 2
String Quartets Nos. 3–5
  (1837–38)

CHOPIN (27)
Impromptu, Op. 29
Nocturne in C minor, Op. 20
Scherzo, No. 2
SCHUMANN (27)
Davidsbündler-Tänze, eighteen
  piano pieces (revised 1850)
p. Études symphoniques, twelve
  symphonic studies for piano
Fantasiestücke for piano, Books
  I and II
THOMAS (26)
La Double échelle, opera
GOUNOD (19)
Scherzo for orchestra

BIZET and BRUCH were born **1838**

BERLIOZ (35)
Benvenuto Cellini, opera
Roméo and Juliet, dramatic
  symphony (1838–39)
BALFE (30)
Falstaff, opera
Diadeste, opera
MENDELSSOHN (29)
Serenade and Allegro gioioso, for
  piano and orchestra
Cello Sonata
Piano Trio No. 1
CHOPIN (28)
Nocturnes, Nos. 11 and 12

(1838–39)
Polonaises Nos. 3 and 4
(1838–39)
Waltz No. 4
NICOLAI (28)
Von Himmel Hoch, overture
SCHUMANN (28)
Kinderscenen, thirteen short piano
  pieces
Kreisleriana, for piano
Novelleten, eight piano pieces
THOMAS (27)
Le Perruquier de la Régence, opera

MUSSORGSKY was born **1839**

ADAM (36)
La Jolie Fille de Gand, ballet
BERLIOZ (36)
Rêverie and Caprice, for violin and
  orchestra
GLINKA (35)
Valse-fantasie, for orchestra
MENDELSSOHN (30)
Ruy Blas, overture
p. Songs Without Words, Book III,
  for piano
CHOPIN (29)
Études, Nos. 25–27
Impromptu, Op. 36
Scherzo, No. 3
Piano Sonata No. 2

SCHUMANN (29)
Nachtstücke, for piano
NICOLAI (29)
Henry II, opera
LISZT (28)
Piano Concerto No. 2
THOMAS (28)
Le Panier fleuri, opera
La Gipsy, ballet
VERDI (26)
Oberto, opera

1840   TCHAIKOVSKY was born; PAGANINI died

DONIZETTI (43)
La Favorita, opera
La Fille du régiment, opera
BERLIOZ (37)
Symphonie Funèbre et Triomphale,
   for chorus, strings and military
   band
GLINKA (36)
Farewell to Petersburg, song cycle
MENDELSSOHN (31)
Lobgesang (Hymn of Praise),
   symphony-cantata (Symphony
   No. 2)
CHOPIN (30)
Ballade, Op. 47 (1840–41)
Fantasia in F minor
Waltz No. 5
NICOLAI (30)
Gildippe ed Odoardo, opera
Il Templario, opera

SCHUMANN (30)
Dichterliebe, song cycle
Frauenliebe und Leben, song cycle
Liederkreiss, nine songs (Heine)
LISZT (29)
Malediction, for piano and strings
   (c.1840)
THOMAS (29)
Carlino, opera
WAGNER (27)
Faust, overture
GADE (23)
Faedrelandets Muser, ballet
Echoes from Ossian, overture
Piano Sonata
GOUNOD (22)
Marche militaire suisse, for
   orchestra
FRANCK (18)
Three Piano Trios, Op. 1

1841   CHABRIER and DVOŘÁK were born

AUBER (59)
Les Diamants de la couronne, opera
ADAM (38)
Giselle, ballet
BALFE (33)
Keolanthe, opera
MENDELSSOHN (32)
Songs Without Words, Books IV
   and VII, for piano
CHOPIN (31)
Nocturnes Nos. 13 and 14
Polonaise No. 5
Prelude No. 25
Waltz No. 12

NICOLAI (31)
Il Proscritto, opera
SCHUMANN (31)
Symphony No. 1, *Spring*
Symphony No. 4 (revised 1851)
Overture, Scherzo and Finale for
   orchestra (*Finale* revised 1845)
Piano Concerto (1841–45)
THOMAS (30)
Le Comte de Carmagnola, opera
GADE (24)
Symphony No. 1

1842   MASSENET and SULLIVAN were born; CHERUBINI died

BERWALD (46)
Symphony No. 2, *Sérieuse*
Symphony No. 3
DONIZETTI (45)
Linda de Chamounix, opera
GLINKA (38)
Russlan and Ludmilla, opera
MENDELSSOHN (33)
Symphony No. 3, *Scottish*
Cello Sonata (1842–43)
Songs Without Words, Book VIII,

   for piano (1842–45)
CHOPIN (32)
Ballade, Op. 52
Impromptu, Op. 51
Polonaise No. 6
Scherzo No. 4
SCHUMANN (32)
Piano Quintet
Piano Quartet
Three String Quartets
Andante and Variations for two

SCHUMANN CONTINUED
pianos, two cellos and horn
(1842?)
Four *Fantasiestücke*, for piano
trio
Liederkreiss, twelve songs
(Eichendorf)
THOMAS (31)
Le Guerillero, opera

VERDI (29)
Nabucco, opera
WAGNER (29)
fp. Rienzi, opera
GADE (25)
Napoli, ballet
Violin Sonata No. 1
FRANCK (20)
Piano Trio No. 4

GRIEG was born   **1843**

DONIZETTI (46)
Maria de Rohan, opera
Don Pasquale, opera
Dom Sébastien, opera
BALFE (35)
The Bohemian Girl, opera
Geraldine, opera
MENDELSSOHN (34)
Athalie, incidental music
String Quartet Pieces, Op. 81
Songs Without Words, Books V
and VI, for piano
CHOPIN (33)
Berceuse, Op. 57
Nocturnes Nos. 15 and 16

SCHUMANN (33)
Das Paradies und die Peri, cantata
LISZT (32)
Valse Impromptu in A♭ major
THOMAS (32)
Angélique et Médor, opera
Mina, opera
VERDI (30)
I Lombardi, opera
WAGNER (30)
fp. The Flying Dutchman, opera
FRANCK (21)
Andante quietoso, for violin and
piano

RIMSKY-KORSAKOV and SARASATE were born   **1844**

BERWALD (48)
A Country Wedding, for organ
(four hands)
BERLIOZ (41)
Roman Carnival Overture
BALFE (36)
The Castle of Aymon, opera
The Daughter of St. Mark, opera
MENDELSSOHN (35)
Violin Concerto

CHOPIN (34)
Piano Sonata No. 3
NICOLAI (34)
Ein Feste Burg, overture with
chorus
VERDI (31)
Ernani, opera
I due Foscari, opera
GADE (27)
In the Highlands, overture

FAURÉ was born   **1845**

BERWALD (49)
Symphony No. 5, *Singulière*
Symphony No. 6
Five Piano Trios
GLINKA (41)
Spanish Overture No. 1, *Jota
Aragonesa*
BALFE (37)
The Enchantress, opera

SCHUMANN (35)
Symphony No. 2 (1845–46)
MENDELSSOHN (36)
Piano Trio No. 2
String Quintet
Songs Without Words, for cello
and piano

CONTINUED

CHOPIN (35)
Cello Sonata, Op. 65
Barcarolle, Op. 60
Polonaise, No. 7
WALLACE (33)
fp. Maritana, opera

VERDI (32)
Alzira, opera
Giovanna d'Arco, opera
WAGNER (32)
fp. Tannhäuser, opera

1846

AUBER (74)
Manon Lescaut, opera
BERLIOZ (43)
The Damnation of Faust, dramatic
  cantata
BALFE (38)
The Bondman, opera
MENDELSSOHN (37)
fp. Elijah, oratorio
String Quartet No. 6
CHOPIN (36)
Nocturnes Nos. 17 and 18
Waltzes Nos. 6–8. Op. 64
  (1846–47)

THOMAS (35)
Betty, ballet
VERDI (33)
Attila, opera
GADE (28)
p. String Quintet
FRANCK (24)
Ruth, oratorio
Ce qu'on entend sur la montagne,
  symphonic poem

1847   MENDELSSOHN died

GLINKA (43)
Greeting to the Fatherland, for
  piano
BALFE (39)
The Maid of Honour, opera
MENDELSSOHN (38)
Lorely, opera (unfinished)
SCHUMANN (37)
Genoveva, opera (1847–48)
Piano Trios Nos. 1 and 2

FLOTOW (35)
Martha, opera
DARGOMIZHSKY (34)
Esmeralda, opera (possibly *c.*1839)
VERDI (34)
Macbeth, opera
I masnadieri, opera
GADE (30)
Symphony No. 3
BORODIN (14)
Flute Concerto (with piano)

1848   DONIZETTI died

BERLIOZ (45)
La Mort d'Ophelie, for two-part
  female chorus (also for voice
  and piano)

GLINKA (44)
Wedding Song (Kamarinskaya),
  fantasia for orchestra
SMETANA (24)
Festive Overture (1848–49)

1849   GODARD was born; STRAUSS, J. (Sr.), CHOPIN and NICOLAI died

MEYERBEER (58)
Le Prophète, opera
ADAM (46)
Le Toréador, opera

NICOLAI (39)
The Merry Wives of Windsor,
  opera

SCHUMANN (39)
Manfred, dramatic poem
Three *Fantasiestücke*, for piano
  and clarinet with violin or
  cello
Adagio and Allegro, for piano and
  horn
LISZT (38)
Héroïde funèbre, for orchestra
  (1849–50)

THOMAS (38)
Le Caïd, opera
VERDI (36)
Luisa Miller, opera
GADE (32)
p. String Octet
BRUCKNER (25)
Requiem in D minor

1850

SCHUMANN (40)
Symphony No. 3, *Rhenish*
Cello Concerto in A minor
LISZT (39)
Prometheus, symphonic poem
Consolations, for piano
Liebesträume, nocturnes for piano

THOMAS (39)
Le Songe d'une nuit d'été, opera
GADE (33)
Mariotta, incidental music
Symphony No. 4
p. Violin Sonata No. 2

d'INDY was born; SPONTINI died   **1851**

SCHUMANN (41)
Piano Trio No. 3
Four *Marchenbilder*, for piano and
  viola (or violin)
Two Violin Sonatas
THOMAS (40)
Raymond, opera
VERDI (38)
Rigoletto, opera
WAGNER (38)
fp. Lohengrin, opera

GOUNOD (33)
Sapho, opera
FRANCK (29)
Le Valet de ferme, opera
BRAHMS (18)
Scherzo in E♭ minor
The first three sets of songs
  (1851–53)

STANFORD was born   **1852**

BERWALD (56)
Three piano trios (1852–54)
ADAM (49)
Si j'étais Roi, opera
BALFE (44)
The Devil's in It, opera
The Sicilian Bride, opera
MENDELSSOHN (posthumous)
fp. Christus, oratorio (unfinished)
LISZT (41)
Hungarian Rhapsodies, Nos. 1–15
GADE (35)
Symphony No. 5
Spring Fantasy, for voices and
  orchestra

GOUNOD (34)
Faust, opera (1852–59)
La Nonne sanglante, opera
  (1852–54)
BRAHMS (19)
Piano Sonata No. 1 (1852–53)
Piano Sonata No. 2
BALAKIREV (15)
*Grande Fantaisie on Russian
  Folksongs*, for piano and
  orchestra
Septet for flute, cello, strings and
  piano

1853   MESSAGER was born

SCHUMANN (43)
Violin Concerto
Märchenerzählungen, four pieces
    for piano, clarinet (or violin)
    and viola
Introduction and Allegro, for piano
Fantasy, for violin
THOMAS (42)
La Tonelli, opera
VERDI (40)
La Traviata, opera
Il Trovatore, opera

OFFENBACH (34)
Le mariage aux lanternes, opera
SMETANA (29)
Festive Symphony (1853–54)
RUBINSTEIN (24)
Melody in F
BRAHMS (20)
Piano Trio No. 1 (1853–54)
Piano Sonata No. 3

1854   CATALANI, HUMPERDINCK, JANÁČEK and MOSKOWSKI were born

MEYERBEER (63)
L'Étoile du nord, opera
BERLIOZ (51)
L'Enfance du Christ, oratorio
SCHUMANN (44)
p. *Albumblätter*, twenty pieces for
    piano
LISZT (43)
Hungaria, symphonic poem
Orpheus, symphonic poem
Les préludes, symphonic poem

BRUCKNER (30)
Solemn Mass in B♭ major
BRAHMS (21)
Piano Concerto No. 1 (1854–58)
Four Ballads for piano
Variations on a Theme by
    Schumann, for piano
BALAKIREV (17)
String Quartet, *Quatour original
    russe* (1854–55)
BIZET (16)
La Prêtresse, one-act opera

1855

BERWALD (59)
Piano Concerto
LISZT (44)
Totentanz, for piano and orchestra
THOMAS (44)
La Cour de Célimène, opera
VERDI (42)
I Vespri siciliani, opera
GADE (38)
p. *Novelleten*, for piano trio
GOUNOD (37)
Symphonies Nos. 1 and 2
Messe solenelle à St. Cecile
LALO (32)
String Quartet
SMETANA (31)
Piano Trio

BRAHMS (22)
Symphony No. 1 begun
    (completed 1876)
Piano Quartet No. 3 begun
    (completed 1875)
SAINT-SAËNS (20)
Symphony No. 1
Piano Quintet
BALAKIREV (18)
Piano Concerto No. 1 (c.1855)
Octet for flute, oboe, horn, piano
    and strings (1855–56)
"Three Forgotten Songs"
BIZET (17)
Symphony in C major
DVOŘÁK (14)
"Forget-Me-Not Polka"
    (1855–56)

CHAUSSON and LIADOV were born; ADAM and SCHUMANN died   **1856**

BERWALD (60)
Two piano quintets (1856–58,
  possibly 1853–54)
ADAM (53)
Le Corsaire, ballet
BERLIOZ (53)
The Trojans, opera (1856–59)
LISZT (45)
Hunnenschlacht, symphonic poem
Tasso, symphonic poem

DARGOMIZHSKY (43)
fp. Russalka, opera
GADE (39)
Symphony No. 6 (*c.*1856)
BRAHMS (23)
Variations on a Hungarian theme,
  for piano
Variations on an original theme,
  for piano
BRUCH (18)
String Quartet

CHAMINADE and ELGAR were born; GLINKA died   **1857**

BALFE (49)
The Rose of Castille, opera
LISZT (46)
Dante Symphony (possibly
  1855–56)
Faust Symphony (possibly
  1854–57)
Mazeppa, tone poem
THOMAS (46)
Le Carnaval de Venise, opera
Psyche, opera
Messe Solenelle
VERDI (44)
Araldo, opera
Simon Boccanegra, opera
WAGNER (44)
Wesendonck Lieder (1857–58)
GOUNOD (39)
Le Médecin malgré lui, opera

BRAHMS (24)
Serenade for Orchestra, in D
  major (1857–58)
Serenade for Orchestra in A
  major (1857–60)
German Requiem (1857–68)
CUI (22)
Scherzo for Orchestra, Nos. 1
  and 2
SAINT-SAËNS (22)
Organ Fantasia No. 1
BIZET (19)
Clovis et Clothilde, cantata
Le Docteur Miracle, operetta
BRUCH (19)
Piano Trio
MUSSORGSKY (18)
Souvenir d'enfance, for piano
DVOŘÁK (16)
Mass in B♭ major (1857–59)

LEONCAVALLO, PUCCINI and SMYTH were born   **1858**

OFFENBACH (39)
Orpheus in the Underworld,
  operetta
FRANCK (36)
Ave Maria, motet
SMETANA (34)
Richard III, symphonic poem
Wallenstein's Camp, symphonic
  poem (1858–59)
CUI (23)
The Caucasian Prisoner, opera

SAINT-SAËNS (23)
Piano Concerto No. 1
BALAKIREV (21)
Overture on Russian Themes
BRUCH (20)
Scherz, List und Rache, opera
MUSSORGSKY (19)
Scherzo for Orchestra
"Edipo" for mixed chorus
  (1858–60)

1859   IPPOLITOV-IVANOV was born

MEYERBEER (68)
Dinorah, opera
BERWALD (63)
p. Cello sonata
LISZT (48)
Hamlet, symphonic poem
Die Ideale, for orchestra
VERDI (46)
Un ballo in maschera, opera
BRAHMS (26)
Marienlieder, for four-part mixed
   choir
String Quartets Nos. 1 and 2
   (1859–73)

CUI (24)
The Mandarin's Son, opera
Tarantella
SAINT-SAËNS (24)
Violin Concerto No. 1
BIZET (21)
Don Procopio, opera
MUSSORGSKY (20)
Marcia di Sciamie, for soloist,
   choir and orchestra
Impromptu Passione, for piano

1860   ALBÉNIZ, CHARPENTIER, WOLF and MAHLER were born;
PADEREWSKI was born (or possibly in 1866)

BALFE (52)
Bianca, opera
LISZT (49)
Fantasy on Hungarian Folk Tunes,
   for piano and orchestra
   (*c*.1860)
THOMAS (49)
Le Roman d'Elvire, opera
GOUNOD (42)
Philémon et Baucis, opera

SMETANA (36)
Haakon Jarl, symphonic poem
   (1860–61)
BRAHMS (27)
String Sextet No. 1, in B♭ major
BRUCH (22)
String Quartet
CHABRIER (19)
Impromptu for piano

1861   ARENSKY, LOEFFLER and MACDOWELL were born

BALFE (53)
The Puritan's Daughter, opera
DARGOMIZHSKY (48)
Baba-Yaga, fantasy for orchestra
GADE (44)
Hamlet, concert overture
Michelangelo, overture
BRAHMS (28)
Piano Quartets Nos. 1 and 2
Variations and Fugue on a
   Theme by Handel, for piano
Soldaten Lieder
Fifteen songs from Magalone
   (1861–68)

PONCHIELLI (27)
La Savoiarda, opera
BALAKIREV (24)
Piano Concerto No. 2 begun
   (resumed 1909)
MUSSORGSKY (22)
Alla marcia notturna, for orchestra
Scherzo and finale, for a
   symphony in D major
DVOŘÁK (20)
String Quintet
RIMSKY-KORSAKOV (17)
Symphony No. 1 (1861–65)

1862   BOËLLMANN, DEBUSSY, DELIUS and GERMAN were born

BERWALD (66)
Estrella de Soria, opera

BERLIOZ (59)
Beatrice et Bénédict, opera

VERDI (49)
La Forza del destino, opera
Inno delle nazioni, for chorus
GOUNOD (44)
La Reine de Saba, opera
SMETANA (38)
On the Seashore, for piano
BORODIN (29)
Symphony No. 1 (1862–67)

BRAHMS (29)
Cello Sonata No. 1 (1862–65)
Piano Studies (Variations on a
    Theme by Paganini), Books I
    and II (1862–63)
DVOŘÁK (21)
String Quartet No. 1
SULLIVAN (20)
The Tempest, incidental music

MASCAGNI and PIERNÉ were born   **1863**

ROSSINI (71)
Petite Messe Solenelle
BALFE (55)
The Armourer of Nantes, opera
Blanche de Nevers, opera
LISZT (52)
Two Concert Studies for piano
BRUCKNER (39)
Symphony in F minor
    (unnumbered)
Overture in G minor
Germanenzug, for chorus and
    brass
SMETANA (39)
The Brandenburgs in Bohemia,
    opera

BRAHMS (30)
Rinaldo, cantata (1863–68)
PONCHIELLI (29)
Roderico, opera
SAINT-SAËNS (28)
Piano Trio No. 1
BIZET (25)
The Pearl Fishers, opera
BRUCH (25)
Die Lorely, opera
MASSENET (21)
Overture de Concert
David Rizzio, cantata

STRAUSS, R. and ROPARTZ were born; MEYERBEER died   **1864**

BALFE (56)
The Sleeping Queen, opera
GADE (47)
Symphonies Nos. 2 and 7
p. Piano Trio in F major
p. Fantasiestücke, for cello and
    piano
Fantasies for clarinet
GOUNOD (46)
Mireille, opera
OFFENBACH (45)
La Belle Hélène, operetta
BRUCKNER (40)
Mass No. 1 in D minor
Symphony in D minor (revised

1869, known as No. 0)
"Um Mitternacht", for male-
    voice chorus
BRAHMS (31)
String Sextet No. 2 (1864–65)
Piano Quintet
BRUCH (26)
Frithjof-Scenen, for solo voices,
    chorus and orchestra (c.1864)
SULLIVAN (22)
L'Ile enchantée, ballet music
Kenilworth, cantata
GRIEG (21)
Album Leaves, for piano
    (1864–78)

DUKAS, GLAZUNOV, SIBELIUS and NIELSEN were born; WALLACE died   **1865**

MEYERBEER (posthumous)
fp. L'Africaine, opera

THOMAS (54)
Marche religieuse, for orchestra

CONTINUED

WAGNER (52)
fp. Tristan und Isolde, music drama
GADE (48)
p. String sextet
GOUNOD (47)
Chant des Compagnons
FRANCK (43)
The Tower of Babel, oratorio
BRAHMS (32)
Trio for piano, violin and horn
BIZET (27)
Ivan the Terrible, opera
Chasse fantastique, for piano

DVOŘÁK (24)
Symphonies Nos. 1 and 2
Cello Concerto in A major
The Cypresses, originally for
    string quartet, later for voice
    and piano
Clarinet Quintet
MASSENET (23)
Suite for Orchestra, No. 1
GRIEG (22)
In Autumn, concert overture
Violin Sonata No. 1

1866   SATIE, CILÈA and BUSONI were born

LISZT (55)
Deux Légendes, for piano
THOMAS (55)
Mignon, opera
DARGOMIZHSKY (53)
The Stone Guest, opera (unfinished)
OFFENBACH (47)
Bluebeard, operetta
La Vie parisienne, operetta
BRUCKNER (42)
Symphony No. 1 (revised 1891)
Mass No. 2 in E minor
SMETANA (42)
The Bartered Bride, opera
SAINT-SAËNS (31)
Suite in D minor, for piano and
    cello (or violin, or viola)
DELIBES (30)
La Source, ballet

BALAKIREV (29)
Symphony No. 1 begun
    (completed 1898)
BIZET (28)
Trois esquisses musicales, for
    piano
TCHAIKOVSKY (26)
Symphony No. 1, *Winter
    Daydreams*
SULLIVAN (24)
In Memoriam Overture
Irish Symphony
Cello Concerto
RIMSKY-KORSAKOV (22)
Overture on Russian Themes
Symphony No. 3 (1866–73)

1867   GIORDANO was born

LISZT (56)
Legend of St. Elizabeth (possibly
    1857–62)
DARGOMIZHSKY (54)
The Triumph of Bacchus, opera-
    ballet
VERDI (54)
Don Carlos, opera
GOUNOD (49)
Roméo et Juliette, opera

OFFENBACH (48)
La Grande Duchesse de Gérolstein,
    operetta
STRAUSS, J. (Jr.) (42)
The Blue Danube Waltz
BORODIN (34)
The Bogatirs, opera-farce
BALAKIREV (30)
Overture on Czech Themes
Thamar, symphonic poem
    (1867–82)
BIZET (29)
The Fair Maid of Perth, opera

MUSSORGSKY (28)
La Disfatta di Sennacherib, for
  chorus and orchestra, first
  version
Symphonic Intermezzo "in modo
  classico"
SULLIVAN (25)
Cox and Box, operetta

GRIEG (24)
Violin Sonata No. 2
Lyric Pieces for piano, Book I
RIMSKY-KORSAKOV (23)
Fantasia on Serbian Themes, for
  orchestra
Sadko, symphonic poem

BANTOCK was born; ROSSINI and BERWALD died **1868**

THOMAS (57)
Hamlet, grand opera
WAGNER (55)
*fp. Die Meistersinger von
  Nürnberg*, opera
OFFENBACH (49)
La Périchole, operetta
BRUCKNER (44)
Mass No. 3, *Grosse Messe*
  (revised 1871 and 1890)
SMETANA (44)
fp. Dalibor, opera
Solemn Prelude for orchestra
STRAUSS, J. (Jr.) (43)
"Tales from the Vienna Woods"
SAINT-SAËNS (33)
Piano Concerto No. 2

BIZET (30)
Symphony in C major, *Roma*
Marche funèbre, for orchestra
Marine, for piano
Variations chromatiques, for piano
BRUCH (30)
Violin Concerto No. 1
MUSSORGSKY (29)
fp. (privately) *Zenitha (The
  Marriage)*, opera
The Nursery, song cycle
  (1868–72)
TCHAIKOVSKY (28)
Fate, symphonic poem
RIMSKY-KORSAKOV (24)
*The Maid of Pskov (Ivan the
  Terrible)*, opera (1868–72)

ROUSSEL was born: BERLIOZ and DARGOMIZHSKY died **1869**

WAGNER (56)
fp. Das Rheingold, music drama
BRUCKNER (45)
Locus iste, motet
BORODIN (36)
Prince Igor, opera begun (left
  unfinished)
Symphony No. 2 begun
  (completed 1876)
BRAHMS (36)
p. Books I and II, of piano studies
  in five books
Eighteen Liebeslieder Waltzes
CUI (34)
William Ratcliffe, opera
SAINT-SAËNS (34)
Piano Concerto No. 3

BALAKIREV (32)
fp. Islamey, piano fantasy
BIZET (31)
Vasco da Gama, symphonic ode
  with chorus
MUSSORGSKY (30)
Boris Godunov, opera (first version
  with piano)
TCHAIKOVSKY (29)
Romeo and Juliet, fantasy overture
  (final version 1880)
SULLIVAN (27)
The Prodigal Son, oratorio
RIMSKY-KORSAKOV (25)
Antar, symphonic suite
GRIEG (24)
Piano Concerto

1870   LEHÁR was born; BALFE died

WAGNER (57)
fp. Die Walküre, music drama
Siegfried Idyll, for orchestra
BRAHMS (37)
Alto Rhapsody, for contralto,
    chorus and orchestra
Triumphlied, for chorus and
    orchestra
SAINT-SAËNS (35)
Introduction and Rondo Capriccioso,
    for violin and orchestra
Mélodies persanes, six songs

DELIBES (34)
Coppélia, ballet
BRUCH (32)
Symphonies Nos. 1 and 2
DVOŘÁK (29)
Dramatic (Tragic) Overture
Three String Quartets
Notturno, for strings
SULLIVAN (28)
Di Ballo, concert overture
FAURÉ (25)
Two vocal duets

1871

VERDI (58)
Aida, opera
GADE (54)
Symphony No. 8
GOUNOD (53)
Saltarello for orchestra
BRUCKNER (47)
Os uisti, motet
STRAUSS, J. (Jr.) (46)
Indigo und die vierzig Rauber,
    operetta
BRAHMS (38)
Schicksalied (Song of Destiny)
SAINT-SAËNS (36)
Marche héroïque, for orchestra
Omphale's Spinning Wheel,
    symphonic poem

BIZET (33)
Jeux d'enfants, for piano duet
Petite Suite d'Orchestre
TCHAIKOVSKY (31)
String Quartet
DVOŘÁK (30)
King and Charcoal Burner, opera
    (first version)
Overture in F major
Piano Trios Nos. 1 and 2
Cello Sonata
MASSENET (29)
Suite for Orchestra No. 2,
    Scènes hongroises

1872   ALFVÉN, SKRIABIN and VAUGHAN WILLIAMS were born

DARGOMIZHSKY (posthumous)
fp. The Stone Guest, opera
FRANCK (50)
Panis Angelicus
LALO (49)
Deux Aubades, for small orchestra
Divertissement, for small
    orchestra
Violin Concerto
BRUCKNER (48)
Symphony No. 2, revised 1891
PONCHIELLI (38)
I Promessi Sposi, opera
SAINT-SAËNS (37)
La Princesse jaune, opera

BIZET (34)
L'Arlésienne, incidental music
Djarmileh, opera
BRUCH (34)
Hermione, opera
Odysseus, cantata
MUSSORGSKY (33)
Khovantschina, opera
TCHAIKOVSKY (32)
Symphony No. 2, *Little Russian*
DVOŘÁK (31)
May Night, nocturne for orchestra
Piano Quintet in A major
GRIEG (29)
Sigurd Jorsalfar, incidental music

VERDI (60)
String Quartet
GOUNOD (55)
Funeral March of a Marionette,
    for orchestra
LALO (50)
Symphonie Espagnole, for violin
    and orchestra
BRUCKNER (49)
Symphony No. 3, *Wagner*
    (revised 1877 and 1888)
BRAHMS (40)
Variations on a Theme by Haydn,
    St. Anthony, for orchestra
PONCHIELLI (39)
Il Parlatore Eterno, opera
Le Due Gemelle, ballet
SAINT-SAËNS (38)
Phaeton, symphonic poem
Cello Concerto No. 1

BIZET (35)
Patrie, overture
DVOŘÁK (32)
Symphony No. 3
Romance, for violin and orchestra
Octet, *Serenade*
String Quartet in A minor
String Quartet in F minor
Violin Sonata
MASSENET (31)
Phedre, concert overture
Suite for Orchestra No. 3,
    Scènes dramatiques
SULLIVAN (31)
The Light of the World, oratorio
FAURÉ (28)
Cantique de Jean Racine

THOMAS (63)
Gille et Gillotin, opera
VERDI (61)
Requiem Mass
GADE (57)
Novelleten, for string orchestra
FRANCK (52)
Redemption, for soprano, chorus
    and orchestra (second edition
    with one orchestral number
    and male chorus added)
BRUCKNER (50)
Symphony No. 4, *Romantic*
    (revised 1880)
SMETANA (50)
The Two Widows, opera
Má Vlast, cycle of six symphonic
    poems (1874–79)
STRAUSS, J. (Jr.) (49)
Die Fledermaus, operetta
PONCHIELLI (40)
I Lituani, opera, revised as *Aldona*
SAINT-SAËNS (39)
Danse macabre, symphonic poem

MUSSORGSKY (35)
Sorochintsky Fair, opera
Night on the Bare Mountain,
    arrangement by Rimsky-
    Korsakov of a passage in
    Sorochintsky Fair
Jesus Navin, for contralto, bass,
    chorus and piano
Pictures from an Exhibition, for
    piano
Sunless, song cycle
TCHAIKOVSKY (34)
Piano Concerto No. 1 (1874–75)
String Quartet
DVOŘÁK (33)
Symphony No. 4
Rhapsody for orchestra, in A minor
String Quartet
MASSENET (32)
Suite for Orchestra No. 4, *Scènes*
    pittoresques
d'INDY (23)
Max et Thecla, symphonic
    overture, Part 2 of Wallenstein
    Trilogy
Jean Hunyade, symphony

1875   COLERIDGE-TAYLOR and RAVEL were born; BIZET died

LALO (52)
Allegro Symphonique
GOLDMARK (45)
The Queen of Sheba, opera
BORODIN (42–46)
String Quartet No. 1 (1875–79)
BRAHMS (42)
Fifteen new Liebeslieder for piano
  duet
String Quartet No. 3
SAINT-SAËNS (40)
Piano Concerto No. 4
BIZET (37)
fp. Carmen, opera
MUSSORGSKY (36–38)
Songs and Dances of Death, song
  cycle (1875–77)
CUI (41)
Angelo, opera
PONCHIELLI (41)
A Gaetano Donizetti, cantata
TCHAIKOVSKY (35)
Symphony No. 3, *Polish*
Swan Lake, ballet
String Quartet

DVOŘÁK (34)
Symphony No. 5
Serenade for Strings
String Quintet, with double-bass
Piano Quartet
Piano Trio
Moravian duets, for voices and
  piano
MASSENET (33)
Eve, oratorio
SULLIVAN (33)
Trial by Jury, operetta
The Zoo, operetta
GRIEG (32)
Peer Gynt, incidental music
RIMSKY-KORSAKOV (31)
Quartet No. 1
FAURÉ (30)
Allegro Symphonique, for orchestra
Suite for Orchestra
Les Djinns, for chorus and
  orchestra
MESSAGER (22)
Symphony

1876   FALLA, WOLF-FERRARI and CARPENTER were born

WAGNER (63)
fp. Siegfried, music drama
fp. Götterdämmerung, music drama
GOUNOD (58)
Cinq-Mars, opera (1876–77)
FRANCK (54)
Les Éolides, symphonic poem
LALO (53)
Cello Concerto
SMETANA (52)
The Kiss, opera
String Quartet No. 1, *From My
  Life*
GOLDMARK (46)
Rustic Wedding, symphony
BRAHMS (43)
Symphony No. 1 (completed)
PONCHIELLI (42)
La Giaconda, opera
SAINT-SAËNS (41)
The Deluge, oratorio

DELIBES (40)
Silvia, ballet
TCHAIKOVSKY (36)
Slavonic March, for orchestra
Variations on a Rococo Theme,
  for cello and orchestra
DVOŘÁK (35)
Piano Concerto in G minor
String Quartet in E major
Piano Trio
Stabat Mater
MASSENET (34)
Suite for Orchestra, No. 5,
  Scènes napolitaines
RIMSKY-KORSAKOV (32)
String Sextet
Quintet for piano and wind
FAURÉ (31)
Violin Sonata in A major
GODARD (27)
Violin Concerto No. 2, *Concerto
  romantique*

d'INDY (25)
Attendez-moi sous l'orme, opera
  (1876–78)
Anthony and Cleopatra, overture
STANFORD (24)
Symphony
LIADOV (21)
Birulki, for piano

WOLF (16–30)
Nachgelassene Werke (1876–90)
DEBUSSY (14–17)
Trio in G minor (1876–79)
STRAUSS, R. (12)
Festmarch, for orchestra, Op. 1

AUBERT, DOHNÁNYI and QUILTER were born **1877**

BRUCKNER (53)
Symphony No. 5 (revised 1878)
BRAHMS (44)
Symphony No. 2
SAINT-SAËNS (42)
Samson and Delilah, opera
Suite for Orchestra
La Jeunesse d'Hercule, symphonic
  poem
TCHAIKOVSKY (37)
Symphony No. 4
Francesca da Rimini, symphonic
  fantasy
Waltz-Scherzo, for violin and
  orchestra
CHABRIER (36)
L'Étoile, opera
DVOŘÁK (36)
The Cunning Peasant, opera
Symphonic Variations for

orchestra
String Quartet in D minor
MASSENET (35)
Le Roi de Lahore, opera
Narcisse, cantata
SULLIVAN (35)
The Sorcerer, operetta
"The Lost Chord", song
STANFORD (25)
Festival Overture
MESSAGER (24)
Don Juan et Haydée, cantata
JANÁČEK (23)
Suite for strings
WOLF (17)
Lieder aus der Jugendzeit
  (1877–78)
Lieder nach verschiedenen Dichtern
  (1877–97)

BOUGHTON was born **1878**

GOUNOD (60)
Marche religieuse, for orchestra
OFFENBACH (59)
Madame Favart, operetta
FRANCK (56)
Cantabile for organ
Fantaisie for organ
Pièce héroïque, for organ
BRUCKNER (54)
Abendzauber, for baritone and
  male chorus
SMETANA (54)
The Secret, opera
Czech Dances
BRAHMS (45)
Piano Concerto No. 2 (1878–81)
Violin Concerto
Violin Sonata No. 1 (1878–79)

SAINT-SAËNS (43)
Symphony No. 2
BRUCH (40)
Violin Concerto No. 2
TCHAIKOVSKY (38)
Violin Concerto
DVOŘAK (37)
Serenade in D minor, for
  orchestra
Slavonic Dances, for orchestra,
  first series
Slavonic Rhapsodies, for orchestra
String Sextet
SULLIVAN (36)
Henry VIII, incidental music
H.M.S. Pinafore, operetta
The Martyr of Antioch, oratorio

CONTINUED

RIMSKY-KORSAKOV (34)
May Night, opera
SARASATE (34)
Zigeunerweisen, orchestral fantasy
FAURÉ (33)
Violin Concerto
GODARD (29)
Les Bijoux de Jeanette, opera
La Tasse, dramatic symphony, for
  solo voices, chorus and
  orchestra
Piano Concerto

d'INDY (27)
The Enchanted Forest, ballad-
  symphony
Quartet in A major for piano and
  strings (1878–88)
MESSAGER (25)
Fleur d'Oranger, ballet
ELGAR (21)
Romance, for violin and piano
  (or orchestra)
Promenades, for wind

1879   IRELAND, RESPIGHI and BRIDGE were born

LISZT (68)
Via Crucis
GADE (62)
En Sommertag paa Landet, for
  orchestra
GOUNOD (61)
The Redemption, oratorio
FRANCK (57)
Béatitudes, cantata
Piano Quintet in F minor
BRUCKNER (55)
String Quartet
BRAHMS (46)
Rhapsody in G minor, for piano
Rhapsody in B minor, for piano
p. Piano Studies, Books III–V
SAINT-SAËNS (44)
Suite Algerienne
Violin Concerto No. 2
MUSSORGSKY (40)
"Song of the Flea", song
TCHAIKOVSKY (39)
Eugene Onegin, opera
Capriccio Italien
Piano Concerto No. 2 (1879–80)
CHABRIER (38)
Une Éducation manquée
DVOŘÁK (38)
Czech Suite for orchestra
Festival March
Polonaise in E♭, for orchestra

Mazurka, for violin and orchestra
Violin Concerto, in A minor
  (1879–80)
String Quartet in E♭ major
MASSENET (37)
Suite for Orchestra No. 6,
  Scènes de féerie
RIMSKY-KORSAKOV (35)
Legend, for orchestra (1879–80)
Sinfonietta on Russian Themes
FAURÉ (34)
Piano Quartet No. 1
GODARD (30)
Scènes poétiques
d'INDY (28)
Le Chant de la Cloche, opera
  (1879–83)
LIADOV (24)
Arabesque, for piano
ELGAR (22)
Harmony Music, for wind
  instruments
Intermezzos, for wind instruments
WOLF (19)
String Quartet (1879–80)
MASCAGNI (16)
Symphony in C minor
STRAUSS, R. (15)
Overture in A minor

1880   BLOCH, INGHELBRECHT, MEDTNER, PIZZETTI were born; OFFENBACH DIED

LISZT (69)
The remaining five Hungarian
  Rhapsodies (*c.*1880)

GADE (63)
Violin Concerto

FRANCK (58)
L'Organiste, fifty-five pieces for
  harmonium
BORODIN (47)
In the Steppes of Central Asia,
  orchestral "picture"
BRAHMS (47)
Academic Festival Overture
Tragic Overture
Piano Trio No. 2 (1880—82)
PONCHIELLI (46)
Il Figliuol Prodigo, opera
SAINT-SAËNS (45)
Violin Concerto No. 3
MUSSORGSKY (41)
Turkish March, for orchestra
Piano Pieces
Five Popular Russian Songs, for
  male chorus
TCHAIKOVSKY (40)
Romeo and Juliet, overture (final
  revision)
Serenade for Strings
CHABRIER (39)
Dix pièces pittoresques, for piano
DVOŘÁK (39)
Symphony No. 6
Violin Sonata
Seven Gipsy Songs
MASSENET (38)
La Vierge, oratorio
SULLIVAN (38)
The Pirates of Penzance, operetta
GRIEG (37)
Two Elegiac Melodies

RIMSKY-KORSAKOV (36)
The Snow Maiden, opera
  (1880—81)
FAURÉ (35)
Berceuse, for violin and piano
GODARD (31)
Symphony
Diane: poème dramatique
d'INDY (29)
Le Camp de Wallenstein,
  symphonic overture, Part 1 of
  Wallenstein Trilogy
JANÁČEK (26)
Dumka, for violin and piano
HUMPERDINCK (26)
Humoreske
CHAUSSON (25)
Les Caprices de Marianne, opera
Joan of Arc, choral
MAHLER (20)
Klagende Lieder
PADEREWSKI (*c*.20)
Violin Sonata
WOLF (20—28)
Eichendorf-Lieder (1880—88)
DEBUSSY (18)
Andante, for piano
Danse bohémienne, for piano
"La Belle au bois dormant", song
  (1880—83)
STRAUSS, R. (16)
Symphony in D minor
String Quartet
BUSONI (14)
String Quartet No. 1 (1880—81)

BARTÓK and ENESCO were born; MUSSORGSKY died   **1881**

LISZT (70)
Mephisto Waltz
GOUNOD (63)
Le Tribut de Zamora, opera
OFFENBACH (posthumous)
fp. The Tales of Hoffman, operetta
FRANCK (59)
Rebecca
LALO (58)
Rhapsodie Norvégienne
BRUCKNER (57)
Symphony No. 6
SMETANA (57)
fp. Libuse, opera

BORODIN (48)
String Quartet No. 2
CUI (46)
Marche solenelle
BRUCH (43)
p. Kol Nidrei, for cello and piano
  (or orchestra)
DVOŘÁK (40)
Legends, for orchestra
String Quartet
MASSENET (39)
Suite No. 7 for orchestra, *Scènes
  alsaciennes*
Hérodiade, opera   CONTINUED

SULLIVAN (39)
Patience, operetta
GRIEG (38)
Norwegian Dances
FAURÉ (36)
Le Ruisseau
Ballade, for piano and orchestra
STANFORD (29)
The Veiled Prophet, opera
DEBUSSY (19)
Fugue for piano
MASCAGNI (18)
Symphony in F major
In Filanda, for voices and
    orchestra

STRAUSS, R. (17)
Violin Concerto in D minor
    (1881–82)
GLAZUNOV (16)
Overture on Greek Themes, No. 1
    (1881–84)
Symphony No. 1
SIBELIUS (16)
Piano Quartet
Piano Trio

1882 GRAINGER, KODÁLY, MALIPIERO, STRAVINSKY and TURINA were born:
RAFF died

THOMAS (71)
Francoise de Rimini
WAGNER (69)
fp. Parsifal, music drama
FRANCK (60)
Hulda, opera (1882–85)
Le Chasseur maudit, symphonic
    poem
LALO (59)
Ballet Suites Nos. 1 and 2,
    Namouna
SMETANA (58)
String Quartet No. 2
BRAHMS (49)
String Quintet No. 1
PONCHIELLI (48)
In Memoria di Garibaldi, cantata
DELIBES (46)
Le Roi s'amuse, incidental music
TCHAIKOVSKY (42)
1812, overture
Piano Trio
DVOŘÁK (41)
My Home, overture
SULLIVAN (40)
Iolanthe, operetta
RIMSKY-KORSAKOV (38)
Piano Concerto (1882–83)
FAURÉ (37)
Romance, for violin and orchestra
La Naissance de Venus

GODARD (33)
Symphonie, ballet
d'INDY (31)
La Mort de Wallenstein, symphonic
    overture, Part 3 of Wallenstein
    Trilogy
STANFORD (30)
Serenade in G, for orchestra
Elegiac symphony
CHAUSSON (27)
Viviane, symphonic poem
Poème de l'amour et de la mer, for
    voice and piano (1882–92)
Piano Trio
IPPOLITOV-IVANOV (23)
Yar-Khmel, for orchestra
MAHLER (22)
Lieder und Gesänge aus der
    Jugendzeit
MACDOWELL (21)
Piano Concerto No. 1
DEBUSSY (20)
Intermezzo, for orchestra
Printemps, for women's choir
    and orchestra
Triomphe de Bacchus, for piano
    duet
Two four-part Fugues, for piano
PIERNÉ (19)
Edith, Cantata
STRAUSS, R. (18)
Horn Concerto No. 1 (1882–83)

GLAZUNOV (17)
Overture on Greek Themes, No. 2
  (1882–85)
String Quartet

BUSONI (16)
Spring, Summer, Autumn, Winter,
  for male voice and orchestra
Il Sabato del villagio, for solo
  voice, chorus and orchestra
Serenata, for cello and piano

BAX, CASELLA, SZYMANOWSKI and WEBERN were born; FLOTOW and **1883**
WAGNER died

BRUCKNER (59)
Symphony No. 7
SMETANA (59)
The Prague Carnival
String Quartet No. 2
STRAUSS, J. (Jr.) (58)
Eine Nacht in Venedig, operetta
BRAHMS (50)
Symphony No. 3
DELIBES (47)
Lakmé, opera
CUI (48)
Suite Concertante, for violin and
  orchestra
CHABRIER (42)
fp. España, orchestral rhapsody
Three *Valses romantiques,* for
  piano duo
DVOŘÁK (42)
Husitská, overture
Scherzo capriccioso, for orchestra
Piano Trio
GRIEG (40)
Lyric Pieces for piano, Book II
FAURÉ (38)
Élégie, in C minor
GODARD (34)
Symphonie Gothique
CATALANI (29)
Dejanire, opera

ELGAR (26)
Une Idyll, for violin and piano
Fugue, for oboe and violin
MAHLER (23)
Lieder eines fahrenden Gesellen,
  song cycle for voice and
  orchestra
WOLF (23)
Penthesilea, symphonic poem
MACDOWELL (22)
Modern Suite, for piano
DEBUSSY (21)
Invocation, for men's chorus and
  orchestra
Le Gladiateur, cantata
PIERNÉ (20)
Le Chemin de l'amour, opera-
  comique
Trois pièces formant suite de concert,
  for orchestra
STRAUSS, R. (19)
Concert Overture
Piano Quartet (1883–84)
GLAZUNOV (18)
Serenade No. 1
String Quartet
BUSONI (17)
Piano Sonata in F minor

GRIFFES was born; SMETANA died **1884**

GADE (67)
Holbergiana Suite
GOUNOD (66)
fp. Mors et Vita, oratorio
FRANCK (62)
Les Djinns, symphonic poem for
  piano and orchestra
Prelude, Chorale et Fugue, for

piano
"Nocturne", song
LALO (61)
Scherzo
BRUCKNER (60)
Symphony No. 8, *Apocalyptic*
  (possibly 1887, revised 1890)
Te Deum

CONTINUED

BRAHMS (51)
Symphony No. 4 (1884–85)
BALAKIREV (47)
Russia, symphonic poem
TCHAIKOVSKY (44)
Mazeppa, opera
Concert-fantasy, for piano and
    orchestra
MASSENET (42)
Manon, opera
SULLIVAN (42)
Princess Ida, operetta
GRIEG (41)
Lyric Pieces for piano, Book III
FAURÉ (39)
Symphony in D minor
    (unpublished)
GODARD (35)
Pedro de Zalamea, opera
Symphonie Orientale
d'INDY (33)
Lied for cello (or viola) and
    orchestra
Saugefleure, orchestral legend

STANFORD (32)
Canterbury Pilgrims, opera
Savonarola, opera
CHAUSSON (29)
Hélène, opera (1884–85)
PUCCINI (26)
Le Villi, opera
PADEREWSKI (*c*.24)
Polish Dances for piano, Books I
    and II
MACDOWELL (23)
Forest Idylls, for piano
DEBUSSY (22)
Suite for Orchestra
Divertissement No. 1 for
    orchestra
Diane au bois, for chorus
L'Enfant prodigue, cantata
STRAUSS, R. (20)
Symphony in F minor
p. Serenade for wind
p. Cello Sonata
GLAZUNOV (19)
Serenade No. 2

1885   BERG, BUTTERWORTH and TAYLOR were born

FRANCK (63)
Symphonic Variations, for piano
    and orchestra
STRAUSS, J. (Jr.) (60)
Zigeunerbaron, operetta
BORODIN (52)
Petite Suite, for piano
Scherzo in A♭, for piano
PONCHIELLI (51)
Marion Delorme, opera
SAINT-SAËNS (50)
Violin Sonata No. 1
TCHAIKOVSKY (45)
Manfred Symphony
CHABRIER (44)
Habanèra, for piano
DVOŘÁK (44)
Symphony No. 7
The Spectre's Bride, cantata
MASSENET (43)
Le Cid, opera

SULLIVAN (43)
The Mikado, operetta
GRIEG (42)
Holberg Suite, for piano or strings
MESSAGER (32)
La Béarnasie, operetta
MACDOWELL (24)
p. Hamlet and Ophelia, symphonic
    poem
DEBUSSY (23)
Almanzor, for chorus
PIERNÉ (22)
Symphonic Overture
Fantaisie-Ballet, for piano and
    orchestra
GLAZUNOV (20)
Stenka Razin, tone poem
SIBELIUS (20)
String Quartet

SCHOECK was born; LISZT and PONCHIELLI died **1886**

FRANCK (64)
Violin Sonata in A major
LALO (63)
Symphony in G minor
GOLDMARK (56)
Merlin
BORODIN (53)
Serenata alla Spagnola (Movement
  in String Quartet "B-La-F")
BRAHMS (53)
Cello Sonata No. 2
Violin Sonatas Nos. 2 and 3
CUI (51)
Deux Morceaux, for cello and
  orchestra
SAINT-SAËNS (51)
Le Carnaval des animaux, for piano
  and orchestra
Symphony No. 3 with organ and
  two pianos
CHABRIER (45)
Gwendoline, opera
DVOŘÁK (45)
Slavonic Dances, for orchestra,
  second series
St. Ludmila, oratorio
SULLIVAN (44)
The Golden Legend, cantata
RIMSKY-KORSAKOV (42)
*Fantasia Concertante on Russian
  Themes*, for violin and
  orchestra
FAURÉ (41)
Piano Quartet No. 2
GODARD (37)
Symphony Légendaire

d'INDY (35)
*Symphony on a French Mountain
  Air*
Suite in D, for trumpet, two flutes
  and string quartet
STANFORD (34)
The Revenge, choral-ballad
MESSAGER (33)
Les deux pigeons, ballet
CATALANI (32)
Edmea, opera
CHAUSSON (31)
Hymne Védique, for chorus and
  orchestra
Solitude dans les bois, for orchestra
DELIUS (24)
Florida Suite, for orchestra
GERMAN (24)
The Rival Poets, operetta
PIERNÉ (23)
Don Luis, opera-comique
STRAUSS, R. (22)
Aus Italien, symphonic fantasia
Macbeth, symphonic poem
  (1886–90)
GLAZUNOV (21)
Symphony No. 2
BUSONI (20)
String Quartet in C minor
Little Suite, for cello and piano
CILÈA (20)
Piano Trio
SATIE (20)
Ogives, for piano

GRANADOS and VILLA-LOBOS were born; BORODIN died **1887**

VERDI (74)
fp. Otello, opera
GADE (70)
p. Violin Sonata No. 3
FRANCK (65)
Prelude, chorale et finale, for
  piano
STRAUSS, J. (Jr.) (62)
Simplizius, operetta
BRAHMS (54)
Double Concerto, for violin, cello

and orchestra
Zigeunerliede
BRUCH (49)
Symphony No. 3
CHABRIER (46)
Le Roi malgré lui, opera
DVOŘÁK (46)
Piano Quintet
Piano Quartet
Terzetto, for two violins and viola

CONTINUED

MASSENET (45)
Parade Militaire
SULLIVAN (45)
Ruddigore, operetta
GRIEG (44)
Violin Sonata No. 3
RIMSKY-KORSAKOV (43)
Capriccio Espagnole, for orchestra
FAURÉ (42)
Pavane, with chorus ad lib
Requiem
d'INDY (36)
Serenade and Valse, for small
    orchestra
Trio for clarinet, cello and piano
STANFORD (35)
Irish symphony
Prelude *Oedipus Rex*
Queen of the Seas, overture
JANÁČEK (33)
Sarka, opera
CHAUSSON (32)
Chant Nuptial
LIADOV (32)
Scherzo, for orchestra
SMYTH (29)
Violin Sonata

IPPOLITOV-IVANOV (28)
Ruth, opera
p. Violin Sonata
WOLF (27)
Italian Serenade, for string quartet,
    later for orchestra
p. Violin Sonata
MACDOWELL (26)
Six Idylls after Goethe, for piano
Six Poems after Heine, for piano
DEBUSSY (25)
*The Blessed Damozel (La Damoiselle
    élue)*, cantata (1887–88)
Cinq Poèmes de Baudelaire,
    songs (1887–89)
PIERNÉ (24)
Piano Concerto
ROPARTZ (23)
La Cloche de morts, for orchestra
GLAZUNOV (22)
Suite Caractèristique (possibly
    1884)
Lyric Poem, for orchestra
CILÈA (21)
Suite for Orchestra
SATIE (21)
Trois sarabandes, for piano

1888

GADE (71–73)
Ulysses, march (1888–90)
GOUNOD (70)
Petite Symphonie, for ten wind
    instruments
FRANCK (66)
Ghisele, opera
Symphony in D minor (1886–88)
Psyche, symphonic poem
LALO (65)
Le Roi d'Ys, opera
CUI (53)
Le Filibustier, opera (1888–89)
TCHAIKOVSKY (48)
Sleeping Beauty, ballet
Hamlet, overture
Symphony No. 5
CHABRIER (47)
Marche joyeuse, for orchestra
SULLIVAN (46)
The Yeoman of the Guard, operetta

GRIEG (45)
Lyric Pieces for piano, Book IV
RIMSKY-KORSAKOV (44)
Russian Easter Festival Overture
Schéhérezade, symphonic suite
FAURÉ (43)
Caligula, incidental music
GODARD (39)
Jocelyn, opera
d'INDY (37)
Fantasie, for oboe and orchestra
STANFORD (36)
Symphony in F major
MESSAGER (35)
Isoline, opera
LIADOV (33)
Mazurka, for orchestra
CHAMINADE (31)
Callirhoe, ballet

MAHLER (28)
Symphony No. 1
Des Knaben Wunderhorn, song
  cycle for voice and orchestra
PADEREWSKI (*c.*28)
Piano Concerto
WOLF (28)
Mörike-Lieder
Goethe-Lieder
MACDOWELL (27)
Lancelot and Elaine, symphonic
  poem
Romance, for cello
Marionettes, for piano
DEBUSSY (26)
Petite Suite, for piano duet
Arabasques 1 and 2, for piano
Ariettes oubliées, songs
DELIUS (26)
Marche caprice, for orchestra
Sleigh Ride, for orchestra
ROPARTZ (24)
Les Landes
Marche de fête

STRAUSS, R. (24)
Don Juan, symphonic poem
p. Violin Sonata
NIELSEN (23)
Little Suite in A minor, for strings
Quintet
Four String Quartets
  (1888–1907)
SIBELIUS (23)
Theme and Variations for quartet
BUSONI (22)
Symphonic Suite
Konzert-Fantasie (*Symphonisches
  Tongedicht*), for piano and
  orchestra
SATIE (22)
Three *Gymnopédies*, for piano
VAUGHAN WILLIAMS (16)
Piano Trio
SUK (14)
Mass in B♭ major

1889

THOMAS (78)
La Tempête, ballet
VERDI (76–85)
Four Sacred Pieces (1889–98)
FRANCK (67)
String Quartet
LALO (66)
Piano Concerto
DVOŘÁK (48)
Symphony No. 8
SULLIVAN (47)
The Gondoliers, operetta
FAURÉ (44)
Shylock, incidental music
Petite pièce, for cello and piano
JANÁČEK (35)
Six Lach Dances
PUCCINI (31)
Edgar, opera
MACDOWELL (28)
Lamia, symphonic poem
Les Orientales, for piano

DEBUSSY (27)
Fantaisie, for piano and orchestra
  (1889–90)
GERMAN (27)
Richard III, incidental music
PIERNÉ (26)
Marche solenelle
Pantomime, for orchestra
ROPARTZ (25)
Carnaval
Cinq pièces brève, for orchestra
STRAUSS, R. (25)
Tod und Verklaerung, symphonic
  poem
GLAZUNOV (24)
Fantasia, *The Forest* (possibly
  1887)
NIELSEN (24)
Symphonic Rhapsody
SIBELIUS (24)
Piano Quintet
Suite for String Trio
String Quartet
Violin Sonata

CONTINUED

BUSONI (23)
String Quartet No. 2
CILEA (23)
Gina, opera

GIORDANO (22)
Marina, opera
SUK (15)
Fantasy, for strings
Piano Trio (1889–90)

1890 MARTINŮ, IBERT and MARTIN were born; GADE and FRANCK died

---

GADE (73)
p. String Quartet
FRANCK (68)
Chorales for organ
BRAHMS (57)
String Quintet No. 2
CUI (55–68)
Three String Quartets in Cm: D:
  E♭ (1890–1913)
TCHAIKOVSKY (50)
The Queen of Spades, opera
DVOŘÁK (49)
Dumka, for piano trio (1890–91)
MASSENET (48)
Visions, symphonic poem
FAURÉ (45)
Cinq mélodies de Verlaine, songs
GODARD (41)
Dante, opera
d'INDY (39)
Karadec, incidental music
String Quartet No. 1
MESSAGER (37)
La Basoche, operetta
CATALANI (36)
Lorely, opera
CHAUSSON (35)
Symphony in B♭ major
LIADOV (35)
Dal tempo antico, for piano
ELGAR (33)
Froissart, concert overture
SMYTH (32)
Anthony and Cleopatra, overture
Serenade in D, for orchestra
IPPOLITOV-IVANOV (31)
Asra, opera
CHARPENTIER (30)
Impressions d'Italie, orchestra suite

WOLF (30)
Spanish Song Book
ARENSKY (29)
A Dream on the Volga, opera
MACDOWELL (29)
Piano Concerto No. 2
Twelve Studies for Piano, Books
  I and II
DEBUSSY (28)
Ballade, for piano
Rêverie, for piano
Suite Bergamasque, for piano
  (1890–1905)
Tarantelle styrienne (Danse), for
  piano
Valse romantique, for piano
GERMAN (28)
Symphony No. 1
MASCAGNI (27)
Cavalleria Rusticana, opera
PIERNÉ (27)
Scherzo Caprice, for piano and
  orchestra
GLAZUNOV (25)
The Sea
Wedding March
Une fête Slav
SIBELIUS (25)
Two Overtures (1890–91)
BUSONI (24)
Konzertstücke for piano
Violin Sonata No. 1
SATIE (24)
Three Gnossiènnes, for piano
RACHMANINOV (17)
Piano Concerto No. 1 (1890–91)
Six songs (1890–93)

BLISS, PROKOFIEV and GRANDJANY were born; DELIBES died   **1891**

BRAHMS (58)
Clarinet Quintet
Piano Trio
BRUCH (53)
Violin Concerto No. 3
DVORÁK (50)
Nature, Life and Love, cycle of
  overtures:
  "Amid Nature"
  "Carnaval"
  "Othello"
Forest Calm, for cello and
  orchestra
Rondo, for cello and orchestra
SULLIVAN (49)
Ivanhoe, opera
GRIEG (48)
Lyric Pieces for piano, Book V
FAURÉ (46)
La Bonne chanson, song cycle
  (1891–92)
d'INDY (41)
Tableaux de voyage
STANFORD (39)
Eden, oratorio
JANÁČEK (37)
The Beginning of a Romance, opera
Rákos Rákóczy, ballet
CHAUSSON (36)
Concerto for piano, violin and
  string quartet
ELGAR (34)
La Capriceuse, for violin and piano
SMYTH (33)
Suite for Strings
WOLF (31)
The Feast of Suhaug, incidental
  music
Italian Song Book, Book I
LOEFFLER (30)
The Nights in the Ukraine, for
  violin and orchestra

MACDOWELL (30)
Suite No. 1 for orchestra
The Lovely Alda, symphonic poem
The Saracens, symphonic poem
DEBUSSY (29)
Rodrigue et Chimène, opera
  (1891–92, unfinished)
Marche écossaise
Mazurka, for piano
Trois mélodies de Verlaine, songs
Deux Romances, songs
GERMAN (29)
Funeral March
MASCAGNI (28)
Solemn Mass
L'Amico Fritz, opera
PIERNÉ (28)
Le Colliers de saphire, ballet
GLAZUNOV (26)
Oriental Rhapsody
NIELSEN (26)
Symphony No. 1
SIBELIUS (26)
Scène de ballet
Piano Quartet
SATIE (25)
Three Préludes from *Les fils des
  étoiles,* for piano
RACHMANINOV (18)
Scherzo for strings
REGER (18)
Piano Trio
Violin Sonata
IVES (17)
Variations on "America", for
  organ
SUK (17)
Dramatic Overture
Piano Quartet

GROFÉ, MILHAUD and HONEGGER were born; LALO died   **1892**

BRAHMS (59)
Fantasien, for piano
SAINT-SAENS (57)
Piano Trio No. 2
DVOŘÁK (52)
Te Deum

TCHAIKOVSKY (52)
Iolanthe, opera
Casse Noisette (Nutcracker), ballet
p. String sextet
MASSENET (50)
Werther, opera   CONTINUED

SULLIVAN (50)
Haddon Hall, opera
RIMSKY-KORSAKOV (48)
fp. Mlada, opera
CATALANI (38)
La Wally, opera
LIADOV (37)
Kukalki, for piano
ELGAR (35)
Serenade for Strings
The Black Knight, cantata
LEONCAVALLO (34)
I Pagliacci, opera
CHARPENTIER (32)
La Vie du poète, cantata
DEBUSSY (30)
Fêtes galantes, songs, first series
DELIUS (30)
Irmelin, opera
GERMAN (30)
Gipsy Suite
Henry VIII, incidental music
MASCAGNI (29)
I Rantzau, opera
PIERNÉ (29)
Les Joyeuses commères de Paris,
   ballet
ROPARTZ (28)
Serenade
STRAUSS, R. (28)
Guntram, opera
DUKAS (27)
Polyeucte, overture

GLAZUNOV (27)
Symphony No. 3 (possibly 1890)
The Kremlin (possibly 1890)
Le Printemps
String Quintet
SIBELIUS (27)
En Saga, symphonic poem
Kullervo, symphonic poem
CILÈA (26)
La Tilda, opera
SATIE (26)
Uspud, ballet
Sonneries de la Rose-Croix, for
   piano
GIORDANO (25)
Mala Vita, opera
BANTOCK (24)
Aegypt, ballet
Fire Worshippers
RACHMANINOV (19)
Prélude and *Danse Orientale*, for
   cello and piano
Five pieces for piano
Intermezzo
REGER (19)
Cello Sonata
SUK (18)
Serenade for Strings
AUBERT (17)
Sous bois, song

1893   BENJAMIN and MOORE were born; GOUNOD, TCHAIKOVSKY and
CATALANI died

VERDI (80)
fp. Falstaff, opera
TCHAIKOVSKY (53)
Symphony No. 6, *Pathétique*
Piano Concerto No. 3
DVOŘÁK (52)
Symphony No. 9, *From the New
   World*
String Quintet
American String Quartet
SULLIVAN (51)
Utopia, Ltd., operetta
GRIEG (50)
Lyric pieces for piano, Book VI

FAURÉ (48)
Dolly Suite, for piano duet
MESSAGER (40)
Madame Chrysanthème, operetta
HUMPERDINCK (39)
Hänsel und Gretel, opera
LIADOV (38)
Une Tabatière à musique, for piano
PUCCINI (35)
Manon Lescaut, opera
SMYTH (35)
Mass in D
ALBÉNIZ (33)
The Magic Opal, opera

PADEREWSKI (c.33)
Polish Fantasy on Original
Themes, for piano and
orchestra
MACDOWELL (32)
Piano Sonata No. 1, *Tragica*
DEBUSSY (31)
String Quartet in G minor
Proses lyriques, songs
GERMAN (31)
Symphony No. 2
Romeo and Juliet, incidental music
The Tempter, incidental music
PIERNÉ (30)
Lizarda, opera-comique
(1893–94)
Bouton d'or, ballet
Le Docteur Blanc, ballet
ROPARTZ (29)
Le Diable couturier, opera
Dimanche breton
String Quartet No. 1
GLAZUNOV (28)
Symphony No. 4

SIBELIUS (28)
Karelia, overture and orchestral
suite
The Swan of Tuonela, symphonic
legend
SATIE (27)
Danses gothiques, for piano
Four Préludes for piano
RACHMANINOV (20)
Aleko, opera
The Rock, fantasy for orchestra
Trio elégiaque
Romance and *Danse hongroise*, for
violin and piano
Suite No. 1 *Fantasy*, for two
pianos
Six songs
SUK (19)
Piano Quintet
RAVEL (18)
Sérénade grotesque, for piano

MOERAN, PISTON, WARLOCK were born; RUBINSTEIN and CHABRIER died   **1894**

BRUCKNER (70)
Symphony No. 9 (unfinished,
fp. 1903)
BRAHMS (61)
Two sonatas for clarinet or viola
and piano
SAINT-SAËNS (59)
Preludes and Fugues for organ
MASSENET (52)
La Navarraise, opera
Thaïs, opera
STANFORD (42)
Symphony in D major, *L'Allegro
ed il pensiero*
MESSAGER (41)
Mirette, operetta
JANÁČEK (40–49)
Jenůfa, opera (1894–1903)
ELGAR (37–39)
King Olaf, cantata (1894–96)
LEONCAVALLO (36)
Serafita, symphonic poem
IPPOLITOV-IVANOV (35)
Armenian Rhapsody (1894–95)

ALBÉNIZ (34)
San Antonio de la Florida
CHARPENTIER (34)
Poèmes chantées, for voice and
piano or orchestra
MAHLER (34)
Symphony No. 2, *Resurrection*
ARENSKY (33)
Raphael, opera
LOEFFLER (33)
Fantasy Concerto, for cello and
orchestra
MACDOWELL (33)
Twelve Virtuoso Studies, for
piano
DEBUSSY (32)
Prélude à l'après-midi d'un faune,
for orchestra
STRAUSS, R. (30)
Also sprach Zarathustra,
symphonic poem
GLAZUNOV (29)
Carnival Overture
"Chopiniana" Suite
String Quartet   CONTINUED

NIELSEN (29)
Symphonic Suite for piano
SIBELIUS (29)
Spring Song, symphonic poem
CILÈA (28)
Cello Sonata
SATIE (28)
*Prélude de la porte héroïque du
ciel*, for piano
GIORDANO (27)
Regina Diaz, opera

SKRIABIN (22)
Piano Concerto
Rêverie, for orchestra
JONGEN (21)
p. String Quartet No. 1
RACHMANINOV (21)
Caprice bohémien, for orchestra
Six piano duets
Seven piano pieces
AUBERT (17)
"Vielle chanson espagnole"

1895   HINDEMITH, ORFF, JACOB, CASTELNUOVO-TEDESCO and SOWERBY were
born; GODARD died

STRAUSS, J. (Jr.) (70)
Waldmeister, operetta
SAINT-SAËNS (60)
Piano Concerto No. 5
BALAKIREV (58)
Ten songs (1895–96)
DVOŘÁK (54)
Suite for orchestra
Cello Concerto
Two String Quartets
SULLIVAN (53)
The Chieftan, operetta
GRIEG (52)
Lyric Pieces for piano, Book VII
RIMSKY-KORSAKOV (51)
Christmas Eve, opera
FAURÉ (50)
Romance, for cello and piano
STANFORD (43)
Suite of Ancient Dances
Piano Concerto No. 1
HUMPERDINCK (41)
Die Sieben Geislein, opera
ELGAR (38)
Organ Sonata in G major
IPPOLITOV-IVANOV (36)
Caucasian Sketches, orchestral
suite
ALBÉNIZ (35)
Enrico Clifford, opera
CHARPENTIER (35)
Impressions fausses, for voice and
orchestra
MAHLER (35)
Symphony No. 3

LOEFFLER (34)
Divertimento, for violin and
orchestra
MACDOWELL (34)
Piano Sonata No. 2, *Eroica*
DELIUS (33)
Over the Hills and Far Away, tone
poem
GERMAN (33)
Symphonic Suite in D minor
MASCAGNI (32)
Guglielmo Ratcliff, opera
Silvano, opera
PIERNÉ (32)
La Coupe enchantée, opera-
comique
Salome, ballet
STRAUSS, R. (31)
Till Eulenspiegel, symphonic poem
GLAZUNOV (30)
Cortège solenelle
Symphony No. 5
SIBELIUS (30)
Cassazione
Lemminkäinen and the Maidens,
symphonic poem
Lemminkäinen in Tuonela,
symphonic poem
Lemminkäinen's Homecoming,
symphonic poem
BUSONI (29)
Suite for Orchestra, No. 2
SATIE (29)
Messe des pauvres
SKRIABIN (23)
Symphony No. 1

RACHMANINOV (22)
Symphony No. 1
HOLST (21)
The Revoke, opera
RAVEL (20)
Menuet antique
WOLF-FERRARI (19)
Violin Sonata

DOHNÁNYI (18)
fp. Piano Quintet
IRELAND (16)
Two pieces for piano
ENESCO (14)
*Ouverture tragica e ouverture
    trionfale*
Four *Sinfonie Scolastiche*
    (1895–96)

HANSON, THOMSON, WEINBERGER, ROBERTSON, GERHARD and   **1896**
SESSIONS were born; THOMAS and BRUCKNER died

GOLDMARK (66)
The Cricket on the Hearth
BRAHMS (63)
Four Serious Songs
SAINT-SAËNS (61)
Violin Sonata No. 2
DVOŘÁK (55)
Four symphonic poems:
    The Watersprite
    The Noonday Witch
    The Golden Spinning-wheel
    The Wood Dove
SULLIVAN (54)
The Grand Duke, operetta
GRIEG (53)
Lyric Pieces for piano, Book VIII
d'INDY (45)
Istar, symphonic variations for
    orchestra
STANFORD (44)
Shamus O'Brien, opera
MESSAGER (43)
Le Chevalier d'Harmenthal,
    operetta
CHAUSSON (41)
Poème, for violin and orchestra
ELGAR (39)
The Light of Life (Lux Christi),
    oratorio
PUCCINI (38)
La Bohème, opera
ALBÉNIZ (36)
Pepita Jiménez, opera
CHARPENTIER (36)
Sérénade à Watteau, for voice and
    orchestra

WOLF (36)
fp. Der Corregidor, opera
Italian Song Book, Book II
MACDOWELL (35)
Indian Suite (Suite No. 2), for
    orchestra
Woodland Sketches, for piano
GERMAN (34)
As You Like It, incidental music
MASCAGNI (33)
Zanetto, opera
STRAUSS, R. (32)
Don Quixote, fantasy variations
    for cello and orchestra
DUKAS (31)
Symphony in C major
GLAZUNOV (31)
Symphony No. 6
BUSONI (30)
Violin Concerto (1896–97)
GIORDANO (29)
Andrea Chénier, opera
ALFVÉN (24)
"Sonata" and "Romance", for
    violin and piano
RACHMANINOV (23)
Six *Moments musicaux*, for piano
Six songs for female or boys'
    voices
Twelve songs
HOLST (22)
Fantasiestücke, for oboe and string
    quartet
Quintet for wind and piano
Four songs
IVES (22)
Symphony No. 1 (1896–98)
Quartet No. 1, *Revival Service*

CONTINUED

SUK (22)
String Quartet No. 1
COLERIDGE-TAYLOR (21)
Symphony in A minor
RAVEL (21)
"Sainte", song

AUBERT (19)
Rimes tendres, song cycle
DOHNÁNYI (19)
Zrinyi, overture

1897   TANSMAN and KORNGOLD were born; BRAHMS and BOËLLMANN died

CUI (62)
p. Five Little Duets, for flute and
    violin with piano
SAINT-SAËNS (62)
Seven Improvisations for Grand
    Organ
DVOŘÁK (56)
"Heroic Song"
MASSENET (55)
Sappho, lyric play
Fantaisie, for cello and orchestra
Marche solenelle
Devant la Madone
SULLIVAN (55)
Te Deum
RIMSKY-KORSAKOV (53)
Three Song Cycles:
    In Spring
    To the Poet
    By the Sea
Piano Trio
FAURÉ (52)
Theme and Variations, for piano
d'INDY (46)
Fervaal, music drama
String Quartet No. 2
MESSAGER (44)
Les P'tites Michu, operetta
CHAUSSON (42)
Chant funèbre
Ballata
Piano Quartet
ELGAR (40)
Imperial March
The Banner of St. George, ballad
    for soprano, chorus and
    orchestra
Sea Pictures, for contralto and
    orchestra
LEONCAVALLO (39)
La Bohème, opera

IPPOLITOV-IVANOV (38)
p. String Quartet
DEBUSSY (35)
Chansons de Bilitis, songs
GERMAN (35)
Hamlet, symphonic poem
Fantasia *In Commemoration*
PIERNÉ (34)
Vendée, opera-comique
L'An Mil, symphonic poem with
    chorus
DUKAS (32)
The Sorcerer's Apprentice,
    symphonic poem
BUSONI (31)
Comedy Overture
CILÈA (31)
L'Arlesiania, opera
SATIE (31)
Deux pièces froids, for piano
ALFVÉN (25)
Symphony No. 1
REGER (24)
Piano Quintet
Cello Sonata
Violin Sonata (1897–98)
HOLST (23)
A Winter Idyll, for orchestra
Clear and Cool, for chorus and
    orchestra
IVES (23–28)
Symphony No. 2 (1897–1902)
AUBERT (20)
Les Noces d'Apollon et d'Urainie,
    cantata
DOHNÁNYI (20)
Symphony No. 1
ENESCO (16)
Rumainian Poem
KODÁLY (15)
Overture for orchestra

SAINT-SAËNS (63)
Preludes and Fugues for organ
SULLIVAN (56)
The Beauty Stone, opera
GRIEG (55)
Symphonic Dances, for orchestra
Lyric Pieces for piano, Book IX
RIMSKY-KORSAKOV (54)
Mozart and Salieri, opera
FAURÉ (53)
Pelléas et Mélisande, incidental
  music
Papillon, for cello and piano
Siciliènne, for cello and piano
Fantaisie, for flute and piano
Andante, for violin and piano
d'INDY (47)
L'Étranger, lyric drama
Medée, incidental music
Chansons et danses, for seven wind
  instruments
STANFORD (46)
Te deum
MESSAGER (45)
Véronique, operetta
HUMPERDINCK (44)
Moorish Rhapsody, for orchestra
CHAUSSON (43)
Soir de fête
ELGAR (41)
Caractacus, cantata
Variations on an original theme,
  Enigma, for orchestra
  (1898–99)
SMYTH (40)
Fantastic, opera

IPPOLITOV-IVANOV (39)
p. Piano Quartet
MACDOWELL (37)
Sea Pieces
MASCAGNI (35)
Iris, opera
STRAUSS, R. (34)
Ein Heldenleben, symphonic poem
SIBELIUS (33)
Symphony No. 1 (1898–99)
King Christian II, incidental music
BUSONI (32)
Violin Sonata No. 2
GIORDANO (31)
Fedora, opera
ALFVÉN (26)
Symphony No. 2 (1898–99)
Elegy, for horn and organ
JONGEN (25)
Fantaisie, for violin and orchestra
HOLST (24)
Ornulf's Drapa, for baritone and
  orchestra
IVES (24–33)
Calcium Light Night, for chamber
  orchestra (1898–1907)
Central Park in the Dark, for
  orchestra (1898–1907)
COLERIDGE-TAYLOR (23)
Ballade, for orchestra
Hiawatha's Wedding Feast, cantata
ENESCO (17)
p. Violin Sonata No. 1

CUI (64)
The Saracen, opera
MASSENET (57)
Cendrillon, opera
Brumaire, overture
SULLIVAN (57)
The Rose of Persia, opera
RIMSKY-KORSAKOV (55)
The Tsar's Bride, opera
CHAUSSON (44)
String Quartet (unfinished)

LIADOV (44)
Slava, for voices, harps and
  pianos
ELGAR (42)
In the South (Alassio), concert
  overture (1899–1904)
Sérénade lyrique, for orchestra
ALBÉNIZ (39)
p. *Catalonia*, for orchestra
ARENSKY (38)
Nal and Damayanti

CONTINUED

DELIUS (37)
Paris — The Song of a Great City,
nocturne for orchestra
GERMAN (37)
The Seasons, symphonic suite
GLAZUNOV (34)
String Quartet
SIBELIUS (34)
Scènes historiques, Suite No. 1
SATIE (33)
Généviève de Brabant, puppet
opera
Jack in the Box, ballet
BANTOCK (31)
String Quartet
JONGEN (26)
Symphony
Violin Concerto
HOLST (25)
Sita, opera (1899–1906)
Walt Whitman, overture

SCHOENBERG (25)
Verklaerte Nacht, for string sextet
(arranged for string orchestra
1917)
SUK (25)
Symphony No. 1 in E major
COLERIDGE-TAYLOR (24)
Solemn Prelude
Death of Minnehaha, cantata
GLIÈRE (24)
Symphony No. 1 (1899–1900)
RAVEL (24)
Pavane pour une Infante défunte,
for piano
AUBERT (22)
Fantaisie, for piano and orchestra
ENESCO (18)
Fantaisie Pastorale

1900 COPLAND and ANTHEIL were born; SULLIVAN died

SAINT-SAËNS (65)
String Quartet
MASSENET (58)
La Terre promisé, oratorio
RIMSKY-KORSAKOV (56)
Legend of Tsar Sultan, opera
FAURÉ (55)
Promethée, lyric tragedy
LIADOV (45)
Polonaise, for orchestra
ELGAR (43)
The Dream of Gerontius, oratorio
LEONCAVALLO (42)
Zaza, opera
PUCCINI (42)
Tosca, opera
IPPOLITOV-IVANOV (41)
Assia
CHARPENTIER (40)
Louise, opera
MAHLER (40)
Symphony No. 4
MACDOWELL (39)
Piano Sonata No. 3, *Norse*
DEBUSSY (38)
Nocturnes, for orchestra and
chorus

GERMAN (38)
Nell Gwynne, incidental music
PIERNÉ (37)
Violin Sonata
ROPARTZ (36)
Five motets
GLAZUNOV (35)
Solenne Overture
SIBELIUS (35)
Finlandia, symphonic poem
BANTOCK (32)
Tone Poem No. 1, *Thalaba the
Destroyer*
VAUGHAN WILLIAMS (28)
Bucolic Suite, for orchestra
RACHMANINOV (27–33)
Twelve songs (1900–06)
REGER (27)
Two *Romances*, for solo
instruments and orchestra
Two String Quartets
Two Clarinet Sonatas
HOLST (26)
Cotswolds Symphony
Suite de Ballet
Ave Maria, for eight-part female
choir

SCHOENBERG (26–39)
Gurre-Lieder, for solo voices, chorus and orchestra (1900–13)
COLERIDGE-TAYLOR (25)
Hiawatha's Departure, cantata
GLIÈRE (25)
String Octet
String Sextet No. 1
String Quartet No. 1

AUBERT (23)
"Suite Brève", for two pianos
"Trois esquisses", for piano
"La Lettre", vocal
BLOCH (20–49)
Helvetia, symphonic fresco for orchestra (1900–29)

FINZI and RUBBRA were born; VERDI died **1901**

DVOŘÁK (60)
fp. Rusalka, opera
GRIEG (58)
Lyric pieces for piano, Book X
FAURÉ (56)
La Voile du bonheur, incidental music
STANFORD (49)
Much Ado About Nothing, opera
Irish Rhapsody No. 1
ELGAR (44)
Cockaigne, overture
Introduction and Allegro, for strings (1901–05)
Pomp and Circumstance Marches Nos. 1–4
Concert Allegro, for piano
SMYTH (43)
The Forest, opera
PADEREWSKI (c.41)
Manru, opera
LOEFFLER (40)
Divertissement Espagnol, for saxophone and orchestra
MACDOWELL (40)
Piano Sonata No. 4, *Keltic*
DEBUSSY (39)
Pour le Piano (possibly 1896)
GERMAN (39)/SULLIVAN (posthumous)
The Emerald Isle (completed by German after Sullivan's death)
MASCAGNI (38)
Le Maschera, opera
PIERNÉ (38)
La Fille de Tabarin, opera-

comique
Poème symphonique, for piano and orchestra
Concertstücke, for harp
STRAUSS, R. (37)
Feuersnot, opera
DUKAS (36)
Piano Sonata in E♭ minor
GLAZUNOV (36)
The Seasons, ballet (possibly earlier)
Symphony No. 2
Cortège, for orchestra
Portraits, for strings
BANTOCK (33)
Tone Poem No. 2, *Dante*
Tone Poem No. 3, *Fifine at the Fair*
SKRIABIN (29)
Symphony No. 2
RACHMANINOV (28)
Piano Concerto No. 2
Cello Sonata
Suite No. 2, for two pianos
IVES (27–30)
Symphony No. 3 (1901–04)
COLERIDGE-TAYLOR (26)
The Blind Girl of Castel-Cuille
Toussaint l'Ouverture, concert overture
Idyll
RAVEL (26)
Jeux d'eau, for piano
Myrrha, cantata
WOLF-FERRARI (25)
p. Piano Quintet
p. Piano Trio

CONTINUED

BLOCH (21)
Symphony in C♯ minor
  (1901–02)
ENESCO (20)
Rumainian Rhapsody, No. 1
Symphonie concertante, for cello
and orchestra
p. Violin Sonata No. 2
KODÁLY (19)
Adagio, for violin (or viola) and
  piano
CASELLA (18)
Pavana, for piano

1902   DURUFLÉ, RODRIGO and WALTON were born

SAINT-SAËNS (67)
Coronation March
Cello Concerto No. 2
MASSENET (61)
Le Jongleur de Notre Dame, opera
Piano Concerto
RIMSKY-KORSAKOV (58)
fp. Kaschey the Immortal, opera
d'INDY (51)
Symphony No. 2 (1902–03)
HUMPERDINCK (51)
Dornroschen
ELGAR (45)
Coronation Ode
Falstaff, symphonic study
  (1902–13)
Dream Children, for piano, or
  small orchestra
MAHLER (42)
Symphony No. 5
Five Rückert Songs
LOEFFLER (41)
Poème, for orchestra
MACDOWELL (41)
Fireside Tales
New England Idylls
DEBUSSY (40)
Pelléas et Mélisande, opera
DELIUS (40)
Appalachia, for orchestra and
  chorus
GERMAN (40)
Merrie England, operetta
PIERNÉ (39)
The Children's Crusade, oratorio
GLAZUNOV (37)
Symphony No. 7
Ballade
NIELSEN (37)
Saul and David, opera
Symphony No. 2, *The Four
  Temperaments*

CILÈA (36)
Adriana Lecouvreur, opera
BANTOCK (34)
Tone Poem No. 4, *Hudibras*
Tone Poem No. 5, *Witch of Atlas*
Tone Poem No. 6, *Lalla Rookh*
The Time Spirit
ROUSSEL (33)
Piano Trio
JONGEN (29)
Fantaisie sur deux Noëls wallons,
  for orchestra
Piano Quartet
RACHMANINOV (29)
The Spring, cantata
REGER (29)
Piano Quintet
Violin Sonata
HOLST (28)
The Youth's Choice, opera
IVES (28–36)
Violin Sonata No. 2 (1902–10)
COLERIDGE-TAYLOR (27)
Meg Blane
GLIÈRE (27)
String Sextet No. 2
RAVEL (27)
Alcyone, cantata
WOLF-FERRARI (26)
p. Piano Trio
p. Violin Sonata
AUBERT (25)
La Légende du Sang
BRIDGE (23)
Berceuse, for violin and small
  orchestra
RESPIGHI (23)
Piano Concerto
BARTÓK (21)
Scherzo for orchestra
ENESCO (21)
Rumainian Rhapsody, No. 2

CUI (68)
Mlle. Fifi, opera
RIMSKY-KORSAKOV (59–61)
The Invisible City of Kitezh, opera
    (1903–05)
Serenade, for cello and piano
d'INDY (52)
Choral Varié, for saxophone and
    orchestra
CHAUSSON (posthumous)
fp. Le Roi Arthus
ELGAR (46)
Symphony No. 2 (*c*.1903–10)
The Apostles, oratorio
PADEREWSKI (*c*.42)
Symphony (1903–07)
DEBUSSY (41)
Le Diable dans le beffroi, libretto
    and musical sketches
Rhapsody, for saxophone,
    contralto and orchestra
Danse sacré et danse profane, for
    harp and strings
D'un cahier d'esquisses, for piano
Estampes, for piano
DELIUS (41)
Sea Drift, for baritone, chorus and
    orchestra
GERMAN (41)
A Princess of Kensington, operetta
DUKAS (38)
Variations, Interlude et Finale,
    on a Theme by Rameau, for
    piano
NIELSEN (38)
Helios, overture
SIBELIUS (38)
Violin Concerto
Romance, for strings
BUSONI (37)
Piano Concerto, with male
    chorus (1903–04)
SATIE (37)
Trois morceaux en forme de poire,
    for piano duet
BANTOCK (35)
Serenade, for four horns
ROUSSEL (34)
Resurrection, for orchestra
Violin Sonata

SKRIABIN (31)
Symphony No. 3, *Divine Poem*
VAUGHAN WILLIAMS (31)
The House of Life, song cycle
RACHMANINOV (30)
Variations on a Theme by
    Chopin, for piano
Ten Preludes for piano
REGER (30)
Gesang der Verklarten, for voice
    and orchestra
HOLST (29)
Indra, symphonic poem
King Estmere, for chorus and
    orchestra
Quintet for wind
IVES (29–34)
Three Places in New England, for
    orchestra (1903–14)
Violin Sonata No. 1 (1903–08)
SCHOENBERG (29)
Pelleas und Melisande, suite for
    orchestra
SUK (29)
Fantasy, for violin and orchestra
COLERIDGE-TAYLOR (28)
The Atonement, oratorio
RAVEL (28)
Schéhérezade, song cycle with
    orchestra
Alyssa, cantata
String Quartet in F major
WOLF-FERRARI (27)
fp. Le Donne curiose, opera
p. Chamber Symphony
La Vita nuova, oratorio
AUBERT (26)
La Momie, ballet
DOHNÁNYI (26)
p. String Quartet
p. Cello Sonata
BARTÓK (22)
Kossuth, tone poem
Violin Sonata
ENESCO (22)
Suite for orchestra
CASELLA (20)
Variations sur une chaconne, for
    piano

1904   DALLAPICCOLA and KABALEVSKY were born; DVOŘÁK died

FAURÉ (59)
Impromptu, for harp
d'INDY (53)
Violin Sonata
STANFORD (52)
Violin Concerto
JANÁČEK (50)
Osud (Fate), opera
LIADOV (49)
Baba Yaga, symphonic poem
PUCCINI (46)
Madama Butterfly, opera
MAHLER (44)
Symphony No. 6
DEBUSSY (42)
La Mer, three symphonic sketches
L'Isle joyeuse, for piano
Masques, for piano
Fêtes galantes, songs (second
   series)
Trois Chansons de France
DELIUS (42)
Koanga, opera
GERMAN (42)
Welsh Rhapsody, for orchestra
ROPARTZ (40)
Cello Sonata No. 1
STRAUSS, R. (40)
Symphonia Domestica
GLAZUNOV (39)
Violin Concerto
SIBELIUS (39)
Symphony No. 3 (1904–07)
Kuolema, incidental music
   (includes "Valse Triste")
GIORDANO (37)
Siberia, opera
ROUSSEL (35–37)
Symphony No. 1, *La poème de la
   forêt* (1904–06)
ALFVÉN (32)
Swedish Rhapsody No. 1,
   Midsommervaka
VAUGHAN WILLIAMS (32)
Songs of Travel
JONGEN (31)
Lalla Rookh, symphonic poem
REGER (31)
String Quartet
Serenade, for flute, violin and

viola
Variations and Fugue on a
   Theme of Beethoven, for two
   pianos
String Trio
Cello Sonata
Violin Sonata
HOLST (30)
The Mystic Trumpeter, for soprano
   and orchestra
IVES (30)
Orchestra Set No. 1 (1904–11)
Thanksgiving and/or Father's Day,
   Part 4 of *Holidays Symphony*
SUK (30)
Symphony in C minor, *Asrael*
   (1904–06)
Prague, symphonic poem
GLIÈRE (29)
String Sextet No. 3
CARPENTER (28)
Improving Songs for Anxious
   Children
AUBERT (27)
The Blue Forest, opera (1904–10)
Chrysothemis, ballet
DOHNÁNYI (27)
p. Serenade, for string trio
BRIDGE (25)
Novelleten, for string quartet
Violin Sonata
BLOCH (24)
Hiver, symphonic poem
   (1904–05)
Printemps, symphonic poem
   (1904–05)
MEDTNER (24)
Nine songs (Goethe)
PIZZETTI (24)
Three Symphonic Preludes to
   Oedipus Rex
BARTÓK (23)
Rhapsody, for piano and orchestra
Burlesca
Piano Quintet
CASELLA (21)
Toccata, for piano

BALAKIREV (68)
Piano Sonata in B minor
BRUCH (67)
Suite on a popular Russian
  melody
d'INDY (54)
Jour d'été a la montagne
HUMPERDINCK (51)
Die Heirat wieder Willen
MAHLER (45)
Symphony No. 7 in E minor
Kindertotenlieder, song cycle for
  voice and orchestra
LOEFFLER (44)
La Mort de Tintagiles, symphonic
  poem for two viole d'amore
  and orchestra
La Villanelle du diable, symphonic
  fantasy for organ and
  orchestra
A Pagan poem, for piano, English
  horn and three trumpets
DEBUSSY (43)
Images, for piano, Book I
DELIUS (43)
A Mass of Life, for solo voices,
  chorus and orchestra
MASCAGNI (42)
Amica, opera
STRAUSS, R. (41)
Salome, opera
GLAZUNOV (40)
Symphony No. 8
Scène dansante
SIBELIUS (40)
Pelléas et Mélisande, incidental
  music
SATIE (39)
 Pousse l'amour, operetta
ROUSSEL (36)
Divertissement, for piano and
  wind quartet
LEHÁR (35)
The Merry Widow, operetta
ALFVÉN (33)
Symphony No. 3
En Skargardssagen, symphonic
  poem

REGER (32)
Sinfonietta, for orchestra
Suite in the Old Style, for violin
  and piano
HOLST (31)
Song of the Night, for violin and
  orchestra
SCHOENBERG (31)
String Quartet No. 1
COLERIDGE-TAYLOR (30)
Five Choral Ballads
GLIÈRE (30)
String Quartet No. 2
RAVEL (30)
Miroirs, for piano
Sonatina, for piano
BRIDGE (26)
Piano Quintet
Phantasie Quartet
Norse Legend, for violin and
piano
IRELAND (26)
Songs of a Wayfarer
RESPIGHI (26)
Re Enzo, comic opera
Notturno, for orchestra
Suite in G major, for string
  orchestra and organ
Burlesca
BARTÓK (24)
Suite No. 1, for orchestra
Suite No. 2, for orchestra
  (revised 1943)
ENESCO (24)
Symphony No. 1
p. String Octet
STRAVINSKY (23)
Symphony in E♭ major
  (1905–07)
CASELLA (22)
Symphony No. 1 (1905–06)
SZYMANOWSKI (22)
Concert Overture
WEBERN (22)
Quartet
BERG (20–23)
Seven "Frühe Lieder", for
  soprano and piano (1905–08)

1906   LUTYENS was born; ARENSKY died

GRIEG (63)
Moods
RIMSKY-KORSAKOV (62)
Le Coq d'Or, opera (1906–7)
FAURÉ (61)
Piano Quintet
La Chanson d'Eve, song cycle
  (1906–10)
d'INDY (55)
Souvenirs, tone poem
LIADOV (51)
Eight Popular Russian Songs, for
  orchestra
ELGAR (49)
The Wand of Youth, suites for
  orchestra (final versions,
  1906–07)
The Kingdom, oratorio
SMYTH (48)
The Wreckers, opera
ALBÉNIZ (46–49)
Ibéria, piano cycle (1906–09)
DELIUS (44)
Piano Concerto
STRAUSS, R. (42)
Elektra, opera (1906–08)
DUKAS (41)
Villanelle, for horn and piano
NIELSEN (41)
fp. Maskarade, opera
SIBELIUS (41)
Pohjola's Daughter, symphonic
  fantasy
SATIE (40)
Passacaille, for piano
Prélude en tapisserie, for piano
BANTOCK (38)
Omar Khayyam
VAUGHAN WILLIAMS (34)
Norfolk Rhapsodies
RACHMANINOV (33)
Francesca da Rimini, opera
The Miserly Knight, opera
Fifteen songs
REGER (33)
Serenade
HOLST (32)
Songs of the West, for orchestra
Two *Songs Without Words*

SCHOENBERG (32)
Chamber Symphonies Nos. 1
  and 2
IVES (32)
The Pond, for flute, harp, piano
  and string quartet
COLERIDGE-TAYLOR (31)
Kubla Khan
RAVEL (31)
Introduction and Allegro, for
  harp, flute, clarinet and string
  quartet
WOLF-FERRARI (30)
fp. School for Fathers, opera
fp. I quatro (sic) rusteghi,
  comedy-opera
QUILTER (29)
To Julia, song cycle
BRIDGE (27)
Three Idylls for string orchestra
String Quartet in E minor
Nine Miniatures for cello and
  piano
IRELAND (27)
Piano Trio No. 1 (*Phantasy Trio*)
BLOCH (26)
Poèmes d'Automne, for voice and
  orchestra
PIZZETTI (26)
String Quartet
KODÁLY (24)
Summer Evening, for orchestra
MALIPIERO (24)
Sinfonia del Mare
BAX (23)
Piano Trio
BERG (21–23)
Piano Sonata (1906–08)
SCHOECK (20)
Serenade, for small orchestra
  (1906–07)

CUI (72)
Matteo Falcone, opera
BALAKIREV (70)
Symphony No. 2 (1906–07)
STANFORD (55)
Stabat Mater
MESSAGER (54)
Fortuno, operetta
ELGAR (50)
Symphony No. 1 (1907–08)
IPPOLITOV-IVANOV (48)
Symphony
MAHLER (47)
Symphony No. 8, *Symphony of a Thousand*
DEBUSSY (45)
Images, for piano, Book II
DELIUS (45)
A Village Romeo and Juliet, opera
Brigg Fair, orchestral rhapsody
Songs of Sunset
GERMAN (45)
Tom Jones, operetta
PIERNÉ (44)
Canzonetta, for clarinet
ROPARTZ (43)
Pastoral and Dance, for oboe and orchestra
Violin Sonata No. 1
DUKAS (42)
Ariadne and Bluebeard, opera
GLAZUNOV (42)
Canto di Destino, overture
NIELSEN (42)
Saga-Drøm, for orchestra (1907–08)
BUSONI (41)
Élégien, for piano
CILÈA (41)
Gloria, opera
GIORDANO (40)
Marcella, opera
ALFVÉN (35)
Swedish Rhapsody No. 2, *Uppsalarapsodi*
VAUGHAN WILLIAMS (35)
Towards the Unknown Region, for chorus and orchestra
In the Fen Country, symphonic impression

JONGEN (34)
Félyane, opera (unfinished)
RACHMANINOV (34)
Symphony No. 2
The Isle of the Dead, symphonic poem
Piano Sonata No. 1
REGER (34)
Variations and Fugue on a Theme of Hiller
HOLST (33)
Somerset Rhapsody, for orchestra
Nine Hymns from the Rig-Veda
SCHOENBERG (33)
String Quartet No. 2
Friede auf Erden, for choir
SUK (33)
A Summer Tale, symphonic poem
GLIÈRE (32)
Symphony No. 2
RAVEL (32)
Rhapsodie espagnole, for orchestra
Pièce en forme de habanera
Cinq mélodies populaires greques, for voice and piano
DOHNÁNYI (30)
p. String Quartet in D major
QUILTER (30)
Serenade, for orchestra
BRIDGE (28)
Isabella, symphonic poem
Trio No. 1, *Phantasie*
RESPIGHI (28)
Fantasy, for piano and orchestra
String Quartet in D major
String Quartet in D minor
MEDTNER (27)
Three Songs (Heine)
BARTÓK (26)
Hungarian Folksongs, for piano
TURINA (25)
Piano Quintet
BAX (24)
Fatherland, for two sopranos, chorus and orchestra
CASELLA (24)
Cello sonata
SZYMANOWSKY (24)
Symphony No. 1
PROKOFIEV (16)
Piano Sonata No. 1 (1907–09)
Four Pieces for piano (1907–11)

1908 MESSIAEN was born; RIMSKY-KORSAKOV, SARASATE and MACDOWELL died

GOLDMARK (78)
A Winter's Tale
FAURÉ (63)
Serenade, for cello and piano
JANÁČEK (54–63)
*Mr. Brouček's Excursion to the
  Moon*, opera (1908–17)
MAHLER (48)
Das Lied von der Erde (The Song
  of the Earth), song cycle with
  orchestra
DEBUSSY (46)
Ibéria, from *Images* for orchestra
The Fall of the House of Usher
  (sketched, uncompleted
  1908–10)
Children's Corner, for piano
Trois chansons de Charles d'Orléans,
  for unaccompanied choir
DELIUS (46)
Dance Rhapsody No. 1, for
  orchestra
In a Summer Garden, for orchestra
PIERNÉ (45)
The Children of Bethlehem,
  oratorio
SIBELIUS (43)
String Quartet in five movements,
  Voces Intimae
BUSONI (42–45)
The Bridal Choice (1908–11)
SATIE (42)
Aperçus désagréables, for piano
  duet
SKRIABIN (36)
Poem of Ecstasy, for orchestra
VAUGHAN WILLIAMS (36)
String Quartet in G minor
REGER (35)
Symphonic Prologue to a Tragedy
Violin Concerto
Piano Trio
Sonata for clarinet, or viola, and
  piano
IVES (34)
The Unanswered Question, for
  orchestra

HOLST (34)
Savitri, opera
Choral Hymns from the Rig-Veda,
  Group I
SCHOENBERG (34)
Buch der hängenden Gärten,
  setting of fifteen poems for
  voice and piano
GLIÈRE (33)
The Sirens, symphonic poem
RAVEL (33)
Gaspard de la nuit, for piano
Ma Mère l'Oye, for piano
FALLA (32)
Pièces espagnoles, for piano
AUBERT (31)
Crépuscles d'Automne, song cycle
QUILTER (31)
Songs of Sorrow
BRIDGE (29)
Dance Rhapsody, for orchestra
Suite for Strings
RESPIGHI (29)
Concerto in the old style, for violin
  and orchestra
MEDTNER (28)
Twelve songs (Goethe)
BARTÓK (27)
Portraits, for orchestra (1907–08)
Violin Concerto No. 1
String Quartet No. 1
KODÁLY (26)
String Quartet No. 1
MALIPIERO (26)
Cello Sonata
STRAVINSKY (26)
Fireworks, for orchestra
Scherzo fantastique
*Lament on the Death of Rimsky-
  Korsakov*, for chorus and
  orchestra
BAX (25)
Lyrical Interlude, for string
  quintet
CASELLA (25)
Symphony No. 2 (1908–09)
Sarabande, for piano or harp

WEBERN (25)
Passacaglia, for orchestra
Entfllieht auf Leichten Kahnan, for
  chorus
Ten Lieder

BERG (23)
An Leukon
VILLA-LOBOS (21)
Recouli, for small orchestra
PROKOFIEV (17–21)
Four pieces for piano (1908–12)

ALBÉNIZ died **1909**

LIADOV (54)
The Enchanted Lake, symphonic
  poem
ELGAR (52)
Elegy, for string orchestra
Violin Concerto (*c*.1909–10)
IPPOLITOV-IVANOV (50)
Treachery
MAHLER (49)
Symphony No. 9
DEBUSSY (47)
Rondes de Printemps, from *Images*
  for orchestra
Rhapsody, for clarinet and
  orchestra (1909–10)
Petite pièce, for clarinet and
  piano, in B♭ major
Préludes for piano, Book I
  (1909–10)
Homage à Haydn, for piano
La plus que lente, for piano
Trois ballades de François Villon,
  songs (1909–10)
Le Promenoir des deux amants,
  songs (1904–10)
GERMAN (47)
Fallen Fairies
STRAUSS, R. (45)
Der Rosenkavalier, opera
  (1909–10)
DUKAS (44)
Prélude élégiaque, for piano
Vocalise
GLAZUNOV (44)
Symphony No. 9 begun
SIBELIUS (44)
Night-ride and Sunrise, tone poem
BUSONI (43)
Berceuse élégiaque
LEHÁR (39)
The Count of Luxemburg, operetta

SKRIABIN (38)
Poem of Fire —Prometheus, for
  orchestra, piano and chorus
VAUGHAN WILLIAMS (37)
A Sea Symphony (Symphony No.
  1), for soloists, chorus and
  orchestra
The Wasps, incidental music
On Wenlock Edge, song cycle
JONGEN (36)
Violin Sonata No. 2
RACHMANINOV (36)
Piano Concerto No. 3
REGER (36)
The 100th Psalm, for voice and
  orchestra
Die Nonnen, for voice and
  orchestra
String Quartet
HOLST (35)
First Suite for Military Band
A Vision of Dame Christian,
  incidental music
Choral Hymns from the Rig-Veda,
  Group II
SCHOENBERG (35)
Five Pieces for Orchestra
  (revised 1949)
Erwartung, monodrama, for
  voice and orchestra
COLERIDGE-TAYLOR (34)
Bon-Bon Suite
GLIÈRE (34–36)
Symphony No. 3, *Ilya Murometz*
RAVEL (34)
Menuet sur le nom d'Haydn, for
  piano
FALLA (33–39)
Nights in the gardens of Spain, for
  piano and orchestra
  (1909–15)

CONTINUED

WOLF-FERRARI (33)
Susanna's Secret, operetta
QUILTER (32)
Seven Elizabethan Lyrics
BRIDGE (30)
Dance Poem, for orchestra
IRELAND (30)
Violin Sonata No. 1
PIZZETTI (29–32)
Phaedra, opera
BARTÓK (28)
For Children, for piano
KODÁLY (27)
Cello Sonata (1909–10)
BAX (26)
Enchanted Summer, for tenor,
  chorus and orchestra
Christmas Carol

CASELLA (26)
Italia, orchestral rhapsody
Orchestral Suite in G major
Notturnino, for piano, or harp
Berceuse triste, for piano
SZYMANOWSKI (26)
Symphony No. 2
WEBERN (26)
Five movements for string quartet
BERG (24)
Four songs (1909–10)
BUTTERWORTH (24)
"I Fear Thy Kisses", song
PROKOFIEV (18)
Sinfonietta (1909–14)
Two Poems, for female voices and
  orchestra (1909–10)
Four Études, for piano

1910   BARBER and SCHUMAN were born: BALAKIREV died

BALAKIREV (73)
Suite on pieces by Chopin
MASSENET (68)
Don Quixote, opera
FAURÉ (65)
Nine preludes
HUMPERDINCK (56)
Koenigskinder, opera
LIADOV (55)
Dance of the Amazons, for
  orchestra
Kikimora, symphonic poem
ELGAR (53)
Romance, for bassoon and
  orchestra
PUCCINI (52)
Girl of the Golden West, opera
MAHLER (50)
Symphony No. 10 begun (left
  unfinished)
NIELSEN (45)
Symphony No. 3, *Espansiva*
  (1910–11)
At a Young Artist's Bier
GIORDANO (43)
Mese Mariano, opera
ROUSSEL (41)
Evocations (1910–11)

VAUGHAN WILLIAMS (38)
*Fantasia on a Theme by Thomas
  Tallis*, for strings
RACHMANINOV (37)
The Bells, choral symphony
Thirteen Piano Preludes
Liturgy of St. John Chrystosum
REGER (37)
Piano Concerto
Piano Quartet
Cello Sonata
String Sextet
HOLST (36)
Beni Mora—Oriental Suite, for
  orchestra
The Cloud Messenger, ode
Choral Hymns for the Rig-Veda,
  Group III
IVES (36–42)
Symphony No. 4 (1910–16)
SCHOENBERG (36–39)
Die Glückliche Hand, music drama
  (1910–13)
SUK (36)
String Quartet No. 2 (1910–11)
COLERIDGE-TAYLOR (35)
Endymion's Dream, for chorus
DOHNÁNYI (33)
Der Schlier der Pierette, ballet
p. Piano Quintet

QUILTER (33)
Three English Dances
Four Songs
RESPIGHI (31)
Semirama, lyric tragedy
BLOCH (30)
fp. Macbeth, opera
MEDTNER (30)
Three songs (Nietsche)
Violin Sonata
BARTÓK (29)
Four Dirges, for piano
Deux Images, for orchestra
MALIPIERO (28)
Sinfonia del Silenzio e della Morte
Impressioni dal vero, I
  (1910—11)
STRAVINSKY (28)
The Firebird, ballet
Petrouchka, ballet (1910—11,
  revised 1946—47)
BAX (27)
In the Faery Hills, symphonic
  poem
Violin Sonata No. 1 (1910—15)

CASELLA (27)
Barcarola, for piano
WEBERN (27)
Six pieces for large orchestra
Four pieces for violin and piano
  (1910—15)
BERG (25)
String Quartet
VILLA-LOBOS (23)
Suite dos canticos sertanejos, for
  small orchestra
PROKOFIEV (19)
Dreams, symphonic poem
Autumnal Sketch, for orchestra
  (revised 1934)
Deux poèmes, for voice and piano
  (1910—11)
MILHAUD (18—23)
La Brèbis égarée, opera
  (1910—15)
KORNGOLD (13)
Piano Trio (1910—13)

MENOTTI was born; MAHLER died **1911**

CUI (76)
The Captain's Daughter, opera
p. Violin Sonata
BRUCH (73)
Concertstücke, for violin
STANFORD (59)
Symphony No. 7
HUMPERDINCK (57)
The Miracle
SMYTH (53)
March of the Women, for
  orchestra
Three Songs of Sunrise, for
  unaccompanied chorus
DEBUSSY (49)
The Martyrdom of St. Sebastian,
  incidental music
GERMAN (49)
Coronation March and Hymn
MASCAGNI (48)
Isabeau, opera

ROPARTZ (47)
Serenade, for string quartet
  (1911—12)
String Quartet No. 2
GLAZUNOV (46)
Piano Concerto
NIELSEN (46)
Violin Concerto
SIBELIUS (46)
Symphony No. 4
Rakastava Suite, for orchestra
Canzonetta, for strings
Valse romantique, for orchestra
SATIE (45)
En habit de cheval, for orchestra
VAUGHAN WILLIAMS (39)
Five Mystical Songs, for baritone,
  chorus and orchestra
JONGEN (38)
S'Arka, ballet
Cello Sonata (1911—12)
RACHMANINOV (38)
Six Études-Tableaux, for piano

CONTINUED

REGER (38)
Eine Lustspielouverture
Die Weihe der Nacht, for chorus
   and orchestra
String Quartet
Violin Sonata
HOLST (37)
Invocations, for cello and
   orchestra
Hecuba's Lament, for chorus and
   orchestra
Second Suite for Military Band
IVES (37)
Browning Overture
The Gong on the Hook and Ladder
Tone-roads No. 1, for chamber
   orchestra (1911–15)
Hallowe'en, for piano and strings
SCHOENBERG (37)
Herzewächse, for soprano, celesta,
   harmonium and harp
COLERIDGE-TAYLOR (36)
Bamboula, rhapsodic dance
Violin Concerto
A Tale of Old Japan, cantata
RAVEL (36)
L'Heure espagnole, opera
Valses nobles et sentimentales, for
   piano, or orchestra
WOLF-FERRARI (35)
fp. The Jewels of the Madonna,
   operetta
AUBERT (34)
Nuit Mauresque (possibly 1907)

QUILTER (34)
Where the Rainbow Ends,
   incidental music
Three Songs of the Sea
BRIDGE (32)
The Sea, for orchestra
BARTÓK (30)
Duke Bluebeard's Castle, opera
Allegro barbaro, for piano
Three *Burlesques*, for piano
ENESCO (30)
Symphony No. 2
STRAVINSKY (29)
The King of the Stars, cantata
TURINA (29)
Quartet
WEBERN (28)
Five pieces for orchestra
   (1911–13)
Two lieder
BUTTERWORTH (26)
Two English Idylls, for small
   orchestra
Six songs from Housman's
   A Shropshire Lad
SCHOECK (25)
Violin Concerto (1911–12)
Dithyrambe, for double chorus
   and orchestra
Erwin und Elmire, incidental
   music (1911–16)
PROKOFIEV (20)
Magdalene, opera (1911–13)
Piano Concerto No. 1 (1911–12)
MILHAUD (19)
Violin Sonata

1912   CAGE and GILLIS were born; COLERIDGE-TAYLOR and MASSENET died

ELGAR (55)
The Music Makers, for contralto,
   chorus and orchestra
IPPOLITOV-IVANOV (53)
The Spy
DEBUSSY (50)
Jeux, poème dansé
Khamma, ballet
Gigues, from *Images* for orchestra
Syrinx, for solo flute
DELIUS (50)
On Hearing the First Cuckoo in

Spring, for orchestra
Song of the High Hills, for
   wordless chorus and orchestra
Summer Night on the River, for
   orchestra
ROPARTZ (48)
La Pays, opera
À Marie endormé
La Chasse du Prince Arthur
STRAUSS, R. (48)
Ariadne auf Naxos, opera, first
   version

DUKAS (47)
La Péri, poème dansé
SIBELIUS (47)
Scènes historiques, Suite No. 2
   for orchestra
Two *Serenades*, for violin
   (1912–13)
BUSONI (46)
Nocturne symphonique
SATIE (46)
*Choses vues à droit et à gauche
   (sans lunettes)*, for violin and
   piano
ROUSSEL (43)
The Spider's Feast, ballet
ALFVÉN (40)
Sten Sture, cantata for male
   voices
VAUGHAN WILLIAMS (40)
Fantasia on Christmas Carols
Phantasy Quintet, for strings
JONGEN (39)
Deux rondes wallons, for orchestra
RACHMANINOV (39)
Fourteen songs
REGER (39)
A Romantic Suite
Konzert im Alten Stil
Romischer Triumphgesang, for
   voice and orchestra
HOLST (38)
Choral Hymns from the Rig-Veda,
   Group IV
IVES (38)
Decoration Day, Part 2 of *Holidays
   Symphony*
Lincoln, the Great Commoner,
   for chorus and orchestra
SCHOENBERG (38)
Pierrot Lunaire, song cycle
GLIÈRE (37)
Chrysis, ballet
RAVEL (37)
Daphnis et Chloé, ballet with
   chorus
CARPENTER (36)
Violin Sonata
BRIDGE (33)
String Sextet

IRELAND (33)
Greater love hath no man, motet
BLOCH (32)
Israel Symphony, for voices and
   orchestra (1912–16)
Prelude and two psalms for high
   voice (1912–14)
MEDTNER (32)
Three *Nocturnes* for piano and
   violin
BARTÓK (31)
Four Pieces for Orchestra
TURINA (30)
La Procesion del Rocio, symphonic
   poem
BAX (29)
Christmas Eve on the Mountains,
   for orchestra
Nympholept, for orchestra
CASELLA (29)
Le Couvent sur l'eau, ballet
   (1912–13)
GRIFFES (28)
The Pleasure Dome of Kubla Khan,
   symphonic poem (1912–16)
Tone Images, for mezzo-soprano
   and piano
BERG (27)
Five Orchestral Songs
BUTTERWORTH (27)
A Shropshire Lad, rhapsody for
   orchestra
Eleven Folk Songs from Sussex
"Bredon Hill" and other songs
TAYLOR (27)
The Siren Song, for orchestra
VILLA-LOBOS (25)
Aglaia, opera
PROKOFIEV (21)
Piano Concerto No. 2
Ballade, for cello and piano
Piano Sonata No. 2
Sarcasms, for piano (1912–14)
Toccata in C major, for piano
MILHAUD (20)
String Quartet No. 1

SAINT-SAËNS (78)
fp. The Promised Land, oratorio
FAURÉ (68)
Pénélope, opera
CHARPENTIER (53)
Julien, opera
DEBUSSY (51)
La Boîte à Joujoux, ballet music
    for piano
Preludes for piano, Book 2
Trois poèmes de Mallarmé, songs
MASCAGNI (50)
Parisina, opera
ROPARTZ (49)
Dans l'ombre de la montagne
Soir sur les Chaumes
STRAUSS, R. (49)
Alpine Symphony
SIBELIUS (48)
Scaramouche, pantomime
Il Bardo, symphonic poem
BUSONI (47)
Indian Fantasy, for piano and
    orchestra
CILÈA (47)
Il Canto della vita, for voice,
    chorus and orchestra
SATIE (47)
Le piège de Medusa, operetta
Chapitres tournés en tous sens, for
    piano
*Croques et agarceries d'un gros
    bonhomme en bois*, for piano
Descriptions automatiques, for
    piano
Embryons desséchés, for piano
Enfantines, children's piano pieces
VAUGHAN WILLIAMS (41)
A London Symphony (Symphony
    No. 2)
JONGEN (40)
Impressions d'Ardennes, for
    orchestra
RACHMANINOV (40)
Piano Sonata No. 2
REGER (40)
Vier Tondichtunger nach Böcklin
Eine Ballettsuite

HOLST (39)
St. Paul's Suite, for strings
Hymn to Dionysus, for choir and
    orchestra
IVES (39)
The Fourth of July, Part 3 of
    Holidays Symphony
Washington's Birthday, Part 1 of
    Holidays Symphony
Over the Pavements, for chamber
    orchestra
FALLA (38)
fp. La Vida brève, opera
CARPENTER (37)
Gitanjali, song cycle
AUBERT (36)
Sillages, three pieces for piano
DOHNÁNYI (36)
Tante Simone, opera
p. Violin Sonata
IRELAND (34)
The Forgotten Rite, for orchestra
Decorations, for piano
Three Dances for piano
Three songs
RESPIGHI (34)
Carnival, overture
BLOCH (33)
Trois poèmes juifs, for orchestra
STRAVINSKY (31)
The Rite of Spring, ballet
BAX (30)
Scherzo for orchestra
CASELLA (30)
Notte di Maggio, for voice and
    orchestra
WEBERN (30)
Six Bagatelles, for string quartet
BERG (28)
Three Orchestral Pieces
    (1913–14)
Four Pieces for clarinet and piano
VILLA-LOBOS (26)
Suite da terra, for small orchestra
Suite for piano
MILHAUD (21)
Suite symphonique No. 1
    (1913–14)

STANFORD (62)
Irish Rhapsody No. 4
MESSAGER (61)
Béatrice, operetta
HUMPERDINCK (60)
Die Marketenderin
LIADOV (59)
Naenia — Dirge
ELGAR (57)
p. Sospiri, for orchestra
Carillon, recitation with orchestra
DEBUSSY (52)
Berceuse héroïque, for piano
DELIUS (52)
North Country Sketches, for
   orchestra
STRAUSS, R. (50)
Die Frau ohne Schatten, opera
   (1914–17)
Josephs-Legende, ballet
NIELSEN (49)
Serenato in vano
SIBELIUS (49)
Symphony No. 5 (1914–15)
Oceanides, symphonic poem
BUSONI (48–50)
Arlecchino, opera (1914–16)
SATIE (48)
*Cinq grimaces pour le "Songe d'une
   nuit d'été"*, for orchestra
Heures séculaires et instantées, for
   piano
Les Pantins dansent, for piano
Sports et divertissements, for piano
Trois valses du précieux dégoûte,
   for piano
Vieux sequins et veilles cuirasses,
   for piano
REGER (41)
Eine Vaterländische Overture
Piano Quartet
Piano Sonata
Variations and fugue on a theme
   of Mozart, for piano
Cello Sonata
HOLST (40)
The Planets, suite for orchestra
   (1914–16)
IVES (40)
Protests, piano sonata

SUK (40)
*Meditation on a Theme of an old
   Bohemian Chorale*, for string
   quartet
RAVEL (39)
Two Hebrew Songs, for soprano
   and orchestra
Piano Trio
QUILTER (37)
A Children's Overture
Four Child Songs
BRIDGE (35)
Summer, tone poem
RESPIGHI (35)
Suite for strings and organ
PIZZETTI (34)
Sinfonia del Fuoco
BARTÓK (33)
The Wooden Prince, ballet
   (1914–16)
Fifteen Hungarian Peasant Songs
   (1914–17)
KODÁLY (32)
Duo for violin and cello
MALIPIERO (32)
Impressioni dal vero, II (1914–15)
STRAVINSKY (32)
Le Rossignol (The Nightingale),
   lyric tale in three acts
Chansons plaisants, for voice and
   small orchestra
Three pieces for string quartet
TURINA (32)
Margot, lyric comedy
BAX (31)
Quintet for piano and strings
   (1914–15)
CASELLA (31–34)
Siciliana and *Burlesca*, for piano
   trio (1914–17)
WEBERN (31)
Three Little Pieces, for cello and
   piano
Four Lieder (1914–18)
TAYLOR (29)
The Chambered Nautilus, for
   chorus and orchestra
The Highwayman, for baritone,
   women's voices and orchestra

CONTINUED

VILLA-LOBOS (27)
Izaht, opera
Ibericarabé, symphonic poem
Dansas dos Indios Mesticos, for
    orchestra
Suite for strings
Suite popular brasiliera, for guitar

PROKOFIEV (23)
Violin Concerto
Scythian Suite, for orchestra
    (1914−15)
The Ugly Duckling, for voice and
    piano
MILHAUD (22)
String Quartet No. 2 (1914−15)
Sonata for two violins and piano
Printemps, for violin and piano

1915   DIAMOND was born; GOLDMARK and SKRIABIN died

SAINT-SAËNS (80)
La Cendre rouge, ten songs
FAURÉ (70−73)
Le Jardin clos, songs (1915−18)
STANFORD (63)
Piano Concerto No. 2
JANÁČEK (61)
Taras Bulba, rhapsody for
    orchestra (1915−18)
ELGAR (58)
Polonia
Une Voix dans le desert, recitation
    with orchestra
DEBUSSY (53)
Cello Sonata
En blanc et noir, for two pianos
Six épigraphes antiques, for piano
Douze études, for piano
ROPARTZ (51)
Divertissement No. 1
BUSONI (49)
Indian Diary
SATIE (49)
Avant-dernières pensées, for piano
GIORDANO (48)
Madame Sans-gêne, opera
BANTOCK (47)
Hebridean Symphony
JONGEN (42)
Suites en deux parties, for viola
    and orchestra
RACHMANINOV (42)
Vesper Mass

REGER (42)
Der Einsiedler, for chorus and
    orchestra
Serenade, for flute, violin, viola,
    or two violins and viola
String Trio
HOLST (41)
Japanese Suite, for orchestra
IVES (41)
Orchestral Set No. 2
Tone-Roads No. 3, for chamber
    orchestra
Concord, piano sonata
GLIÈRE (40)
Trizna, symphonic poem
RAVEL (40)
Three songs for unaccompanied
    choir
CARPENTER (39)
Adventures in a Perambulator, for
    orchestra
Concertino for piano and
    orchestra
FALLA (39)
fp. El Amor Brujo, ballet
DOHNÁNYI (38)
Violin Concerto No. 1
BRIDGE (36)
The Open Air and *The Story of My*
    Heart, for orchestra
Lament, for strings
String Quartet in G minor
IRELAND (36)
Preludes for piano
RESPIGHI (36)
Sinfonia drammatica

BLOCH (35)
Schelomo, for cello and orchestra
  (1915–16)
PIZZETTI (35–41)
Deborah and Jael, opera
  (1915–21)
BARTÓK (34)
Rumanian Christmas Songs, for
  piano
Rumanian Folk Dances, for piano
String Quartet No. 2 (1915–17)
ENESCO (34)
Suite for orchestra
KODÁLY (33)
Sonata for unaccompanied cello
STRAVINSKY (33)
Rénard, burlesque
TURINA (33)
Evangelio, symphonic poem
BAX (32)
Violin Sonata No. 2
Légende, for violin and piano
Maiden with the Daffodils, for
  piano
Winter Waters, for piano

SZYMANOWSKI (32)
Symphony No. 3, *Song of the
  Night* (1915–16)
WEBERN (32–34)
Four Lieder (1915–17)
GRIFFES (31)
Fantasy Pieces, for piano
Three Tone Pictures, for piano
SCHOECK (29)
Trommelschlage
VILLA-LOBOS (28)
String Quartets Nos. 1 and 2
BLISS (24)
Piano Quartet (*c.*1915)
String Quartet (*c.*1915)
PROKOFIEV (24)
Chout, ballet, revised 1920
The Gambler, opera, revised 1928
Cinq poésies, for voice and piano
Visions fugitives, for piano
  (1915–17)
CASTELNUOVO-TEDESCO (20)
Copias
HANSON (19)
Prelude and Double Fugue, for
  two pianos

BUTTERWORTH killed in action, GRANADOS drowned when the "Sussex" **1916**
was torpedoed, REGER died

---

d'INDY (65–67)
Sinfonia brève de ballo gallico
STANFORD (64)
The Critic, opera
SMYTH (58)
The Boatswain's Mate, opera
IPPOLITOV-IVANOV (57)
Ole the Norseman
LOEFFLER (55)
Hora Mystica, symphony with
  men's voices
DEBUSSY (54)
Ode à la France, for chorus
  (1916–17)
Sonata for flute, viola and harp
DELIUS (54)
Dance Rhapsody No. 2, for
  orchestra
Violin Concerto

NIELSEN (51)
Symphony No. 4, *Inextinguishable*
Chaconne, for piano
Theme and Variations, for piano
SIBELIUS (51)
Everyman, incidental music
BUSONI (50–58)
Doktor Faust, opera (1916–24)
SATIE (50)
Parade, ballet
JONGEN (43)
String Quartet No. 2
RACHMANINOV (43)
Nine *Études-Tableaux*, for piano
  (1916–17)
Six songs
REGER (43)
Quintet in A major
DOHNÁNYI (39)
Variations on a Nursery Song, for
  piano and orchestra

CONTINUED

QUILTER (39)
Three songs of William Blake
BRIDGE (37)
"A Prayer", for chorus
BLOCH (36)
String Quartet No. 1
MEDTNER (36–38)
Piano Concerto No. 1 (1916–18)
BARTÓK (35)
Suite for piano
GRAINGER (34)
In a Nutshell, for piano and
    orchestra
KODÁLY (34)
String Quartet No. 2 (1916–17)
STRAVINSKY (34)
Berceuse du chat, for voice and
    three clarinets
TURINA (34)
Navidad, incidental music
BAX (33)
Elegy Trio, for flute, viola and
    harp
Ballade, for violin and piano
Dream in Exile, for piano
CASELLA (33)
Elegia Eroica
Pagine di Guerra
Pupazzetti
GRIFFES (32)
The Kairn of Koridwen, dance
    drama
Roman Sketches, for orchestra
Two Sketches on Indian Themes,
    for string quartet

VILLA-LOBOS (29)
Symphony No. 1, *The Unforseen*
Three Symphonic poems
    Centauro de Ouro
    Miremis
    Naufragio de Kleonica
Sinfonietta on a Theme by Mozart
Marcha religiosa No. 1, for
    orchestra
Cello Concerto
String Quartet No. 3
BLISS (25)
Two pieces for clarinet and piano
PROKOFIEV (25)
Symphony No. 1, *Classical*
    (1916–17)
HONEGGER (24)
String Quartet No. 1 (1916–18)
Violin Sonata (1916–18)
MILHAUD (24)
String Quartet No. 3
SOWERBY (21)
Woodwind Quintet
HANSON (20)
Symphonic Prelude
Piano Quintet
KORNGOLD (19)
Der Ring des Polykrates, opera
    buffe
TANSMAN (19)
Symphony No. 1
WALTON (14)
Piano Quartet

pre **1917**

HINDEMITH
Cello Concerto No. 1

1917   ARNELL was born; CUI died

FAURÉ (72)
Violin Sonata No. 2
ELGAR (60)
fp. The Spirit of England, for voices
    and orchestra
Le Drapeau Belge, recitation with
    orchestra
Fringes of the Fleet, song cycle

PUCCINI (59)
La Rondine, opera
DEBUSSY (55)
Violin Sonata
DELIUS (55)
Eventyr, for chorus and orchestra

MASCAGNI (54)
Lodoletta, opera
Satanic Rhapsody
ROPARTZ (53)
Musiques au jardin
Violin Sonata No. 2
BUSONI (51)
Turandot, opera
Die Brautwahl, orchestral suite
JONGEN (44)
Tableaux pittoresques, for orchestra
HOLST (43)
Hymn of Jesus, for chorus and
 orchestra
A Dream of Christmas
SUK (43)
Harvestide, symphonic poem
RAVEL (42)
Le Tombeau de Couperin, for piano
CARPENTER (41)
Symphony No. 1
AUBERT (40)
Tu es Patrus, for chorus and
 organ
Six poèmes arabes (possibly 1907)
BRIDGE (38)
Cello Sonata
IRELAND (38)
Violin Sonata No. 2
Piano Trio No. 2
The Cost, songs
RESPIGHI (38)
The Fountains of Rome,
 symphonic poem
Old Airs and Dances for Lute,
 transcribed for orchestra,
 Series I
Violin Sonata in B minor
KODÁLY (35)
Seven piano pieces (1917–18)
MALIPIERO (35)
Armenia
Ditirambo Tragico
STRAVINSKY (35)
The Soldier's Tale, opera-ballet
Les Noces, cantata-ballet
 (1917–23)
Song of the Nightingale,
 symphonic poem
Song of the Haulers on the Volga

TURINA (35)
La Adultera penitente, incidental
 music
BAX (34)
Between Dusk and Dawn, ballet
Symphonic Variations, for piano
 and orchestra
November Woods, symphonic
 poem
Moy Well (An Irish Tone Poem),
 for two pianos
Tintagel, symphonic poem
An Irish Elegy, for English horn,
 harp and strings
SZYMANOWSKI (34)
Violin Concerto No. 1
String Quartet
WEBERN (34)
Six Lieder, with instruments
 (1917–21)
Five Lieder (1917–22)
GRIFFES (33)
Sho-Jo, pantomimic drama
BERG (32)
Wozzeck, opera (1917–21)
SCHOECK (31)
Don Ranudo de Colibrados
 (1917–18)
VILLA-LOBOS (30)
Amazonas, ballet for orchestra
Uirapurú, ballet
Symphony No. 2, *The Ascension*
Five symphonic poems:
 Fantasma
 Lobishome
 Iara
 Saci Perêrê
 Tedio de alvorada
Sexteto mistico, for flute, clarinet,
 saxophone, harp, celesta and
 double-bass
String Quartet No. 4
PROKOFIEV (26)
Piano Concerto No. 3 (1917–21)
Piano Sonatas Nos. 3 and 4
Seven, they are seven, for voices
 and orchestra
MILHAUD (25)
Symphony for small orchestra,
 No. 1, *Le Printemps*

CONTINUED

WARLOCK (23)
An Old Song, for small orchestra
HINDEMITH (22)
Three Pieces for cello and piano
SOWERBY (22)
Piano Concerto No. 1 (revised 1919)
Serenade, for string quartet
Comes Autumn Time, for organ

HANSON (21)
Symphonic Legend
Concerto da camera, for piano and string quartet
POULENC (18)
Rapsodie nègre, for cello, piano, flute and string quartet

1918   BERNSTEIN and ROCHBERG were born; DEBUSSY died

SAINT-SAËNS (83)
Fantasia No. 3, for organ
FAURÉ (73)
Cello Sonata No. 1
Une Châtelaine et sa tour, for harp
d'INDY (67)
Sarabande et Minuet, for piano and instruments
ELGAR (61)
Piano Quintet in A minor (1918–19)
String Quartet in E minor
Violin Sonata
PUCCINI (60)
Il Trittico, three one-act operas:
  Suor Angelica
  Il Tabarro
  Gianni Schicchi
DELIUS (56)
A Song Before Sunset
ROPARTZ (54)
Piano Trio
Cello Sonata No. 2 (1918–19)
NIELSEN (53)
Pan and Syrinx, for orchestra
SATIE (52)
Socrates, symphonic drama for four sopranos and chamber orchestra
BANTOCK (50)
Pibroch, for cello and piano, or harp
ALFVÉN (46)
Symphony No. 4 (1918–19)
JONGEN (45)
p. Serenade tendre, for string quartet
p. Serenade triste, for string quartet

CARPENTER (42)
Four Negro Songs
IRELAND (39)
Leaves from a Child's Sketchbook
RESPIGHI (39)
Il Tramonto, for mezzo-soprano and string quartet
BLOCH (38)
Suite for Viola (1918–19)
Suite for Viola and Piano (1918–19)
PIZZETTI (38)
Violin Sonata
BARTÓK (37)
The Miraculous Mandarin, ballet (1918–19)
GRAINGER (36)
Children's March
MALIPIERO (36)
Pantea, ballet
L'Orfeide, opera (1918–21)
Grottesco, for small orchestra
STRAVINSKY (36)
Ragtime, for eleven instruments
Four Russian Songs
TURINA (36)
Poema en forma de canciones, for voice and piano
BAX (35)
String Quartet No. 1
Folk Tale, for cello and piano
GRIFFES (34)
Poem, for flute and orchestra
Piano Sonata
TAYLOR (33)
Portrait of a Lady, for eleven instruments
SCHOECK (32)
Das Wandbild

VILLA-LOBOS (31)
Jesus, opera
Vidapura, oratorio
Marcha religiosa, Nos. 3 and 7
MARTINŮ (28)
Czech Rhapsody
BLISS (27)
Madame Noy, for soprano and
    instruments
MILHAUD (26)
L'Homme et son desir, ballet
Symphony for small orchestra,
    No. 2, *Pastorale*
Sonata for flute, oboe, clarinet
    and piano
String Quartet No. 4

HINDEMITH (23)
String Quartet No. 1
Violin Sonatas Nos. 1 and 2
GERHARD (22)
Piano Trio
*L'Infantament Meravellos de
    Shahrazade*, for voice and piano
POULENC (19)
Trois mouvements perpetuelles,
    for piano
Sonata for piano (four hands)
Sonata for two clarinets
Toréador, songs (1918–32)

LEONCAVALLO died **1919**

FAURÉ (74)
Fantaisie, for piano and orchestra
Mirages, songs
MESSAGER (66)
Monsieur Beaucaire, opera
HUMPERDINCK (65)
Gaudeamus
JANÁČEK (65)
Katya Kabanova, opera (1919–21)
*The Diary of a Young Man Who
    Disappeared*, song cycle
ELGAR (62)
Cello Concerto
DELIUS (57)
Fennimore and Gerda, opera
GERMAN (57)
Theme and Six Variations for
    orchestra
PIERNÉ (56)
Piano Quintet
Cello Sonata
MASCAGNI (56)
Si, opera
BUSONI (53)
Concertino for clarinet and small
    orchestra
SATIE (53)
Four *Petites pièces montées*, for
    small orchestra
Nocturnes, for piano
BANTOCK (51)
Colleen, viola sonata

ROUSSEL (50)
Symphony No. 2 (1919–21)
Impromptu for harp
JONGEN (46)
Poème héroïque, for violin and
    orchestra
HOLST (45)
Ode to Death
Festival Te Deum
IVES (45–53)
Orchestral Set No. 3 (1919–27)
SUK (45)
Legend of Dead Victors
Towards a New Life
GLIÈRE (44)
Imitation of Jezekiel, symphonic
    poem
CARPENTER (43)
Birthday of the Infanta, ballet
FALLA (43)
fp. *The Three-Cornered Hat*, ballet
Fantasia bética, piano solo
AUBERT (42)
La Habanera, symphonic poem
DOHNÁNYI (42)
Suite in F♯ minor
BRIDGE (40–50)
The Christmas Rose, opera
    (1919–29)
IRELAND (40)
The Holy Boy, prelude for piano,
    later orchestrated
Summer Evening, for piano

CONTINUED

RESPIGHI (40)
La Boutique fantasque, ballet
ENESCO (38)
Symphony No. 3, with organ and chorus
KODÁLY (37)
Serenade, for two violins and viola
MALIPIERO (37–39)
Tre Commedie Goldiane, opera (1919–21)
BAX (36)
Harp Quintet
Piano Sonatas Nos. 1 and 2
What the Minstrel Told Us, for piano
GRIFFES (35)
Nocturnes, for orchestra
TAYLOR (34)
Through the Looking-Glass, Suite for chamber orchestra
SCHOECK (33)
Venus, opera (1919–20)
VILLA-LOBOS (32)
Zoé, opera
Symphony No. 3, *The War*
Symphony No. 4, *The Victory*
Dansa frenetica, for orchestra
BLISS (28)
As You Like It, incidental music
Rhapsody, for solo voices and instruments
Piano Quintet

PROKOFIEV (28)
The Love of Three Oranges, opera
The Fiery Angel, opera
Overture on Hebrew Themes, for piano, clarinet and string quartet
HONEGGER (27)
Violin Sonata, No. 2
Dance of the Goat, for flute
MILHAUD (27)
Suite symphonique No. 2, *Protée*
Machines agricoles, songs
MOERAN (25)
Three piano pieces
HINDEMITH (24)
Cello Sonata
Viola Sonata
Sonata for Solo Viola
SOWERBY (24)
Trio for flute, viola and piano
HANSON (23)
Symphonic Rhapsody
KORNGOLD (22)
Much Ado About Nothing, incidental music
POULENC (20)
Le Bestaire, song cycle
Cocardes, songs
SHOSTAKOVICH (13)
Scherzo for orchestra
Eight preludes for piano

1920 FRICKER and SHAPERO were born; BRUCH and GRIFFES died

FAURÉ (75)
Masques et Bergamasques, suite for orchestra
d'INDY (69)
Le Poème de rivages (1920–21)
Légende de St. Christophe
JANÁČEK (66)
Ballad of Blanik, symphonic poem
SMYTH (62)
Dreamings
DELIUS (58)
Hassan, incidental music
PIERNÉ (57)
Paysages franciscains

BUSONI (54)
Divertimento, for flute and orchestra
Sonatina No. 6 for piano
SATIE (54)
La Belle excentrique, for orchestra
VAUGHAN WILLIAMS (48)
Shepherd of the Delectable Mountains, opera
The Lark Ascending, for violin and orchestra
Three preludes for organ
Suite de ballet, for flute and piano
Mass in G minor (1920–21)

RAVEL (45)
La Valse, choreographic poem for
orchestra
Sonata for violin and cello
(1920–22)
CARPENTER (44)
A Pilgrim Vision, for orchestra
DOHNÁNYI (43)
Hitvallas, for tenor, chorus and
orchestra
IRELAND (41)
Piano Sonata
Three London pieces, for piano
RESPIGHI (41)
Scherzo Veneziano, choreographic
comedy
Dance of the Gnomes
BLOCH (40)
Violin Sonata No. 1
BARTÓK (39)
Eight Improvisations on Peasant
Songs
MALIPIERO (38)
Oriente immaginario
STRAVINSKY (38)
Pulcinella, ballet suite
Symphonies for Wind Instruments
Concertino for string quartet
TURINA (38)
Sinfonia Sevillana
Danzas fantasticas
BAX (37)
The Truth About Russian Dancers,
ballet
The Garden of Fand, symphonic
poem
Summer Music, for orchestra
Four pieces for piano
BERG (35)
Das Wein, concert aria (possibly
1929)
VILLA-LOBOS (33)
Symphony No. 5, *The Peace*
Dansa diabolica, for orchestra
Chôros No. 1
BLISS (29)
The Tempest, overture and
interludes (1920–21)
Two Studies for Orchestra
Concerto for piano, tenor voice,
strings and percussion (revised

as Concerto for two pianos
and orchestra, 1924)
Conversations, for chamber
orchestra
Rout, for soprano and chamber
orchestra, revised for full
orchestra 1921
PROKOFIEV (29)
Five *Songs Without Words*, for
voice and piano
HONEGGER (28)
Pastorale d'été, for orchestra
Viola Sonata
Cello Sonata
MILHAUD (28)
Le Boeuf sur le toit, ballet
Ballade, for piano and orchestra
Five *Études*, for piano and
orchestra
Serenade (1920–21)
String Quartet No. 5
Printemps, six pieces for piano
BENJAMIN (27)
Three Impressions, for voice and
string quartet
MOERAN (26)
Theme and Variations for piano
Piano Trio in E minor
Ludlow Town, song cycle
CASTELNUOVO-TEDESCO (25)
La Mandragola, opera (1920–23)
Cipressi
SOWERBY (25)
Cello Sonata
The Edge of Dreams, song cycle
HANSON (24)
Before the Dawn, symphonic poem
Exaltation, symphonic poem
KORNGOLD (23)
The Dead City, opera
CHÁVEZ (21)
Symphony
Piano Sonata No. 1
POULENC (21)
Five Impromptus for piano
Suite in C major, for piano
SHOSTAKOVICH (14)
Five Preludes for piano

1921   ARNOLD and SHAPEY were born; SAINT-SAËNS and HUMPERDINCK died

FAURÉ (76)
Piano Quintet No. 2
JANÁČEK (67)
Violin Sonata
MASCAGNI (58)
Il Piccolo Marat, opera
STRAUSS, R. (57)
Schlagobers, ballet
DUKAS (56)
La Plainte, au loin, du faune, for
    piano
BUSONI (55)
Elegy, for clarinet and piano
Romance and Scherzo for piano
GIORDANO (54)
Giove a Pompeii
VAUGHAN WILLIAMS (49)
A Pastoral Symphony (Symphony
    No. 3)
HOLST (47)
The Perfect Fool, opera
The Lure, ballet
GLIÈRE (46)
Cossacks of Zaporozh, symphonic
    poem
CARPENTER (45)
Krazy Kat, ballet
FALLA (45)
*Homage pour la tombeau de
    Debussy*, for guitar
AUBERT (44)
Dryade, symphonic poem
QUILTER (44)
Three Pastoral Songs
Five Shakespeare Songs
IRELAND (42)
Mai-Dun, symphonic rhapsody
Land of Lost Content, song cycle
RESPIGHI (42)
Adagio with Variations, for cello
    and orchestra
BLOCH (41–43)
Piano Quintet (1921–23)
MEDTNER (41)
Sonata-Vocalise No. 1
PIZZETTI (41)
Cello Sonata
BARTÓK (40)
Violin Sonata No. 1

ENESCO (40)
Oedipus, opera (begun *c*.1921)
Violin Concerto
GRAINGER (39)
Molly on the Shore, for solo piano
MALIPIERO (39)
Impressioni dal vero, III
    (1921–22)
STRAVINSKY (39)
Mavra, opera buffe (1921–22)
TURINA (39)
Canto a Sevilla, song cycle
BAX (38)
Symphony No. 1 (1921–22)
Of a Rose I sing, for small chorus,
    harp, cello and double-bass
Viola Sonata
Mater Ora Filium, for
    unaccompanied chorus
CASELLA (38)
A Notte Alta
VILLA-LOBOS (34)
Malazarte, opera
Quartet for harp, celesta, flute
    and saxophone, with women's
    voices
MARTINŮ (31)
Istar, ballet
BLISS (30)
A Colour Symphony (1921–22,
    revised 1932)
Mêlée fantasque, for orchestra
    (revised 1965)
PROKOFIEV (30)
Five Songs
HONEGGER (29)
Horace Victorieux, "mimed
    symphony"
Sonatina for clarinet and piano
    (1921–22)
King David, oratorio
MILHAUD (29)
Symphony No. 3 for small
    orchestra, *Sérénade*
Symphony No. 4 for strings,
    Ouverture, Chorale, Étude
Saudades de Brasil, dance suite
    for orchestra

MOERAN (27)
In the Mountain Country,
  symphonic impression
On a May Morning, for piano
HINDEMITH (26)
Chamber Music No. 1 (1921–22)
SOWERBY (26)
Symphony No. 1
Violin Sonata No. 1
CASTELNUOVO-TEDESCO (25)
Thirty-three Shakespeare Songs

HANSON (25)
Concerto for organ, strings and
  harp
CHÁVEZ (22)
El Fuego neuvo, ballet
String Quartet No. 1
RUBBRA (20)
The Secret Hymnody, for chorus
  and orchestra
SHOSTAKOVICH (15)
Theme with Variations, for
  orchestra

FOSS and HAMILTON were born **1922**

FAURÉ (77)
Cello Sonata No. 2
L'Horizon chimerique, songs
d'INDY (71)
Le rêve de Cynias (1922–23)
DELIUS (60)
Pagan Requiem (possibly
  1914–16)
STRAUSS, R. (58)
Intermezzo, opera (1922–23)
NIELSEN (57)
Symphony No. 5
Quintet for wind
SIBELIUS (57)
Suite caractéristique
BANTOCK (54)
Song of Songs
JONGEN (49)
Rhapsody, for piano and
  instruments
HOLST (48)
Fugal Overture No. 1
GLIÈRE (47)
Comedians, ballet (also in 1930)
RAVEL (47)
Berceuse sur le nom Fauré
FALLA (46)
El Retablo de Maese Pedro, opera
Seven Spanish Popular Songs
DOHNÁNYI (45)
The Tower of the Voivod
QUILTER (45)
As You Like It, incidental music

BRIDGE (43)
Sir Roger de Coverley, for string
  quartet, or orchestra
Piano Sonata (1922–25)
RESPIGHI (43)
The Sleeping Beauty, musical fable
Concerto Gregoriano, for violin
  and orchestra
BLOCH (42)
In the Night, for piano
Poems of the Sea, for piano
  (1922–24)
PIZZETTI (42)
Lo Straniero, opera
Requiem
BARTÓK (41)
Violin Sonata No. 2
GRAINGER (40)
Shepherd's Hey, for solo piano
STRAVINSKY (40)
Octet for wind (1922–23)
BAX (39)
The Happy Forest, symphonic
  poem
SCHOECK (36)
Élégie, song cycle (1922–23)
IBERT (32)
Ballad of Reading Gaol, ballet
Ports of Call (Escales), orchestral
  suite
MARTINŮ (32)
Three Symphonic poems:
  The Grove of Satyrs
  Shadows
  Vanishing Midnight

CONTINUED

MILHAUD (30)
La Création du monde, ballet
  (1922–23)
Symphony No. 5, for small wind
  orchestra
Three *Rag-Caprices*
String Quartet No. 6
MOERAN (28)
Rhapsody No. 1
Three Fancies, for piano
WARLOCK (28)
Serenade for Frederick Delius, for
  orchestra
HINDEMITH (27)
String Quartets Nos. 2 and 3
Suite for Klavier
Sonata for Solo Viola
Die Junge Magd, song cycle
SOWERBY (27)
Ballad of King Estmere, for two
  pianos and orchestra
From the Northlands, for piano
GERHARD (26)
Seven Haï-Ku, for voice and five
  instruments

HANSON (26)
Symphony No. 1, *Nordic*
TANSMAN (25)
Sextour, ballet
POULENC (23)
Sonata for clarinet and bassoon
Sonata for trumpet, horn and
  trombone
Chanson à boire, for a cappella
  male choir
ANTHEIL (22)
Symphony No. 1
Airplane Sonata, for piano
Sonata Sauvage, for piano
WALTON (20)
fp. (privately) *Façade*, for reciter
  and chamber ensemble
SHOSTAKOVICH (16)
Two Fables of Krilov, for mezzo-
  soprano and orchestra
Suite in F♯ minor, for two pianos
Three Fantastic Dances, for piano

1923 LIGETI and MENNIN were born

FAURÉ (78)
Piano Trio
JANÁČEK (69)
Quartet No. 1
ELGAR (66)
fp. King Arthur, incidental music
SMYTH (65)
Fête galante, opera
Soul's Joy, for unaccompanied
  chorus
IPPOLITOV-IVANOV (64)
Mtzyry (1923–24)
LOEFFLER (62)
Avant que tu ne t'en ailles, poem
PIERNÉ (60)
Cydalise and the Satyr, ballet
SIBELIUS (58)
Symphony No. 6
SATIE (57)
Ludions, songs
BUSONI (56)
Ten Variations on a Chopin
  prelude

BANTOCK (55)
Pagan Symphony
ALFVÉN (51)
Bergakungen, pantomime drama
VAUGHAN WILLIAMS (51)
Old King Cole, ballet
HOLST (49)
Choral Symphony (1923–24)
Fugal Overture No. 2
SCHOENBERG (49)
Serenade, for septet and baritone
GLIÈRE (48–50)
Shahk-Senem, opera (1923–25)
FALLA (47–50)
Concerto for harpsichord, flute,
  oboe, clarinet, violin and cello
  (1923–26)
AUBERT (46)
La Nuit ensorcelée, ballet
IRELAND (44)
Cello Sonata

RESPIGHI (44)
Belfagor, lyric comedy
La Primavera, lyric poem for
 soloists, chorus and orchestra
BLOCH (43)
Baal Shem, for violin and piano
Melody, for violin and piano
Enfantines, for piano
Five Sketches in Sepia, for piano
Nirvana, for piano
BARTÓK (42)
Dance Suite, for orchestra
KODÁLY (41)
Psalmus Hungaricus, for tenor,
 chorus and orchestra
TURINA (41)
Jardin de oriente
BAX (40)
Romantic Overture, for small
 orchestra
Saga Fragment, for piano, strings,
 trumpet and cymbals
Piano Quartet
Oboe Quintet
Cello Sonata
CASELLA (40)
Concerto for string quartet
 (1923–24)
BERG (38–40)
Chamber Concerto (1923–25)
TAYLOR (38)
A Kiss in Xanadu, pantomime
 for two pianos
VILLA-LOBOS (36)
Suite for voice and viola
BLISS (32)
String Quartet (1923–24)
Ballads of the Four Seasons, song
 cycle
The Women of Yueh, song cycle

PROKOFIEV (32)
Piano Sonata No. 5
HONEGGER (31)
Chant de joie
MILHAUD (31)
Symphony No. 6, for soprano,
 contralto, tenor and bass soli,
 oboe and cello
WARLOCK (29)
The Curlew, song cycle
HINDEMITH (28)
String Quartet No. 4
Kleine Sonata for viola d'amore
 and klavier
Sonata for solo cello
HANSON (27)
North and West, symphonic poem
Lux Aeterna, symphonic poem
 with viola obbligato
String Quartet
ROBERTSON (27)
Overture
SESSIONS (27)
The Black Maskers, incidental
 music
THOMSON (27)
Two sentimental tangoes
CHÁVEZ (24)
Piano Sonata No. 2
POULENC (24)
Les Biches, ballet
ANTHEIL (23)
Violin Sonata No. 1
Ballet mécanique (1923–24,
 revised 1953)
COPLAND (23)
As it fell upon a day, for soprano,
 flute and clarinet
SHOSTAKOVICH (17)
Piano Trio No. 1

BUSONI, FAURÉ, PUCCINI and STANFORD died **1924**

FAURÉ (79)
String Quartet
d'INDY (73)
Piano Quintet
JANÁČEK (70)
The Cunning Little Vixen, opera
The Makropoulos Affair, opera
 (1924–26)
Miade, Suite for wind

ELGAR (67)
fp. Pageant of Empire
ROPARTZ (60)
String Quartet No. 3 (1924–25)
STRAUSS, R. (60–63)
The Egyptian Helen, opera
 (1924–27)

CONTINUED

DUKA S (59)
Sonnet de Ronsard, for voice and
   piano
SIBELIUS (59)
Symphony No. 7
SATIE (58)
Mercure, ballet
Relâche, ballet
GIORDANO (57)
La Cena delle beffe, opera
BANTOCK (56)
The Seal-woman, opera
VAUGHAN WILLIAMS (52)
Hugh the Drover, opera
HOLST (50)
At The Boar's Head, opera
Terzetto, for flute, oboe and viola
SCHOENBERG (50)
Quintet for Wind
GLIÈRE (49)
Two Poems for soprano and
   orchestra
For the Festival of the Comintern,
   fantasy for wind orchestra
March of the Red Army, for wind
   orchestra
RAVEL (49)
Tzigane, for violin and piano
RESPIGHI (45)
Concerto in the Mixo-Lydian mode,
   for orchestra
The Pines of Rome, symphonic
   poem
Old Airs and Dances for Lute,
   second series
Doric, String Quartet
BLOCH (44)
Concerto Grosso for strings with
   piano obbligato (1924–25)
In The Mountains (Haute Savoie),
   for string quartet
Night, for string quartet
Three Landscapes, for string
   quartet
Three Nocturnes, for piano trio
Violin Sonata No. 2, *Poème
   mystique*
Exotic Night, for violin and piano
From Jewish Life, for cello and
   piano
Méditation hébraïque, for cello and
   piano

MEDTNER (44)
Violin Sonata
BARTÓK (43)
Five Village Scenes, for female
   voice and piano
STRAVINSKY (42)
Concerto for piano and wind
Piano Sonata
BAX (41)
Symphony No. 2 (1924–25)
Cortège, for orchestra
String Quartet No. 2 (1924–25)
CASELLA (41)
La Giara, ballet
Partita, for piano (1924–25)
SZYMANOWSKI (41)
Prince Potemkin, incidental music
WEBERN (41)
Five canons for voice, clarinet
   and bass-clarinet
Six "Volkstexte"
SCHOECK (38)
Penthesiles (1924–25)
VILLA-LOBOS (37)
Chôros, Nos. 2 and 7
BLISS (33)
Masks I–IV, for piano
PROKOFIEV (33)
Symphony No. 2 (1924–25)
Quintet for oboe, clarinet, violin,
   viola and double-bass
HONEGGER (32)
Mouvement symphonique No. 1,
   Pacific 231
MILHAUD (32)
Les Malheurs d'Orphée, opera
Esther de Carpentras (1924–25)
BENJAMIN (31)
Pastoral Fantasy for string quartet
Sonatina for violin and piano
MOORE (31)
The Pageant of P.T. Barnum,
   suite for orchestra
MOERAN (30)
Rhapsody No. 2
HINDEMITH (29)
Piano Concerto
Chamber Music No. 2
Sonata for solo violin
Das Marienleben, song cycle
SOWERBY (29)
Synconata, for jazz orchestra

TANSMAN (27)
Sinfonietta
GERSHWIN (26)
Rhapsody in Blue, for piano and
orchestra
CHÁVEZ (25)
Sonatina for violin and piano
Sonatina for cello and piano
POULENC (25)
Promenade, for piano
Poèmes de Ronsard (1924–25)
COPLAND (24)
Symphony for organ and
orchestra
FINZI (23)
Severn Rhapsody

RUBBRA (23)
Double Fugue for orchestra
SEIBER (19)
String Quartet No. 1
Sarabande and Gigue, for cello and
piano
Missa Brevis, for unaccompanied
chorus
SHOSTAKOVICH (18)
Symphony No. 1 (1924–25)
Scherzo, for orchestra
Prelude and Scherzo, for string
octet (1924–25)

BERIO and BOULEZ were born; SATIE died   **1925**

d'INDY (74)
Diptyque méditerranéen (1925–26)
Cello Sonata
JANÁČEK (71)
Sinfonietta (1925–26)
Concertino for seven instruments
STANFORD (posthumous)
fp. The Travelling Companion,
opera
LOEFFLER (64)
Memories of my Childhood, for
orchestra
DELIUS (63)
Caprice and Elegy, for cello and
orchestra
NIELSEN (60)
Symphony No. 6, *Simple*
SIBELIUS (60)
Tapiola, symphonic poem
ROUSSEL (56)
Pour une fête de printemps, tone
poem
Serenade, for harp, flute, violin,
viola and cello
Jouers de flûte, for flute and piano
Violin Sonata
Segovia, for guitar
VAUGHAN WILLIAMS (53)
Concerto accademico, for violin
and string orchestra
Flos Campi, suite for viola, chorus
and small orchestra
Sancta Civitas, oratorio

GLIÈRE (50)
Cleopatra, ballet
RAVEL (50)
L'Enfant et les sortilèges, opera
CARPENTER (49)
Skyscrapers, ballet
AUBERT (48)
Capriccio, for violin and orchestra
QUILTER (48)
The Rake, ballet suite
Five Jacobean Lyrics
BLOCH (45)
Prélude (Recueillement), for string
quartet
PIZZETTI (45–47)
Fra Gherado, opera (1925–27)
GRAINGER (43)
Country Gardens, for orchestra
KODÁLY (43)
*Meditations on a theme of
Debussy*, for piano
MALIPIERO (43)
Filomela a l'infatuato, opera
Merlino maestro d'organi, opera
(1925–28)
Il Mistero de Venezia, opera
(1925–28)
STRAVINSKY (43)
Serenade in A major, for piano
BAX (42)
Piano Sonata No. 3
WEBERN (42)
Three Lieder   CONTINUED

TAYLOR (40)
Fantasy on Two Themes, for
orchestra
Jurgen, for orchestra
Circus Days, for jazz orchestra
BERG (40)
Lyric Suite, for string quartet
(1925–26)
VILLA-LOBOS (38)
Chôros Nos. 3, 8 and 10
IBERT (35)
Concerto for cello and wind
instruments
Scherzo féerique
MARTINŮ (35)
On Tourne, ballet
Half-Time, symphonic poem
Piano Concerto No. 1
PROKOFIEV (34)
Pas d'acier, ballet (1925–26)
Divertimento for orchestra
(1925–29)
HONEGGER (33)
Judith, opera
Concertino for piano and
orchestra
MILHAUD (33)
String Quartet No. 7
Deux Hymnes
BENJAMIN (32)
Three Mystical Songs, for
unaccompanied chorus
MOERAN (31)
Summer Valley, for piano
HINDEMITH (30)
Concerto for orchestra
Chamber Music Nos. 3 and 4
ORFF (30)
Prelude for orchestra

SOWERBY (30)
From the Northland, for orchestra
Monotony, for jazz orchestra
The Vision of Sir Launfal, for
chorus and orchestra
CASTELNUOVO-TEDESCO (29)
Le danze del re David, for piano
HANSON (29)
The Lament of Beowulf, for chorus
TANSMAN (28)
La Nuit Kurde, opera (1925–27)
Symphony No. 2
GERSHWIN (27)
Piano Concerto
CHÁVEZ (26)
Energia, for nine instruments
POULENC (26)
Napoli Suite, for piano
COPLAND (25)
Grogh, ballet
Dance Symphony
Music for the Theater, suite for
small orchestra
RUBBRA (24)
La Belle Dame sans merci, for
orchestra and chorus
Violin Sonata No. 1
WALTON (23)
Portsmouth Point, overture
BERKELEY (22)
"The Thresher", for voice and
piano
LAMBERT (20)
Romeo and Juliet, ballet
(1925–26)
SEIBER (20)
Serenade, for six wind instruments
Sonata da Camera, for violin and
cello

1926   BROWN, FELDMAN and HENZE were born

PUCCINI (posthumous)
fp. Turandot, opera
JANÁČEK (72)
Capriccio, for piano and wind
Festliche Messe
SMYTH (68)
Entente Cordiale, opera
Sleepless Dreams, for chorus and
orchestra
A Spring Canticle, for chorus and

orchestra
ROPARTZ (62)
Romance and Scherzino, for violin
and orchestra
NIELSEN (61)
Flute Concerto
SIBELIUS (61)
The Tempest, incidental music
HOLST (52)
The Golden Goose, choral ballet

GLIÈRE (51)
Red Poppy, ballet (1926–27)
RAVEL (51)
Chansons madécasses, for voice, flute, cello and piano
BRIDGE (47)
String Quartet No. 3
BLOCH (46)
America: An Epic Rhapsody, for orchestra
Four Episodes for chamber orchestra
MEDTNER (46)
Piano Concerto No. 2 (1926–27)
BARTÓK (45)
Piano Concerto No. 1
Three Village Scenes, for chorus and orchestra
Cantata Profana, for tenor and baritone soli, chorus and orchestra
Out of Doors, suite for piano
Mikrokosmos, for piano (1926–37)
Nine Little Pieces for piano
Piano Sonata
KODÁLY (44)
Háry János, opera
MALIPIERO (44)
L'esilio dell' eroe, five symphonic impressions
TURINA (44)
La oracion del torero, for string quartet
Piano Trio
CASELLA (43)
Introduction, Aria and Toccata, for orchestra
Concerto Romano, for organ and orchestra
Adieu à la vie, for voice and orchestra
Scarlattiana
SZYMANOWSKI (43)
Harnasie, ballet
Stabat Mater
WEBERN (43)
Two Lieder
TAYLOR (41)
The King's Henchman, opera
VILLA-LOBOS (39)
Chôros Nos. 4, 5, 6 and 6bis.

IBERT (36)
Jeux, for orchestra
MARTIN (36)
Rythmes, three symphonic movements
BLISS (35)
Hymn to Apollo, for orchestra (revised 1965)
Introduction and Allegro for orchestra (revised 1937)
MILHAUD (34)
Le Pauvre matelot, opera
MOERAN (32)
Irish Love Song, for piano
PISTON (32)
Three Pieces for flute, clarinet and bassoon
Piano Sonata
WARLOCK (32)
Capriol Suite, for strings
HINDEMITH (31)
Cardillac, opera
SOWERBY (31)
Mediaeval Poem, for organ and orchestra
HANSON (30)
Pan and the Priest, symphonic poem
Organ Concerto
THOMSON (30)
Sonata da Chiesa, for five instruments
TANSMAN (29)
Piano Concerto No. 1
HARRIS (28)
Impressions of a rainy day, for string quartet
CHÁVEZ (27)
Los cuatro soles, ballet
POULENC (27)
Trio for oboe, bassoon and piano
Chansons gaillardes
ANTHEIL (26)
Jazz Symphonietta, for twenty-two instruments
COPLAND (26)
Piano Concerto
DURUFLÉ (24)
Scherzo for organ
WALTON (24)
Siesta, for orchestra

CONTINUED

LAMBERT (21)
Pomona, ballet
Poems by Li-Po

SEIBER (21–23)
Divertimento, for clarinet and
  string quartet (1926–28)
SHOSTAKOVICH (20)
Piano Sonata No. 1

1927

d'INDY (76)
Concerto for piano, flute, cello
  and string quartet
"Suites en parties", for harp,
  flute, viola and cello
JANÁČEK (73)
From the House of the Dead, opera
(1927–28)
Glagolitic Mass
SMYTH (69)
Concerto for violin and horn
PIERNÉ (64)
Sophie Arnould, opera-comique
NIELSEN (62)
En Fantasirejse til Faerøerne,
  rhapsodic overture
ROUSSEL (58)
Piano Concerto
VAUGHAN WILLIAMS (55)
Along the Field, eight songs for
  voice and violin
RACHMANINOV (54)
Piano Concerto No. 4
HOLST (53)
The Morning of the Year, choral
  ballet
Egdon Heath, symphonic poem
The Coming of Christ, mystery
  play
SCHOENBERG (53)
String Quartet No. 3
AUBERT (50)
p. *Noël pastoral*, for piano and
  orchestra
p. Violin Sonata
BRIDGE (48)
Enter Spring, for orchestra
IRELAND (48)
Sonatina, for piano

RESPIGHI (48)
The Sunken Bell, opera
Church Windows, symphonic
  impressions
The Birds, suite for small
  orchestra
Three Botticelli Pictures, for
  orchestra
Brazilian Impressions, for
  orchestra
BARTÓK (46)
String Quartet No. 3
GRAINGER (45)
Shallow Brown
Irish Tune from County Derry
STRAVINSKY (45)
Oedipus Rex, opera-oratorio
BAX (44)
Violin Sonata No. 3
CASELLA (44)
Concerto for Strings
Cello Sonata No. 2
WEBERN (44)
String Trio
IBERT (37)
Angélique, opera
MARTINŮ (37)
Le Raid merveilleux, ballet
  (1927–28)
La Revue de cuisine, ballet
La Bagarre, symphonic poem
BLISS (36)
Oboe Quintet
Four Songs, for high voice and
  violin
HONEGGER (35)
Antigone, lyric drama
MILHAUD (35)
Violin Concerto No. 1
Carnival of Aix, for piano and
  orchestra
PISTON (33)
Symphonic Piece

CASTELNUOVO-TEDESCO (32)
Piano Concerto No. 1
HINDEMITH (32)
Chamber Music, No. 5
ORFF (32)
Concertino for wind
HANSON (31)
Heroic Elegy, for chorus and
orchestra
SESSIONS (31)
Symphony No. 1
WEINBERGER (31)
Schwanda the Bagpiper, opera
TANSMAN (30)
Piano Concerto No. 2
HARRIS (29)
Concerto for clarinet, piano and
string quartet
CHÁVEZ (28)
"HP", ballet

POULENC (28)
Concert champêtre, for harpsichord
and orchestra (1927–28)
Deux novelettes, for piano
(1927–28)
Airs chantés (1927–28)
DURUFLÉ (25)
Triptyque, for piano
WALTON (25)
Viola Concerto
Sinfonia concertante, for piano
and orchestra
KHACHATURIAN (24)
Poèm, for piano
ALWYN (22)
Five Preludes for Orchestra
LAMBERT (22)
Music for Orchestra
Elegiac Blues
SHOSTAKOVICH (21)
The Nose, opera (1927–28)
The Age of Gold, ballet (1927–30)
Symphony No. 2, *October*
Aphorisms, for piano

KORTE, MUSGRAVE and STOCKHAUSEN were born; JANÁČEK died **1928**

JANÁČEK (74)
String Quartet No. 2, *Intimate
Pages*
ELGAR (71)
fp. Beau Brummell, incidental
music
IPPOLITOV-IVANOV (69)
Episodes from Schubert's Life
LOEFFLER (67)
Intermezzo, *Clowns*
ROPARTZ (64)
Rhapsody, for cello and orchestra
NIELSEN (63)
Clarinet Concerto
BANTOCK (60)
Pilgrim's Progress
LEHÁR (58)
Frederica, operetta
ALFVÉN (56)
Manhem, cantata for male voices
VAUGHAN WILLIAMS (56)
Sir John in Love, opera
Te Deum, in G major

JONGEN (55)
Pièce symphonique, for piano and
orchestra
HOLST (54)
Moorside Suite, for brass band
SCHOENBERG (54)
Variations for orchestra
GLIÈRE (53)
String Quartet No. 3
RAVEL (53)
Bolero, for orchestra
CARPENTER (52)
String Quartet
BRIDGE (49)
Rhapsody, for two violins and
viola
RESPIGHI (49)
Toccata, for piano and orchestra
PIZZETTI (48)
Concerto dell'estate

CONTINUED

BARTÓK (47)
Rhapsodies Nos. 1 and 2, for violin and orchestra
Rhapsody No. 1 for cello and piano
String Quartet No. 4

GRAINGER (46)
Colonial Songs
Over the Hills and Far Away

STRAVINSKY (46)
Apollo Musagetes, ballet
Le Baiser de la fée, ballet

TURINA (46)
Ritmos, choreographic fantasy

BAX (45)
Symphony No. 3 (1928–29)
Sonata for two pianos
Sonata for violin and harp

CASELLA (45)
La Donna serpente, opera (1928–31)
Violin Concerto

WEBERN (45)
Symphony for small orchestra

BERG (43–49)
Lulu, opera (1928–34)

SCHOECK (42–44)
Vom Fischer und syner Fru, dramatic cantata (1928–30)

VILLA-LOBOS (41)
Chôros, Nos. 11 and 14

MARTINŮ (38)
Les Lames de Couteau, opera
The Soldier and the Dancer, opera
Échec au roi, ballet
Concertino for piano (left hand) and chamber orchestra
Entr'acte
La Rapsodie

BLISS (37)
Pastoral: Lie strewn the white flocks, for mezzo-soprano, chorus, flute, drums and string orchestra

PROKOFIEV (37)
The Prodigal Son, ballet
Symphony No. 3

HONEGGER (36)
Mouvement symphonique No. 2, Rugby

MILHAUD (36)
Christophe Columb, opera (revised 1956)
Cantate pour louer le Seigneur

MOORE (35)
A Symphony of Autumn
Moby Dick, for orchestra

HINDEMITH (33)
Concerto for organ and chamber orchestra
Chamber Music, No. 6

ORFF (33)
Entrata (revised 1940)

SOWERBY (33)
Symphony No. 2

GERHARD (32)
Wind Quintet

THOMSON (32)
Symphony on a Hymn Tune

TANSMAN (31)
Lumières

GERSHWIN (30)
An American in Paris, for orchestra

HARRIS (30)
Piano Sonata

POULENC (29)
Trois pièces, for piano

ANTHEIL (28)
Transatlantic, opera (1928–29)

COPLAND (28)
Symphony No. 1

DURUFLÉ (26)
Prélude, recitatif et variations, for flute, viola and piano

LAMBERT (23)
Piano Sonata (1928–29)

SHOSTAKOVICH (22)
Six romances on words by Japanese poets, for tenor and orchestra (1928–32)
Film music

MESSIAEN (20)
Fugue in D minor for orchestra
La Banquet céleste, for organ
Le Banquet eucharistique

d'INDY (78)
String Sextet
GIORDANO (62)
Il Re, opera
ROUSSEL (60)
Symphony No. 3 (1929–30)
LEHÁR (59)
The Land of Smiles, operetta
VAUGHAN WILLIAMS (57)
Benedicite, for soprano, chorus
and orchestra
JONGEN (56)
Passacaille et Gigue, for orchestra
Suite for viola and orchestra
HOLST (55)
The Tale of the Wandering Scholar,
opera
Concerto for two violins
Twelve songs
SCHOENBERG (55)
Von Heute auf Morgen, opera
DOHNÁNYI (52)
A Tenor, opera
BRIDGE (50)
Trio No. 2
IRELAND (50)
Ballade, for piano
RESPIGHI (50)
The Festivals of Rome, orchestral
suite
BLOCH (49)
Abodah, for violin and piano
PIZZETTI (49)
Rondo veneziano, for orchestra
GRAINGER (47)
English Dance
MALIPIERO (47)
Torneo notturno, opera
STRAVINSKY (47)
Capriccio, for piano and orchestra
TURINA (47)
Triptico
BAX (46)
Overture, Elegy and Rondo, for
orchestra
Legend, for viola and piano
BERG (44)
Three Pieces for Orchestra

VILLA-LOBOS (42)
Introdução aos Chôros, for
orchestra
Chôros Nos. 9, 12 and 13
Suite sugestiva, for voice and
orchestra
Twelve studies for guitar
IBERT (39)
Persée et Andromédée, opera
MARTINŮ (39)
Journée de bonté, opera
The Butterfly that stamped, ballet
BLISS (38)
Serenade, for baritone and
orchestra
PROKOFIEV (38)
Symphony No. 4 (1929–30,
revised 1947)
MILHAUD (37)
Viola Concerto
Concerto for percussion and
small orchestra
BENJAMIN (36)
Concerto quasi una fantasia, for
piano and orchestra
MOORE (36)
Violin Sonata
PISTON (35)
Suite No. 1 for orchestra
SOWERBY (34)
Cello Concerto (1929–34)
Prairie, symphonic poem
Florida Suite, for piano
THOMSON (33)
Five Portraits, for four clarinets
WEINBERGER (33)
Christmas, for orchestra
TANSMAN (32)
Le cercle etèrnal, ballet
HARRIS (31)
American Portraits, for orchestra
POULENC (30)
Aubade, for piano and instruments
Hommage à Roussel, for piano
Eight piano Nocturnes
(1929–38)
COPLAND (29)
Symphonic Ode (revised 1955)
Vitebsk, for piano trio

CONTINUED

RUBBRA (28)
Triple Fugue, for orchestra
DURUFLÉ (27)
Prélude, Adagio and Chorale, for
   organ
KABALEVSKY (25)
Piano Concerto No. 1
String Quartet in A minor
LAMBERT (24)
The Rio Grande, for chorus, piano
   and orchestra

SHOSTAKOVICH (23)
Symphony No. 3, *The 1st of May*
MESSIAEN (21)
Préludes, for piano
BARBER (19)
Serenade for string orchestra, or
   string quartet

1930   WARLOCK died

d'INDY (79)
String Quartet No. 4
Suite for flute obbligato, violin,
   viola, cello and harp
Piano Trio No. 2, in the form of
   a suite
ELGAR (73)
Pomp and Circumstance March,
   No. 5
Severn Suite, for brass band, or
   orchestra
SMYTH (72)
The Prison, for unaccompanied
   chorus
DELIUS (68)
A Song of Summer
STRAUSS, R. (66–68)
Arabella, opera (1930–32)
VAUGHAN WILLIAMS (58)
Prelude and Fugue for orchestra
Job, a Masque for Dancing, for
   orchestra
JONGEN (57)
Sonata Eroica
RACHMANINOV (57)
Three Russian Folksongs, for
   chorus and orchestra (possibly
   1927)
HOLST (56)
Choral Fantasia
Hammersmith, prelude and
   scherzo for orchestra
AUBERT (53)
Feuilles d'images
BRIDGE (51)
Oration, "concert elegiaco" for
   cello

IRELAND (51)
Piano Concerto
RESPIGHI (51)
Metamorphosen modi XII, theme
   and variations for orchestra
PIZZETTI (50)
Piano Concerto
BARTÓK (49)
Piano Concerto No. 2 (1930–31)
GRAINGER (48)
Lord Peter's Stable-boy
Spoon River
To a Nordic Princess
KODÁLY (48)
Dances of Marosszek, for piano
MALIPIERO (48)
La Bella ed il mostro, opera
STRAVINSKY (48)
Symphony of Psalms, for chorus
   and orchestra
BAX (47)
Symphony No. 4
Overture to a picaresque comedy,
   for orchestra
Winter Legends, for piano and
   orchestra
CASELLA (47)
Serenade for small orchestra
WEBERN (47)
Quartet for violin, clarinet,
   saxophone and piano
TAYLOR (45)
Peter Ibbetson, opera
VILLA-LOBOS (43)
Bachianas Brasilieras, Nos. 1
   and 2

IBERT (40)
Le Roi d'Yvetot, opera
Divertissement, for chamber
  orchestra
MARTINŮ (40)
Serenade, for chamber orchestra
Violin Sonata No. 1
BLISS (39)
Morning Heroes, symphony for
  orator, chorus and orchestra
PROKOFIEV (39)
Sur le Borythène (On the Dnieper),
  ballet
Four Portraits, symphonic suite
  (1930–31)
String Quartet No. 1
HONEGGER (38)
Les aventures du roi pausole,
  light opera
Symphony No. 1
MILHAUD (38)
Maximilien, opera
MOORE (37)
Overture on an American theme
PISTON (36)
Flute Sonata
HINDEMITH (35)
Concert music, for piano, brass
  and harps
ORFF (35)
Catulli Carmina, for chorus and
  orchestra (revised 1943)
SOWERBY (35)
Organ Symphony
HANSON (34)
Symphony No. 2, *Romantic*
SESSIONS (34)
Piano Sonata No. 1

THOMSON (34)
Violin Sonata
WEINBERGER (34)
The Beloved Voice, opera
Bohemian Songs and Dances, for
  orchestra
TANSMAN (33)
Triptyque, for string orchestra
HARRIS (32)
String Quartet No. 1
CHÁVEZ (31)
Sonata for horns
POULENC (31)
Épitaphe, song
COPLAND (30)
Piano Variations
DURUFLÉ (28)
Suite for organ
KABALEVSKY (26)
Poem of Struggle, for chorus and
  orchestra
ALWYN (25)
Piano Concerto
SHOSTAKOVICH (24)
*Lady Macbeth of the Mtsensk
  District*, opera
The Bolt, choreographic spectacle
  (1930–31)
Film music
MESSIAEN (22)
Les Offrandes oubliées, for
  orchestra
Simple chant d'une âme
Diptyque, for organ
BRITTEN (17)
Hymn to the Virgin

WILLIAMSON was born; d'INDY and NIELSON died **1931**

ELGAR (74)
p. Nursery Suite, for orchestra
NIELSEN (66)
Commotio, for organ
PIERNÉ (68)
*Divertissement sur un thème
  pastorale*, for orchestra
Fantaisie basque, for violin
CILÈA (65)
Suite for orchestra

ROUSSEL (62)
Bacchus and Ariadne, ballet
VAUGHAN WILLIAMS (59)
Symphony No. 4 (1931–34)
Piano Concerto
In Windsor Forest, cantata
SUK (57)
Mass in B♭ major
RAVEL (56)
Piano Concerto in G major
Piano Concerto for the left hand   CONTINUED

BRIDGE (52)
Phantasm, rhapsody for piano
  and orchestra
IRELAND (52)
Songs Sacred and Profane
PIZZETTI (51–55)
Oreseolo, opera (1931–35)
BARTÓK (50)
Forty-four duos for two violins
GRAINGER (49)
The Nightingale and the Two Sisters
KODÁLY (49)
The Spinning Room, lyric scenes
  (1931–32)
Theater Overture
Pange lingua, for chorus and
  organ
MALIPIERO (49)
Concerto for Orchestra
STRAVINSKY (49)
Violin Concerto
TURINA (49)
Rapsodia sinfonica, for piano and
  strings
Piano Quartet
BAX (48)
Symphony No. 5 (1931–32)
The Tale the Pine Trees Knew,
  symphonic poem
Nonet for flute, oboe, clarinet,
  harp and strings
String Quintet
CASELLA (48–52)
Introduction, corale e marcia, for
  woodwind (1931–35)
SZYMANOWSKI (48)
Symphonie concertante, for piano
  (1931–32)
VILLA-LOBOS (44)
String Quartet No. 5
MARTIN (41)
Chaconne, for cello and piano
Violin Sonata
MARTINŮ (41)
Spaliček, ballet
Partita (Suite No. 1)
Cello Concerto
BLISS (40)
Clarinet Quintet

PROKOFIEV (40)
Piano Concerto No. 4 for the left
  hand
GROFÉ (39)
Grand Canyon Suite, for orchestra
HONEGGER (39)
Cries of the World, choral-
  orchestral
Amphion
1001 Nights
BENJAMIN (38)
The Devil Take Her, comic opera
PISTON (37)
Suite for oboe and piano
HINDEMITH (36)
The Unceasing, oratorio
SOWERBY (36)
Passacaglia, Interlude and Fugue,
  for orchestra
THOMSON (35)
Four Portraits, for violin and
  piano
Serenade, for flute and violin
Quartet No. 1
Stabat Mater
WEINBERGER (35)
Passacaglia, for orchestra
TANSMAN (34)
Symphony No. 3, *Symphony
  concertante*
Concertino, for piano
GERSHWIN (33)
Second Rhapsody
HARRIS (33)
Toccata, for orchestra
POULENC (32)
Bagatelle, for violin and piano
Troi poèmes de Louise Lalanne,
  songs
Nine songs
ANTHEIL (31)
Helen Retires, opera
RUBBRA (30)
Piano Concerto
Violin Sonata No. 2
WALTON (29)
fp. Belshazzar's Feast, for baritone,
  chorus and orchestra
LAMBERT (26)
Concerto for piano and nine
  instruments

SHOSTAKOVICH (25)
Hamlet, incidental music
MESSIAEN (23)
Le Tombeau resplendissant

BARBER (21)
School for Scandal, overture
Dover Beach, for voice and string
quartet
MENOTTI (20)
Variations on a Theme of Schumann,
for piano

GOEHR was born **1932**

DELIUS (70)
Prelude to Irmelin
MASCAGNI (69)
Pinotta, opera
ROUSSEL (63)
Quartet
ALFVÉN (60)
Spamannen, incidental music
Vi, incidental music
VAUGHAN WILLIAMS (60)
Magnificat
RACHMANINOV (59)
Variations on a Theme by
Corelli, for piano
SCHOENBERG (58)
Moses und Aron, opera
CARPENTER (56)
Patterns, for piano and orchestra
Song of Faith, for chorus and
orchestra
IRELAND (53)
A Downland Suite, for brass band
RESPIGHI (53)
Belkis, Queen of Sheba, ballet
Mary of Egypt, mystery play
Airs and Dances for Lute, 3rd
series
GRAINGER (50)
Blithe Bells
MALIPIERO (50)
Violin Concerto
Sette Invenzione
Inni
STRAVINSKY (50)
Duo concertante, for viola and
piano
BAX (49)
Cello Concerto
Sinfonietta
A Northern Ballad, for orchestra
(1932–33)
Piano Sonata No. 4

CASELLA (49)
La Favola d'Orfeo, opera
Sinfonia for clarinet, trumpet and
piano
SZYMANOWSKI (49)
Violin Concerto No. 2 (1932–33)
SCHOECK (46)
Praeludium
VILLA-LOBOS (45)
Caixinha de Bôas Festas, ballet
IBERT (42)
Donogoo, for orchestra
Paris, symphonic suite
MARTINŮ (42)
Sinfonia for two orchestras
Les Rondes
PROKOFIEV (41)
Piano Concerto No. 5
HONEGGER (40)
Mouvement symphonique No. 3
(1932–33)
Sonatina for violin and cello
MILHAUD (40)
String Quartet No. 8
BENJAMIN (39)
Violin Concerto
MOERAN (38)
Farrago, suite for orchestra
HINDEMITH (37)
Philharmonic Concerto
SOWERBY (37)
Piano Concerto No. 2
THOMSON (36)
Quartet No. 2
WEINBERGER (36)
The Outcasts of Poker Flat, opera
TANSMAN (35)
La Grand Ville, ballet
Two Symphonic Movements

CONTINUED

HARRIS (34)
Chorale for strings
Fantasy, for piano and woodwind
  quintet
String Sextet
CHÁVEZ (33)
String Quartet No. 2
POULENC (33)
Concerto for two pianos and
  orchestra
Sextet for piano and wind
  (1932–40)
Intermezzo, in D minor for piano
Improvisations for piano
  (1932–43)
Le bal masqué, cantata
KHACHATURIAN (29)
String Quartet
Trio for clarinet, violin and piano
Violin Sonata
KABALEVSKY (28)
Symphonies Nos. 1 and 2

SHOSTAKOVICH (26)
From Karl Marx to our own days,
  symphonic poem with voices
Twenty-four Preludes for piano
  (1932–33)
Film music
MESSIAEN (24)
Hymne au Saint Sacrement, for
  orchestra
Apparition de l'Église Étérnelle,
  for organ
Fantaisie burlesque, for piano
BARBER (22)
Cello Sonata
BRITTEN (19)
Sinfonietta for chamber orchestra
Phantasy Quartet, for oboe and
  strings
GOULD (19)
Chorale and Fugue in Jazz

1933 PENDERECKI was born

IPPOLITOV-IVANOV (74)
The Last Barricade (1933–34)
ROPARTZ (69)
Sérénade champêtre
GLAZUNOV (68)
Epic Poem
VAUGHAN WILLIAMS (61)
The Running Set, for orchestra
JONGEN (60)
Symphonie concertante, for organ
  and orchestra
La légende de Saint-Nicholas, for
  children's chorus and
  orchestra
HOLST (59)
Brook Green, suite for strings
Lyric Movement for viola and
  strings
CARPENTER (57)
Sea Drift, symphonic poem
IRELAND (54)
Legend, for piano and orchestra
BLOCH (53)
Avodath Hakodesh, sacred service
  for baritone, chorus and
  orchestra

PIZZETTI (53)
Cello Concerto (1933–34)
KODÁLY (51)
Dances of Galantá, for orchestra
MALIPIERO (51)
La favola del figlio cambiato, opera
STRAVINSKY (51)
Suite italienne, for cello and piano
TURINA (51)
Piano Trio
BAX (50)
Sonatina for cello and piano
CASELLA (50)
Concerto for violin, cello, piano
  and orchestra
VILLA-LOBOS (46)
Pedra Bonita, ballet
MARTIN (43)
Four Short Pieces for guitar
MARTINŮ (43)
The Miracle of Our Lady, opera
BLISS (42)
Viola Sonata
PROKOFIEV (42)
Cello Concerto (1933–38)
Chant symphonique, for orchestra

MILHAUD (41)
Piano Concerto No. 1
BENJAMIN (40)
Prima Donna, comic opera
MOORE (40)
String Quartet
PISTON (39)
Concerto for Orchestra
String Quartet No. 1
CASTELNUOVO-TEDESCO (38)
Sonata for guitar, *Homage to Boccherini*
HANSON (37)
The Merry Mount, opera
TANSMAN (36)
Partita, for string orchestra
HARRIS (35)
Symphony No. 1
String Quartet No. 2
CHÁVEZ (34)
Symphony No. 1, *Sinfonia de Antigona*
Soli, No. 1 for oboe, clarinet, trumpet and bassoon
Cantos de Mexico
POULENC (34)
Feuillets d'album, for piano
Villageoises, for piano
COPLAND (33)
Symphony No. 2, *Short Symphony*
FINZI (32)
A Young Man's Exhortation, song cycle

RUBBRA (32)
Bee-Bee-Bei, opera
BERKELEY (30)
Violin Sonata No. 2 (*c.*1933)
KHACHATURIAN (30)
Symphony No. 1 (1933–34)
Dance Suite
KABALEVSKY (29)
Symphony No. 3
SHOSTAKOVICH (27)
Concerto No. 1 for piano, string orchestra and trumpet
The Human Comedy, incidental music (1933–34)
MESSIAEN (25)
L'Ascension, for organ
Mass for eight sopranos and four violins
BARBER (23)
Music for a Scene from Shelley
CAGE (21)
Sonata for solo clarinet
BRITTEN (20)
A Boy was Born, for unaccompanied voices
Friday Afternoons, twelve children's songs with piano (1933–35)
Two Part-songs for chorus and piano

BIRTWHISTLE and (MAXWELL) DAVIES were born; DELIUS, ELGAR and **1934**
HOLST died

IPPOLITOV-IVANOV (75)
Catalan Suite
DELIUS (72)
Songs of Farewell, for chorus and orchestra
PIERNÉ (71)
Fragonard, ballet
Giration, ballet
STRAUSS, R. (70)
Symphony for wind instruments
ROUSSEL (65)
Symphony No. 4
Sinfonietta for Strings

VAUGHAN WILLIAMS (62)
Fantasia on "Greensleeves", for orchestra
Suite for viola and small orchestra
SCHOENBERG (60)
Suite in G for strings
RACHMANINOV (61)
Rhapsody on a Theme by Paginini, for piano and orchestra
CARPENTER (58)
Piano Quintet
FALLA (58)
Fanfare for wind and percussion

CONTINUED

IRELAND (55)
A Comedy Overture, for brass
    band
RESPIGHI (55)
La Fiamma, melodrama
Concerto for oboe, horn, violin,
    double-bass, piano and string
    orchestra
BLOCH (54–56)
A Voice in the Wilderness,
    symphonic poem for cello and
    orchestra (1934–36)
BARTÓK (53)
String Quartet No. 5
KODÁLY (52)
Jesus and the Merchants, for
    chorus and orchestra
MALIPIERO (52)
Symphony No. 1
Piano Concerto No. 1
STRAVINSKY (52)
Persephone, for speaker, singers
    and orchestra
BAX (51)
Symphony No. 6
Concerto for flute, oboe, harp
    and string quartet
Octet for horn, strings and piano
Clarinet Sonata
CASELLA (51)
Cello Concerto (1934–35)
Notturno e Tarentella, for cello
WEBERN (50)
Concerto for nine instruments
IBERT (44)
Diane de Poitiers, ballet
Concertino da camera, for alto
    saxophone and small orchestra
MARTIN (44)
Piano Concerto No. 1
MARTINŮ (44)
Inventions
BLISS (43)
Things to Come, suite for
    orchestra, from music for the
    film
PROKOFIEV (43)
Lieutenant Kijé, symphonic suite
    with baritone ad lib
Egyptian Night, symphonic suite

HONEGGER (42)
Sémiramis, ballet
Cello Concerto
String Quartet No. 2 (1934–36)
MOERAN (40)
Nocturne, for baritone, chorus
    and orchestra
PISTON (40)
Prelude and Fugue for organ
HINDEMITH (39)
Mathis der Maler, opera, also
    symphony
ORFF (39)
Bayerische Musik
GERHARD (38)
Ariel, ballet
THOMSON (38)
Four Saints in Three Acts, opera
WEINBERGER (38)
A Bed of Roses, opera
GERSHWIN (36)
Cuban Overture
HARRIS (36)
Symphony No. 2
*When Johnny Comes Marching
    Home*, overture
Songs for Occupations, for chorus
Piano Trio
POULENC (35)
Two Intermezzi for piano
Presto, Badinage, Humoresque, for
    piano
Eight *Chansons polonaises*
Four *Chansons pour enfants*
    (1934–35)
COPLAND (34)
Hear Ye! Hear Ye!, ballet
Statements, for orchestra
RUBBRA (33)
Sinfonia concertante, for piano and
    orchestra
Rhapsody, for violin
RODRIGO (32)
Cantico de la Esposa, for voice and
    piano
WALTON (32)
Escape Me Never, ballet from the
    film
fp. Symphony No. 1 (first three
    movements only)

BERKELEY (31)
Three pieces for two pianos
  (1934–38)
Polka for piano
SEIBER (29)
Eva Spielt mit Puppen, opera
String Quartet No. 2 (1934–35)
TIPPETT (29)
String Quartet No. 1
SHOSTAKOVICH (28)
Bright Stream, comedy ballet
Suite for Jazz Orchestra, No. 1
Cello Sonata
Film music

SCHUMAN (24)
Choreographic Poem, for seven
  instruments
CAGE (22)
Six short Inventions for seven
  instruments
BRITTEN (21)
Simple Symphony, for string
  orchestra
Suite for violin and piano
Holiday Diary, for piano
Te Deum
LUTOSLAWSKI (21)
Piano Sonata

MAW was born; BERG, DUKAS, IPPOLITOV-IVANOV, LOEFFLER and SUK died   **1935**

PIERNÉ (72)
Images, ballet
MASCAGNI (72)
Nero, opera
STRAUSS, R. (71)
The Silent Woman, opera
Der Friedenstag, opera (1935–36)
VAUGHAN WILLIAMS (63)
Five Tudor Portraits, choral suite
CARPENTER (59)
Danza, for orchestra
FALLA (59)
Pour le tombeau de Paul Dukas,
  for piano
BLOCH (55)
Piano Sonata
STRAVINSKY (53)
Concerto for two pianos
TURINA (53)
Serenade, for quartet
BAX (52)
The Morning Watch, for chorus
  and orchestra
Overture to Adventure, for
  orchestra
WEBERN (52)
Das Augenlicht, for chorus and
  orchestra
Three Lieder
BERG (50)
Violin Concerto
IBERT (45)
Gonzaque, opera
MARTIN (45)
Rhapsody for strings

MARTINŮ (45)
The Suburban Theatre, opera
Le Jugement de Paris, ballet
Concertino No. 2, for piano
BLISS (44)
Music for Strings
PROKOFIEV (44)
Romeo and Juliet, ballet
  (1935–36)
Violin Concerto No. 2
Musiques d'enfants, for piano
MILHAUD (43)
Cello Concerto No. 1
String Quartet No. 9
BENJAMIN (42)
Heritage, for orchestra
Romantic Phantasy, for violin,
  viola and orchestra
MOORE (42)
White Wings, opera
PISTON (41)
String Quartet No. 2
Piano Trio No. 1
HINDEMITH (40)
Concerto for Orchestra
Viola Concerto, *Der
  Schwanendreher*
ORFF (40)
Carmina Burana, scenic cantata
  (1935–36)
HANSON (39)
Drum Taps, for baritone, chorus
  and orchestra
SESSIONS (39)
Violin Concerto   CONTINUED

GERSHWIN (37)
Porgy and Bess, opera
CHÁVEZ (36)
Symphony No. 2, *Sinfonia India*
Obertura Republicana
POULENC (36)
Margot, incidental music
Suite française, for chamber
    orchestra
Cinq poèmes (Eluard)
"A sa guitare" (Ronsard)
ANTHEIL (35)
Dreams, ballet
FINZI (34)
Introit, for violin and orchestra
    (revised 1945)
DURUFLÉ (33)
Three Dances for Orchestra

BERKELEY (32)
Overture for Orchestra
Jonah, oratorio
String Quartet No. 1
Étude, Berceuse, Capriccio, for
    piano
How Love Came In, for voice and
    piano
RAWSTHORNE (30)
Viola Sonata (revised 1954)
SHOSTAKOVICH (29)
Symphony No. 4 (1935–36)
Five fragments for small orchestra
MESSIAEN (27)
La nativité du Seigneur, nine
    meditations for organ
SCHUMAN (25)
Symphony No. 1 for eighteen
    instruments
DIAMOND (20)
Partita for oboe, bassoon and
    piano

1936   BENNETT was born; GERMAN, GLAZUNOV and RESPIGHI died

STRAUSS, R. (72)
Daphne, opera
GLAZUNOV (71)
Saxophone Concerto
ROUSSEL (67)
Rhapsodie flamande
Concertino for Cello
VAUGHAN WILLIAMS (64)
Riders to the Sea, one-act opera
The Poisoned Kiss, romantic
    extravaganza, for voices and
    orchestra
Dona nobis pacem, cantata
JONGEN (63)
Triptyque, three suites for
    orchestra
RACHMANINOV (63)
Symphony No. 3
SCHOENBERG (62)
Violin Concerto
CARPENTER (60)
Violin Concerto
WOLF-FERRARI (60)
Il campiello, opera
QUILTER (59)
Julia, opera

IRELAND (57)
London Overture, for orchestra
MEDTNER (56)
Violin Sonata, *Sonata Epica*
BARTÓK (55)
*Music for Strings, Percussion and
    Celesta*
Petite Suite for piano
KODÁLY (54)
Te Deum
MALIPIERO (54)
Julius Caesar, opera
Symphony No. 2, *Elegiaca*
BAX (53)
Concerto for bassoon, harp and
    string sextet
String Quartet No. 3
WEBERN (53)
Variations for Piano
TAYLOR (51)
Lucrece, for string quartet
VILLA-LOBOS (49)
Bachianas brasilieras, No. 4, for
    piano

MARTIN (46)
Symphony for Full Orchestra
(1936–37)
Danse de la peur, for two pianos
and small orchestra
String Trio
MARTINŮ (46)
Juliette: or The Key to Dreams,
opera (1936–37)
BLISS (45)
Kenilworth Suite, for brass
PROKOFIEV (45)
Peter and the Wolf, for narrator
and orchestra
Russian Overture
Cantata for the twentieth
anniversary of the October
Revolution (1936–37)
HONEGGER (44)
Nocturne
String Quartet No. 3
MILHAUD (44)
Suite provençale
MOORE (43)
The Headless Horseman, opera
CASTELNUOVO-TEDESCO (41)
Concerto for two guitars and
orchestra
Concertino, for harp and chamber
orchestra
Tarantella
ORFF (41)
Olympischer Reigen
SOWERBY (41)
Organ Concerto No. 1
SESSIONS (40)
String Quartet No. 1
TANSMAN (39)
Viola Concerto
Two Intermezzi
GERSHWIN (38)
Three Preludes for piano
HARRIS (38)
Symphony for Voices
Time Suite, for orchestra
Prelude and Fugue for string
orchestra
Piano Quintet

POULENC (37)
Litanies à la Vierge noire, for
voices and organ
Petites voix, for children's choir
Seven songs for a cappella choir
Les soirées de Nazelles, for piano
ANTHEIL (36)
Course, dance score
COPLAND (36)
El salon Mexico, for orchestra
FINZI (35)
Interlude, for oboe and string
quartet
Earth, Air and Rain, song cycle
RUBBRA (35)
Symphony No. 1
BERKELEY (33)
Five short pieces for piano
KHACHATURIAN (33)
Piano Concerto
KABALEVSKY (32)
Piano Concerto No. 2
ALWYN (31)
Marriage of Heaven and Hell,
choral work
LAMBERT (31)
Summer's Last Will and Testament,
for chorus and orchestra
RAWSTHORNE (31)
Concerto for clarinet and string
orchestra
TIPPETT (31)
Piano Sonata (1936–37,
revised 1942)
SHOSTAKOVICH (30)
Salute to Spain, incidental music
Four Romances on verses of
Pushkin, for bass and piano
Film music
BARBER (26)
Symphony No. 1
Adagio for strings (arranged from
String Quartet No. 1)
String Quartet No. 1
SCHUMAN (26)
String Quartet No. 1
MENOTTI (25)
Trio for a Housewarming Party,
for flute, cello and piano
GILLIS (24)
Four Moods in Three Keys, for
chamber orchestra CONTINUED

BRITTEN (23)
Our Hunting Fathers, song cycle
Soirées musicales, suite
GOULD (23)
Little Symphony
Symphonette No. 2

DIAMOND (21)
TOM, ballet
Violin Concerto No. 1
Psalm, for orchestra
Concerto for string quartet
Cello Sonata
BERIO (11)
Pastorale

1937 BEDFORD and NILSSON were born; GERSHWIN, PIERNÉ, RAVEL, ROUSSEL and SZYMANOWSKI died

PIERNÉ (74)
Gulliver in Lilliput
ROPARTZ (73)
Requiem, with orchestra
BANTOCK (69)
King Solomon
ROUSSEL (68)
String Trio
ALFVÉN (65)
Swedish Rhapsody No. 3,
    Dalarapsodi
VAUGHAN WILLIAMS (65)
Festival Te Deum
SCHOENBERG (63)
String Quartet No. 4
AUBERT (60)
Les fêtes d'été
RESPIGHI (posthumous)
fp. Lucrezia, opera
BRIDGE (58)
String Quartet No. 4
IRELAND (58)
These Things Shall Be, for baritone,
    chorus and orchestra
Green Ways, for piano
BLOCH (57)
Violin Concerto (1937–38)
Evocations, symphonic suite
ENESCO (56)
Suite villageoise, for orchestra
MALIPIERO (55)
Piano Concerto No. 2
Cello Concerto
STRAVINSKY (55)
Jeu de cartes, ballet
BAX (54)
Violin Concerto
A London Pageant, for orchestra
Northern Ballad, No. 2 for
    orchestra

CASELLA (54)
Concerto for Orchestra
Il deserto tentato, oratorio
TAYLOR (52)
Ramuntcho, opera
Casanova, ballet
SCHOECK (51)
Massimilla Doni, opera
VILLA-LOBOS (50)
Currupira, ballet
Sabastiao
Descobrimento do Brasil, four
    suites for chorus and orchestra
MARTINŮ (47)
Alexandra bis, opera
Comedy on the Bridge, opera
IBERT/HONEGGER (47/45)
L'Aiglon, opera
BLISS (46)
Checkmate, ballet
GROFÉ (45)
Broadway at Night
Symphony in Steel
MILHAUD (45)
Cantate de la paix
BENJAMIN (44)
Overture to an Italian comedy, for
    orchestra
Nightingale Lane, for two voices
    and piano
MOERAN (43)
Symphony in G minor
PISTON (43)
Symphony No. 1
Concertino, for piano and chamber
    orchestra
HINDEMITH (42)
Symphonic Dances, for orchestra
Organ Sonatas Nos. 1 and 2

ORFF (42)
Der Mond, opera (1937–38)
THOMSON (41)
Filling Station, ballet
WEINBERGER (41)
Wallenstein, opera
TANSMAN (40)
Bric-a-Brac
Fantasy, for cello
Fantasy, for violin
HARRIS (39)
Symphony No. 3
String Quartet No. 3
POULENC (38)
Deux marches et un intermède, for
   chamber orchestra
Mass in G major
Sécheresses, cantata
Bourée d'Auvergne, for piano
Tel jour telle nuit, songs
RUBBRA (36)
Symphony No. 2
String Quartet
WALTON (35)
Crown Imperial, coronation march
In Honour of the City, for chorus
   and orchestra
BERKELEY (34)
Domini est terra, for chorus and
   orchestra
Mont Juic, suit of Catalan dances
   for orchestra (with Britten)
KHACHATURIAN (34)
Song of Stalin, for chorus and
   orchestra
DALLAPICCOLA (33)
Volo di Notte, opera (1937–38)
LAMBERT (32)
Horoscope, ballet

RAWSTHORNE (32)
Theme and Variations, for two
   violins
TIPPETT (32)
A Song of Liberty
SHOSTAKOVICH (31)
Symphony No. 5
MESSIAEN (29)
Poèmes pour Mi, for voice and
   orchestra
BARBER (27)
First Essay for Orchestra
SCHUMAN (27)
Symphony No. 2
String Quartet No. 2
Choral étude
MENOTTI (26)
Amelia al Ballo, opera
GILLIS (25)
The Woolyworm, symphonic
   satire
The Crucifixion, for solo voices,
   narrator, chorus and orchestra
The Panhandle, suite
*Thoughts Provoked on Becoming a
   Prospective Papa*, suite
BRITTEN (24)
Mont Juic, suite of Catalan
   dances for orchestra (with
   Berkeley)
Variations on a Theme of Frank
   Bridge, for strings
On This Island, song cycle
GOULD (24)
Piano Concerto
Spirituals for orchestra
DIAMOND (22)
Variations for small orchestra
Quintet for flute, string trio and
   piano

1938

STRAUSS, R. (74–76)
The Love of Danae, opera
   (1938–40)
BANTOCK (70)
Aphrodite in Cyprus, symphonic
   ode
VAUGHAN WILLIAMS (66)
The Bridal Day, masque
Serenade to Music, for sixteen solo

voices and orchestra
JONGEN (65)
Hymne à la Meuse, for chorus and
   orchestra
GLIÈRE (63)
Harp Concerto
IRELAND (59)
Piano Trio No. 3

CONTINUED

PIZZETTI (58–62)
L'Oro, opera (1938–42)
BARTÓK (57)
Violin Concerto No. 2
Sonata for two pianos and
  percussion
Contrasts, for clarinet, violin and
  piano
KODÁLY (56)
Variations on a Hungarian
  Folksong, for orchestra
  (1938–39)
MALIPIERO (56)
Anthony and Cleopatra, opera
Triple concerto for violin, cello
  and piano
STRAVINSKY (56)
Dumbarton Oaks, concerto for
  sixteen instruments
WEBERN (55)
String Quartet
SCHOECK (52)
Das Schloss Durande, opera
  (1938–39)
VILLA-LOBOS (51)
Bachianas brasilieras Nos. 3 and 6
String Quartet No. 6
IBERT (48)
La Famille cardinal, opera (with
  Honegger)
Capriccio, for ten instruments
MARTIN (48)
Le Vin herbe (Der Zaubertrank)
  opera (1938–41)
Ballade, for saxophone, strings,
  piano and percussion
Sonata da chiesa
MARTINŮ (48)
Concerto for two string
  orchestras, piano and timpani
Concerto grosso for orchestra
Tre ricercare, for orchestra
Quartet No. 5
Madrigals for women's voices
BLISS (47)
Piano Concerto
PROKOFIEV (47)
Alexander Nevsky, cantata
  (1938–39)

HONEGGER (46)
La Famille cardinal, opera (with
  Ibert)
La Danse des morts, for solo
  voices, chorus and orchestra
Joan of Arc at the stake, incidental
  music
MILHAUD (46)
Medée, opera
BENJAMIN (45)
Two Jamaican pieces for
  orchestra:
  Jamaican Song
  Jamaican Rumba
Cotillon Suite, for orchestra
Sonatina for cello and piano
MOORE (45)
Dedication, for chorus
PISTON (44)
The Incredible Flutist, ballet
CASTELNUOVO-TEDESCO (43)
Auvassin et Nicolette, for voice,
  instruments and marionettes
HINDEMITH (43)
Nobilissima visione, ballet
SOWERBY (43)
Theme in Yellow, for orchestra
Clarinet Sonata
HANSON (42)
Symphony No. 3
ROBERTSON (42)
Piano Quintet
WEINBERGER (42)
Variations on *Under the Spreading
  Chestnut Tree*, for orchestra
SESSIONS (41)
Scherzino and March, for orchestra
TANSMAN (41)
La toison d'or, opera
Symphony No. 4
HARRIS (40)
Soliloquy and Dance, for viola and
  piano
CHÁVEZ (39)
Concerto for four horns
POULENC (39)
Concerto for organ, strings and
  timpani
Four Penitential Motets
  (1938–39)

COPLAND (38)
An Outdoor Overture
Billy the Kid, ballet
RUBBRA (37)
Prism, ballet music
BERKELEY (35)
The Judgement of Paris, ballet
Introduction and Allegro, for
two pianos and orchestra
DALLAPICCOLA (34)
Canti di prigionia, for chorus and
instruments (1938–41)
KABALEVSKY (34)
Colas Breugnon, opera
Vasilek, ballet
RAWSTHORNE (33)
Symphonic Studies for orchestra
TIPPETT (33)
Concerto for Double String
Orchestra (1938–39)
LUTYENS (32)
String Quartets Nos. 1 and 2
Partita for two violins
Sonata for solo viola

SHOSTAKOVICH (32)
Suite for Jazz Orchestra, No. 2
String Quartet No. 1
Film music
CAGE (26)
Metamorphosis, for piano
GILLIS (26)
The Raven
BRITTEN (25)
Piano Concerto No. 1 in D major
LUTOSLAWSKI (25)
Symphonic Variations
DIAMOND (23)
Cello Concerto
Music for double string orchestra,
brass and timpani
Heroic Piece, for small orchestra
Elegy in memory of Ravel, for
brass, harps and percussion
Piano Quartet
SHAPERO (18)
Three Pieces for Three Pieces, for
woodwind trio
FOSS (16)
Four two-voice Inventions for
piano
Three Goethe-Lieder

1939

VAUGHAN WILLIAMS (67)
Five Variants of Dives and Lazarus,
for strings and harp
JONGEN (66)
Ouverture-Fanfare, for orchestra
SCHOENBERG (65)
Kol Nidrei
WOLF-FERRARI (63)
Dama Boba, opera
IRELAND (60)
Concertino pastorale, for strings
BARTÓK (58)
Divertimento for Strings
String Quartet No. 6
KODÁLY (57)
Concerto for Orchestra
The Peacock Variations, for
orchestra
MALIPIERO (57)
Ecuba, opera
BAX (56)
Symphony No. 7

CASELLA (56)
Sinfonia (1939–40)
WEBERN (56)
First Cantata (Jone)
VILLA-LOBOS (52)
New York Skyline, for orchestra
MARTIN (49)
Three Ballades, for instruments
MARTINŮ (49)
Field Mass
PROKOFIEV (48)
Simeon Kotko, opera
Zdravitsa, cantata
Piano Sonata No. 6 (1939–40)
Piano Sonata No. 7 (1939–42)
Piano Sonata No. 8 (1939–44)
MILHAUD (47)
Symphony No. 1 for full orchestra
King René's Chimney, for wind
quartet

CONTINUED

MOORE (46)
The Devil and Daniel Webster,
  opera
PISTON (45)
Violin Concerto No. 1
Violin Sonata
CASTELNUOVO-TEDESCO (44)
Guitar Concerto
Violin Concerto No. 2, *The*
  Prophets
HINDEMITH (44)
Violin Concerto
SOWERBY (44)
Forsaken of Man, cantata
SESSIONS (43)
Pages from a Diary, for piano
KORNGOLD (42)
Die Kathrin, opera
HARRIS (41)
Symphony No. 4
String Quartet
CHÁVEZ (40)
Four nocturnes for voice and
  orchestra
POULENC (40)
Fiançailles pour rire, songs
RUBBRA (38)
Symphony No. 3
RODRIGO (37)
Concierto de Aranjuez, for guitar
  and orchestra
WALTON (37)
Violin Concerto
BERKELEY (36)
Serenade for string orchestra
Five songs (1939–40)
KHACHATURIAN (36)
Happiness, ballet
Masquerade, incidental music
KABALEVSKY (35)
Symphony No. 4
ALWYN (34)
Violin Concerto
Rhapsody, for piano quartet
Sonata-Impromptu, for violin and
  viola

RAWSTHORNE (34)
String Quartet No. 1
TIPPETT (34)
Fantasia on a Theme by Handel,
  for piano and orchestra
  (1939–41)
A Child of Our Time, oratorio
  (1939–41)
LUTYENS (33)
Three pieces for orchestra
String Trio
SHOSTAKOVICH (33)
Symphony No. 6
Film music
MESSIAEN (31)
Les corps glorieux, for organ
BARBER (29)
Violin Concerto
SCHUMAN (29)
American Festival Overture
Prelude for Voices
String Quartet No. 3
Quartettino, for four bassoons
MENOTTI (28)
The Old Maid and the Thief, opera
CAGE (27)
Imaginary Landscape, No. 1
First Construction (In metal),
  for percussion sextet
GILLIS (27)
An American Symphony
  (Symphony No. 1) (1939–40)
BRITTEN (26)
Violin Concerto in D minor
  (revised 1958)
Canadian Carnival, for orchestra
  (1939–40)
Ballad of Heroes, for voices and
  orchestra
Les Illuminations, song cycle
GOULD (26)
Symphonette No. 3
Jericho, for concert band
ARNELL (22)
String Quartet No. 1
SHAPERO (19)
Trumpet Sonata

1940

STRAUSS, R. (76)
Capriccio, opera (1940–41)

VAUGHAN WILLIAMS (68)
Six Choral Songs — to be sung in

VAUGHAN WILLIAMS CONTINUED
time of war
Valiant for truth, motet
CARPENTER (64)
Symphony No. 2
FALLA (64)
Homenajes, for orchestra
BRIDGE (61)
Rebus, for orchestra
Vignettes de danse, for small
    orchestra
Divertimento for flute, oboe,
    clarinet and bassoon
PIZZETTI (60)
Symphony in A major
MALIPIERO (58)
La vita e'sogno, opera
STRAVINSKY (58)
Symphony in C
WEBERN (57)
Variations for Orchestra
VILLA-LOBOS (53)
Preludes for guitar
Saudades da juventude, Suite I
MARTINŮ (50)
Military March
BLISS (49)
Seven American Poems, for low
    voice and piano
PROKOFIEV (49)
The Duenna, opera (1940–41)
Cinderella, ballet (1940–44)
MILHAUD (48)
String Quartet No. 10, *Birthday*
BENJAMIN (47)
Sonatina for chamber orchestra
PISTON (46)
Chromatic Study for Organ
HINDEMITH (45)
Symphony in E♭ major
Cello Concerto No. 2
The Four Temperaments, for piano
    and strings
Harp Sonata
SOWERBY (45)
Symphony No. 3
GERHARD (44)
Don Quixote, ballet (1940–41)
ROBERTSON (44)
Prelude, Scherzo and Ricercare,
    for orchestra
String Quartet

WEINBERGER (44)
Saxophone Concerto
Song of the High Seas, for
    orchestra
KORNGOLD (43)
Songs of the Clown
Four Shakespeare Songs
HARRIS (42)
Western Landscape, ballet
American Creed, for orchestra
Ode to Truth, for orchestra
Challenge, for baritone, chorus
    and orchestra
Evening Piece, for orchestra
String Quintet
CHÁVEZ (41)
Antigona, ballet
Piano Concerto
Xochipili-Macuilxochitl, for
    Mexican orchestra
POULENC (41)
Histoire de Babar le petit éléphant,
    for piano and narrator
    (1940–45)
Mélancolie, for piano
Cello Sonata
Banalities, songs
COPLAND (40)
Quiet City, suite for trumpet,
    English horn and strings
FINZI (39)
Dies natalis, cantata
DURUFLÉ (38)
Andante and Scherzo for
    orchestra
WALTON (38)
The Wise Virgins, ballet
BERKELEY (37)
Symphony No. 1
Sonatina for recorder and piano
Four Concert Studies, Set I, for
    piano
Five Housman songs, for tenor
    and piano
KHACHATURIAN (37)
Violin Concerto
KABALEVSKY (36)
The Golden Spikes, ballet
The Comedians Suite, for small
    orchestra

CONTINUED

ALWYN (35)
Masquerade, overture
Divertimento for solo flute
LAMBERT (35)
Dirge, for voices and strings
SEIBER (35)
Besardo Suite No. 1
LUTYENS (34)
Midas, ballet, for string quartet
  and piano
Chamber Concertos Nos. 1 and 2
  (1940–41)
SHOSTAKOVICH (34)
King Lear, incidental music
Piano Quintet in G minor
Three pieces for solo violin
BARBER (30)
*A Stop-watch and an Ordnance
  Map*, for male chorus and
  orchestra
SCHUMAN (30)
Secular Cantata No. 1, *This is
  our time*
GILLIS (28)
A Symphony of Faith (Symphony
  No. 2)
A Symphony of Free Men
  (Symphony No. 3) (1940–41)
Portrait of a Frontier Town

BRITTEN (27)
Paul Bunyan, operetta (1940–41,
  revised 1974)
Sinfonia da requiem
Diversions on a Theme, for piano
  (left hand) and orchestra
Seven Sonnets of Michangelo, for
  tenor and piano
GOULD (27)
Latin-American Symphonette
A Foster Gallery, for orchestra
DIAMOND (25)
Symphony No. 1
Concerto for small orchestra
Quartet No. 1
ARNELL (23)
Violin Concerto
SHAPERO (20)
String Quartet
FOSS (18)
Music for *The Tempest*
Two Symphonic Pieces
Four Preludes for flute, clarinet
  and bassoon

1941 BRIDGE and PADEREWSKI died

VAUGHAN WILLIAMS (69)
England, My England, for baritone,
  chorus and orchestra
JONGEN (68)
Ouverture de fête, for orchestra
La Cigale et le fourmi, for
  children's choir
RACHMANINOV (68)
Three Symphonic Dances, for
  orchestra
SCHOENBERG (67)
Variations and Recitative, for
  organ
CARPENTER (65)
Song of Freedom, for chorus and
  orchestra
IRELAND (62)
Sarnia, for piano
Three Pastels, for piano
O Happy Land, song

BARTÓK (60)
Concerto for two pianos and
  percussion
MALIPIERO (59)
I Capriccio di Callot, opera
  (1941–42)
WEBERN (58–60)
Second Cantata (Jone)
  (1941–43)
TAYLOR (56)
Processional, for orchestra
MARTIN (51)
Sonata da chiesa, for flute and
  string orchestra
BLISS (50)
String Quartet

PROKOFIEV (50)
War and Peace, opera (1941–42)
Suite for Orchestra, *1941*
A Summer's Day, suite for small
  orchestra
Symphonic March
String Quartet No. 2
HONEGGER (49)
Symphony No. 2 for strings and
  trumpet
MILHAUD (49)
Clarinet Concerto
Piano Concerto No. 2
Concerto for two pianos
Four Sketches
MOORE (48)
Village Music, suite for small
  orchestra
PISTON (47)
Sinfonietta, for orchestra
ORFF (46)
Die Kluge, opera (1941–42)
SOWERBY (46)
Poem, for viola with organ or
  orchestra
GERHARD (45)
Hommaje a Pedrell, symphony
SESSIONS (45)
Montezuma, opera (1941–62)
THOMSON, (45)
Symphony No. 2
WEINBERGER (45)
Lincoln Symphony
Czech Rhapsody, for orchestra
The Bird's Opera, for orchestra
KORNGOLD (44)
Psalm, for voices and orchestra
HARRIS (43)
From this Earth, ballet
Acceleration, for orchestra
Violin Sonata
POULENC (42)
Les animaux modèles, ballet
La Fille du jardinier, incidental
  music
Exultate Deo, for voices
Salve Regina, for voices
COPLAND (41)
Piano Sonata

RUBBRA (40)
Symphony No. 4
The Morning Watch, for choir and
  orchestra
WALTON (39)
Scapino, overture
RAWSTHORNE (36)
The Creel Suite, for piano duet
SEIBER (36)
Besardo Suite No. 2, for strings
Pastorale and Burlesque, for flute
  and strings (1941–42)
Transylvanian Rhapsody
Fantasy, for cello and piano
TIPPETT (36)
String Quartet No. 2 (1941–42)
LUTYENS (35)
Five Intermezzi for Piano
SHOSTAKOVICH (35)
The Gamblers, opera
Symphony No. 7, *Leningrad*
MESSIAEN (33)
Quatour pour la fin du temps, for
  violin, clarinet, cello and piano
SCHUMAN (31)
Symphonies Nos. 3 and 4
Newsreel, suite for orchestra
CAGE (29)
Double Music, for percussion
GILLIS (29)
The Night Before Christmas, for
  narrator and orchestra
BRITTEN (28)
Scottish Ballad, for two pianos
  and orchestra
Matinées musicales, for orchestra
String Quartet
GOULD (28)
Lincoln Legend
LUTOSLAWSKI (28)
Symphony No. 1 (1941–47)
Variations on a Theme of Paganini,
  for two pianos
DIAMOND (26)
The Dream of Audubon, ballet
ARNELL (24)
String Quartet No. 2
BERNSTEIN (23)
Symphony No. 1, *Jeremiah*
  (1941–44)
Clarinet Sonata (1941–42)

CONTINUED

FRICKER (21)
Three Piano Preludes (1941–44)
SHAPERO (21)
Nine-minute Overture
Piano Sonata (four hands)

FOSS (19)
Allegro concertante
Dance Sketch
Duo for cello and piano

1942

ROPARTZ (78)
De Profundis, with orchestra
STRAUSS, R. (78)
Horn Concerto No. 2
ALFVÉN (70)
Symphony No. 5
VAUGHAN WILLIAMS (70)
Coastal Command, orchestral
    suite
SCHOENBERG (68)
Piano Concerto
GLIÈRE (67)
Concerto for coloratura soprano
CARPENTER (66)
Symphony No. 3
IRELAND (63)
Epic March
MEDTNER (62)
Piano Concerto No. 3, *Ballade*
    (1942–43)
PIZZETTI (62)
Piano Sonata
MALIPIERO (60)
Minnie la candida, opera
STRAVINSKY (60)
Danses concertantes
Norwegian Moods
Polka for Circus Elephants
CASELLA (59)
Paganiniana
VILLA-LOBOS (55)
Bachianas brasilieras, No. 7, for
    orchestra
String Quartet No. 7
PROKOFIEV (51)
Flute Sonata
Ballad of an Unknown Boy,
    cantata
MARTIN (52)
*Die Weise von Liebe und Tod des
    Cornets*, for voice and
    orchestra (1942–43)
MARTINŮ (52)
Symphony No. 1

MILHAUD (50)
String Quartet No. 11
BENJAMIN (49)
Concerto for oboe and strings
MOORE (49)
Quintet for woodwinds and horn
MOERAN (48)
Violin Concerto
PISTON (48)
Fanfare for the Fighting French
Flute Quintet
Interlude, for viola and piano
GERHARD (46)
Violin Concerto (1942–45)
SESSIONS (46)
Duo for violin and piano
THOMSON (46)
Canon for Dorothy Thomson
The Mayor La Guardia Waltzes
KORNGOLD (45)
Prayer, for tenor, chorus and
    orchestra
Tomorrow, song
TANSMAN (45)
Symphony No. 2
HARRIS (44)
What so proudly we hail, ballet
Symphony No. 5
Piano Concerto, with band
CHÁVEZ (43)
Toccata for percussion
    instruments
POULENC (43)
Violin Sonata (1942–43)
Chansons villageoises
ANTHEIL (42)
Symphony No. 4
COPLAND (42)
Rodeo, ballet
fp. A Lincoln Portrait, for
    narrator and orchestra
Danzon Cubano

FINZI (41)
Prelude and Fugue for string
  trio
Let us Garlands Bring, songs
DURUFLÉ (40)
Prélude et Fugue sur l'nom Alain,
  for organ
RODRIGO (40)
Concierto Heroico, for piano and
  orchestra
WALTON (40)
Prelude and Fugue (The Spitfire),
  for orchestra
BERKELEY (39)
String Quartet No. 2
Sonatina for violin and piano
KHACHATURIAN (39)
Gayane, ballet
Symphony No. 2
DALLAPICCOLA (38)
Marsia, ballet (1942–43)
Five *Frammente de Saffo*
KABALEVSKY (38)
Before Moscow, opera
People's Avengers, suite for chorus
  and orchestra
Our Great Fatherland, cantata
ALWYN (37)
Concerto Grosso No. 1
LAMBERT (37)
Aubade héroïque, for orchestra
RAWSTHORNE (37)
Piano Concerto No. 1
SEIBER (37)
Balaton, opera
La Blanchisseuse, ballet music
TIPPETT (37)
Two madrigals: *The Source,* and
  The Windhover
LUTYENS (36)
Three symphonic preludes
Nine bagatelles for cello and
  piano
Two songs (Auden)

SHOSTAKOVICH (36)
Native Leningrad, suite
Piano Sonata No. 2
*Six Romances on verses of English
  poets,* for bass and piano
BARBER (32)
Second Essay for Orchestra
SCHUMAN (32)
Piano Concerto
Requiescat
Secular Cantata No. 2, *A Free
  Song*
MENOTTI (31)
The Island God, opera
CAGE (30)
Wonderful Widow of 18 Springs,
  for voice and closed piano
GILLIS (30)
Three Sketches for strings
BRITTEN (29)
A Ceremony of Carols, for treble
  voices and harp
Hymn to St. Cecilia, for
  unaccompanied voices
FINE (28)
Music for *Alice in Wonderland*
DIAMOND (27)
Symphony No. 2
Concerto for two solo pianos
ARNELL (25)
Symphony No. 2
BERNSTEIN (24)
Seven Anniversaries, for piano
  (1942–43)
SHAPERO (22)
Violin Sonata
FOSS (20)
The Prairie, for soloists, chorus
  and orchestra
Clarinet Concerto (later arranged
  as Piano Concerto No. 1)

RACHMANINOV died **1943**

ROPARTZ (79)
Indiscret, ballet
Petit Symphonie
VAUGHAN WILLIAMS (71)
Symphony No. 5

JONGEN (70)
Piano Concerto
SCHOENBERG (69)
Ode to Napoleon, for speaker,
  strings and piano

CONTINUED

CARPENTER (67)
The Anxious Bugler, for orchestra
IRELAND (64)
Fantasy Sonata, for clarinet and
  piano
BARTÓK (62)
Concerto for Orchestra
MALIPIERO (61)
L'allegra brigata, opera
BAX (60)
Work in Progress, overture
CASELLA (60)
Concerto for strings, piano and
  percussion
Harp Sonata
TAYLOR (58)
Christmas Overture
MARTIN (53)
Sechs Monologe aus Jedermann,
  for voice and piano
MARTINŮ (53)
Symphony No. 2
In Memory of Lidice, for orchestra
Concerto for two pianos
Violin Concerto
IBERT (53)
String Quartet in C
HONEGGER (51)
Jour de fête suisse, suite
MILHAUD (51)
Bolivar, opera
MOORE (50)
In Memoriam, symphonic poem
MOERAN (49)
Rhapsody No. 3, for piano and
  orchestra
PISTON (49)
Symphony No. 2
Prelude and Allegro, for organ
  and strings
Passacaglia, for piano
HINDEMITH (48)
Cupid and Psyche, overture
*Symphonic Metamorphoses on a
  theme by Weber*
Ludus Tonalis, for piano
ORFF (48)
Catulli Carmina (revised version)
HANSON (47)
Symphony No. 4, *Requiem*

THOMSON (47)
Flute Sonata
TANSMAN (46)
Symphony No. 6, *In Memoriam*
Symphonic études
HARRIS (45)
Cantata for chorus, organ and
  brass
Mass for male chorus and organ
POULENC (44)
Figure humaine, cantata
Metamorphoses, songs
Deux poèmes, songs
Montparnasse, song
COPLAND (43)
Violin Sonata
RODRIGO (41)
Concierto de estio, for violin and
  orchestra
WALTON (41)
The Quest, ballet
Henry V, incidental music
BERKELEY (40)
Divertimento for orchestra
String Trio
DALLAPICCOLA (39)
Sex Carmina Alcaei, for soprano
  and instruments
ALWYN (38)
Pastoral Fantasia, for viola and
  strings
SEIBER (38)
Fantasia concertante, for violin
  and strings (1943–44)
TIPPETT (38)
Boyhood's End, song cycle
Plebs angelica, motet for double
  chorus
SHOSTAKOVICH (37)
Symphony No. 8
MESSIAEN (35)
Visions de l'Amen, for two pianos
Rondeau, for piano
SCHUMAN (33)
Symphony No. 5, for strings
William Billings, overture
Prayer in Time of War, for
  orchestra

CAGE (31)
She is Asleep, for percussion,
 voice and prepared piano
Amores, for prepared piano and
 percussion
Perilous Night, for prepared
 piano (1943–44)
GILLIS (31)
Symphony No. 4
Prairie Poem
BRITTEN (30)
Prelude and Fugue for strings
Rejoice in the Lamb, festival
 cantata
Serenade, song cycle

GOULD (30)
Symphonies Nos. 1 and 2
Viola Concerto
Interplay, for piano and orchestra
Concertette, for viola and
 orchestra
DIAMOND (28)
Quartet No. 2
ARNELL (26)
Symphony No. 1
BERNSTEIN (25)
I Hate Music, five songs for
 soprano
ARNOLD (22)
Beckus the Dandipratt, overture
Larch Trees, symphonic poem
FOSS (21)
Paradigm, for percussion

TAVENER was born; CHAMINADE and SMYTH died   **1944**

VAUGHAN WILLIAMS (72)
Symphony No. 6 (1944–47)
Concerto for oboe and strings
A Song of Thanksgiving, for
 soprano, chorus and orchestra
String Quartet No. 2
JONGEN (71)
Bourée, for orchestra
IRELAND (65)
A Maritime Overture, for military
 band
BLOCH (64)
Suite symphonique
PIZZETTI (64)
Violin Concerto
BARTÓK (63)
Sonata for unaccompanied violin
MALIPIERO (62)
Symphony No. 3, *delle campane*
STRAVINSKY (62)
Élégie, for solo viola
Sonata for two pianos
CASELLA (61)
Missa Solemnis, *Pro pace*
BAX (60)
Legend, for orchestra
VILLA-LOBOS (57)
Bachianas brasilieras, No. 8, for
 orchestra
String Quartet No. 8

IBERT (54)
Suite elisabethaine, for orchestra
Trio for violin, cello and harp
MARTIN (54)
Petite symphonie concertante
 (1944–45)
Passacaglia, for organ
In terra pax, oratorio
MARTINŮ (54)
Symphony No. 3
Cello Concerto (1944–45)
BLISS (53)
Miracle in the Gorbals, ballet
The Phoenix, march
"Auvergnat" for voice and piano
PROKOFIEV (53)
Symphony No. 5
MILHAUD (52)
Symphony No. 2 for full
 orchestra
Suite française
Jeux de printemps
BENJAMIN (51)
Symphony No. 1 (1944–45)
MOORE (51)
Down East Suite, for violin with
 piano or orchestra
MOERAN (50)
Overture for a Masque
Sinfonietta

CONTINUED

PISTON (50)
Fugue on a Victory Tune
Partita, for violin, viola and organ
HINDEMITH (49)
Hérodiade, for speaker and
　chamber orchestra
ORFF (49)
Die Bernauerin (1944–45)
SOWERBY (49)
Classic Concerto, for organ and
　strings
Violin Sonata No. 2
Canticle of the Sun, cantata
GERHARD (48)
Alegrias, ballet suite
Pandora, ballet (1944–45)
ROBERTSON (48)
Rhapsody, for piano and
　orchestra
American Serenade, for string
　quartet
SESSIONS (48)
Symphony No. 2 (1944–45)
THOMSON (48)
Suite No. 1, *Portraits*
Suite No. 2
TANSMAN (47)
Symphony No. 7
Partita, for piano and orchestra
Le roi qui jouait le fou
HARRIS (46)
Symphony No. 6
CHÁVEZ (45)
Hija de Colquide, ballet
String Quartet No. 3
POULENC (45)
La Mamelles de Tiresias, opera
　buffe
La Nuit de la Saint-Jean,
　incidental music
La Voyageur sans bagage,
　incidental music
Un Soir de niege, cantata
COPLAND (44)
Appalachian Spring, ballet
RUBBRA (43)
Soliloquy, for cello and orchestra
BERKELEY (41)
"Lord, when the sense of Thy
　sweet grace", for mixed chorus
　and orchestra

KHACHATURIAN (41)
Concerto for violin and cello
Masquerade Suite
DALLAPICCOLA (40)
Il Prigioniero, opera (1944–48)
Due liriche de Anacreonte
　(1944–45)
KABALEVSKY (40)
The Family of Taras, opera
　(c.1944)
RAWSTHORNE (39)
Street Corner Overture
SEIBER (39)
Notturno, for horn and strings
TIPPETT (39)
Symphony No. 1 (1944–45)
"The Weeping Babe", motet
LUTYENS (38)
Suite gauloise, for small orchestra
SHOSTAKOVICH (38)
Russian River, suite
*Eight English and American
　Folksongs*, for low voice and
　orchestra
Piano Trio No. 2
String Quartet No. 2
Children's Notebook, for piano
Film music
MESSIAEN (36)
Vingt regards sur l'enfant Jésus,
　for piano
BARBER (34)
Symphony No. 2 (revised 1947)
Capricorn Concerto, for flute,
　oboe, trumpet and strings
Excursions, for piano
SCHUMAN (34)
Circus, overture
Te Deum
MENOTTI (33)
Sebastian, ballet
CAGE (32)
A Book of Music, for two prepared
　pianos
Three Dances for two amplified
　prepared pianos (1944–45)
GILLIS (32)
Symphony No. 5 (1944–45)
*A Short Overture to an Unwritten
　Opera*
The Alamo, symphonic poem

BRITTEN (31)
Festival Te Deum
GOULD (31)
Concerto for Orchestra
FINE (30)
The Choral New Yorker, cantata
DIAMOND (29)
The Tempest, incidental music
Rounds, for string orchestra
ARNELL (27)
Symphony No. 3
BERNSTEIN (26)
Fancy Free, ballet
On the Town, dance episodes

FRICKER (24)
Piano Prelude
SHAPERO (24)
Three amateur sonatas, for piano
ARNOLD (23)
Horn Concerto
*Variations on a Ukrainian
  Folksong*, for piano
FOSS (22)
The Heart Remembers, ballet
Within These Walls, ballet
Symphony
Ode

BARTÓK and MASCAGNI died, WEBERN was accidentally shot dead **1945**

STRAUSS, R. (81)
Metamorphoses, for twenty-three
  solo instruments
Oboe Concerto
VAUGHAN WILLIAMS (75)
Story of a Flemish Farm,
  orchestral suite
SCHOENBERG (71)
Prelude to a *Genesis* suite
CARPENTER (69)
The Seven Ages, for orchestra
BLOCH (65)
String Quartet No. 2
BARTÓK (64)
Piano Concerto No. 3
Viola Concerto
KODÁLY (63)
Missa Brevis
STRAVINSKY (63)
Symphony in Three Movements
BAX (62)
Legend-Sonata, for cello and piano
TAYLOR (60)
Elegy, for orchestra
SCHOECK (59)
Sommernacht
Suite in A for strings
VILLA-LOBOS (58)
Piano Concerto No. 1
Bachianas brasilieras, Nos. 5 and 9
Fantasia for cello
MARTIN (55)
Golgotha, oratorio (1945–48)

MARTINŮ (55)
Symphony No. 4
Thunderbolt P-47
BLISS (54)
Baraza, concert piece for piano
  and orchestra, with men's
  voices ad lib
PROKOFIEV (54)
Symphony No. 6 (1945–47)
Piano Sonata No. 9 (1945–47)
MILHAUD (53)
The Bells, ballet
Cello Concerto No. 2
String Quartet No. 12, *In memory
  of Fauré*
BENJAMIN (52)
From San Domingo, for orchestra
Red River Jig, for orchestra
Elegy, Waltz and Toccata, for
  viola and orchestra
MOORE (52)
Symphony in A major
MOERAN (51)
Cello Concerto
PISTON (51)
Sonata for violin and harpsichord
HINDEMITH (50)
Piano Concerto
JACOB (50)
Symphony No. 2
Clarinet Concerto
ORFF (50)
Astutuli (1945–46)
SOWERBY (50)
Trumpet Sonata

CONTINUED

GERHARD (49)
The Duenna, opera (1945–47)
HANSON (49)
Serenade for flute, strings, harp
  and orchestra
ROBERTSON (49)
Punch and Judy, overture
KORNGOLD (48)
Violin Concerto
String Quartet No. 3
TANSMAN (48)
Concertino, for guitar and
  orchestra
HARRIS (47)
Piano Concerto No. 1
CHÁVEZ (46)
Piramide
POULENC (46)
Le Soldat et la sorciére, incidental
  music
Chansons françaises, for choir
FINZI (44)
Farewell to Arms, for tenor and
  small orchestra
BERKELEY (42)
Piano Sonata
Violin Sonata
Six piano preludes
Festival Anthem, for mixed choir
  and organ
KHACHATURIAN (42)
Solemn Overture *To the End of
  the War*
DALLAPICCOLA (41)
Ciaccona, Intermezzo e Adagio,
  for cello
ALWYN (40)
Concerto for oboe, harp and
  strings
RAWSTHORNE (40)
Cortèges, fantasy overture
SEIBER (40)
Phantasy, for flute, horn and
  strings

TIPPETT (40)
String Quartet No. 3 (1945–46)
LUTYENS (39)
Chamber Concerto No. 3
Five Little Pieces for Clarinet and
  Piano
SHOSTAKOVICH (39)
Symphony No. 9
Two songs
Film music
BARBER (35)
Cello Concerto
SCHUMAN (35)
Undertow, ballet
MENOTTI (34)
Piano Concerto in A minor
GILLIS (33)
To an Unknown Sailor,
  symphonic poem
BRITTEN (32)
Peter Grimes, opera
String Quartet No. 2
The Holy Sonnets of John Donne,
  for voice and piano
GOULD (32)
Harvest, for vibraphone, harp
  and strings
Ballad, for band
DIAMOND (30)
Symphonies Nos. 3 and 4
ARNELL (28)
String Quartet No. 3
BERNSTEIN (27)
Hashkivenu, for voices and organ
SHAPERO (25)
Serenade, for string orchestra
FOSS (23)
Song of Anguish, for voice and
  piano, or orchestra
MENNIN (22)
Concertino for flute, strings and
  percussion

1946   FALLA died

VAUGHAN WILLIAMS (74)
Partita, for double string
  orchestra (1946–48)
Introduction and Fugue for two
  pianos

DOHNÁNYI (69)
Piano Concerto No. 2
QUILTER (69)
Tulips, for chorus and orchestra

IRELAND (67)
fp. Satyricon Overture
BLOCH (66–68)
Concerto symphonique, for piano
MALIPIERO (64)
Symphony No. 4, *In Memoriam*
STRAVINSKY (64)
Ebony Concerto, for clarinet and
  orchestra
Concerto in D for strings
BAX (63)
Te Deum
Gloria
MARTIN (56)
Overture to Racine's *Athalie*
BLISS (55)
Adam Zero, ballet
HONEGGER (54)
Symphony No. 3, *Liturgique*
Symphony No. 4, *Deliciae
  basiliensis*
MILHAUD (54)
Symphony No. 3, *Hymnus
  ambrosianus*
Piano Concerto No. 3
Violin Concerto No. 2
String Quartet No. 13
BENJAMIN (53)
Caribbean Dance, for orchestra
MOORE (53)
Quintet for clarinet and strings
MOERAN (52)
Fantasy Quartet for oboe and
  strings
PISTON (52)
Divertimento, for nine instruments
HINDEMITH (51)
*When Lilacs in the Dooryard
  Bloomed*, requiem
SESSIONS (50)
Piano Sonata No. 2
KORNGOLD (49)
The silent serenade, comedy with
  music
Cello Concerto
HARRIS (48)
Accordion Concerto
Concerto for two pianos
POULENC (47)
Two songs
COPLAND (46)
Symphony No. 3

BERKELEY (43)
Nocturne for orchestra
Introduction and Allegro for solo
  violin
Five songs
RUBBRA (43)
Missa cantauriensis, for double
  choir
DALLAPICCOLA (42)
Two pieces for orchestra
  (1946–47)
ALWYN (41)
Suite of Scottish Dances
RAWSTHORNE (41)
Prisoner's March, for orchestra
TIPPETT (41)
Little Music, for strings
SHOSTAKOVICH (40)
String Quartet No. 3
BARBER (36)
Medea: the Cave of the Heart,
  ballet
MENOTTI (35)
The Medium, opera
CAGE (34)
Sonatas and Interludes for
  Prepared Pianos (1946–48)
GILLIS (34)
Symphony No. $5\frac{1}{2}$, *Symphony
  for Fun* (1946–47)
BRITTEN (33)
The Rape of Lucretia, opera
Variations and Fugue on a
  Theme of Purcell (*A Young
  Person's Guide to the Orchestra*)
GOULD (33)
Minstrel Show, for orchestra
Symphony No. 3
FINE (32)
Fantasia, for string trio
Violin Sonata
DIAMOND (31)
Quartet No. 3
Violin Sonata
ARNELL (29)
Piano Concerto
Piano Trio
BERNSTEIN (28)
Facsimile, ballet
FRICKER (26)
Four Fughettas for two pianos

CONTINUED

ARNOLD (25)
Symphony for strings
SHAPEY (25)
String Quartet No. 1
Piano Sonata
FOSS (24)
Song of Songs, for voice and
  orchestra
Composer's Holiday, for violin
  and piano
MENNIN (23)
Symphony No. 3

BOULEZ (21)
Piano Sonata No. 1
Sonatina for flute and piano
Le Visage nuptial, for voices and
  chamber orchestra
BERIO (21)
Four Popular Songs (1946–47)
HENZE (20)
Chamber concerto, for solo piano,
  solo flute and strings
Sonata for violin and piano

1947   CASELLA died

ROPARTZ (83)
Divertissement No. 2
SCHOENBERG (73)
A Survivor from Warsaw, cantata
AUBERT (70)
Offrande
KODÁLY (65)
Viola Concerto
String Quartet
MALIPIERO (65)
Symphony No. 5, *Concertante in
  eco*
Symphony No. 6, *degli archi*
STRAVINSKY (65)
Orpheus, ballet
BAX (64)
Two Fanfares for the Wedding of
  Princess Elizabeth and Prince
  Philip
Morning Song, for piano and
  small orchestra
Epithalamium, for chorus and
  organ
SCHOECK (61)
Cello Concerto
MARTIN (57)
Trois chants de Noël, for voice,
  flute and piano
MARTINŮ (57)
Quartet No. 7
PROKOFIEV (56)
The Story of a Real Man, opera
  (1947–48)
MILHAUD (55)
Symphony, *1848*
Concerto for marimba and
  vibraphone

BENJAMIN (54)
Ballade for strings
MOORE (54)
Farm Journal, suite for chamber
  orchestra
PISTON (53)
Symphony No. 3
String Quartet No. 3
HINDEMITH (52)
Symphonia serena (possibly 1946)
Clarinet Concerto
ORFF (52)
Antigone, opera (1947–48)
SOWERBY (52)
Symphony No. 4
ROBERTSON (51)
Trilogy, for orchestra
SESSIONS (51)
fp. The Trial of Lucullus, opera
THOMSON (51)
The Seine at Night, for orchestra
The Mother of us all, opera
KORNGOLD (50)
Symphonic Serenade, for strings
Five songs for middle voice
TANSMAN (50)
Music for Orchestra
Isiah the Prophet
HARRIS (49)
Quest, for orchestra
POULENC (48)
Flute Sonata
ANTHEIL (47)
Symphony No. 5 (1947–48)
FINZI (46)
Ode for St. Cecilia's Day (possibly
  1950)

RUBBRA (46)
Festival Overture
Symphony No. 5 (1947–48)
Cello Sonata
DURUFLÉ (45)
Requiem, for solo voices, chorus,
  organ and orchestra
RODRIGO (45)
Four *Madrigales amatorias*, for
  voice and piano
WALTON (45)
Hamlet, incidental music
String Quartet in A minor
BERKELEY (44)
Piano Concerto
Four Poems of St. Teresa of Avila,
  for contralto and orchestra
Stabat Mater
"The Lowlands of Holland", for
  voice and piano
KHACHATURIAN (44)
Symphonie-Poème
ALWYN (42)
Manchester Suite, for orchestra
Piano Sonata
Three songs (Louis MacNiece)
RAWSTHORNE (42)
Concerto for oboe and string
  orchestra
TIPPETT (42)
The Midsummer Marriage, opera
LUTYENS (41)
The Pit, dramatic scene for voices
  and orchestra
Viola Concerto
Chamber Concertos Nos. 4 and 5
SHOSTAKOVICH (41)
Violin Concerto No. 1 (1947–48)
Poem of the Motherland, cantata
Film music
MESSIAEN (39)
Turangalîla, symphony
BARBER (37)
Knoxville: Summer of 1915,
  ballet suite for voice and
  orchestra
SCHUMAN (37)
Night Journey, ballet
Violin Concerto
MENOTTI (36)
The Telephone, opera
Errand into the Maze, ballet

GILLIS (35)
Symphony No. 6
Dude Ranch
Three Short Pieces, for strings
BRITTEN (34)
Albert Herring, opera
Canticle No. 1, "My beloved is
  mine"
Prelude and Fugue for organ
GOULD (34)
Fall River Legend, ballet
DIAMOND (32)
Romeo and Juliet, incidental
  music
Violin Concerto No. 2
Piano Sonata
ARNELL (30)
Punch and the Child, ballet
Harpsichord Concerto
BERNSTEIN (29)
Symphony No. 2, *The Age of
  Anxiety*, for piano and
  orchestra (1947–49)
Five Pieces for Piano (1947–48)
FRICKER (27)
Wind Quintet
String Quartet in one movement
Sonata for Organ
Three Sonnets of Cecco Angiolier,
  for tenor and seven
  instruments
Two Madrigals
SHAPERO (27)
Piano Sonata No. 1
ARNOLD (26)
Violin Sonata
Viola Sonata
Children's Suite, for piano
SHAPEY (26)
Piano Quintet
FOSS (25)
String Quartet
MENNIN (24)
Fantasia for String Orchestra
BERIO (22)
Petite Suite for piano
BOULEZ (22)
Soleil des eaux, for voices and
  orchestra
Piano Sonata No. 2 (1947–48)

CONTINUED

HENZE (21)
Symphony No. 1 (first version)
Violin Concerto No. 1
Concertino for piano and wind
  orchestra with percussion

String Quartet No. 1
Five Madrigals for small mixed
  choir and eleven solo
  instruments

1948   GIORDANO, LEHÁR and WOLF-FERRARI died

STRAUSS, R. (84)
Duet concertino, for clarinet,
  bassoon and strings
CARPENTER (72)
Carmel Concerto
AUBERT (71)
Le Tombeau de Chateaubriande
QUILTER (71)
The Sailor and His Lass, for
  soloist, chorus and orchestra
KODÁLY (66)
Czinka Panna, opera
MALIPIERO (66)
Mondi celeste e infernali, opera
  (1948–49)
Symphony No. 7, *delle canzoni*
Piano Concerto No. 3
STRAVINSKY (66)
Mass, for chorus and double
  wind quintet
MARTIN (58)
Ballade, for cello and piano
Eight piano preludes
MARTINŮ (58)
Piano Concerto No. 3
BLISS (57)
The Olympians, opera (1948–49)
PROKOFIEV (57)
The Stone Flower, ballet
  (1948–53)
MOORE (55)
The Emperor's New Clothes, opera
  for children
MOERAN (54)
Serenade in G major
PISTON (54)
Toccata, for orchestra
Suite No. 2 for orchestra
HINDEMITH (53)
Concerto for trumpet, bassoon
  and strings
Septet for wind instruments
HANSON (52)
Piano Concerto

ROBERTSON (52)
Violin Concerto
THOMSON (52)
Wheatfield at Noon, for orchestra
Acadian Songs and Dances
TANSMAN (51)
Music for Strings
HARRIS (50)
Elegy and Paean, for viola and
  orchestra
CHÁVEZ (49–51)
Violin Concerto (1948–50,
  revised 1962)
POULENC (49)
Quatre petites prières (St. Francis),
  for choir
ANTHEIL (48)
McKonkey's Ferry, overture
Symphony No. 6
Serenade, for string orchestra
Piano Sonata No. 4
Songs of Experience, for voice and
  piano
COPLAND (48)
Concerto for clarinet and strings,
  with harp and piano
RUBBRA (47)
The Buddha, suite for flute, oboe,
  violin, viola and cello
RODRIGO (46)
Ausencias de Dulcinea, for bass,
  four sopranos and orchestra
BERKELEY (45)
Concerto for two pianos and
  orchestra
DALLAPICCOLA (44)
Quattro liriche di Antonio Machado,
  for soprano and piano
KABALEVSKY (44)
Violin Concerto
ALWYN (43)
Three Winter Poems, for string
  quartet

RAWSTHORNE (43)
Violin Concerto No. 1
Clarinet Quartet
SEIBER (43)
Johnny Miner, radio opera
String Quartet No. 3, *Quartetto lyrico* (1948–51)
TIPPETT (43)
Suite in D major
LUTYENS (42)
Chamber Concerto No. 6
Three Improvisations, for piano
Aptote, for solo violin
Nine songs
SHOSTAKOVICH (42)
From Jewish Folk Poetry, song cycle
Film music
BARBER (38)
String Quartet No. 2
Piano Sonata
SCHUMAN (38)
Symphony No. 6
GILLIS (36)
Saga of a Prairie School
BRITTEN (35)
St. Nicholas, for voices and instruments
GOULD (35)
Serenade of Carols
FINE (34)
Toccata concertante
Partita for wind quintet
DIAMOND (33)
Chaconne, for violin and piano
ARNELL (31)
Symphony No. 4

BERNSTEIN (30)
Four Anniversaries, for piano
FRICKER (28)
Symphony No. 1
Rondo Scherzoso, for orchestra
SHAPERO (28)
Symphony for Classical Orchestra
The Travellers, for orchestra
ARNOLD (27)
Festival Overture
The Smoke, overture
Symphonic Suite
Sonatina for flute and piano
FOSS (26)
Oboe Concerto
Ricordare, for orchestra
Capriccio, for cello and piano
HAMILTON (26)
Symphonic Variations for string orchestra
Quintet for clarinet and string quartet
HENZE (22)
The Magic Theatre, opera
Chorus of the Captured Trojans, for chorus and orchestra
Chamber Sonata, for piano, violin and cello (revised 1963)
Lullaby of the Blessed Virgin, for boys' choir and instruments
The Reproach, concert aria for voice and instruments
Whispers from the Heavenly Death, cantata
KORTE (20)
String Quartet No. 1

STRAUSS, R. and TURINA died   **1949**

VAUGHAN WILLIAMS (77)
Fantasia (quasi variazione) on "Old 104th", for piano, chorus and orchestra
An Oxford Elegy, for speaker, chorus and small orchestra
Folksongs of the Four Seasons, cantata
SCHOENBERG (75)
Fantasia, for violin and piano
QUILTER (72)
Love at the Inn, opera

BLOCH (69)
Scherzo fantasque, for piano
PIZZETTI (69)
Vanna Lupa, opera
IBERT (59)
Étude-Caprice, pour un Tombeau de Chopin, for solo cello
MARTIN (59)
Concerto for seven wind instruments

CONTINUED

PROKOFIEV (58)
Winter Bonfire, suite for narrator, boys' chorus and orchestra (1949–50)
Cello Sonata
HONEGGER (57)
Concerto da camera
MILHAUD (57)
Piano Concerto No. 4
String Quartets Nos. 14 and 15 (can be played together as octet)
BENJAMIN (56)
The Tale of Two Cities, opera (1949–50)
Valses Caprices, for clarinet and piano
PISTON (55)
Piano Quintet
Duo for violin and cello
HINDEMITH (54)
Horn Concerto
Concerto for woodwind, harp and orchestra
Organ Sonata No. 2
SOWERBY (54)
Ballade, for English horn and strings
THOMSON (53)
Cello Concerto
TANSMAN (52)
Ricercari
Tombeau de Chopin, for strings
HARRIS (51)
Kentucky Spring, for orchestra
POULENC (50)
Piano Concerto
FINZI (48)
Clarinet Concerto
Before and After Summer, song cycle
RODRIGO (47)
Concierto galante, for cello and orchestra
WALTON (47)
Violin Sonata
BERKELEY (46)
Colonus' Praise, for chorus and orchestra
Three Mazurkas for piano
Scherzo for piano

DALLAPICCOLA (45)
Job, mystery play (1949–50)
Tre poemi, for soprano and chamber orchestra
KABALEVSKY (45)
Cello Concerto
ALWYN (44)
Symphony No. 1
RAWSTHORNE (44)
Concerto for string orchestra
Cello Sonata
SEIBER (44)
Andantino and pastorale, for clarinet and piano
Ulysses, cantata (possibly 1946–47)
LUTYENS (43)
String Quartet No. 3
SHOSTAKOVICH (43)
Ballet Suite No. 1, for orchestra
String Quartet No. 4
The Song of the Forests, oratorio
Film music
SCHUMAN (39)
Judith, ballet
BRITTEN (36)
The Little Sweep (Let's Make an Opera)
Spring Symphony, for voices and orchestra
A Wedding Anthem, for voices and organ
LUTOSLAWSKI (36)
Overture for Strings
FINE (35)
The Hourglass, choral cycle
DIAMOND (34)
Timon of Athens, symphonic portrait
L'âme de Debussy, song cycle
BERNSTEIN (31)
La bonne cuisine, song cycle
Two love songs
ROCHBERG (31)
Symphony No. 1
Night Music, for chamber orchestra
FRICKER (29)
Concerto for violin and small orchestra, No. 1 (1949–50)
Prelude, Elegy and Finale, for string orchestra

ARNOLD (28)
Clarinet Concerto
SHAPEY (28)
String Quartet No. 2
Three Essays on Thomas Wolfe,
   for piano
FOSS (27)
*The Jumping Frog of Calvares
   County*, opera
Piano Concerto No. 2
HAMILTON (27)
Symphony No. 1
String Quartet No. 1
MENNIN (26)
Symphony No. 4, *The Cycle*, for
   choir and orchestra
The Christmas Story, cantata

BERIO (24)
Magnificat
BOULEZ (24)
Livre pour cordes, for string
   orchestra
Livre pour quatour, for string
   quartet
HENZE (23)
Ballet Variations
Jack Pudding, ballet
Symphony No. 2
Symphony No. 3 (1949–50)
Apollo et Hyazinthus, for
   harpsichord, contralto and
   eight solo instruments
Variations for piano
Serenade, for solo cello

CILÈA and MOERAN died   **1950**

STRAUSS, R. (posthumous)
Four Last Songs
VAUGHAN WILLIAMS (78)
Concerto grosso, for string
   orchestra
The Sons of Light, cantata
Sun, Moon, Stars and Man, song
   cycle
DOHNÁNYI (73)
Twelve studies for piano
BLOCH (70)
Concertino for viola, flute and
   strings
PIZZETTI (70)
Ifigenia, opera
ENESCO (69)
Vox Maris, symphonic poem
MALIPIERO (68)
Symphony in one movement
Piano Concerto No. 4
BAX (67)
Concertante for orchestra with
   piano (left hand)
TAYLOR (65)
Restoration Suite, for orchestra
MARTIN (60)
Violin Concerto (1950–51)
Five Ariel Songs, for chamber
   choir
BLISS (59)
String Quartet No. 2

PROKOFIEV (59)
Sinfonia concertante, for cello and
   orchestra (reworking of the
   1933–38 cello concerto)
MOORE (57)
Giants in the Earth, opera
PISTON (56)
Symphony No. 4
HINDEMITH (55)
Sinfonietta
Requiem for Those we Love
   (possibly 1946)
JACOB (55)
Sinfonietta in D major
A Goodly Heritage, cantata
ORFF (55)
Trionfo di Afrodite
SOWERBY (55)
Christ Reborn, cantata
GERHARD (54)
Impromptus for piano
TANSMAN (53)
Phèdre, ballet
POULENC (51)
Stabat Mater
ANTHEIL (50)
Volpone, opera
COPLAND (50)
Piano Quartet
Twelve Poems of Emily Dickinson,
   for voice and piano

CONTINUED

FINZI (49)
Intimations of Immortality, for
  tenor, chorus and orchestra
BERKELEY (47)
Sinfonietta for orchestra
Elegy for violin and piano
Toccata for violin and piano
Theme and Variations for solo
  violin
KHACHATURIAN (47)
Cello Concerto
LAMBERT (45)
Tiresias, ballet
RAWSTHORNE (45)
Symphony No. 1
TIPPETT (45)
Heart's Assurance, song cycle
LUTYENS (44)
Concertante, for five players
SHOSTAKOVICH (44)
Two Romances on verse by
  Mikhail Lermontov, for voice
  and piano
Twenty-four Preludes and Fugues
  for piano
Film music
MESSIAEN (42)
Le merle noir, for piano and flute
Messe de la Pentecôte
SCHUMAN (40)
String Quartet No. 4
MENOTTI (39)
The Consul, opera
CAGE (38)
String Quartet in Four Parts
BRITTEN (37)
Lachrymae, for viola and piano
Five Flower Songs, for
  unaccompanied chorus
GOULD (37)
Family Album, for orchestra
LUTOSLAWSKI (37)
Concerto for Orchestra (1950–54)
DIAMOND (35)
Piano Concerto
Chorale, for chorus
Quintet for two violas, two cellos,
  and clarinet
ARNELL (33)
Symphony No. 5
String Quintet

BERNSTEIN (32)
Prelude, Fugue and Riffs, for jazz
  combo and orchestra
FRICKER (30)
Symphony No. 2 (1950–51)
Concertante No. 1, for English
  horn and strings
Violin Sonata
Four Impromptus (1950–52)
ARNOLD (29)
Symphony No. 1
Serenade for small orchestra
Eight English Dances
String Quartet No. 1 (possibly
  1946)
SHAPEY (29)
Violin Sonata
HAMILTON (28)
Clarinet Concerto
MENNIN (27)
Symphony No. 5
Violin Concerto
Canto and Toccata, for piano
Five Pieces for Piano
BERIO (25)
Concertino for solo clarinet, solo
  violin, harp, celeste and strings
Opus Number Zoo, for woodwind
  quintet and narrator (revised
  1970)
HENZE (24)
Rosa Silber, ballet
Piano Concerto No. 1
Symphonic Variations, for piano
  and orchestra
STOCKHAUSEN (22)
Chore für Doris, for choir
Choral, for choir
Three Lieder, for voice and
  chamber orchestra

VAUGHAN WILLIAMS (79)
Pilgrim's Progress, for soloists,
  chorus and orchestra
Romance in D♭, for harmonica
SCHOENBERG (77)
De Profundis, for a cappella choir
BLOCH (71)
Cinq Pièces hébraïques
String Quartet No. 3 (1951–52)
MALIPIERO (69)
Sinfonia del zodiaco
STRAVINSKY (69)
The Rake's Progress, opera
Mass, for horns and orchestra
SCHOECK (65)
Horn Concerto
Festlichen Hymnus
IBERT (61)
Sinfonia concertante
MARTIN (61)
Concerto for cembalo and small
  orchestra (1951–52)
PROKOFIEV (60)
Symphony No. 7 (1951–52)
HONEGGER (59)
Symphony No. 5, *Di Tre Re*
Monopartita, for orchestra
MILHAUD (59)
The Seven-branched candelabra
BENJAMIN (58)
Orlando's Silver Wedding, ballet
PISTON (57)
String Quartet No. 4
HINDEMITH (56)
Die Harmonie der Welt, symphony
JACOB (56)
Concerto for Flute
Fantasia on Songs of the British
  Isles
SOWERBY (56)
Concert Piece, for organ and
  orchestra
GERHARD (55)
Concerto for piano and strings
HANSON (55)
Fantasia on a Theme of youth, for
  piano and strings
SESSIONS (55)
String Quartet No. 2

THOMSON (55)
Five Songs of William Blake, for
  baritone and orchestra
KORNGOLD (54)
Symphony in F♯ major
TANSMAN (54)
Symphony No. 8
HARRIS (53)
Cumberland Concerto, for
  orchestra
Symphony No. 7
CHÁVEZ (52)
Symphony No. 3
ANTHEIL (51)
Eight Fragments from Shelley, for
  chorus
COPLAND (51)
Pied Piper, ballet
RUBBRA (50)
Festival Te Deum
String Quartet No. 2
BERKELEY (48)
Gibbons Variations, for voices,
  strings and organ
Three Greek songs, for voice and
  piano
DALLAPICCOLA (47)
Canti di Liberazione, for chorus
  and orchestra (1951–55)
ALWYN (46)
Concerto Grosso No. 2
Festival March
RAWSTHORNE (46)
Piano Concerto No. 2
Concertante pastorale, for flute,
  horn and strings
SEIBER (46)
Concertino for clarinet and strings
The Seasons
LUTYENS (45)
Penelope, music drama
Requiem for the Living
Nativity, for soprano and strings,
  or organ
SHOSTAKOVICH (45)
Ballet Suite No. 2, for orchestra
Ten poems on texts by
  revolutionary poets, for chorus
Film music

CONTINUED

MENOTTI (40)
Amahl and the Night Visitors, opera
Apocalypse, for orchestra
CAGE (39)
Concerto for prepared piano and chamber orchestra
Imaginary Landscape, No. 4
Music of Changes, for piano
BRITTEN (38)
Billy Budd, opera
Six Metamorphoses after Ovid, for solo oboe
GOULD (38)
The Battle Hymn of the Republic
LUTOSLAWSKI (38)
Little Suite, for orchestra
Silesian Triptych, for voice and orchestra
DIAMOND (36)
Symphony No. 6
Quartet No. 4
Piano Trio
Mizmor L'David, for voices, organ and orchestra
The Midnight Meditation, song cycle
ARNELL (34)
Harlequin in April, ballet
String Quartet No. 4
BERNSTEIN (33)
"Afterthought", song
FRICKER (31)
Canterbury Prologue, ballet
Viola Concerto
Concertante No. 2, for three pianos, strings and timpani
SHAPERO (31—38)
Concerto for Orchestra (1951—58)

ARNOLD (30)
Sussex, overture
Concerto for piano duet and strings
Sonatina for clarinet and piano
Sonatina for oboe and piano
SHAPEY (30)
Fantasy, for orchestra
String Quartet No. 3
Cantata
HAMILTON (29)
Clerk Saunders, ballet
Symphony No. 2
Flute Quartet
Piano Sonata (revised 1971)
MENNIN (28)
Canzona, for band
BERIO (26)
Two Pieces for Violin and Piano
BOULEZ (26)
fp. Polyphonie X, for eighteen instruments
HENZE (25)
Boulevard Solitude, lyric drama
A Country Doctor, radio opera
Labyrinth, choreographic fantasy
The Sleeping Princess, ballet
FELDMAN (25)
Intersection I
Projections I and II
STOCKHAUSEN (23)
Formel, for orchestra
Kreuzspiel, for instrumental ensemble
Sonatine, for violin and piano
GOEHR (19)
Piano Sonata (1951—52)
Songs of Babel

1952

VAUGHAN WILLIAMS (80)
Sinfonia Antarctica (Symphony No. 7)
AUBERT (76)
Cinéma
DOHNÁNYI (75)
Violin Concerto No. 2
Harp Concerto

BLOCH (72)
Sinfonia brève
Concerto Grosso, for string quartet and string orchestra
STRAVINSKY (70)
Cantata on old English texts
MALIPIERO (70)
Violin Concerto

SCHOECK (66)
Befreite Sehnsucht, song cycle
MARTIN (62)
La Tempête, opera (1952–55)
HONEGGER (60)
Suite archaïque
PROKOFIEV (61)
Cello Concertino
BLISS (61)
The Enchantress, scena for
  contralto and orchestra
Piano Sonata
MOORE (59)
Cotillion Suite, for string orchestra
PISTON (58)
Fantasy, for English horn, harp
  and strings
HINDEMITH (57)
Symphony in B♭ for military
  band
Sonata for four horns
SOWERBY (57)
String Trio
GERHARD (56)
Symphony No. 1 (1952–53)
THOMSON (56)
Sea Piece with Birds, for orchestra
KORNGOLD (55)
Sonnet to Vienna, song
RUBBRA (51)
Viola Concerto
FINZI (51)
Love's Labour Lost, suite
RODRIGO (50)
Four *Villancicos*, for voice and
  piano
Four *Villancicos*, for chorus
  "Canciones de Navidad"
BERKELEY (49)
Flute Concerto
Four Ronsard Sonnets, Set I, for
  two tenors and piano
DALLAPICCOLA (48)
Quaderno musicale di Annalibera,
  for piano
Goethe-Lieder
KABALEVSKY (48)
Piano Concerto No. 3
Cello Sonata
RAWSTHORNE (47)
Canticle of Man, chamber cantata

TIPPETT (47)
"Dance Clarion Air", madrigal
LUTYENS (46)
String Quartets Nos. 4–6
SHOSTAKOVICH (46)
Ballet Suite No. 3, for orchestra
String Quartet No. 5
Four Monologues on verses of
  Pushkin, for bass and piano
*The Sun Shines Over Our
  Motherland*, cantata
MENOTTI (41)
Violin Concerto
CAGE (40)
Water Music
Williams Mix
4′ 33″ (tacet) for piano, in four
  movements
BRITTEN (39)
Canticle No. 2, "Abraham and
  Isaac", for contralto, tenor
  and piano
GOULD (39)
Dance Variations, for two pianos
  and orchestra
FINE (38)
String Quartet
Mutability, song cycle
BERNSTEIN (35)
Trouble in Tahiti, opera
Wonderful Town
ROCHBERG (34)
String Quartet No. 1
Twelve bagatelles, for piano
FRICKER (32)
Concerto for piano and small
  orchestra (1952–54)
String Quartet No. 2
ARNOLD (31)
Curtain Up
Three Shanties, for wind quintet
SHAPEY (31)
Symphony No. 1
Quartet for oboe and string trio
Oboe Sonata
Suite for piano
FOSS (30)
Parable of Death, for narrator,
  tenor and orchestra
HAMILTON (30)
Bartholomew Fair, overture
Violin Concerto

CONTINUED

MENNIN (29)
Concertato for orchestra, *Moby Dick*
Quartet No. 2
BERIO (27)
Allez Hop, for voice, mime and dance
Five Variations, for piano (1952–53)
BOULEZ (27)
fp. Structures, for two pianos, Book I
BROWN (26)
Folio and Four Systems, for piano and orchestra
Music for Violin, Cello and Piano

HENZE (26)
King Stag, opera (1952–55)
The Idiot, ballet-pantomime
Quintet for wind instruments
String Quartet No. 2
STOCKHAUSEN (24)
Spiel, for orchestra
Punkte, for orchestra (1952–53)
Kontrapunkte, for ten instruments (1952–53)
Schlagtrio, for piano and timpani
Klavierstücke I–IV
Étude, musique concrete

1953 BAX, JONGEN, QUILTER and PROKOFIEV died

DOHNÁNYI (76)
Stabat Mater
PIZZETTI (73)
Cagliostro, opera
STRAVINSKY (71)
Septet
Three songs from Shakespeare, for mezzo-soprano and piano
BAX (70)
Coronation March
MARTINŮ (63)
The Marriage, opera
BLISS (62)
Processional, for orchestra and organ
HONEGGER (61)
Christmas Cantata
MILHAUD (61)
David, opera
MOORE (60)
Piano Trio
ROBERTSON (57)
The Book of Mormon, oratorio
SESSIONS (57)
Sonata for solo violin
KORNGOLD (56)
Straussiana, for orchestra
Theme and Variations for orchestra
HARRIS (55)
Piano Concerto No. 2
Abraham Lincoln walks at midnight, chamber cantata

CHÁVEZ (54)
Symphony No. 4, *Sinfonia romantica*
Symphony No. 5, *Symphony for Strings*
POULENC (54)
Dialogues des Carmelites, opera
Sonata for two pianos
ANTHEIL (53)
Capital of the World, ballet
WALTON (51)
Coronation Te Deum
Orb and Sceptre, coronation march for orchestra
BERKELEY (50)
Suite for orchestra
ALWYN (48)
Symphony No. 2
The Magic Island, symphonic prelude
SEIBER (48)
Three pieces for cello and orchestra
TIPPETT (48)
Piano Concerto (1953–55)
Divertimento for chamber orchestra, *Sellinger's Round* (1953–55)
Fantasia concertante on a Theme by Corelli, for strings

LUTYENS (47)
Three songs and incidental
music for Group Theater's
Homage to Dylan Thomas
SHOSTAKOVICH (47)
Ballet Suite No. 4
Symphony No. 10
Concertino, for two pianos
MESSIAEN (45)
Reveil des oiseaux, for piano and
orchestra
BARBER (43)
Souvenirs, ballet suite
SCHUMAN (43)
The Mighty Casey, baseball opera
Voyage, for piano
CAGE (41)
*Music for piano — "4–84 for 1–84
Pianists"* (1953–56)
BRITTEN (40)
Gloriana, opera
Winter Words, songs
GOULD (40)
Inventions for four pianos and
orchestra
ARNELL (36)
The Great Detective, ballet
Lord Byron, symphonic portrait
ROCHBERG (35)
Chamber Symphony, for nine
instruments

FRICKER (33)
Violin Concerto No. 2, *Rapsodie
concertante*
ARNOLD (32)
Homage to the Queen, ballet
Symphony No. 2
Oboe Concerto
Violin Sonata No. 2
SHAPEY (32)
String Quartet No. 4
Cello Sonata
LIGETI (30)
String Quartet
MENNIN (30)
Symphony No. 6
BERIO (28)
Chamber Music, for female voice,
clarinet, cello and harp
BROWN (27)
"25 Pages—from 1 to 25 pianos"
HENZE (27)
The End of a World, radio opera
Ode to the Westwind, for cello
and orchestra
MUSGRAVE (25)
A Tale for Thieves, ballet
A Suite of Bairnsangs, for voice
and piano
STOCKHAUSEN (25)
Elektronische Studie, I
HODDINOTT (24)
fp. Fugal Overture, for orchestra
fp. Nocturne, for orchestra

1954

VAUGHAN WILLIAMS (82)
Concerto for bass tuba and
orchestra
Violin Sonata in A minor
This Day (Hodie), cantata
DOHNÁNYI (77)
American Rhapsody
KODÁLY (72)
Spartacus, ballet
STRAVINSKY (72)
In Memoriam Dylan Thomas, for
voice, trombones and string
quartet
TAYLOR (69)
The Dragon, opera

BLISS (63)
A Song of Welcome, for solo
voices, chorus and orchestra
MILHAUD (62)
Harp Concerto
PISTON (60)
Symphony No. 5
SOWERBY (59)
All on a Summer's Day, for
orchestra
Fantasy, for trumpet and organ
SESSIONS (58)
The Idyll of Theocritus, for soprano
and orchestra

CONTINUED

THOMSON (58)
Concerto for flute, strings and
  percussion
HARRIS (56)
Fantasy, for piano and orchestra
POULENC (55)
Bucolique, for orchestra
Matelote provençale, for orchestra
COPLAND (54)
The Tender Land, opera
FINZI (53)
Grand Fantasia and Toccata, for
  piano and orchestra
RUBBRA (53)
Symphony No. 6
RODRIGO (52)
Concert-Serenade, for harp and
  orchestra
WALTON (52)
Troilus and Cressida, opera
BERKELEY (51)
A Dinner Engagement, opera
Nelson, opera
Trio for violin, horn and piano
Sonatina for piano duet
KHACHATURIAN (51)
Spartacus, ballet
DALLAPICCOLA (50)
Piccola musica notturna, for
  orchestra
ALWYN (49)
Lyra angelica, for harp and
  strings
RAWSTHORNE (49)
Practical Cats, for speaker and
  orchestra
String Quartet No. 2
SEIBER (49)
Elegy, for solo violin and small
  orchestra
To Poetry, song cycle
LUTYENS (48)
Infidelio, seven scenes for voices
  and instruments
Valediction, for clarinet and piano
SHOSTAKOVICH (48)
Festival Overture
*Five Romances (Songs of Our
  Days)*, for bass and piano
Film music

BARBER (44)
Prayers of Kiekegaard, for soprano,
  chorus and orchestra
MENOTTI (43)
The Saint of Bleeker Street, opera
CAGE (42)
34′ 46.776″ for a pianist, for
  prepared piano
BRITTEN (41)
The Turn of the Screw, opera
Canticle No. 3, "Still Falls the
  Rain", for tenor, chorus and
  piano
LUTOSLAWSKI (41)
Dance Preludes, first version for
  clarinet and piano
DIAMOND (40)
Sinfonia concertante
Sonata for solo violin
BERNSTEIN (36)
Serenade for violin, strings and
  percussion
Five Anniversaries, for piano
On the Waterfront, film score
ROCHBERG (36)
David the Psalmist, cantata
Three psalms, for chorus
FRICKER (34)
Dance Scene, for orchestra
Nocturne and Scherzo, for piano
  (four hands)
ARNOLD (33)
Sinfonietta No. 1
Concerto for flute and strings
Harmonica Concerto
Organ Concerto
The Tempest, incidental music
SHAPEY (33)
Concerto for clarinet with six
  instruments
Sonata Variations, for piano
HAMILTON (32)
String Octet
*Four Border Songs and the Fray
  of Suport*
Songs of Summer, for soprano
  and piano
BERIO (29)
Nones, for orchestra
Variations for chamber orchestra
Mutations, electronic music

BOULEZ (29)
Le marteau sans maître, for alto
  voice and six instruments
MUSGRAVE (26)
Cantata for a Summer's Day
STOCKHAUSEN (26)
Elektronische Studie, II
Klavierstücke V–X

HODDINOTT (23)
fp. Concerto for clarinet and
  string orchestra
GOEHR (22)
Fantasia for orchestra (revised
  1958)
Fantasias for clarinet and piano
BENNETT (18)
Piano Sonata
Sonatina for flute

ENESCO, HONEGGER and ROPARTZ died   **1955**

VAUGHAN WILLIAMS (83)
Symphony No. 8
MARTIN (65)
Études, for string orchestra
  (1955–56)
MARTINŮ (65)
Three frescoes
BLISS (64)
Violin Concerto
*Meditations on a Theme of John
  Blow*, for orchestra
Elegiac Sonnet, for tenor, string
  quartet and piano
MILHAUD (63)
Symphonies Nos. 5 and 6
PISTON (61)
Symphony No. 6
ORFF (60)
Der Sänger der Vorwelt
Comoedia de Christi resurrectione
GERHARD (59)
Concerto for harpsichord, strings
  and percussion (1955–56)
String Quartet No. 1 (1955–56)
HANSON (59)
Symphony No. 5, *Sinfonia sacrae*
SESSIONS (59)
Mass, for unison male voices and
  organ
TANSMAN (58)
Capriccio
Le Sermant, opera
Concerto for Orchestra
ANTHEIL (55)
Cabezza de Vacca, cantata
  (1955–56)

COPLAND (55)
Symphonic Ode
A Canticle of Freedom, for chorus
  and orchestra (revised 1965)
FINZI (55)
Cello Concerto
RUBBRA (54)
Piano Concerto
RODRIGO (53)
Fantasia para un Gentilhombre, for
  guitar (*c.*1955)
WALTON (53)
Johannesburg Festival Overture
Richard III, incidental music
BERKELEY (52)
Suite from *Nelson*, for orchestra
Concerto for flute, violin, cello
  and harpsichord (or piano)
Sextet, for clarinet, horn and
  string quartet
Concert Study in E♭, for piano
Crux fidelis, for solo tenor and
  mixed chorus
Look up sweet Babe, for soprano
  and mixed chorus
Salve Regina, for voices and
  organ
KHACHATURIAN (52)
Three Suites for Orchestra
DALLAPICCOLA (51)
An Mathilde, cantata
KABALEVSKY (51)
Nikita Vershinin, opera
ALWYN (50)
Autumn Legend, for English horn
  and strings
RAWSTHORNE (50)
Madame Chrysanthème, ballet

CONTINUED

TIPPETT (50)
Sonata for four horns
LUTYENS (49)
Music for Orchestra, I
Capriccii, for two harps and
  percussion
Nocturnes, for violin, guitar and
  cello
Sinfonia for organ
SHOSTAKOVICH (49)
Film music
SCHUMAN (45)
Credendum, for orchestra
CAGE (43)
26' 1.499" for a string player
BRITTEN (42)
Hymn to St. Peter
Alpine Suite, for recorder trio
GOULD (42)
Jekyll and Hyde Variations, for
  orchestra
Derivations, for clarinet and band
LUTOSLAWSKI (42)
Dance Preludes, second version
  for clarinet and instruments
FINE (41)
Serious Song and Lament, for
  string orchestra
ARNELL (38)
Love in Transit, opera
ROCHBERG (37)
Duo concertante, for violin and
  cello
FRICKER (35)
Litany, for double string orchestra
Musick's Empire, for chorus and
  small orchestra
The Tomb of St. Eulalia, for
  counter-tenor, gamba and
  harpsichord
Horn sonata
SHAPERO (35)
Credo, for orchestra

ARNOLD (34)
Tam O'Shanter, overture
Little Suite for Orchestra, No. 1
Serenade, for guitar and strings
John Clare, cantata
FOSS (34)
Griffelkin, opera
The Gift of the Magi, ballet
SHAPEY (34)
Challenge — the Family of Man,
  for orchestra
Piano Trio
BOULEZ (30)
Symphonie mecanique
HENZE (29)
Symphony No. 4
Quattro Poemi, for orchestra
Three Symphonic Studies
  (revised 1964)
KORTE (27)
Concertato on a Choral theme, for
  orchestra
MUSGRAVE (27)
The Abbot of Drimock, chamber
  opera
Five Love Songs, for soprano and
  guitar
STOCKHAUSEN (27)
Gruppen, for three orchestras
Zeitmasze, for oboe, flute,
  English horn, clarinet and
  bassoon
Gesang de Jünglinge, electronic
  music
HODDINOTT (26)
fp. Symphony No. 1
DAVIES (21)
Stedman Doubles, for clarinet and
  percussion
Trumpet Sonata

1956   CHARPENTIER and FINZI died

VAUGHAN WILLIAMS (84)
Symphony No. 9 (revised 1958)
Two organ preludes, *Romanza*
  and *Toccata*
Epithalamion, cantata
  (1956–57)

Ten Blake Songs, for tenor and
  oboe
A Vision of Aeroplanes, motet
STRAVINSKY (74)
Canticum sacrum

MARTIN (66)
Overture in Homage to Mozart
BLISS (65)
Edinburgh Overture
MILHAUD (64)
Symphony No. 7
MOORE (63)
The Ballad of Baby Doe, opera
PISTON (62)
Serenata, for orchestra
Quintet for wind
CASTELNUOVO-TEDESCO (61)
All's Well that Ends Well, opera
JACOB (61)
Piano Concerto No. 2
Sextet
Piano Trio
ORFF (61)
Nanie and Dithyrambe, with choir
GERHARD (60)
Nonet for eight winds and
  accordion
HANSON (60)
*Elegy in Memory of Serge
Koussevitsky*, for orchestra
SESSIONS (60)
Piano Concerto
HARRIS (58)
Folk Fantasy for Festivals, for
  piano and choir
POULENC (57)
Le travail du peintre, song cycle
"Deux mélodies", songs
FINZI (55)
In Terra Pax, for chorus and
  orchestra
Eclogue, for piano and strings
RUBBRA (55)
Symphony No. 7
WALTON (54)
Cello Concerto
BERKELEY (53)
Ruth, opera
KHACHATURIAN (53)
Ode of Joy, for voices and
  orchestra
DALLAPICCOLA (52)
*Concerto per la notte di natale
dell'anno*
Cinque canti, for baritone and
  eight instruments

KABALEVSKY (52)
Symphony No. 5
Romeo and Juliet, symphonic
  suite
ALWYN (51)
Symphony No. 3
RAWSTHORNE (51)
Violin Concerto No. 2
TIPPETT (51)
Symphony No. 2 (1956–57)
LUTYENS (50)
*Chorale for Orchestra (Hommage à
  Stravinsky)*
Three Duos (horn and piano;
  cello and piano; violin and
  piano) (1956–57)
In the Temple of a Bird's Wing,
  for baritone and piano
SHOSTAKOVICH (50)
Katerina Ismailova, opera
String Quartet No. 6
Spanish Songs, for soprano and
  piano
Film music
MESSIAEN (48)
Oiseaux exotiques, for piano,
  wind and percussion
BARBER (46)
Summer Music, for woodwind
  quintet
SCHUMAN (46)
New England Triptych, for
  orchestra
MENOTTI (45)
*The Unicorn, the Gorgon and the
  Manticore*, ballet
GOULD (43)
Santa Fé Saga, for band
Dialogue, for piano and strings
BRITTEN (43)
The Prince of the Pagodas, ballet
Antiphon, for choir and organ
DIAMOND (41)
Sonata for solo cello
ARNELL (39)
Landscape and Figures, for
  orchestra
BERNSTEIN (38)
Candide
ROCHBERG (38)
Sinfonia fantasia

CONTINUED

FRICKER (36)
Suite for harpsichord
Cello sonata
ARNOLD (35)
The Dancing Master, opera
The Open Window, opera
Solitaire, ballet suite
A Grand Overture
SHAPEY (35)
Mutations No. 1, for piano
FOSS (34)
Psalms, with orchestra
HAMILTON (34)
Scottish Dances
Sonata for chamber orchestra
MENNIN (33)
Cello Concerto
Sonata concertante, for violin
  and piano
BERIO (31)
Allelujah, I and II, for orchestra
String Quartet
Perspectives, electronic music

HENZE (30)
Maratona, ballet
Ondine, ballet (1956–57)
Concerto per il Marigny, for piano
  and seven instruments
Five Neapolitan Songs, for voice
  and chamber orchestra
STOCKHAUSEN (28)
Klavierstücke XI
HODDINOTT (27)
fp. Septet for wind, strings and
  piano
GOEHR (24)
String Quartet No. 1 (1956–57)
DAVIES (21)
Five pieces for piano
NILSSON (19)
Frequenzen, for eight players
  (*c.*1956)

1957   KORNGOLD, SCHOECK and SIBELIUS died

MALIPIERO (75)
Piano Quintet
STRAVINSKY (75)
Agon, ballet
Threni (Lamentations of Jeremiah),
  for soloists, chorus and
  orchestra (1957–58)
MARTIN (67)
La mystère de la Nativité, oratorio
  (1957–59)
BLISS (66)
Discourse, for orchestra, first
  version (recomposed 1965)
MILHAUD (65)
Symphony No. 8, *Rhodanienne*
Oboe Concerto
Aspen Serenade
MOORE (64)
Gallantry, a soap opera
PISTON (63)
Viola Concerto
SOWERBY (62)
The Throne of God, for chorus and
  orchestra
GERHARD (61)
Don Quixote, ballet suite

SESSIONS (61)
Symphony No. 3
THOMSON (61)
The Lively Arts, Fugue
WEINBERGER (61)
Préludes religieuses et profanes,
  for organ
POULENC (58)
Elegy, for horn and piano
COPLAND (57)
Orchestral Variations
Piano Fantasy
RUBBRA (56)
In Memoriam Maraie matris Dei,
  cantata
WALTON (55)
Partita, for orchestra
BERKELEY (54)
"Sweet was the Song", for
  voices and organ
Sonatina for guitar
KHACHATURIAN (54)
Lermontov Suite

DALLAPICCOLA (53)
Requiescat, for chorus and
    orchestra (1957—58)
ALWYN (52)
Elizabethan Dances, for orchestra
RAWSTHORNE (52)
Violin Sonata
LUTYENS (51)
Six Tempi for Ten Instruments
Variations for solo flute
De Amore, cantata
SHOSTAKOVICH (51)
Symphony No. 11, *The Year
    1905*
Piano Concerto No. 2
SCHUMAN (47)
Prologues, for chorus and
    orchestra
CAGE (45)
Piano Concerto (1957—58)
Winter Music: for 1—20 Pianists
BRITTEN (44)
Noye's Fludde, mystery play
Songs from the Chinese, for high
    voice and guitar
GOULD (44)
Declaration Suite
LUTOSLAWSKI (44)
Five songs
DIAMOND (42)
The World of Paul Klee, for
    orchestra
ARNELL (40)
The Angels, ballet
BERNSTEIN (39)
West Side Story, film score
FRICKER (37)
Octet, for flute, clarinet, bassoon,
    horn, violin, viola, cello and
    double-bass
Piano Variations
A Vision of Judgment, oratorio
ARNOLD (36)
Symphony No. 3
Toy Symphony
Four Scottish Dances, for
    orchestra
SHAPEY (36)
String Quartet No. 5, with female
    voices (1957—58)
Rhapsodie, for oboe and piano
Duo for viola and piano

FOSS (35)
Behold! I built an house
HAMILTON (35)
Five Love Songs, for tenor and
    orchestra
Cantata for tenor and piano
BERIO (32)
Divertimento for Orchestra
Serenata, for flute and fourteen
    instruments
El mar la mar, for voices and
    instruments
Momenti, electronic sound
BOULEZ (32)
Doubles, for orchestra
Poésie pour pouvoir, for reciter,
    orchestra and tape
Deux improvisations sur Mallarmé,
    for soprano and instrumental
    ensemble
Piano Sonata No. 3
FELDMAN (31)
Pieces for four pianos
HENZE (31)
Nocturnes and arias, for soprano
    and orchestra
Sonata per archi (1957—58)
HODDINOTT (28)
fp. Rondo Scherzoso, for trumpet
    and piano
WILLIAMSON (26)
Piano Sonata No. 1
GOEHR (25)
The Deluge, cantata
Capriccio, for piano
BIRTWHISTLE (23)
Refrains and Choruses, for flute,
    oboe, clarinet, bassoon and
    horn
DAVIES (23)
St. Michael, sonata for seventeen
    wind instruments
Alma redemptoris mater, for six
    wind instruments
MAW (22)
Sonatina, for flute and piano
BENNETT (21)
Five Pieces for Orchestra
String Quartet No. 3
Violin Sonata
Sonata for solo violin

CONTINUED

BENNETT CONTINUED
Sonata for solo cello
Four improvisations for violin

NILSSON (20)
Kreutzungen, for instrumental
  ensemble
Buch der Veränderungen
Mädchentotenlieder (1957—58)

1958   VAUGHAN WILLIAMS died

VAUGHAN WILLIAMS (86)
The First Nowell, for soloist,
  chorus and orchestra
Four last songs, for voice and
  piano
Vocalises, for soprano and
  clarinet
PIZZETTI (78)
Murder in the Cathedral, opera
MARTIN (68)
Overture in Rondo
Pseaumes de Genève, for mixed
  choir, children's voices, organ
  and orchestra
BLISS (67)
The Lady of Shalott, ballet
MILHAUD (66)
Violin Concerto No. 3, *Concerto
  royal*
PISTON (64)
Psalm and Prayer of David, for
  chorus and seven instruments
CASTELNUOVO-TEDESCO (63)
The Merchant of Venice, opera
Saul
HINDEMITH (63)
Octet
JACOB (63)
Diversions, for woodwind and
  strings
Old Wine in New Bottles, for
  wind instruments
Suite for recorder and string
  quartet
Miniature string quartet
ORFF (63)
Oedipus, der Tyrann
HANSON (62)
Mosaics, for orchestra
SESSIONS (62)
Symphony No. 4
String Quintet
CHÁVEZ (59)
Inventions, No. 1 for piano

POULENC (59)
La voix humaine, lyric tragedy
  (monodrama for soprano)
RUBBRA (57)
Oboe Sonata
Pezzo ostinato, for solo harp
BERKELEY (55)
Concerto for piano and double
  string orchestra
Five Poems by W.H. Auden, for
  voice and piano
KHACHATURIAN (55)
Sonatina for piano
RAWSTHORNE (53)
Halle Overture
SEIBER (53)
Permutazione a cinque, for flute,
  oboe, clarinet, horn and
  bassoon
*Portrait of the Artist as a Young
  Man*, chamber cantata
TIPPETT (53)
King Priam, opera (1958—61)
Crown of the Year, for chorus and
  orchestra
Prelude, Recitative and Aria, for
  flute, oboe and harpsichord
LUTYENS (52)
Piano e Forte, for piano
SHOSTAKOVICH (52)
Moscow, Cheremushki, musical
  comedy
BARBER (48)
Vanessa, opera
MENOTTI (47)
Maria Golovin, opera
CAGE (46)
Fontana Mix
Variations I
BRITTEN (45)
Nocturne, for tenor, seven obbli-
  gato instruments and strings
Sechs Hölderlin-Fragmente, song
  cycle

GOULD (45)
Rhythm Gallery, for narrator and orchestra
St. Lawrence Suite, for band
LUTOSLAWSKI (45)
Funeral Music, for strings
Three Postludes (1958–63)
DIAMOND (43)
Woodwind Quintet
ARNELL (41)
Moonflowers, opera
ROCHBERG (40)
Symphony No. 2
Cheltenham Concerto, for chamber orchestra
Dialogues, for clarinet and piano
FRICKER (38)
Comedy Overture
Toccata for piano and orchestra (1958–59)
SHAPERO (38)
On Green Mountain, for jazz combo
ARNOLD (37)
Sinfonietta No. 2
SHAPEY (37)
Ontogeny, for orchestra
Walking Upright, song cycle
FOSS (36)
Symphony of Chorales
HAMILTON (36)
Overture 1912
Concerto for jazz trumpet and orchestra
Sonata for solo cello
LIGETI (35)
Apparitions, for orchestra (1958–59)
Artikulation, for tape
MENNIN (35)
Piano Concerto
BERIO (33)
Tempi concertati, for flute, violin, two pianos and other instruments (1958–59)
Differences, for five instruments and tape
Sequence I, for flute
Theme (Homage to Joyce), electronic music

HENZE (32)
Der Prinz von Homburg, opera
Three Dithyrambs, for chamber orchestra
Chamber Music
Three Tentos, for guitar
KORTE (30)
The Story of the Flutes, tone poem
MUSGRAVE (30)
Obliques, for orchestra
String Quartet
A Song for Christmas, for voice and piano
HODDINOTT (29)
fp. Harp Concerto
fp. Four Welsh Dances, for orchestra
fp. Concertino for viola and small orchestra
fp. Serenade, for string orchestra
WILLIAMSON (27)
Santiago de Espada, overture
Piano Concerto No. 1
GOEHR (26)
La Belle Dame sans merci, ballet
PENDERECKI (25)
Emanations, for two string orchestras
Epithaphiom on the death of Artur Malawski, for string orchestra and timpani
The Psalms of David, for chorus and instruments
DAVIES (24)
Stedman Caters (revised 1968)
Sextet
MAW (23)
Nocturne, for mezzo-soprano and chamber orchestra
NILSSON (21)
Stunde eines Blocks, for soprano and six players
Zwanzig Gruppen für Blaser, for piccolo, oboe and clarinet (1958–59)
Quantitaten, for piano

MALIPIERO (77)
Sei poesie di Dylan Thomas, for soprano and ten instruments
Musica da Camera, for wind quintet
STRAVINSKY (77)
Movements, for piano and orchestra
Double Canon for string quartet
Epitaphium, for flute, clarinet and harp
PISTON (65)
Concerto for two pianos and orchestra
Three New England Sketches, for orchestra
SOWERBY (64)
Ask of the Covenant, cantata
GERHARD (63)
Symphony No. 2
HANSON (63)
Summer Seascapes
THOMSON (63)
Collected Poems
Fugues and Cantilenas, for orchestra
HARRIS (61)
Give me the splendid silent sun, cantata
POULENC (60)
Gloria, for voices and orchestra
COPLAND (59)
Dance Panels, ballet
RUBBRA (58)
Violin Concerto
BERKELEY (56)
Overture for Light Orchestra
Sonatina for two pianos
"So sweet love seemed", for voice and piano
DALLAPICCOLA (55)
Dialoghi, for cello and orchestra
ALWYN (54)
Symphony No. 4
RAWSTHORNE (54)
Symphony No. 2, *A pastoral symphony*
SEIBER (54)
Improvisation for Jazz Band and Symphony Orchestra

LUTYENS (53)
Quincunx, for solo voices and orchestra
SHOSTAKOVICH (53)
Cello Concerto No. 1
BARBER (49)
A Hand of Bridge, opera, for four solo voices and chamber orchestra
SCHUMAN (49)
Three Moods, for piano
BRITTEN (46)
Cantata Academica, *Carmen basiliense*, for solo voices, chorus and orchestra
Missa brevis
LUTOSLAWSKI (46)
Dance Preludes, third version for instruments
DIAMOND (44)
Symphony No. 7
ARNELL (42)
Paralyzed Princess, operetta
ROCHBERG (41)
La bocca della verita, for oboe and piano
String Quartet No. 2
FRICKER (39)
Serenade No. 1, for flute, clarinet, bass-clarinet, viola, cello and harp
Serenade No. 2, for flute, oboe and piano
ARNOLD (38)
Guitar Concerto
Oboe Quartet
Six Songs of William Blake, for voice and strings
SHAPEY (38)
Violin Concerto
Rituals, for orchestra
Soliloquy, for narrator, string quartet and percussion
Evocation, for violin, piano and percussion
Form, for piano
FOSS (37)
Introductions and Goodbyes, opera
HAMILTON (37)
Sinfonia for two orchestras
Écossaise, for orchestra

BERIO (34)
Quaderni I, II and III from *Epifanie*
  for orchestra (1959–63)
BOULEZ (34)
fp. Tombeau, for orchestra
FELDMAN (33)
Atlantis, for chamber orchestra
HENZE (33)
Elegy for Young Lovers, opera
  (1959–61)
The Emperor's Nightingale, ballet
Piano Sonata
KORTE (31)
For a Young Audience, for
  orchestra
Fantasy, for violin and piano
MUSGRAVE (31)
Triptych, for tenor and orchestra
STOCKHAUSEN (31)
Carré, for four orchestras and
  four choirs
Refrain, for piano, celesta and
  percussion
Zyklus, for one percussionist
Kontakte, electronic sound
HODDINOTT (30)
fp. Nocturne and Dance, for harp
  and orchestra
fp. Piano Sonata No. 1

GOEHR (27)
Hecuba's Lament, for orchestra
  (1959–61)
Variations for flute and piano
Four songs from the Japanese
Sutter's Gold, cantata
  (1959–60)
PENDERECKI (26)
Strophes, for soprano, narrator
  and ten instruments
BIRTWHISTLE (25)
Monody for Corpus Christi, for
  soprano, flute, horn and
  violin
Précis, for piano
DAVIES (25)
Prolation, for orchestra
Ricercare and doubles on "To
  many a well"
Five motets
BENNETT (23)
The Approaches of Sleep
NILSSON (22)
*Und die Zeiger seiner Augen wurden
  langsam züruckgedreht*, for solo
  voices, chorus and mixed
  media
Ein irrender Sohn, for voice and
  instruments

ALFVÉN, BENJAMIN, DOHNÁNYI and SEıBER died   **1960**

KODÁLY (78)
Symphony in C
MALIPIERO (78)
String Quartet No. 3
STRAVINSKY (78)
Monumentum pro Gesualdo, for
  orchestra
MARTIN (70)
Drey minnelieder, for soprano and
  piano
BLISS (69)
Tobias and the Angel, opera
MILHAUD (68)
Symphony No. 10
PISTON (66)
Symphony No. 7
Violin Concerto No. 2
ORFF (65)
Ludus de nato Infante mirijucus

GERHARD (64)
Symphony No. 3, *Collages*
String Quartet No. 2 (1960–62)
SESSIONS (64)
Divertimento, for orchestra
THOMSON (64)
Requiem Mass
Mass for solo voice and piano
(with orchestra 1962)
WEINBERGER (64)
Aus Tirol
CHÁVEZ (61)
Love Propitiated, opera
POULENC (61)
Elegy, for two pianos
COPLAND (60)
Nonet for strings
DURUFLÉ (58)
Four motets on Gregorian themes,
  for a cappella choir   CONTINUED

WALTON (58)
Symphony No. 2
fp. Anon. in Love, six songs for
tenor and guitar
BERKELEY (57)
A Winter's Tale, suite for
orchestra
Prelude and Fugue for clavichord
*Improvisation on a Theme of
Falla*, for piano
Missa brevis
KHACHATURIAN (57)
Rhapsody, for violin and orchestra
Ballade, for bass with orchestra
DALLAPICCOLA (56)
Ulisse, opera (1960–68)
KABALEVSKY (56)
Overture pathétique, for orchestra
The Spring, symphonic poem
Major-minor études, for cello
Camp of Friendship, songs
SEIBER (55)
Invitation, ballet
A Three-cornered fanfare
LUTYENS (54)
Wind Quintet
SHOSTAKOVICH (54)
*Novorossiysk Chimes (The Fire of
Eternal Glory)*, for orchestra
String Quartets Nos. 7 and 8
Satires (Pictures of the Past), for
soprano and piano
Film music
MESSIAEN (52)
Chronochromie
BARBER (50)
Toccata festiva, for organ and
orchestra
SCHUMAN (50)
Symphony No. 7
CAGE (48)
Cartridge Music
Theater Piece, for 1–8 Performers
BRITTEN (47)
A Midsummer Night's Dream,
opera
FINE (46)
Diversion, for orchestra
DIAMOND (45)
Symphony No. 8
Quartet No. 5

ROCHBERG (42)
Time-Span, for orchestra
FRICKER (40)
Symphony No. 3
SHAPERO (40)
Partita, for piano and orchestra
ARNOLD (39)
Rinaldo and Armida, ballet
Symphony No. 4
Song of Simeon, nativity play
SHAPEY (39)
Dimensions, for soprano and
twenty-three instruments
De profundis, for solo double-bass
and instruments
Movements, for woodwind
quartet
Five, for violin and piano
This Day, for voice and piano
FOSS (38)
Time Cycle, four songs with
orchestra
HAMILTON (38)
Piano Concerto
LIGETI (37)
Atmospheres, for orchestra
BERIO (35)
Circles, for voice, harp and two
percussion
BOULEZ (35)
fp. Pli selon pli, for soprano and
orchestra
FELDMAN (34)
Durations I–V (1960–61)
HENZE (34)
Antifone, for orchestra
KORTE (32)
Quintet for oboe and strings
MUSGRAVE (32)
Trio for flute, oboe and piano
Colloquy, for violin and piano
Monologue, for piano
HODDINOTT (31)
fp. Concerto No. 1 for piano,
wind and percussion
Sextet for flute, clarinet, bassoon,
violin, viola and cello
PREVIN (31)
Overture to a Comedy, for
orchestra

PENDERECKI (27)
Anaklasis, for strings and
    percussion groups
String Quartet No. 1
BIRTWHISTLE (26)
The World is Discovered, for
    instrumental ensemble
DAVIES (26)
O Magnum Mysterium, for
    chorus, instruments and organ

MAW (25)
Five Epigrams, for unaccompanied
    chorus
BENNETT (24)
Journal, for orchestra
Calendar, for chamber ensemble
Winter Music, for flute and piano
    (or orchestra)
NILSSON (23)
Szene I
Reaktionen, for four percussionists

GRAINGER died   **1961**

MARTIN (71)
Monsieur de Pourceaugnac, opera
    (1961–62)
MOORE (68)
Wings of the Dove, opera
PISTON (67)
Symphonic Prelude
JACOB (66)
Trombone Concerto
Fantasia on Scottish Tunes
HANSON (65)
Bold Island, suite
THOMSON (65)
A Solemn Music, for orchestra
WEINBERGER (65)
Eine walserouverture
TANSMAN (64)
Psalms, for tenor, chorus and
    orchestra
HARRIS (63)
Canticle to the Sun, cantata
CHÁVEZ (62)
Symphony No. 6
Soli No. 2, for wind quintet
POULENC (62)
La dame de Monte Carlo,
    monologue for soprano and
    orchestra
RUBBRA (60)
Cantata da camera (Crucifixus
    pro nobis)
WALTON (59)
Gloria, for solo voices, chorus
    and orchestra
BERKELEY (58)
Concerto for violin and chamber
    orchestra
Five pieces for violin and orchestra

KHACHATURIAN (58)
Piano Sonata
KABELEVSKY (57)
Rondo for violin and piano
RAWSTHORNE (56)
Concerto for ten instruments
*Improvisations on a theme by
    Constant Lambert*, for orchestra
TIPPETT (56)
Magnificat and Nunc Dimittis
Three songs for Achilles, for voice
    and guitar
LUTYENS (55)
Symphonies for solo piano,
    winds, harps and percussion
Catena, cantata
SHOSTAKOVICH (55)
Symphony No. 12, *1917*
BARBER (51)
Dies Natalis, choral preludes
CAGE (49)
Atlas eclipticalis, for orchestra
    (1961–62)
Variations II
Music for Carillon No. 4
BRITTEN (48)
Cello Sonata
War Requiem
LUTOSLAWSKI (48)
Jeux vénitiens
FINE (47)
Romanza, for wind quintet
DIAMOND (46)
Nonet, for three violins, three
    violas and three cellos
ARNELL (44)
Brass Quintet

CONTINUED

ROCHBERG (43)
Songs of Innocence and Experience,
 for soprano and chamber
 orchestra
FRICKER (41)
Twelve studies for piano
Cantata for tenor and chamber
 ensemble (1961–62)
ARNOLD (40)
Symphony No. 5
Divertimento No. 2, for full
 orchestra
SHAPEY (40)
Incantations, for soprano and ten
 instruments
Discourse, for flute, clarinet,
 violin and piano
FOSS (39)
Echoi, for clarinet, cello, piano
 and percussion (1961–63)
LIGETI (38)
Fragment, for eleven instruments
Volumina, for organ (1961–62)
BERIO (36)
Visage, electronic music with
 voice
BOULEZ (36)
Structures, for two pianos,
 Book II
BROWN (35)
Available Forms II
HENZE (35)
Six absences, pour le clavecin

KORTE (33)
Symphony No. 2
Four Blake Songs, for voices and
 piano
MUSGRAVE (33)
Serenade, for five instruments
Sir Patrick Spens, for tenor and
 guitar
HODDINOTT (32)
fp. Piano Concerto No. 2
fp. Violin Concerto
WILLIAMSON (30)
Organ Concerto
GOEHR (29)
Violin Concerto (1961–62)
Suite for six instruments
PENDERECKI (28)
Fluorescences, for orchestra
Dimensions of Time and Silence,
 for choir and orchestra
Polymorphia
Threnody, for fifty-two stringed
 instruments
Kanon, for strings and tape
DAVIES (27)
String Quartet
Te Lucis Ante Terminius, for
 choir and chamber orchestra
MAW (26)
Essay, for organ (revised 1963)
BENNETT (25)
The Ledges, opera
Suite française, for small orchestra
Oboe sonata
NILSSON (24)
Szene II

1962   IBERT and IRELAND died

STRAVINSKY (80)
The Flood, opera
Abraham and Isaac, for baritone
 and orchestra
BLISS (71)
The Beatitudes, cantata
MILHAUD (70)
Symphony No. 12
MOORE (69)
The Greenfield Christmas Tree, a
 Christmas entertainment

PISTON (68)
Lincoln Center, Festival overture
String Quartet No. 5
JACOB (67)
News from Newtown, cantata
ORFF (67)
Ein Sommernachtstraum
GERHARD (66)
Concert for Eight
THOMSON (66)
A Joyful Fugue, to follow *A
 Solemn Music*
Pange lingua, for organ

TANSMAN (65)
Resurrection, for orchestra
Six symphonic studies for
  orchestra
HARRIS (64)
Symphonies Nos. 8 and 9
POULENC (63)
Sept repons des ténébres, for
  soprano, chorus and orchestra
Clarinet Sonata
Oboe Sonata
COPLAND (62)
Connotations, for orchestra
Down a Country Lane, for
  orchestra
WALTON (60)
*fp. A Song for the Lord Mayor's
Table*, song cycle
BERKELEY (59)
Batter My Heart, for soprano,
  chorus, organ and chamber
  orchestra
Sonatina, for oboe and piano
"Autumn's Legacy", for voice
  and piano
KHACHATURIAN (59)
Cello Sonata
DALLAPICCOLA (58)
Preghiere, for baritone and
  chamber orchestra
KABALEVSKY (58)
Cello Sonata
Requiem (1962–63)
RAWSTHORNE (57)
Medieval Diptych, for baritone
  and orchestra
Divertimento for chamber
  orchestra
Quintet for piano and wind
Piano trio
SEIBER (posthumous)
p. Violin Sonata
TIPPETT (57)
Concerto for orchestra
  (1962–63)
Praeludium, for brass, bells and
  percussion
Piano Sonata No. 2
Songs for Ariel
LUTYENS (56)
Music for Orchestra II
Five bagatelles for piano

SHOSTAKOVICH (56)
Symphony No. 13, *Babi-Yar*
BARBER (52)
Piano Concerto
Andromache's Farewell, for
  soprano and orchestra
SCHUMAN (52)
Song of Orpheus, fantasy for cello
  and orchestra
LUTOSLAWSKI (49)
Trois poèmes d'Henri Michaux,
  for chorus and orchestra
  (1962–63)
FINE (48)
Symphony No. 2
DIAMOND (47)
This Sacred Ground, for baritone,
  choruses and orchestra
Quartet No. 6
ARNELL (45)
String Quartet No. 5
ARNOLD (41)
Concerto for two violins and
  strings
SHAPEY (41)
Convocation, for chamber group
Chamber Symphony for ten solo
  players
Piece for violin and instruments
Birthday Piece, for piano
HAMILTON (40)
Arias for small orchestra
Sextet
LIGETI (39)
Poème symphonique, for one
  hundred metronomes
Aventures, for three singers and
  seven instruments
Nouvelles aventures, for three
  singers and seven instruments
  (1962–63)
BERIO (37)
Passaggio, messa in scena for
  soprano, two choirs and
  instruments
BROWN (36)
Novara, for instrumental ensemble
FELDMAN (36)
The Swallows of Salangan, for
  chorus and instruments
Last Pieces, for piano

CONTINUED

HENZE (36)
In re cervo, opera
Les Caprices de Marianne,
    incidental music
Symphony No. 5
Novae de Infinito laudes, cantata
KORTE (34)
Ceremonial Prelude and Passacaglia,
    for band
Nocturne and March, for band
MUSGRAVE (34)
Chamber Concerto No. 1
The Phoenix and the Turtle, for
    small chorus and orchestra
STOCKHAUSEN (34)
Momente, for voices and
    instruments (1962–64)
HODDINOTT (33)
fp. Symphony No. 2
fp. Variations for flute, clarinet,
    harp and string quartet
fp. Rebecca, for unaccompanied
    voices
GOEHR (30)
A Little Cantata of Proverbs
Two Choruses, for mixed choir a
    cappella
PENDERECKI (29)
Stabat Mater

BIRTWHISTLE (28)
Chorales for Orchestra (1962–63)
DAVIES (28)
First fantasia on an "In Nomine"
    of John Taverner, for orchestra
Sinfonia for chamber orchestra
Leopardi Fragments, for voices
    and instruments
MAW (27)
Chamber Music for five
    instruments
Scenes and Arias, for voices and
    instruments
Our Lady's Song, for
    unaccompanied voices
BENNETT (26)
London Pastoral Fantasy, for
    tenor and chamber orchestra
Sonata No. 2 for solo violin
Fantasy, for piano
Three Elegies, for choir
NILSSON (25)
Entree, for orchestra and tape
Szene III
TAVENER (18)
Piano Concerto (1962–63)
Three Holy Sonnets, for voice
    and orchestra

1963   HINDEMITH and POULENC died

STRAVINSKY (81)
In Memoriam Aldous Huxley,
    variations for orchestra
    (1963–64)
MARTIN (73)
Le quatre éléments, symphonic
    studies (1963–64)
BLISS (72)
Belmont Variations, for brass band
A Knot of Riddles, for baritone
    and eleven instruments
Mary of Magdala, cantata
MILHAUD (71)
Pacem in terris, for choir and
    orchestra
PISTON (69)
*Variations on a theme of Edward
    Burlinghame Hill*, for orchestra
Capriccio, for harp and string
    orchestra

CASTELNUOVO-TEDESCO (68)
Song of Songs
JACOB (68)
Suite for brass band
GERHARD (67)
The Plague, for speaker, chorus
    and orchestra
Hymnody, for eleven players
HANSON (67)
For the First Time, for orchestra
SESSIONS (67)
Psalm 140, for soprano and
    organ, or orchestra
TANSMAN (66)
Six movements for string
    orchestra
HARRIS (65)
*Epilogue to Profiles in Courage:
    J.F.K.*, for orchestra
Salute to Death

WALTON (61)
Variations on a theme of Hindemith,
  for orchestra
BERKELEY (60)
Four Ronsard Sonnets, for tenor
  and orchestra
KABALEVSKY (59)
Three Songs of Revolutionary
  Cuba
Three songs
Five songs (1963–64)
RAWSTHORNE (58)
Carmen Vitale, for soprano,
  chorus and orchestra
LUTYENS (57)
Music for Orchestra III
Encomion, for chorus, brass and
  percussion
String Quintet
Fantasie Trio, for flute, clarinet
  and piano
Wind Trio
Présages, for solo oboe
The Country of the Stars, motet
SHOSTAKOVICH (57)
Overture on Russian and Kirghiz
  Folk Themes
Film music
MESSIAEN (55)
Sept Haï-Kaï
SCHUMAN (53)
Symphony No. 8
MENOTTI (52)
Labyrinth, opera
The Last Savage, opera
Death of the Bishop of Brindisi,
  cantata
CAGE (51)
Variations III and IV
BRITTEN (50)
Symphony for cello and orchestra
Cantata misericordium, for tenor,
  baritone, string quartet, string
  orchestra, piano, harp and
  timpani
DIAMOND (48)
Quartet No. 7
ARNELL (46)
Musica pacifica
BERNSTEIN (45)
Symphony No. 3, *Kaddish*

ROCHBERG (45)
Piano Trio
FRICKER (43)
O longs désirs, songs for soprano
  and orchestra
ARNOLD (42)
Little Suite for Orchestra No. 2
SHAPEY (42)
Brass Quintet
String Quartet No. 6
Seven, for piano (four hands)
HAMILTON (41)
Sonatas and Variants, for ten
  wind instruments
Nocturnes with Cadenza, for piano
LIGETI (40)
Requiem (1963–65)
MENNIN (40)
Symphony No. 7 (1963–64)
Canto, for orchestra
BERIO (38)
Sincronie, for string quartet
  (1963–64)
Sequence II, for harp
BROWN (37)
Times Five, for orchestra
From Here, for chorus and
  orchestra
FELDMAN (37)
Christian Wolff in Cambridge
HENZE (37)
Adagio, for clarinet, horn,
  bassoon and string quintet
Ariosi, for soprano, violin and
  orchestra
Los Caprichos, for orchestra
Lucy Escott Variations, for piano
  or harpsichord
Being Beauteous, cantata
Cantata della fiaba estrema
KORTE (35)
Southwest, dance overture
Prairie Song, for trumpet and
  band
Introductions, for brass quintet
Mass for Youth, with orchestra or
  keyboard
MUSGRAVE (35)
The Five Ages of Man, for chorus
  and orchestra
STOCKHAUSEN (35)
Plus Minus   CONTINUED

HODDINOTT (34)
fp. Sinfonia for string orchestra
fp. Divertimento for oboe, clarinet,
   horn and bassoon
WILLIAMSON (32)
Our Man in Havana, opera
Elevamini Symphony
GOEHR (31)
Little Symphony
Little Music for Strings
Virtutes, cycle of songs and
   melodies for chorus, piano
   duet, and percussion
DAVIES (29)
Veni Sancte Spiritus, for soloists,
   chorus and small orchestra
Seven *"In Nomine"*, for
   instruments (1963–65)

MAW (28)
Round, for children's choir, mixed
   choir and piano
The Angel Gabriel, for
   unaccompanied voices
BEDFORD (26)
Piece for Mo, for instrumental
   ensemble
Two Poems, for chorus
NILSSON (26)
Versuchungen, for orchestra
TAVENER (19)
Three Sections, from T.S. Eliot's
   "The Four Quartets" for tenor
   and piano (1963–64)

1964

MALIPIERO (82)
Symphony No. 8
In Time of Daffodils, for solo
   voices and instruments
STRAVINSKY (82)
Elegy for J.F.K., for baritone (or
   mezzo-soprano) and three
   clarinets
Fanfare for a new theater, for two
   trumpets
MARTIN (74)
Pilate, cantata
BLISS (73)
*Homage to a Great Man (Winston
   Churchill)*, march for
   orchestra
The Golden Cantata
GROFÉ (72)
World's Fair Suite
MILHAUD (72)
La mère coupable, opera
   (1964–65)
String Septet
PISTON (70)
Sextet for stringed instruments
Piano Quartet
SOWERBY (69)
Symphony No. 5
Piano Sonata
SESSIONS (68)
Symphony No. 5

THOMSON (68)
Autumn Concertino, for harp,
   strings and percussion
The Feast of Love, for baritone
   and orchestra
TANSMAN (67)
Il usignolo di Boboli, opera
HARRIS (66)
Horn of Plenty, for orchestra
Duo for cello and piano
CHÁVEZ (65)
Resonancias, for orchestra
Tambuco, for percussion
COPLAND (64)
Emblems for a symphonic band
Music for a Great City, for
   orchestra
RUBBRA (63)
String Quartet No. 3
Improvisation for solo cello
BERKELEY (61)
Diversions, for eight instruments
"Songs of the Half-light", for
   high voice and guitar
Mass for five voices
DALLAPICCOLA (60)
Quattro liriche di Antonio Machado,
   for soprano and orchestra
Parole di San Paolo, for voice and
   instruments

KABALEVSKY (60)
Cello Concerto No. 2
Rhapsody for piano and
   orchestra
ALWYN (59)
Concerto Grosso, No. 3
RAWSTHORNE (59)
Symphony No. 3
Elegiac Rhapsody, for strings
TIPPETT (59)
Prologue and Epilogue, for choir
   and orchestra
LUTYENS (58)
Music for Piano and Orchestra
Music for Wind
Scena, for violin, cello and
   percussion
SHOSTAKOVICH (58)
String Quartets Nos. 9 and 10
The Execution of Stepan Razin,
   cantata
MESSIAEN (56)
Couleurs de la cité céleste
SCHUMAN (54)
Symphony No. 9
String Trio
MENOTTI (53)
Martin's Lie, opera
BRITTEN (51)
Cello Suite No. 1
Curlew River, parable for church
   performance
GOULD (51)
*World War I: Revolutionary
   Prelude, Prologue* (1964–65)
Marches: Formations, for band
Festive Music, for off-stage
   trumpet and orchestra
LUTOSLAWSKI (51)
String Quartet
DIAMOND (49)
Quartet No. 8
We Two, song cycle
FRICKER (44)
Symphony No. 4 (1964–66)
ARNOLD (43)
Sinfonietta No. 3
Water Music
FOSS (42)
Elytres, for orchestra

HAMILTON (42)
Organ Concerto
Cantos, for orchestra
Jubilee, for orchestra
BOULEZ (39)
fp. Figures — Doubles — Prismes,
   for orchestra
Éclat, for fifteen instruments
BROWN (38)
Corroborree, for two or three
   pianos
HENZE (38)
The Young Lord, comic opera
Tancredi, ballet
Divertimenti for two pianos
Choral Fantasy
KORTE (36)
Diablerie, for woodwind quintet
MUSGRAVE (36)
The Decision, opera (1964–65)
STOCKHAUSEN (36)
Mikrophonie I
Mixtur, for five orchestral groups
   and electronics
HODDINOTT (35)
fp. Jack Straw, overture
fp. Harp Sonata
fp. Intrada, for organ
fp. Sarum Fanfare, for organ
fp. Toccata all Giga, for organ
fp. Danegeld, for unaccompanied
   voices
WILLIAMSON (33)
The Display, dance symphony
The Merry Wives of Windsor,
   incidental music
Piano Concerto No. 3
Sinfonia concertante, for piano,
   trumpets and orchestra
Variations for cello and piano
Elegy J.F.K., for organ
Three Shakespeare Songs, for
   voice and guitar (or piano)
GOEHR (32)
*Five Poems and an Epigram of
   William Blake*, for chorus
PENDERECKI (31)
Sonata for cello and orchestra
BIRTWHISTLE (30)
Three Movements with Fanfares,
   for orchestra
Entr'actes and Sappho Fragments,   CONTINUED

BIRTWHISTLE CONTINUED
for soprano and instruments
*Description of the Passing of a
Year*, narration for mixed
choir a cappella
DAVIES (30)
Second Fantasia on John
Taverner's "In Nomine", for
orchestra
Shakespeare Music
MAW (29)
One Man Show, comic opera
Corpus Christi Carol
Balulalow, for unaccompanied
voices

BENNETT (28)
The Mines of Sulphur, opera
Jazz Calendar, ballet
Aubade, for orchestra
String Quartet No. 4
Nocturnes, for piano
BEDFORD (27)
A Dream of Seven Lost Stars, for
choir and chamber orchestra
(1964–65)
NILSSON (27)
La Bran, for choir and orchestra
TAVENER (20)
The Cappemakers, for narrators,
solo voices, chorus and
instruments

1965

KODÁLY (83)
Variations for piano
MALIPIERO (83)
Costellazioni, for piano
MARTIN (75)
Cello Concerto (1965–66)
PISTON (71)
Symphony No. 8
Pine Tree Fantasy, for orchestra
Ricercare, for orchestra
JACOB (70)
Festival Te Deum
SOWERBY (70)
Solomon's Garden, for chorus and
orchestra
GERHARD (69)
Concerto for orchestra
SESSIONS (69)
Piano Sonata No. 3
HARRIS (67)
Symphony No. 10
Rhythm and Spaces, for string
orchestra
CHÁVEZ (66)
Violin Concerto No. 2
Soli No. 3, for bassoon, trumpet,
viola, timpani and orchestra
Inventions No. 2, for violin, viola
and cello
RUBBRA (64)
Inscape, suite for chorus, strings
and harp

RODRIGO (63)
Sonata Pimpante, for violin and
piano (1965–66)
WALTON (63)
The Twelve, for chorus and
orchestra
BERKELEY (62)
Partita, for chamber orchestra
Three songs for four male voices
KHACHATURIAN (62)
Concerto-Rhapsody, for cello and
orchestra
KABALEVSKY (61)
Symphonic Prelude
Rondo for cello and piano
RAWSTHORNE (60)
Tankas of the Four Seasons, for
tenor and chamber ensemble
Concertante, for violin and piano
TIPPETT (60)
Vision of St. Augustine, for
baritone, chorus and orchestra
The Shires Suite, for chorus and
orchestra (1965–70)
LUTYENS (59)
The Numbered, opera
The Valley of Hatsu-Se, for solo
voice and instruments
SHOSTAKOVICH (59)
Five Romances on texts from
Krokodil magazine, for bass
and piano

MESSIAEN (57)
La Transfiguration de notre Seigneur Jésus-Christ (1965–69)
CAGE (53)
Variations V
BRITTEN (52)
Gemini Variations, for flute, violin and piano (four hands)
Songs and Proverbs of William Blake, for voice and piano
The Poet's Echo, for voice and piano
Voices for Today, for chorus
LUTOSLAWSKI (52)
Paroles tissées, for voice and instruments
BERNSTEIN (47)
Chichester Psalms, for chorus and orchestra
ROCHBERG (47)
Music for the Magic Theater
Zodiac, for orchestra
Black Sounds, for winds and percussion
Contra Mortem et Tempus, for violin, flute, clarinet and piano
La bocca della verita, for violin and piano
FRICKER (45)
Four *Dialogues*, for oboe and piano
Ricercare for organ
Four songs for soprano and piano (or orchestra)
ARNOLD (44)
Five *Fantasies*, for bassoon: clarinet: flute: horn: oboe
SHAPEY (44)
String Trio
Configurations, for flute and piano
FOSS (43)
Fragments of Archilochos, for chorus, speaker, soloists and chamber ensemble
HAMILTON (43)
String Quartet No. 2
Dialogues, for soprano and instruments
Aubade, for solo organ

BERIO (40)
Laborintus II, for voices, instruments and tape
Rounds, for cembalo
Sequence III, for solo voice
BROWN (39)
String Quartet
Nine Rarebits, for one or two harpsichords
FELDMAN (39)
De Kooning, for piano trio, horn and percussion
Journey to the End of Night, for soprano and four wind instruments
Four Instruments
HENZE (38)
The Bassarids, opera
In Memoriam: The White Rose, for chamber orchestra
KORTE (37)
String Quartet No. 2
Aspects of Love, songs
MUSGRAVE (37)
Festival Overture
Excursions, for piano (four hands)
STOCKHAUSEN (37)
Stop, for orchestra
Mikrophonie II
Solo (1965–66)
HODDINOTT (36)
fp. Concerto grosso No. 1
fp. Aubade and Scherzo, for horn and strings
fp. Dives and Lazarus, cantata
WILLIAMSON (34)
The Happy Prince, opera
Violin Concerto
Concerto grosso, for orchestra
Sinfonietta
Symphonic Variations, for orchestra
Concerto for two pianos and wind quintet
Four North-Country Songs, for voice and orchestra
GOEHR (33)
Pastorals, for orchestra
PENDERECKI (32)
Capriccio, for oboe and strings

CONTINUED

BIRTWHISTLE (31)
Tragoedia, for instrumental
    ensemble
Ring a Dumb Carillon, for soprano,
    clarinet and percussion
Carmen Paschale, motet for
    mixed chorus and organ
DAVIES (31)
Revelation and Fall, for soprano
    and instruments
The Shepherd's Calendar, for singer
    and instruments
Shall I die for mannes sake, for
    soprano and alto voices and
    piano
Ecce manus tradentis, for mixed
    choir and instruments
MAW (30)
String Quartet

BENNETT (29)
Symphony No. 1
Trio for oboe, flute and clarinet
Diversions, for piano
BEDFORD (28)
This One for You, for orchestra
Music for Albion Moonlight, for
    soprano and instruments
"O now the drenched land
    awakes", for baritone and
    piano duet
NILSSON (28)
*Litanei uber das verlorene
    Schlagzeug*
TAVENER (21)
Chamber Concerto (revised
    1968)
The Whale, for chorus and
    orchestra (1965–66)
Cain and Abel, cantata

1966   TAYLOR died

MALIPIERO (84)
Symphony No. 9
STRAVINSKY (84)
Requiem Canticles, for solo voices,
    chorus and orchestra
MOORE (73)
Carry Nation, opera
PISTON (72)
Variations for cello and
    orchestra
Piano Trio No. 2
CASTELNUOVO-TEDESCO (71)
Sonata for cello and harp
JACOB (71)
Oboe Sonata
Variations on a theme of
    Schubert
SOWERBY (71)
Symphonia brevis, for organ
GERHARD (70)
Epithalium, for orchestra
Gemini, for violin and piano
HANSON (70)
Summer Seascape
ROBERTSON (70)
Piano Concerto
SESSIONS (70)
Symphony No. 6
Six Pieces for Cello

THOMSON (70)
Lord Byron, opera (1966–68)
*Fantasy in Homage to an Earlier
    England*, for orchestra
The Nativity, for soloists, chorus
    and orchestra (1966–67)
Étude, for cello and piano
TANSMAN (69)
Concertino, for oboe and chamber
    orchestra
CHÁVEZ (67)
Soli No. 4, for brass trio
WALTON (64)
Missa brevis
KHACHATURIAN (63)
Suite for Orchestra, No. 4
KABALEVSKY (62)
The Motherland, cantata
ALWYN (61)
Derby Day, overture
RAWSTHORNE (61)
Cello Concerto
Sonatine, for flute, oboe and
    piano
String Quartet No. 3
TIPPETT (61)
The Knot Garden, opera
    (1966–70)

LUTYENS (60)
The Fall of the Leafe, for oboe
and string quartet
Music for Three, for flute, oboe
and piano
Akapotik Rose, for soprano and
instruments
And Suddenly It's Evening, for
tenor and instruments
SHOSTAKOVICH (60)
Cello Concerto No. 2
String Quartet No. 11
Preface . . ., for bass and piano
BARBER (56)
Anthony and Cleopatra, opera
CAGE (54)
Variations VI
BRITTEN (53)
The Burning Fiery Furnace,
parable for church performance
The Golden Vanity, for boys and
piano
GOULD (53)
Columbia, for orchestra
Venice, audiograph for two
orchestras
DIAMOND (51)
Quartets Nos. 9 and 10
ARNELL (49)
Robert Flaherty, portrait
FRICKER (46)
Three Scenes, for orchestra
The Day and the Spirits, for
soprano and harp (1966–67)
Fantasy for viola and piano
SHAPEY (45)
Partita, for violin and thirteen
players
Poème, for violin and piano
Mutations No. 2, for piano
Partita, for solo violin
FOSS (44)
Discrepancy, for twenty-four wind
instruments
HAMILTON (44)
Five Scenes, for trumpet and
piano
Flute Sonata
Threnos, for organ
LIGETI (43)
Cello Concerto
Lux aeterna

BERIO (41)
*Il cambattimento de Tancredi e
Clorinda*, for voices, violins
and continuo
Sequence IV, for piano
Sequence V, for trombone
BROWN (40)
Modules 1 and 2, for orchestra
FELDMAN (40)
First Principles (1966–67)
HENZE (39)
Double Concerto for oboe, harp
and strings
Fantasia for Strings
Muses of Sicily, for chorus,
pianos, wind instruments and
timpani
MUSGRAVE (38)
Nocturnes and Arias, for orchestra
Chamber Concertos Nos. 2 and 3
STOCKHAUSEN (38)
Adieu, for wind quintet
Hymnen, for mixed media
Telemusik, electronic music
HODDINOTT (37)
fp. Pantomime, overture
fp. Piano Concerto No. 3
fp. Variants, for orchestra
fp. Concerto grosso, No. 2
fp. String Quartet No. 1
fp. Piano Sonata No. 4
WILLIAMSON (35)
Julius Caesar Jones, opera
The Violins of St. Jacques, opera
Sun Into Darkness, ballet
Five Preludes for piano
Two Organ Epitaphs for Edith
Sitwell
Six English Lyrics, for voice and
piano
GOEHR (34)
Arden Muss Sterben (Arden Must
Die), opera
BIRTWHISTLE (32)
Punch and Judy, opera (1966–67)
Verses, for clarinet and piano
DAVIES (32)
Notre Dame des fleurs, for solo
voices and instruments
Five carols

CONTINUED

MAW (31)
Sinfonia for small orchestra
The Voice of Love, song cycle
BENNETT (30)
Epithalamion, for voices and
  orchestra
Childe Rolande, for voice and
  piano

BEDFORD (29)
That White and Radiant Legend,
  for soprano, speaker and
  instruments
Piano Piece I

1967   AUBERT and KODÁLY died

KODÁLY (85)
Laudes Organi, for chorus and
  organ
MALIPIERO (85)
Symphony No. 10
Carnet de Notes, for chamber
  orchestra
Cassazione, for string sextet
MARTIN (77)
String Quartet
BLISS (76)
River Music, for unaccompanied
  choir
PISTON (73)
Clarinet Concerto
JACOB (72)
Concerto for Band
Six miniatures
Animal Magic, cantata
SOWERBY (72)
Organ Concerto No. 2
Dialogue, for organ and piano
Organ Passacaglia
GERHARD (71)
Symphony No. 4, *New York*
HANSON (71)
Dies Natalis, for orchestra
SESSIONS (71)
Symphony No. 7
THOMSON (71)
Shipwreck and Love Scene, from
  "Don Juan", for tenor and
  orchestra
HARRIS (69)
Symphony No. 11
CHÁVEZ (68)
Inventions No. 3, for harp
COPLAND (67)
Inscape, for orchestra

DURUFLÉ (65)
Mass *Cum jubilo*, for baritone,
  choir, organ and orchestra
RODRIGO (65)
Concierto andaluz, for four guitars
  and orchestra
WALTON (65)
The Bear, opera
BERKELEY (64)
Castaway, opera
Oboe Quartet
Nocturne for harp
Signs in the Dark, for voices and
  strings
KABALEVSKY (63)
Recitative and Rondo, for piano
RAWSTHORNE (62)
Overture for Farnham
Theme, Variations and Finale, for
  orchestra
Scena rustica, for soprano and
  harp
The God in the Cave, cantata
LUTYENS (61)
*Time Off? Not the ghost of a
  chance*, charade
Novenaria, for orchestra
Scroll for Li-Ho, for violin and
  piano
Helix, for piano (four hands)
SHOSTAKOVICH (61)
Violin Concerto No. 2
Funeral—Triumphcl Prelude, for
  orchestra
October, symphonic poem
Seven Romances on poems of
  Alexander Blok, for soprano
  and piano trio
Spring, Spring, for bass and piano
Film music

MENOTTI (56)
Canti della lontananza, song cycle
CAGE (55)
H P S C H D (1967–69)
BRITTEN (54)
The Building of the House,
overture
Cello Suite No. 2
GOULD (54)
Vivaldi Gallery, for string quartet
or divided orchestra
LUTOSLAWSKI (54)
Symphony No. 2
DIAMOND (52)
Choral Symphony, *To Music*
Violin Concerto No. 3
Hebrew Melodies, song cycle
ARNELL (50)
Sections, for piano and orchestra
FRICKER (47)
Seven Counterpoints for
Orchestra
Episodes I, for piano (1967–68)
Ave Maris Stella, for male voices
and piano
Cantilena and Cabaletta, for solo
soprano (1967–68)
ARNOLD (46)
Symphony No. 6
Peterloo, for orchestra
Concert Piece, for piano and
percussion
Trevelyan Suite, for wind band
SHAPEY (46)
Partita-Fantasy, for cello and
sixteen players
Reyem, for flute, violin and
piano
Deux, for two pianos
For Solo Trumpet
Songs of Ecstasy, for soprano,
tape and instruments
FOSS (45)
Cello Concerto
Baroque Variations, for orchestra
Phorion, for orchestra, electronic
organ, harpsichord and guitar
HAMILTON (45)
Agamemnon, opera (1967–69)
Royal Hunt of the Sun, opera
(1967–69)

LIGETI (44)
Lontana, for orchestra
Two Studies for Organ
(1967–69)
MENNIN (44)
Piano Sonata
BERIO (42)
Rounds, for piano
Sequence VI, for viola
O King, for voice and five players
BROWN (41)
Event—Synergy II (1967–68)
FELDMAN (41)
Chorus and Instruments
In Search of an Orchestration
HENZE (40)
Piano Concerto No. 2
Telemanniana, for orchestra
Moralities, three scenic cantatas
MUSGRAVE (39)
Concerto for Orchestra
Music for horn and piano
Impromptu, for flute and oboe
STOCKHAUSEN (39)
Prozession, for mixed media
HODDINOTT (37)
fp. Organ Concerto
fp. Night Music, for orchestra
fp. Clarinet Sonata
fp. Suite for harp
WILLIAMSON (36)
Dunstan and the Devil, opera
Pas de Quatre, ballet
The Moonrakers, cassation
Serenade, for instruments
Sonata for two pianos
GOEHR (35)
String Quartet No. 2
Warngedichte, for voice and piano
PENDERECKI (34)
Pittsburgh Overture, for wind and
percussion
Dies Irae, oratorio
DAVIES (33)
Antechrist, for chamber ensemble
Hymnos, for clarinet and piano
MAW (32)
Sonata for strings and two horns
Double Canon for Igor Stravinsky

CONTINUED

BENNETT (31)
A Penny for a Song, opera
Symphony No. 2
Wind Quintet
The Music That Her Echo Is, song
  cycle
BEDFORD (30)
Trona for Twelve, instrumental
  ensemble
Five, for five strings
18 Bricks Left on April 21st, for
  two electric guitars

NILSSON (30)
Revue, for orchestra
TAVENER (23)
Grandma's Footsteps, for chamber
  orchestra
Three Surrealist Songs
  (1967–68)

1968   CASTELNUOVO-TEDESCO and SOWERBY died

MALIPIERO (86)
Gli eroi di Bonaventura
Flute Concerto
MARTIN (78)
Piano Concerto No. 2
Maria-Triptychon, for soprano,
  solo violin and orchestra
JACOB (73)
Divertimento
Suite for bassoon and string
  quartet
GERHARD (72)
Libra, for flute, clarinet, violin,
  guitar, piano and percussion
HANSON (72)
Symphony No. 6
SESSIONS (72)
Symphony No. 8
TANSMAN (71)
Four Movements for orchestra
HARRIS (70)
Concerto for amplified piano,
  brasses and percussion
Piano Sextet
RUBBRA (67)
Symphony No. 8
Violin Sonata No. 3
Advent Cantata
RODRIGO (66)
Concierto madrigal, for two guitars
  and orchestra
WALTON (66)
Capriccio burlesca, for orchestra
BERKELEY (65)
Theme and variations for piano
  duet
The Windhover, for mixed choir

KABALEVSKY (64)
Sisters, opera
Colas Breugnon, revised version
RAWSTHORNE (63)
Concerto for two pianos and
  orchestra
Trio for flute, viola and harp
LUTYENS (62)
Essence of Our Happiness, for
  voices and orchestra
A Phoenix, for soprano and
  instruments
Horai, for violin horn and piano
Epithalanium, for organ (soprano
  solo optional)
The Egocentric, for voice and
  piano
The Tyme Doth Flete, for
  unaccompanied voices
SHOSTAKOVICH (62)
String Quartet No. 12
Sonata, for violin and grand
  piano
MENOTTI (57)
Help, help, the Globolinks,
  children's opera
BRITTEN (55)
The Children's Crusade, for
  children's voices and
  orchestra
The Prodigal Son, parable for
  church performance
GOULD (55)
Troubador Music, for four guitars
  and orchestra
LUTOSLAWSKI (55)
Livre pour orchestre

ARNELL (51)
The Food of Love, overture
Nocturne: Prague 1968, for
  mixed media
ROCHBERG (50)
Symphony No. 3, *A 20th-
  century Passion*
Tableaux, for soprano and eleven
  players
FRICKER (48)
Concertante No. 4, for flute, oboe,
  violin and strings
Refrains, for solo oboe
Gladius Domini, toccata for organ
Six Pieces for organ
Magnificat, for solo voices, choir
  and orchestra
Some Serious Nonsense, for tenor
  and instruments
HAMILTON (46)
Pharsalia, opera
LIGETI (45)
Ramifications, for string
  orchestra (1968–69)
Ten Pieces for wind quintet
String Quartet No. 2
Continuum, for harpsichord
MENNIN (45)
Cantata de virtute (1968–69)
BERIO (43)
Sinfonia
Queste vuol dire che, for three
  female voices, small choir and
  tape
BOULEZ (43)
fp. Domaines, for clarinet and
  twenty-one instruments
FELDMAN (42)
*False Relationships and the
  Extended Ending*, for two
  chamber groups
Vertical Thoughts 2
HENZE (41)
Essay on Pigs, for voice and
  orchestra
The Raft of the "Medusa",
  oratorio
KORTE (40)
Symphony No. 3
Matrix, for instruments
May the Sun Bless Us, for male
  voices, brass and percussion

MUSGRAVE (40)
Beauty and the Beast, ballet
  (1968–69)
Clarinet Concerto
STOCKHAUSEN (40)
Aus den Sieben Tagen, fifteen
  compositions for ensemble
Für Kommende Zeiten, for
  ensemble
Kurzwellen, for piano and
  amplified instruments
Spiral, for mixed media
Stimmung, for six vocalists
HODDINOTT (39)
fp. Symphony No. 3
fp. Sinfonietta 1
fp. Fioriture, for orchestra
fp. Divertimenti for eight
  instruments
fp. Nocturnes and Cadenzas, for
  clarinet, violin and piano
fp. Piano Sonata No. 5
fp. Roman Dream, for soprano
  and instruments
fp. An Apple Tree and a Pig, for
  unaccompanied voices
WILLIAMSON (37)
The Growing Castle, opera
Knights in Shining Armour,
  cassation
The Snow Wolf, cassation
Piano Quintet
From a Child's Garden, twelve
  poems for voice and piano
GOEHR (36)
Naboth's Vineyard, dramatic
  madrigal
Romanza, for cello and orchestra
PENDERECKI (35)
The Devils of Loudon, opera
String Quartet No. 2
Capriccio for Seigfried Palm, for
  solo cello
BIRTWHISTLE (34)
Nomos, for four amplified wind
  instruments and orchestra
Linoi, for clarinet and piano
DAVIES (34)
L'Homme Armé, for speaker (or
  singer) and chamber ensemble

CONTINUED

BENNETT (32)
All the King's Men, children's
    opera
Piano Concerto
Crazy Jane, for soprano and
    instruments

BEDFORD (31)
Gastrula, for orchestra
Pentomino, for wind quintet
Piano Piece II
"Come in here, child", for
    soprano and amplified piano
TAVENER (24)
In Alium, for soprano and
    orchestra

1969

MARTIN (79)
Erasme Monumentum, for
    orchestra and organ
Poèmes de la mort, for solo male
    voices and three electric
    guitars
BLISS (78)
*The World is Charged with the
    Grandeur of God*, for chorus
    and wind
Miniature Scherzo for piano
Angels of the Mind, song cycle
JACOB (74)
Redbridge Variations
Piano Quartet
ORFF (74)
De Temporum fine comoedia,
    cantata (1969–71)
GERHARD (73)
Leo, chamber symphony
TANSMAN (72)
Hommage à Erasme de Rotherdam,
    for orchestra
Concertino, for flute and chamber
    orchestra
HARRIS (71)
Symphony No. 12
CHÁVEZ (70)
Clio, Symphonic ode
Discovery, for orchestra
Fuego olimpico, suite for orchestra
RUBBRA (68)
Missa brevis
BERKELEY (66)
Symphony No. 3
Windsor Variations, for piano duet
RAWSTHORNE (64)
Triptych, for orchestra

LUTYENS (63)
Isis and Osiris, lyric drama
String Trio
The Tides of Time, for double-bass
    and piano
The Dying of the Sun, for guitar
Temenos, for organ
SHOSTAKOVICH (63)
Symphony No. 14
BARBER (59)
Despite and Still, song cycle
SCHUMAN (59)
In Praise of Shahn, canticle for
    orchestra
CAGE (57)
Cheap Imitation
BRITTEN (56)
Suite for harp
"Who are these children?", for
    tenor and piano
GOULD (56)
Soundings
LUTOSLAWSKI (56)
Cello Concerto (1969–70)
DIAMOND (54)
Music for Chamber Orchestra
FRICKER (49)
Saxophone Quartet
Praeludium, for organ
FOSS (47)
Geod, for orchestra, with optional
    voices
HAMILTON (47)
Circus, for two trumpets and
    orchestra
LIGETI (46)
Chamber Concertante, for thirteen
    instruments (1969–70)

BERIO (44)
Opera
Modification (Hornpipe) for five
  instruments
Sequence VII, for oboe
FELDMAN (43)
*On Time and the Instrumental
  Factor*, for orchestra
BROWN (42)
Modules 3, for orchestra
HENZE (42)
Symphony No. 6
Compases, for viola and twenty-
  two players (1969–70)
El Cimarrón, recital for four
  musicians (1969–70)
KORTE (41)
Facets, for saxophone quartet
Dialogues, for saxophone and
  tape
MUSGRAVE (41)
Memento vitae, for orchestra
  (1969–70)
Night Music, for chamber
  orchestra
Soliloquy, for guitar and tape
STOCKHAUSEN (41)
Fresco, for four orchestral groups
For Dr. K., for instruments
Pole für 2 (1969–70)
Expo für 3 (1969–70)
HODDINOTT (40)
fp. Symphony No. 4
fp. Divertimento, for orchestra
fp. Sinfonietta 2
fp. Horn Concerto
fp. Nocturnes and Cadenzas, for
  cello and orchestra
fp. Investiture Dances, for
  orchestra
fp. Black Bart, for voices and
  orchestra
fp. Violin Sonata No. 1
WILLIAMSON (38)
Lucky Peter's Journey, comedy
  with music
The Brilliant and the Dark, choral-
  operatic sequence
Symphony No. 2

GOEHR (37)
Konzertstücke, for piano and small
  orchestra
Nonomiya, for piano
Paraphrase on a Monteverdi
  madrigal, for solo clarinet
PENDERECKI (36)
Utrenja, for solo voices, choirs,
  and orchestra (1969–71)
BIRTWHISTLE (35)
Down by the Greenwood Side,
  dramatic pastoral
Verses for ensemble, for
  instrumental ensemble
Medusa, for instrumental
  ensemble (1969–70)
Ut Heremita Solus, arrangement
  of instrumental motet
Hoquetus David (Double Hoquet),
  arrangement of instrumental
  motet
Cantata for soprano and
  instrumental ensemble
DAVIES (35)
St. Thomas Wake, for orchestra
Worldes Bliss, for orchestra
Eight Songs for a Mad King, for
  male singer and chamber
  ensemble
Vesalii icones, for dancer, solo
  cello and ensemble
Eram quasi Agnus, instrumental
  motet
MAW (34)
The Rising of the Moon, opera
  (1969–70)
BENNETT (33)
A Garland for Marjory Fleming,
  for soprano and piano
BEDFORD (32)
The Tentacles of the Dark Nebula,
  for tenor and instruments
TAVENER (25)
Celtic Requiem, for voices and
  orchestra

MALIPIERO (88)
Symphony No. 11
MARTIN (80)
Three Dances, for oboe, harp,
    string quintet and string
    orchestra
BLISS (79)
Cello Concerto
JACOB (75)
A York Symphony, for orchestra
A Joyful Noise, for brass band
The Pride of Youth, for brass band
SESSIONS (74)
Rhapsody, for orchestra
*When Lilacs Last in the Dooryard
    Bloom'd*, cantata
RUBBRA (69)
Piano Trio No. 2
WALTON (68)
*Improvisations on an Impromptu
    of Britten*, for orchestra
BERKELEY (67)
Dialogues, for cello and chamber
    orchestra
String Quartet No. 3
Theme and Variations, for guitar
DALLAPICCOLA (66)
Sicut umbra
Tempus aedificandi
ALWYN (65)
Sinfonietta for strings
RAWSTHORNE (65)
Oboe Quartet
TIPPETT (65)
Symphony No. 3 (1970–72)
Songs for Dov, for voice and
    orchestra
LUTYENS (64)
Anerca, for narrator, guitars and
    percussion
Vision of Youth, for soprano and
    instruments
In the Direction of the Beginning,
    for voice and piano
Oda a la Tormenta, for mezzo-
    soprano and piano
Verses of Love, for unaccompanied
    voices

SHOSTAKOVICH (64)
March of the Soviet Militia, for
    wind orchestra
String Quartet No. 13
Loyalty, for male chorus
Film music
MENOTTI (59)
The Leper, drama
Triplo concerto a tre, symphonic
    piece
BRITTEN (57)
Owen Wingrave, opera
ROCHBERG (52)
Mizmor L'Piyus, for bass-baritone
    and small orchestra
Songs of Krishna, for soprano and
    piano
FRICKER (50)
Paseo, for guitar
The Roofs, for soprano and
    percussion
HAMILTON (48)
Alastor, for orchestra
Voyage, for horn and chamber
    orchestra
Epitaph for this world and time,
    for three choirs and three
    organs
BERIO (45)
Memory, for electric piano and
    electric cembalo
BOULEZ (45)
Multiples, for orchestra
fp. Cummings ist der Dichter, for
    voices and instruments
FELDMAN (44)
Madam Press died last week at 90
The Viola in My Life, I, II and III
BROWN (43)
Syntagm III, for instrumental
    ensemble
KORTE (42)
Gestures, for electric brass,
    percussion, piano and band
Psalm XIII, for chorus and tape
MUSGRAVE (42)
Elegy, for viola and cello
From one to another, for viola
    and tape
Impromptu No. 2 for flute,
    oboe and clarinet

STOCKHAUSEN (42)
Mantra, for two pianists
HODDINOTT (41)
fp. The Sun, the Great Luminary of the Universe, for orchestra
fp. Sinfonietta 3
fp. Violin Sonata No. 2
fp. Cello Sonata
fp. Fantasy for harp
GOEHR (38)
Symphony in one movement
Concerto for eleven instruments
Sonata about Jerusalem
Shadowplay 2, music theater for tenor and instruments
PENDERECKI (37)
Kosmogonia, for solo voices, chorus and orchestra
BIRTWHISTLE (36)
Four Interludes from a Tragedy, for clarinet and tape
Nenia on the Death of Orpheus, for soprano and instruments
Prologue, for tenor and instruments
DAVIES (36)
Taverner, opera
BENNETT (34)
Guitar Concerto
BEDFORD (33)
The Garden of Love, for instrumental ensemble
The Sword of Orion, for instrumental ensemble
NILSSON (33)
Attraktionen, for string quartet
TAVENER (26)
Nomine Jesu, for voices and orchestra
Coplas, for voices and tape

RAWSTHORNE, ROBERTSON and STRAVINSKY died   **1971**

MARTIN (81)
Requiem (1971–72)
BLISS (80)
Two Ballads for women's chorus and small orchestra
Triptych, for piano
JACOB (76)
Rhapsody for three hands (piano)
SESSIONS (75)
Concerto for viola and cello
COPLAND (71)
Duo for flute and piano
BERKELEY (68)
"Palm Court Waltz", for orchestra, or piano duet
In Memoriam Igor Stravinsky, for string quartet
"Duo" for cello and piano
Introduction and Allegro, for double-bass and piano
Chinese Songs, for voice and piano
DALLAPICCOLA (67)
Tempus destruendi
RAWSTHORNE (66)
Quintet for piano, clarinet, horn, violin and cello
LUTYENS (65)
Dirge for the Proud World, for soprano, counter-tenor, harpsichord and cello
Driving Out the Death, for oboe and string trio
Islands, for narrator, solo voices and instrumental ensemble
Requiescat (Igor Stravinsky 1971), for soprano and string trio
The Tears of Night, for voices and instruments
SHOSTAKOVICH (65)
Symphony No. 15
BARBER (61)
The Lovers, for baritone, chorus and orchestra
MENOTTI (60)
fp. The Most Important Man in the World, opera
BRITTEN (58)
Cello Suite No. 3
Canticle IV, "Journey of the Magi"
GOULD (58)
Suite for tuba and three horns

CONTINUED

ARNELL (54)
I think of all soft limbs, for
mixed media
BERNSTEIN (53)
Mass, theater piece for singers,
players and dancers
FRICKER (51)
*Sarabande in memoriam Igor
Stravinsky*
Nocturne, for chamber orchestra
Concertante No. 5, for piano and
string quartet
A Bourrée for Sir Arthur Bliss, for
cello
Intrada, for organ
HAMILTON (49)
Violin Concerto No. 2, *Amphion*
LIGETI (48)
Melodien, for orchestra
Horizont, for recorder
MENNIN (48)
Sinfonia for Orchestra
BERIO (46)
Bewegung I and II, for orchestra
Ora, for voice, instruments and
small orchestra
Autre fois, for flute, clarinet and
harp
Agnus, for two sopranos and
three clarinets
Amores, for voices and
instruments
FELDMAN (45)
Chorus and Orchestra I
The Viola in My Life IV
Three clarinets, cello and piano
Rothko Chapel
I Met Heine . . .
HENZE (44)
Violin Concerto No. 2
Heliogabalus imperator, for
orchestra (1971–72)
KORTE (43)
I think you would have understood,
for mixed media
Remembrances, for flute and tape
MUSGRAVE (43)
Horn Concerto
Primavera, for soprano and flute
STOCKHAUSEN (43)
Sternklang, for five groups
Trans, for orchestra

HODDINOTT (42)
fp. The Tree of Life, for solo voices,
chorus, organ and orchestra
fp. Concertino, for trumpet, horn
and orchestra
fp. Oboe Concerto
fp. Horn Sonata
fp. Violin Sonata No. 3
fp. Out of the Deep, motet
WILLIAMSON (40)
Genesis, cassation
The Stone Wall, cassation
Death of Cuchulain, for five male
voices and percussion
Peace Pieces, for organ
In Place of Belief, settings of ten
poems, for voices and piano
duet
PENDERECKI (38)
Actions, for jazz ensemble
De Natura Sonoris, II, for winds,
percussion and strings
Prélude (1971), for winds,
percussion and double-basses
BIRTWHISTLE (37)
An Imaginary Landscape, for
orchestra
The Fields of Sorrow, for voices
and instruments
Meridian, for voices and
instruments
Chronometer, for eight-track
electronic tape
DAVIES (37)
From Stone to Thorn, for mezzo-
soprano and instruments
MAW (36)
*Epitaph — Canon in memory of Igor
Stravinsky*, for flute, clarinet
and harp
BEDFORD (34)
Nurse's Song with Elephants, for
singer and ten acoustic
guitars
*Star Clusters, Nebulae and Places
in Devon*, for mixed double
chorus and brass
With One Hundred Kazoos, for
instrumental ensemble and
kazoos
"Some Stars Above Magnitude
2.9", for soprano and piano

TAVENER (27)
In memoriam Igor Stravinsky, for
two alto flutes, organ and

bells
Responsorium, for voices and
flutes

GROFÉ died   **1972**

MARTIN (82)
Ballade, for viola, wind orchestra,
cembalo, harp and timpani
BLISS (81)
Metamorphic Variations, for
orchestra
Three songs
JACOB (77)
Double-bass Concerto
Tuba Suite
Psalm 103
COPLAND (72)
Three Latin-American Sketches
WALTON (70)
Sonata for string orchestra
Jubilate Deo, for double chorus
and organ
Five bagatelles for guitar
BERKELEY (69)
Four Concert Studies for piano,
set 2
"Hymn for Shakespeare's
Birthday", for mixed choir
and organ
Three Latin motets, for five-part
choir
TIPPETT (67)
Piano Sonata No. 3 (1972–73)
LUTYENS (66)
The Linnet from the Leaf, for
voices and instrumental groups
Voice of Quiet Waters, for chorus
and orchestra
Counting Your Steps, for chorus,
flutes and percussion
Chimes and Cantos, for voice and
instruments
Dialogo, for tenor and lute
Plenum I, for piano
SHOSTAKOVICH (66)
String Quartet No. 14
LUTOSLAWSKI (59)
Preludes and Fugue, for thirteen
solo strings

ROCHBERG (54)
String Quartet No. 3
Electrikaleidoscope
Ricordanza, for cello and piano
FRICKER (52)
Introitus, for orchestra
Ballade, for flute and piano
Fanfare for Europe, for trumpet
Come Sleep, for contralto, alto
flute and bass-clarinet
Seven Little Songs for Chorus
FOSS (50)
Ni bruit, ni vitesse, for pianos and
percussion
Cave of the Winds, for wind
quintet
HAMILTON (50)
Commedia, concerto for orchestra
Palinodes, for solo piano
Descent of the Celestial City, for
chorus and organ
LIGETI (49)
Kylwyria, opera
Double Concerto for flute, oboe
and orchestra
BERIO (47)
Concerto for two pianos and
orchestra (1972–73)
E Vó, for soprano and
instruments
Recital I (for Cathy), for mezzo-
soprano and instruments
BOULEZ (47)
. . . Explosante-fixe . . ., for
ensemble and live electronics
(1972–74)
FELDMAN (46)
Cello and Orchestra
Chorus and Orchestra II
Voice and Instruments
Voices and Instruments
Pianos and Voices I and II

CONTINUED

BROWN (45)
Time Spans, for orchestra
New Piece: Loops, for chorus
and/or orchestra
Sign Sounds, for instrumental
ensemble
MUSGRAVE (44)
The Voice of Ariadne, chamber
opera (1972–73)
STOCKHAUSEN (44)
Alphabet für Liege
Am Himmel Wander Ich . . .,
Indianerlieder
Ylem, for nineteen players/
singers
HODDINOTT (43)
fp. Aubade, for small orchestra
fp. Piano Sonata No. 6
fp. The Hawk is Set Free, for
orchestra
WILLIAMSON (41)
The Red Sea, opera
Symphony No. 3, *The Icy Mirror*,
for solo voices, chorus and
orchestra
Partita for Viola, on themes of
Walton
The Musicians of Bremen, for six
male voices
Love the Sentinel, for
unaccompanied voices
PENDERECKI (39)
Partita, for harpsichord, five solo
instruments (amplified) and
orchestra
Canticum canticorum Salomonis
(Song of Songs), for sixteen-
voice chorus, chamber
orchestra and dance pair
BIRTWHISTLE (38)
The Triumph of Time, for
orchestra
*Tombeau — In memoriam Igor
Stravinsky*, for flute, clarinet,
harp and string quartet
Dinah and Nick's Love Song, for

instruments
La Plage, for soprano and
instruments
Epilogue — Full Fathom Five, for
baritone and instruments
DAVIES (38)
Blind Man's Buff, masque
*Canon in memory of Igor
Stravinsky*, for instrumental
ensemble
Fool's Fanfare, for speaker and
instruments
Hymn to St. Magnus, for
soprano and chamber
ensemble
Tenebrae super Gesualdo, for
mezzo-soprano, guitar and
chamber ensemble
MAW (37)
Concert Music for Orchestra
Five Irish Songs, for chorus
BENNETT (36)
Commedia II, for flute, cello and
piano
BEDFORD (35)
An Easy Decision, for soprano
and piano
Holy Thursday with Squeakers, for
soprano and instruments
Spillihpnerak, for viola
*When I Heard the Learned
Astronomer*, for tenor and
instruments
TAVENER (28)
Variations on "Three Blind Mice",
for orchestra
Ultimos ritos, for voices and
orchestra with amplified
instruments
Ma fin est mon commencement,
for voices and instruments
Canciones espanolas, for voices
and instruments
*Little Requiem for Father Malachy
Lynch*

1973   MALIPIERO died

MARTIN (83)
Polyptyque, for violin and two
small string orchestras

Fantasy on Flamenco rhythms, for
piano

JACOB (78)
Saxophone Quartet
ORFF (78)
Rota, for chorus and instruments
THOMSON (77)
Cantata based on Nonsense
  Rhymes
BERKELEY (71)
Antiphon, for string orchestra
Voices of the Night, for orchestra
Sinfonia concertante, for oboe
  and orchestra
ALWYN (68)
Symphony No. 5, *Hydriotaphia*
LUTYENS (67)
One and the Same, scena for
  soprano, speaker, two female
  mimes, male mime and
  instrumental ensemble
The Waiting Game, three scenes
  for mezzo-soprano, baritone
  and small orchestra
Rape of the Moone, for wind octet
Laudi, for soprano and
  instruments
Roads, for two sopranos, counter-
  tenor, baritone and bass
Plenum II, for solo oboe
Plenum III, for string quartet
Tre, for solo clarinet
SHOSTAKOVICH (67)
Six poems of Maria Tsvetaeva,
  suite for contralto and piano
BARBER (63)
fp. String Quartet
SCHUMAN (63)
Concerto on Old English Rounds,
  for solo viola, women's
  chorus and orchestra
MENOTTI (62)
fp. Suite for two cellos and piano
BRITTEN (60)
Death in Venice, opera
ARNELL (56)
Astronaut One, for mixed media
FRICKER (53)
Gigue for cello
The Grove of Dodona, for six flutes
ARNOLD (52)
Symphony No. 7
FOSS (51)
MAP, a musical game

MENNIN (50)
fp. Symphony No. 8
BERIO (48)
Eindrücke, for orchestra
  (1973–74)
Still, for orchestra
. . . Points on the Curve to Find . . .,
  for piano and twenty-two
  instruments
Linea, for two pianos, vibraphone
  and marimba
FELDMAN (47)
String Quartet and Orchestra
Voices and cello
For Frank O'Hara
BROWN (46)
Centering, for solo violin and ten
  instruments
MUSGRAVE (45)
Viola Concerto
STOCKHAUSEN (45)
Inori, for soloist and orchestra
  (1973–74)
HODDINOTT (44)
fp. Symphony No. 5
fp. The Floore of Heav'n, for
  orchestra
WILLIAMSON (42)
The Winter Star, cassation
Concerto for two pianos and
  strings
Ode to Music, for chorus, echo
  chorus and orchestra
Pietà, for soprano, oboe, bassoon
  and piano
Canticle of Fire, for chorus and
  organ
Little Carols of the Saints, five
  organ pieces
The World at the Manger, cantata
PENDERECKI (40)
Symphony
BIRTWHISTLE (39)
Grimethorpe Aria, for brass band
Five Choral Preludes arranged
  from Bach, for soprano and
  instrumental ensemble
Chanson de geste, for solo
  sustaining instrument and
  tape

CONTINUED

DAVIES (39)
Fiddlers at the Wedding, for mezzo-soprano and chamber orchestra (1973–74)
Stone Litany, for mezzo-soprano and orchestra
Scottish Dances, for instrumental ensemble
MAW (38)
Serenade, for chamber orchestra
Life Studies, for fifteen solo strings
Personae, for piano
BENNETT (37)
Concerto for Orchestra
Viola Concerto
Commedia III and IV
Scena I and II
Alba, for organ

BEDFORD (36)
A Horse, His Name was Hunry Fencewaver Walkins, for instrumental ensemble
Jack of Shadows, for solo viola and instruments
Pancakes . . ., for wind quintet
Variations on a Rhythm by Mike Oldfield, for percussion
TAVENER (29)
Thérèse, opera (1973–76)
Requiem for Father Malachy

1974   MARTIN and MILHAUD died

BLISS (84)
Orchestral prelude *Lancaster*
MARTIN (84)
Et la vie l'emporta, chamber cantata
JACOB (79)
Sinfonia brevis
Havant Suite, for chamber orchestra
Quartet for clarinets
BERKELEY (72)
Guitar Concerto
Suite for Strings
Herrick Songs, for voices and harp
WALTON (72)
Cantico del sole
Magnificat and Nunc Dimittis
LUTYENS (68)
The Winter of the World, for orchestras
Kareniana, for instrumental ensemble
SHOSTAKOVICH (68)
String Quartet No. 15
Four verses of Capitan Lebjadkin, for bass and piano
Suite on verses of Michelangelo Buonarotti, for bass and piano
BRITTEN (61)
Suite on English Folk Tunes, for orchestra
Canticle V, "The death of Narcissus", for tenor and harp
A Birthday Hansel, for voice and harp
DIAMOND (59)
fp. Quartet No. 10
BERNSTEIN (56)
Dybbuk, ballet
ROCHBERG (56)
Imago mundi, for orchestra
FRICKER (54)
Spirit Puck, for clarinet and percussion
Trio-Sonata for organ
Two Petrarch Madrigals
FOSS (52)
fp. Orpheus, for viola, cello (or guitar) and orchestra
HAMILTON (52)
The Cataline Conspiracy, opera
Piano Sonata No. 2
BERIO (49)
Per la dolce memoria di quel giorno, ballet
Aprés visage, for orchestra and tape
Calmo, for soprano and instruments
Chorus, for voices and instruments

BOULEZ (49)
Rituel, in memoriam Maderna, for
   orchestra in eight groups
FELDMAN (48)
Instruments, I
Voice and Instruments, II
KORTE (46)
Libera me, four songs
MUSGRAVE (46)
Space Play, concerto for nine
   instruments
STOCKHAUSEN (46)
Atmen gibt das leben . . . , for
   mixed choir
Herbstmusik
Vortrag über Hu, for solo voice
HODDINOTT (45)
fp. The Beach of Falesa, opera
fp. Ritornelli, for solo trombone,
   winds and percussion
WILLIAMSON (43)
The Glitter Gang, cassation
PENDERECKI (41)
The Dream of Jacob
BIRTWHISTLE (40)
Chorales from a Toyshop, for
   variable orchestration

DAVIES (40)
Miss Donnithorne's Maggot, for
   mezzo-soprano and chamber
   orchestra
Dark Angels, for soprano and
   guitar
All Sons of Adam, motet for
   instrumental ensemble
BENNETT (38)
Spells, for soprano, chorus and
   orchestra
Love Spells, for soprano and
   orchestra
Four-piece Suite, for two pianos
Sonnet Sequence, for tenor and
   strings
Time's Whiter Series, for counter-
   tenor and lute
BEDFORD (37)
Star's End, for rock instruments
   orchestra
Twelve Hours of Sunset, for
   chorus and orchestra
The Golden Wine is Drunk, for
   sixteen solo voices
Because he liked to be at home, for
   tenor, recorder and harp

BLISS, DALLAPICCOLA, GRANDJANY and SHOSTAKOVICH died   **1975**

BLISS (85)
Shield of Faith, cantata
JACOB (80)
Concerto for organ, strings and
   percussion
Rhapsody, for piano
Fantasy Sonata, for organ
HARRIS (77)
Symphony No. 14
SESSIONS (76)
Three Choruses on Biblical texts
BERKELEY (73)
Quintet for piano and wind
LUTYENS (69)
Eos, for small orchestra
Fanfare for a Festival, for three
   trumpets and three trombones
Pietà, for harpsichord
Ring of Bone, for solo piano
SHOSTAKOVICH (69)
The Dreamers, ballet
Sonata for viola and grand piano

BRITTEN (62)
Phaedra, dramatic cantata for
   mezzo-soprano and small
   orchestra
String Quartet No. 3
BERNSTEIN (57)
Seven Dances from *Dybbuk*
Suite No. 1 from *Dybbuk*
ROCHBERG (57)
Violin Concerto
FRICKER (55)
Symphony No. 5
String Quartet No. 3
HAMILTON (53)
Sea Music, for chorus and string
   quartet
Violin Sonata No. 1
Cello Sonata No. 2
Te Deum

CONTINUED

BERIO (50)
Il malato immaginario, incidental
   music
La ritirata notturna di Madrid, for
   orchestra
Sequence VIII, for percussion
Sequence IX, for violin
FELDMAN (49)
Piano and Orchestra
Instruments II
Four Instruments, for piano,
   violin, viola and cello

MUSGRAVE (47)
Orfeo I and II, for flute, strings
   and tape
STOCKHAUSEN (47)
Musik im bauch
Tierkreis (Zodiac)
HODDINOTT (46)
fp. Landscapes, for orchestra
DAVIES (41)
Ave maris stella
BENNETT (39)
Violin Concerto
Oboe Quartet

This timeline enables the reader to see at a glance when each composer was born and died, as well as who was contemporary with whom. Horizontal lines begin with the year of a composer's birth, and end with that of his death. At the end of each line, the composer's age at death is also given.

Composers are listed chronologically in the left-hand column of each page, according to their dates of birth. Where all the composers born within a century cannot be listed on a single page, the latter part of the century is displayed in full overleaf and any timelines which have to be repeated are printed in gray.

The column following a composer's name shows, in almost every case, the country of his birth. Many composers became citizens of and/or ended their lives in some other country (notably the United States). Stravinsky, for example, achieved the right to four passports—Russian, French, British and American. The compilers feel, however, that the country of a composer's birth is usually of greatest interest.

The abbreviations indicate:

Als:	Alsace	Hol:	Holland
Aust:	Australia	Hun:	Hungary
Aus:	Austria	I:	Italy
Bel:	Belgium	Mex:	Mexico
Braz:	Brazil	Nor:	Norway
Cz:	Czechoslovakia	Pol:	Poland
Den:	Denmark	Rum:	Rumania
Fin:	Finland	R:	Russia
F:	France	Sp:	Spain
G:	Germany	Swe:	Sweden
G.B.:	Great Britain	Swi:	Switzerland
	(including Ireland)	U.S.A.:	United States

	1500	1505	1510	1515	1520	1525	1530	1535	1540	1545

TALLIS Thomas/GB
GABRIELLI Andrea/I
PALESTRINA Giovanni/I
BYRD William/GB

	1550	1555	1560	1565	1570	1575	1580	1585	1590	1595

TALLIS Thomas/GB 1505–1585 (80)
GABRIELLI Andrea/I 1510–1586 (76)
PALESTRINA Giovanni/I 1525–1594 (69)
BYRD William/GB
MORLEY Thomas/GB
GABRIELLI Giovanni/I
FARNABY Giles/GB 1560–1600 (40)
CAMPIAN Thomas/GB
SWEELINCK Jan P./Ho.
BULL John/GB
DOWLAND John/GB
MONTEVERDI Claudio/I
FRESCOBALDI Girolamo/I
GIBBONS Orlando/GB
SCHÜTZ Heinrich/G

		1600	1605	1610	1615	1620	1625	1630	1635	1640	1645

BYRD William/GB — 1543–1623 (80)

MORLEY Thomas/GB — 1557–1603 (46)

GABRIELLI Giovanni/I — 1557–1612 (55)

CAMPIAN Thomas/GB — 1562–1620 (58)

SWEELINCK Jan P./Ho. — 1562–1621 (59)

BULL John/GB — 1563–1628 (65)

DOWLAND John/GB — 1563–1626 (63)

MONTEVERDI Claudio/I — 1567–1643 (76)

FRESCOBALDI Girolamo/I — 1583–1643 (60)

GIBBONS Orlando/GB — 1583–1625 (42)

SCHÜTZ Heinrich/G

LULLY Jean-Batiste/F

BUXTEHUDE Dietrich/Den

BLOW John/GB

	1650	1655	1660	1665	1670	1675	1680	1685	1690	1695

TELEMANN Georg/G

RAMEAU Jean P./F

BACH Johann Sebastian/G

HANDEL George F./G

SCARLATTI Domenico/I

PORPORA Niccolò A./I

LECLAIR Jean-Marie/F

SCHÜTZ Heinrich/G — 1585–1672 (87)

LULLY Jean-Batiste/F — 1632–1687 (55)

BUXTEHUDE Dietrich/Den

BLOW John/GB

CORELLI Arcangelo/I

PURCELL Henry/GB — 1659–1695 (36)

SCARLATTI Alessandro/I

COUPERIN François/F

ALBINONI Tommaso/I

VIVALDI Antonio/I

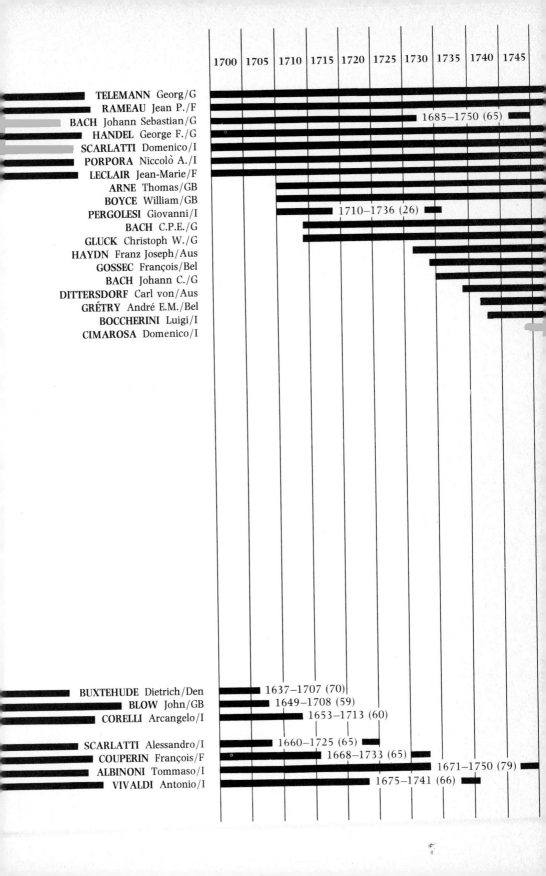

	1700	1705	1710	1715	1720	1725	1730	1735	1740	1745

TELEMANN Georg/G
RAMEAU Jean P./F
BACH Johann Sebastian/G   1685–1750 (65)
HANDEL George F./G
SCARLATTI Domenico/I
PORPORA Niccolò A./I
LECLAIR Jean-Marie/F
ARNE Thomas/GB
BOYCE William/GB
PERGOLESI Giovanni/I   1710–1736 (26)
BACH C.P.E./G
GLUCK Christoph W./G
HAYDN Franz Joseph/Aus
GOSSEC François/Bel
BACH Johann C./G
DITTERSDORF Carl von/Aus
GRÉTRY André E.M./Bel
BOCCHERINI Luigi/I
CIMAROSA Domenico/I

BUXTEHUDE Dietrich/Den   1637–1707 (70)
BLOW John/GB   1649–1708 (59)
CORELLI Arcangelo/I   1653–1713 (60)

SCARLATTI Alessandro/I   1660–1725 (65)
COUPERIN François/F   1668–1733 (65)
ALBINONI Tommaso/I   1671–1750 (79)
VIVALDI Antonio/I   1675–1741 (66)

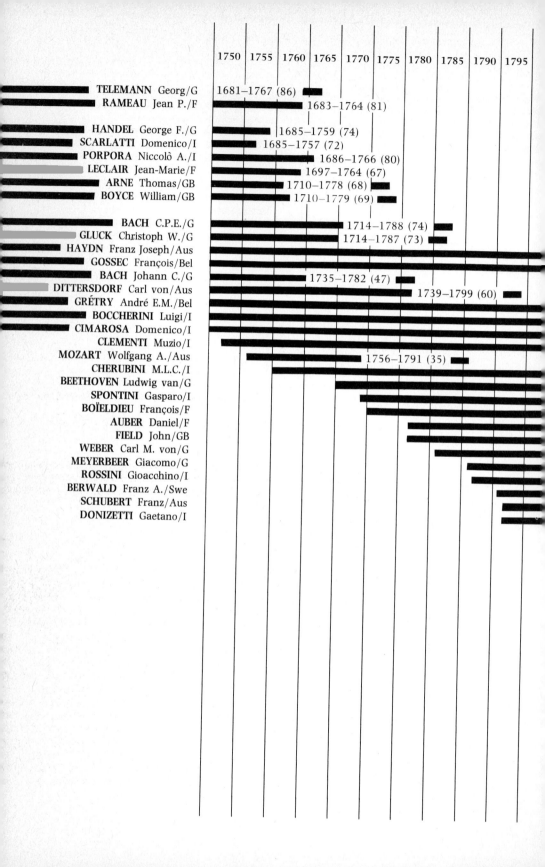

	1750	1755	1760	1765	1770	1775	1780	1785	1790	1795

TELEMANN Georg/G   1681–1767 (86)
RAMEAU Jean P./F   1683–1764 (81)

HANDEL George F./G   1685–1759 (74)
SCARLATTI Domenico/I   1685–1757 (72)
PORPORA Niccolò A./I   1686–1766 (80)
LECLAIR Jean-Marie/F   1697–1764 (67)
ARNE Thomas/GB   1710–1778 (68)
BOYCE William/GB   1710–1779 (69)

BACH C.P.E./G   1714–1788 (74)
GLUCK Christoph W./G   1714–1787 (73)
HAYDN Franz Joseph/Aus
GOSSEC François/Bel
BACH Johann C./G   1735–1782 (47)
DITTERSDORF Carl von/Aus   1739–1799 (60)
GRÉTRY André E.M./Bel
BOCCHERINI Luigi/I
CIMAROSA Domenico/I
CLEMENTI Muzio/I
MOZART Wolfgang A./Aus   1756–1791 (35)
CHERUBINI M.L.C./I
BEETHOVEN Ludwig van/G
SPONTINI Gasparo/I
BOÏELDIEU François/F
AUBER Daniel/F
FIELD John/GB
WEBER Carl M. von/G
MEYERBEER Giacomo/G
ROSSINI Gioacchino/I
BERWALD Franz A./Swe
SCHUBERT Franz/Aus
DONIZETTI Gaetano/I

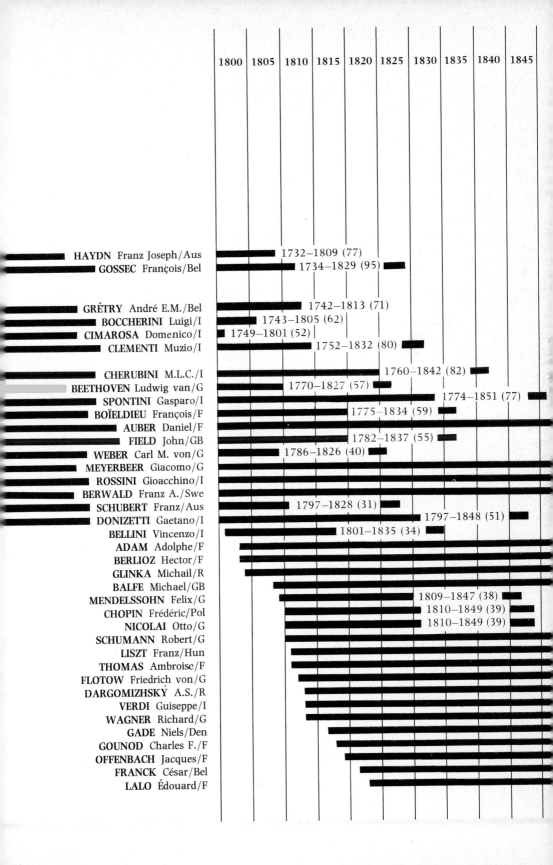

	1800	1805	1810	1815	1820	1825	1830	1835	1840	1845

HAYDN Franz Joseph/Aus — 1732–1809 (77)
GOSSEC François/Bel — 1734–1829 (95)

GRÉTRY André E.M./Bel — 1742–1813 (71)
BOCCHERINI Luigi/I — 1743–1805 (62)
CIMAROSA Domenico/I — 1749–1801 (52)
CLEMENTI Muzio/I — 1752–1832 (80)

CHERUBINI M.L.C./I — 1760–1842 (82)
BEETHOVEN Ludwig van/G — 1770–1827 (57)
SPONTINI Gasparo/I — 1774–1851 (77)
BOÏELDIEU François/F — 1775–1834 (59)
AUBER Daniel/F
FIELD John/GB — 1782–1837 (55)
WEBER Carl M. von/G — 1786–1826 (40)
MEYERBEER Giacomo/G
ROSSINI Gioacchino/I
BERWALD Franz A./Swe
SCHUBERT Franz/Aus — 1797–1828 (31)
DONIZETTI Gaetano/I — 1797–1848 (51)
BELLINI Vincenzo/I — 1801–1835 (34)
ADAM Adolphe/F
BERLIOZ Hector/F
GLINKA Michail/R
BALFE Michael/GB
MENDELSSOHN Felix/G — 1809–1847 (38)
CHOPIN Frédéric/Pol — 1810–1849 (39)
NICOLAI Otto/G — 1810–1849 (39)
SCHUMANN Robert/G
LISZT Franz/Hun
THOMAS Ambroise/F
FLOTOW Friedrich von/G
DARGOMIZHSKỲ A.S./R
VERDI Guiseppe/I
WAGNER Richard/G
GADE Niels/Den
GOUNOD Charles F./F
OFFENBACH Jacques/F
FRANCK César/Bel
LALO Édouard/F

	1800	1805	1810	1815	1820	1825	1830	1835	1840	1845

AUBER Daniel/F
MEYERBEER Giacomo/G
ROSSINI Gioacchino/I
BERWALD Franz A./Swe
SCHUBERT Franz/Aus — 1797–1828 (31)
DONIZETTI Gaetano/I — 1797–1848 (51)
BELLINI Vincenzo/I — 1801–1835 (34)
ADAM Adolphe/F
BERLIOZ Hector/F
GLINKA Michail/R
BALFE Michael/GB
MENDELSSOHN Felix/G — 1809–1847 (38)
CHOPIN Frédéric/Pol — 1810–1849 (39)
NICOLAI Otto/G — 1810–1849 (39)
SCHUMANN Robert/G
LISZT Franz/Hun
THOMAS Ambroise/F
FLOTOW Friedrich von/G
DARGOMIZHSKY A.S./R
VERDI Guiseppe/I
WAGNER Richard/G
GADE Niels/Den
GOUNOD Charles F./F
OFFENBACH Jacques/F
FRANCK César/Bel
LALO Édouard/F
BRUCKNER Anton/Aus
SMETANA Bedřich/Cz
STRAUSS Johann (Jr.)/Aus
GOLDMARK Karl/Hun
BORODIN Alexander/R
BRAHMS Johannes/G
PONCHIELLI Amilcare/I
CUI César/R
SAINT-SAËNS Camille/F
DELIBES Léo/F
BALAKIREV Mily/R
BIZET Georges/F
BRUCH Max/G
MUSSORGSKY Modeste/R
TCHAIKOVSKY Peter I./R
CHABRIER Emmanuel/F
DVOŘÁK Antonin/Cz
MASSENET Jules E.F./F
SULLIVAN Arthur/GB
GRIEG Edvard H./Nor
RIMSKY-KORSAKOV N./R
SARASATE Pablo/Sp
FAURÉ Gabriel/F
GODARD Benjamin/F

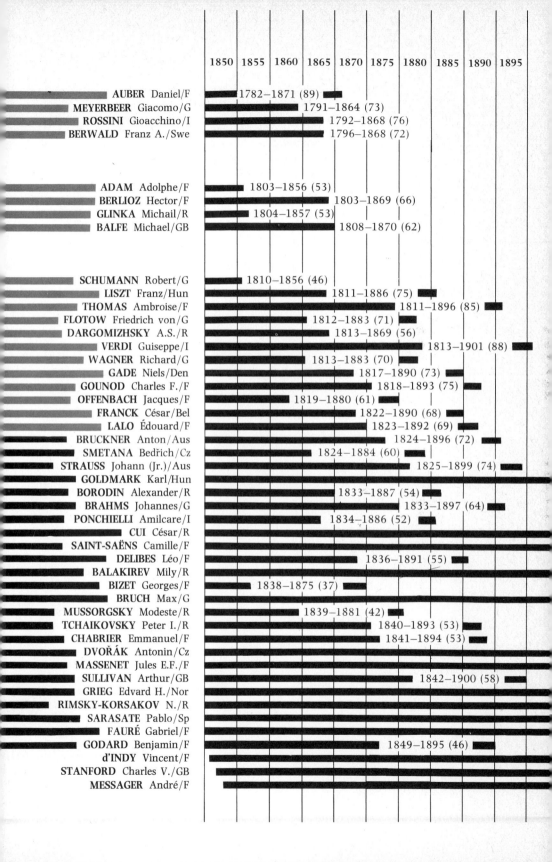

	1850	1855	1860	1865	1870	1875	1880	1885	1890	1895

AUBER Daniel/F — 1782–1871 (89)
MEYERBEER Giacomo/G — 1791–1864 (73)
ROSSINI Gioacchino/I — 1792–1868 (76)
BERWALD Franz A./Swe — 1796–1868 (72)

ADAM Adolphe/F — 1803–1856 (53)
BERLIOZ Hector/F — 1803–1869 (66)
GLINKA Michail/R — 1804–1857 (53)
BALFE Michael/GB — 1808–1870 (62)

SCHUMANN Robert/G — 1810–1856 (46)
LISZT Franz/Hun — 1811–1886 (75)
THOMAS Ambroise/F — 1811–1896 (85)
FLOTOW Friedrich von/G — 1812–1883 (71)
DARGOMIZHSKY A.S./R — 1813–1869 (56)
VERDI Guiseppe/I — 1813–1901 (88)
WAGNER Richard/G — 1813–1883 (70)
GADE Niels/Den — 1817–1890 (73)
GOUNOD Charles F./F — 1818–1893 (75)
OFFENBACH Jacques/F — 1819–1880 (61)
FRANCK César/Bel — 1822–1890 (68)
LALO Édouard/F — 1823–1892 (69)
BRUCKNER Anton/Aus — 1824–1896 (72)
SMETANA Bedřich/Cz — 1824–1884 (60)
STRAUSS Johann (Jr.)/Aus — 1825–1899 (74)
GOLDMARK Karl/Hun
BORODIN Alexander/R — 1833–1887 (54)
BRAHMS Johannes/G — 1833–1897 (64)
PONCHIELLI Amilcare/I — 1834–1886 (52)
CUI César/R
SAINT-SAËNS Camille/F
DELIBES Léo/F — 1836–1891 (55)
BALAKIREV Mily/R
BIZET Georges/F — 1838–1875 (37)
BRUCH Max/G
MUSSORGSKY Modeste/R — 1839–1881 (42)
TCHAIKOVSKY Peter I./R — 1840–1893 (53)
CHABRIER Emmanuel/F — 1841–1894 (53)
DVOŘÁK Antonin/Cz
MASSENET Jules E.F./F
SULLIVAN Arthur/GB — 1842–1900 (58)
GRIEG Edvard H./Nor
RIMSKY-KORSAKOV N./R
SARASATE Pablo/Sp
FAURÉ Gabriel/F
GODARD Benjamin/F — 1849–1895 (46)
d'INDY Vincent/F
STANFORD Charles V./GB
MESSAGER André/F

	1850	1855	1860	1865	1870	1875	1880	1885	1890	1895

LALO Édouard/F — 1823–1892 (69)

BRUCKNER Anton/Aus — 1824–1896 (72)

SMETANA Bedřich/Cz — 1824–1884 (60)

STRAUSS Johann (Jr.)/Aus — 1825–1899 (74)

GOLDMARK Karl/Hun

BORODIN Alexander/R — 1833–1887 (54)

BRAHMS Johannes/G — 1833–1897 (64)

PONCHIELLI Amilcare/I — 1834–1886 (52)

CUI César/R

SAINT-SAËNS Camille/F

DELIBES Léo/F — 1836–1891 (55)

BALAKIREV Mily/R

BIZET Georges/F — 1838–1875 (37)

BRUCH Max/G

MUSSORGSKY Modeste/R — 1839–1881 (42)

TCHAIKOVSKY Peter I./R — 1840–1893 (53)

CHABRIER Emmanuel/F — 1841–1894 (53)

DVOŘÁK Antonin/Cz

MASSENET Jules E.F./F

SULLIVAN Arthur/GB — 1842–1900 (58)

GRIEG Edvard H./Nor

RIMSKY-KORSAKOV N./R

SARASATE Pablo/Sp

FAURÉ Gabriel/F

GODARD Benjamin/F — 1849–1895 (46)

d'INDY Vincent/F

STANFORD Charles V./GB

MESSAGER André/F

CATALANI Alfredo/I — 1854–1893 (39)

HUMPERDINCK Engelbert/G

JANÁČEK Leoš/Cz

CHAUSSON Ernest/F — 1855–1899 (44)

LIADOV Anatol/R

CHAMINADE Cécile/F

ELGAR Edward/GB

LEONCAVALLO Ruggero/I

PUCCINI Giacomo/I

SMYTH Ethel/GB

IPPOLITOV-IVANOV Mikhail/R

ALBÉNIZ Isaac/Sp

CHARPENTIER Gustave/F

WOLF Hugo/Aus

PADEREWSKI Ignacy/Pol

MAHLER Gustav/Aus

ARENSKY Anton/R

LOEFFLER Charles/Als

MACDOWELL Edward/USA

BOËLLMANN Léon/F — 1862–1897 (35)

DEBUSSY Claude/F

DELIUS Frederick/GB

GERMAN Edward/GB

MASCAGNI Pietro/I

PIERNÉ Gabriel/F

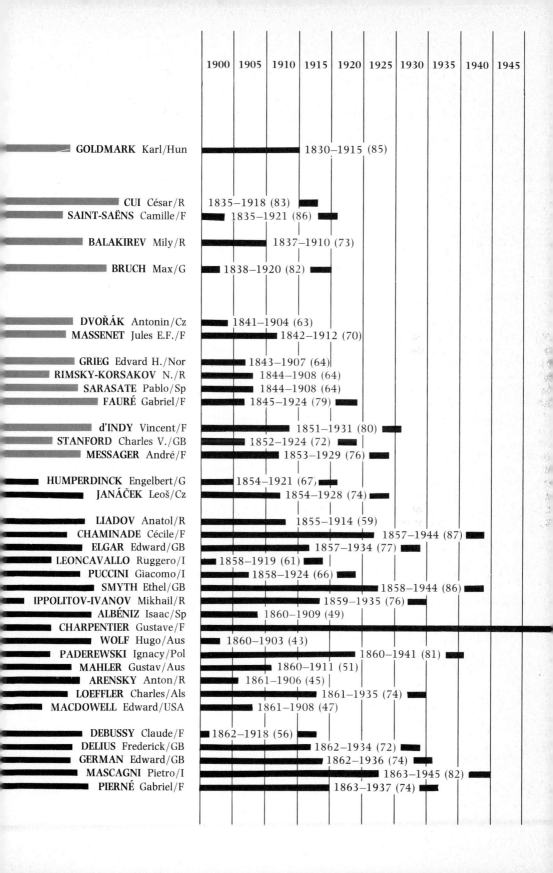

	1900	1905	1910	1915	1920	1925	1930	1935	1940	1945

GOLDMARK Karl/Hun — 1830–1915 (85)

CUI César/R — 1835–1918 (83)
SAINT-SAËNS Camille/F — 1835–1921 (86)

BALAKIREV Mily/R — 1837–1910 (73)

BRUCH Max/G — 1838–1920 (82)

DVOŘÁK Antonin/Cz — 1841–1904 (63)
MASSENET Jules E.F./F — 1842–1912 (70)

GRIEG Edvard H./Nor — 1843–1907 (64)
RIMSKY-KORSAKOV N./R — 1844–1908 (64)
SARASATE Pablo/Sp — 1844–1908 (64)
FAURÉ Gabriel/F — 1845–1924 (79)

d'INDY Vincent/F — 1851–1931 (80)
STANFORD Charles V./GB — 1852–1924 (72)
MESSAGER André/F — 1853–1929 (76)

HUMPERDINCK Engelbert/G — 1854–1921 (67)
JANÁČEK Leoš/Cz — 1854–1928 (74)

LIADOV Anatol/R — 1855–1914 (59)
CHAMINADE Cécile/F — 1857–1944 (87)
ELGAR Edward/GB — 1857–1934 (77)
LEONCAVALLO Ruggero/I — 1858–1919 (61)
PUCCINI Giacomo/I — 1858–1924 (66)
SMYTH Ethel/GB — 1858–1944 (86)
IPPOLITOV-IVANOV Mikhail/R — 1859–1935 (76)
ALBÉNIZ Isaac/Sp — 1860–1909 (49)
CHARPENTIER Gustave/F
WOLF Hugo/Aus — 1860–1903 (43)
PADEREWSKI Ignacy/Pol — 1860–1941 (81)
MAHLER Gustav/Aus — 1860–1911 (51)
ARENSKY Anton/R — 1861–1906 (45)
LOEFFLER Charles/Als — 1861–1935 (74)
MACDOWELL Edward/USA — 1861–1908 (47)

DEBUSSY Claude/F — 1862–1918 (56)
DELIUS Frederick/GB — 1862–1934 (72)
GERMAN Edward/GB — 1862–1936 (74)
MASCAGNI Pietro/I — 1863–1945 (82)
PIERNÉ Gabriel/F — 1863–1937 (74)

| | 1850 | 1855 | 1860 | 1865 | 1870 | 1875 | 1880 | 1885 | 1890 | 1895 |

STANFORD Charles V./GB
MESSAGER André/F
CATALANI Alfredo/I — 1854–1893 (39)
HUMPERDINCK Engelbert/G
JANÁČEK Leoš/Cz
CHAUSSON Ernest/F — 1855–1899 (44)
LIADOV Anatol/R
CHAMINADE Cécile/F
ELGAR Edward/GB
LEONCAVALLO Ruggero/I
PUCCINI Giacomo/I
SMYTH Ethel/GB
IPPOLITOV-IVANOV Mikhail/R
ALBÉNIZ Isaac/Sp
CHARPENTIER Gustave/F
WOLF Hugo/Aus
PADEREWSKI Ignacy/Pol
MAHLER Gustav/Aus
ARENSKY Anton/R
LOEFFLER Charles/Als
MACDOWELL Edward/USA
BOËLLMANN Léon/F — 1862–1897 (35)
DEBUSSY Claude/F
DELIUS Frederick/GB
GERMAN Edward/GB
MASCAGNI Pietro/I
PIERNÉ Gabriel/F
STRAUSS Richard/G
ROPARTZ Guy/F
DUKAS Paul/F
GLAZUNOV Alexander/R
SIBELIUS Jean/Fin
NIELSON Carl A./Den
SATIE Erik/F
CILÈA Francesco/I
BUSONI Ferruccio/I
GIORDANO Umberto/I
BANTOCK Granville/GB
ROUSSEL Albert/F
LEHÁR Franz (Ferencz)/Hun
ALFVÉN Hugo/Swe
SKRIABIN Alexander/R
VAUGHAN WILLIAMS Ralph/GB
RACHMANINOV Sergei/R
REGER Max/G
JONGEN Joseph/Bel
HOLST Gustav T./GB
SCHOENBERG Arnold/Aus
SUK Josef/Cz
IVES Charles/U.S.A.
COLERIDGE-TAYLOR Samuel/GB
RAVEL Maurice/F
GLIÈRE Reinhold/R

	1900	1905	1910	1915	1920	1925	1930	1935	1940	1945

STANFORD Charles V./GB — 1852–1924 (72)
MESSAGER André/F — 1853–1929 (76)

HUMPERDINCK Engelbert/G — 1854–1921 (67)
JANÁČEK Leoš/Cz — 1854–1928 (74)

LIADOV Anatol/R — 1855–1914 (59)
CHAMINADE Cécile/F — 1857–1944 (87)
ELGAR Edward/GB — 1857–1934 (77)
LEONCAVALLO Ruggero/I — 1858–1919 (61)
PUCCINI Giacomo/I — 1858–1924 (66)
SMYTH Ethel/GB — 1858–1944 (86)
IPPOLITOV-IVANOV Mikhail/R — 1859–1935 (76)
ALBÉNIZ Isaac/Sp — 1860–1909 (49)
CHARPENTIER Gustave/F
WOLF Hugo/Aus — 1860–1903 (43)
PADEREWSKI Ignacy/Pol — 1860–1941 (81)
MAHLER Gustav/Aus — 1860–1911 (51)
ARENSKY Anton/R — 1861–1906 (45)
LOEFFLER Charles/Als — 1861–1935 (74)
MACDOWELL Edward/USA — 1861–1908 (47)

DEBUSSY Claude/F — 1862–1918 (56)
DELIUS Frederick/GB — 1862–1934 (72)
GERMAN Edward/GB — 1862–1936 (74)
MASCAGNI Pietro/I — 1863–1945 (82)
PIERNÉ Gabriel/F — 1863–1937 (74)
STRAUSS Richard/G — 1864–1949 (85)
ROPARTZ Guy/F
DUKAS Paul/F — 1865–1935 (70)
GLAZUNOV Alexander/R — 1865–1936 (71)
SIBELIUS Jean/Fin
NIELSON Carl A./Den — 1865–1931 (66)
SATIE Erik/F — 1866–1925 (59)
CILÈA Francesco/I — 1866–1950 (84)
BUSONI Ferruccio/I — 1866–1924 (58)
GIORDANO Umberto/I — 1867–1948 (81)
BANTOCK Granville/GB — 1868–1946 (78)
ROUSSEL Albert/F — 1869–1937 (68)
LEHÁR Franz (Ferencz)/Hun — 1870–1948 (78)
ALFVÉN Hugo/Swe
SKRIABIN Alexander/R — 1872–1915 (43)
VAUGHAN WILLIAMS Ralph/GB
RACHMANINOV Sergei/R — 1873–1943 (70)
REGER Max/G — 1873–1916 (43)
JONGEN Joseph/Bel
HOLST Gustav T./GB — 1874–1934 (60)
SCHOENBERG Arnold/Aus
SUK Josef/Cz — 1874–1935 (61)
IVES Charles/U.S.A.
COLERIDGE-TAYLOR Samuel/GB — 1875–1912 (37)
RAVEL Maurice/F — 1875–1937 (62)
GLIÈRE Reinhold/R

	1875	1880	1885	1890	1895	1900	1905	1910	1915	1920

CHARPENTIER Gustave/F
STRAUSS Richard/G
ROPARTZ Guy/F
DUKAS Paul/F
GLAZUNOV Alexander/R
SIBELIUS Jean/Fin
NIELSON Carl A./Den
SATIE Erik/F — 1866–1925 (59)
CILÈA Francesco/I
BUSONI Ferruccio/I — 1866–1924 (58)
GIORDANO Umberto/I
BANTOCK Granville/GB
ROUSSEL Albert/F
LEHÁR Franz (Ferencz)/Hun
ALFVÉN Hugo/Swe
SKRIABIN Alexander/R — 1872–1915 (43)
VAUGHAN WILLIAMS Ralph/GB
RACHMANINOV Sergei/R
REGER Max/G — 1873–1916 (43)
JONGEN Joseph/Bel
HOLST Gustav T./GB
SCHOENBERG Arnold/Aus
SUK Josef/Cz
IVES Charles/U.S.A.
COLERIDGE-TAYLOR Samuel/GB — 1875–1912 (37)
RAVEL Maurice/F
GLIÈRE Reinhold/R
FALLA Manuel de/Sp
WOLF-FERRARI Ermanno/I
CARPENTER John Alden/U.S.A.
AUBERT Louis/F
DOHNÁNYI Ernst von/Hun
QUILTER Roger/GB
IRELAND John/GB
RESPIGHI Ottorino/I
BRIDGE Frank/GB
BLOCH Ernest/Swi
MEDTNER Nicholas/R
PIZZETTI Ildebrando/I
BARTÓK Béla/Hun
ENESCO Georges/Rum
GRAINGER Percy Aldridge/Aust
KODÁLY Zoltán/Hun
MALIPIERO Gian Francesco/I
STRAVINSKY Igor/R
TURINA Joaquín/Sp
BAX Arnold Trevor/GB
CASELLA Alfredo/I
SZYMANOWSKI Karol/Pol
WEBERN Anton von/Aus
GRIFFES Charles/U.S.A. — 1884–1920 (36)
BERG Alban/Aus
TAYLOR Deems/U.S.A.
BUTTERWORTH George/GB — 1885–1916 (31)

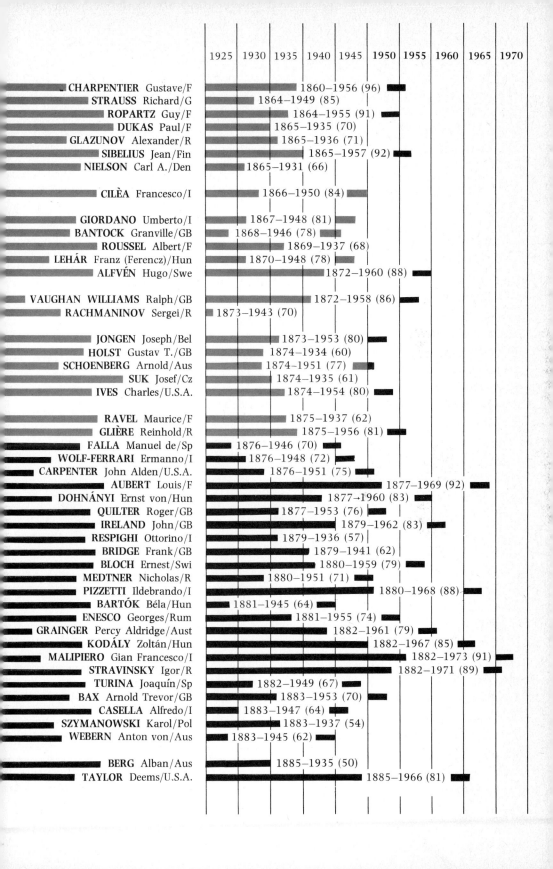

	1925	1930	1935	1940	1945	1950	1955	1960	1965	1970

CHARPENTIER Gustave/F — 1860–1956 (96)
STRAUSS Richard/G — 1864–1949 (85)
ROPARTZ Guy/F — 1864–1955 (91)
DUKAS Paul/F — 1865–1935 (70)
GLAZUNOV Alexander/R — 1865–1936 (71)
SIBELIUS Jean/Fin — 1865–1957 (92)
NIELSON Carl A./Den — 1865–1931 (66)

CILÈA Francesco/I — 1866–1950 (84)

GIORDANO Umberto/I — 1867–1948 (81)
BANTOCK Granville/GB — 1868–1946 (78)
ROUSSEL Albert/F — 1869–1937 (68)
LEHÁR Franz (Ferencz)/Hun — 1870–1948 (78)
ALFVÉN Hugo/Swe — 1872–1960 (88)

VAUGHAN WILLIAMS Ralph/GB — 1872–1958 (86)
RACHMANINOV Sergei/R — 1873–1943 (70)

JONGEN Joseph/Bel — 1873–1953 (80)
HOLST Gustav T./GB — 1874–1934 (60)
SCHOENBERG Arnold/Aus — 1874–1951 (77)
SUK Josef/Cz — 1874–1935 (61)
IVES Charles/U.S.A. — 1874–1954 (80)

RAVEL Maurice/F — 1875–1937 (62)
GLIÈRE Reinhold/R — 1875–1956 (81)
FALLA Manuel de/Sp — 1876–1946 (70)
WOLF-FERRARI Ermanno/I — 1876–1948 (72)
CARPENTER John Alden/U.S.A. — 1876–1951 (75)
AUBERT Louis/F — 1877–1969 (92)
DOHNÁNYI Ernst von/Hun — 1877→1960 (83)
QUILTER Roger/GB — 1877–1953 (76)
IRELAND John/GB — 1879–1962 (83)
RESPIGHI Ottorino/I — 1879–1936 (57)
BRIDGE Frank/GB — 1879–1941 (62)
BLOCH Ernest/Swi — 1880–1959 (79)
MEDTNER Nicholas/R — 1880–1951 (71)
PIZZETTI Ildebrando/I — 1880–1968 (88)
BARTÓK Béla/Hun — 1881–1945 (64)
ENESCO Georges/Rum — 1881–1955 (74)
GRAINGER Percy Aldridge/Aust — 1882–1961 (79)
KODÁLY Zoltán/Hun — 1882–1967 (85)
MALIPIERO Gian Francesco/I — 1882–1973 (91)
STRAVINSKY Igor/R — 1882–1971 (89)
TURINA Joaquín/Sp — 1882–1949 (67)
BAX Arnold Trevor/GB — 1883–1953 (70)
CASELLA Alfredo/I — 1883–1947 (64)
SZYMANOWSKI Karol/Pol — 1883–1937 (54)
WEBERN Anton von/Aus — 1883–1945 (62)

BERG Alban/Aus — 1885–1935 (50)
TAYLOR Deems/U.S.A. — 1885–1966 (81)

	1875	1880	1885	1890	1895	1900	1905	1910	1915	1920

FALLA Manuel de/Sp
WOLF-FERRARI Ermanno/I
CARPENTER John Alden/U.S.A.
AUBERT Louis/F
DOHNÁNYI Ernst von/Hun
QUILTER Roger/GB
IRELAND John/GB
RESPIGHI Ottorino/I
BRIDGE Frank/GB
BLOCH Ernest/Swi
MEDTNER Nicholas/R
PIZZETTI Ildebrando/I
BARTÓK Béla/Hun
ENESCO Georges/Rum
GRAINGER Percy Aldridge/Aust
KODÁLY Zoltán/Hun
MALIPIERO Gian Francesco/I
STRAVINSKY Igor/R
TURINA Joaquín/Sp
BAX Arnold Trevor/GB
CASELLA Alfredo/I
SZYMANOWSKI Karol/Pol
WEBERN Anton von/Aus
GRIFFES Charles/U.S.A. 1884–1920 (36)
BERG Alban/Aus
BUTTERWORTH George/GB 1885–1916 (31)
TAYLOR Deems/U.S.A.
SCHOECK Othmar/Swi
VILLA-LOBOS Heitor/Braz
MARTIN Frank/Swi
MARTINŮ Bohuslav/Cz
IBERT Jacques/F
BLISS Arthur/GB
PROKOFIEV Sergei/R
GRANDJANY Marcel/F
GROFÉ Ferde/U.S.A.
MILHAUD Darius/F
HONEGGER Arthur/Swi
BENJAMIN Arthur/Aust
MOORE Douglas/U.S.A. 1893–
MOERAN Ernest J./GB
PISTON Walter/U.S.A. 1894–
WARLOCK Peter/GB
HINDEMITH Paul/G
ORFF Carl/G 1895–
JACOB Gordon/GB 1895–
CASTELNUOVO-TEDESCO Mario/I
SOWERBY Leo/U.S.A.
GERHARD Roberto/Sp
HANSON Howard/U.S.A. 1896–
THOMSON Virgil/U.S.A. 1896–
WEINBERGER Jaromir/Cz
ROBERTSON Leroy/U.S.A.

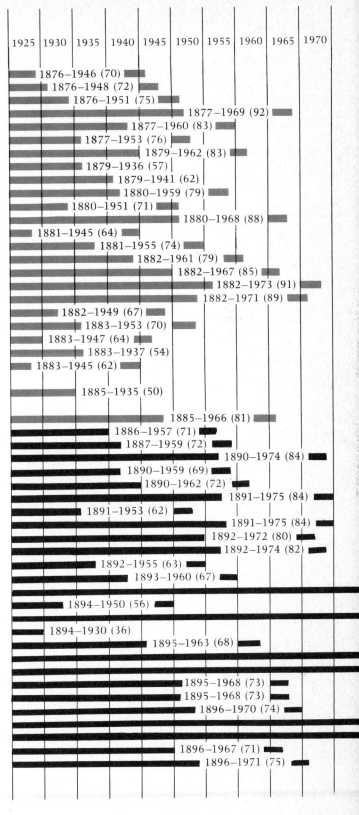

	1925	1930	1935	1940	1945	1950	1955	1960	1965	1970

FALLA Manuel de/Sp — 1876–1946 (70)
WOLF-FERRARI Ermanno/I — 1876–1948 (72)
CARPENTER John Alden/U.S.A. — 1876–1951 (75)
AUBERT Louis/F — 1877–1969 (92)
DOHNÁNYI Ernst von/Hun — 1877–1960 (83)
QUILTER Roger/GB — 1877–1953 (76)
IRELAND John/GB — 1879–1962 (83)
RESPIGHI Ottorino/I — 1879–1936 (57)
BRIDGE Frank/GB — 1879–1941 (62)
BLOCH Ernest/Swi — 1880–1959 (79)
MEDTNER Nicholas/R — 1880–1951 (71)
PIZZETTI Ildebrando/I — 1880–1968 (88)
BARTÓK Béla/Hun — 1881–1945 (64)
ENESCO Georges/Rum — 1881–1955 (74)
GRAINGER Percy Aldridge/Aust — 1882–1961 (79)
KODÁLY Zoltán/Hun — 1882–1967 (85)
MALIPIERO Gian Francesco/I — 1882–1973 (91)
STRAVINSKY Igor/R — 1882–1971 (89)
TURINA Joaquín/Sp — 1882–1949 (67)
BAX Arnold Trevor/GB — 1883–1953 (70)
CASELLA Alfredo/I — 1883–1947 (64)
SZYMANOWSKI Karol/Pol — 1883–1937 (54)
WEBERN Anton von/Aus — 1883–1945 (62)

BERG Alban/Aus — 1885–1935 (50)

TAYLOR Deems/U.S.A. — 1885–1966 (81)
SCHOECK Othmar/Swi — 1886–1957 (71)
VILLA-LOBOS Heitor/Braz — 1887–1959 (72)
MARTIN Frank/Swi — 1890–1974 (84)
MARTINŮ Bohuslav/Cz — 1890–1959 (69)
IBERT Jacques/F — 1890–1962 (72)
BLISS Arthur/GB — 1891–1975 (84)
PROKOFIEV Sergei/R — 1891–1953 (62)
GRANDJANY Marcel/F — 1891–1975 (84)
GROFÉ Ferde/U.S.A. — 1892–1972 (80)
MILHAUD Darius/F — 1892–1974 (82)
HONEGGER Arthur/Swi — 1892–1955 (63)
BENJAMIN Arthur/Aust — 1893–1960 (67)
MOORE Douglas/U.S.A.
MOERAN Ernest J./GB — 1894–1950 (56)
PISTON Walter/U.S.A.
WARLOCK Peter/GB — 1894–1930 (36)
HINDEMITH Paul/G — 1895–1963 (68)
ORFF Carl/G
JACOB Gordon/GB
CASTELNUOVO-TEDESCO Mario/I — 1895–1968 (73)
SOWERBY Leo/U.S.A. — 1895–1968 (73)
GERHARD Roberto/Sp — 1896–1970 (74)
HANSON Howard/U.S.A.
THOMSON Virgil/U.S.A.
WEINBERGER Jaromir/Cz — 1896–1967 (71)
ROBERTSON Leroy/U.S.A. — 1896–1971 (75)

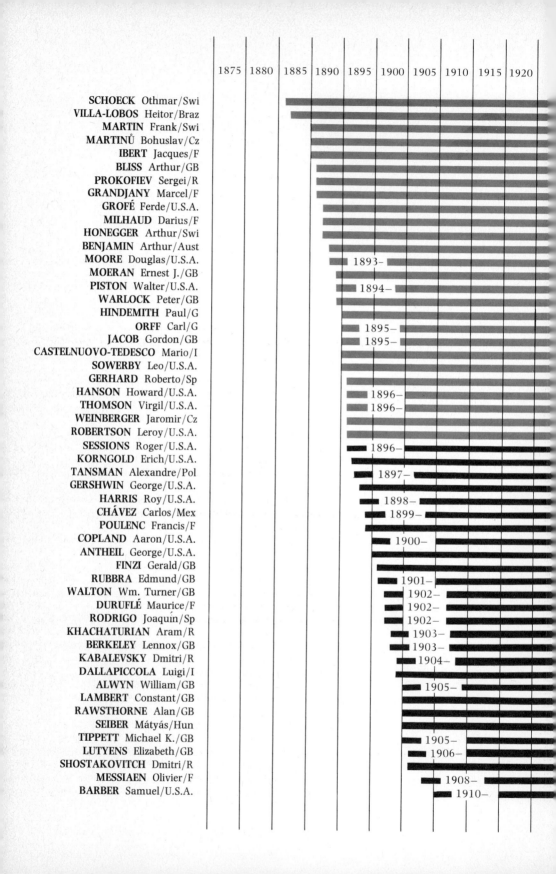

	1875	1880	1885	1890	1895	1900	1905	1910	1915	1920

SCHOECK Othmar/Swi
VILLA-LOBOS Heitor/Braz
MARTIN Frank/Swi
MARTINŮ Bohuslav/Cz
IBERT Jacques/F
BLISS Arthur/GB
PROKOFIEV Sergei/R
GRANDJANY Marcel/F
GROFÉ Ferde/U.S.A.
MILHAUD Darius/F
HONEGGER Arthur/Swi
BENJAMIN Arthur/Aust
MOORE Douglas/U.S.A.   1893–
MOERAN Ernest J./GB
PISTON Walter/U.S.A.   1894–
WARLOCK Peter/GB
HINDEMITH Paul/G
ORFF Carl/G   1895–
JACOB Gordon/GB   1895–
CASTELNUOVO-TEDESCO Mario/I
SOWERBY Leo/U.S.A.
GERHARD Roberto/Sp
HANSON Howard/U.S.A.   1896–
THOMSON Virgil/U.S.A.   1896–
WEINBERGER Jaromir/Cz
ROBERTSON Leroy/U.S.A.
SESSIONS Roger/U.S.A.   1896–
KORNGOLD Erich/U.S.A.
TANSMAN Alexandre/Pol   1897–
GERSHWIN George/U.S.A.
HARRIS Roy/U.S.A.   1898–
CHÁVEZ Carlos/Mex   1899–
POULENC Francis/F
COPLAND Aaron/U.S.A.   1900–
ANTHEIL George/U.S.A.
FINZI Gerald/GB
RUBBRA Edmund/GB   1901–
WALTON Wm. Turner/GB   1902–
DURUFLÉ Maurice/F   1902–
RODRIGO Joaquín/Sp   1902–
KHACHATURIAN Aram/R   1903–
BERKELEY Lennox/GB   1903–
KABALEVSKY Dmitri/R   1904–
DALLAPICCOLA Luigi/I
ALWYN William/GB   1905–
LAMBERT Constant/GB
RAWSTHORNE Alan/GB
SEIBER Mátyás/Hun
TIPPETT Michael K./GB   1905–
LUTYENS Elizabeth/GB   1906–
SHOSTAKOVITCH Dmitri/R
MESSIAEN Olivier/F   1908–
BARBER Samuel/U.S.A.   1910–

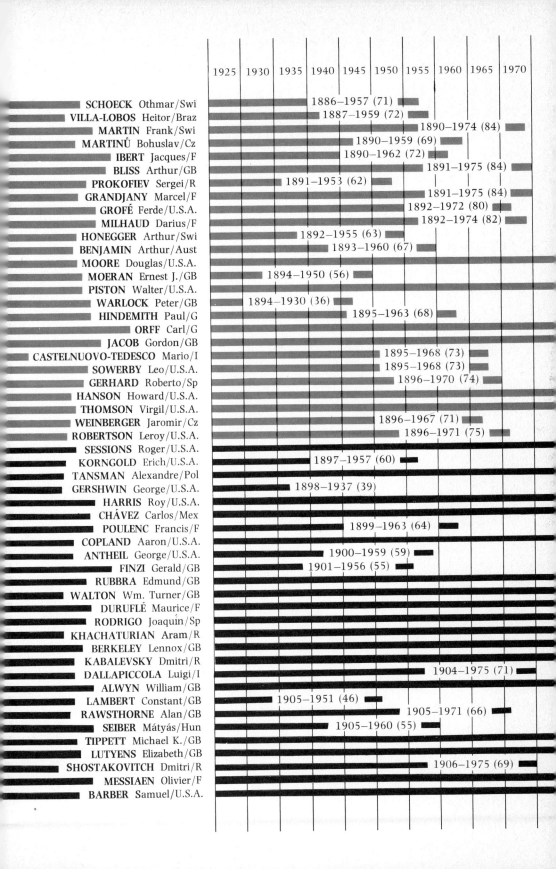

	1925	1930	1935	1940	1945	1950	1955	1960	1965	1970

SCHOECK Othmar/Swi — 1886–1957 (71)
VILLA-LOBOS Heitor/Braz — 1887–1959 (72)
MARTIN Frank/Swi — 1890–1974 (84)
MARTINŮ Bohuslav/Cz — 1890–1959 (69)
IBERT Jacques/F — 1890–1962 (72)
BLISS Arthur/GB — 1891–1975 (84)
PROKOFIEV Sergei/R — 1891–1953 (62)
GRANDJANY Marcel/F — 1891–1975 (84)
GROFÉ Ferde/U.S.A. — 1892–1972 (80)
MILHAUD Darius/F — 1892–1974 (82)
HONEGGER Arthur/Swi — 1892–1955 (63)
BENJAMIN Arthur/Aust — 1893–1960 (67)
MOORE Douglas/U.S.A.
MOERAN Ernest J./GB — 1894–1950 (56)
PISTON Walter/U.S.A.
WARLOCK Peter/GB — 1894–1930 (36)
HINDEMITH Paul/G — 1895–1963 (68)
ORFF Carl/G
JACOB Gordon/GB
CASTELNUOVO-TEDESCO Mario/I — 1895–1968 (73)
SOWERBY Leo/U.S.A. — 1895–1968 (73)
GERHARD Roberto/Sp — 1896–1970 (74)
HANSON Howard/U.S.A.
THOMSON Virgil/U.S.A.
WEINBERGER Jaromir/Cz — 1896–1967 (71)
ROBERTSON Leroy/U.S.A. — 1896–1971 (75)
SESSIONS Roger/U.S.A.
KORNGOLD Erich/U.S.A. — 1897–1957 (60)
TANSMAN Alexandre/Pol
GERSHWIN George/U.S.A. — 1898–1937 (39)
HARRIS Roy/U.S.A.
CHÁVEZ Carlos/Mex
POULENC Francis/F — 1899–1963 (64)
COPLAND Aaron/U.S.A.
ANTHEIL George/U.S.A. — 1900–1959 (59)
FINZI Gerald/GB — 1901–1956 (55)
RUBBRA Edmund/GB
WALTON Wm. Turner/GB
DURUFLÉ Maurice/F
RODRIGO Joaquín/Sp
KHACHATURIAN Aram/R
BERKELEY Lennox/GB
KABALEVSKY Dmitri/R
DALLAPICCOLA Luigi/I — 1904–1975 (71)
ALWYN William/GB
LAMBERT Constant/GB — 1905–1951 (46)
RAWSTHORNE Alan/GB — 1905–1971 (66)
SEIBER Mátyás/Hun — 1905–1960 (55)
TIPPETT Michael K./GB
LUTYENS Elizabeth/GB
SHOSTAKOVITCH Dmitri/R — 1906–1975 (69)
MESSIAEN Olivier/F
BARBER Samuel/U.S.A.

	1875	1880	1885	1890	1895	1900	1905	1910	1915	1920

SESSIONS Roger/U.S.A.   1896–
KORNGOLD Erich/U.S.A.
TANSMAN Alexandre/Pol   1897–
GERSHWIN George/U.S.A.
HARRIS Roy/U.S.A.   1898–
CHÁVEZ Carlos/Mex   1899–
POULENC Francis/F
COPLAND Aaron/U.S.A.   1900–
ANTHEIL George/U.S.A.
FINZI Gerald/GB
RUBBRA Edmund/GB   1901–
WALTON Wm. Turner/GB   1902–
DURUFLÉ Maurice/F   1902–
RODRIGO Joaquín/Sp   1902–
KHACHATURIAN Aram/R   1903–
BERKELEY Lennox/GB   1903–
KABALEVSKY Dmitri/R   1904–
DALLAPICCOLA Luigi/I
ALWYN William/GB   1905–
LAMBERT Constant/GB
RAWSTHORNE Alan/GB
SEIBER Mátyás/Hun
TIPPETT Michael K./GB   1905–
LUTYENS Elizabeth/GB   1906–
SHOSTAKOVITCH Dmitri/R
MESSIAEN Olivier/F   1908–
BARBER Samuel/U.S.A.   1910–
SCHUMAN William/U.S.A.   1910–
MENOTTI Gian-Carlo/U.S.A.   1911–
CAGE John/U.S.A.   1912–
GILLIS Don/U.S.A.   1912–
BRITTEN Benjamin/GB   1913–
LUTOSLAWSKI Witold/Pol   1913–
GOULD Morton/U.S.A.   1913–
FINE Irving/U.S.A.
DIAMOND David Lee/U.S.A.   1915–
ARNELL Richard/GB   1917–
BERNSTEIN Leonard/U.S.A.   1918–
ROCHBERG George/U.S.A.   1918–
FRICKER Peter R./GB   1920
SHAPERO Harold/U.S.A.   1920
ARNOLD Malcolm/GB   1921
SHAPEY Ralph/U.S.A.   1921
HAMILTON Ian/GB
FOSS Lukas/U.S.A.
MENNIN Peter/U.S.A.
LIGETI György/Hun

	1925	1930	1935	1940	1945	1950	1955	1960	1965	1970

SESSIONS Roger/U.S.A.

KORNGOLD Erich/U.S.A. — 1897–1957 (60)

TANSMAN Alexandre/Pol

GERSHWIN George/U.S.A. — 1898–1937 (39)

HARRIS Roy/U.S.A.

CHÁVEZ Carlos/Mex

POULENC Francis/F — 1899–1963 (64)

COPLAND Aaron/U.S.A.

ANTHEIL George/U.S.A. — 1900–1959 (59)

FINZI Gerald/GB — 1901–1956 (55)

RUBBRA Edmund/GB

WALTON Wm. Turner/GB

DURUFLÉ Maurice/F

RODRIGO Joaquín/Sp

KHACHATURIAN Aram/R

BERKELEY Lennox/GB

KABALEVSKY Dmitri/R

DALLAPICCOLA Luigi/I — 1904–1975 (71)

ALWYN William/GB

LAMBERT Constant/GB — 1905–1951 (46)

RAWSTHORNE Alan/GB — 1905–1971 (66)

SEIBER Mátyás/Hun — 1905–1960 (55)

TIPPETT Michael K./GB

LUTYENS Elizabeth/GB

SHOSTAKOVITCH Dmitri/R — 1906–1975 (69)

MESSIAEN Olivier/F

BARBER Samuel/U.S.A.

SCHUMAN William/U.S.A.

MENOTTI Gian-Carlo/U.S.A.

CAGE John/U.S.A.

GILLIS Don/U.S.A.

BRITTEN Benjamin/GB

LUTOSLAWSKI Witold/Pol

GOULD Morton/U.S.A.

FINE Irving/U.S.A. — 1914–1962 (48)

DIAMOND David Lee/U.S.A.

ARNELL Richard/GB

BERNSTEIN Leonard/U.S.A.

ROCHBERG George/U.S.A.

FRICKER Peter R./GB

SHAPERO Harold/U.S.A.

ARNOLD Malcolm/GB

SHAPEY Ralph/U.S.A.

1922 **HAMILTON** Ian/GB

1922 **FOSS** Lukas/U.S.A.

1923 **MENNIN** Peter/U.S.A.

1923 **LIGETI** György/Hun

BOULEZ Pierre/F — 1925–

BERIO Luciano/I — 1925–

BROWN Earle/U.S.A. — 1926–

FELDMAN Morton/U.S.A. — 1926–

HENZE Hans Werner/G — 1926–

MUSGRAVE Thea/GB — 1928–

	1875	1880	1885	1890	1895	1900	1905	1910	1915	1920

SCHUMAN William/U.S.A.   1910–

MENOTTI Gian-Carlo/U.S.A.   1911–

CAGE John/U.S.A.   1912–

GILLIS Don/U.S.A.   1912–

BRITTEN Benjamin/GB   1913–

LUTOSLAWSKI Witold/Pol   1913–

GOULD Morton/U.S.A.   1913–

FINE Irving/U.S.A.

DIAMOND David Lee/U.S.A.   1915–

ARNELL Richard/GB   1917–

BERNSTEIN Leonard/U.S.A.   1918

ROCHBERG George/U.S.A.   1918

FRICKER Peter R./GB   19

SHAPERO Harold/U.S.A.   19

ARNOLD Malcolm/GB   1

SHAPEY Ralph/U.S.A.   1

HAMILTON Ian/GB

FOSS Lukas/U.S.A.

MENNIN Peter/U.S.A.

LIGETI György/Hun

	1925	1930	1935	1940	1945	1950	1955	1960	1965	1970

SCHUMAN William/U.S.A.
MENOTTI Gian-Carlo/U.S.A.
CAGE John/U.S.A.
GILLIS Don/U.S.A.
BRITTEN Benjamin/GB
LUTOSLAWSKI Witold/Pol
GOULD Morton/U.S.A.
FINE Irving/U.S.A. — 1914–1962 (48)
DIAMOND David Lee/U.S.A.
ARNELL Richard/GB
BERNSTEIN Leonard/U.S.A.
ROCHBERG George/U.S.A.
FRICKER Peter R./GB
SHAPERO Harold/U.S.A.
ARNOLD Malcolm/GB
SHAPEY Ralph/U.S.A.
1922 HAMILTON Ian/GB
1922 FOSS Lukas/U.S.A.
1923 MENNIN Peter/U.S.A.
1923 LIGETI György/Hun
BOULEZ Pierre/F 1925–
BERIO Luciano/I 1925–
BROWN Earle/U.S.A. 1926–
FELDMAN Morton/U.S.A. 1926–
HENZE Hans Werner/G 1926–
MUSGRAVE Thea/GB 1928–
KORTE Karl/U.S.A. 1928–
STOCKHAUSEN Karlheinz/G 1928–
PREVIN André/U.S.A. 1929–
HODDINOTT Alun/GB 1929–
WILLIAMSON Malcolm/Aust 1931–
GOEHR Alexander/G 1932–
PENDERECKI Krzysztof/Pol 1933–
BIRTWHISTLE Harrison/GB 1934–
DAVIES Peter Maxwell/GB 1934–
MAW Nicholas/GB 1935–
BENNETT Richard R./GB 1936–
BEDFORD David/GB 1937–
NILSSON Bo/Swe 1937–
TAVENER John/GB 1944–